Issues for
Debate in American
Public Policy

Issues for
Debate in American
Public Policy

FIFTH EDITION

CQ PRESS

A Division of Congressional Quarterly Inc. Washington, D.C.

SELECTIONS FROM THE CQ RESEARCHER

CQ Press
1255 22nd Street, N.W., Suite 400
Washington, D.C. 20037

(202) 729-1900; toll-free, 1-866-4CQ-PRESS (1-866-427-7737)
www.cqpress.com

⊗ The paper used in this publication exceeds the requirements of the American National Standard for Information Sciences—Permanence of Paper for Printed Library Materials, ANSI Z39.48-1992.

Printed and bound in the United States of America

08 07 06 05 04   5 4 3 2

A CQ Press College Division Publication

Director	Brenda Carter
Acquisitions editor	Charisse Kiino
Marketing analyst	Bonnie Erickson
Production editor	Belinda Josey
Cover designer	Kimberly Glyder
Composition	Circle Graphics
Print buyer	Margot Ziperman
Sales manager	James Headley

ISSN: 1543-3889
ISBN: 1-56802-889-X

Contents

Annotated Contents

The 16 *CQ Researcher* reports reprinted in this book have been reproduced essentially as they appeared when first published. In the few cases in which important new developments have since occurred, updates are provided in the overviews highlighting the principal issues examined.

EDUCATION

Rising College Costs

Tuition and fees at public colleges soared a record 14 percent in 2003, continuing a quarter-century trend of higher-education costs rising faster than inflation. The average total cost of attending a private school jumped to $26,854 annually—far beyond the means of most American families. The size of federal grants to students has not kept pace with rising prices, and state appropriations to colleges have not adjusted to burgeoning enrollments. Colleges have asked for increased government spending on higher education, but Republican congressional leaders are instead considering penalizing schools that raise prices, arguing that the schools are wasting money. To cope with the financial crunch, more and more colleges are turning to innovative uses of technology to reduce costs.

Combating Plagiarism

In 2003, 48 University of Virginia students quit or were expelled for plagiarism. *New York Times* reporter Jayson Blair plagiarized or fabricated parts of more than three-dozen articles. Best-selling historians Doris Kearns Goodwin and Stephen Ambrose were accused of stealing from other writers. Journalists and educators consider plagiarism a growing problem. Many believe that the Internet is partly to blame because it makes copying published material so easy. Studies show that 90 percent of college students know plagiarism is wrong, but educators say many do it anyway because they do not think they will get caught or because in today's ethical climate they consider plagiarism trivial compared to well-publicized instances of political and corporate dishonesty. Other educators note that high-school students do not understand or have never been taught about copyright regulations and how to properly cite sources.

HEALTH CARE

Medicare Reform

Medicare—the federal health-insurance program for the elderly and disabled—was established in 1965, and in 2003 lawmakers considered and passed the most significant changes to the program's history. The proposed reforms will allow Medicare's 41 million beneficiaries to obtain prescription-drug coverage through private health-insurance plans and private insurers to play an expanded role in delivering health services to seniors. Republicans and Democrats were far apart on the issue: Republicans wanted to inject market competition into the Medicare system, asserting that it was the only way to control rising program costs. Democrats, however, wanted to protect Medicare's core fee-for-service program and its principle of equal benefits for all. On December 8, 2003, President George W. Bush signed into law the Medicare Prescription Drug, Improvement and Modernization Act, the negotiation of which stands out as one of the most significant health-policy debates in years.

Drug Company Ethics

Questions about the business practices of the pharmaceutical industry are growing along with the sector's unprecedented profits. Critics contend that drugmakers put profit margins before human needs and in the process sometimes jeopardize public safety. Consumer advocates and federal regulators complain of skyrocketing drug prices, misleading ads and cutthroat litigation. They also accuse the industry of buying influence in Washington to keep legislators, regulators and low-priced competitors at bay. The drug companies insist that such criticism is overblown, arguing that strong competition in the industry is evidenced by the billions of dollars companies spend each year developing new products as well as the meteoric rise in generic drugs. The national spotlight on drugmakers intensified as lawmakers debated Medicare reform in 2003.

SOCIAL POLICY

Affirmative Action

Should colleges consider race in admissions? A showdown over the use of race in college admissions ended with the U.S. Supreme Court issuing split decisions on the matter. The rulings involved suits brought by white applicants to the University of Michigan's undergraduate college and law school who had been rejected for admission and then challenged university policies that gave an advantage to minority applicants. The university argued that the policies were needed to ensure racial and ethnic diversity on campus. The Court upheld the law school's admissions policy, which considered each applicant individually, but ruled against the undergraduate school's, which it held operated too much like a racial quota system. Officials at Michigan and other elite universities felt that the rulings would result in only minor changes in admissions policies, but Justice Sandra Day O'Connor expressed the belief that minority preferences will be obsolete in 25 years.

Gay Marriage

Gay-rights advocates are intensifying efforts to gain legal recognition for same-sex unions, but the campaign is facing strong opposition from social conservatives. Supporters of same-sex marriage argue that gay and lesbian couples need and deserve the same symbolic and practical benefits for their relationships as are enjoyed by heterosexuals. Opponents hold that recognizing same-sex unions will hurt traditional families at a time when marriage is already suffering from a high divorce rate and other social trends. These opposing groups also disagree sharply on the effects of raising children in gay households. In February 2004, the Massachusetts Supreme Court upheld its November 2003 ruling by confirming that only the full rights of marriage—as opposed to civil unions—are consistent with the state constitution. Meanwhile, President George W. Bush continued to seek a constitutional amendment and other measures through federal law to define marriage solely as the union of a man and a woman.

Race in America

Many people believe that the end of legal discrimination gave blacks the same chance of success as other Americans, and by any measure, African-Americans' social, economic and political standing has vastly improved since the civil rights upheavals of the 1950s and 1960s. Yet by the same measures—income, accumulation of wealth, life expectancy, education and so on—blacks lag far behind whites. Many African-Americans (and not a few whites) hold that discrimination, whether resulting from institutional practice or deliberate prejudice, prevents them from attaining jobs and homes equal to those enjoyed by whites. The 2003 Supreme Court decision upholding affirmative action in education heartened many blacks, but racially tinged incidents, such as those in Cincinnati, Benton Harbor, Michigan and Tulia, Texas, serve as reminders of the still unfolding, troubled history of race in American society.

Abortion Debates

The battle lines in the abortion issue remain clearly drawn more than 30 years after the Supreme Court's controversial *Roe v. Wade* decision established a constitutional right to the procedure. Anti-abortion groups continue to urge Congress and state legislatures to regulate abortion practices, while abortion-rights supporters counter that the measures undercut women's reproductive freedom. At the urging of President George W. Bush, Congress passed a ban on a late-term procedure that opponents call "partial-birth" abortion. The Supreme Court struck it down, holding that it violates *Roe v. Wade*. Legislative fights, however, continue unabated in the states, where more than 300 anti-abortion laws have been enacted since 1995. Meanwhile, both sides are girding for a fight should Bush have the opportunity to make an appointment to the Supreme Court.

ENVIRONMENT

SUV Debate

Sport-utility vehicles have become icons of American consumption in the past decade, changing the look of

the nation's highways. Few consumer products have attracted such adulation as well as scorn. Fans of the trucklike passenger vehicles love their spacious interiors, rugged appearance and high-off-the-ground seating. Critics see them as gas-guzzling, turnover-prone behemoths that spew pollutants and endanger the occupants of smaller cars. Like minivans, SUVs are categorized by the government as light trucks, which are held to less stringent fuel-efficiency and safety standards than cars. The Bush administration has ordered automakers to increase light-truck mileage efficiency by 1.5 miles per gallon—to 22.2 miles per gallon—during the 2005–2007 model years, but environmentalists say that is not enough.

Air Pollution Conflict

Environmentalists are outraged over Bush administration policies that they say weaken the landmark Clean Air Act. President George W. Bush's proposed "Clear Skies" initiative would allow industries to buy pollution credits from cleaner plants as an alternative to installing equipment to reduce emissions. The administration also has relaxed a long-standing rule requiring older power plants to install modern pollution-control technology when they modernize. Plant operators say the changes will make it easier to reduce harmful emissions. Environmentalists contend that they will merely reverse improvements in air quality hard won over the past three decades. Meanwhile, several smog-ridden states threatened to sue the Environmental Protection Agency following an announcement in November 2003 that it was dropping more than 50 investigations into violations of anti-pollution rules.

CIVIL LIBERTIES, CIVIL RIGHTS AND JUSTICE

Civil Liberties Debates

The administration of George W. Bush has faced strong criticism from the left and the right for its legal tactics concerning civil liberties in its war on terrorism. Critics charge the administration with infringing on constitutional rights by holding two U.S. citizens as "enemy combatants" without access to lawyers. Hundreds of foreigners captured in Afghanistan are also being held at the Guantanamo Naval Base in Cuba for trial before military tribunals. Some members of Congress are rethinking provisions of the USA Patriot Act, the sweeping law passed after the September 11 attacks that expanded the government's search-and-surveillance powers in terrorism cases. Attorney General John Ashcroft has vigorously defended the law as an essential counterterrorism tool. So far, courts have generally upheld the administration's actions, but several legal challenges were pending in 2004, including three before the Supreme Court.

School Desegregation

In May 2004, the nation celebrated the 50th anniversary of *Brown v. Board of Education,* the Supreme Court's landmark decision declaring racial segregation in public schools unconstitutional. It is widely held, however, that the promise of equal educational opportunity for all offered by the once-controversial ruling remains unfulfilled. Today, an increasing percentage of African-American and Latino students attend schools with mostly other minorities—a situation that critics blame on recent Supreme Court decisions easing judicial supervision of desegregation plans. Black and Latino students also lag far behind whites in academic achievement. School desegregation advocates call for stronger steps to break down racial and ethnic isolation and to upgrade schools that serve minority students. Critics of mandatory desegregation, however, think that more accountability, stricter academic standards and parental choice will do more to improve education for all students.

BUSINESS AND THE ECONOMY

Media Ownership

Media companies are expanding rapidly, integrating broadcast television, cable, radio, newspapers, books, magazines and the Internet under their roofs. Five conglomerates control most prime-time television programming, and one company—Clear Channel—dominates radio. Yet, in the paradox of today's media landscape, consumers have more choices than ever, although critics say too many choices are low-brow offerings, like "reality" TV. Meanwhile, such newcomers as satellite radio and Web bloggers keep sprouting. As media companies push to grow even larger, a nationwide debate rages over whether there is enough diversity of content and ownership. In June 2003, the Federal Communications Commission relaxed its media-ownership rules. Congress approved less sweeping changes in 2004.

Exporting Jobs

The U.S. economy is recovering, but employment continues to lag. Experts blame some of the joblessness on the job-exporting phenomenon known as offshoring. Well-trained, low-wage workers in India, China and other developing countries, along with the widespread availability of high-speed Internet connections, make exporting American jobs attractive. In addition, millions of foreign professionals have entered the U.S. workforce using temporary visas, while millions more undocumented foreign workers from Mexico and other parts of Latin America have found low-wage jobs in the United States thanks to lax immigration and border-control policies. Offshoring proponents claim that paying lower wages reduces the cost of goods and raises profits, ultimately enabling U.S. companies to create better-paying jobs for Americans. Critics counter that offshoring simply eliminates good jobs.

FOREIGN POLICY

Democracy in the Arab World

The monarchs and presidential strongmen who have governed Arab states since the mid-20th century have been reluctant to share power, allow free elections or permit popular dissent. Following the overthrow of Iraqi president Saddam Hussein in April 2003, President George W. Bush vowed to establish a working democracy in Iraq and to promote free elections throughout the Middle East. Efforts at democratization face daunting obstacles, however, including the Arab world's limited experience with self-rule, the huge income gap between rich and poor and the increasing appeal of radical Islamist movements. Although some experts see encouraging signs in a few countries, prospects for democracy appear dim in many others, including Egypt and Saudi Arabia, two major U.S. allies.

Nuclear Proliferation and Terrorism

The recent discovery of a global black market in nuclear weapons and related technology has intensified concerns that so-called rogue nations and organizations like Osama bin Laden's al Qaeda network might acquire nuclear devices. A network run by the "father" of Pakistan's atomic bomb, A. Q. Khan, sold nuclear-weapons materials to Iran and North Korea, which have refused to sign the Nuclear Non-Proliferation Treaty. Virtually all the other nations of the world are signatories. President George W. Bush responded to the revelations about Khan's network with a plan to strengthen international anti-proliferation efforts, including calling on the U.N. Security Council to require all states to criminalize proliferation of components that could be used to make weapons of mass destruction. While arms experts commended the president for focusing on proliferation, some thought that his proposals did not go far enough.

Preface

In this important and possibly pivotal era of American public policymaking, instructors can draw from countless controversial public policy issues to inspire classroom debate. Should the right to abortion be limited or overturned? Should same-sex unions be legally recognized? Do low-paid foreign workers hurt or help the economy? Only comprehensive and balanced examinations of such issues lead to constructive debates that weigh the intricate and at times convoluted dynamics of public policy. These kinds of exchanges engage students in class but also draw them into the public agenda that affects them beyond the classroom walls. By examining their thoughts on important issues, students begin to define their role as active participants in public policy.

The fifth edition of *Issues for Debate in American Public Policy,* an up-to-the minute collection of 16 reports from *The CQ Researcher,* illustrates just how broadly contentious policy issues affect citizens and the government they elect. *The Researcher,* a weekly policy backgrounder that provides balanced coverage of meaningful issues on the public agenda, brings complicated topics down to earth by fully explaining difficult concepts in plain English. Each report chronicles and analyzes current and past legislative and judicial activities as well as possible future actions, whether at the local, state or federal level. *Issues for Debate* is designed to promote in-depth discussion, facilitate further research and help readers think critically and formulate their own positions on crucial issues.

This collection is divided into seven areas of public policy concern. The pieces were chosen to expose students to a diversity of issues, ranging, for example, from civil rights to foreign policy. We are gratified to know that *Issues for Debate* is appealing to audiences inside and outside of education. Teachers are using it as a supplement in introductory public policy and American government courses, and active citizens, journalists and business and government leaders are turning to it to better understand key issues, actors and policy positions.

THE CQ RESEARCHER

The CQ Researcher was founded in 1923 as *Editorial Researcher Reports* and was sold primarily to newspapers as a research tool. The magazine was renamed and redesigned in 1991 as *The CQ Researcher*. While it is still used by hundreds of newspapers, some of which reprint all or part of each issue, high school, college and public libraries are now the *Researcher*'s main subscribers, making students, not journalists, its primary audience.

The *Researcher*'s staff writers—all highly experienced journalists—sometimes compare the experience of writing a *Researcher* report to drafting a college term paper. Indeed, there are many similarities: Each report is as long as many term papers—about 11,000 words—and is written by one person without any significant outside help. One of the key differences is that the writers interview leading experts and government officials for each issue. The *Researcher* won the American Bar Association's coveted Silver Gavel award for magazines in 2002 for a series of nine reports on civil liberties and other legal issues.

Like students, staff writers begin the creative process by choosing a topic. Working with the *Researcher*'s editors, the writer identifies a subject that has public policy implications and for which there is significant controversy. After a topic is selected, the writer embarks on a week or two of intense research. Articles are clipped, books ordered and information gathered from a variety of sources, including interest groups, universities and the government. Once the writer is well informed about the subject, he or she begins interviewing academics, officials, lobbyists and people working in the field. Each report usually requires a minimum of ten to fifteen interviews, although some issues covering especially complicated subjects call for more. After much reading and interviewing, the writer develops a detailed outline. Only then does the writing begin.

CHAPTER FORMAT

Each issue of the *Researcher,* and therefore each selection in this book, is structured in the same way. Each begins with an overview, which briefly touches on the areas that will be explored in greater detail in the rest of the chapter. The next section, "Issue Questions," chronicles important and current debates on the topic under discussion. It is structured around a number of key questions, such as "Is democracy taking root in the Arab world?" "Should Congress give the government additional powers in anti-terrorism cases?" This section is the core of each chapter: The questions raised are often controversial and usually the subject of much debate among those who work in and think about the field. Hence, the answers presented are never conclusive but detail the range of opinion on the topic.

Following "Issue Questions" is the "Background" section, which provides a history of the issue being examined. This look back includes important legislative measures, executive actions and court decisions that illustrate how current policy has evolved. Next, the section "Current Situation" examines contemporary policy issues, legislation under consideration and legal action being taken. Each selection concludes with "Outlook," a section that addresses possible actions and outcomes for the next five to ten years, such as new regulations, court rulings and initiatives from Capitol Hill and the White House.

Each report contains additional features that augment the main text: two or three sidebars that examine issues related to the topic, a pro versus con debate by two experts, a chronology of key dates and events, and an annotated bibliography detailing major sources used by the writer.

ACKNOWLEDGMENTS

We wish to thank many people for helping to make this collection a reality. Tom Colin, managing editor of *The CQ Researcher,* gave us his enthusiastic support and cooperation as we developed this fifth edition. He and his talented staff of editors and writers have amassed a first-class library of *Researcher* reports, and we are fortunate to have access to that rich cache. We also thankfully acknowledge the advice and feedback from current readers and are gratified by their success with the book.

Some readers of this collection may be learning about the *Researcher* for the first time. We expect that many readers will want regular access to this excellent weekly research tool. Anyone interested in subscription information or a no-obligation free trial of the *Researcher* can contact CQ Press at www.cqpress.com or 1-866-4CQ-Press (1-866-427-7737, toll-free).

We hope that you will be pleased by the fifth edition of *Issues for Debate in American Public Policy*. We welcome your feedback and suggestions for future editions. Please direct comments to Charisse Kiino, CQ Press, 1255 22nd Street, N.W., Suite 400, Washington, D.C. 20037, or *ckiino@cqpress.com.*

—*The Editors of CQ Press*

Contributors

Adriel Bettelheim is editor for social policy at *CQ Weekly*, where he previously covered science and technology. He is the author of *Aging in America A to Z* (CQ Press, 2001) and was a member of *The CQ Researcher* team that won the 1999 Society of Professional Journalists Award for Excellence for a 10-part series on health care. He has a bachelor's degree in chemistry from Case Western Reserve University.

Thomas J. Colin, managing editor of *The CQ Researcher,* has been a magazine and newspaper journalist for more than 25 years. Before joining Congressional Quarterly in 1991, he was a reporter and editor at the *Miami Herald* and *National Geographic* and editor in chief of *Historic Preservation.* He holds a bachelor's degree in English from the College of William and Mary and in journalism from the University of Missouri.

Mary H. Cooper specializes in environmental, energy and defense issues. Before joining *The CQ Researcher* as a staff writer in 1983, she was a reporter and Washington correspondent for the Roman daily *l'Unità.* She is the author of *The Business of Drugs* (CQ Press, 1990) and a contract translator-interpreter for the State Department. Cooper graduated from Hollins College with a degree in English.

Alan Greenblatt is a staff writer at *Governing* magazine. He previously covered elections, agriculture and military spending for *CQ Weekly,* where he won the National Press Club's Sandy Hume

Memorial Award for Excellence in Journalism. He graduated from San Francisco State University in 1986 and received a master's degree in English literature from the University of Virginia in 1998.

Brian Hansen is a former staff member of *The CQ Researcher* who specializes in environmental issues. He previously reported for the *Colorado Daily* in Boulder and the Environment News Service. His honors include the Scripps Howard Foundation award for public service reporting and the Education Writers Association award for investigative reporting. He holds a bachelor's degree in political science and a master's in education from the University of Colorado.

David Hatch is a freelance writer in Arlington, Virginia, who specializes in media, advertising and consumer issues. A former reporter in the Crain Communications Washington bureau, he holds a bachelor's degree in English from the University of Massachusetts, Amherst.

Benton Ives-Halperin covers House floor votes for *CQ.com,* a Congressional Quarterly online publication, and is a former assistant editor of *The CQ Researcher.* He graduated from the University of Virginia with a bachelor's degree in English.

Kenneth Jost, associate editor of *The CQ Researcher,* graduated from Harvard College and Georgetown University Law Center, where he is an adjunct professor. He is the author of the *Supreme Court Yearbook* and editor of the *Supreme Court A to Z* (both published by CQ Press). He was a member of *The CQ Researcher* team that won the 2002 American Bar Association Silver Gavel Award.

Tom Price is a freelance writer in Washington, D.C., who focuses on education, technology and business. Previously he was a correspondent in the Cox Newspapers Washington Bureau and chief politics writer for the *Journal Herald* in Dayton, Ohio, and for the *Dayton Daily News.* He is the author of three major studies on politics and the Internet published by the Foundation for Public Affairs and of *Washington, D.C. for Dummies.* His work has appeared in the *New York Times, Time, Rolling Stone* and other publications. He earned a bachelor's degree in journalism at Ohio University.

1

Rising College Costs

Tom Price

Incoming freshmen gather for their next orientation event at the University of Illinois Urbana-Champaign campus last June. Democratic Illinois Gov. Rod Blagojevich signed legislation in July guaranteeing that the tuition for in-state undergraduate students will not be raised at a state institution beginning in 2004. Across the country, tuition and fees at public colleges soared a record 14 percent this year.

From *The CQ Researcher,*
December 5, 2003.

The average undergraduate racks up student debts totaling about $18,000.[1] And then there's Erin Sandonato.

In 1997, she launched her college career at Georgia Southern University, in Statesboro, confident she would not be straining her family's pocketbook.

As a Georgia high-school graduate with at least a "B" average, she qualified for the state's HOPE scholarship program, which pays for tuition, fees and books at any public university in Georgia.

But when her parents moved to Florida, Sandonato transferred to the University of Central Florida to be closer to them. Since their income was too high to let her qualify for Florida grants — but not high enough to pay all her bills — she worked full time.

"Physically and financially, I just couldn't work 40 hours a week and take a full class load," she recalls. So after her sophomore year, she dropped out and worked for a year and a half, waiting tables and clerking in a mall.

When Sandonato returned to classes, her energy and bankroll replenished, she picked Broward Community College in Fort Lauderdale because "it was a lot less expensive" than a four-year university.

Last spring, she finally finished her bachelor's degree in public relations at the University of West Florida, in Fort Myers. Now she ponders how to pay back the $45,000 in debt she says she acquired during her six undergraduate years.

"I would have been a lot better off financially if I had stayed in Georgia," she says. "I had absolutely no idea the financial obligations that college actually has until I was in the middle of it."

College prices have been steadily rising, and millions of students like Sandonato are feeling the pinch. Indeed, her story touches on many of the major issues accompanying the soaring price of higher education, including the:

- Plight of middle-income families;
- Trend away from need-based financial aid and toward merit-based aid;
- Strains of combining work with study;
- Burden of debt;
- Difficulty in understanding the complexity of tuition pricing; and the
- Relatively low tuitions at public institutions — especially community colleges.

Tuition and fees at public colleges and universities — which award most U.S. bachelor's degrees — soared by 14.1 percent from the last academic year to this year, according to the College Board's annual report on higher-education prices, released Oct. 21. That was the sharpest increase in at least three decades, and it followed a 10 percent hike last year — the steepest since 1981. Community colleges increased tuition and fees by 13.8 percent, while costs at private four-year schools rose 6 percent.[2]

The increases raise the total cost — tuition, fees and room and board — of attending a residential, four-year state school by 9.8 percent and 5.7 percent at private institutions. The cost of attending an elite private university now can approach an eye-popping $40,000 a year, while the average private school costs $26,854 (of which $19,710 is for tuition and fees). In-state students at public four-year institutions pay an average of $10,636 (including $4,694 for tuition and fees).

These increases are just the latest hikes in a quarter-century trend of higher-education prices rocketing far above the inflation rate. Over the last decade, tuition increases at public, private and two-year institutions exceeded inflation by between 22 and 47 percent.

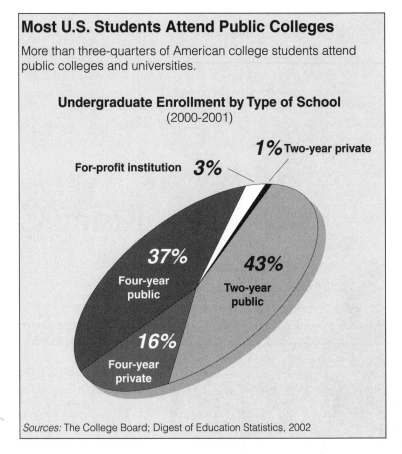

Most U.S. Students Attend Public Colleges

More than three-quarters of American college students attend public colleges and universities.

Undergraduate Enrollment by Type of School
(2000-2001)

1% Two-year private
For-profit institution *3%*
37% Four-year public
43% Two-year public
16% Four-year private

Sources: The College Board; Digest of Education Statistics, 2002

As prices rise, critics charge that colleges are wasting money on extravagant facilities, overpaid administrators and underworked faculty. Some students complain that reductions in course offerings are preventing them from graduating on time. And high-school graduates from lower-income families are finding it harder to get to college at all.

With Congress preparing to reauthorize the Higher Education Act — the primary source of federal aid for higher education — leaders of the House Education and Workforce Committee issued a report in September bluntly demanding cuts in the cost of higher education.[3]

"Decades of uncontrolled cost increases are pushing the dream of a college degree further out of reach of needy students," declared "The College Cost Crisis" report. "The crisis requires a dramatic response."

Sen. Judd Gregg, R-N.H., chairman of the Senate Health, Education, Labor and Pensions Committee, issued a similar warning at the panel's first hearing on reauthorization on Oct. 16.

Costs Rose Faster at Private Schools

The inflation-adjusted cost of a four-year education at a private university more than doubled since the mid-1970s and jumped 75 percent at public schools.

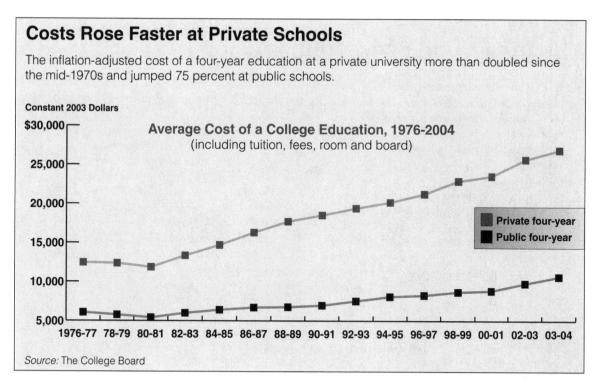

Constant 2003 Dollars

Average Cost of a College Education, 1976-2004
(including tuition, fees, room and board)

Private four-year
Public four-year

1976-77 78-79 80-81 82-83 84-85 86-87 88-89 90-91 92-93 94-95 96-97 98-99 00-01 02-03 03-04

Source: The College Board

"While tuition goes up and up, and more and more students are priced out of a college education, colleges are finding it hard to achieve efficiencies in the delivery of education," Gregg said. "Achieving greater efficiency needs to become a priority for colleges, so that a quality postsecondary education is available to everyone."

But college leaders argue that the tuition price hikes aren't as bad as they seem because financial aid lowers the "net price" that students actually pay. Furthermore, they say, more state and federal funding would reduce the need for future price increases.

College officials also insist that, despite what critics say, they are cutting costs, both through traditional steps — such as work-force reductions — and innovations in management, teaching and application of technology. (*See sidebar, p. 14.*)

Educators note, however, that state appropriations to higher-education institutions have not kept up with enrollment increases, especially since the weakening national economy began putting strains on state tax receipts beginning in about 2001.[4]

"The states have been running away from higher education," complains Terry Hartle, senior vice president for

government and public affairs at the American Council on Education. "In 1980, about 48 percent of the revenue at public colleges came from state appropriations. In 2000, it was only 35 percent."

College budgets also have been squeezed by the stock market collapse — which crunched endowments — and the sputtering economy, which has taken a toll on fundraising. Donations to colleges declined by 1.2 percent in 2002, the first drop in 14 years.[5]

As rising college prices have outpaced student aid, the proportion of American high-school graduates enrolling in college also has dropped — to 61.7 percent in 2001 from a peak of 67 percent in 1997. In 2000, the United States fell to 13th place compared with other nations in the percentage of the population studying for a bachelor's degree or higher and seventh place in the proportion pursuing a lesser degree.[6]

Still, more money is available in grants and loans today than at any time in history. Nearly $40 billion in grants was shared by nearly half of the nation's students in the 2002-03 academic year. But advocates for the poor worry that a trend away from basing aid on need is reducing assistance available to lower-income students.

Loans Provide Most Financial Aid

More financial aid — $105 billion — was available to U.S. college students last year than ever before. More than half of the aid was in the form of loans, and $48 billion came from grants.[1] Students also received and earned more than $1 billion from college work-study jobs. In addition, federal tax breaks saved students and their parents more than $5 billion.

The federal government provides about two-thirds of all student aid, most in the form of loans. Colleges and universities themselves pass out the biggest proportion of scholarships and other grants — more than $20 billion. State governments, which provide operating support to state colleges and universities, also distribute more than $5 billion in grants. Private-sector loans total nearly $7 billion a year.

Here are the top sources of student aid:[2]

Pell Grants — The federal government's primary contribution of grants to lower-income students totaled more than $11.7 billion last year. Most go to undergraduates, although some are awarded to postgraduates enrolled in teacher-certification programs. Pell Grant recipients often receive other forms of aid as well. The maximum grant this academic year is $4,050, the minimum $400. The average grant last year was $2,421.[3] A grant's size is based on a student's financial circumstances and the cost of attending his school. The program is named for former Sen. Claiborne Pell, D-R.I.

Subsidized Stafford Loans — The largest, single, source of federal education aid totaled more than $22.3 billion last year. They are awarded on the basis of student need. The maximum provided in a year ranges from $2,625 for a freshman to $8,500 for a graduate student. The federal government pays the interest until six months after the student stops attending school at least half time, and the student doesn't have to begin repaying the loan until then. Payment can be deferred longer, or even forgiven, for graduates who take certain public-service jobs. The program is named for former Sen. Robert T. Stafford, R-Vt.

Unsubsidized Stafford Loans — These loans are similar to the subsidized Stafford loans, but the government does not pay the interest, and the maximum loan available is $18,500 for a graduate student. Borrowers can postpone repaying the loan until after they leave school. The same deferment and forgiveness provisions apply.

PLUS Loans — These unsubsidized federal loans are made to parents. Repayment begins when the loan is made. The variable interest rate is capped at 9 percent. Deferment or forgiveness for public-service employment is available.

Perkins Loans — The federal government and a higher-education institution jointly finance these loans, which are awarded by the school to needy students. Undergraduates can borrow up to $4,000 annually, graduate students up to $6,000. Repayment begins nine months after the student stops attending school at least half time. Repayment can be deferred or forgiven if the student takes certain public-service employment. The

Because grants and college price tags vary widely, however, the averages paint only a fuzzy picture of how individual students fare, making it difficult for families to make informed financial decisions about college. The confusion can lead lower-income families to give up on higher education, even though grants and loans could make it affordable. At the same time, many middle-income families feel overburdened because they don't qualify for substantial grants.

As the size of individual grants lags behind the price increases, students like Sandonato are graduating with ever-higher debt loads, and a sense that working their way through school robbed them of an essential part of college life.

Sandonato talks wistfully of having wanted to "experience college not just in the classroom but in activities outside of the classroom." Instead, she says, she had time only to "work full time, take classes and worry about exams."

As families, university administrators and members of Congress wrestle with the issue of rising college costs, here are some of the questions they are debating:

Are tuitions rising because colleges waste money?

When *The New York Times* reported recently on opulent new amenities at American colleges, leaders of the House Education Committee quickly sent copies to every rep-

program is named for the late Rep. Carl D. Perkins, D-Ky.

Supplemental Educational Opportunity Grants — Undergraduate students with exceptional financial need are eligible for these grants, which range from $100 to $4,000 a year and are funded by the federal government and awarded by colleges and universities.

Work-Study — Colleges disperse these funds for the federal government to students who work to pay a portion of their college expenses. Students must be paid at least the minimum wage, and schools are encouraged to place students in public-service jobs or jobs related to their course of study, often on campus. The amount a student can earn is based on financial need.

HOPE Scholarship Tax Credits — First- or second-year college students — or their parents — can use these credits to reduce their federal income tax payments by up to $1,500 a year, depending on financial need, college costs and other available financial aid.[4]

Lifetime Learning Credit — Tax credits of up to $1,000 are available to students who are beyond the second year of college or are taking classes parttime to upgrade their job skills. Amounts depend on financial need, college costs and other available financial aid.[5]

Institutional Grants — Colleges offer these scholarships from their own funds. Some are based on financial need. Others, awarded on merit, go to athletes, outstanding scholars and other students who are particularly attractive to college admissions and financial-aid officers. On private campuses, nearly 60 percent of students received institutional grants last year.

State Grants — States are shifting away from awarding grants on the basis of need: 90 percent of all state grants a decade ago were need-based, compared with 76 percent last year. While state grants overall are only one-third the size of the federal grant programs, state grants have grown twice as fast over the last decade. Grants vary from state to state. Georgia's HOPE program, for instance, pays for tuition, fees and books at any public higher-education institution in the state for any graduate of a Georgia high school with at least a "B" average who maintains a "B" average and Georgia residency while in college.[6] New York's Tuition Assistance Program, which awards annual scholarships worth up to $5,000, is based on need.[7]

---

[1] "Trends in Student Aid, 2003," The College Board. Available online at http://www.collegeboard.com/prod_downloads/press/cost03/cb_trends_aid_2003.pdf

[2] Unless otherwise noted, financial aid information is from the U.S. Education Department Web site: http://www.ed.gov/finaid/landing.jhtml?src=rt

[3] Statistics from "Trends in Student Aid, 2003," and the Education Department Web site, *op. cit.*

[4] Department of Education, "The HOPE Scholarship and Lifetime Learning Credits;" online at http://ed.gov/offices/OPE/PPI/HOPE/index.html

[5] *Ibid.*

[6] Georgia Student Finance Commission, "Georgia's Hope Scholarship Program." Available online at http://www.gsfc.org/HOPE/Index.cfm

[7] New York Higher Education Services Corp., "Tuition Assistance Program: New York's TAP Can Help You Pay for College!" Available online at http://www.hesc.com/bulletin.nsf/0/3CA243796A98D19D85256D88006B4AD3?OpenDocument&a=PF

---

resentative and to journalists who cover education. In a cover letter, Chairman John A. Boehner, R-Ohio, and Higher Education Subcommittee Chairman Howard "Buck" McKeon, R-Calif., lamented "the increasing availability of lavish facilities on campuses across America and how this trend is driving up the cost of higher education."[7]

Similarly, when the College Board's latest report on college prices noted the relationship between declining state appropriations and rising tuition at public schools, Boehner immediately issued a statement decrying higher education's reluctance to admit its own responsibility for the soaring cost of college.

"Hyperinflation in college costs has been pummeling parents and students for more than a decade," he said, "and the problem has not been a lack of spending by the states or federal government. Even when states were increasing their investment in higher education in recent years, college tuition was skyrocketing."

Referring to the *Times* report, Boehner charged that "extravagant spending by institutions for everything from super-size Jacuzzis and sunbathing decks to massage facilities and rock-climbing walls is contributing significantly to the soaring cost of college."

Adding to the allegations of extravagance are periodic reports about high-paid athletic coaches and college presidents, along with questions about generous faculty salaries and light workloads.

The Chronicle of Higher Education has reported that four private college presidents earned more than $800,000 in 2002, and 27 earned at least $500,000, for example. A dozen state education executives also were members of the "half-million-dollar club," and two liberal arts college presidents earned more than $400,000.[8]

Such reports make college administrators and their supporters cringe. They say many students (and parents) want fancy amenities, and that colleges must compete for the best students.

At the same time, they insist that institutions have to pay top dollar to get top-quality executives. But, they point out, in the context of total college costs, presidential pay has no real impact on prices. And besides, relatively few institutions acquire lavish recreational facilities or extravagantly paid executives anyway, they say.

It's not fair to compare college prices to the overall inflation rate, college executives add, because educational institutions are labor intensive with unique expenses.

"Higher education is a people-heavy business," says Travis Reindl, director of state policy analysis at the American Association of State Colleges and Universities. "And it's not just about paying them. It's also about employee benefits. Look at where health-care costs have gone in the last few years. Talk about being above the rate of inflation!"

Colleges also come under fire because of the seemingly light workloads enjoyed by high-priced, tenured faculty. A 1998 survey by the National Center for Education Statistics (NCES) concluded that the average classroom-teaching load was 11 hours a week.[9]

But while professors may spend only 11 hours in the classroom, according to the NCES survey, they work an additional 45.6 hours each week on research, administration, advising students and other duties.[10]

Because colleges are so labor intensive, they have trouble increasing productivity, says Naomi Richman, manager of the higher-education rating team at Moody's Investors Service.

"In most areas of the economy, you have productivity gains over time, so a factory can produce the same amount of widgets at lower cost," she says. "If teachers are teaching 20 kids in the classroom, if they [start teaching 30], that's considered watering down the product."

Many college employees also require expensive tools, pointed out Ronald Ehrenberg, director of the Cornell Higher Education Research Institute. "Theoretical scientists, who in a previous generation required only desks and pencils and papers, now often require supercomputers," Ehrenberg noted. "Experimental scientists increasingly rely on sophisticated laboratory facilities that are increasingly expensive to build and operate."[11]

Moreover, college executives tend to be paid less than their counterparts in private industry, according to Sandy Baum, a Skidmore College economics professor who analyzes higher-education finance for the College Board. For most teachers, she adds, "making a decision to be a faculty member is a decision that money is not what your life is about." Teachers "work very hard," she says. "They put a lot of time into their teaching and research — and research is a very important part of what faculty members do."

"I don't think higher education has done a very good job of explaining its efforts to hold down costs," University System of Maryland Chancellor William Kirwan said at a roundtable hosted by McKeon's subcommittee on Sept. 30. Because of recent state subsidy cuts, "we eliminated 800 positions — about 4 percent of our staff. We have not had raises for faculty and staff going on three years."

Nevertheless, some education scholars say colleges could still make themselves more efficient. "There's less innovation in higher education" than in other organizations, says Patrick M. Callan, president of the National Center for Public Policy and Higher Education. "Recessions usually force choices on organizations and squeeze out excess. But in higher education, we simply shift the [burden to pay] onto the students."

Carol Twigg, executive director of Rensselaer Polytechnic Institute's Center for Academic Transformation, is demonstrating how innovation with information technology can cut costs and improve teaching effectiveness. (*See sidebar, p. 14.*) The center is helping colleges redesign courses to cut the time teachers spend lecturing, grading tests and carrying out administrative tasks. Retooling the teaching process is enabling teachers to teach more students and in most cases teach them more effectively.

Thirty demonstration projects have cut costs an average of 40 percent, Twigg says. Meanwhile, "significant increases in student learning" were measured in 22 of the projects, and the others matched the effectiveness of traditional teaching methods.

Should government increase funding for higher education?

Nearly $12 billion was appropriated during the 2002-2003 academic year for Pell Grants, the primary source of federal grants for low-income students. (*See sidebar, p. 4.*)[12] The amount represents a 48 percent inflation-adjusted increase in a decade.

"If anyone told me 15 years ago that we'd have $12 billion in Pell Grants by now," Callan says, "I'd have said we'd probably pretty much have solved the problems of access to education."

But the access is not there, spurring debate about whether state and federal governments are short-changing America's institutions of higher education. Even though federal spending on higher-education grants has increased substantially, it has not kept pace with rapidly rising college prices and enrollments.

The inflation-adjusted price of attending college — tuition, fees and room and board — rose between 32 and 39 percent over the last 10 years, with the smallest percentage increase occurring at public four-year institutions and the highest at public two-year schools. And while Pell Grant expenditures jumped 48 percent during that decade, the number of grant recipients rose only 20 percent. As a result, the average Pell Grant pays a smaller portion of the average student's expenses than it did a decade ago.[13]

Last year, the average Pell Grant was $2,421, enough to pay a live-at-home student's tuition and fees at the typical community college. But it paid just a quarter of the average tuition, fees, room and board at four-year state schools, and covered only about one-tenth of those charges at the average private college.[14]

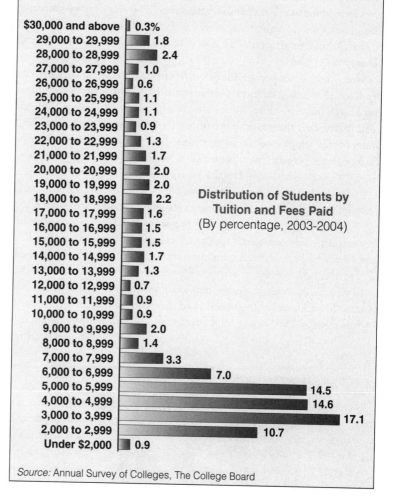

Most Students Pay Less Than $7,000

Two-thirds of the full-time undergraduates at American four-year colleges pay less than $7,000 a year in tuition and fees. About 14 percent spend at least $20,000.

Distribution of Students by Tuition and Fees Paid
(By percentage, 2003-2004)

Tuition and Fees	Percentage
$30,000 and above	0.3%
29,000 to 29,999	1.8
28,000 to 28,999	2.4
27,000 to 27,999	1.0
26,000 to 26,999	0.6
25,000 to 25,999	1.1
24,000 to 24,999	1.1
23,000 to 23,999	0.9
22,000 to 22,999	1.3
21,000 to 21,999	1.7
20,000 to 20,999	2.0
19,000 to 19,999	2.0
18,000 to 18,999	2.2
17,000 to 17,999	1.6
16,000 to 16,999	1.5
15,000 to 15,999	1.5
14,000 to 14,999	1.7
13,000 to 13,999	1.3
12,000 to 12,999	0.7
11,000 to 11,999	0.9
10,000 to 10,999	0.9
9,000 to 9,999	2.0
8,000 to 8,999	1.4
7,000 to 7,999	3.3
6,000 to 6,999	7.0
5,000 to 5,999	14.5
4,000 to 4,999	14.6
3,000 to 3,999	17.1
2,000 to 2,999	10.7
Under $2,000	0.9

Source: Annual Survey of Colleges, The College Board

And the $4,050 maximum available under a Pell Grant — available only to dependent students from families whose income is around $20,000 or less — falls far short of most students' expenses, says Reindl of the American Association of State Colleges and Universities. "The size of available grants declines as family income rises, up to $50,000, at which point, "you're pretty much out of it," Reindl explains.

As a result, more students are borrowing more money: Loans comprised 54 percent of student aid last year, up from about 45 percent a decade earlier. In the huge California community-college system alone, more than 90,000 students or potential students dropped out or failed to enroll this academic year because of tuition hikes and course cuts caused by inadequate state support, according to Chancellor Thomas Nussbaum. "The very idea of what public higher education should be is being eroded," he complained. "That's 100,000 people. Gone."[15]

Meanwhile, state appropriations — the largest source of revenue for public colleges — have not kept up with enrollment increases either. In fact, as enrollments have been increasing, the states' share of higher-education budgets has dipped to "a dangerously low point," College Board president and former West Virginia Gov. Gaston Caperton said at an Oct. 21 press conference.

Over the last three years, states faced a collective $200 billion budget gap, largely due to already enacted tax cuts, the sluggish economy and pressures from a growing anti-tax movement.[16] As a result, about half the states reduced higher-education appropriations for the current academic year by an average of 5 percent.

In Kentucky, for example, the state's contribution to Murray State University's general fund dropped from 64.5 percent in 2001-02 to 58.4 percent in 2003-04,

university President F. King Alexander said.[17] At the University System of Maryland over the last decade, as enrollment climbed 25 percent, state support did not keep up, Chancellor Kirwan noted.

Higher-education advocates want the state and federal governments to jack up their education spending, particularly for Pell Grants and other aid to lower-income students. The Coalition for Better Student Loans — including financial-aid administrators, parents, lenders and higher-education organizations — wants federal loan programs for other students enhanced as well. The group asked Congress for larger subsidized loans, reduced fees, more flexible repayment options and an additional $1 billion to forgive loans to graduates who take hard-to-fill jobs at modest pay, such as teaching in low-income communities.

Many state officials would increase higher-education spending if their state budgets would allow it, and leading congressional Democrats want to raise federal assistance. But Republican leaders in Congress are skeptical about the need for more U.S. aid for higher education.

The federal government provided two-thirds of all student aid last year: $15.8 billion in grants, $1.2 billion in work-study funds, $5.4 billion in tax credits and $49 billion in guaranteed and subsidized loans.[18] Those amounts represent a substantial increase above inflation in all categories over the decade, the GOP lawmakers note.

"We have been putting more and more money into higher education, and we just can't keep up" with rising college prices, McKeon says. "We fall further and further behind as the schools increase their tuition and fees, and as the states lower their help for schools."

The pattern makes McKeon wonder if raising federal aid to students actually encourages colleges to raise prices so they can gobble up the federal increase. Boehner entertains similar thoughts about state spending decisions. "It does seem pretty clear that the more the federal government was doing, the states looked over and said, 'Maybe we don't have to do as much,' " Boehner says.

The Bush administration appears to be of a similar mind. "The color of change is not always green," Deputy Assistant Education Secretary Jeffrey Andrade told an independent advisory committee on financial aid in April. "I urge the committee not to take the easy way out and argue that all we need is money."[19]

AP Photo/Gene Boyars

Freshmen Lauren Bassos, left, and Jennifer Buono attend Brookdale Community College in Lincroft, N.J., instead of a four-year college. Community and online institutions are becoming increasingly popular as costs at four-year public and private schools outpace inflation.

Size of Pell Grants Has Dropped

The total amount spent on Pell Grants for low-income students has risen over the last 30 years (top graph), but due to rising enrollments the inflation-adjusted amount of the maximum grant (bottom graph) has declined since peaking in 1975-76.

Expenditures (in $ billions)

Federal Pell Grant Expenditures
(1973-2003, in constant 2003 dollars)

Amount of grant

Maximum Pell Grant Awards Per Student
(1973-2003, in constant 2003 dollars)

Source: The College Board

Should colleges be penalized for raising prices?

House Republicans want to take a stick to rising college prices.

The Affordability in Higher Education Act, introduced by McKeon in October, would deny some federal funds to institutions that raise tuition and fees substantially above the overall inflation rate.[20]

The measure would establish a "College Affordability Index," defined as twice the Consumer Price Index. If a college raised tuition and fees by more than the index over a two-year period — with some exceptions — it would be required to explain to the U.S. Education Department the reasons for the price hike and provide a plan for holding down prices in the future.

If the college continued to exceed the index for three more years, it would lose any federal student aid dispersed on campus, such as work-study funds and Perkins loans. The federal government would continue to offer students direct aid, such as Pell Grants and Stafford loans, although the size of the loans could be restricted.

"The federal government should not have to automatically subsidize hyperinflation in college costs," Education and Workforce Committee aide David Schnittger argues.

McKeon describes the threat to cut federal aid as about the only weapon Congress can wield against price increases. "There is no pressure on [colleges] to keep their rates down," he explains. "What's their incentive? I come from the retail business. When customers didn't come in, I had to get them in by lowering prices, holding sales. Colleges and universities don't have that mentality."

But as Callan points out and as a former clothing store owner like McKeon can appreciate, when demand goes up in a free market, there is no natural incentive to lower prices. "Higher education is kind of in the driver's seat right now," Callan says. "Families that have a generation or two of experience with college understand that the worst thing that could happen to your child is not to go to college. We're sort of the cartel that controls access to the middle class, and we're taking the opportunity to leverage up prices, as any private-sector, for-profit enterprise would.

"Right now, hardly any college that's very attractive feels that it's going to lose enrollment by raising prices."

Nevertheless, McKeon insists that Congress is determined to get colleges to hold tuition down. "We're serious about doing it," he says, and the measure must "have teeth . . . or it's not going to work."

Even some opponents of the legislation acknowledge the congressional frustration that's driving McKeon's proposal. "I sympathize," says Peter Magrath, president of the National Association of State Universities and Land Grant Colleges. "I think he is right to raise the issue. He's got our attention, and rightly so."

Callan says that while he doesn't support McKeon's proposal, "It's kind of hard to argue against it. [Funding] is the only leverage the federal government has."

But Magrath, Callan and others point out that the measure amounts to a form of federal price control, normally opposed by Republicans and conservatives. Price controls never work, the educators argue, adding that McKeon's plan also would hurt innocent students. (For his part, McKeon contends that his proposal is not a form of price control because it does not prevent colleges

> **"Higher education is kind of in the driver's seat right now. Families that have a generation or two of experience with college understand that the worst thing that could happen to your child is not to go to college. We're sort of the cartel that controls access to the middle class, and we're taking the opportunity to leverage up prices, as any private-sector, for-profit enterprise would. "**
>
> — **Patrick M. Callan,**
> President, National Center for
> Public Policy and Higher Education

from raising fees if they are willing to accept cuts in federal aid.)

"Increases in tuition in community colleges are the direct result of cutbacks in state appropriations," says George Boggs, president and chief executive officer of the American Association of Community Colleges. "It doesn't make any sense to penalize those colleges or their students — who are among the most needy students in higher education — because of something they can't control."

"If you throw schools out of the [federal aid] programs, that just means there isn't money for the students," argues Reindl, of the American Association of State Colleges and Universities. "And your stick is going to come down disproportionately on the lower-income students."

The American Council on Education's Hartle points out that the problem with college finances is multi-

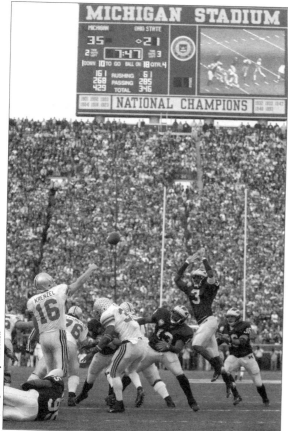

The Ohio State Buckeyes play the Michigan Wolverines in front of 112,118 fans at Michigan Stadium on Nov. 22. Critics oppose big athletic programs as well as lavish college facilities like Jacuzzis and rock-climbing walls. But educators say sports programs and fancy amenities cost relatively little and are necessary to attract students.

After publicly floating his idea early in the year, McKeon tweaked the final version of the bill to address criticism that his focus on the percentage of price increases would discriminate against the least expensive institutions.

As introduced, the bill would exempt the least expensive quarter of institutions in each higher-education category (community colleges, public four-year institutions, private four-year institutions and so forth). It also would exempt schools whose price increases only exceeded the index by less than $500.

McKeon acknowledges that pegging the index at twice the inflation rate was arbitrary. "It's a number I kind of picked," he said at the press conference during which he unveiled the bill. "We could have said three times or one time. We said twice, thinking that would be conservative."

BACKGROUND

Exclusive Clubs

For 300 years, America's college campuses remained fairly exclusive venues, even though Ann Radcliffe set up a scholarship fund at Harvard College in 1643, the North Carolina General Assembly chartered a state university in 1789 and the Morrill Act supplied federal support for practical education at public universities in 1862.[21]

By 1869, approximately 52,000 students were enrolled at U.S. colleges — about as many as now attend the University of Texas in Austin. About 9,300 of the students were awarded bachelor's degrees the following spring, and one got a Ph.D [22]

In 1901, access to education broadened with the opening of the first public "junior" college, in Joliet, Ill. — a partnership of the University of Chicago and Joliet Township High School.[23] The number of two-year schools grew rapidly, and by 1940 students were studying on 575 two-year campuses across the country. But most were private institutions, and many were highly selective.[24]

Congress' decision after World War II to underwrite college educations for returning veterans established today's widespread belief that every American should be able to attend college and the federal government should help make that possible. The Servicemen's Readjustment

pronged, caused by decisions made by many parties, including state and federal governments, students' families and colleges themselves. "McKeon is saying to colleges and universities: 'It's your problem; you solve it.' But taking a four-cornered financing scheme, and expecting one corner to fix the concerns, doesn't make a great deal of sense."

In addition, warns Skidmore's Baum, McKeon's idea of capping tuition could make colleges less accessible to the needy because colleges provide aid for disadvantaged students from tuition proceeds. "If you are going to be penalized for raising your tuition too much," she explains, "a good strategy would be to cut tuition and not spend money on need-based aid."

CHRONOLOGY

1800s *Federal government steps into public higher education.*

1862 Congress passes the Morrill Act to help states establish public universities.

1869 About 52,000 students are enrolled in U.S. colleges.

1900-1960 *Higher education begins to become mass education.*

1901 University of Chicago and Joliet Township High School establish first public junior college, in Joliet, Ill.

1939 College enrollment hits 1.5 million.

1940 Students take courses at 575 two-year colleges. Most are private institutions; many are highly selective.

1944 Congress passes "GI Bill," giving returning World War II veterans the wherewithal to attend college.

1947 College enrollment hits 2.3 million.

1950 Students pay less than 9 percent of cost of public college education.

1952 For first time, more students attend public colleges than private ones.

1959 College enrollment hits 3.6 million.

1960-1980 *Federal government becomes a big-time higher-education bankroller.*

1963 Congress authorizes $1.2 billion for three years of college construction projects, 40 percent earmarked for community and technical colleges.

1964 Federal work-study program begins. Four-year public college tuition and fees average less than $300 a year.

1965 Congress passes Higher Education Act, creating Guaranteed Student Loans, later named for Sen. Robert T. Stafford, R-Vt. For the first time, a majority of high school graduates goes on to college.

1969 College enrollment reaches 8 million, an unprecedented and unrepeated 122 percent increase in 10 years.

1972 Congress establishes federal grants for lower-income students, later named for Sen. Claiborne Pell, D-R.I.

1976 Tuition and fees for one year cost about $600 at average public four-year college.

1978 Middle-class students share in federal assistance, as Congress expands eligibility for Pell Grants and makes student loans available for all income levels.

1980-2003 *College prices skyrocket and governments provide more aid to middle and upper classes.*

1980 Parent Loans for Undergraduate Students — PLUS Loans — enable parents to borrow for their children's education, regardless of family income. States appropriate 44 percent of state colleges' spending.

1990 College enrollment hits 13.8 million.

1993 Georgia establishes HOPE Scholarship Program for "B"-or-better students regardless of financial need, establishing model for other states and federal government.

1997 Federal government provides more federal aid for middle class through tax credits, deductions for student loan interest and tax-free college savings accounts. Two-thirds of high school graduates attend college — a historical high.

1999 State appropriations to public colleges drop to 32.3 percent of the schools' budgets. Students' share of public college cost rises to 18.5 percent.

2000 Colleges enroll 15.3 million.

2001 Percentage of high-school grads attending college drops to 61.7.

2002 Need-blind state grants account for 24 percent of all state grants, up from 10 percent 10 years earlier.

2003 Tuition and fees at public four-year colleges average $4,694, more than 15 times higher than in 1964. Private four-year colleges average $19,710, two-year public schools, $1,905.

Act of 1944 — known as the GI Bill — provided that aid, and vets by the millions grabbed at the opportunity.

By 1947, college attendance had soared to 2.3 million from 1.5 million in 1939. A growing proportion of students became the first from their families to study beyond high school. By 1952, public institutions eclipsed private schools as the primary place to earn a degree as working- and middle-class students took advantage of lower public school tuition. That trend would accelerate in succeeding decades.

The returning soldiers also fathered children in record numbers, setting the stage for another enrollment boom that a generation later would combine with President Lyndon B. Johnson's Great Society programs to make federal funds even more important to higher education.

The Soviet Union's 1957 launch of the first satellite, *Sputnik*, spurred Congress to pass the National Defense Education Act the next year. The bill created the National Defense Student Loan Program for studying in fields considered critical to the national defense, such as math, science and foreign languages. The loans — the first federal aid to students who were not military veterans — later were renamed National Direct Student Loans.

In 1963, the Higher Education Facilities Act authorized $1.2 billion in federal spending over three years for college and university construction projects, with 40 percent set aside to help states build new community and technical colleges. In 1964, Congress passed the Economic Opportunity Act, which created the college work-study program within its anti-poverty provisions.

In 1965, for the first time, the number of public two-year community colleges exceeded the number of public four-year schools, although — as today — full-time-equivalent enrollment (FTE) remained higher at the four-year institutions. Thanks to their affordability, convenient locations and evening classes, community colleges attracted lower-income, live-at-home students and older working students.

Also that year, Congress passed the Higher Education Act, which today remains the primary source of federal money for colleges, universities and their students. The law authorized Education Opportunity Grants, allocated to colleges for distribution among lower-income students, and created Guaranteed Student Loans, which later were named for Sen. Robert T. Stafford, R-Vt.

President Bush, House Education Committee Chairman John Boehner, R-Ohio, and Sen. Edward M. Kennedy, D-Mass., share a laugh before Bush signed the landmark No Child Left Behind Act last January at Hamilton High School, in Hamilton, Ohio. Boehner has been critical of colleges and universities for not holding costs down.

In 1972, Congress established direct federal grants to lower-income students, later named for a key supporter, Sen. Claiborne Pell, D-R.I. The federal government also began to provide matching funds for state financial-aid plans and created the Student Loan Marketing Association (now known as SLM Corp., or Sallie Mae) to facilitate the student-borrowing market by buying and selling the debts.

Need-Blind Aid

With middle-class families increasingly complaining about rising college prices, Congress in 1978 passed the Middle Income Student Assistance Act, which expanded eligibility for Pell Grants and made federal loans available to students of all income levels. In the late '80s and throughout the '90s, Congress created several tax benefits to mitigate higher-education expenses — measures that benefit the middle and upper classes more than the poor.

To counter a "brain drain" of promising students leaving their home states for college, several states created scholarship programs that weren't based on need. Some were available to any high-school graduate who qualified for college. Others were merit-based.

Some advocates for the poor warned that providing aid for the middle class would divert aid from the poor and make it more difficult for needy students to attend college. But tax breaks and merit scholarships "have

Innovation Cuts Costs — and Improves Teaching

The Math Emporium at Virginia Polytechnic Institute and State University in Blacksburg, Va., is open 24 hours a day, nearly 365 days a year. Sprawling over the vast, acre-plus first floor of a remodeled department store, the facility provides math students with 500 desktop computers. Opened in 1997, the facility enabled Tech to redesign its math courses to cut costs, free teachers from routine work and turn out better-educated, happier students.

Up the East Coast in Connecticut, Fairfield University biology students participate in interactive computer exercises during lectures and use their laptops — rather than scalpels — to dissect animals during lab sessions. By conveying information more efficiently, computers have cut the time students must spend in introductory courses, thus reducing the Jesuit school's need for adjunct professors.

Down south at Florida Gulf Coast University in Fort Myers — the self-proclaimed "fastest growing public university in the nation" — the introductory Understanding the Visual and Performing Arts class is taught with CD-ROMs, videotapes and Web pages. The electronic tools enable each faculty member to teach more students while giving students a more vivid understanding of the arts. The electronic approach has cut the use of adjunct teachers and boosted average student grades by a full letter.[1]

Across the country, colleges and universities are seeking to innovate their way to lower costs — and many are dis-

The Mathematics Technology Learning Center at the University of Alabama offers 240 computers 70 hours a week. The program has boosted passing grades in intermediate algebra by 50 percent.

Courtesy University of Alabama

covering they can improve educational quality at the same time. The trend has mounted a frontal assault on the traditional notion that colleges can't become more productive because faculty can teach only a certain number of students at a time.

"Higher-education leaders say you can't do anything about costs because they honestly believe it," says Carol Twigg, executive director of the Center for Academic Transformation at Rensselaer Polytechnic Institute in upstate New York. Innovators are "trying to change the nature of the conversation and say 'you can reduce costs, and there are lots of ways you can do it.'"

Wielding grants from the Pew Charitable Trusts, the center is encouraging schools to apply technology to the cause of academic productivity. "Higher education has a flawed production mode," Twigg says. "We teach classes in repetitive little cells. With the typical freshman English course or algebra course in a large institution, you've got 50 classes with 50 faculty members all doing the exact same thing — standing in front of a class of 30 students."

But much content delivery can be shifted from faculty lectures to interactive computer programs, she says. The computers can quiz the students and immediately tell them how well they're grasping the subject matter. The students can work with the computers whenever it's most convenient while interacting with teachers when they need personalized help.

"You utilize technology to take on tasks the technology can take on and free up faculty time and enable them to do other things," Twigg explains.

About half of the class hours in community colleges and a third in four-year institutions are consumed in just 25 core courses, Twigg says. Many are introductory courses with high failure rates — 50 to 60 percent at community colleges and from 15 to 40 percent at

The 500-computer Math Emporium at Virginia Polytechnic Institute and State University in Blacksburg, Va., helps cut costs, free teachers from routine work and turn out better students.

four-year schools. Making these courses less labor-intensive and more effective can have a huge impact on college costs and student success.

Virginia Tech is a leader in course redesign. The Mathematics Department began computer teaching in two freshman calculus courses in 1992. The approach proved so popular and effective that the department began redesigning other courses. Five years later, the Emporium was launched.

Tech math students can use any Internet connection to access self-paced tutorials, teachers' notes and streaming video lectures. In the Emporium, they can get around-the-clock help from faculty members and tutors.

Tech, Fairfield and Florida Gulf Coast are among 30 schools that received $200,000 Pew grants to work with Twigg's program. The redesigned courses have reduced costs an average 40 percent, Twigg says, while doing a better job of teaching than traditional courses.

On 22 of the campuses, students in redesigned courses tested better than students in traditional courses, she says. At the eight other schools, the students scored about the same.

On benchmark exams at Fairfield, for instance, students in redesigned courses got 88 percent of the questions correct compared with 79 percent in traditional courses. The redesigned courses experienced a 3 percent dropout rate compared with 8 percent in previous years. Eighty-five percent of students enrolled for a second semester of biology after taking the redesigned first-semester course, up from 75 percent.

At Florida Gulf Coast, 54 percent of students in the redesigned course earned "A" or "B" grades, up from 31 percent in the traditional course. "D"s and "F"s dropped to 21 percent from 45 percent.

But course redesign is not the only cost-cutting innovation on campus. Members of the Wisconsin Association of Independent Colleges and Universities, for instance, are collaborating on back-office operations to tap economies of scale they can't produce individually. The schools anticipate savings on such areas as health insurance, information technology, purchasing, travel management, billing, staff training and financial administration.[2]

Other institutions are offering tuition discounts to encourage students to take evening, weekend and summer classes to make better use of facilities.

Meanwhile, the cell phone is playing an increasingly important role on campuses, as it is everywhere else. Long-distance calling from dormitory telephones has faded as a source of college revenue now that most students carry their own cell phones. During the 2001-02 academic year, for instance, Miami University of Ohio's phone income dropped $300,000.

So schools are taking a new tack: This year, in an effort to recoup its losses, Miami joined a growing number of schools that — like the corner grocery store — are selling cell phone plans to their students.[3]

[1] Information about these and other innovative uses of information technology can be found on the Web site of the Center for Academic Transformation, Rensselaer Polytechnic Institute: http://center.rpi. edu.

[2] Rolf Wegenke, president, Wisconsin Association of Independent Colleges and Universities, testimony before the House Education and the Workforce Committee, 21st Century Competitiveness Subcommittee, July 10, 2003. Available online at http://edworkforce. house.gov/hearings.

[3] Mary Beth Marklein, "Colleges Catch Cellphone Wave," *USA Today*, Oct. 29, 2003, p. 5D.

become enormously popular with middle-class families who also tend to be voters," notes Sandra Ruppert, a program director with the Education Commission of the States. Need-blind state grants increased from 10 percent of all state grants in 1992 to 24 percent in 2002.[25]

The combination of new federal-aid provisions, expanded state facilities and the arrival on campus of the Baby Boomers sent enrollments skyrocketing — from 3.6 million in the fall of 1959 to 8 million in 1969, an unprecedented 122 percent jump that would never be surpassed. Over the next 30 years, growing at slower rates, enrollments reached 15.3 million in 2000.

From an enclave for the elite, the college campus evolved into the normal next stop for the typical high-school graduate. In 1965, for the first time, a majority of high-school grads enrolled in college. By 1997, two-thirds were taking that step.

Federal financial aid soared along with enrollments. Spending on Pell Grants, for instance, rose from $48 million in the 1973-74 academic year to the current $11.7 billion. During the 30-year period, the minimum grant increased faster than inflation — from $50 to $400 this year, as did the maximum grant, which went up from $452 to $4,050. But, because of year-to-year fluctuations in funding, inflation-adjusted grants generally had more purchasing power in the '70s than today, and the minimum grants were worth more through most of the '90s than they are now.

State appropriations to public colleges also tended to increase over the years, with variations among the states according to economic conditions. From 1980-81 to 1999-2000, for instance, state appropriations increased from $19 billion to nearly $51 billion, a pace more than a third faster than inflation.

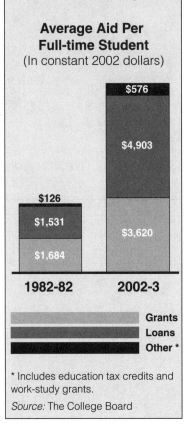

Students Borrow More Today

Loans account for nearly 55 percent of the average student's $9,099 aid package today compared with 45 percent 20 years ago.

Average Aid Per Full-time Student
(In constant 2002 dollars)

1982-82
- $126 Other
- $1,531 Loans
- $1,684 Grants

2002-3
- $576 Other
- $4,903 Loans
- $3,620 Grants

Grants
Loans
Other *

* Includes education tax credits and work-study grants.
Source: The College Board

Yet college spending rose even faster. Four-year state colleges spent $34.7 billion in 1980-81 and nearly $125 billion in 1999-2000, an increase more than 50 percent above the inflation rate. Even accounting for rising enrollments, spending-per-student exceeded inflation by a third on both four-year and two-year campuses.

Thus, even though state appropriations went up, states' share of college budgets declined from 44 percent in 1980-81 to 32.3 percent in 1999-2000. And, in the last few years, declining tax receipts have led many states to reduce appropriations.

So students — or their parents — have had to make up the difference. When the first Baby Boomers hit campus in 1964, average tuition and fees were less than $300 a year at public four-year schools, and the full cost of tuition, fees, room and board was less than $1,000.[26]

Since then, according to a College Board study, the full price for a four-year degree has increased at more than twice the inflation rate on private campuses and at 75 percent above inflation at public schools.[27] Over the last decade, tuition at public four-year schools rose four times faster than the median family income.[28]

Thus, as states' share of college budgets declined, the proportion covered by students' tuition and fees more than doubled, from less than 9 percent in 1950 to 18.5 percent in 1999. The rest was covered by federal and local governments, private gifts, endowment earnings and charges for products and services, such as room and board.

In the final analysis, public schools no longer offer the same bargain for middle-class students they did when the first boomers plunked down $300 for tuition and fees. And federal grants for lower-income students don't cover as large a portion of college charges as they did in the program's early years.

CURRENT SITUATION

Democratic Proposals

As Congress prepares to reauthorize the Higher Education Act in 2004, Democrats are rolling out expensive, new spending proposals, but Republican leaders aren't interested in significant hikes.

Meanwhile, realizing they aren't likely to get much from the current administration and Congress, college executives are searching for new ways to cut costs and raise funds. At the same time, schools in several states are fending off lawsuits aimed at undoing recent price hikes.

"Just as Social Security is a promise of retirement security to senior citizens, just as Medicare is a promise of health security to senior citizens, so we should make education security a promise to every young American," Sen. Edward M. Kennedy, D-Mass., said in introducing the College Quality, Affordability and Diversity Improvement Act, on Oct. 28. "If you work hard, if you finish high school, if you are admitted to a college, we should guarantee that you can afford the cost of the four years it takes to earn a degree."[29]

Introducing the similar College Opportunity for All Act in the House on Sept. 25, Rep. George Miller, D-Calif., lamented, "too many low- and middle-income students and their families are struggling with soaring college costs, taking on mountains of debt and working long hours that hurt their academics and overall college experience." His bill would "increase college opportunities for millions of Americans through smart investments and innovations," he said.[30]

Kennedy and Miller — the senior Democrats on the Senate and House education committees — want to:

- Increase the size of Pell Grants;
- Expand the work-study program;
- Forgive more of the loans for graduates who take public-service jobs;
- Allow borrowers to refinance loans at lower rates; and
- Allow working students to earn more money before having their aid reduced.

Miller's bill would establish a pilot program of year-round Pell Grants for students who want to complete their studies quicker, raise the maximum Pell Grant from the current $4,050 to $11,600 by 2011 and raise the maximum public-service loan forgiveness from $5,000 to $17,500.

Kennedy would raise the maximum Pell Grant to $4,500 immediately and make more students eligible. He would raise the maximum loan forgiveness to $15,000 and would increase the value of federal tax credits and deductions for college expenses.

The Senate legislation also would offer additional federal funds to states that don't cut their appropriations to colleges by more than 10 percent in a year. It would waive antitrust laws to allow the secretary of Education to convene a "college cost summit," at which educators could negotiate agreements for holding down prices. It also would require colleges to publish clear information about their prices and financial-aid practices, so students could get a better picture of actual charges.

Kennedy estimated the cost of his bill at $15 billion a year and said he would cover most of the costs by repealing tax breaks on dividends and capital gains and by reducing lenders' profits from student loans.

The Democrats' bills respond to educators' contentions that "Congress can best serve students and their

Vanderbilt University Chancellor Gordon Gee earns $852,023. He is one of four presidents of private universities who were paid more than $800,000, according to *The Chronicle of Higher Education*. Educators say they have to pay top dollar to get top executives and that, in the context of total college costs, presidential pay has little impact on prices.

families by renewing the federal government's commitment to fully funding student aid programs," as National Association of Independent Colleges and Universities President David Warren put it.

"The federal government's role is to provide student aid," Skidmore's Baum says, "and the federal government should be putting more money into need-based student aid so lower-income students could go to college."

College Board President Caperton argued, "If we do not turn the national conversation back to investment in education and away from tax reduction, [President Bush's] "No Child Left Behind" campaign slogan will become just an empty phrase."

GOP Proposals

Republican leaders in Congress disagree. Boehner, for instance, charged that Kennedy's bill "lets colleges and universities continue to accept billions of dollars a year in federal subsidies without any new accountability to parents, students and taxpayers, despite evidence that questionable spending practices by institutions are contributing significantly to exploding costs."

The House Education and Workforce Committee probably will not address student aid until it completes work on McKeon's Affordability in Higher Education Act, committee aide Schnittger says. Besides penalizing institutions for raising prices above a certain point, McKeon's bill would encourage innovative efforts to hold down college costs and would try to make college-pricing information more understandable to students and parents.

In contrast to the Democrats' proposals, McKeon said, "I don't think we need to be looking at new money to incentivize" colleges to innovate. "That's not in the cards."

Under McKeon's plan, the Education Department would gather and publish information about individual institutions' charges and financial-aid practices. The information would be made public — probably on the department's Web site — in an "easily accessible and understandable" manner that would enable students and parents to compare the expenses they would likely face on different campuses. Boehner said the bill would "arm consumers with more information" as they decide where to attend college.

The General Accounting Office — Congress' non-partisan investigating agency — would study colleges

that have succeeded in becoming more affordable and report findings by mid-2010.

A demonstration project would allow the department to waive regulations for up to 100 institutions that innovate to reduce prices, and the Education secretary would identify federal policies that impede innovation. "Information is power," Boehner added. "When you give consumers more access to information, that can help drive change in the marketplace. Colleges should have an obligation to provide useful, easy-to-use and understandable information so students and parents can make this monumental decision with all the facts in hand."

The GOP bill responds to a 1998 report by the congressionally created National Commission on the Cost of Higher Education, which found that most colleges have "permitted a veil of obscurity to settle over their basic financial operations." The commission, composed primarily of educators, said that colleges "must be affordable and more accountable."[31]

However, the bill does not respond to the call for more federal financial-aid. Nevertheless, McKeon said when his subcommittee takes up financial-aid legislation, it will consider raising the borrowing limits on student

> "Hyperinflation in college costs has been pummeling parents and students for more than a decade . . . Extravagant spending by institutions for everything from super-size Jacuzzis and sunbathing decks to massage facilities and rock-climbing walls is contributing significantly to the soaring cost of college."
>
> — Rep. John H. Boehner, R-Ohio, Chairman, House Education Committee

loans. He also hopes to "put more money into Pell Grants" by increasing the number of grants, not increasing their individual value.

Noting that Pell Grant spending has more than doubled since 1996 and rose by more than $1.7 billion between 2001 and 2002 alone, McKeon predicts, "the criticism they'll give is we're not putting in enough. No matter what we do, that will be the criticism."

Colleges Cut Costs

Well aware of the congressional majority's sentiment, college executives have intensified efforts to cut costs, even as they imposed record-setting price hikes for the current academic year. "If American Airlines hired an outside consultant to tell them how to increase profits, and the suggestion was only to raise prices, the consultant probably would be fired," Mark Yudof, chancellor of the Texas University System, said of the need for colleges to do more than hike tuition.[32]

Murray State University President Alexander described cutbacks typical of those implemented by colleges across the country.[33] Over the last three years, he said, his Kentucky school:

- Froze and eliminated faculty positions;
- Eliminated positions for administrators, professionals, support staff and graduate assistants;
- Closed the campus television station;
- Reduced the number of classes;
- Halted heating and cooling system upgrades;
- Reduced travel; and
- Restricted overtime.

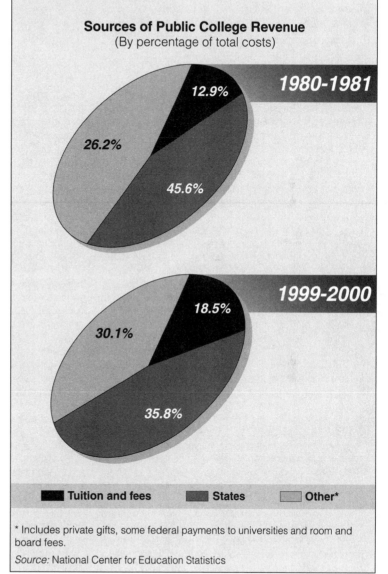

Students' Share of College Costs Rose

Over the past 20 years, the share of college costs paid by state governments dropped by a fifth while students' share (tuition and fees) jumped by more than 40 percent.

Sources of Public College Revenue
(By percentage of total costs)

1980-1981

12.9%
26.2%
45.6%

1999-2000

18.5%
30.1%
35.8%

■ Tuition and fees   ■ States   □ Other*

* Includes private gifts, some federal payments to universities and room and board fees.

Source: National Center for Education Statistics

Colleges also are exploring innovative ways to reduce expenses and increase revenues. "Colleges need to think about quality in ways that don't start with the assumption that cost-effectiveness and quality are always in

Should the federal government penalize colleges and universities for significant tuition increases?

YES
Rep. Howard "Buck" McKeon, R-Calif.
Chairman, House Education Subcommittee
on Higher Education

Written for The CQ Researcher, November, 2003

America's higher-education system is in crisis as a result of explosive price increases that are jeopardizing the dream of a college education for millions of students across America. According to the Advisory Committee on Student Financial Assistance, cost factors prevent 48 percent of all qualified, low-income high-school graduates from attending a four-year college and 22 percent from attending any college at all. At this rate, by the end of the decade, over 2 million qualified students will miss out on the opportunity to go to college.

As chairman of the House Subcommittee on 21st Century Competitiveness, I have made college affordability a top priority. In 1997, I created the National Commission on the Cost of Higher Education to study tuition increases and rising administrative costs and to make policy recommendations on how to hold down these increases. Throughout my eight-year chairmanship, I have worked hard to increase the maximum Pell Grant from $2,000 to $4,050 and have fought to drive down interest rates to make student loans more affordable. Nevertheless, tuition has not dropped, but instead has skyrocketed beyond our most liberal projections.

To place higher education back within the reach of our nation's youth, last month I introduced the Affordability in Higher Education Act. The measure, among other things, sanctions colleges and universities that boldly increase tuition and fees at hyper-inflationary rates year after year. My bill states that, beginning in 2008, if an institution increases its tuition and fees more than twice the rate of inflation for an interval of three years, it could be removed from participation in programs within Title IV of the Higher Education Act, which would exclude them from receiving direct aid through their students' Pell Grants and Stafford and Direct Loans.

It is a shame that tuition has spiraled so far out of the reach of America's students that it is necessary to introduce legislation to penalize colleges into compliance. However, drastic times call for drastic measures. My legislation will give colleges plenty of time to react before any sanctions are imposed (in 2011).

I hope that no schools are sanctioned as a result of my bill. However, I refuse to sit idly by and endlessly subsidize colleges without holding them accountable for extraordinary price increases that prevent our nation's brightest from pursuing higher education.

NO
Travis Reindl
Director, State Policy Analysis, American
Association of State Colleges and Universities

Written for The CQ Researcher, November, 2003

Sanctioning institutions for tuition increases will not change state or campus behavior. Thirty years ago, federal lawmakers put financial aid in the hands of students rather than institutions. As a result, any significant attempt to use federal student aid as a "carrot" or a "stick" will disproportionately impact students.

Such an approach fails to recognize basic realities: In the public sector, most colleges do not set their own tuition rates. Those rates are largely influenced by state funding (which has fallen more than $3 billion over the past two fiscal years).

Moreover, making the Department of Education responsible for hundreds of institutional-management reviews does not seem to be the most effective use of scarce federal resources, particularly with a Pell Grant shortfall approaching $3 billion.

Washington can, however, help students and their families through improved institutional disclosure and consumer information. By moving beyond "sticker prices" and percentage increases to metrics such as average/median net price and average/median loan debt per graduate, the federal government can equip students and families with data about how institutions are spending their money and about what the average student can expect to pay at a particular campus.

Making such information broadly available will result in better-informed consumers and more accountable institutions — a true "win-win." More important, the Department of Education and other agencies already collect value-added data elements such as those listed above, so there is no good reason why they couldn't — or shouldn't — be disseminated as soon as possible.

By focusing on areas where it does not have effective leverage, Congress also leaves aside the types of fundamental policy questions that Higher Education Act reauthorization is meant to engage. For example, what is Congress' priority in federal student-aid programs — ensuring access or subsidizing choice? At what point does excessive student indebtedness become a drag on the formation of economic and social capital?

These and other questions deserve to be tackled by lawmakers, particularly as the aging of the Baby Boomers threatens an unprecedented strain on the federal budget, and student borrowing/debt reaches record levels.

College affordability is a crucial issue, and members such as Rep. Howard "Buck" McKeon deserve credit for their persistence and candor. Congress, however, should focus its limited time, energy and resources where they will yield the greatest result.

Should governments reduce financial aid for middle-income students in order to provide more college grants to the poor?

YES
Sandy Baum
Economics Professor, Skidmore College

Co-author, "Trends in College Pricing" and "Trends in Student Aid," Published annually by the College Board
Written for The CQ Researcher, November 2003

Providing adequate aid to qualified low-income students should be a high priority for the federal government. The diversion of student subsidies in recent years away from low-income students and toward middle-income students reduces both our economic efficiency and the equity of our society.

To be efficient, public subsidies must alter behavior in socially meaningful ways. While middle-income students face pressures meeting the rapidly rising price of a college education, it is usually their choice of institution — rather than their access to higher education — that is at issue. In contrast, for low-income students the question often is whether or not they will go to college at all and, if they do enroll, whether they will graduate.

College attendance rates disturbingly correlate with family income. While virtually all high-income students with the highest test scores go to college, about a quarter of those from low-income families with the same test scores do not. And those low-income students who do go to college disproportionately attend two-year colleges and are much less likely to earn bachelor's degrees.

Denying educational opportunity to qualified students not fortunate enough to be born into comfortable financial circumstances is unfair under almost any reasonable definition of equity, but it also reduces our economy's productive capacity. College graduates earn more than high-school graduates, contribute more to society and receive fewer social services.

In recent years, the federal government has aimed an increasing portion of higher-education subsidies at more affluent families through tax preferences for college savings and other tax-based policies. This shifting focus of federal policy, along with the movement of states away from need-based aid, reduces the effectiveness of student subsidies.

There are many areas of federal expenditures more deserving of cuts than middle-income student assistance — and elimination of recent tax cuts for the most fortunate Americans would certainly be a better trade-off. But grants for low-income students must be at the top of the higher-education policy agenda.

NO
Scott Ross
*Executive Director,
Florida Student Association*

Written for The CQ Researcher, November 2003

The concept of need-based financial aid should not be ignored by either the federal or state governments, but it should not be created at the expense of middle-income students.

Three groups of students attend college in this country. The first is made up of students who generally have the means to attend college at their own or their parents' expense. They generally do not require financial aid. The second group includes those unable to pay for any of their education. Through the Free Application for Federal Student Aid (FAFSA), these students are deemed to have financial need and are usually awarded significant funds to pursue their education.

Middle-income students comprise the third group, which includes the majority of students applying to college. They usually cannot obtain any financial aid because their parents or providers earn just enough to exclude them from receiving any need-based financial aid.

To create more need-based financial aid at the expense of these middle-income students would be devastating to thousands of students who want to pursue their education. When most of these students seek help, the only answer they are given is, "Take out a student loan."

While nobody can argue that student loans have become an almost necessary part of financing a student's education, these middle-income students are being sent into the work force with debt that is almost unmanageable. This tremendous debt load forces students to seek employment entirely based on financial reward and prevents them from accepting jobs in education or other critical jobs.

The cost of education in the United States is rising at an astronomical rate. Each and every day, some of our best and brightest students are being "priced out" of an opportunity to attend college.

If we continue to neglect middle-income students and ask them to take on a financial burden that is beyond their means, we are essentially choosing one student over another, thus contradicting the actual intent of need-based financial aid: to give all students an opportunity to pursue their educational dreams.

direct opposition," says Callan of the National Center for Public Policy and Higher Education.

The American Association of Community Colleges' Boggs sees two-year schools' approaches to the challenge as "very innovative and creative and entrepreneurial." Community colleges are partnering with other institutions, businesses, industries and governments, Boggs explains. "They have offered classes on weekends and evenings for a long time. A growing number are putting courses online — or at least information, study guides and other materials to help the students in the traditional program."

In Charlotte, N.C., for example, Boggs says, Central Piedmont Community College recruited businesses to sponsor courses. And two-year schools are cooperating with high schools on what Callan describes as "increasing student productivity" — encouraging students to take courses for college credit while still in high school.

Gov. Mark Warner, D-Va., wants all of his state's public high schools to take part in what he calls "a dramatic reform" of the senior year.

"For students not going on to higher education, we'll work with them to get an industry-recognized certificate" in a trade, such as auto mechanics, Warner said of his Senior Year Plus proposal. "For the college-bound, we'll offer every high-school senior the opportunity to acquire a full semester of college credit" through dual college-high school enrollment and advanced-placement courses. "It will save $5,000 on college costs for the family, $3,000 for the state."

Callan calls it an example of how actions to address the cost problem can also be "educationally compelling" ideas. "We have a huge amount of research that says the senior year in high school is a horrible waste of time," Callan explains. "When kids who are ready to do college work are offered the chance, we find the families and the students jump at it. It cuts costs, and it educationally makes sense."

Some institutions are being forced to make their prices more appealing to students and parents. For instance, a recent Illinois law guarantees that the tuition for instate undergraduate students will not be raised at a state institution once they enroll.[34] Other state legislatures have imposed — and later lifted — price freezes or caps in the past. Gov. Robert Ehrlich, Jr., R-Md., said he may propose a cap on tuition at state schools, possibly tying it to inflation. State budget cuts in Maryland led

public institutions to raise tuition by as much as 21 percent this year and to contemplate another 20 percent hike for next year.[35]

And students in at least four states have asked courts to roll back college-price increases. Students in Maryland and California allege that state institutions breached contracts by raising prices after students had enrolled on the basis of lower advertised charges. The California court has not ruled. A judge granted summary judgment for the University of Maryland, and the students have appealed.

Students and alumni won their suit in Missouri, where a 19th-century law required that "all youths resident of the state" be admitted to the University of Missouri "without payment of tuition." The university didn't charge tuition until 1987, and the legislature repealed the law in 2001, after the suit was filed. But the trial court ruled in favor of about 114,000 students who paid tuition in the interim, and the state Supreme Court refused the university's appeal. Robert Herman, the plaintiffs' lawyer in the class-action suit, says the university owes the plaintiffs "well over $1 billion."

The court has not decided on a remedy. Herman suggests paying the plaintiffs with vouchers that they could use to purchase university services over time. Some might donate their awards back to the university, he says. Others might use the vouchers to pay for their children's education, to take classes themselves or to "sell them on eBay."

OUTLOOK

Tight Budgets

College soothsayers don't like what they're reading in their tea leaves. Converging trends dictate that upward pressures on college costs will endure for the foreseeable future. Educators will have to find innovative ways to hold down costs in order to avoid pricing ever-larger numbers of potential students out of the higher-education market.

Republican leaders in Congress oppose any significant increase in federal aid to higher education, and states won't find it easy to raise their appropriations to colleges.

In fact, higher education's declining share of state budgets is in danger of becoming a permanent phenomenon, "rather than a temporary adjustment to cyclical

> **"States, and higher education in particular, are likely to face very tight budget conditions for the next decade. All but a handful of states will find it impossible to maintain current levels of public services within their existing tax structures."**
>
> — **Dennis Jones**,
> President, National Center for
> Higher Education Management Systems

state fiscal problems," economists Thomas J. Kane and Peter R. Orszag wrote in a recent Brookings Institution report.[36]

"States, and higher education in particular, are likely to face very tight budget conditions for the next decade," said Dennis Jones, president of the National Center for Higher Education Management Systems. "All but a handful of states will find it impossible to maintain current levels of public services within their existing tax structures."[37]

Colleges' declining share of state budgets is widely attributed to increased state spending on K-12 education and increased costs for Medicaid, law enforcement and prisons at a time of strong opposition to tax increases and support for tax cuts. Unlike the federal government, every state but Vermont is constitutionally required to balance its books.[38]

"Higher education is a discretionary part of the budget, and that's not true for Medicaid, corrections, police and that type of stuff," says Magrath, of the National Association of State Universities and Land Grant Colleges.

In addition, says the Education Commission of the States' Ruppert, legislators are "well aware that there are other sources of revenue for colleges in tuition and fees and donations and endowments and grants."

Legislators, therefore, find it easier to balance tight budgets on higher education's back. And "this danger is likely to become even more pronounced in the future because of further projected increases in Medicaid costs and because of demographic shifts over the next decade and beyond," Kane and Orszag wrote.

The Congressional Budget Office estimates that Medicaid will consume 2.8 percent of gross domestic product in 2030 — up from 1.2 percent now — as the Baby Boomers grow old and the cost of health care continues to rise. The states' Medicaid burden will jump substantially as well, they added, and as a result, "state support for higher education is likely to come under increasing pressure, even as state revenues recover."

As this is occurring, notes Callan of the National Center for Public Policy and Higher Education, "In 2009 we're going to have the biggest high-school graduating class in the history of the country." And they will be "the poorest as well as the most ethnically and racially heterogeneous generation of students to appear on the doorstep of American higher education."[39]

The increase in enrollments will require more staff and facilities, and the lower-income students will be more likely to need remedial education and, therefore, be more expensive to educate. And they will need financial aid.

Callan worries: "If we continue the trajectory of cost increases and price increases for much longer, there will not be enough financial aid — even in the most generous circumstances — to cover the needs."

NOTES

1. Sandy Baum, Skidmore College economics professor and College Board analyst, quoted during an Oct. 21 press conference.

2. All figures on college prices in this section are from "Trends in College Pricing 2003," College Board; Oct. 21, 2003; www.collegeboard.com.

3. Rep. John Boehner, R-Ohio, and Rep. Howard "Buck" McKeon, R-Calif., "The College Cost Crisis," House Committee on Education and the Workforce, Sept. 3, 2003; http://edworkforce. house.gov.

4. For background, see William Triplett, "State Budget Crises," *The CQ Researcher*, Oct. 3, 2003, pp. 821-844.

5. Goldie Blymenstyk, "Donations to Colleges Decline for the First Time Since 1988," *The Chronicle of Higher Education*, March 21, 2003, p. 29.

6. Sandra S. Ruppert, "Closing the College Participation Gap," Education Commission of the States, October 2003, p. 2. Available online at www.communitycollegepolicy.org.

7. Greg Winter, "Jacuzzi U? A Battle of Perks to Lure Students," *The New York Times*, Oct. 5, 2003, p. A1.

8. Blymenstyk, *op. cit.*

9. Linda J. Zimbler, "Background Characteristics, Work Activities, and Compensation of Faculty and Instructional Staff in Postsecondary Institutions: Fall 1998," Department of Education, National Center for Education Statistics; http://nces.ed.gov/pubs 2001/2001152.pdf.

10. *Ibid.*

11. Address to 2003 annual meeting of the American Educational Finance Association; www.ilr.cornell.edu/cheri/wp/cheri_wp32.pdf.

12. "Trends in Student Aid, 2003," The College Board; www.collegeboard.com.

13. "Trends in College Pricing," *op. cit.*

14. *Ibid.*

15. Scott Jaschik, "Match the Mission To the Tuition," *The Washington Post*, Oct. 26, 2003, p. B1.

16. Triplett, *op. cit.*

17. F. King Alexander, testimony before House Education and Workforce 21st Century Competitiveness Subcommittee, Sept. 23, 2003; http://edworkforce.house.gov.

18. "Trends in Student Aid," *op. cit.*

19. Stephen Burd, "Bush's Next Target?" *The Chronicle of Higher Education*, July 11, 2003, p. A18.

20. 108th Congress, First Session, H.R. 3311, the Affordability in Education Act of 2003; http://frwebgate.access.gpo.gov.

21. "Ann Radcliffe Trust," in Handbook for Students 2002-2003, Faculty of Arts and Sciences, Harvard University; www.registrar.fas.harvard.edu/handbooks; William S. Powell, "Carolina — A Brief History," University of North Carolina at Chapel Hill, www.unc.edu/about/history.html; for background, see Scott W. Wright, "Community Colleges," *The CQ Researcher*, April 21, 2000, p. 338.

22. Enrollment figures are from the "Digest of Education Statistics, 2002," U.S. Department of Education, National Center for Education Statistics; http://nces.ed.gov/pubs2003/digest02/index.asp.

23. Wright, *op. cit.*

24. Historical information in this section is derived in part from: Wright, *op. cit.*; Mary H. Cooper, "Paying for College," *The CQ Researcher*, Nov. 20, 1992, pp. 1001-1024; "History of Student Financial Aid," from the Web site FinAid: The Smart Student Guide to Financial Aid, www.finaid.org. "The Higher Education Act: A History," *The Chronicle of Higher Education*, July 11, 2003, p. A8.

25. Financial aid information is from "Trends in Student Aid," *op. cit.*

26. Unless otherwise noted, college finance information comes from "Digest of Education Statistics, 2002," *op. cit.*

27. "Trends in College Pricing," *op. cit.*

28. Ruppert, *op. cit.*, p. 4.

29. 108th Congress, First Session, S 1793, College Quality, Affordability, and Diversity Improvement Act of 2003; http://frwebgate.access.gpo.gov.

30. 108th Congress, First Session, HR 3180, College Opportunity for All Act; http://frwebgate.access.gpo.gov.

31. "Straight Talk About College Costs and Prices: The Final Report and Supplemental Material from the National Commission on the Cost of Higher Education," American Council on Education/Oryx Press, 1998; www.acenet.edu/washington/college_costs/1998/07july/straight_talk.html.

32. Quoted in Sara Hebel, "The Future of Tuition," *The Chronicle of Higher Education*, Sept. 19, 2003, p. A10.

33. Alexander, *op. cit.*

34. Susan C. Thomson, "SIU Plans for Freeze on Tuition Beginning Next Year," *St. Louis Post-Dispatch*, Sept. 12, 2003, p. B1.

35. Lori Montgomery and Amy Argetsinger, "Ehrlich Says He May Seek Tuition Cap At Colleges," *The Washington Post*, Oct. 31, 2003, p. B1.

36. Thomas J. Kane and Peter R. Orszag, "Higher Education Spending: The Role of Medicaid and the Business Cycle," Brookings Institution Policy Brief No. 124, September 2003; http://www.brookings.org.

37. Dennis Jones, "State Shortfalls Projected Throughout the Decade," National Center for Public Policy and Higher Education, February 2003; www.highereducation.org/pa_0203/index.html.

38. Ruppert, *op. cit.*, p. 4.

39. Patrick M. Callan, "A Different Kind of Recession," College Affordability In Jeopardy, a supplement of *National Crosstalk*, National Center for Public Policy and Higher Education, Feb. 11, 2003; www.highereducation.org/reports.

BIBLIOGRAPHY

Books

Cohen, Arthur M., and Florence B. Brawer, *The American Community College*, 4th ed., Jossey-Bass, 2002.
This standard reference by a UCLA higher-education professor (Cohen) and the research director of the Center for the Study of Community Colleges (Brawer) analyzes the history and contributions of community colleges.

Ehrenberg, Ronald G., *Tuition Rising: Why College Costs So Much*, Harvard University Press, 2002.
The director of Cornell's Higher Education Research Institute delineates causes of escalating college price increases, including the costs of buildings, personnel, supplies, technology and the desire to score well in *U.S. News & World Report's* annual college review.

McPherson, Michael S., and Morton Owen Schapiro, *The Student Aid Game*, Princeton University Press, 1997.
Current (Schapiro) and former (McPherson) college presidents explore the intricacies of higher-education finance and lay out policy options for governments and institutions.

Pittinsky, Matthew (ed.), *The Wired Tower: Perspectives on the Impact of the Internet on Higher Education*, Financial Times Prentice Hall, 2002.
As chairman and a founder of Blackboard Inc., a major supplier of information technology to education, Pittinsky speaks from experience. Other contributors include college administratiors and financiers.

Articles

"Education Life," *The New York Times*, Nov. 9, 2003. Available, for a fee, at www.nytimes.com/indexes/ 2003/11/09/edlife/index.html.
This issue of *The Times'* education section contains several timely stories about rapidly rising college prices and the debate about what should be done.

"The Future of Tuition," *The Chronicle of Higher Education*, Sept. 19, 2003.
This special report in the weekly higher-education journal provides both news reports and several commentaries on such topics as the "public-private quality gap," aid for the poor and inadequate college planning and budgeting.

"Holding on to HOPE," *The Atlanta Journal and Constitution*, Sept. 9-11, 2003.
This three-day series about Georgia's HOPE scholarship program for "B"-or-better students says it is running out of money. HOPE gives most of its aid to Georgians who would attend college anyway, the report says.

"Learning the Hard Way," *Newsweek*, Sept. 15, 2003, p. 50.
A survey of global education conditions asserts that despite lamentations about problems facing U.S. colleges, it's instructive to observe how they are envied elsewhere.

Reports and Studies

Boehner, John, and Howard McKeon, "The College Cost Crisis," House Committee on Education and the Workforce, Sept. 3, 2003. Available at http:// edworkforce.house.gov/issues/108th/education/higher education/CollegeCostCrisisReport.pdf.
Committee Chairman Boehner and McKeon, who chairs the Higher Education Subcommittee, argue that colleges overcharge.

Jones, Dennis, "State Shortfalls Projected Throughout the Decade," National Center for Public Policy and Higher Education, February 2003. Available at www.highereducation.org/pa_0203/ index.html.
The president of the National Center for Higher Education Management Systems warns that public colleges shouldn't expect significant increases in state support over the next 10 years. Most states will not even be able to maintain current services with existing tax structures, he says.

"Straight Talk About College Costs and Prices: The Final Report and Supplemental Material from the National Commission on the Cost of Higher Education," American Council on Education/Oryx Press, 1998.
A congressionally mandated commission warns: "If colleges and universities do not take steps to reduce their costs, policymakers at the federal and state levels will intervene and take up the task for them."

"Trends in College Pricing 2003," *The College Board.* **Available at www.collegeboard.com/prod_ downloads/press/cost03/cb_trends_pricing_2003.pdf.**
This is the most-quoted annual report on the cost of attending college.

"Trends in Student Aid, 2003," *The College Board.* **Available at www.collegeboard.com/prod_down loads/press/cost03/cb_trends_aid_2003.pdf.**
A companion to "Trends in College Pricing" summarizes recent and historical information about grants and loans.

For More Information

American Association of Community Colleges, 1 Dupont Circle, N.W., Suite 410, Washington, DC 20036-1193; (202) 728-0200; www.aacc.nche.edu. The primary advocacy organization for the nation's community colleges.

American Association of State Colleges and Universities, 1307 New York Ave., N.W., Washington, DC 20005-4704; (202) 293-7070; www.aascu.org. Represents more than 430 public colleges and universities in the United States and its territories; lobbies for programs that strengthen academic quality, promote access and inclusion and facilitate educational innovation.

American Council on Education, 1 Dupont Circle, N.W., Suite 800, Washington, DC 20036-1193; (202) 939-9300; www.acenet.edu. Conducts and publishes research and lobbies on issues relating to women and minorities in higher education and management of higher-education institutions.

College Board, 45 Columbus Ave., New York, NY 10023-6992; (212) 713-8000; www.collegeboard.com. Promotes high learning standards, equity of opportunity and financial support for needy college students.

Education Commission of the States, 700 Broadway, Suite 1200, Denver, CO 80203-3460; (303) 299-3600; www.ecs.org. A clearinghouse that provides state policy-makers and education leaders with independent research and analysis on issues facing all levels of the education system.

Education and Workforce Committee, U.S. House of Representatives. The GOP-led panel maintains a Web site, "College Cost Central," which it calls "A Resource for Parents, Students, & Taxpayers Fed Up With the High Cost of Higher Education;" available at http://edworkforce.house.gov/issues/108th/education/highereducation/collegecostcentral.htm.

Institute for Higher Education Policy, 1320 19th St., N.W., Suite 400, Washington, DC 20036; (202) 861-8223; www.ihep.com. Studies the rising costs of a college education and government regulatory issues facing colleges and universities.

National Association for Equal Opportunity in Higher Education, 8701 Georgia Ave., Suite 200, Silver Spring, MD 20910; (301) 650-2440; www.nafeo.org. Represents public and private historically black colleges and universities.

National Association of Independent Colleges and Universities, 1025 Connecticut Ave., N.W., Suite 700, Washington, DC 20036-5405; (202) 785-8866; www.naicu.edu. Represents private colleges and universities on policy issues such as student aid, taxation and government regulation.

National Association of State Universities and Land Grant Colleges, 1 Dupont Circle N.W., Suite 710, Washington DC 20036; (202) 778-0818; www.nasulgc.org. Serves as a clearinghouse for issues involving public higher education.

National Center for Public Policy and Higher Education, 152 North Third St., Suite 705, San Jose, CA 95112; (408) 271-2699; www.highereducation.org. An independent, nonpartisan think tank that promotes public policies that enhance students' opportunities to pursue high-quality education and training beyond high school.

United Negro College Fund, 8260 Willow Oaks Corporate Dr., Fairfax, VA 22031; 1 (800) 331-2244; www.uncf.org. Represents private, historically black colleges and universities.

2

Combating Plagiarism

Brian Hansen

AP Photo/Janet Hostetter

Best-selling author Doris Kearns Goodwin is among several well-known writers who have faced plagiarism charges. Goodwin recently acknowledged her publisher had paid an undisclosed sum to settle plagiarism charges. Many educators say the Internet is partly to blame for student plagiarism. Others say high schools aren't teaching students how to avoid it. Meanwhile, some media critics say news organizations haven't been doing enough to crack down on plagiarism and other forms of journalistic fraud.

From *The CQ Researcher,*
September 19, 2003.

S usan Maximon, a social-studies teacher at Fairview High School in Boulder, Colo., knows teenage writing when she sees it. So a bright red flag went up last year when one of her 11th-grade students turned in a research paper teeming with $10 words.

"I knew he didn't write it," Maximon says. "It was filled with big words and expressions that he never used and probably didn't even understand."

Robert Rivard, editor of the *San Antonio Express-News*, had a similar revelation last April as he was reading a *New York Times* article about the mother of an American soldier missing in Iraq. "I was bewildered," Rivard recalls. "I thought I'd read it before." He had — in his own paper — eight days earlier. That's why *The Times'* story by Jayson Blair sounded so familiar.

"It suddenly dawned on me that it was an act of plagiarism," Rivard says. "It was subtly changed and manipulated, but it was clearly" by *Express-News* reporter Macarena Hernandez.

In the Fairview High case, the student confessed after Maximon confronted him with evidence his paper was nearly identical to one available on the Internet. Maximon gave him a zero for the assignment.

Blair's case was not resolved so quietly. The 27-year-old resigned on May 1, shortly after Rivard alerted *Times* editors. They soon discovered that Blair had plagiarized, fabricated or otherwise falsified parts of at least three-dozen articles. "He fabricated comments. He concocted scenes. He lifted material from other newspapers and wire services," *The Times* said in a front-page, 14,000-word mea culpa published on May 11.[1]

The much-publicized scandal dealt a devastating blow to the 152-year-old *Times*, widely considered the greatest newspaper in the world. Some experts worried that Blair had tarnished the reputations of all news organizations. "In a lot of people's minds, *The Times* is the bell cow of American journalism," said Don Wycliff, public editor of the *Chicago Tribune*. "They'll think, 'Well, if it's done there, you know it's done everywhere.' "[2]

Derived from the Latin word *plagiarius* ("kidnapper"), plagiarism can range from purloining someone else's reportage or buying a prewritten term paper and turning it in as one's own to copying a few sentences from a book or Web site without citing the source.[3] According to the authoritative Modern Language Association, plagiarism is "a form of cheating that has been defined as the false assumption of authorship: the wrongful act of taking the product of another person's mind, and presenting it as one's own."[4] (*See box, p. 45.*)

Most Students Say Plagiarism Is Wrong

Many educators say today's students don't understand what plagiarism is or don't consider it as serious cheating. But according to a recent survey, nearly 90 percent of college students strongly view major acts of plagiarism as unethical.

It is Wrong To:	Students' Ethical Views on Acts of Plagiarism		
	Strongly Agree or Somewhat Agree	**Neither Agree nor Disagree**	**Somewhat Disagree or Strongly Disagree**
Hand in Someone Else's Writing as One's Own	89.1%	7.0%	3.9%
Use the Internet to Copy Text to Hand in as One's Own	89.3%	7.7%	3.1%
Purchase Papers From Print Term-Paper Mills	89.1%	6.8%	4.1%
Purchase Papers From Online Term-Paper Mills	89.8%	6.1%	4.1%

Source: Patrick M. Scanlon and David R. Neumann, "Internet Plagiarism Among College Students," *Journal of College Student Development,* May/June 2002.

Although plagiarism among high school and college students is not new, some educators say students today are more likely to plagiarize because of the Internet. "Kids have always plagiarized, but the Web has made it a lot easier," says Joyce Valenza, a librarian at Springfield Township High School in Erdenheim, Pa. "It's given them an enormous resource for finding materials that they don't think their teachers can verify as not their own."

"Academic honesty is the cornerstone of college learning and liberal education and, indeed, is a continuing problem that colleges face," says Debra Humphreys, vice president of communications and public affairs at the Association of American Colleges and Universities. "Our members are facing different challenges than in the past as a result of the Internet. Problems related to plagiarism on campus parallel problems in the larger society, such as newspaper plagiarism scandals and illegal file sharing of music and movies."

Moreover, Internet resources are widely considered to be free for the taking. "There's a belief among young people that materials found online are free, or are somehow inherently different from something you buy at a record store or get out of a book or magazine," says John Barrie, president of TurnItIn.com, an Oakland, Calif., firm that sells software that helps thousands of schools detect plagiarism. "Kids download music from the Internet even though it's a form of intellectual-property theft. It's naive to think that attitude is not going to have a large impact on plagiarism at educational institutions."

"On a given day, we process between 10,000 and 15,000 student papers, and about 30 percent are less than original," Barrie says.

Recent studies indicate that 40 percent of college students have plagiarized material at least once. (*See graph, p. 31.*) Although plagiarism is not a crime, authors and musicians who think they have been plagiarized can sue for copyright infringement. To win damages, a plaintiff must typically prove that the plagiarism harmed "the potential market for, or value of," their copyrighted work.[5]

Last April, French jazz pianist Jacques Loussier sued the rapper Eminem for $10 million, claiming his hit song "Kill You" borrowed heavily from Loussier's 20-year-old song "Pulsion." The suit is pending. Even former Beatle George Harrison was successfully sued for plagiarism (*see p. 39*).

In addition to musicians, several best-selling historians have run into plagiarism problems, including Doris Kearns Goodwin and Stephen Ambrose. Goodwin acknowledged in January her publisher had paid an undisclosed sum in 1987 to settle allegations that Goodwin's *The Fitzgeralds and the Kennedys* contained plagiarized text from Lynne McTaggart's *Kathleen Kennedy: Her Life and Times*.

Ambrose was criticized for not putting quotation marks around passages in his celebrated World War II book *The Wild Blue* that were identical to passages in *Wings of Morning*, an earlier chronicle by University of Pennsylvania history Professor Thomas Childers. Ambrose had cited Childers' book in his footnotes and claimed the mistake was inadvertent. Journalists later found unquoted passages from other authors in at least six of Ambrose's other books, but he vigorously denied he was a plagiarist. "I stand on the originality of my work," he wrote last May, just before his death. "The reading public will decide whether my books are fraudulent and react accordingly."[6]

Punishments for students who plagiarize range from failing grades on individual assignments to flunking an entire course — or worse. Some schools have revoked degrees from people whose plagiarism came to light months or years after they graduated. At other schools — especially those with strict honor codes — plagiarism can be grounds for suspension or expulsion.

For example, at the University of Virginia — famous for its tough honor code — 48 students quit or were expelled for plagiarism between April 2001 and November 2002. The university revoked the degrees of three of the plagiarists who had graduated before their cases were adjudicated by the student-run Honor Committee. "The cases ranged from the wholesale copying of entire papers to copying a few sentences here and there," says Nicole Eramo, special assistant to the com-

How Much Plagiarism?

High-school students plagiarize significantly more than college students, according to several studies in which students are asked to "self-report" copying. Although plagiarism appears to have remained relatively stable during the past 40 years, Donald McCabe of Rutgers University thinks it is actually far more prevalent today because many students don't consider cut-and-paste Internet copying as cheating. In addition, McCabe notes other types of dishonesty — such as cheating on exams — have skyrocketed.

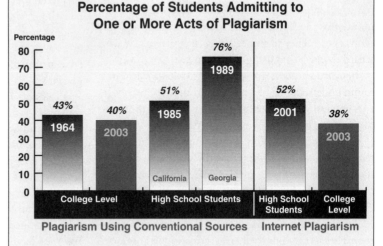

Percentage of Students Admitting to One or More Acts of Plagiarism

Sources: W.J. Bowers, "Student Dishonesty and Its Control in College," Columbia University, 1964; Donald McCabe, unpublished study, Rutgers University, 2003; Donald McCabe, "Cheating: Why Students Do It and How We Can Help Them Stop," *American Educator*, winter 200l; B. Brandes, "Academic Honesty: A Special Study of California Students," 1986; Fred Schab, "Schooling Without Learning: Thirty Years of Cheating in High School," *Adolescence*, Vol. 23, 1991.

mittee. "Most of our students are fairly intolerant of that type of cheating."

However, some experts say educators are going overboard in trying to root out plagiarism. Rebecca Moore Howard, an associate professor of writing and rhetoric at Syracuse University, blames the crackdown more on "hysteria" than real understanding of the issues. She says plagiarism is frequently the result of students not knowing — or never having been taught — how to properly cite sources.

"All writers appropriate language from other sources and reshape it as their own, but inexperienced writers don't do that very well," Howard says. "They don't realize that what they're doing is plagiarism."

According to University of Colorado freshman Liz Newton, "It was kind of unclear at my high school what plagiarism really was. You were just kind of expected to know what it was and not do it."

"The perception [among college professors] is that students are no longer learning about plagiarism adequately at the high-school level, so there's an education and re-education process that needs to take place," says renowned academic-integrity researcher Donald McCabe. Some high-school teachers themselves "don't even understand" what constitutes plagiarism in the digital age, adds the Rutgers University professor and founder of the Center for Academic Integrity at Duke University. "They're still catching up, particularly with regard to plagiarism using the Internet."

Because students are arriving at college without a sound understanding of what plagiarism is, some colleges and universities are spending more time than they used to teaching newly arriving students how to avoid it. "There's a concerted effort across campus for courses that require any kind of writing to really work with students so they understand what plagiarism is," says Fran Ebbers, librarian at St. Edward's University, in Austin, Texas. "We've had university-wide discussions about this."

As plagiarism scandals plague campuses and newsrooms across the country, here is a closer look at some of the questions being debated:

Has the Internet increased the incidence of student plagiarism?

In the past, students who plagiarized first had to spend hours poring over dusty library books to find material to copy, then retype it. If they bought material from a term-paper mill, they had to wait for it to arrive through the mail.

Today, students surfing the Web can access millions of documents on every subject imaginable — without leaving their desks. With the click of a mouse, they can electronically "cut and paste" text — a few sentences or entire documents — into their "own" work.

Experts generally agree that the Internet and other modern technologies have made plagiarism easier. They disagree, however, about whether the new technologies encourage more students to plagiarize. Louis Bloomfield, a University of Virginia physics professor who two years ago accused 158 students of submitting plagiarized term papers, says technology is partly to blame. "Plagiarism has become so easy," he says, "It's everywhere, and if you think you don't have it going on in your institution, you're naive."

But Jim Purdy, assistant director of the Center for Writing Studies at the University of Illinois, Urbana-Champaign, says the Internet is simply not creating vast numbers of new student plagiarizers. "Based on my personal experiences," he says, "this fear is being blown somewhat out of proportion."

Over the years, researchers have tried to quantify the incidence of plagiarism and other forms of academic cheating.[7] Most of the studies are based on surveys in which students "self-report" their behaviors. Taken at face value, the studies generally belie the notion that the advent of the Internet has led to an increase in academic plagiarism.

Professor W. J. Bowers of Columbia University documented the incidence of plagiarism and academic cheating among college students 40 years ago — long before the advent of the Internet. In a 1964 survey, Bowers found that 43 percent of the respondents acknowledged plagiarizing at least once.[8]

In a recent survey of 18,000 U.S. college students by Rutgers University's McCabe, 38 percent of respondents acknowledged engaging in one or more instances of Internet-facilitated "cut-and-paste" plagiarism. But notably, a slightly bigger group — 40 percent — said they had plagiarized using conventional books, journals and other sources.

In another recent study, Rochester Institute of Technology (RIT) professors Patrick Scanlon and David Neumann found that the number of students who admitted to Internet plagiarism was about the same as during the pre-Internet era.[9] "Our study indicates that some of the estimates of Internet-facilitated plagiarism are overblown," Scanlon says. "We didn't find evidence of the epidemic of Internet plagiarism that's been touted in the popular press. If anything, the numbers for plagiarism have actually gone down [from the pre-Internet era], or it's a wash."

According to Scanlon and Neumann, nearly 25 percent of the students admitted to plagiarizing from the Internet: 16.5 percent "sometimes" cut and paste text from an Internet source without citation, 8 percent do so "often." The study found that 6 percent "sometimes" buy papers from online term-paper mills and 2.3 percent do so "often."

Notably, the respondents thought other students plagiarized much more frequently than they did. For example, while only 8 percent "often" took text from Internet sources without citation, 54.4 percent believed their peers often did so. "That's consistent with studies of other kinds of things," Scanlon says. "People will overestimate behaviors in others that they themselves are not taking part in."

Significantly more plagiarism is self-reported by high-school students. Of the 2,294 juniors surveyed by McCabe in 2000-2001, for example, 52 percent said they had "copied a few sentences from a Web site without footnoting them," and 16 percent acknowledged turning in papers "obtained in large part from a term-paper mill or Web site."[10] McCabe contends that many high-school students plagiarize more than their college counterparts because they don't fully understand what plagiarism is or how to avoid it. But others do it because they believe they won't get caught, he says.

However, pre-Internet era studies also found high incidences of high-school plagiarism. In a 1985 California survey, 51 percent of the students admitted plagiarizing.[11] And 76 percent of the highschoolers surveyed by a University of Georgia researcher in 1989 admitted to copying "word for word" out of a book.[12]

Critics maintain there is much more Internet-facilitated plagiarism occurring today than self-reporting studies indicate, because many students — at both the high-school and college levels — either don't understand or refuse to admit that copying from the Web is wrong.

"A lot of kids don't understand that they can't cut and paste text from the Internet into their own papers

New York Times Executive Editor Howell Raines, center, and Managing Editor Gerald Boyd, right, resigned under pressure from Publisher Arthur Sulzberger Jr., left, in the wake of the scandal involving rogue reporter Jayson Blair.

[without citing the source]," says Leigh Campbell-Hale, a social-studies teacher at Boulder's Fairview High School. "I even had one kid say to me, 'If I pay for a paper I bought online, it's mine.' "

McCabe found similar attitudes in his recent college survey: 44 percent of the students considered minor, cut-and-paste Internet plagiarism as "trivial" cheating or not cheating at all.

Kids dismiss Internet plagiarism as trivial because they have bought into the "techie" culture, which holds that anything found on the Web is "free" — that copyright laws do not apply on the Internet, according to some experts. Students regard Internet plagiarism much like downloading music files, they say. But as the music industry's recent copyright-infringement suit indicates, such piracy is considered intellectual-property theft.[13]

"A lot of high-school and college students don't see that as a problem at all," says librarian Ebbers, at St. Edward's University.

Jill Vassilakos-Long, a librarian at California State University, San Bernardino, has a slightly different view. "A lot of students would agree that plagiarism and downloading music are theft, but they see them as victimless crimes."

Confronting Plagiarism Can Pose Risk

Punishments for plagiarism usually are meted out without incident. But occasionally, things get ugly — for the accusers. Teachers and professors who impose harsh consequences on plagiarizing students sometimes face unpleasant consequences from their students, parents and unsupportive colleagues and administrators.

Law Professor John L. Hill, for example, was sued, verbally harassed and had his house vandalized after he filed plagiarism complaints against five law students at St. Thomas University in Miami, Fla., in 1995. But "the worst part" of the ordeal was the lack of support from colleagues and school officials, recalls Hill, who now teaches law at Indiana University in Indianapolis.

Hill says the five students incorporated materials from the *Stanford Law Review* and other publications into their own papers without attribution. One student copied "about 30 pages" of text — original footnotes and all. "It was pretty clear-cut," Hill recalls. "It was verbatim plagiarism."

Thus Hill was shocked when his own colleagues and the student-run honor committee did not support him. "A number of faculty just refused to accept that [plagiarism] was a significant problem," Hill says. "One colleague insisted I was on a 'witch hunt.' And the president of the university ordered the dean to punt — to basically do nothing — because he didn't want to deal with any possible legal implications."

When the students refused to admit wrongdoing, Hill referred them to the honor committee. Shortly thereafter, Hill says he started getting harassing phone calls, his house was egged and his front door was twice ripped from its hinges. During the trial proceedings, students booed and hissed at him. One of the defendants even tried to taint Hill as a plagiarist. "They tore apart everything I'd ever written in the hope of finding some plagiarism, which they didn't," Hill says. "I was really portrayed as the bad guy."

Ultimately, two of the cases were dismissed and a third student was acquitted. A fourth student pleaded guilty, and the final defendant was convicted on a split vote. For punishments, the two guilty students were ordered to write five-page papers on plagiarism.

Later, one of the convicted plagiarists sued Hill and the university for "loss of ability to obtain a job as an attorney."[1]

Some educators refrain from pursuing student plagiarizers because they fear either litigation or lack of support from administrators wishing to avoid negative publicity.[2] But Hill says he'd do the same thing again. "It was an unpleasant experience, to say the least," Hill says, "but I just wouldn't feel good about letting something like [plagiarism] ride."

Christine Pelton, a biology teacher at Piper High School in Piper, Kan., had a similar experience in 2001 after assign-

But the music industry blames online music-sharing and downloading in part for a 26 percent drop in CD sales and a 14 percent drop in revenues. "Our industry is being ravaged by piracy," said Zack Horowitz, president and chief operating officer of Universal Music Group.[14]

There are non-economic repercussions as well, says Barrie, of TurnItIn.com. "A lot of students bust their derrières to get into the best university or medical school or law school, but some get out-competed by students who cheat," he says. "I have zero sympathy for that. Students should be held accountable for what they do."

Moreover, if plagiarism were allowed to go unchecked, the impact on society could be catastrophic, according to Lawrence M. Hinman, director of the Values Institute at the University of San Diego. Hinman says trust is fundamental to the social, political and eco-

nomic fabric of any successful society. "Without trust in public and business institutions outside the family, an economy stops developing after a certain point," he says.

Researchers, for their part, acknowledge that self-reporting studies may underrepresent the true size of the plagiarism problem, given students' wide-ranging views on the morality of the activity.

"It's a moving target as far as students are concerned as to what actually constitutes plagiarism," says Rutgers' McCabe. "When I debrief a small percentage of them [after a survey], some of them say, 'Yeah, I did that, but I don't consider it cheating, so I didn't check it off.' "

Should teachers use plagiarism-detection services?

Many schools use private companies to ferret out student plagiarism. Chicago-based Glatt Plagiarism Services —

ing her 10th-graders to write scientific reports about leaves. The project represented half of the semester's grade, so students had to do well to pass the course. Pelton spelled that out in a contract she had her students and their parents sign. Section No. 7 warned, "Cheating and plagiarism will result in the failure of the assignment."

After checking her students' reports with TurnItIn. com, a plagiarism-detection service, Pelton concluded that 28 of her 118 students — one-quarter of the entire sophomore class — had plagiarized from Internet sites, books or each other. Pelton flunked them all. Outraged parents demanded that Pelton change the grades, arguing she hadn't adequately explained what constitutes plagiarism. Pelton, noting the contract, adamantly denied the charge. "I made a big point of telling them [that plagiarism] would cause them to fail," she said. "I gave them ample warning."[3]

When Pelton refused to change the grades, the parents went to the school board. On Dec. 11, 2001, the board and District Superintendent Michael Rooney decreed that the project would count for only 30 percent of the students' semester grades. All the students who would have failed due to plagiarism would now pass.

Rooney announced the policy change the following morning. Pelton was furious that her authority had been stripped away. "I went to my class and tried to teach the kids, but they were whooping and hollering and saying, 'We don't have to listen to you anymore,' " she said.[4]

Pelton immediately resigned, telling Rooney that she couldn't work in a district that didn't support her. "I knew I couldn't teach," she later recalled. "I left at noon and didn't come back."[5]

At least nine other Piper teachers quit in protest. The town's residents, many of whom had supported Pelton throughout the ordeal, ousted one school board member in a special recall election. Another board member resigned and a third did not seek re-election. Rooney also resigned under pressure last year.

Pelton, who opened a home day-care center after the plagiarism imbroglio, was honored last year with a certificate of appreciation from Kansas lawmakers. "I knew what I did that day would have an impact on my future," she said of her decision to resign. "Students not only need the building blocks of learning, but [also] morals and values."[6]

---

[1] For background, see Carolyn Kleiner and Mary Lord, "The Cheating Game," *U.S. News & World Report*, Nov. 22, 1999, p. 55.

[2] For background, see Kathy Koch, "Cheating in Schools," *The CQ Researcher*, Sept. 22, 2000, pp. 745-768.

[3] Quoted in Richard Jerome and Pam Grout, "Cheat Wave: School Officials Let Plagiarists Off Easy, So Teacher Christine Pelton Quit — Sending Her Town into a Tizzy," *Time*, June 17, 2002, p. 83.

[4] Quoted in Diane Carroll, "Plagiarism Dispute Divides a School District," *The Kansas City Star*, Jan. 29, 2002, p. A1.

[5] Quoted in Bill Lagattuta, "Paying the Piper," CBS News' "48 Hours," May 31, 2002.

[6] Quoted in "House Honors Teacher Who Resigned in Plagiarism Incident," The Associated Press, May 6, 2002.

whose clients include DePaul University and the U.S. Naval Academy — operates on the premise that students should be able to reproduce any document they actually wrote. After the company's software eliminates every fifth word of a suspected plagiarist's paper, the student is then asked to fill in the blanks to prove authorship. The program calculates a "plagiarism probability score" based on the number of correct responses, the time it took a student to complete the task and other factors.

"We authenticate authorship using techniques of cognitive science," said company founder Barbara Glatt. "It's easy and accurate."[15]

The system developed by TurnItIn.com functions like a supercharged search engine, comparing students' papers to documents residing in three places: public portions of the Internet; a proprietary database of books, journals and newspapers; and a proprietary database of all the student-authored papers ever submitted to it by all its clients. An "originality report" prepared for every paper checked by TurnItIn.com tells instructors what percent of the paper, if any, matches text ("strings" of approximately eight words or more) in other documents.

"An instructor can sit down with a student and say, 'Please explain to me why 82 percent of your paper came from this book or Web site,' " Barrie says. "Instructors no longer have to rely on gut feelings when they suspect plagiarism. There is just no way to sneak plagiarized material through our system — no way."

But some educators consider detection services as superficial "quick fixes" that allow teachers to sidestep the issues that caused their students to plagiarize in the first place. "Teachers who get too caught up acting like detectives ignore what they really ought to be doing as teachers, which is talking to students about things like originality and using sources correctly," says RIT's Scanlon. "Using a plagiarism checker gives you a reason to avoid having those conversations."

Syracuse's Howard agrees, adding that lazy teachers are also partly to blame for the plagiarism problem. "Giving students canned, mindless assignments that have no meaning for them just invites plagiarism," Howard says. "Those assignments are so mind-deadening that students who have not managed their time well may look for papers online, because they're not getting anything out of the experience anyway."

Howard says teachers who use plagiarism-detection services risk alienating their students — especially the honest ones — by sending the message that everyone is a potential plagiarist. She likens teachers who use the services to employers who subject their employees to mandatory drug testing.

"Using [detection services] to certify students' honesty, paper by paper, what that does to pedagogy is, to me, just horrific," Howard says.

Howard and other critics also contend that copying students' papers into TurnItIn.com's "proprietary" database and providing them to clients violates students' privacy rights and amounts to unauthorized copying and distribution of their intellectual property.

But many teachers say they inform their students at the start of a course that their work will be copied, retained and perhaps used as "evidence" by the detection service. However, some schools, including the University of California, Berkeley, have refused to use TurnItIn due to concerns about privacy and copyright violations.

"There probably were ways we could have done it legally, but given all the questions, the administration here just felt that it really didn't want to go in that direction," says Mike Smith, Berkeley's assistant chancellor for legal affairs.

Barrie maintains that his company is on "very solid legal ground" and uses students' papers only in ways authorized by the U.S. Copyright Act.[16] "The thousands of institutions that are currently our clients all sign an agreement with us, and we wouldn't have one client if what we were doing was illegal," Barrie says.

Are news organizations doing enough to guard against plagiarism and other types of journalistic fraud?

The Jayson Blair scandal has prompted news organizations everywhere to re-examine their ethics policies.

The Miami Herald, for example, was one of many newspapers that revamped its policy regarding the use of wire-service copy in articles written by staff reporters. *The Herald's* new policy requires reporters to more clearly distinguish the wire copy from their own text and tell readers specifically where it came from. Executive Editor Tom Fiedler says he was surprised that some of his reporters didn't think such attribution was necessary.

"They thought if it was on the wires, it was fair game" for them to use without attribution, Fiedler says.

Other news organizations clarified or changed their policies regarding the use of datelines, which traditionally indicate where the reporter actually worked on the story. New York-based Bloomberg News had bucked convention and used datelines to reflect where a story's action occurred, regardless of the reporter's physical location. But Bloomberg changed its policy after *The Times* revealed Blair had falsified datelines to conceal the fact that he hadn't traveled to the scene. Bloomberg Editor-in-chief Matthew Winkler said his organization had decided the old policy "could be misleading."[17]

Still other organizations revamped their policies regarding the use of unnamed or "anonymous" sources. Quotes that Blair fabricated and attributed to law-enforcement officials while covering the sniper case prompted a prosecutor in the case to call a news conference to deny the made-up assertions. Many experts were shocked when *The Times* conceded this spring that Blair's editors never asked him to identify his anonymous sources.

"That's just unbelievable," says Thomas Kunkel, dean of Blair's alma mater, the University of Maryland School of Journalism. "If I've got a reporter making accusations [like Blair did] on the front page of *The New York Times*, if I'm the editor, I'm going to want to know where they're coming from."

Rivard discourages the use of anonymous sources at the *San Antonio Express-News*. But if they are used, their identities must be revealed to senior editors. "If a reporter came in and said, 'I've got something but I can't tell you who the source is,' we wouldn't publish it," Rivard says.

At the *Seattle Times*, the Blair affair prompted editors to revive the paper's old system of newsroom "accuracy checks," in which news sources are contacted and asked about the accuracy, fairness and completeness of the paper's coverage.

"Accuracy is our prime directive," Executive Editor Michael Fancher wrote in a June 15 column announcing he was resurrecting the old policy. "Each of us in the newsroom has a personal responsibility to the highest standards of integrity and honesty, starting with devotion to accuracy in all our work."[18]

But no news organization did more to shore up its ethical standards than *The New York Times*. Shortly after the Blair scandal broke, Assistant Managing Editor Allan Siegal was asked to form a committee to determine why Blair hadn't been stopped sooner. The so-called Siegal Committee of 25 *Times* staffers and three distinguished outside journalists began its work in mid-May.

Heads also rolled at *The Times*. On June 5, Executive Editor Howell Raines and Managing Editor Gerald Boyd both resigned under pressure from Publisher Arthur Sulzberger Jr. On July 14, op-ed columnist Bill Keller, a former *Times* managing editor, became executive editor. On June 30, his first day on the job, Keller unveiled the committee's report and announced that he would accept its major recommendations, which he said would "improve the way we run the newsroom" and "protect our precious credibility."[19]

Among its many recommendations, the report suggested the appointment of a "public editor" — a position known at other newspapers as an ombudsman — to deal with reader complaints and write periodic columns about the *Times'* "journalistic practices." Keller said the public editor "can make us more sensitive on matters of fairness and accuracy, and enhance our credibility." [20] Keller also tapped Siegal as the paper's new "standards editor," who will establish journalistic standards and educate staffers on accuracy and ethics.

Geneva Overholser, a former editor of the *Des Moines Register* and a one-time ombudsman at *The Washington Post*, calls the *Times'* decision to appoint a public editor "a terrific first step. [It's] something that could have been helpful to them in the difficulties of the last few months."[21]

But *Washington Post* columnist Robert J. Samuelson thinks the *Times* still doesn't get it. "No place in American journalism is so smug and superior as *The New York Times*," he wrote on Aug. 13. "It [is] this conceit — the belief that *The Times* must be right because it is *The Times* and sets the rules — that ultimately caused the Jayson Blair debacle. Until that conceit is purged, *The Times* will remain vulnerable to similar blunders."[22]

In addition, Samuelson groused, "The public editor's appointment will last for a year and be reviewed; the editor's independence is compromised by being responsible to the executive editor; and it's unclear how often the public editor will write."

Rivard and other experts say news organizations are not doing enough to guard against plagiarizing reporters. "I think plagiarism is a bigger problem in American journalism today than many of us [in the media] have understood or acknowledged," he says. "The development of the Web may be the single, most important factor in both spawning an environment where plagiarism is committed more and where people succumb to that weakness more."

Kelly McBride, an ethics instructor at the St. Petersburg, Fla.-based Poynter Institute for journalism, says few news organizations devote much time to training their reporters to recognize and avoid plagiarism. "I don't think there's much conversation about plagiarism in most newsrooms, other than 'don't do it,' " McBride says.

Trudy Lieberman, a contributing editor at the *Columbia Journalism Review* and a media ethics instructor at New York University, agrees. Lieberman says journalistic plagiarism persists, in part, because news organizations don't deal with plagiarizing reporters in a consistent manner. "Plagiarism is acceptable at some organizations but not at others," Lieberman says. "Somebody can plagiarize and still be 'king of the hill' if they're a good columnist or someone the organization wants to keep. But more marginal employees [who get caught plagiarizing] may be asked to leave. There doesn't seem to be a standard punishment for journalistic plagiarism at all."

Michael Richards and Clay Calvert, professors of journalism and law at Pennsylvania State University, argue in a forthcoming article that rogue journalists —

and their employers — should be legally liable for plagiarism and other journalistic fraud.[23]

In the Blair case, according to Richards, *The Times* acted negligently and perpetrated fraud on its readers because it "ignored the warning signs" that Blair was filing demonstrably false stories. "*The Times'* top editors knew they had a problem, but they chose to ignore it," he says. "They abrogated their responsibility by ignoring the warning signs."[24]

But the University of Maryland's Kunkel and other experts point out that no news organization is safe from a rogue reporter. "Somebody who wants to undermine the system can do it very easily," Kunkel says. "You can say what you want and put in all kinds of safeguards, but basically, it's a system that depends on the trustworthiness of the reporters."

BACKGROUND

Imitation Encouraged

Plagiarism has not always been regarded as unethical. In fact, for most of recorded history, drawing from other writers' works was encouraged. This view was grounded in the belief that knowledge of the human condition should be shared by everyone, not owned or hoarded. The notion of individual authorship was much less important than it is today.

"Writers strove, even consciously, to imitate earlier great works," wrote authors Peter Morgan and Glenn Reynolds in their 1997 book *The Appearance of Impropriety*. "That a work had obvious parallels with an early work — even similar passages or phrases — was a mark of pride, not plagiarism. Imitation was bad only when it was disguised or a symptom of laziness. It was not denounced simply on the grounds of being 'unoriginal.'"[25]

Examples of this tradition abound in literature. In ancient Greece, for example, writers such as Homer, Plato, Socrates and Aristotle borrowed heavily from earlier works. "Aristotle lifted whole pages from Democritus," wrote Alexander Lindey in his 1952 book *Plagiarism and Originality.*

Novelist and former Vassar College English Professor Thomas Mallon agrees that the concept of originality was radically different centuries ago. "Jokes about out-and-out literary theft go back all the way to Aristophanes

and "The Frogs" [a play written in 405 B.C.], but what we call plagiarism was more a matter for laughter than litigation," Mallon wrote in his 1989 book *Stolen Words: Forays into the Origins and Ravages of Plagiarism.* "The Romans rewrote the Greeks. Virgil is, in a broadly imitative way, Homer, and for that matter, typologists can find most of the Old Testament in the New."

The Greek concept of imitation — known as *mimesis* — continued to influence writers during the Middle Ages. According to Syracuse's Howard, the Catholic Church promoted the medieval emphasis on mimesis because it was concerned with spreading the message of God. "The individual writer in this economy of authorship is beside the point, even a hindrance," Howard writes in her 1999 book *Standing in the Shadow of Giants: Plagiarists, Authors, Collaborators.* "Instead, the writer voices God's truth . . . and participates in the tradition of that truth-telling. Even in patron-sponsored writing for the purpose of entertainment, the writer's identity and originality are only tangentially at issue. Plagiarism was a concern that seldom arose."

Rise of Copyright

Attitudes about plagiarism began to change in the 16th century, as the Protestant Reformation swept across Western Europe. The notion that salvation could be attained without adhering to strict Catholic sacraments gave new importance to the concepts of originality and individual thought. These ideals were spread far and wide through the use of the printing press — invented in 1440 — and new copyright laws, which advanced the notion that individual authorship was good and that mimesis was bad.

Notably, religious reformers like Martin Luther were among the staunchest opponents of the new copyright laws — first proposed in the late 1400s — because they believed human learning should circulate unrestricted for the common good and betterment of mankind.

"Much like defenders of Internet freedoms of access and speech today, Luther and others objected that copyright laws would limit the free circulation of ideas and knowledge that had been made so widely and instantly available . . . [by] the printing press," scholar C. Jan Swearingen wrote in a 1999 essay.[26]

Passage of the first copyright laws — in England in 1710 and in the United States in 1790 — transformed writing into a viable economic pursuit. Mimesis was no

C H R O N O L O G Y

Before 1600 *Writers are encouraged to draw from others' works until printing press is invented and authorship becomes a profession.*

1700-1900 *Copyright laws make plagiarism an issue for schools, publishing houses and other institutions.*

1710 England passes first copyright law.

1790 Congress passes first U.S. copyright law.

1890s Plagiarism is commonplace at many colleges and universities.

1900-1990 *Schools, news organizations and other institutions struggle with plagiarism.*

1964 Thirty percent of the college students polled by Rutgers University researcher Donald McCabe admit plagiarizing at least once.

1971 Beatle George Harrison is sued for plagiarizing a copyrighted song and ordered to pay $587,000 in damages.

1972 Boston University successfully sues several Massachusetts-based term-paper mills for fraud. The following year, the Massachusetts legislature outlaws term-paper sales in the state.

September 1987 Sen. Joseph Biden Jr., D-Del., abandons his presidential bid after reporters catch him plagiarizing speeches from other politicians.

1989 University of Georgia researcher Fred Schab finds that 76 percent of high-school students have copied material "word for word" out of a book without attributing it.

1990-Present *The advent of the Internet makes committing plagiarism easier than ever. But experts disagree as to whether or not the invention is creating more plagiarists than would otherwise exist.*

1997 Boston University sues to prohibit term-paper mills from operating via the Internet. The court dismisses the suit, saying the mills did not violate federal racketeering laws, as the university alleged.

April 1998 *Boston Globe* columnist Mike Barnicle resigns amid allegations he plagiarized and fabricated articles.

May 1998 *The New Republic* fires writer Stephen Glass for fabricating an article and later finds that he had plagiarized or fabricated at least two-dozen other articles.

February 2001 Researcher McCabe finds that 52 percent of high-school juniors admitted to copying "a few sentences from a Web site without footnoting them." Sixteen percent said they had turned in a paper "obtained in large part from a term-paper mill or Web site."

April 2001 University of Virginia physics Professor Louis Bloomfield refers 158 cases of alleged plagiarism to the school's student-run Honor Committee.

January 2002 Best-selling authors Stephen Ambrose and Doris Kearns Goodwin are accused of plagiarism. Both claim they did so unintentionally.

May 2002 A multi-campus survey concludes that the incidence of Internet-facilitated plagiarism among college students is no greater than the level of "conventional" copying in the pre-Internet era.

Feb. 5, 2003 In an address to the United Nations Security Council, Secretary of State Colin Powell cites a British government report detailing Iraq's efforts to conceal alleged weapons of mass destruction. The report is later found to be based largely on outdated plagiarized articles from the Internet.

May 1, 2003 Reporter Jayson Blair resigns from *The New York Times* after getting caught plagiarizing an article from the *San Antonio Express-News*.

May 11, 2003 *The New York Times* publishes a 14,000-word account of Blair's plagiarism and other acts of journalistic fraud.

June 5, 2003 *New York Times* Executive Editor Howell Raines and Managing Editor Gerald Boyd resign in wake of the Blair scandal.

Rogue Reporter at *The New York Times*

We have to stop Jayson from writing for *The Times*. Right Now." When Jonathan Landman, the metropolitan editor of *The New York Times*, wrote that now-famous e-mail message to two newsroom colleagues in April 2002, he had good reason for concern. Jayson Blair, a young reporter on his staff, was making numerous mistakes and was behaving erratically.

But *Times* officials didn't stop Blair. In fact, they assigned the 27-year-old to the prestigious national desk, where he covered high-profile stories such as the Washington, D.C., sniper case. Blair's work on those stories was nothing short of a "journalistic disaster," declares a report by 25 *Times* staffers and three outside journalists. Known as the Siegal Committee report, it concludes that Landman's "stop Jayson" e-mail was just one of several red flags about Blair that were ignored by top management at the *Times*.[1]

Blair resigned from the *Times* last May 1, two days after *The San Antonio Express-News* accused him of plagiarizing an *Express-News* story about the mother of a Texas soldier missing in Iraq. In the days that followed, *Times* journalists uncovered problems in dozens of other articles by Blair.[2] Besides lifting materials from other newspapers and wire services, Blair fabricated comments and scenes and otherwise misled readers about what he allegedly witnessed. Today, Blair is widely regarded as one of the most notorious plagiarists and fabricators in journalism history.

Blair reportedly exhibited poor journalistic ethics before the *Times* first hired him in June 1998. He had attended the University of Maryland in the mid-1990s and served as editor of the school's newspaper, *The Diamondback*, from 1996 to 1997. This summer, after the *Times* published a 14,000-word account of Blair's ethical breaches, some 30 former Maryland students said his "disgraceful behavior at *The New York Times* resembled a recurring pattern we witnessed when he worked at *The Diamondback*."[3]

But Blair received good reviews from his professors, who helped him land an internship at the *Times* in June 1998. Blair had a "strong start" at the paper, though he

occasionally had problems with reliability, the Siegal Committee found. *The Times* gave Blair another internship the following summer. After that, the paper hired him as an "intermediate" reporter, meaning he would be closely supervised for up to three years.

Blair performed well for about a year. But in fall 2000, he started making frequent errors. Nevertheless, he became a regular staff reporter in early 2001, almost two years before his probationary period ended. "I think race was the decisive factor in his promotion," Landman told the Siegal Committee.[4]

But Gerald Boyd, the then-deputy managing editor who had recommended Blair's promotion, said it was "absolute drivel" that he had disregarded the reporter's mistakes on account of his race. Like Blair, Boyd is also African-American. "Did I pat [Blair] on the back? Did I say 'hang in there'? Yes, but I did that with everybody," Boyd said after the scandal broke.[5]

That fall, Blair claimed his problems stemmed from the anguish of losing a cousin in the Sept. 11 terrorist attacks. In fact, he did not, *The Times* discovered after he resigned.

In February 2002, with Blair's mistakes mounting, Boyd warned the young reporter that he was "blowing a big opportunity." Blair, who said he was struggling with serious "personal problems," was granted a leave of absence. "When he returned, so did his errors," the Siegal report declares. Blair was warned that his job was in peril, and his editors began supervising him closely. Blair resented the short-leash approach and asked to be transferred to another department. Landman reluctantly sent him to the sports desk, warning the editor there to "be careful" with the young reporter.[6]

Blair's sports stint was short-lived. On Oct. 20, 2002, *Times* officials assigned him to a team of reporters covering the sniper shootings. *The Times* had been scooped on some developments in the story, and Boyd and Howell Raines, the paper's executive editor — thought Blair, who was familiar with the D.C. suburbs, could help bolster the paper's coverage. *Times* National Editor Jim

Roberts, who was in charge of the coverage team, says no one warned him about Blair's bad track record. "This was an invitation to disaster," the Siegal Committee declared.

Blair's stories about the sniper case contained numerous factual errors, fabricated or plagiarized quotes and other problems, the *Times'* internal investigation found. In a Dec. 22, 2002, article, for example, Blair wrote that "all the evidence" pointed to [Lee] Malvo as the triggerman in the attacks." The piece drew strong criticism from a prosecutor in the case, who called a press conference and denounced much of the report as "dead wrong."[7]

Former *New York Times* reporter Jayson Blair committed plagiarism and other forms of journalistic fraud in more than three-dozen articles.

AFP Photo/Courtesy New York Times

Times' computerized photo archives. But knowing that Roberts did not buy his explanation, Blair resigned.[8]

A few weeks later, Blair told *The New York Observer* his actions stemmed, in part, from a host of personal problems and that he had turned to alcohol and cocaine in an effort to cope. When he finally got caught, he said, he was pretty desperate. "I was either going to kill myself or I was going to kill the journalist persona," he said. "So Jayson Blair the human being could live, Jayson Blair the journalist had to die."[9]

Blair authored a short narrative about his experiences at *The Times* for the October 2003 issue of *Jane* magazine. He is also writing a book about his experiences; the working title reportedly is *Burning Down My Master's House: My Life at The New York Times.*

Still, *The Times* kept Blair on the high-profile national staff when the war in Iraq started. Blair's home-front reports about the war, like his sniper stories, were riddled with factual errors and fabricated quotes. In a March 27 piece, for example, Blair claimed to have traveled to Palestine, W. Va., to interview family members of then-missing Pvt. Jessica Lynch. Blair wrote that Lynch's father "choked up as he stood on his porch here overlooking the tobacco fields and cow pastures." In fact, the porch overlooks no such thing. According to *The Times*, Blair never visited the Lynch home, but instead tried to concoct the scene by drawing details from other published news accounts.

Blair was finally tripped up when the *San Antonio Express-News* complained in April that Blair had plagiarized a *News* article about the family of a soldier from Los Fresnos, Texas. Roberts called Blair into his office and asked him to describe what he had seen in Texas. Blair did so in great detail, describing the family's white stucco house, the red Jeep in the driveway, and the roses blooming in the yard. In fact, Blair had not gone to Texas, but instead had viewed pictures of the house stored in the

[1] The Siegal Committee's "Report of the Committee on Safeguarding the Integrity of Our Journalism," was published on July 28, 2003. It is available on *The New York Times* Web site at www.nytco.com.

[2] For background, see Dan Barry, *et. al.*, "Correcting the Record: Times Reporter Who Resigned Leaves Long Trail of Deception," *The New York Times*, May 11, 2003.

[3] Quoted in the Siegal Committee report, *op. cit.*

[4] *Ibid.*

[5] Quoted in Howard Kurtz, "To the Editors: How Could This Happen? N.Y. Times Staff, Execs in 'Painful and Honest' Meeting Over Plagiarism Fiasco," *The Washington Post*, May 15, 2003, p. C1.

[6] Quoted in the Siegal Committee report, *op. cit.*

[7] For background, see Matthew Barakat, "Prosecutor Denies Teen Was Sole Sniper," The Associated Press Online, Dec. 23, 2002.

[8] See Barry, *op. cit.*

[9] Quoted in Sridhar Pappu, "So Jayson Blair Could Live, the Journalist Had to Die," *The New York Observer*, May 26, 2003, p. 1.

longer tolerated or encouraged — in fact it was illegal. "No longer was a writer supposed to build on top of the structures left by earlier figures; now one was supposed to sweep the ground clear and build from scratch," Morgan and Reynolds write. "Once money was involved, people became more vigilant for copying, whether real or imagined."[27]

Mallon agrees. "Plagiarism didn't become a truly sore point with writers until they thought of writing as their trade," he writes in *Stolen Words*. "The writer, a new professional, was invented by a machine [the printing press]. Suddenly his capital and identity were at stake. Things were now competitive and personal, and when writers thought they'd been plundered they fought back."[28]

'Fertile Ground'

Meanwhile, other forces were creating "fertile ground for plagiarism" at America's colleges and universities, explains Sue Carter, an associate professor of English at Ohio's Bowling Green State University. Admissions started rising dramatically in the mid-1800s, in part because schools began accepting women for the first time. As enrollments increased, schools began requiring students to present more of their work in writing, rather than orally, as they had in the past, Carter says.

"At Harvard . . . by the 1890s, first-year students wrote a new paper every two weeks as well as one short paper six days a week for the entire academic year," Carter wrote in a 1999 article on the history of plagiarism. "In such a climate . . . students may have felt plagiarism to be a viable option."[29]

Aside from the sheer volume of writing, students also may have felt pushed toward plagiarism because many schools assigned unimaginative, "canned topics" for those papers, Carter says. "Some students believed it was OK to cheat because the teachers weren't doing their jobs. For them, it made sense to plagiarize."

To be sure, not all the student plagiarism of the mid-19th century was intentional. There were no universally agreed-upon guidelines for using sources properly. Writer's manuals didn't appear until the late 19th or early 20th centuries. "It's not like there was an *MLA Handbook* or a *Chicago Manual of Style*," Carter says. "Students knew they couldn't claim another person's words as their own, but there was nothing to give them specific, concrete guidelines about avoiding plagiarism, such as using quotation marks or footnotes."

Still, students who were so inclined in the mid-1800s could easily obtain completed papers from fraternity houses or "term-paper mills" that set up shop near many universities. A graduate student who taught writing at Harvard in the 1890s even sold term papers himself, Carter says.

Inadvertent academic plagiarism began to level off in the 1920s, as specialized handbooks began to appear providing guidelines on the correct use of sources. Even so, the number of students who patronized term-paper mills continued to grow. Calling themselves academic "research" companies, they advertised in campus newspapers and "alternative" publications and often employed graduate students to do the writing.

In Boston in the 1960s and '70s, for example, term papers were hawked on street corners and from Volkswagen buses, says Kevin Carleton, assistant vice president for public relations at Boston University (BU). "You could find them in Kenmore Square and Harvard Square and at Boston College and Northeastern University," Carleton says.

In 1972, BU sued several local term-paper mills for fraud and won an injunction prohibiting them from operating. The following year, the Massachusetts legislature banned the sale of term papers. Today, 16 states ban term-paper mills, according to the Denver-based National Conference of State Legislatures.

But BU wasn't so successful in 1997 when it tried to use federal anti-racketeering laws to prohibit all term-paper mills from using the fledgling Internet. A federal court dismissed the university's suit on the grounds that the Internet-based mills could not be prosecuted under the racketeering law. The judge also ruled that the university could not prove that it had been substantially harmed by the mills, since it could name only one student who tried to pass off an Internet-purchased paper as his own.

The mills named in the suit had planned to mount a free-speech defense, but they didn't have to use it. "We prepared a very strong First Amendment stance," said Boston lawyer Harvey Schwartz, who represented two of the operations. "This case was about academic freedom on the Internet."[30]

Second Chances

As in the literary and academic worlds, attitudes toward plagiarism also have changed over time in the realm of journalism. "Twenty or 30 years ago, there was plenty of plagiarism, embellishment and other ethical shortcuts," said Howard Kurtz, media critic for *The Washington Post*. "But they didn't always come to light, in part because journalists were reluctant to expose one another."[31]

The University of Maryland's Kunkel agrees. "When I first broke into the business 30 years ago, I worked with a guy who once in a while made up quotes and things," Kunkel recalls. "It was in high-school sports, and he sort of viewed it as saving everybody's time because the quotes were so predictable and innocuous. I don't think his editors knew, but it was pretty common knowledge in newsrooms around the county that there were people who did stuff like that."

In 1972, for example, the now-defunct *National Observer* fired journalist Nina Totenberg for lifting without attribution several paragraphs from a *Washington Post* profile of Rep. Thomas P. "Tip" O'Neill, D-Mass., who was about to become House majority leader. "I was in a hurry. I used terrible judgment," Totenberg said in a 1995 interview. "I should have been punished. I have a strong feeling that a young reporter is entitled to one mistake and to have the holy bejeezus scared out of her to never do it again."[32]

Totenberg got a second chance and today is a well-regarded legal-affairs correspondent for National Public Radio.

Other high-profile cases in which admitted or alleged plagiarists returned to journalism after their work was questioned include:

- **Mike Barnicle** — the legendary *Boston Globe* columnist resigned in 1998 amid allegations of plagiarism and fabricating articles. Today he writes a column for the *New York Daily News* and frequently appears on MSNBC's "Hardball" and other television programs.
- **Elizabeth Wurtzel** — was fired by *The Dallas Morning News* in 1988 for plagiarism. Wurtzel went on to write for prestigious magazines such as *New York* and *The New Yorker*. She has also written two best-selling books, *Prozac Nation: Young and Depressed in America* (1994) and *Bitch: In Praise of Difficult Women* (1999).
- **Marcia Stepanek**, who was fired by *Business Week* magazine in January 2001 for plagiarizing a *Washington Post* article on computer privacy.

Stepanek said she did not intend to plagiarize. "I was sloppy with my notes but nothing more," she said.[33] Today, she is the executive editor of *CIO Insight*, a magazine for information-technology professionals.

Stephen Glass, who was fired by *The New Republic* in 1998 for plagiarizing and fabricating articles, also has cashed in on his wrongdoing. His "novel" about his exploits, *The Fabulist*, was published in May. It recounts the misadventures of a young writer named Stephen Glass who gets fired from a Washington, D.C.-based magazine for making up news stories and features. The protagonist — like the real Glass — even creates bogus voice-mail recordings and Web sites to conceal his deceit. A movie about the young reporter's deceptions, "Shattered Glass," is slated to open next month.

Charles Lane, the editor who fired Glass from *The New Republic* in 1998, said he was stunned "that someone could do what Steve did and cash in on it."[34]

"Being disgraced is not so bad these days," said McBride, at the Poynter Institute. "In our society . . . people can capitalize on values [such as] cleverness, creativity, glibness, sharp-tongued wit and cynicism. It really says something about the entertainment society we live in — in that world, we don't really care how smarmy you are."[35]

CURRENT SITUATION

Plagiarism and Politics

From time to time, plagiarism ensnares politicians as well. Sen. Joseph Biden Jr., D-Del., for example, was forced to abandon his quest to become his party's 1988 presidential nominee when sleuthing reporters caught him delivering campaign speeches containing phrases plagiarized from other American and British politicians. The senator also faced allegations he had plagiarized a paper during law school. In dropping out of the race, Biden acknowledged that he "made some mistakes," but claimed the media "exaggerated" his missteps.[36]

In recent months, critics have assailed President Bush and British Prime Minister Tony Blair over revelations that they touted two bogus reports about Iraq's alleged weapons of mass destruction (WMD) — one found to contain plagiarized materials and the other based on forged documents — to win support for attacking Iraq.

The report containing plagiarized materials was posted on Blair's official Web site on Feb. 3, 2003.[37] Among other things, it claimed to provide "up-to-date details" of Iraq's efforts to conceal its alleged weapons of mass destruction from U.N. weapons inspectors. Secretary of State Colin Powell cited the report in his Feb. 5, 2003, address to the U.N. Security Council, saying, "I would call my colleagues' attention to the fine paper that the United Kingdom distributed yesterday which describes in exquisite detail Iraqi deception activities."[38]

Within hours, news organizations discovered that the report that Powell had cited was based largely on out-of-date magazine articles from the *Middle East Review* and other journals that had been plagiarized — typographical errors and all — from the Internet.[39]

In an interview with *The New York Times*, a spokesman for Blair acknowledged that the report was, indeed, a "pull-together of a variety of sources." The spokesman added that "we should . . . have acknowledged which bits came from public sources and which bits came from other sources."[40]

Reporters quickly tracked down the author of one of the plagiarized articles, Ibrahim al-Marashi, who said British officials had not asked permission to incorporate his work into their intelligence dossier. Al-Marashi, who had written the article as a postgraduate student at the Monterey Institute of International Studies in Monterey, Calif., said he believed his work was accurate, but he told a *New York Times* reporter, "Had they [British officials] consulted me, I could have provided them with more updated information."[41]

In a later interview, al-Marashi said British officials distorted his work to make the Iraqi threat appear more serious than he believed it to be. "It connected me with the . . . case for going to war," al-Marashi said this summer. "It was never my intention to have it support such an argument to provide evidence to go to war."[42]

To date, none of the WMD described by President Bush and Prime Minister Blair have been found in Iraq.

'Poisonous Atmosphere'

Some journalists say news organizations have gone overboard in their effort to enforce tougher, new ethical standards in the wake of the Jayson Blair scandal.

Many point to the trouble that befell Rick Bragg, a Pulitzer Prize-winning *New York Times* reporter. Bragg angrily resigned from the paper on May 28, five days after *The Times* published an editor's note saying an article he had written the previous June had relied too heavily on the work of an uncredited freelance journalist, J. Wesley Yoder. *The Times* stated in its editor's note that the article, which described the lives of oystermen on Florida's Gulf Coast, should have carried Yoder's byline as well as Bragg's. *The Times* suspended Bragg for two weeks as a result of the incident.

Bragg readily admitted that he had done little firsthand reporting on the story, and said he didn't tell his editors about Yoder's contribution to the story because it was *The Times'* practice not to credit freelancers. "It would have been nice for [Yoder] to share a byline, or at least a tagline, but that's not the policy," he told the *Columbia Journalism Review* on May 23. "I don't make the policies."[43]

Yoder saw it that way as well. "This is what stringers do — the legwork," he said. "I did most of the reporting and Rick wrote it. Rick tried to bring the piece alive, to take the reader there, and he did a darn good job of it."[44]

In an interview a few days later, Bragg blamed his suspension on the "poisonous atmosphere" that he said had developed at *The Times* following the Jayson Blair incident. "Obviously, I'm taking a bullet here; anyone with half a brain can see that," he told *The Washington Post's* Kurtz. "Reporters are being bad-mouthed daily. I hate it. It makes me sick."[45]

Bragg quit the paper. But his defense — that it was a common and accepted practice at *The Times* for correspondents to rely on the work of unattributed freelancers, stringers and interns — didn't sit well with some of his colleagues. Peter Kilborn, a reporter in *The Times'* Washington bureau, chastised Bragg in an e-mail to the newspaper's national desk. "Bragg's comments in defense of his reportorial routines are outrageous," Kilborn wrote. "I hope there is some way that we as correspondents . . . can get the word out . . . that we do not operate that way. Bragg says he works in a poisonous atmosphere. He's the poison."[46]

Despite his rocky departure from *The Times*, Bragg landed on his feet. He has negotiated a $1 million deal to write a book about Pvt. Jessica Lynch — about whom Jayson Blair had falsified one of his reports. (*See sidebar, p. 41.*)

Action in Schools

Teachers and schools across the country are taking a variety of steps to combat plagiarism. Some school districts have policies for dealing with plagiarism at the elementary, middle school and secondary school levels. The Springfield Township School District in Erdenheim, Pa., for example, defines plagiarism as "Direct copying of the work of another submitted as the student's own." Under the district's policy, plagiarism includes "Lack of in-text or in-project documentation; Documentation that does not check out or does not match Works Cited/ Works Consulted;" and "Work that suddenly appears on final due date without a clear provenance."

"We believe that we must not only teach the ethics and mechanics of documentation, but we must also hold students accountable for the ethical use of the ideas and words of others," the district's policy states. "Plagiarism, in any form, is unethical and unacceptable."

Lawrence High School in Fairfield, Maine, requires students and parents to sign a plagiarism policy every year that defines plagiarism and lays out the consequences for violators. First-time offenders get three options: rewrite the plagiarized paper within a week; write an entirely different paper within a week; or receive a zero on the rejected paper. Subsequent offenses receive automatic zeroes. The policy also outlines procedures in which students can challenge plagiarism allegations.

"School faculty members and administrators should take special care to define [plagiarism] and explain how to avoid it," Kelley R. Taylor, general counsel of the National Association of Secondary School Principals (NASSP), wrote in a recent issue of *Principal Leadership*,

How to Avoid Plagiarism

"Plagiarism involves two kinds of wrong," according to the Modern Language Association (MLA). "Using another person's ideas, information, or expressions without [acknowledgment] constitutes intellectual theft. Passing off another person's ideas, information, or expressions as your own . . . constitutes fraud." Here are the MLA's plagiarism guidelines for writers:

You have plagiarized if you:

- Took notes without differentiating summaries, paraphrases or quotations from others' work or ideas and then presented wording from the notes as if they were your own.
- Copied text from the Web and pasted it into your paper without quotation marks or citation.
- Presented facts without saying where you found them.
- Repeated or paraphrased wording without acknowledgment.
- Took someone's unique or particularly apt phrase without acknowledgment.
- Paraphrased someone's argument or presented someone's line of thought without acknowledgment.
- Bought or otherwise acquired a research paper and handed in part or all of it as your own.

To avoid plagiarism:

- List the writers and viewpoints discovered in your research and use the list to double-check the material in your report before turning it in.
- While taking notes, keep separate and distinct your own ideas, summaries of others' ideas or exact wording from other people's work.
- Identify the sources of all exact wording, paraphrases, ideas, arguments and facts that you borrow.

Source: Joseph Gibaldi, *The MLA Handbook for Writers of Research Papers*, Sixth Edition, Modern Language Association of America, 2003.

the NASSP's journal. "Teach your faculty members to teach students what plagiarism is and how to avoid it with proper references and source citations."[47]

Taylor says teachers can do a number of things in their classrooms to combat plagiarism, such as structuring writing assignments so students have to revise their work and requiring students to turn in annotated bibliographies, to show they are familiar with their sources.

Many college professors and administrators, though, complain that high schools aren't doing enough to teach students about plagiarism. "I don't know what's going

Should educators use commercial services to combat plagiarism?

YES John Barrie
President, TurnItIn.com

Written for The CQ Researcher, September 2003

I spent more than 10 years researching how our brains create a conscious representation of the world, and the take-home message is that we draw from the past to create the present. Academic endeavors work in a similar manner. Students from elementary school to postgraduate are constantly learning from and building upon the corpus of prior work from their peers, authors of books or journal articles, lectures from faculty or from information found on the Internet. One of the best methods for learning involves collaboration or peer review among groups of students in order to share ideas and criticism regarding course material.

Subsequent intellectual accomplishments of students — or academics — are sometimes measured by their ability to distill weeks, months or years of hard work into a manuscript of original thought. For example, a high-school student might compose a book report about Othello while a college undergrad might write a manuscript regarding the sublime philosophy of Nietzsche. In either case, the faculty is attempting to ascertain whether that student has understood the course material. The problem begins when faculty cannot determine whether a student wrote a term paper or plagiarized it from other sources. But is that a problem?

TurnItIn receives about 15,000 papers per day from students in 51 countries writing across the curriculum, and about 30 percent of those papers are less than original. This is supported by the largest-ever study of plagiarism involving more than 18,000 students on 23 campuses. The study (released this month by Rutgers University Professor Donald McCabe) concluded that nearly 40 percent of college undergraduates admitted to plagiarizing term papers using information cut-and-pasted from the Internet.

This raises the obvious question: "Why is Internet plagiarism growing exponentially in the face of honor codes, vigilant faculty and severe punishments ranging all the way to expulsion?" The answer: The status quo doesn't work, and our society's future leaders are rapidly building a foundation of shaky ethics while cheating their way to a degree.

The real shame is that while some administrators shirk their responsibility to face the problem or are in complete dereliction of their duty as educators by not demanding original work from all students, ethical, hard-working students are being out-competed by their cheating peers — and it's an outrage.

Digital plagiarism is a digital problem and demands a digital solution, whether it's TurnItIn or otherwise. No one wants to live in a society populated by Enron executives.

NO Rebecca Moore Howard
Associate Professor of Writing and Rhetoric, Syracuse University

Written for The CQ Researcher, September 2003

Teaching, not software, is the key to preventing plagiarism. Today's students can access an array of electronic texts and images unimaginable just 20 years ago, and students' relationship to the practice of information-sharing has changed along with the technology.

But today's students lack extensive training and experience in working carefully from print sources, and they may not understand that they need to learn this skill. They may also find it difficult to differentiate between kinds of sources on the Internet. With information arriving as a cacophony of electronic voices, even well-intentioned students have difficulty keeping track of — much less citing — who said what.

Moreover, the sheer volume of available information frequently leaves student writers feeling that they have nothing new to say about an issue. Hence too many students — one in three, according to a recent survey conducted by Rutgers University Professor Donald McCabe — may fulfill assignments by submitting work they have not written.

Were we in the throes of widespread moral decay, capture-and-punishment might provide an appropriate deterrent. We are, however, in the midst of a revolution in literacy, and teachers' responses must be more complex. They must address the underlying issues: students' ability to conduct research, comprehend extended written arguments, evaluate sources and produce their own persuasive written texts, in explicit dialogue with their sources.

Classrooms must engage students in text and in learning — communicating a value to these activities that extends beyond grades earned and credentials accrued. McCabe, who is a founder of the renowned Center for Academic Integrity at Duke University, recommends pedagogy and policies that speak to the causes of plagiarism, rather than buying software for detection and punishment. In a 2003 position statement, the Council of Writing Program Administrators urges, "Students should understand research assignments as opportunities for genuine and rigorous inquiry and learning." The statement offers extensive classroom suggestions for teachers and cautions that using plagiarism-catching software may "justify the avoidance of responsible teaching methods."

Buying software instead of revitalizing one's teaching means that teachers, like students, have allowed the electronic environment to encourage a reductive, automated vision of the educational experience. As one of my colleagues recently remarked, "The 'world's leading plagiarism-prevention system' is not TurnItIn.com — it's careful pedagogy."

on in high schools. Some students don't seem to be prepared to do proper citation and research" at the college level, says Ronald Stump, vice chancellor of student affairs at the University of Colorado at Boulder. "I don't want to paint every high school in the same way, but a lot of students do seem to be surprised" when they get accused of plagiarism.

Most Colorado professors talk to their classes about plagiarism or include warnings about it on their course syllabi, Stump says. Like many schools, the university has a student-run honor committee that disseminates information about plagiarism and adjudicates plagiarism cases referred to it by school faculty. Penalties for plagiarism range from a letter saying a student broke the honor code to expulsion. In addition, plagiarists frequently are required to attend academic-integrity classes, says Allison Jennings, 21, a political science major and the director of adjudication for the university's honor code council. "It really discusses how not to plagiarize," Jennings says of the class. "It's really about education."

The University of Virginia also goes to great lengths to educate students about plagiarism, says Eramo, of the school's Honor Committee. While most professors educate and warn their students about plagiarism, the specifics of the warnings vary. "They often will put statements on their syllabi about what plagiarism is and what they will and will not accept, and what kinds of citation requirements they have," Eramo says. "But it definitely varies from faculty member to faculty member."

Eramo says the Honor Committee is trying to get faculty members to understand that not every student has the same understanding of what plagiarism is and how to avoid it. "So many students are coming here without that knowledge, and the faculty are sort of expecting them to have it, and they don't," Eramo says.

The Honor Committee has its own plagiarism-education program, Eramo says. Students who attend the summer orientation session, for example, get a 20-minute presentation about the honor system that includes information on plagiarism. Each fall, Honor Committee staff visit every dormitory and speak to students about the consequences for plagiarism and other forms of cheating. The committee also hosts voluntary round-table discussions about the honor code during the year.

OUTLOOK

Internet Blamed

Although the Jayson Blair scandal sent a loud wake-up call to all reporters and editors, academics and working journalists alike say journalism will continue, nonetheless, to be occasionally tainted by plagiarizing reporters. Many blame the ease of plagiarizing from the Internet and the demands of online journalism's round-the-clock deadline pressure.

Before the Internet, reporters' deadlines typically fell only once a day, notes the University of Maryland's Kunkel. Today, however, reporters for both print and electronic news outlets are often expected to break stories on their employers' Web sites as soon as possible, and update them whenever the circumstances change. The pressure-packed environment tempts some reporters to plagiarize, he says. "Some plagiarizing is certainly driven by [deadline] pressure," says Kunkel, who adds that "computers and electronic databases have made it easy — maybe too easy — to co-opt other people's work."

The San Antonio Express-News's Rivard agrees. "People who might not have copied something out of another newspaper in the pre-electronic era can now get an extraordinary amount of information about any topic, anytime, using the Internet," Rivard says. "It's easy to abuse that kind of access."

Others downplay the connection between plagiarism and online journalism. "We do operate under more pressure than in the past, but that's no excuse for failing to follow the protections and guidelines that should be in place for ensuring the integrity of a story," says *The Miami Herald's* Fiedler. "We would never tell our reporters to cut corners or not verify something in order to get it online quickly — we just don't do that."

Fiedler does not believe the Blair scandal will permanently alter the public's perception of the media. "Most readers who followed it did not leap to some drastically dark conclusion that the credibility of the media is now gone," he says. "If they were skeptical of what they saw in the media [before the scandal] they just added a count to their indictment. But if they tended to give the media generally good marks for credibility, I think they will continue to do so."

Kunkel, ultimately, also is optimistic. "American journalism has never been more professional than it is today, and the instances of plagiarism are probably rarer than ever," he says. "But when somebody like Jayson Blair gets exposed, there's such an uproar that everybody believes the industry is going to hell in a handbasket. That's not so."

A similar debate promises to continue raging over plagiarism in education. Some experts say the problem is only going to get worse until students change their perception of the Internet. Rutgers' McCabe says many feel that material found on the Internet is in the public domain and that they may freely "cut and paste" it into their own papers.

"A large number of students understand that adults — teachers and others — think that [cut-and-paste plagiarism] is wrong, but they don't think it is," McCabe says. "Whether they believe it's wrong or not, they're trying to make the argument that it's not cheating."

Other experts say schools should combat plagiarism — not by focusing on detection and interdiction — but by better clarifying what plagiarism is in a digital age. "As teachers, we really own the problem," says Springfield Township High School librarian Valenza. "At our school, we're really trying to develop a culture where kids understand what plagiarism is and how to avoid it."

The Rochester Institute's Scanlon agrees. "We seem to be turning over to computers a problem that's supposedly caused by computers and the Internet, and I'm not so sure that's wise," he says. "Plagiarism is not a technological problem — it's a problem that has to do with ethical behavior and the correct use of sources. And it existed long before the advent of the Internet."

NOTES

1. Quoted in Dan Barry *et al.*, "Correcting the Record: Times Reporter Who Resigned Leaves Long Trail of Deception," *The New York Times*, May 11, 2003, p. A1.

2. Quoted in Peter Johnson, "Media Weigh In On 'Journalistic Fraud,' " *USA Today*, May 12, 2003, p. A1.

3. The *Oxford English Dictionary* defines plagiarism as "the wrongful appropriation or purloining, and publication as one's own, of the ideas, or the expression of the ideas (literary, artistic, musical, mechanical, etc.) of another.

4. Alexander Lindey, *Plagiarism and Originality* (1952), in Joseph Gibaldi, *MLA Handbook for Writers of Research Papers*, 6th ed. (2003), p. 66.

5. The effect that a plagiarized work has on the market value of a copyrighted work is a key provision of the Copyright Act of 1976. For background, see Kenneth Jost, "Copyright and the Internet," *The CQ Researcher*, Sept. 29, 2000, pp. 769-792.

6. Quoted in Stephen Ambrose, "Accusations of Plagiarism Deserve an Honest Reply," Newhouse News Service, May 2, 2002.

7. For background, see Kathy Koch, "Cheating in Schools," *The CQ Researcher*, Sept. 22, 2000, pp. 745-768.

8. Donald McCabe and Linda Trevino, "What We Know About Cheating in College: Longitudinal Trends and Recent Developments," *Change*, January/February 1996, pp. 29-33.

9. See Patrick M. Scanlon and David R. Neumann, "Internet Plagiarism Among College Students," *Journal of College Student Development*, May/June 2002, pp. 375-384.

10. See Donald McCabe, "Cheating: Why Students Do It and How We Can Help them Stop," *American Educator*, winter 2001, pp. 38-43.

11. See B. Brandes, "Academic Honesty: A Special Study of California Students," California State Department of Education, 1986.

12. See Fred Schab, "Schooling Without Learning: Thirty Years of Cheating in High School," *Adolescence*, Vol. 23 (1991), pp. 681-687.

13. Amy Harmon, "261 Lawsuits Filed on Music Sharing," *The New York Times*, Sept. 9, 2003, p. A1. See also John Leland, "Beyond File-Sharing, A Nation of Copiers," *The New York Times*, Sept. 14, 2003, Sec. 9, p. 1.

14. Bruce Orwall, *et al.*, "Music Industry Presses 'Play' on Plan to Save Its Business," *The Wall Street Journal*, Sept. 9, 2003, p. A1.

15. Quoted in Tom Anderson, "Software Tattles on Academic Plagiarists," *The Oakland* [California] *Tribune*, Feb. 4, 2002.

16. For more information on U.S. copyright law, see Jost, *op. cit.* A detailed legal brief addressing copy-

right-related questions directed against TurnItIn.com is at www.turnitin.com/static/legal/legal_document.html.

17. Quoted in Howard Kurtz, "Rick Bragg Quits at New York Times," *The Washington Post*, May 29, 2003, p. C1.

18. Quoted in Michael R. Fancher, "Newspaper Bringing Back System of Accuracy Checks," *The Seattle Times*, June 15, 2003, p. A2.

10. Keller's memo and the Siegal report are available at: www.nytco.com.

20. *Ibid.*

21. Quoted in Howard Kurtz, "N.Y. Times to Appoint Ombudsman," *The Washington Post*, July 31, 2003, p. C1.

22. Robert J. Samuelson, "Smug Journalism," *The Washington Post*, Aug. 13, 2003, p. A27.

23. The article will be published this fall in the *Fordham Intellectual Property, Media and Entertainment Law Journal.*

24. Quoted in Cynthia Cotts, "Can The Times be Sued?" *The Village Voice*, Sept. 10, 2003.

25. Quoted in Peter W. Morgan and Glenn H. Reynolds, *The Appearance of Impropriety: How the Ethics Wars Have Undermined American Government, Business, and Society* (1997).

26. See C. Jan Swearingen, "Originality, Authenticity, Imitation and Plagiarism: Augustine's Chinese Cousins," in Lise Buranen and Alice M. Roy (eds.), *Perspectives on Plagiarism and Intellectual Prosperity in a Postmodern World* (1999), pp. 19-30.

27. Morgan and Reynolds, *op. cit.*

28. Quoted in Thomas Mallon, *Stolen Words: Forays into the Origins and Ravages of Plagiarism* (1989), pp. 3-4.

29. Quoted in Sue Carter Simmons, "Compelling Notions of Authorship: A Historical Look at Students and Textbooks on Plagiarism and Cheating," in Lise Buranen and Alice M. Roy (eds.), *Perspectives on Plagiarism and Intellectual Property in a Postmodern World* (1999), pp. 41-51.

30. Quoted in Ralph Ranalli, "Judge Drops BU Lawsuit Against Web 'Paper Mills,'" *The Boston Herald*, Dec. 8, 1998, p. A14.

31. Quoted in Kathy Koch, "Journalism Under Fire," *The CQ Researcher*, Dec. 25, 1998, pp. 1121-1144.

32. Quoted in Trudy Lieberman, "Plagiarize, Plagiarize, Plagiarize . . . Only Be Sure To Call It Research," *Columbia Journalism Review*, July/August 1995, p. 21.

33. Quoted in Howard Kurtz, "Stephen Glass Waits for Prime Time to Say 'I Lied,' " *The Washington Post*, May 7, 2003, p. C1.

34. Quoted in Howard Kurtz, "Business Week Fires Writer for Plagiarism; Story on Computer Privacy Was Similar to Post Article," *The Washington Post*, Feb. 10, 2001, p. C3.

35. Quoted in Maria Puente, "Disgrace, Dishonor, Infamy: They're Not So Bad Anymore," *USA Today*, May 22, 2003, p. D1.

36. Quoted in David Espo, "Biden Quits Races, Cites 'Exaggerated Shadow' of Mistakes," The Associated Press, Sept. 23, 1987.

37. The report can be viewed online at www.number10.gov.uk/files/pdf/Iraq.pdf.

38. A transcript is available at: www.state.gov/secretary/rm/2003/17300.htm.

39. For background, see Sarah Lyall, "Britain Admits That Much of Its Report on Iraq Came From Magazines," *The New York Times*, Feb. 8, 2003, p. A9.

40. *Ibid.*

41. *Ibid.*

42. Quoted in Ben Russell, "Government Risked My Life by Copying Iraq Study," *The* [London] *Independent*, June 20, 2003, p. 10.

43. Quoted in Geoffrey Gray, "More Trouble at The Times: Rick Bragg Suspended," *Columbia Journalism Review* (online version), May 23, 2003.

44. *Ibid.*

45. Quoted in Howard Kurtz, "Suspended N.Y. Times Reporter Says He'll Quit," *The Washington Post*. May 27, 2003, p. C1.

46. Kilborn's e-mail was quoted in Seth Mnookin, "Firestorm in the Newsroom: The Times's National Staff Defends Their Reporting Methods," *Newsweek* (online version), May 28, 2003.

47. Kelley R. Taylor, "Cheater, cheater . . ." *Principal Leadership*, April 2003, pp. 74-78.

BIBLIOGRAPHY

Books

Buranen, Lise, and Alice M. Roy (eds.), *Perspectives on Plagiarism and Intellectual Property in a Postmodern World*, State University of New York Press, 1999.
Essays by scholars and copyright attorneys on copyright law, changing attitudes toward plagiarism and strategies for dealing with academic plagiarism.

Glass, Stephen, *The Fabulist*, Simon & Schuster, 2003.
A fictionalized account of the author's infamous career at *The New Republic*, where he was exposed as a plagiarist and journalistic fraud in 1998.

Howard, Rebecca Moore, *Standing in the Shadow of Giants: Plagiarists, Authors, Collaborators*, Ablex, 1999.
A professor of writing and rhetoric at Syracuse University chronicles attitudes toward plagiarism since ancient times, maintaining academic plagiarism is frequently inadvertent.

Lathrop, Ann, and Kathleen Foss, *Student Cheating and Plagiarism in the Internet Era: A Wake-Up Call*, Libraries Unlimited, 2000.
This discussion deals with how students use the Internet to download term papers and purloin text from online sources. Lathrop is a professor emeritus at California State University, Long Beach; Foss is a librarian at the Los Alamitos Unified School District.

Mallon, Thomas, *Stolen Words: Forays into the Origins and Ravages of Plagiarism*, Ticknor & Fields, 1989.
A novelist and a former English professor discusses plagiarism in literature and popular culture, maintaining society is generally too lax in prosecuting plagiarists.

Articles

Ambrose, Stephen, "Accusations of Plagiarism Deserve an Honest Reply," Newhouse News Service, May 2, 2002.
The best-selling historian defends himself against the plagiarism allegations that dogged him in the final months of his life.

Barry, Dan, *et. al.*, "Correcting the Record: Times Reporter Who Resigned Leaves Long Trail of Deception," *The New York Times*, May 11, 2003, p. A1.
This is *The Times'* internal account of Jayson Blair, the rogue reporter who plagiarized and fabricated dozens of articles. A companion piece documents problems *The Times* found in 39 articles by Blair.

Edmundson, Mark, "How Teachers Can Stop Cheaters," *The New York Times*, Sept. 9, 2003, p. A29.
Some professors think teachers need to stop looking exclusively for technological solutions to the problem of plagiarism in schools.

Kumar, Anita, "High-Tech Sleuthing Catches College Cheats," *The St. Petersburg Times*, Aug. 31, 2003, p. A1.
A journalist interviews educators who say plagiarism-detection services are desperately needed and those who argue they are the wrong way to deal with plagiarism.

Kurtz, Howard, "To the Editors: How Could This Happen? N.Y. Times Staff, Execs in 'Painful and Honest' Meeting Over Plagiarism Fiasco," *The Washington Post*, May 15, 2003, p. C1.
The Washington Post's media critic chronicles how *New York Times* staffers reacted with shock and anger after Jayson Blair was exposed as a fraud.

Lyall, Sarah, "Britain Admits That Much of Its Report on Iraq Came From Magazines," *The New York Times*, Feb. 8, 2003, p. A9.
Reporter Lyall documents how the British government plagiarized articles for its official report about Iraq's efforts to hide its weapons of mass destruction.

Puente, Maria, "Disgrace, Dishonor, Infamy: They're Not So Bad Anymore," *USA Today*, May 22, 2003, p. D1.
Reporter Puente writes about disgraced journalists who wrote books and articles after committing journalistic fraud.

Studies and Reports

McCabe, Donald, "Cheating: Why Students Do It and How We Can Help them Stop," *American Educator*, **winter 2001.**
A management professor at Rutgers University and an expert on academic cheating documents how and why high-school students engage in plagiarism.

Scanlon, Patrick M., and David R. Neumann, "Internet Plagiarism Among College Students," *Journal of College Student Development*, **May/June 2002, pp. 375-384.**
Professors of communication at the Rochester Institute of Technology conclude that the Internet has not caused a dramatic increase in plagiarism.

Siegal, Allan M., (ed.), "Report of the Committee on Safeguarding the Integrity of Our Journalism," *The New York Times*, **July 28, 2003; www.nytco.com.**
Times staffers and outside journalists recommend a number of changes following the Jayson Blair scandal; the report is available at www.nytco.com.

For More Information

American Library Association, 50 E. Huron, Chicago, IL 60611; (800) 545-2433; www.ala.org. Publishes articles about how educators can detect and prevent plagiarism.

Berkman Center for Internet and Society at Harvard Law School, Baker House, 1587 Massachusetts Ave., Cambridge, MA 02138; (617) 495-7547; http://cyber.law.harvard.edu. The center's Web site contains numerous articles about plagiarism in the Internet age.

Center for Academic Integrity, Duke University, Box 90434, Durham, NC 27708; (919) 660-3045; www.academicintegrity.org. A consortium of 200 colleges and universities concerned about academic plagiarism.

Center for Excellence in Teaching and Learning, New Library Building LE-G60, 1400 Washington Ave., Albany, NY 12222; (518) 437-3920; www.albany.edu/cetl. The center's Web site discusses avoiding plagiarism and has plagiarism-detection software available for downloading.

Center for the Study of College Student Values, Florida State University, 113 Stone Building, Tallahassee, FL 32306-4452; (850) 644-6446; www.collegevalues.org. Publishes the *Journal of College and Character* and studies ethical issues.

Council of Writing Program Administrators, P.O. Box 8101, North Carolina State University, Raleigh, NC 27695-8105; (919) 513-4080; www.ilstu.edu/~ddhesse/wpa. This national association provides Web resources for preventing plagiarism.

Poynter Institute for Media Studies, 801 Third St. South, St. Petersburg, FL 33701-4920; (888) 769-6837; www.poynter.org. Conducts classes for journalism students, teachers and professionals. Poynter columnist Jim Romenesko tracks plagiarism in journalism. The nonprofit institute owns Congressional Quarterly Inc.

TurnItIn.com, 1624 Franklin St., 7th Floor, Oakland, CA 94612; (510) 287-9720; www.turnitin.com. A leading provider of plagiarism-detection services.

3

Medicare Reform

Adriel Bettelheim

Seniors' prescription-drug costs would be covered — at least in part — under legislation to overhaul Medicare being debated by Congress. With drug prices skyrocketing and an election year looming, lawmakers are trying to hammer out a compromise between House and Senate versions of the measure. Some 12 million elderly Americans do not have drug coverage.

LingTee Hailey, a 75-year-old Nashville retiree, seems like exactly the kind of person Washington policymakers want to help when they discuss overhauling the federal Medicare program. To treat her high blood pressure and macular degeneration, an eye condition that can lead to blindness, Hailey takes prescription drugs that cost her $2,400 per year — a steep price considering her only source of income is $16,000 in Social Security payments.

But when the former architectural designer studies the proposals under discussion in the House and Senate that would add a prescription-drug benefit to Medicare, she gets angry. Even after paying a $420 annual premium and deductible, elderly Americans like Hailey likely would have to spend thousands of dollars before government coverage pays for all or the vast majority of her drug bills.

"There's a huge gap where you have to pay the entire thing," an irate Hailey exclaims. "People who can't afford it now certainly can't afford [the cost-sharing arrangement]."[1]

Finding a way to help Hailey and other seniors is the biggest task facing 17 influential House members and senators, who began negotiations on July 15 to write legislation that would make the most significant structural changes to Medicare in its 38-year history. At an annual cost of $269 billion, the Medicare program — which provides health-insurance protection to virtually every American who reaches age 65 — is the second-most-expensive federal domestic program after Social Security.

Medicare expenditures as a percentage of gross domestic product are projected to rise from the current 2.6 percent to 5.3 percent in 2035 and 9.3 in 2077, according to the program's trustees.

From *The CQ Researcher,*
August 22, 2003.

Program costs have risen due to the growing demand for services like home health care and technologically advanced procedures like organ transplants, joint replacements and new cancer treatments. Waste, fraud and abuse on the part of some providers have added to higher costs as well.

With health-care spending growing faster than the overall economy, it is increasingly difficult to offer quality care at affordable prices and still control rising Medicare costs. Covering seniors' prescription drugs would only add to the spiraling costs: Retail drug prices jumped more than three times the rate of inflation between 1998 and 2000.[2]

"If we were creating the Medicare program today, we would model it after what consumers are receiving in today's health-care marketplace: more choices and better benefits," Thomas A. Scully, administrator of the Centers for Medicare and Medicaid Services, told the Senate Finance Committee on June 6. "Not only is it important to offer modern, innovative health-care choices for seniors, but to do so in a way that is fiscally responsible."

After years of blaming each other for Medicare's woes and using the issue as a political cudgel in elections, Republicans and Democrats early in the current 108th Congress concluded that it was in their respective interests to revamp the entitlement program, which currently serves 41 million elderly and disabled Americans.

The lawmakers who assembled on July 15 for ceremonial handshakes pledged to work in a bipartisan fash-

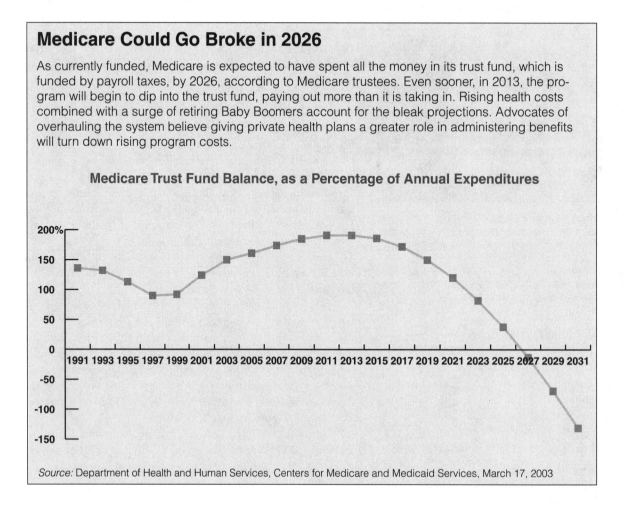

Medicare Could Go Broke in 2026

As currently funded, Medicare is expected to have spent all the money in its trust fund, which is funded by payroll taxes, by 2026, according to Medicare trustees. Even sooner, in 2013, the program will begin to dip into the trust fund, paying out more than it is taking in. Rising health costs combined with a surge of retiring Baby Boomers account for the bleak projections. Advocates of overhauling the system believe giving private health plans a greater role in administering benefits will turn down rising program costs.

Medicare Trust Fund Balance, as a Percentage of Annual Expenditures

Source: Department of Health and Human Services, Centers for Medicare and Medicaid Services, March 17, 2003

ion. But they still have very different visions of how the program should work when the first Baby Boomers become eligible for benefits in 2010. Those differences may yet scuttle efforts to produce a final bill for President Bush to sign. But the fact that leaders of both major political parties are considering overhauling arguably the most popular legacy of former President Lyndon B. Johnson's Great Society speaks volumes about the shifting national debate over health care and social policy.

Both the House and Senate plans would allow seniors to get Medicare-subsidized prescription drugs in 2006, either through special drug-only insurance policies or all-inclusive private health plans. Between 2004 and 2006, they could obtain interim subsidized drug coverage through privately offered drug-discount cards. The sweeping House and Senate blueprints would also encourage seniors to enroll in private managed-care health plans — such as preferred provider organizations (PPOs) or health-maintenance organizations (HMOs) — as an alternative to Medicare's government-provided fee-for-service system. (*See glossary, p. 65.*)

But because both Congress and the Bush administration have agreed to cap spending on Medicare overhaul at $400 billion over the next 10 years, revising the system will require painful trade-offs. For instance, some Medicare beneficiaries will have to pay higher out-of-pocket costs for drugs. And seniors in certain geographic regions may have fewer options for obtaining health coverage. And one of the bills would cause a fundamental shift away from Medicare's core principle of equal benefits for all.

Most policymakers believe the system must be changed because Medicare cannot survive the demographic surge of retiring Baby Boomers. On March 17, Medicare's trustees forecast that the payroll-tax-funded

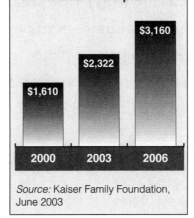

Spending on Rx Drugs Likely to Increase

Seniors will spend 36 percent more on prescription drugs by 2006, the year Congress proposes creating new Medicare drug benefits.

Average Per Capita Annual Drug Spending by Medicare Recipients

$1,610 — 2000
$2,322 — 2003
$3,160 — 2006

Source: Kaiser Family Foundation, June 2003

program will exhaust its trust-fund money by 2026 — four years earlier than was projected last year. In addition, the report said, Medicare will begin to dip into the trust fund, by paying out more than it is taking in, by 2013 — three years earlier than projected last year. Rising drug and other health costs combined with a dramatic increase in the number of beneficiaries account for the revised estimates.[3]

Critics of the overhaul efforts say that while Medicare should be modernized to improve its long-term viability, the House and Senate plans rely too heavily on private insurers and market forces to cut costs and deliver benefits. This could lead to many seniors seeing their coverage curtailed or reduced due to insurers' business decisions, critics say. They also want policymakers to heed the risks of a competitive market and strengthen the traditional government-run Medicare system, which allows beneficiaries to choose which doctors they see.

"Medicare is a viable program," says Marilyn Moon, a senior fellow at the Urban Institute, a nonpartisan Washington think tank. "In terms of meeting the needs of those it is intended to serve, and in terms of future affordability, the program can continue to succeed. It is neither unsustainable nor fatally flawed."

Overhauling the system this year, however, would signal that both political parties are willing to make tough choices to address the needs of an influential group of voters.* It also would deliver immediate relief to the approximately 12 million Medicare beneficiaries who don't have drug coverage provided through employer-sponsored health plans or individual policies.

---

* If lawmakers do not reach an agreement on reform this year, they will have to start all over next year drafting plans, holding hearings and markups — making chances for success very slim.

How Much Competition Is Enough?

Discussions about revamping Medicare inevitably turn to the thorny question of how to inject market competition into the system and control the program's rising costs. It is a conundrum that divides Republicans and most Democrats and is arguably the most difficult element of the current negotiations over overhauling the program.

The House-passed plan assumes a much greater role for private health insurers than the Senate plan and revives the controversial concept of "premium support," which was endorsed in 1999 by a bipartisan commission studying proposals to overhaul the system. Fittingly, one of the commission's co-chairmen was current House Ways and Means Committee Chairman Bill Thomas, R-Calif., who helped draft the House version of the Medicare overhaul legislation and now heads the House-Senate conference on the measure. The other co-chair was Sen. John Breaux, D-La., a conservative Democrat and one of the current Senate conferees.

> **Defenders of traditional Medicare worry that healthier and wealthier seniors will gravitate to private plans, leaving sicker and poorer seniors in the traditional system.**

In an effort to trigger competition between private plans, the pending premium-support proposal would have the federal government subsidize some of the out-of-pocket costs that beneficiaries would have to pay to join private health plans. Beneficiaries who prefer to buy more expensive plans would have to pay more out of their own pockets, while those who opt for plans with lower premiums could save both themselves and the federal government money.

Premium support also would help pay some of the costs for Medicare's traditional fee-for-service program, allowing it to compete on equal footing with the private plans. The fee-for-service system pays physicians and other health-care providers for Medicare services, as they are provided to beneficiaries.

The House bill would require private health plans to bid against each other to offer Medicare services in geographic regions established by the government. The three lowest

But policymakers still will have to overcome sharp divisions if they are to combine aspects of a bipartisan Senate Medicare drug bill and a considerably more conservative House version crafted virtually with no Democratic input. More important, lawmakers must convince seniors that any revised system will meet their health needs and be worth paying for — or face a potentially devastating political backlash in next year's presidential and congressional elections.

Such conundrums have made Medicare and other forms of national health insurance a political flashpoint ever since former President Harry S Truman's unsuccessful effort to create a national health-insurance system in 1949-50. For nearly a generation, Democrats and their allies in labor pressed for a system that would pro-

vide coverage for seniors, only to be rebuffed by congressional Republicans and the influential American Medical Association (AMA), which felt it would lead to standardization of care and government overregulation of the medical profession. It was only after a Democratic landslide in 1964 that Congress became willing to pass authorizing legislation.

Since then, Medicare has been a public-policy paradox: a beloved government-run program that actually provides much less in the way of benefits than most private health plans. In the 1980s and '90s Congress beefed up benefits, adding coverage of flu and pneumonia vaccinations, as well as mammograms to detect breast cancer. As part of the 1997 Balanced Budget Act, lawmakers added more preventive coverage, including screening for

bidders would win the right to offer service modeled on preferred provider organizations (PPOs). Medicare beneficiaries could select between traditional Medicare fee-for-service or one of the three private options.

In areas where competition exists, the House plan would require the traditional Medicare system to compete directly on price against the private plans, beginning in 2010. The government would review all of the bids and establish a weighted average cost of care, by which it would establish payment rates. Traditional Medicare would have to provide services according to those rates. If the cost of any participating plan, including Medicare, exceeded the established rate, beneficiaries would have to make up the extra amount through out-of-pocket payments.

Defenders of traditional Medicare worry that healthier and wealthier seniors will gravitate to private plans, leaving sicker, poorer seniors in the traditional system. Those beneficiaries' medical bills are likely to rise faster, making it likely that costs under the traditional system will exceed the established rates.

A group of 37 Senate Democrats served notice to President Bush on July 8 that they would not support any conference agreement that includes the House language on competition or otherwise "coerce [beneficiaries] into leaving conventional Medicare to enroll in HMOs [health maintenance organizations] and private plans." In a letter to Bush, the senators additionally said they would oppose an agreement that would force seniors "to choose between giving up their doctor or face higher premiums to stay in the current Medicare program."[1]

The statement was designed to assuage labor unions, consumer groups and other traditional Democratic allies that the traditional fee-for-service program would be protected in negotiations.

But conservative lawmakers had similarly drawn their own line earlier. On June 25 a group of 42 House Republicans wrote Speaker J. Dennis Hastert, R-Ill., that they would not support any final compromise unless it promotes private health plans.

The members identified "cost-saving, market-based measures" in the House-passed plan as essential to their support, and demanded that any final bill include the House language. "Should this reform be removed or weakened, we cannot, as a matter of responsible public policy, support a bill to add a prescription-drug benefit to Medicare, which would accelerate the insolvency of this vital program," the lawmakers wrote.[2]

The Senate bill treats competition differently, allowing private plans to compete against each other but not charge beneficiaries more than traditional Medicare until 2009. After that, plans could compete with each other in ways similar to the method outlined in the House bill. However, the plans could not compete directly against Medicare. The Senate bill also contains a provision favored by Democrats that would offer a government-run drug benefit in those areas where there are not at least two private plans offering drug benefits.

---

[1] See Rebecca Adams, "Criticism of Medicare Bill Is Growing on Both Sides of Aisle in the Senate," *CQ Today*, July 9, 2003, p. 15.

[2] See Adam Graham-Silverman, "House Conservatives Draw Line on Conference Report," *CQ Today*, June 27, 2003, online at www.cq.com.

---

prostate and colorectal cancer and coverage for managing diabetes.

The push to enact legislation this year and dramatically reshape the program was driven by forecasts of huge federal budget deficits in the coming decade, and the realization by both parties that Congress may never again be in a position to target as much as $400 billion for Medicare overhaul. No less a figure than Sen. Edward M. Kennedy, D-Mass., a liberal lion and staunch defender of government entitlements, threw his support behind the bipartisan Senate plan early in the debate, giving it an immediate air of credibility. Though the plan goes against Kennedy's wishes by providing incentives for seniors to join private health plans to obtain Medicare drug coverage, it also would allow similar drug

coverage for seniors who remain in Medicare's traditional fee-for-service system.[4]

The Senate bill represents "a major breakthrough in our effort to give senior citizens the prescription-drug coverage under Medicare they need and deserve," Kennedy says.

President Bush made overhauling Medicare his top domestic policy priority in his 2003 State of the Union address and could reap significant political benefits from any agreement struck by Congress. Overhauling Medicare would allow Bush to take credit for delivering results on an issue on which Democrats have traditionally scored high with voters. And any negative fallout will only likely materialize well after the 2004 elections — another factor driving some politicians to cut a deal this year.

As congressional negotiators debate ways to overhaul the Medicare system, here are some of the questions they are asking:

Will adding Medicare drug coverage help most seniors?

The debate over drug coverage for the elderly elicits powerful images, such as the ailing senior on a fixed income cutting pills in half to make the medicine last longer or elderly residents of border states taking bus trips into Canada and Mexico to buy low-priced prescription drugs. Politicians cite such real-life circumstances as they debate how to balance the needs of an aging population that is using more and more prescription drugs with those of a Medicare system whose drug spending is expected to grow by 10 percent annually over the next decade.

Though seniors comprise only 13 percent of the nation's population, they account for 42 cents of every dollar spent on prescription drugs, according to the liberal-leaning Washington advocacy group Families USA. Nine in 10 Medicare beneficiaries use prescription drugs, at an average annual cost of $2,322. Advocates for the elderly fear medical inflation will hike those out-of-pocket costs dramatically at a time when many cash-squeezed companies are considering reducing drug coverage for retirees.[5]

The Medicare overhaul plans under discussion would allow seniors to obtain prescription-drug coverage in two main ways: by joining a new managed-care network similar to a PPO — which most seniors do not now have — or by remaining in the traditional Medicare program and buying a separate drug-only insurance plan, an option that does not exist now.[6]

Supporters say the coverage will provide a safety net by subsidizing the average senior's drug bills and providing so-called catastrophic coverage for the lion's share of expenses for the sickest beneficiaries. Low-income beneficiaries would receive extra subsidies.

"[The overhaul plan] is like a shot of legislative botox," says House Energy and Commerce Committee Chairman Billy Tauzin, R-La., whose panel helped draft that chamber's Medicare drug bill. "It will rejuvenate an antiquated program by eliminating the old-age lines of a different era and give it a fresh new look and appeal."

But many question how much the new drug benefit would help seniors. Both the House and Senate proposals contain so many gaps — due mostly to budget constraints — that seniors may feel cheated and unwilling to pay for the new benefit. The House plan, for example, would require seniors to pay monthly premiums of about $35 and an annual deductible of $250. In exchange, the government would pay 80 percent of drug costs from $251 to $2,000, but seniors would pay drug costs from $2,001 to $4,900. Only after a senior paid $3,500 out-of-pocket would Medicare cover all further drug costs. The Senate plan contains a similar coverage gap, known in health-care parlance as a "doughnut hole."

GOP leaders stress that very few seniors would fall into the coverage gaps. Yet the Kaiser Family Foundation, a health-care think tank, estimates that in 2006 a third of Medicare recipients will probably fall within the House's doughnut hole.[7] One such senior is Hailey, the Nashville retiree who was upset the proposed drug benefit does not offer continuous coverage.

"The best we are offering is an on-again, off-again discount plan that provides at least as much confusion as it does coverage," says Senate Minority Leader Tom Daschle, D-S.D., who blames Republican tax cuts for leaving Congress with insufficient funds to create across-the-board coverage for drug costs. "The drug benefit is drastically underfunded. As a result, seniors will be forced to pay high deductibles and face large gaps in coverage."

Others worry that struggling employers could stop offering prescription-drug coverage to their retirees, transferring the burden to the new government plan and leaving the retirees with potentially skimpier benefits. Aware of the threat of so-called employer crowd-out, lawmakers already have larded both the House and Senate bills with billions of dollars in subsidies to employers to continue retiree coverage.

Most employers expect to retain benefits for seniors already receiving them, according to surveys by the Kaiser Family Foundation and others. But some — already hurt by rising health-care costs — are planning reduced coverage for future retirees. Lawmakers worry that the promise of government coverage may entice some companies to scale back or drop their private coverage sooner.

"You don't want to replace private dollars with public dollars," says House Ways and Means Committee Chairman Bill Thomas, R-Calif., chairman of the House-Senate Medicare drug conference.

Closely watching the debate are seniors such as Darlene Vierow, 70, of Evans, Colo., who doubts the bank where she used to work will cover her drug costs indefinitely and hopes Congress will create a Medicare drug benefit. The bank's share of her medical insurance, including drug coverage, totals $6,000 — an amount she expects to exhaust in two years. Vierow suffers from migraines, osteoporosis and high cholesterol, requiring medicine that would cost her more than $500 out-of-pocket per month without coverage. Vierow's story is featured on the Web site of AARP, the influential seniors' lobby. While it has not taken a formal position on a specific overhaul plan, the AARP is urging Congress to preserve the traditional Medicare system.[8]

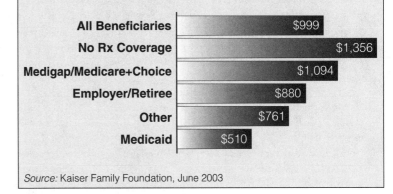

Uninsured Americans Pay More for Drugs

About 12 million elderly Americans don't have prescription-drug coverage. Many tend to be older and sicker than seniors who have coverage through employer-sponsored plans or privately purchased policies and, as a result, spend more out-of-pocket for drugs.

Average Out-of-pocket Drug Spending by Medicare Beneficiaries, by Source of Drug Coverage

All Beneficiaries	$999
No Rx Coverage	$1,356
Medigap/Medicare+Choice	$1,094
Employer/Retiree	$880
Other	$761
Medicaid	$510

Source: Kaiser Family Foundation, June 2003

Beyond employer subsidies, many lawmakers are adding elements to the Medicare plans to further address seniors' rising drug costs without taking the more dramatic and politically controversial step of imposing price controls. Both the House and Senate bills, for example, would streamline the Food and Drug Administration (FDA) process for approving less-expensive generic equivalents of brand-name drugs. The bills would restrict brand-name drug companies to apply for only one 30-month stay to protect their patents from generic drugmakers' challenges. Under current law, brand-name drugmakers can file multiple stays.

Another provision would allow licensed drug wholesalers, pharmacists and doctors to import U.S. drugs shipped or manufactured abroad, where they often sell for less. The House plan, in particular, contains controversial language, strenuously opposed by the drug industry, allowing consumers to import FDA-approved prescription drugs from Canada. If imports from Canada are deemed safe by the Institute of Medicine, an arm of the National Academy of Sciences, the provision could be expanded to cover drugs made in FDA-approved facilities in 25 industrialized countries.

Opponents fear the provision could trigger a flood of counterfeit or ineffective medications into the U.S. mar-

ket. But with public frustration over skyrocketing drug prices building, many policymakers are demanding a solution that delivers price breaks to seniors. During House debate, importation supporter Gil Gutknecht, R-Minn., held up two packages of the breast cancer drug tamoxifen. "Why is it that Americans have to spend $260 for this life-saving drug," he asked, "when Germans can buy it for $60?"[9]

Are private insurance companies that stand to play a bigger role in Medicare willing to administer benefits?

For years, Republicans have advocated an expanded role for private insurance companies in Medicare, believing they are better equipped to control the program's growth than a government bureaucracy. GOP lawmakers are so convinced of this that they have compromised with Democrats and agreed to add prescription-drug coverage for the first time since Medicare was created in 1965.

But most Democrats and some Republicans remain skeptical about private companies' willingness to participate, pointing to unsuccessful attempts to steer beneficiaries into managed-care plans since 1998. Many question the wisdom of relying heavily on private insur-

Discriminating Against the Rich?

Much of the current Medicare system's appeal lies in its universal nature: Anyone who reaches age 65 is eligible, regardless of income. If he were old enough, even Bill Gates, the world's richest person, would be able to receive subsidized health care under the program.

But current congressional efforts to overhaul the program are tempting policymakers to consider restricting benefits for wealthier seniors. The House version of the bill, for instance, would gradually phase out federal subsidies for so-called catastrophic prescription-drug coverage for beneficiaries with incomes of $60,000 or higher.

The concept is technically called "income relating," but it is more widely — and incorrectly — known as "means testing." * Congress has debated the option at least three times since the late 1980s during discussions on entitlement reform. But lawmakers generally worry about alienating wealthier seniors, who tend to vote in higher numbers than other age groups. The Bush administration opposes income relating.

Income relating is again being considered because President Bush and Congress agreed to limit spending on Medicare overhaul to $400 billion over a decade. Advocates of the idea argue that without some income criteria, an individual like billionaire Gates, co-founder of Microsoft Corp., would be eligible for the same benefits as an uninsured, impoverished senior.

"There's a notion that it's OK to consider using the money for the people who are most in need," said Republican pollster Bill McInturff, adding that many of the most affluent seniors have private benefits and are not in need of additional assistance.[1]

Substantial opposition to the idea still exists, in part because it would tinker with Medicare's core principle of equal benefits for all workers who contribute to the program through payroll taxes. Lawmakers who want to retain the core principle, such as Sen. Edward M. Kennedy, D-Mass., additionally worry that income relating will make Medicare appear more like a program targeted to the needy instead of a middle-class entitlement, making it less politically popular and potentially vulnerable to future budget cuts.

Kennedy engaged in a rare shouting match with Sen. Dianne Feinstein, D-Calif., on the Senate floor on June 26, after Feinstein unsuccessfully tried to attach an amendment to the Senate Medicare bill that would charge higher premiums for some wealthier recipients.

Congress' most well-known experiment with income relating took place in 1988, when lawmakers passed

ers to pay for drugs and meet other important health needs of elderly Americans.[10]

"There hasn't been any insurance company I'm aware of that says they want to participate in this," says Ira S. Loss, senior health-care analyst for Washington Analysis Corp., a financial consulting firm. "This could be a benefit that no one comes to."[11]

Many seniors in recent years have been stung by steep premium increases from their Medicare managed-care plans, or by companies' decisions to withdraw from Medicare altogether, claiming program reimbursements were too low to provide them with a sufficient profit.

William Cornelius, a 74-year-old Baldwin, Pa., retiree, learned in late 2002 that he was facing a nearly fivefold increase in his Medicare HMO premiums. "This thing is running wild. It's totally out of control," he said. "How can you afford it if it continues down this road, if they keep raising [premiums] by these exorbitant percentages?" Eventually, Cornelius switched to a rival plan whose premium was about four times what his old plan cost.[12]

Congress expanded Medicare's managed-care program and renamed it Medicare+Choice in the 1997 Balanced Budget Act. Lawmakers hoped that encouraging more beneficiaries to join private plans would both save money and give seniors a more complete package of health coverage. To encourage the development of managed care in outlying areas, where Medicare reimbursements traditionally are lower and private plans have been reluctant to serve beneficiaries, Congress authorized creation of networks of doctors, hospitals and other health providers who could band together to offer insurance.

Instead, dozens of private plans withdrew from the program, complaining the government was setting low reimbursement rates and that it made little business sense

the Medicare Catastrophic Coverage Act. It dramatically expanded Medicare benefits but charged affluent beneficiaries extra for limiting their annual out-of-pocket medical expenses. The bill passed by large margins. Fewer than half of Medicare beneficiaries were subject to the extra tax.

However, the new fee caused an uproar, culminating in an incident in which then-Ways and Means Chairman Dan Rostenkowski, D-Ill., was chased by a group of angry seniors after a meeting in his Chicago district. The next year, lawmakers took the unprecedented step of repealing the law.

In 1995, Congress tried to charge Medicare beneficiaries with incomes above $60,000 more for their Part B coverage.** But the provision was wrapped in a broader budget-reconciliation bill that was vetoed by then-President Bill Clinton. Two years later, the Senate Finance Committee

Microsoft Chairman Bill Gates — the world's richest person — is entitled to receive Medicare at age 65, but some lawmakers want to restrict benefits for wealthier seniors in the federally subsidized program.

included language in its version of a budget-reconciliation bill linking Medicare beneficiaries' Part B insurance deductibles to their incomes.

The theory was that the change would alter seniors' behavior, making them think twice about spending their own money on health services. Clinton endorsed the idea, and it was included in the final Senate version of the budget bill. However, the idea was dropped in conference in the face of strong opposition from House lawmakers.

---

[1] See Bob Benenson, "Tying Benefits to Income a Tap Dance On Politically Deadly 'Third Rail,' " *CQ Weekly*, June 7, 2003, p. 1362.

* Means testing refers to the practice of specifically targeting an entitlement to individuals below a certain income level, as is the case with the nation's welfare program. Income relating allows all individuals to obtain the same benefit, but charges well-heeled recipients more.

** Medicare Part B is an optional package covering physicians' office visits and outpatient services available to individuals 65 and older willing to pay monthly premiums, an annual deductible and co-payments.

to continue administering the benefits. As of January, an estimated 2.4 million seniors had been forced to join another Medicare+Choice plan or return to the government-run Medicare system because their original plan had left the program. Many of the seniors joined a managed-care plan specifically to obtain prescription drug coverage not offered in traditional Medicare.

Those skeptical about the current overhaul efforts say private companies, by their nature, must create shareholder profits and thus are more focused on the bottom line than on patients' needs. Democrats, in particular, note that Medicare managed-care plans have not been able to make enough money to justify remaining in the program, even after Congress gave them more funds in 1999 and 2000 to cushion their needs.

There also is evidence suggesting managed-care plans may not be holding down costs as well as they depict. A

Commonwealth Fund study in August found out-of-pocket costs for Medicare managed-care enrollees will increase by 10 percent in 2003. The study found the average enrollee in a Medicare+Choice plan is spending $1,964, twice the 1999 average. The increase was largely attributable to higher managed-care premiums, physician and hospital co-payments and prescription drug co-payments. Managed-care plans disputed the findings.

The Center for Medicare and Medicaid Services' Scully says such fallout won't happen under the current Medicare-overhaul proposals. Both plans envision a cost-sharing arrangement in which the private plans and the government share in any cost savings or overruns beyond specified levels, giving private plans an incentive to consistently keep costs down and to remain in the program.

Moreover, Scully argues, the plans involved will be preferred provider organizations (PPOs), which are more flexible than older forms of managed care — such as health-maintenance organizations — and better at coordinating health services. Scully and other Bush administration officials say government data suggest the most efficient plans can offer the same benefits as the government-run Medicare system for an average of 2.3 percent less.*

"The private marketplace has developed an efficient and effective model of health plans that meets the needs of enrollees and purchasers, as well as providers, in specific local markets," Scully says.

Both overhaul plans call on health insurers to bid against each other to offer PPO-type coverage in one of 10 geographic regions. But insurers are lobbying hard to change the legislative language, because they fear that the regions could be too large, making it onerous to offer a standard package of coverage over a wide area. Some companies may not be licensed to operate in all the states in a geographic region or lack provider networks across a particular region. Without such relationships, it would be difficult to offer a continuum of services to a potential enrollee.

The insurers also take issue with lawmakers' plans to limit to three the number of plans serving a particular region. Insurers contend it will cost millions of dollars to assemble provider networks and to make a competitive bid. They also argue that any company that wants to devote the resources to compete to offer benefits should be allowed to do so.

"I think there is a long way to go before [insurers] say, 'Oh yeah, count me in,' " says Donald Young, president of the Health Insurance Association of America, a trade group representing insurers who offer health, disability, long-term care and other forms of coverage.[13]

But even if insurers' changes, like single-state regions, are adopted, there are few assurances they will remain in the program. All expect to constantly re-evaluate the business climate to gauge whether it makes sense to participate.

"There's nothing to hold them in the market long-term, so there's no way to ensure that seniors will get stable, predictable coverage over time," says Patricia Neuman, director of the Medicare Policy Project at the Kaiser Family Foundation. "It's just real uncertain."

Can the traditional Medicare system compete with private health plans?

The notion of Medicare "competing" with private health plans seems contradictory, at first. After all, the pending overhaul plans envision Medicare designing a system specifically to encourage managed-care plans to play a more prominent role in the program. Government efforts to then have the traditional program vie against these private insurers would appear to be self-defeating.

However, Medicare still would continue to operate its traditional program, which embraces a so-called "fee-for-service" model in which doctors and other health-care providers bill the government for services provided. Patients generally can obtain care from any licensed provider, and the government pays a predetermined portion of costs after the patient has paid an annual deductible.

The big question is whether traditional Medicare can survive once private insurers, with their coordinated provider networks and cost controls, administer benefits to seniors. This conundrum is at the heart of the debate over the overhaul efforts and is sparking the sharpest ideological differences between Republicans and Democrats.

"The end result will be that Medicare as we know it will wither on the vine," Democrats on the House Energy and Commerce Committee wrote in dissenting views in the committee report on the House overhaul plan. The lawmakers fear private plans will skim off well-heeled beneficiaries, leaving the poorest and sickest Medicare recipients in the traditional program, driving up its costs even faster. House overhaul efforts, they said, are "an ideological experiment in which our nation's seniors are the guinea pigs, with no real cost savings or improvement in Medicare's outlook."[14]

Competition issues have dominated Medicare debates since the National Bipartisan Commission on the Future of Medicare in 1999 studied a concept known as "premium support." Developed by academics, it encourages competition between private health plans by paying a portion of a participant's premium. Medicare beneficia-

---

* PPOs — the most prevalent form of managed care — limit costs by steering patients to physicians and other health providers who agree to accept discounted prices in exchange for seeing more patients. Unlike HMO patients, PPO participants can go outside the network for care, usually after paying an annual deductible and higher co-payments.

CHRONOLOGY

1910s-1920s *Early efforts to develop health-insurance systems for workers prove ahead of their time.*

1912-1920 Labor groups unsuccessfully encourage legislatures to establish government-run health insurance.

1930s-1950s *Great Depression and the New Deal prompt the first large-scale debate over a national health-insurance system.*

1934 President Franklin D. Roosevelt focuses on creating the Social Security system after doctors object to national health insurance.

1945-1949 President Harry S Truman, on several occasions, calls for compulsory national health insurance for all. Congressional Republicans, physicians' groups and other medical-care providers resist the effort.

1950s *Influential medical groups warn Congress that federal health insurance would lead to government control of health care and prove exorbitantly expensive. Meanwhile, the growth of private insurance brings hospital coverage to about 60 percent of the population.*

1960s *Democratic-controlled Congress works with President Lyndon B. Johnson to establish the Medicare system.*

1960 With pressure mounting from organized labor and other groups to address seniors' health costs, House Ways and Means Committee Chairman Wilbur Mills, D-Ark., strikes a deal with the American Medical Association, leading to passage of a law covering health costs of the indigent elderly who do not qualify for welfare.

1964 After Johnson sweeps to re-election, and Democrats bolster their majorities in both houses of Congress, the Ways and Means panel begins hearings on a national health-insurance system.

1965 Johnson signs Medicare bill into law on July 30 at the Independence, Mo., home of Truman, who is signed up as the program's first beneficiary.

1970s-1990s *Congress expands the program, but cannot contain its costs.*

1972 Medicare is expanded to cover certain disabled persons and those with end-stage renal disease.

1983 The program begins reimbursing hospitals based on a patient's diagnosis rather than the actual treatments he received.

1988 Congress expands Medicare benefits, but wealthier seniors rebel against higher premiums they must pay to help defray the costs, forcing Congress to repeal the law the next year.

1991 Congressional Budget Office warns the program is unprepared to deal with the eligibility of Baby Boomers beginning in 2010.

1995 Medicare spending represents one of every five health-care dollars spent — up from 11 percent in 1970.

1997 Congress passes the Balanced Budget Act, creating a Medicare managed-care option known as Medicare+Choice, and cuts $115 million over five years — nearly equal to all previous cuts combined.

1999 National Bipartisan Commission on the Future of Medicare disbands after a year without agreeing on how to overhaul the program.

2000s *New overhaul proposals emerge in the House and Senate.*

2003 President Bush proposes to spend $400 billion over 10 years to overhaul Medicare. . . . The House and Senate pass overhaul bills adding a prescription-drug benefit and increasing the role of private health plans in delivering Medicare benefits. . . . Lawmakers began conference negotiations on the two bills in July.

ries who want to purchase more expensive plans would have to pay more out-of-pocket, while those who opt for plans with lower premiums would save both themselves and the federal government money. The federal government would also pay a portion of costs for Medicare's fee-for-service program, making it compete against private plans on an equal footing. The concept is resurfacing during current talks on overhauling the system. (*See sidebar, p. 56.*)

Defenders of traditional Medicare are particularly incensed at language in the House bill — staunchly backed by conservative lawmakers — requiring traditional fee-for-service plans to compete directly on price against private plans, beginning in 2010, in regions where competition between private plans already exists. The government would consider all of the bids and establish a weighted average, to be used to set payment rates. Traditional Medicare would have to be able to provide services according to those rates. If the cost of any plan, including Medicare, exceeded the established rate, beneficiaries would have to make up the extra amount through out-of-pocket payments.

This system would theoretically reward efficiency because a plan that can keep its costs below the weighted average would still be guaranteed to receive the average payment and could offer additional services and benefits, or discounts on drugs, to attract more beneficiaries.

Democrats and some moderate Republicans fear this will make the fee-for-service system unaffordable because wealthier, healthier seniors will opt to pay for more generous benefits. That will leave sicker, low-income beneficiaries lumped together in a traditional Medicare system whose care costs could exceed the weighted average if the beneficiaries' medical costs rise faster than those in the private plans.

Republican supporters of the proposal, however, depict Medicare as an efficient, cost-effective system that will be able to compete with private plans. They note that government-run Medicare has considerably lower administrative costs than private health plans, as well as more clout negotiating discounts with providers. PPO plans' administrative expenses are 8 to 13 percent of expenditures, compared with 2 percent or less for Medicare, according to a Centers for Medicare and Medicaid Services analysis this year. The GOP lawmakers, nevertheless, believe private plans will be able to

squeeze new efficiencies out of the health market in the next decade and beyond.[15]

The most contentious issues during the House-Senate conference will probably revolve around making the traditional program compete with private plans. House conservatives have already promised to veto any conference agreement that does not include a provision that sets up direct competitive bidding between traditional Medicare and private health plans. Democrats, meanwhile, have vowed to oppose any final bill that contains the House language and are backing alternative Senate language allowing private plans to compete against each other to serve regions, but not directly against the government-run system.

"You have two sides that have drawn a line in the sand, and those lines are very far apart," Robert L. Laszewski, a health policy analyst, told *The Washington Post.* "It's not simply numbers. It's a fundamental difference . . . I think the only thing they can agree to is to do nothing at all."[16]

BACKGROUND

Evolution of Medicare

Medicare was established around the notion of equal benefits for all at a time when nearly half of U.S. senior citizens' incomes were below federal poverty levels, and many could not obtain private insurance. Its roots extend to early 20th-century efforts by a group of University of Wisconsin economists — known as the American Association for Labor Legislation — to persuade state legislators to enact laws providing broad hospital and medical benefits to workers and their dependents, particularly low-income workers. By 1917, such bills had been introduced in 12 states, and interest groups such as the AMA, the National Association of Manufacturers and the American Hospital Association (AHA) appeared receptive to the proposal.

However, between 1918 and 1920, momentum shifted against the idea, in part due to a still-prevalent Jeffersonian view that government mostly existed to promote private enterprise and self-reliance. Another line of thinking at the time embraced "social Darwinism," which applied Charles Darwin's scientific views to social relations and found justification for the notion of "every man for himself." Progressives additionally were divided

Glossary of Medicare Terms

Catastrophic coverage — Health insurance for the most expensive illnesses and conditions. It sets annual limits on potential out-of-pocket expenses, beyond which insurance pays all or the vast majority of costs.

Deductible — The amount a patient pays out-of-pocket each year before insurance coverage kicks in. Medicare's Part A deductible for hospital insurance is $840 in 2003 (more for hospital stays beyond 60 days). The optional Part B deductible for doctors' office visits is $100 per year, after which beneficiaries pay 20 percent of the Medicare-approved amount for services.

Drug card — An interim way of financing a drug benefit until proposed structural reforms take effect. Overhaul advocates would like to give beneficiaries drug cards, offered by private health plans, providing discounts for outpatient drugs at participating pharmacies. As envisioned, the cards would be used from 2004 to 2006, at which times a permanent Medicare drug benefit would come into existence.

Income relating — The concept of requiring wealthier Medicare beneficiaries to pay more for their coverage. The controversial idea has been revived during current negotiations on the future of the program.

Managed care — Any health system that combines the delivery and financing of health-care services. There are many different varieties of managed-care plans, including the oldest form: health-maintenance organizations (HMOs), which give patients less freedom to choose their health-care providers and obtain care outside of health plans. In general, managed-care plans give patients access to a network of health-care providers who have agreed to accept certain negotiated rates in exchange for seeing more patient volume. Some more-restrictive plans have "gate-keepers," or doctors who must preapprove treatments by specialists in order to keep costs down. The least restrictive

— and most prevalent — managed-care plans are preferred provider organizations (*see below*).

Medicare — The federal program established in 1965 that provides health insurance to individuals age 65 and over and the disabled. The program is financed by payroll taxes and offers hospital insurance with optional coverage for outpatient doctor visits and other care.

Medicare+Choice — A federal program created by Congress in 1997 authorizing managed-care plans to serve Medicare recipients, as an alternative to Medicare's traditional fee-for-service system. Many seniors choose the managed-care option because the plans typically offer more generous benefits, including drug coverage, which is not offered by traditional Medicare.

Medicare Part A — Medicare's hospitalization insurance, which covers inpatient care at hospitals and skilled-nursing facilities. Also covers hospice care and some home health care.

Medicare Part B — Optional health insurance that covers doctors' office visits, outpatient medical and surgical services, supplies and occupational therapy.

Preferred provider organizations (PPOs) — A managed-care plan that limits costs by steering patients to health-care providers who have agreed to accept discounted prices in the hope of getting more patient visits. PPOs are less restrictive than HMOs and older forms of managed care, which means they place fewer restrictions on the type of care that plan beneficiaries can receive. Advocates of overhauling Medicare want PPOs to administer new drug benefits.

Premiums — Fees usually paid each month for health insurance. Medicare has always charged a premium for its optional Part B coverage; it stands at $58.70 per month in 2003. Overhaul plans envision monthly premiums of about $35 for new drug coverage. The vast majority of seniors do not pay Part A premiums.

---

between rooting out abuses that victimized workers and establishing a variety of new social-welfare programs.[17]

Sentiment began to shift back in favor of a government-provided safety net during the Depression and the early days of Franklin D. Roosevelt's "New Deal." In 1934, Roosevelt convened a Cabinet Committee on Economic Security to study all forms of social insurance,

including health insurance. However, the prospect of a government-run health-insurance system triggered quick and fervent protests from doctors, who viewed it as an attempt to institutionalize medical care and regulate their profession.

Pressure from the AMA was felt acutely in Congress, where there was little interest-group pressure in favor of creating a national health-insurance system. Secretary of Labor Frances Perkins, an influential voice in the administration, argued that under the existing economic circumstances the White House would be wise to spend its political capital on creating what became the Social Security System. Roosevelt, taking the cautious route, heeded the advice and put health insurance on the back burner, though the topic continued to generate significant debate.

After World War II, Roosevelt's successor, Truman, enthusiastically revived the push for national health insurance, though he had not previously made his ideas on the subject known. Truman sent Congress a draft bill in November 1945 making it a cornerstone of a social-policy package he called the "Fair Deal." But the increasingly conservative bent of the postwar Congress, and Truman's lack of prestige at the time, conspired to defeat the effort.

In 1946, voters elected a Republican-controlled Congress, and organized labor turned its attention to fighting the Taft-Hartley law, which imposed new restrictions on unions. By 1948, Truman concluded government health insurance would have to be considered an "ultimate aim" instead of an immediate possibility.

Final Battles

The final round of political battles on the issue began in 1957, when the AFL-CIO mobilized its 14 million members for an all-out fight to create health insurance for Social Security beneficiaries. Despite AMA and AHA opposition, congressional hearings the next two years brought new attention to the worrisome economic plight of American seniors and convinced some lawmakers that the private insurance market could not give many the coverage they needed. Figures such as House Speaker Sam Rayburn, D-Texas, and then-Senate Majority Leader Johnson joined a lobbying campaign for a national system, while Republicans sought alternatives, such as federal subsidies for private insurers to cover the aged poor.

It was left to Rep. Wilbur Mills, D-Ark., chairman of the powerful House Ways and Means Committee, to begin developing a compromise. He worked with the AMA to expand payments to providers under state aid programs, creating a category of assistance called "medical indigency" for elderly citizens who did not qualify for welfare but still needed help with their medical bills.

The agreement became a rallying point and was codified in legislation that cleared Congress and was signed into law in 1960.

But creation of the limited program did not tamp down sentiment for a full-fledged national health-insurance program. President John F. Kennedy was determined to press for a congressional showdown but soon became consumed with Cold War events. Nevertheless, public debate intensified, with doctors' groups trying to blunt the momentum and organized labor and the insurance industry promoting new low-cost private insurance programs for individuals over 65.

However, sentiment for national health insurance continued to grow. Such disparate groups as the National Council of Churches, union retiree organizations and grass-roots seniors' groups mobilized by the national Democratic Party — such as the National Council of Senior Citizens — vocally pressed for a new system.

The outcome of the 1964 elections assured creation of Medicare. Johnson, who became president after Kennedy's 1963 assassination, was returned to office by the largest plurality in the nation's history, while Democrats picked up 38 House seats and two in the Senate. With lopsided majorities in both Houses, Mills and his allies began to cobble together a measure creating the modern Medicare program. The legislation added Title XVIII to the 1935 Social Security Act. The authorizing legislation also created Medicaid, a separate program for the poor under age 65.

The resulting Medicare system consists of several parts. Part A, which covers hospitalization, is free to all Americans eligible for Social Security. Financed by a special payroll tax on both employers and workers, it covers inpatient hospital treatment, skilled nursing-home care and some home health and hospice care. Most hospitals are reimbursed predetermined amounts based on the average cost of treating a condition.

Medicare also offers an optional package of services known as Part B that covers doctors' office visits and outpatient services. It is available to anyone 65 or older willing to pay monthly premiums, an annual deductible and co-payments. Part B pays for physical or occupational therapists, certain home health services, medical equipment, prosthetics and doctors' visits. It also covers preventive services, such as certain vaccinations, screening for cervical, colorectal and prostate cancer and mammograms.

Health-care experts deem the Part B package a bargain in the current marketplace because recipients only pay about one-quarter of what the covered services are worth, with the remainder subsidized by federal taxpayers.[18]

Benefits Added

In 1972, Congress made individuals with end-stage renal disease eligible for coverage for such services as dialysis and kidney transplantation. In 1997, lawmakers added Part C, known as Medicare+Choice, allowing expanded health-care options for those enrolled in Parts A and B, including the ability to enroll in private managed-care plans. The private plans try to attract customers by offering services not provided under "traditional" Medicare, such as prescription drugs, eyeglasses and hearing aids. However, many plans have pulled out of the program, dissatisfied with the level of reimbursements Medicare provides.

Medicare's benefit package still resembles a typical circa-1965 health insurance package. It pays for most "medically necessary care," but excludes many preventive measures and all long-term care, except rehabilitation in a nursing home after a hospital stay. It also excludes hearing, vision, dental and foot care or prescription drugs, except those administered in a doctor's office. Medicare also lacks "stop loss" coverage, a central component of private plans that limits the amount patients must pay out-of-pocket for their share of covered medical bills each year.

Whenever lawmakers have added benefits, they have simultaneously taken steps to control costs. In 1983 Congress created a hospital reimbursement system that based payments on a patient's diagnosis rather than on what the hospital actually did to treat the patient. Payments were set based on what the average hospital would spend to treat a patient with the same condition, with some allowances for geographic variations.

Though the new system brought hospital spending under better control, payments to physicians soared 15 to 18 percent annually in the 1980s — a symptom, critics contend, of overcompensation for surgery, diagnostic tests and other procedures. To control costs lawmakers in 1989 adopted a system that paid according to the time, training and skill needed to perform a given procedure, with adjustments for overhead. Medicare also set targets for spending increases based on inflation, changes in the number of beneficiaries and other factors.

Senate Majority Leader Bill Frist, R-Tenn., a heart-transplant surgeon, will be a key negotiator as conferees work out differences between House and Senate versions of a proposed Medicare-overhaul bill. Majority Whip Mitch McConnell, R-Ky., looks on.

Getty Images/Stefan Zaklin

Revising payment systems eased some financial pressure, but policymakers generally agreed that a longer-term solution would entail gradually moving beneficiaries away from Medicare's fee-for-service system. The creation of Medicare+Choice in 1997 tried to persuade seniors to give up their choice of doctors and hospitals in exchange for enhanced benefits offered by providers in private health-plan networks. Medicare pegged payments to private plans at 95 percent of the cost of caring for the average beneficiary — a move designed to save the program money. However, studies soon revealed that healthier beneficiaries who tended to live longer switched to private plans, increasing Medicare's long-term costs. And many private plans withdrew from the program after government efforts to cap payment increases, leaving millions of seniors searching for new health-care arrangements.

Earlier this year, the Bush administration continued to look to private health plans for solutions when it unveiled a draft Medicare-overhaul plan offering a new prescription-drug benefit only to those seniors who left the traditional Medicare system and enrolled in managed-care plans. That proposal quickly drew the ire of influential Republicans and Democrats from rural states, who recalled the reluctance of private insurers to serve their regions after the creation of Medicare+Choice. Senate Finance Committee Chairman Charles E. Grassley, R-Iowa, and ranking Democrat Max Baucus of Montana — responsible for shepherding Medicare legislation through that chamber — insisted that seniors who remain in traditional Medicare be offered an equivalent drug benefit. The inclusion of that guarantee in the Senate bill won the support of some Democrats. But it remains a sore point with conservative politicians, who believe the addition of a drug benefit will dramatically boost mandatory government spending unless significant market reforms are introduced into the Medicare system.

"[Such] reforms are essential to make the current program sustainable," write Joseph Antos and Jagadeesh Gokhale, scholars at the conservative American Enterprise Institute in Washington. "With their abandonment, the prescription-drug benefit that is about to be signed into law will be the most fiscally irresponsible legislation in U.S. history."[19]

CURRENT SITUATION

Conference Hurdles

If Congress and the administration are to overhaul Medicare this year, they must overcome deep philosophical differences and significant bureaucratic challenges.

The House-Senate talks are likely to continue through at least early fall and are aimed at reconciling two very different Medicare plans. The House plan would focus its drug coverage on seniors with lower drug costs. Beneficiaries would meet a $250 deductible, after which Medicare would pay 80 percent of drug costs up to $2,000. After that, seniors would pay for their drug costs until they had spent $3,500 out-of-pocket, at which point Medicare would cover all further drug costs.

The House bill also would require wealthier seniors to pay more before they could receive catastrophic coverage — a controversial element known as "income relating" that both Democrats and the Bush administration oppose. (*See sidebar, p. 60.*)

Not surprisingly, the Senate bill is more bipartisan, given the political difficulties of passing any Medicare legislation in a chamber where Republicans have 51 seats and Democrats 48, with one independent. It would require seniors to pay a $275 deductible, after which

Retirees demonstrate against plans to overhaul Medicare at a June 25 rally in Washington, D.C. Seniors fear increasing the role of private health plans will give elderly Americans fewer options in choosing doctors and hospitals.

Medicare would pay half of their drug costs up to $4,500 a year. Medicare would then stop offering coverage until a senior paid out-of-pocket costs of $3,700. At that point, the government would pay 90 percent of costs.

The biggest differences between the two bills deal with the differing roles of government and the private sector in delivering health benefits. The most contentious aspect involves the House plan's requirement that the traditional Medicare system begin competing with private health plans in specified geographic regions beginning in 2010, to be phased in over five years. (*See sidebar, p. 56.*)

The provision was written to turn Medicare into a so-called "defined-contribution" program, in which the government's financial liability is fixed. Conservatives believe this ultimately will hold down program costs. Traditional Medicare is a "defined-benefit" system, in which the government guarantees patients a certain level of care, irrespective of how much it costs.

The Senate would allow more limited competition. For five years, beginning in 2009, some private plans could bid against each other on price, but not against the traditional Medicare system. Before that time, private plans could bid against each other, but their payments would be limited by the rates for traditional Medicare. The theory is the private plans could get a lot of new business administering benefits; if they offer more generous packages than traditional Medicare, they could, in theory, peel off seniors from the fee-for-service system, especially healthier and wealthier seniors.

Will pending Medicare proposals help elderly Americans?

YES
Sen. Bill Frist, R-Tenn.
Majority Leader, U.S. Senate

From a speech on the Senate floor, June 10, 2003

[Our] goal is twofold: to strengthen and improve Medicare and, at the same time, provide meaningful prescription-drug benefits to seniors and Americans with disabilities. . . . [O]ver the next 30 years, we will have a doubling in the number of seniors, but in terms of workers actually paying into the program itself, that will be falling off continually over time. Thus, we need to take this opportunity . . . to modernize the program so seniors and individuals with disabilities will continue to get good care and hopefully improve that care in this environment where we have to address the issues of solvency and sustainability.

Some [say] Medicare denies some seniors coverage. [W]e will make sure this coverage is available to every senior everywhere. We will specifically . . . ensure access in rural areas. We will be creating public-private partnerships that will offer choice — again, it is voluntary — but will be offering choice for all seniors in every corner of America.

Seniors might ask: Do I have to give up what I have now? Are you forcing me into some new system? The answer is no. This is a voluntary program. All of us will be able to look every senior in their eyes and say: You can keep exactly what you have now if that is what you want. We will be able for the first time to say there are options that include choices you may not have today in Medicare, such as preventive care, such as chronic-disease management.

The fact is, the current program is fragmented. It does not provide adequate coverage. . . . [I]t does not adequately cover preventive care. It does not cover disease management or chronic-disease management. As we all know, it does not cover outpatient prescription drugs. I do believe good health depends on giving seniors good options, the opportunity to choose the plan that best meets their needs.

Seniors deserve care that keeps them healthy by incorporating preventive measures. Seniors deserve care that protects them from catastrophic out-of-pocket expenses. America's seniors should have the ability to see the doctor they choose, even if that doctor is outside the network. America's seniors deserve a system that focuses on their needs to keep them healthy and not just to respond to acute, episodic illness.

Since 1965, Medicare has admirably served a generation of America's seniors. We owe tomorrow's seniors no less. That will take a response in this body to give seniors access to the care they truly deserve. I look forward to working with my colleagues to strengthen and improve Medicare.

NO
Sen. Debbie Stabenow, D-Mich.
Member, Special Committee on Aging

From a speech on the Senate floor, June 11, 2003

[T]here is much work left to be done by this body before we have prescription-drug coverage that, in fact, meets the needs and the desires of the seniors of America.

All of the prescription-drug plans [under discussion] involve private insurance first. If private insurance is available in your state or region, if there are two or more companies there . . . you would have to choose one of those two private insurance plans. . . . [S]eniors, potentially every year, would get paperwork in the mail about two different insurance companies . . . and would have to wade through the paperwork and decide which of the two is best for them. The next year, if those two companies were not both available . . . the senior would have the ability to go to a backup plan — something administered through Medicare. Then the next year, if there were two companies that decided they wanted to try their hand in covering Medicare prescription drug[s] in their region, [seniors] could not get the Medicare plan anymore; they would have to pick between those two companies.

Potentially, this could happen every single year. Seniors are not asking for more paperwork or more choices of insurance companies. There is a better way to do this: to give people more choices, but make sure one of the choices is traditional Medicare.

I [am] quite amazed that we are even talking about structuring a plan this way when . . . Medicare has been rising in cost about 5 percent a year, and private insurance is going up 15 to 20 percent a year. . . . This approach uses a more expensive model — arguably, putting more dollars into the pockets of insurance companies. . . .

Why are we going through all this convoluted process? Well, I think there are two reasons. [Some] believe we should move to private insurance, [and] some don't believe we should have universal health coverage under Medicare. I disagree.

[In addition] . . . a very large and powerful prescription-drug lobby, . . . I believe, at all costs, wants to make sure our . . . 40 million seniors and disabled people . . . are not in one insurance plan together, who could then negotiate big discounts in prices. By dividing folks up into lots of different insurance plans, making it more confusing for people to stay in traditional Medicare and get prescription-drug help, and trying in every way to move people more to managed care, the prescription-drug companies know they will not [be forced] to substantially lower their prices for seniors.

The Bush administration has not endorsed one plan over the other, but officials told conservative lawmakers privately that the White House will work in conference to bend any final bill its way — presumably to more closely resemble the House bill. The administration has taken pains not to appear to be micromanaging the negotiations, or doing anything to antagonize Democrats. However, many observers predict that President Bush will have to get involved at some point and make personal appeals to lawmakers in order to win votes.

"Clearly, this is going to be very difficult," said Gail Wilensky, who ran the Medicare program during the administration of former President George Bush. The conferees "are knowledgeable, smart, tough individuals, and it will be a real battle as to how it plays out. It will be very important how the White House comes down."[20]

Floor Drama

The negotiations could easily unravel. The political challenges were evident during a tumultuous June 27 House debate on its version of the legislation. With Democrats nearly unanimously opposed to the bill, House GOP leaders faced defections from some their own moderates, who feared the competition provisions in the bill could gut traditional Medicare. They also faced a rebellion from about two-dozen conservatives who withheld their votes, arguing the bill did not do enough to promote competition and would merely boost government spending by adding a drug benefit.

On the pivotal vote, Majority Leader Tom DeLay, R-Texas, and Majority Whip Roy Blunt, R-Mo., focused on a handful of wavering party members, holding the vote open until they could wear down enough members to declare victory. At about 2:30 a.m., about a half-hour after the allotted time for the House vote had expired, Rep. Jo Ann Emerson, R-Mo., left a small group of Republicans and picked up a green ballot, signifying a "yea" vote. Democrats groaned as she walked to the well and cast the ballot. The lighted board above the floor showed more yes votes than no's for the first time. The speaker promptly banged the gavel, closing the vote. Republicans won, 216-215, with one member — Ernest Istook, R-Okla. — voting present.[21]

There was no such drama in the Senate, where the bipartisan bill passed by a wide majority of 76-21. Many of the Democrats who had misgivings but voted for the

President Bush discusses health care with senior citizens during a rally at Sun City, Fla. Bush's call to spend $400 billion over 10 years to update Medicare spurred the current talks.

AFP Photo/Tannen Maury

bill could vote against a more conservative conference agreement later.* But since only 51 votes are needed to approve a compromise, the White House can afford to lose a dozen or more Democratic votes and still prevail.

Ways and Means Committee Chairman Thomas is chairman of the conference, by virtue of his committee's jurisdiction over the issue and his party's control of both the House and Senate. The 61-year-old lawmaker is regarded both as one of the smartest and most prickly members of Congress. Recently, he offered a tearful apology on the House floor after calling the Capitol police to break up a meeting of Ways and Means Democrats.

---

* The conferees include Senate bill authors Grassley and Baucus, as well as Majority Leader Bill Frist, R-Tenn., Minority Leader Tom Daschle, D-S.D., Budget Committee Chairman Don Nickles, R-Okla., and Sens. Orrin G. Hatch, R-Utah, John D. Rockefeller IV, D-W.Va., and John B. Breaux, D-La. Of the group, Daschle and Rockefeller are the most vocal opponents of the GOP proposals, with Baucus and Breaux likely to support a bipartisan compromise, if it does not veer too far toward the House position.

House conferees include Tauzin and ranking Democrat John D. Dingell of Michigan, ranking Ways and Means Committee Democrat Charles B. Rangel of New York, DeLay, and Reps. Michael Bilirakis, R-Fla., Nancy L. Johnson, R-Conn., and Marion Berry, D-Ark.

Already, he has accused several of the Democratic negotiators of hypocrisy for signing a letter that publicly urged bipartisan compromise while privately insisting that most elements of the existing system survive.[22]

"It becomes much more difficult to make something happen when people on the conference sign letters" suggesting they would not support a bill without certain provisions, Thomas said after a meeting at the White House between conferees and President Bush. "You have to practice bipartisanship all of the time, not just in front of the cameras."

Democrats worry that Thomas will not tolerate dissent but will bend the conference toward the House position, particularly with respect to premium support and competition between traditional Medicare and private health plans. "There is a growing fear within the Democratic side in the Senate that this is going to turn very badly when Bill Thomas puts his loving arms around it in the conference," says Sen. Richard J. Durbin, D-Ill., who voted for the Senate bill, despite misgivings about whether it will undermine the traditional program.

Lobbyists could also insert special provisions in what would be the biggest health-care measure in years. For example, Breaux, backed by large hospital chains, inserted language in the Senate bill preventing doctors from referring patients to new facilities in which they have ownership interests. The move is designed to steer business away from so-called "specialty hospitals" that deal with one type of practice, such as orthopedics, and that community hospitals say skim profitable specialties, leaving them with high-cost treatments like emergency care.[23]

Both bills boost payments to certain providers, such as rural hospitals and doctors. Alaska, for example, would get a $45 million demonstration project to increase program reimbursements — the work of Senate Appropriations Committee Chairman Ted Stevens, R-Alaska.

With so much at stake, lawmakers expect considerable horse-trading, particularly to prevent conservative Republicans from defecting like they did before the House floor vote. "There have been no commitments [to conservatives] about conference," Grassley said. "We're going into conference with everything on the table, and we'll just have to work our way through it."

OUTLOOK

More Debates Expected

Though both parties have endorsed Medicare overhaul with lightning speed by Washington standards, many expect future battles over the program, since many of the compromises so far are designed to spawn future debates.

If an added drug benefit triggers further program growth, Republicans are prepared to respond with next-generation proposals that would, for example, limit those who qualify for benefits or link the level of benefits to participants' incomes. Tying benefits to incomes "directs most of the help to the people who need help," says Rep. Jim McCrery, R-La., a House Ways and Means Committee member.

But it also could bolster Democratic contentions that Republicans' real goal is to dismantle Medicare over time. Democrats worry that a targeted, less universal Medicare benefit will make the program resemble welfare, eroding congressional and public support.

"When a senior citizen enters a hospital, Medicare pays the same amount for their care whether they are a pauper or a millionaire," Sen. Kennedy says. "Medicare is for all senior citizens who paid into the program during their working years — not just some senior citizens. And it should stay that way."

Democrats hope to use the coverage gaps in any compromise plan as justification for future increases in Medicare spending, in the hope of creating gap-free drug benefits for all seniors. The strategy would put Republicans in the position of arguing that more government spending on seniors would be a budget-buster and expose the U.S. Treasury to the brunt of future drug-price increases.[24]

"The gap or 'doughnut hole' reduces protection just at the time when many of those who are most in need are expecting some relief," says the Urban Institute's Moon. "The basic problem is that $400 billion is not enough to provide a well-designed prescription-drug benefit."

But no one really knows how seniors will respond to a revamped system. Establishing new coverage options, in which beneficiaries would have to select from three managed-care plans or the traditional Medicare system, would be likely to spawn confusion, according to many experts. Considerable backlash could also develop if cost-cutting companies drop guarantees they will continue paying retirees' health bills into the future, figuring seniors could get equivalent coverage from the government.

Moreover, seniors could decide the extra out-of-pocket expenses for the new benefits are not worth the cost. Such a scenario doomed a 1988 Medicare catastrophic-coverage law that proposed a tax surcharge on certain wealthy beneficiaries.

Hoping to avoid a repeat, GOP strategists are urging Republican lawmakers not to hype the proposed drug benefit, but merely depict it as an alternative or a safety option for those without coverage. Others don't expect a negative reaction but worry that seniors may want even more generous benefits.

Members of Congress "will find out that they're not off the hook on this at all," said Robert Blendon, a pollster at the Harvard School of Public Health.[25]

NOTES

1. Quoted in Sheryl Gay Stolberg, "Medicare Plan Far From Cure-All, Irate Retirees Find," *The New York Times*, June 26, 2003, p. A1.

2. Pharmaceutical companies blame rising research costs for the large price hikes, but critics attribute them to higher company spending on what they say is excessive direct-to-consumer advertising and higher industry profit margins. For background, see David Hatch, "Drug Company Ethics," *The CQ Researcher*, June 6, 2003, pp. 521-544. Also see "Prescription Drug Trends: A Chartbook Update," Kaiser Family Foundation, November 2001, pp. 7-8.

3. See Centers for Medicare and Medicaid Services, "2003 Annual Report of the Boards of Trustees of the Hospital Insurance and Supplementary Medical Insurance Trust Funds," March 17, 2003. For background on drug prices, see Hatch, *ibid.*

4. For background, see Congressional Research Service, "Medicare Prescription Drug and Reform Legislation," RL31966, June 19, 2003 (update).

5. See Families USA, "Out of Bounds: Rising Prescription Drug Prices for Seniors," 2003.

6. For background, see David Nather and Rebecca Adams, "Medicare Rewrite: Prescription For Disappointing Everyone," *CQ Weekly*, July 5, 2003, pp. 1690-1696.

7. See Kaiser Family Foundation, "Medicare and Prescription Drug Spending Chartpack," June 2003.

8. See Sarah Lueck, "Medicare Drug Benefit Is a Mixed Bag for the Elderly," *The Wall Street Journal*, July 14, 2003, p. B1.

9. See Mike Dorning, "Bill Gives Boost to Reducing Drug Costs," *Chicago Tribune*, July 26, 2003, p. A1.

10. For background, see Rebecca Adams, "GOP Pushes Private Coverage," *CQ Weekly*, Nov. 23, 2002, pp. 3071-3072.

11. Quoted in "As Medicare Conference Approaches, Lobbyists Ready to Kick Into Gear," *CQ Weekly*, July 5, 2003, pp. 1692-1693.

12. Quoted in Pamela Gaynor, "No Panacea," *Pittsburgh Post-Gazette*, Dec. 22, 2002, p. F1.

13. *Ibid.*

14. See House Committee Report 108-178, Part I.

15. See Mary Agnes Carey, "Private Medicare Health Plans Already Being Tested," *CQ Today*, June 16, 2003, p. 8.

16. Quoted in Amy Goldstein, "Medicare Talks Moving Slowly," *The Washington Post*, July 27, 2003, p. A12.

17. For background, see Peter A. Corning, "The Evolution of Medicare, From Idea to Law," Social Security Administration, 1969. Available online at http://www.ssa.gov/history/corning.html.

18. For background, See Julie Rovner, *Health Care Policy and Politics A to Z*, CQ Press (2000), pp. 121-126.

19. See Joseph Antos and Jagadeesh Gokhale, "The Medicare Prescription Drug Benefit Is Bad for America's Health," American Enterprise Institute, *On The Issues*, July 2003.

20. See Rebecca Adams and Mary Agnes Carey, "Compromise Will Come Hard In Medicare-Overhaul Conference," *CQ Weekly*, June 28, 2003, pp. 1611-1617.

21. See Jonathan Allen and Adam Graham-Silverman, "Hour by Hour, Vote by Vote, GOP Breaks Tense Tie," *CQ Weekly*, June 28, 2003, pp. 1614-1615.

22. See David Nather, "Contrite Chairman Does Not Quell Calls for more GOP Comity," *CQ Weekly*, July 26, 2003, pp. 1885-1888.

23. See Laurie McGinley and Sarah Lueck, "Medicare Bill: Prescription for Politics," *The Wall Street Journal*, July 14, 2003, p. A4.

24. For background, see Mary Agnes Carey, "Plans for Targeted Benefits Deepen Medicare Debate," *CQ Weekly*, June 7, 2003, pp. 1358-1363.

25. See Nather and Adams, *op. cit.*

BIBLIOGRAPHY

Books

Jost, Timothy S., *Disentitlement: The Threats Facing Our Public Health Programs and a Right-Based Response*, Oxford University Press, 2003.
A law professor examines how deficiencies in private health insurance have hindered the ability to finance health care for U.S. citizens and what American policymakers can learn from national health insurance and social insurance in other countries.

Morrison, Ian, *Health Care in the New Millennium: Vision, Values and Leadership*, Jossey-Bass, 2000.
A futurist and health-care analyst explores managed care and market-driven reforms in the U.S. health system and why escalating costs continue to plague the marketplace.

Oberlander, Jonathan, *The Political Life of Medicare*, University of Chicago Press, 2003.
An accessible history of the Medicare program by a professor of social medicine details the bipartisan consensus the program has enjoyed for decades and how it has been overlooked in recent policy disputes.

Articles

"Medicare Drug Benefit Is a Mixed Bag for the Elderly," *The Wall Street Journal*, July 14, 2003, p. B1.
A package of articles examines Medicare beneficiaries' concerns that proposed coverage is too skimpy and the various choices facing employers, who can decide to trim or even eliminate retiree health coverage.

Adams, Rebecca, "Medicare Prescription Benefit Just One Part of Overhaul," *CQ Weekly*, Jan. 18, 2003, pp. 150-153.
This year's Medicare debate probably will go beyond adding a drug benefit to the entitlement program. It is also likely to include a proposal for the largest overhaul in the program's 38-year history.

Goldstein, Amy, and Helen Dewar, "Medicare Bills Pass in Congress; Prescription Drug Benefit Is Key To Biggest Changes In 38 Years," *The Washington Post*, June 27, 2003, p. A1.
Details the political jockeying that led to near-simultaneous House and Senate passage of Medicare drug bills and the differences between the plans.

Nather, David, and Rebecca Adams, "Medicare Rewrite: Prescription For Disappointing Everyone?" *CQ Weekly*, July 5, 2003, pp. 1690-1696.
Beyond political compromises, negotiators trying to reconcile Medicare drug proposals in Congress will assess whether a revamped program addresses seniors' needs.

Toner, Robin, "Medicare: Battleground for a Bigger Struggle," *The New York Times*, July 20, 2003, p. WK1.
The differences in Medicare-overhaul plans illustrate Republicans' and Democrats' profoundly different visions of social-welfare programs and of government in general.

Reports and Studies

Congressional Research Service, "Medicare Prescription Drug Provisions of S1, as Passed by the Senate, and HR1, as Passed by the House," July 11, 2003.
A detailed, nonpartisan analysis of provisions in House and Senate Medicare-overhaul plans.

General Accounting Office, "Medicare: Observations on Program Sustainability and Strategies to Control Spending on Any Proposed Drug Benefit," April 9, 2003.
In conjunction with House Ways and Means Committee hearings on overhauling Medicare, this report examines the challenges of adding a drug benefit to Medicare in the context of the program's current and projected financial condition.

Gold, Marsha, and Lori Achman, "Average Out-of-Pocket Health Care Costs for Medicare+Choice Enrollees Increase 10 Percent in 2003," Mathematica Policy Research Inc./The Commonwealth Fund, August 2003.
The average Medicare managed-care enrollee is spending 10 percent more than last year and double the levels of four years ago, raising questions about private health plans' ability to control costs.

Kaiser Family Foundation, "The Current Medicare Prescription Drug Debate: Briefing Charts," July 15, 2003.
A series of briefing charts, prepared by a nonpartisan health-care think tank, with background information on prescription-drug use and spending among senior citizens, recent survey data on employers' likely reaction to a Medicare drug benefit and an overview of pending Medicare legislation.

Shea, Dennis G., Bruce C. Stuart and Becky Briesacher, "Caught in Between: Prescription Drug Coverage of Medicare Beneficiaries Near Poverty," The Commonwealth Fund, August 2003.
Researchers from Pennsylvania State University and the University of Maryland conclude that pending Medicare-overhaul proposals passed by the House and Senate would only slightly reduce the drug costs of a couple living at 160 percent of the federal poverty level.

For More Information

AARP, 601 E St., NW, Washington, DC 20049; (888) 687-2277; www.aarp.org. Influential seniors lobby urging policymakers to strengthen the traditional Medicare system.

American Association of Health Plans, 1129 20th St., NW, Suite 600, Washington, DC 20036; (202) 778-3200; www.aahp.org. This trade group representing private health plans supports Medicare privatization.

American Medical Association, 515 N. State St., Chicago, IL 60610; (800) 621-8335; www.ama-assn.org. A physicians group opposed to creation of the original Medicare program, now actively involved in influencing the debate over overhauling it.

Centers for Medicare and Medicaid Services, 7500 Security Blvd., Baltimore, MD 21244-1850; (410) 786-3000; http://www.cms.hhs.gov. The Department of Health and Human Services branch responsible for administering Medicare.

Consumers Union, 1666 Connecticut Ave., NW, Suite 310, Washington, DC 20009-1039; (202) 462-6262; www.consumersunion.org. A consumers' group that backs efforts to lower consumers' drug prices but opposes Republican-led efforts to overhaul Medicare.

Families USA, 1334 G St., NW, Washington, DC 20005; (202) 628-3030; www.familiesusa.org/site/PageServer?pagename=Medicaid_Index. A nonprofit organization "dedicated to the achievement of high-quality, affordable health care for all Americans."

Health Insurance Association of America, 1201 F. St, NW, Suite 500, Washington, DC 20004; (202) 824-1600; www.hiaa.org. A prominent trade organization representing managed-care firms that would play a more prominent role delivering benefits in a revamped Medicare system.

Pharmaceutical Research and Manufacturers Association, 1100 15th St., NW, Washington, DC 20005; (202) 835-3400; www.phrma.org. The drug industry's trade association opposes price controls on prescription drugs and importation of foreign drugs.

4

Drug Company Ethics

David Hatch

Thousands of Americans shop for drugs in Los Algodones, Mexico, where a cluster of 28 pharmacies offers savings of up to 70 percent on prescription drugs. Critics of U.S. drugmakers complain about high drug prices, misleading ads and anti-competitive behavior, but drug companies say the billions of dollars they spend developing new products and the meteoric rise in generic drugs prove competition is thriving.

Getty Images/Ann Summa

This past March, Bristol-Myers Squibb, one of the world's biggest drug companies, settled federal charges that it had engaged in a decade of misconduct to block competition from low-cost generic drugs.

The illegal conduct "protected nearly $2 billion in annual sales at a high cost to cancer patients and other consumers," the Federal Trade Commission (FTC) said, forcing Americans "to overpay by hundreds of millions of dollars for important and often life-saving medications."

Bristol agreed to stop hindering competition for three of its blockbuster drugs, including two anti-cancer drugs, Taxol and Platinol, and the anti-anxiety medication BuSpar.[1] Bristol's anti-competitive behavior had included paying more than $70 million to a rival drug company to keep its generic version of BuSpar off the market; deceiving the U.S. Patent and Trademark Office; and filing "baseless" patent-infringement lawsuits, the FTC said.

The misconduct was extraordinary, even by pharmaceutical-industry standards, says Joe Simons, director of the FTC's Bureau of Competition. "It was conduct going on over a long period of time and quite pervasive," he says. "We're very concerned where generics are being kept out of the market, and prices to consumers are significantly higher than they need to be."

The commission's complaint may have been unusual in its sweeping scope, but it was far from the first time drugmakers have come under fire in recent years. Indeed, federal regulators — along with numerous senior citizens' groups and consumer advocates — routinely criticize drugmakers' increasingly aggressive tactics to win

From *The CQ Researcher*, June 6, 2003.

product approval, promote medications, block competitors and stave off regulation.

Some critics say drugmakers' methods are so excessive that tougher oversight of the industry is needed, including strict price controls and curbs on advertising and marketing.

But the pharmaceutical industry says it is guilty of nothing more than savvy, if hard-nosed, business practices, especially in the highly competitive battle between brand-name and generic drugs, which now command 47 percent of the entire prescription-drug market.[2] Moreover, the drugmakers point out, they spend billions of dollars on research every year and save countless lives with the medications they develop.

"The U.S. has the most innovative pharmaceutical industry in the world, bar none," says Jeff Trewhitt, a spokesman for the Pharmaceutical Research and Manufacturers of America (PhRMA).

"Eighty-five of the 95 new biotechnology medicines approved by the Food and Drug Administration [FDA] since 1982 have been researched, developed and produced by U.S.-based companies," Trewhitt says. The United States is able to develop so many new drugs, he says, because other countries impose price controls, which make drugs less expensive in those countries but also stifle innovation.[3]

The industry's success translates into big profits: U.S. drugmakers boasted a 17 percent return on revenue in 2002 — the highest profits of any industry.[4] Americans spent $140.6 billion on prescription drugs in 2001, three times more than a decade earlier, according to the Kaiser Family Foundation. The figure is projected to grow by more than 200 percent by 2012 — to $445 billion. As a percentage of overall health-care costs, U.S. spending on prescription drugs is projected to grow from 11 percent in 2001 to 17 percent in 2012.[5]

But the success comes with intense oversight. Nearly every aspect of the business draws scrutiny from government and nonprofit watchdogs, and pharmaceutical companies are being hit with huge class-action lawsuits and fines. In addition, safety recalls of prescription drugs are on the increase: In the last five years, 13 medications have been pulled off the market; many others legally remain on pharmacy shelves despite nagging questions. Heavily advertised Celebrex and Vioxx, for example, are still sold although they are dogged by safety concerns, as

well as evidence that some over-the-counter pain relievers work equally well.[6]

Some of the drug industry's critics are also critical of the FDA, the lead regulator of the pharmaceutical industry, for its close ties to drugmakers.[7] Half of the agency's budget comes from industry user fees, and some members of its advisory committees, which make recommendations on drug approval, have business ties to pharmaceutical companies and thus potential conflicts of interest.[8] The FDA's critics include the General Accounting Office (GAO), which chastised the agency for what it said was lax oversight of drug-company advertising. Advertising by the industry grew rapidly after the agency relaxed its ad guidelines in 1997, effectively giving the industry a green light to advertise heavily on television.

Many lawmakers worry that the ad glut is prompting consumers to seek drugs they may not need — raising both the nation's overall health-care bill and taxpayers' costs for government-subsidized health-care programs. Other critics question whether the burgeoning cost of advertising is contributing to the increasing prices for prescription drugs, which are rising faster than inflation.

Drugmakers wield enormous influence in Washington through a vast lobbying force, generous campaign contributions and strong political connections to the Bush administration. Critics say that groups funded by drug companies purport to be consumer organizations representing seniors but are actually front groups carrying the industry's message on television and elsewhere, sometimes creating confusion that critics say is intentional. (*See sidebar, p. 77.*) And with drug companies generously funding many academic institutions that evaluate medications, questions also have been raised about the objectivity of certain test results.

Critics also note the drug industry receives several tax breaks for its research and development (R&D) efforts, although much of the research that pharmaceutical companies rely on to develop new drugs is culled from government-funded studies, mainly at the National Institutes of Health (NIH). But PhRMA emphasizes that drug companies spent $32 billion last year on research, far more than NIH's entire operating budget.

Although the makers of brand-name drugs come in for much of the criticism and regulatory action, generic-drug companies also get their share. While they offer competition and lower prices, some have been charged with colluding with brand-name drug companies or each

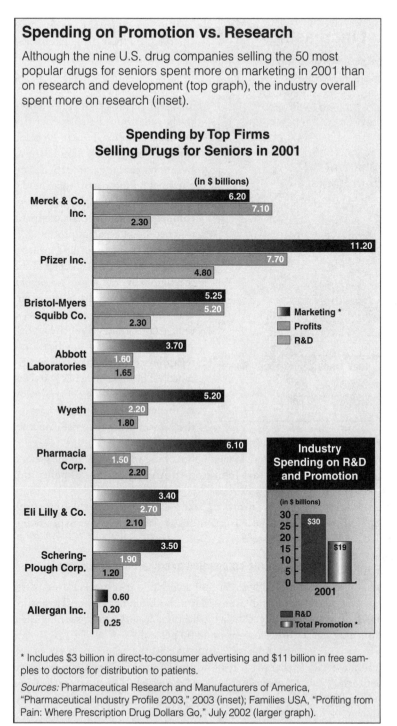

Spending on Promotion vs. Research

Although the nine U.S. drug companies selling the 50 most popular drugs for seniors spent more on marketing in 2001 than on research and development (top graph), the industry overall spent more on research (inset).

Spending by Top Firms Selling Drugs for Seniors in 2001

(in $ billions)

Merck & Co. Inc.
- 6.20
- 7.10
- 2.30

Pfizer Inc.
- 11.20
- 7.70
- 4.80

Bristol-Myers Squibb Co.
- 5.25
- 5.20
- 2.30

■ Marketing *
■ Profits
■ R&D

Abbott Laboratories
- 3.70
- 1.60
- 1.65

Wyeth
- 5.20
- 2.20
- 1.80

Pharmacia Corp.
- 6.10
- 1.50
- 2.20

Eli Lilly & Co.
- 3.40
- 2.70
- 2.10

Schering-Plough Corp.
- 3.50
- 1.90
- 1.20

Allergan Inc.
- 0.60
- 0.20
- 0.25

Industry Spending on R&D and Promotion

(in $ billions)

	2001
$30	$19

■ R&D
□ Total Promotion *

* Includes $3 billion in direct-to-consumer advertising and $11 billion in free samples to doctors for distribution to patients.

Sources: Pharmaceutical Research and Manufacturers of America, "Pharmaceutical Industry Profile 2003," 2003 (inset); Families USA, "Profiting from Pain: Where Prescription Drug Dollars Go," July 2002 (larger graph).

"The FTC has as many problems with generics as it does with the brand-name manufacturers," says Sarah Lenz Lock, a senior attorney at AARP (formerly the American Association of Retired Persons).

Lately, the spotlight on the industry has been even more intense as lawmakers prepare to renew a critical debate over adding a prescription-drug benefit to Medicare, an issue taking on added importance with a presidential election looming next year. The proposed new benefit appears to have wide support, including from the pharmaceutical industry. Debate centers mostly on how it should be structured and what it should cover.

President Bush, backed by drug companies, wants to offer sizable drug coverage for senior citizens in private health plans, but only a modest benefit under Medicare. The approach creates an incentive for seniors to switch from federally funded Medicare to private insurance and leaves drugmakers with the most bargaining power over prices, critics say.

Democrats, some Republicans and the AARP would prefer to have the benefit under Medicare, but they recognize that private plans will likely have a role if a consensus is to be reached on a drug benefit.

Fueling the push for prescription-drug coverage are skyrocketing costs for medications in the United States. In 2000, the average retail price of a prescription drug was $45.79 — more than twice the 1990 price tag. The average retail price of a brand-name drug in 2000 was $65.29 — more than triple the cost of a generic.

other to keep lower-priced products off the market, thus keeping prices artificially high.

Prices for retail drugs increased more than three times the inflation rate from 1998 to 2000.[9]

Generics' Share of Market Increasing

Low-cost generic drugs accounted for nearly half of the U.S. drug market in 2000 — more than double their share in 1984. Generics are expected to overtake brand-name prescription drugs by 2005. The rise is largely attributable to legislation favorable to generic drugmakers and efforts by the health-care industry to cut costs.

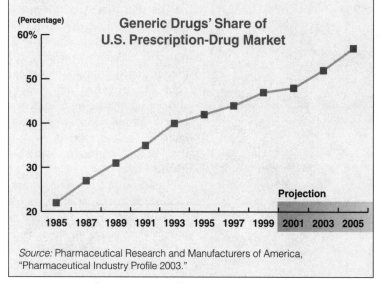

(Percentage)

Generic Drugs' Share of U.S. Prescription-Drug Market

Projection

1985 1987 1989 1991 1993 1995 1997 1999 2001 2003 2005

Source: Pharmaceutical Research and Manufacturers of America, "Pharmaceutical Industry Profile 2003."

But other patent ploys have emerged. As their drug patents are about to expire, pharmaceutical companies often create patent-protected successors that are virtually identical to the originals — effectively extending the patent, critics say. Schering-Plough used the tactic with its allergy medication Claritin. Before its patent expired, Schering obtained a fresh patent for a nearly identical drug, Clarinex. It now competes without generic competition because it is patent protected.

Arnold S. Relman and Marcia Angell, former editors-in-chief of the prestigious *New England Journal of Medicine*, maintain that pharmaceutical companies, faced with pressure to boost profits, rely on such low-risk strategies to develop medications, regardless of their medical significance. "They use their R&D dollars to imitate top-selling drugs already on the market or to find new uses for their own blockbusters," the two physicians wrote recently.[10]

"It's a blatant abuse of the whole spirit of the generic law," says John Rother, AARP's director of policy and strategy.

As lawmakers take a closer look at regulation of the pharmaceutical industry, here are some issues being discussed:

Are drug companies overcharging Americans?

Faced with $1,500 a year in out-of-pocket drug costs, Bill and Ginny Mayer, both 68, of Monroe Township, N.J., get their medications from Canada, slashing their drug costs by up to 50 percent.[11]

Industry critics like Rother say the lower prices charged abroad prove U.S. drug companies overcharge Americans. Indeed, the House Government Reform Committee says drug prices in the United States are 55 percent higher than prices for the same drugs in the United Kingdom.[12]

Prescriptions are cheaper overseas because — unlike in the United States — most foreign governments con-

To make matters worse for U.S. consumers, prices for the exact same drugs — made by the same companies — are significantly lower in other countries, which strictly control drug prices. The higher U.S. prices have led some to charge drugmakers with price gouging. Perhaps not surprisingly, the increases also have fueled a growing trend among seniors and others of buying medications via the Internet or in other countries, often by driving across the border into Mexico or Canada. The Bush administration has cracked down on the practice, warning consumers that the products may be unsafe. It's also threatening legal action against organizations that help U.S. citizens import drugs.

Meanwhile, drug companies play cat-and-mouse with regulators while trying to sidetrack competitors. A few years ago, the FTC cracked down on brand-name companies paying generics to settle patent-infringement litigation and stay off the market. "We tend not to see the patent-settlement problem anymore," says Simons of the FTC.

trol prices. In the United States, however, "We let [drug companies] price at what the market will bear," says Gary Claxton, director of the Healthcare Marketplace Project at the Kaiser Family Foundation.

In Canada, for example, individual provinces negotiate with pharmaceutical companies to determine how much they can charge through the national health program.

However, according to a recent report from the Cato Institute, "Simplistic comparisons between drug costs in the United States and those in other countries have little value. Economic wealth, exchange rates, product-liability rules, price controls and other factors all contribute to the price of drugs."[13]

While drugs in Canada are generally considered safe, even supporters of drug reimportation warn that potentially dangerous counterfeit drugs are sometimes sold in other countries, particularly where regulatory oversight is lax.

Lower prices in Canada partly reflect a weak Canadian dollar and a faltering local economy, Cato argued. "Canadians also benefit from less, and less expensive, product-liability litigation," it said. Another factor contributing to price disparities is the fact that patent protection for brand-name pharmaceuticals is not as extensive in Canada and Mexico.

Industry supporters also say such price controls stifle innovation by reducing incentives for drugmakers to pursue costly research to create new medicines.

But, industry critics say U.S. companies are not developing major, new, innovative drugs but are primarily reworking existing blockbuster formulas. Citing FDA documents, Relman and Angell pointed out that only 23 percent of newly approved drugs are "significant improvements" on existing products. "Many of these drugs would be more accurately described as modest, incremental improvements," they wrote.[14]

As proof that U.S. drug-pricing practices are unfair, others cite the fact that domestic drug prices have increased far faster than inflation. In a study of 50 drugs used by senior citizens, the health-care advocacy group Families USA found that prices for nearly three-quarters of the drugs rose faster than inflation from 2001 to 2002. Prices for more than a third of the drugs rose three or more times faster than inflation.[15]

For instance, the price for a 10 mg dose of the cholesterol-lowering drug Lipitor jumped 13.5 percent, more than five times the inflation rate, according to the report. The price for Celebrex, an anti-inflammatory, rose 9.4 percent, more than triple the inflation rate, and the price for the hypertension drug Metoprolol rose nearly eight times faster. Increases were even more dramatic over longer periods. From 1992 to 2002, the price of Furosemide, a diuretic made by Mylan, rose 338.7 percent — more than 11 times the inflation rate.

PhRMA defends the price increases, emphasizing that industry investment in R&D has expanded from roughly $1 billion a year in the 1970s to $32 billion in 2002. It says the average cost of researching, developing and introducing a new drug is $802 million.[16] "Higher rewards provide the incentive to take on higher risks," the Cato Institute said in its report, adding that drug companies develop about 90 percent of new medicines, with the NIH developing the rest.[17]

But critics note that PhRMA's cost estimate came from the Tufts (University) Center for the Study of Drug Development, which receives industry funding. In fact, the consumer group Public Citizen contends that the estimate is not fully representative of industry spending, since only a few newly approved drugs were considered.[18]

PhRMA says the estimate is an average and that the center's funding is inconsequential.

Michael Gluck, a professor of health policy at Georgetown University, notes that taxpayers essentially subsidize much of the drug industry's research through their funding of the National Institutes of Health, whose scientists conduct research that becomes the basis for new medications and sometimes later go to work for the industry.

Ron Pollack, executive director of Families USA, thinks pharmaceutical companies are raising prices to "unaffordable" and "improper" levels to plow more money into increased promotion and advertising. "They make more on profits than they spend on research and development," he says. Eight of nine major pharmaceutical companies reviewed by the group last year spent twice as much on marketing, advertising and administration as they spent on R&D. (*See graph, p. 77*)[19]

And prices stay high when pharmaceutical companies succeed in blocking generic competitors, according to the group. "Every day that brand-name manufacturers can avoid competition from generics, they stand to make

Industry Critics Warn of 'Front' Groups

True or false: The following organizations represent senior citizens: United Seniors Association; the Seniors Coalition; the 60 Plus Association.

If you answered true, critics of the drug industry would say you are among the millions of Americans who have been fooled. The organizations may seem to be watchdogs protecting seniors, but they are really "front" groups that accept drug-company funding and tout industry positions, the critics say.

"I don't think that's illegal, but it's perhaps unethical because you're not being straight about who you're really representing," says John Rother, director of policy and strategy at the AARP (formerly American Association of Retired Persons).

David Herman, executive director of the Seniors Coalition, denies his group is a front, even though up to 20 percent of its money comes from drug companies. "There's nothing to hide," he says. "We're not going to apologize for receiving unrestricted money." His group occasionally differs with the Pharmaceutical Research and Manufacturers of America (PhRMA) on policy issues, he adds.

Echoing drugmakers, all three of the Virginia-based groups strongly support President Bush's proposal on Medicare reform, even though AARP and other watchdogs say it isn't generous enough. The 60 Plus Association criticizes AARP for everything from shortening its name to suing drugmakers. It also objects to amending the so-called Hatch-Waxman Act, a position held by brand-name

drug companies. Critics say loopholes in the 1984 law allow drugmakers to extend their patents.

While the three groups claim to be nonpartisan, they describe themselves as conservative, and critics say they almost exclusively support Republicans. The 60 Plus Association's Web site notes its president, Jim Martin, has known President Bush since 1968. Charles Jarvis, chairman of United Seniors, served as deputy undersecretary of the Interior in the Reagan and Bush administrations and as campaign chairman for GOP presidential candidate Gary Bauer, according to Public Citizen.[1]

PhRMA spokesman Jeff Trewhitt won't say whether his organization helps finance the groups. Herman acknowledges receiving "unrestricted" funding, and Jarvis said in a statement, "We will aggressively seek support from every single, individual association and business that agrees with our market-based approach to solutions for every senior in America."

Frank Clemente, director of Public Citizen's Congress Watch, says the Virginia groups had been independent until PhRMA sought ties with them after taking heat during the Clinton administration for creating a front group, Citizens for Better Medicare (CBM), from scratch. The group, which was headed by PhRMA's former advertising director, spent about $65 million on television ads opposing Clinton's Medicare reform plan and had ties to the Virginia-based groups.[2]

PhRMA insists CBM wasn't a front. "We helped to found it, and we helped to fund it," Trewhitt acknowledges, adding

millions of dollars," Families USA said in a recent report.[20]

But the Cato Institute report argued: "Prices for U.S. pharmaceuticals are not excessive relative to the benefits they offer. Drugs have contributed to the sharp reduction in mortality rates from many diseases, including AIDS."[21]

Rother sees other factors at play: New medications invariably enter the market at high prices, he says, and Americans are consuming — and therefore buying — more drugs than ever before. "I think there's a discomfort with out-and-out price controls in the United States," he says.

Should the government restrict drug advertising?

During a recent broadcast of the "CBS Evening News," which has strong viewership among over-50 Americans, almost one-fourth of the ads were for prescription drugs. Spots appearing during the May 29 newscast touted Nexium and Prevacid, two competing heartburn medications, the allergy remedy Allegra and the various contributions of pharmaceutical giant Pfizer. "Meeting humanity's greatest challenges: that's the heritage of an original American company," the Pfizer ad said.

Drug companies spent $2.7 billion[22] on "direct-to-consumer" (DTC) ads in 2001 — three times as much

that 90 other organizations had ties to it and thousands joined as members.

The New York Times reported United Seniors spent up to $13 million during the 2002 election season on TV ads in 20 congressional districts. Democrats say the spots were designed to help GOP candidates.[3] Rother says the pharmaceutical industry is skirting campaign-finance laws by using ads run by such groups to back GOP positions. "There's no money for anyone to counter them on TV, so it definitely has an impact," he says.

Jarvis describes the United Seniors Association as non-partisan and says its ads encourage both Democrats and Republicans to support "a tangible prescription-drug benefit under Medicare now."

The groups don't mention their drug-industry connections on their Web sites or in ads, omissions that critics say are intentional. AARP says some of its members thought United Seniors ads were sponsored by AARP. The groups' financing is "all a matter of public record," says Pfizer spokesman Nehl Horton. "I don't buy that anyone's hiding anything."

All three organizations claim to speak for millions of older Americans, although as recently as 2001 none of the three listed any revenue from membership dues on their tax returns, the *AARP Bulletin* reported recently.[4]

The drug industry has relied on other groups to spread its message. The hundreds of health officials who formed hepatitis C coalitions in 11 states in the late 1990s actually were part of a marketing effort by Schering-Plough to promote an $18,000-a-year treatment for the disease, according to *The Washington Post.* "The drugmaker's campaign offers a vivid look at a public-

relations tactic gaining currency in corporate America: the use of 'Astroturf,' or 'grass tops' — groups posing as authentic local organizations to promote a product or political aim," the paper said.[5]

Three years ago, a consumer activist representing Citizens for the Right to Know and two other grass-roots organizations told lawmakers at a Senate hearing on prescription drugs that pharmacies — and not drug companies — are responsible for costly medications. The notion that drugmakers gouge consumers is "completely unfounded," Elizabeth Helms testified.

But Helms was hardly an objective voice. "What her audience did not hear was that she also works full time for a public-relations company whose clients include the Pharmaceutical Research and Manufacturers of America," *The New York Times* reported, noting PhRMA had provided start-up funding for the group.[6]

---

[1] See "United Seniors Association: Hired Guns for PhRMA and Other Corporate Interests," Public Citizen, July 2002.

[2] See Executive Summary of "Citizens for Better Medicare: The Truth Behind the Drug Industry's Deception of America's Seniors," Public Citizen, July 20, 2000.

[3] See Robin Toner, "The 2002 Campaign: The Drug Industry. Democrats See a Stealthy Drive by Drug Industry to Help Republicans," *The New York Times*, Oct. 20, 2002, p. A20.

[4] See Bill Hogan, "Consumer Alert," *AARP Bulletin*, February 2003.

[5] See Robert O'Harrow Jr., "Grass Roots Seeded by Drugmaker; Schering-Plough Uses 'Coalition' to Sell Costly Treatment," *The Washington Post*, Sept. 12, 2000, p. A1.

[6] See Jeff Gerth and Sheryl Gay Stolberg, "With Quiet, Unseen Ties, Drug Makers Sway Debate," *The New York Times*, Oct. 5, 2000, p. A1.

---

as the $791 million they spent in 1996.[23] The total included $1.6 billion spent for TV commercials, up from $220 million in 1996. The FDA's relaxation of its ad guidelines in 1997, softening disclosure requirements for TV spots, helped spur the growth.

The industry's advertising money was apparently well spent: Heavily advertised drugs are the drugmakers' biggest sellers, and most ads are for medications that must be taken repeatedly, offering the greatest sales opportunities, according to a recent GAO report.[24]

Consumer advocates and other industry critics say the increase in drug ads has created an "ad glut," particularly on television, which they say prompts patients to request

prescriptions they don't need — escalating overall health-care costs. They also blame the increased ad spending for rising drug prices.

Drug companies insist that the price hikes are needed to finance increased spending on research — not advertising. The Cato Institute argues that advertising actually promotes price competition and lower prices by boosting competition. "The suppression of ads might aid some market leaders in the industry, but it would not benefit consumers," Cato said in a recent report.[25]

But critics point out that many drug companies have boosted spending on advertising faster than they've increased spending on creating new products. Indeed,

Spending on Advertising Skyrocketed

Drug companies spent about $2.5 billion on direct-to-consumer advertising in 2000, or nearly 10 times more than in 1994. The percentage spent on print ads declined significantly during the period while the percentage spent on TV correspondingly increased.

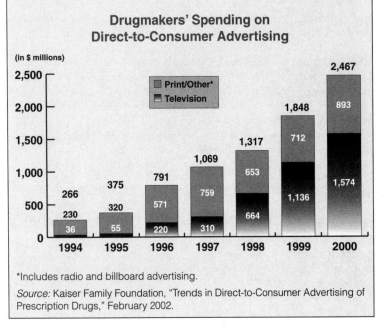

Drugmakers' Spending on Direct-to-Consumer Advertising

(in $ millions)

Legend:
- Print/Other*
- Television

Year	Total	Television	Print/Other*
1994	266	36	230
1995	375	55	320
1996	791	220	571
1997	1,069	310	759
1998	1,317	664	653
1999	1,848	1,136	712
2000	2,467	1,574	893

*Includes radio and billboard advertising.

Source: Kaiser Family Foundation, "Trends in Direct-to-Consumer Advertising of Prescription Drugs," February 2002.

spending on DTC drug advertising by the nine top drug-makers for seniors grew 145 percent from 1997 to 2001, while R&D spending rose only 59 percent, according to the GAO.[26]

While advertising spending may be rising faster than research expenditures for some companies, PhRMA points out that drug companies overall spend far more on R&D than they do on advertising. Moreover, PhRMA says, drug advertising is educational. It cites a 2001 report in *Prevention* magazine showing that 80 percent of Americans find the advertising informative.[27] "We certainly believe that there is a clear benefit to advertising," says spokesman Trewhitt.

"Advertising does not compete with R&D; rather, the two are complementary," the Cato Institute said. "Marketing hikes revenues and investment returns, making more money available for — and increasing the incentive for — R&D."[28]

Advertising executives are quick to agree. "A tremendous amount of this information is possibly the difference between life and death for these patients," says Dan Jaffe, executive vice president of the Association of National Advertisers. The ads "empower" Americans to talk to their doctors about diabetes, high cholesterol, kidney disease and other ailments, he says.

Some of the industry's sharpest critics concede the point — to a degree. Rother of AARP says some ads, such as those for cholesterol-lowering drugs, prompt people to see their doctors and take medication. But he thinks many ads are misleading: "We believe the ads should give consumers more information about appropriateness and about alternatives."

AARP worries, for example, that Celebrex and Vioxx ads do not mention that less-expensive, over-the-counter drugs are equally effective. "When studies show that 96 percent of people would get just as much pain relief from ibuprofen, that's a pretty relevant fact," Rother says. Including such information in the ads would result in lower public expenditures, because people could choose cheaper alternatives.

Doctors also worry that ads do not provide balanced views of risks and benefits, he says. "That suggests to me that we may need to do more in the way of the guidance about how to communicate the benefits and risks effectively," he says. The FDA may require more disclosure in print ads, but not in TV spots, an FDA official said on condition of anonymity.

If the FDA feels an ad is misleading, it sends "regulatory" letters to drug companies. Since 1997, the agency has issued repeated regulatory letters to several companies, including 14 such letters to GlaxoSmithKline, six to Schering Plough, five to Merck and four to Pfizer regarding Lipitor. "The advertisements gave the false impression that Lipitor can reduce heart disease and falsely claimed that Lipitor is safer than competitors," the GAO said about Pfizer's ads.[29]

But the GAO complained that such letters "do not completely deter pharmaceutical companies from making misleading claims in subsequent advertisements." Moreover, Rep. Henry A. Waxman, D-Calif., a longtime critic of both the agency and the industry, complained last October in a letter to Health and Human Services (HHS) Secretary Tommy G. Thompson that FDA enforcement actions against drug advertisers dropped 50 percent last year, even as drug ads were increasing. In a March 31 response, McClellan said the agency is stepping up enforcement and sending out some regulatory letters more quickly.

McClellan points out, however, that studies show DTC ads can aid consumers, and few doctors surveyed by the FDA felt pressured by their patients to prescribe heavily advertised drugs, as some critics have claimed.

But DTC advertising, it turns out, is only the tip of the pharmaceutical promotional spear. Drug companies spend far more marketing their products directly to doctors — with freebies that include meals, exotic junkets, education and drug samples. In 2001, of the $19.1 billion spent on promotional activities — $15 billion was for marketing to doctors.[30]

Rother says drug companies on average spend about $7,000 per doctor marketing directly to physicians. "It's a huge phenomenon, and that's money that gets built into the cost structure of the whole enterprise," he says. To dampen the criticism about marketing to physicians, PhRMA has adopted a voluntary code of conduct that sets limits on how much drug companies can pay for meals for doctors, consulting fees and trips, and continuing education; it also advises against certain activities, such as paying for entertainment.

Meanwhile, HHS in April issued stricter guidelines directing drugmakers not to offer doctors gifts and other rewards in exchange for administering their drugs. Giving gifts or making payments strictly to influence business could violate federal anti-kickback statutes, the guidelines warn.

But drugmakers haven't given up easily in their efforts to frame the debate over ethics. Two years ago, when the American Medical Association launched a $1 million campaign to increase doctors' awareness of its existing ethics guidelines, it was major pharmaceutical companies — including Bayer, Eli Lilly, GlaxoSmithKline, Merck and Pfizer — that picked up $675,000 of the tab.[31]

In recent years, lawmakers in Congress have introduced various measures to regulate drug-company advertising, including bills to boost FDA fines for running false or misleading ads and reduce or eliminate tax deductions for advertising and marketing expenditures. Democrats Sen. Debbie Stabenow, Mich., and Reps. Jerrold Nadler, N.Y., and Patrick Kennedy, R.I., have offered measures to reduce or eliminate the tax deductions that drug companies take for their advertising and marketing expenditures.

Jaffe says removing the tax deduction from prescription-drug advertising is tantamount to taxing speech.

Does the drug industry wield too much influence in Washington?

Just how powerful is the pharmaceutical industry? Consider this: More drug-industry lobbyists walk the halls of Capitol Hill than lawmakers — at least 600 vs. 535 senators and representatives.

And some of the most powerful members of the Bush administration are former drug-company executives, including Defense Secretary Donald Rumsfeld — former chairman of G.D. Searle, now part of Pfizer — and just-resigned White House Budget Director Mitch Daniels, a former senior vice president at Eli Lilly.[32]

"This is probably one of the most — if not the most — influential industries in Washington," says Frank Clemente, director of Public Citizen's Congress Watch. "We can't even get a generic-drug bill passed. These guys are just very hard to beat; we see it all the time."

Over the years, the pharmaceutical industry's powerful lobby in Washington has proven quite adept at thwarting all manner of legislative threats. Rep. Tom Allen, D-Maine, co-chairman of the House Affordable Medicines Task Force, has offered bills tying U.S. drug prices to the lowest prices in other industrialized countries, but the measures never passed, says Claxton of the Kaiser Family Foundation.

But Pfizer spokesman Nehl Horton cites last year's Senate passage of the legislation favorable to generic drugmakers (see p. 93) as evidence that lobbyists for brand-name companies don't always win: The proposed legislation has not been enacted into law. Moreover, he says, lobbying is necessary to educate lawmakers about a complex business and to ensure that industry views are considered. "People put the term 'influence' on it as if

C H R O N O L O G Y

1900-1930s *Congress passes key laws regulating pharmaceutical firms.*

1906 The Food and Drugs Act bans interstate commerce in mislabeled or adulterated food, beverages and drugs.

1930 The Food and Drug Administration (FDA) is established.

1938 The landmark Food, Drug and Cosmetic Act establishes the modern system of drug regulation after 100 deaths due to untested pediatric medication.

1940-1960s *Congress tightens the restrictions on drug efficacy and safety.*

1962 Amendments to the Food, Drug and Cosmetic Act require FDA-approved drugs to be safe and effective, creating current drug marketing standards and regulations.

1962 The sleeping pill thalidomide is blamed for causing terrible birth defects in babies. Outrage strengthens support for tougher drug regulation.

1966 The Fair Packaging and Labeling Act requires all consumer products sold through interstate commerce to be accurately and informatively labeled, including packaging for drugs.

1970-1980s *New laws and tax credits encourage research and development and the rise of generic drugs.*

1981 Economic Recovery Act provides tax credits for research to qualifying firms that increase their R&D expenditures in a given tax year.

1983 Orphan Drug Act creates economic incentives for drug companies to fight rare diseases, or conditions affecting up to 200,000 Americans.

1984 Drug Price Competition and Patent Restoration Act, known as Hatch-Waxman, facilitates introduction of generics and extends brand-name patents.

1988 FDA becomes an agency of the Department of Health and Human Services, with its own commissioner.

1990s *Drugmakers get a break on patent protection from Congress and international trade negotiators.*

1992 Prescription Drug User Fee Act requires FDA to collect user fees from pharmaceutical companies to supplement its annual federal appropriations. The funding is used to review new drug applications.

1994 Uruguay Round Agreements Act extends U.S. patents on pharmaceuticals from 17 years after a patent is issued to 20 years after a patent application is filed.

1997 Food and Drug Administration Modernization Act adds six months of patent protection for medications tested on children. It also expands the FDA's user-fee program.

2000-2003 *Federal regulators crack down on anti-competitive behavior as drug companies roll out blockbuster prescription drugs.*

2002 Senate passes the Greater Access to Affordable Pharmaceuticals Act, which closes perceived loopholes in Hatch-Waxman Act used by brand-name companies to block generics from entering the marketplace.

March 2003 Federal Trade Commission fines Bristol-Myers Squibb Co. for anti-competitive behavior against generic drugmakers spanning a decade, sending a strong warning to drug companies to curb abusive business practices. . . . President Bush proposes broad outline for new Medicare drug benefit, setting the stage for legislative debate on an issue affecting more than 40 million seniors.

April 16, 2003 Pfizer and Pharmacia merge to become the world's largest pharmaceutical company. Its portfolio includes the blockbuster prescription medications Celebrex, Lipitor, Zoloft and Viagra, the erectile-dysfunction treatment that began the trend of "lifestyle drugs," and the over-the-counter hair-growth ointment Rogaine.

there's something wrong with it," he says. "We live in a democracy that allows and encourages people to make their views known."

Clemente claims drug companies spend more on federal lobbying than any other industry. Drug companies spent $177 million on lobbying in 1999 and 2000, about $50 million more than the insurance and telecommunications industries.[33]

Yet the pharmaceutical industry is not the largest campaign contributor in Washington. The industry trailed 10 other sectors — including entertainment and real estate — in contributions to federal candidates and political parties in 2002, according to the Center for Responsive Politics. Of the drugmakers' $20.6 million in contributions, 79 percent went to Republicans. PhRMA, the industry's top contributor, donated nearly $3.2 million, of which 95 percent landed in Republican coffers.[34]

During the 2000 presidential election, the drug industry's $26.7 million in donations included at least $850,000 in contributions to the Bush-Cheney inaugural committee, according to the center.

The industry's influence extends beyond its checkbook. Dozens of former lawmakers or lawmakers' relatives have lobbied for the industry, including former Republican National Committee Chairman Haley Barbour; Linda Daschle, wife of Senate Minority Leader Tom Daschle, D-S.D; Scott Hatch, son of Senate Judiciary Committee Chairman Orrin G. Hatch, R-Utah, and Anthony Podesta, the brother of President Bill Clinton's former chief of staff, John Podesta.[35]

The industry's influence also reaches deep into the FDA. Because many members of key drug-approving advisory committees have connections to drugmakers, critics say the industry has too much influence over the agency's regulatory process. For instance, half of the FDA's budget comes from industry user fees, they point out. "I don't know any other agency that's funded by the very industry that it regulates," says Matt Keller, legislative director for the watchdog group Common Cause.

Critics think the FDA's close relationship with drug companies makes it lax on regulation. According to the *Los Angeles Times*, FDA regulators sometimes feel pressure from higher-ups within the agency to approve drugs, even if they have safety concerns. "People are aware that turning something down is going to cause problems with [officials] higher up in the FDA, maybe

more problems than it's worth," an FDA regulator said after departing the agency.[36]

Drug companies say conflict-of-interest allegations regarding FDA advisory panel members are overblown. Before members can participate in meetings, they're screened for potential conflicts of interest and excluded if necessary, the FDA said.

In addition, says PhRMA's Trewhitt, if panel members with ties to the industry were eliminated, there wouldn't be enough candidates for the committees. Pfizer's Horton says the panels rely on the expert opinions of industry representatives.

Moreover, FDA committees reject drugs roughly 20 percent of the time, according to John Treacy, an official at the FDA's Center for Drug Evaluation and Research.

Critics say drug companies manipulate the regulatory process in other ways. Larry D. Sasich, a pharmacist and research analyst with Public Citizen, says companies sometimes spin the results of drug trials, either by leaving important information out or by emphasizing insignificant data. "We have seen puff pieces [in medical journals] years before a drug appears before an FDA committee," he says.

BACKGROUND

Cracking Down

Drug companies have been fighting with regulators for centuries.

"Adulteration and misbranding of foods and drugs had long been a fixture in the American cultural landscape," the FDA says. By the late 1800's, charlatans peddling a worthless assortment of wonder drugs and potions abounded, with even the most reputable companies dabbling in deceit.[37]

In 1937, a Tennessee drug company sold an untested pediatric medication that caused 100 deaths, mostly in children. The ensuing public outrage triggered congressional approval of the landmark 1938 Food, Drug and Cosmetic Act, requiring new drugs to be shown safe before marketing — and beginning a new era of government regulation of pharmaceuticals.

Since then, the industry has been accused of a variety of questionable practices, including failing to develop medications with only a few potential users or those that might compete with existing, high-priced drugs.[38] For example, research has indicated that steroids — which cost about $50 — might be a possible cure for sepsis, a potentially lethal condition for which the only approved drug, Eli Lilly's Xigris, costs $7,000 a dose. However, neither Lilly — which spent millions developing Xigris — nor other companies have conducted the expensive research needed to prove that steroids, for which the patents have expired, are an effective treatment.[39]

In 1984, Congress passed the so-called Hatch-Waxman Act, which established guidelines designed to make it easier for generics to enter the market and granted brand-name drug companies additional market exclusivity for their products under certain conditions.

One of the most controversial provisions in Hatch-Waxman is the "30-month stay," a period during which drug companies can resolve patent disputes. But the Generic Pharmaceutical Association says brand-name companies use it to file new last-minute patents — as Bristol-Myers Squibb did with BuSpar — that act as "bait" to get generic companies to challenge the late filings. When a generic company takes the bait and challenges the filing, the brand-name company can then sue for patent infringement, automatically triggering the 30-month delay on the market entry of the generic.

In early 2002, Congress renewed until 2007 a program that gives drug companies an extra six months of patent exclusivity for brand-name drugs in exchange for agreeing to test the medications for use by children.[40]

Companies also sometimes do not fully vet new uses for old drugs, leading to potentially dangerous consequences. For example, Schering-Plough said on May 30 it may face criminal indictments from federal prosecutors over allegations that it promoted drugs for unapproved

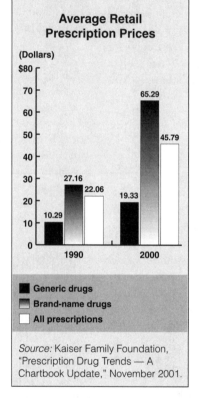

Brand-Name Prices Rose the Most

Prices for all prescription drugs doubled in the past decade, but the rate of increase was higher for brand-name drugs, which were more than three times as costly as generics in 2000.

Average Retail Prescription Prices

(Dollars)

- 1990: Generic drugs 10.29; Brand-name drugs 27.16; All prescriptions 22.06
- 2000: Generic drugs 19.33; Brand-name drugs 65.29; All prescriptions 45.79

■ Generic drugs
▨ Brand-name drugs
□ All prescriptions

Source: Kaiser Family Foundation, "Prescription Drug Trends — A Chartbook Update," November 2001.

uses, illegally provided doctors with research grants to prescribe its drugs, and submitted false pricing information so Medicaid would pay too much for its drugs.[41]

Warner-Lambert, now part of Pfizer, was accused of marketing the epilepsy drug Neurontin in the mid-1990s for unapproved uses rather than subjecting it to additional testing. Whistleblower David P. Franklin resigned from his position as a medical liaison for the company after concluding that it was illegally promoting "off-label" uses of the medication and providing financial incentives to doctors to prescribe it.

Pfizer, which acquired Warner-Lambert in 2000, said it is not responsible for pre-acquisition behavior and doesn't promote drugs in that manner. Pfizer is trying to negotiate a settlement with Franklin and the government prosecutors who subsequently sued the company.[42] In February, a coalition of public-interest groups also sued Pfizer and its Parke-Davis subsidiary, for improperly promoting off-label use of Neurontin.

"We are outraged to find that once again a major drug company has decided it is above the law and can market its drug by any means necessary," said Ahaviah Glaser, director of the Boston-based Prescription Access Litigation Project (PAL), which seeks to make prescription drugs affordable.[43] The group says the company tried to market Neurontin for more than a dozen ailments, ranging from bipolar disorder to migraines, and sought to exploit loopholes in federal laws banning the marketing of drugs for unapproved uses. The group's suit also alleges that Parke-Davis, formerly a division of Warner-Lambert, hired ghostwriters to pen scientific articles praising the off-label uses of Neurontin and then paid physicians to put their names to the articles.

In Texas, Wyeth Pharmaceuticals allegedly hired inexperienced lawyers who had just been elected to the state legislature in a ploy to delay their lawsuits involving the weight-loss regimen fen-phen, which caused heart and lung damage in some patients. Texas and a few other states allow lawyer-legislators to delay trials they are involved in when legislatures go into session.[44]

According to Craig McDonald, director of the watchdog group Texas for Public Justice, "One day you're a small-town lawyer doing wills and divorces. You get elected to the legislature and the next day you're a lucratively paid, high-priced corporate lawyer working on complex product-liability cases. But you're not really working. What you're doing is filing a single piece of paper."[45]

State Rep. Steve Wolens, D-Dallas, agreed. "Why would you hire a lawyer who's been a lawyer for five minutes to represent you in a complicated drug case?" he asked. "You wouldn't, except for the fact that they just got elected to the Texas legislature."[46]

Anti-Competitive Acts

Meanwhile, the FTC is hopeful that its action this year against Bristol-Myers Squibb will deter future anti-competitive behavior by it and other companies. Under its settlement with the FTC, Bristol agreed not to seek late listings of patents or 30-month delays of generic competitors. If Bristol violates the restrictions, the FTC can confiscate any profits from the violations and fine the firm $11,000 a day.

"The chances that they could do anything [illegal] would be pretty limited," says the FTC's Simons.

The FTC reprimand helped propel settlement of a class-action suit alleging that Bristol acted improperly to extend its patent on BuSpar. PAL sued on behalf of thousands of plaintiffs, and was later joined by AARP and attorneys general from dozens of states. The company eventually agreed to pay $535 million in damages.

AARP also has joined PAL in a class-action suit alleging Schering-Plough paid two firms $75 million not to sell a generic equivalent of its blood-pressure medication K-Dur. A third class-action lawsuit by the group alleged that AstraZeneca, maker of the breast-cancer drug Tamoxifen, colluded with Barr Laboratories to protect the price of Tamoxifen. While on appeal, a settlement was reached in which Barr agreed not to manufacture its own generic of the drug for 10 years while AstraZeneca

Members of Congress and the United Seniors Association flank House Speaker J. Dennis Hastert, R-Ill., during a Capitol Hill rally on May 1, 2002, calling for improved prescription-drug benefits.

pays Barr $21 million and supplies it with Tamoxifen for sale as a lower-priced generic.

Despite such actions, the FTC acknowledges it has limited anti-competitive regulatory authority. For example, it is powerless against pharmaceutical companies patenting so-called "me-too" drugs — slight variations of competing blockbusters marketed to cash in on their popularity.

"There's nothing obviously anti-competitive about it," Simons says, adding that similar products are permitted under the patent laws. "If the FDA approves the drug, there's really nothing for the Federal Trade Commission to do," he says, unless a company uses deception to persuade customers to switch to the new drug.

Industry advocates say having similar drugs on the market is beneficial because competition drives prices down, and slightly varied drugs can affect the body in different ways.

The FTC also grapples with collusion among generics. "One pays the other, rather than the two of them competing and driving the price down. With only one competing, the price is higher and they can share the additional profits," Simons explains.

Last June the agency charged Dublin-based Elan and Toronto-based Biovail — companies that manufacture generic and branded pharmaceuticals — with agreeing not to compete in the market with generic offerings of Bayer's blood-pressure remedy Adalat. In a consent decree, the

Third World Testing Draws Criticism

Facing growing financial and regulatory pressure, pharmaceutical companies are exporting many of their drug trials to the Third World, where costs are lower, regulations are less stringent — or nonexistent — and there's a vast pool of desperate potential test subjects.

The globalization of drug trials increased at a rapid clip during the 1990s, when applications from overseas researchers seeking U.S. Food and Drug Administration (FDA) approval for new drugs increased 16-fold, according to a Department of Health and Human Services (HHS) report.[1]

While the practice often saves lives and speeds up drug approvals, it also can exploit the world's most vulnerable people by subjecting them to controversial testing procedures usually prohibited in the West, critics say, such as giving sick control-group patients placebos when known effective treatments are available.

"It could be considered murder," said Doctors Without Borders physician Evariste Lodi, after a 10-year-old meningitis patient in Kano, Nigeria, died in 1996 after Pfizer researchers gave her only the experimental antibiotic Trovan, while effective alternative treatments were available nearby. "The patient died because [the doctor] refused to help."[2]

Thirty Nigerian families later sued Pfizer, claiming that the testing caused brain damage, paralysis or death in their children, that they were never informed their children were receiving experimental drugs and that the testing violated U.S. and international laws.[3] The FDA Office of Criminal Investigations also reportedly opened a probe of the incident.[4]

Pfizer insists its experiment was "well conceived, well executed and saved lives," and was conducted with the approval of both Nigerian authorities and the families of the treated patients.[5] But a Nigerian doctor who oversaw the Trovan experiment later told a *Washington Post* reporter that a key ethics-approval document wasn't created until a year after the experiment, and was backdated to make it appear to have been signed before the trial began. Use of Trovan, which was never approved for children, was later linked to fatal liver failure and was severely restricted in the United States. The European Union eventually banned it altogether.[6]

Other allegations have surfaced in recent years of illiterate and impoverished people in Africa, Asia and Eastern Europe unknowingly agreeing to testing, signing contracts they don't understand or accepting opportunities to travel that had strings attached.

Drug companies say they often are forced to conduct clinical trials overseas because not enough patients in the West have medical conditions "of interest." Plus, while the average American fills more than 10 prescriptions a year, only one in 350 is willing to participate in a clinical trial for a new drug.[7] "Recruitment of patients is a major challenge," says John T. Kelly, senior vice president for scientific and regulatory affairs at the Pharmaceutical Research and Manufacturers of America (PhRMA).

In 2001, HHS created an office to monitor foreign experiments by U.S. researchers, and a presidential panel recommended that safeguards be established for American scientists testing drugs in Third World countries. A House panel the same year adopted a bill that would have more tightly regulated foreign drug trials by American companies.[8]

The FDA says foreign clinical studies presented to support new drug applications must meet U.S. testing standards and satisfy ethical standards outlined by the World Medical Association's 2000 international treaty, the

companies agreed not to engage in anti-competitive behavior with generic competitors.

CURRENT SITUATION

Lawsuits Up

Drug recalls have increased nearly 4 percentage points in recent years, growing from 1.6 percent during the period from 1993 to 1996 to 5.3 percent from 1997 to 2000, according to the GAO.[47]

In recent years, the FDA has recalled the diabetes treatment Rezulin, which caused serious liver failure and death in some users; Pondimin, part of the fen-phen weight-loss regimen; and Redux, which caused heart-valve damage in some patients. The prescription antihistamine Seldane, which caused heart attacks when used with other prescribed drugs, also was dropped from circulation.[48]

Declaration of Helsinki. Under the declaration, experimental therapies should be tested against "best current" treatments, and placebos should be avoided except when there is no effective treatment. Moreover, potential risks should be explained to participants before they take part in a trial.

According to Caroline Loew, assistant vice president for international regulatory affairs at PhRMA, drug companies would be foolish to conduct research overseas that does not comply with FDA rules, because the drug wouldn't be approved. "Companies that are investing $800 million in every single drug are not going to waste money on trials that don't meet [the FDA's] exacting standards," she said.[9]

PhRMA adopted its own new guidelines last fall to help standardize clinical trials. Among the recommendations: Testing must satisfy local laws, and study results must be reported in an accurate and timely fashion. "All participation in a clinical trial is based on informed consent, freely given without coercion," the guidelines say.[10]

But critics complain that both the PhRMA and Helsinki guidelines are voluntary, and many countries have few laws or enforcement mechanisms to oversee clinical research. "It is largely unregulated. The companies will tell you otherwise, but it's not true," says Peter Lurie, deputy director of the Health Research Group at Public Citizen, a watchdog group.

Lurie wants institutional review boards, the FDA or the United Nations to more carefully scrutinize overseas drug testing. The FDA often doesn't learn about overseas research until after it has been conducted. The host countries should also "exert more control," he says.

Lurie and others charge that some drug companies use poor countries as cheap testing zones for potential blockbuster drugs that are actually targeted at patients in lucrative markets back home. "The diseases that are of most interest [to the drug companies] are mainly the degenerative diseases — arthritis, obesity, heart disease — the diseases of people in the developed world," says South African bioethicist Dr. Solomon Benatar.[11]

Millions of people die every year in the Third World from diseases like malaria, which are uncommon in wealthy countries and thus attract little drug-research money, say critics. Although thousands of clinical trials are conducted around the world every year, only 0.3 percent of the industry's research budget was spent on the handful of drugs approved over the last two decades for tropical diseases.[12]

If drug companies really wanted to help the world's most needy people, critics say, they'd do more research on tropical diseases, slash drug prices in developing countries and permit greater generic competition.

"Some research should be done in developing countries, but it should be done on diseases prevalent in those areas," says Lurie. "No one should look at this research as a substitute for moving drugs into the developed world."

---

[1] Sonia Shah, "Globalizing Clinical Research: Big PhRMA Tries Out First World Drugs on Unsuspecting Third World Patients," *The Nation*, July 1, 2002.

[2] Joe Stephens, "The Body Hunters: As Drug Testing Spreads, Profits and Lives Hang in the Balance," *The Washington Post*, Dec. 17, 2000, p. A1.

[3] Shah, *op. cit.*

[4] Joe Stephens, "Pfizer Experiment Spurs Criminal Probe," *The Washington Post*, Sept. 8, 2001.

[5] *Ibid.*

[6] *Ibid.*

[7] Shah, *op. cit.* See also Roger Thurow and Scott Miller, "As U.S. Balks on Medicine Deal, African Patients Feel the Pain," *The Wall Street Journal*, June 2, 2003, p. A1.

[8] Stephens, *op. cit.*, Sept. 8, 2001.

[9] Shah, *op. cit.*

[10] "PhRMA Adopts Principles For Conduct Of Clinical Trials And Communication Of Clinical Trial Results," press release, June 20, 2002; posted at www.phrma.org.

[11] Shah, *op. cit.*

[12] *Ibid.*

In March, the FDA asked the makers of three rheumatoid-arthritis medications to warn patients about a possible link to incurable lymph cancer. The three drugs — Amgen's Enbrel, Johnson & Johnson's Remicade and Abbott Lab's Humira — could have combined sales of more than $2 billion this year.[49]

Some critics blame the industry's extraordinary influence in Washington for getting questionable drugs passed. "This track record is totally unacceptable," said Curtis Furberg, a professor of public-health sciences at Wake Forest University. "The patients are the ones paying the price. They're the ones developing all the side effects, fatal and non-fatal."[50]

Other critics say the companies are not testing their drugs sufficiently. "Are there systemic problems with the drug companies? The answer to that, in some cases, is yes," said Dr. David Egilman, a public health professor at Brown University who consults for lawyers suing the industry.[51] The Cato Institute says the FDA is actually too slow to approve drugs, and that delays over the years have caused far more deaths than recalled medications ever did.[52]

Sensing that drugmakers are as vulnerable to litigation as tobacco companies, some trial lawyers have begun aggressively filing class-action lawsuits on behalf of tens of thousands of plaintiffs against major companies like Pfizer and Bristol-Myers. The plaintiff pools for such suits are enormous, the trial lawyers say, largely because drugs for chronic conditions like depression and diabetes — which are taken by millions of people for years on end — have vastly increased the pool of potential plaintiffs if the drugs cause problems.[53]

The trial lawyers insist they're only going after dangerous drugs that the FDA and manufacturers should be protecting the public from.

In addition, because drug companies only conduct clinical trials on a few thousand subjects over a relatively short period of time before a drug is approved, potential rare side effects sometimes only surface once a drug has been in circulation for a long time.

The upswing in litigation is forcing the industry to spend several billion dollars a year defending itself. Wyeth alone has earmarked $14 billion since 1997 to defend itself against product litigation.[54]

But industry advocates say pharmaceuticals have never been safer, side effects occur with all medications and more drugs are consumed today than ever before. And prescription drugs provide a relatively inexpensive means of offsetting much larger health-care costs, they say.

"Increases in drug utilization seem to be driven primarily by the fact that health-care organizations, physicians and patients find many of the newer drugs to be extremely valuable," John Calfee, a resident scholar at the American Enterprise Institute, a Washington think tank, testified before Congress two years ago.

Meanwhile, drug companies have won some recent legal and public-opinion victories. Legal experts were surprised, for example, when a Texas jury in March rejected a plaintiff's request for $560 million in damages after he developed several medical problems linked to Bayer's since-recalled anti-cholesterol drug Baycol. Philip Beck, Bayer's defense attorney, said the verdict proved the company had not acted recklessly. Nevertheless, the

company still faces about 8,400 lawsuits over the problematic drug.[55]

Regulatory Action

With a new commissioner at the FDA, observers are carefully watching to see how the agency moves to tighten regulation of the pharmaceutical industry. There are signs that McClellan, the economist and physician who took the FDA helm in November, is willing to lock horns with drugmakers on some issues, but many are still skeptical that the agency will abandon what they see as a light-handed approach to regulation.

In a controversial move, McClellan has sought to shift some blockbuster medications from prescription-only to over-the-counter availability. Drug companies, such as Pfizer and Aventis, are resisting the proposal, arguing that the change could result in unsafe use of their products. The FDA says only drugs that are considered safe and can be administered without a doctor's supervision are being considered for the switch.

Critics of the plan say the approach benefits employers and insurers more than consumers, who would no longer have some of the medications they depend on covered by health plans.

In January, the agency announced it was speeding up the drug-approval process, in part by reducing multiple-agency reviews. FDA officials insist they're not lowering their safety standards but simply streamlining the process. In announcing the move, the agency cited a recently published Tufts University study showing that $100 million in development costs per approved drug could be saved by cutting total clinical development and regulatory review time by about 25 percent, the agency said in a release.[56]

"Certainly the faster the approval process, the better the potential for getting important new drugs to market, and thereby helping people," says Pollack of Families USA. "It's a balancing act, because we do want faster approval of drugs, but only if adequate testing has taken place."

The FDA is also heading the Bush administration's crackdown on the importation of prescription drugs from other countries, over the Internet or through mail order. The agency insists it is motivated by concerns that drugs in other countries could be unsafe because the agency cannot monitor how they're shipped, stored and dispensed. But critics think the administration is trying

Should Americans be allowed to purchase drugs from other countries?

YES Rep. Bernard Sanders, I-Vt.
Co-Chair, House Prescription Drug Task Force

From testimony, before government reform subcommittee on wellness and human rights, April 3, 2003

More and more Americans . . . cannot afford the outrageously high prices the pharmaceutical industry is charging them. While Americans pay the highest prices in the world for their medicine, the pharmaceutical industry — which receives huge tax breaks and subsidies from the U.S. government — continues to be the most profitable industry in this country and provides huge compensation packages to their executives.

To protect their profits . . . the industry has spent hundreds of millions in the last few years on campaign contributions, lobbying and advertising. [T]he pharmaceutical industry is the greediest industry in this country, and will do anything to protect their interests at the expense of the well-being of the American people.

In recent years Americans have begun to express their disgust and anger with the . . . high cost of prescription drugs by utilizing the marketplace. When they understand that they can purchase the same exact medicine in Canada for up to 90 percent lower prices . . . they are flock[ing] into that market. Up to 1 million Americans are either going across the border to buy their medicine or . . . are using the Internet.

And what has been the response of the drug companies? They are working with their political allies to stop Americans from buying prescription drugs in Canada. Glaxo has begun limiting their supplies to Canada. . . . The FDA has begun cracking down on businesses [that] help Americans purchase low-cost prescription drugs. The . . . drug companies and their allies, including the FDA, [say] they are concerned about the "safety" issue. [But,] all of the medicine being provided to Americans by registered pharmacies in Canada is highly regulated. The Canadian drug-regulatory system is quite as strong as . . . in the United States. Interestingly, despite the fact that 1 million Americans now buy medicine in Canada, there is not, to the best of my knowledge, one instance in which adulterated or unsafe medicine has been sold to an American. [Meanwhile,] one out of five Americans are not taking their medicine because of the high price. [T]hat is the safety issue . . . the FDA should be looking at.

In the 2002 election cycle the industry contributed over $6 million to the Democratic Party and over $18 million to the Republican Party. This is payback time. Tragically, the FDA and this administration have chosen to represent the interest of the industry and not the American people.

NO Alan F. Holmer
President and CEO, Pharmaceutical Research and Manufacturers of America

Written for The Cq Researcher, June 1, 2003

Thanks to continued innovation, more and more Americans are benefiting from prescription medicines — and every American should have full access to these important advances. But exposing seniors to potentially counterfeit, sub-potent or adulterated medicines is not the solution.

Legislation to allow importation of medicine from other countries would short-circuit existing safeguards that already allow importation. The MEDS Act of 2000 said that for drug importation to be legal, the secretary of Health and Human Services (HHS) must demonstrate to Congress that implementation of the law would not risk public health and safety, and that it would significantly reduce costs for U.S. consumers.

HHS secretaries of the last two administrations, one Democrat and one Republican, said they could not make this assertion. More recently, FDA Commissioner Mark McClellan has said: "The situation remains 'buyer beware,' and that's not a good way to assure public health."

These concerns have been borne out by a recent instance of unapproved drugs entering the United States. On May 20, FDA officials warned that unapproved versions of an erectile-dysfunction drug were shipped to U.S. consumers from a foreign country. It also is useful to recall why in 1987 Congress passed the Prescription Drug Marketing Act, which regulates distribution of medicines in the United States. In 1984 over 1 million counterfeit birth control pills had been shipped from Panama to Miami and New York. In 1985, 1,800 bottles of a counterfeit antibiotic were shipped from Singapore to Miami and Boston.

No American wants to return to those days. The United States has the world's safest medicine supply. That's because the FDA safeguards the process from beginning to end, even making sure the product is stored and shipped safely. But the FDA can't ensure the safety of medicines from outside our borders.

Nor should any American who hopes for new and better medicines want to import a foreign government's price controls. In foreign countries, price controls have led to the marked decline of pharmaceutical companies' ability to discover new medicines. This deprives patients of the full benefits of prescription medicines, which make up just 10 cents of each health care dollar in the United States.

The right solution to better access is to pass prescription-drug coverage for seniors and disabled persons under Medicare. Pharmaceutical companies also offer free medicines to needy Americans through patient-assistance programs, which helped 5.5 million people last year with more than $1.5 billion worth of drugs.

to protect the business interests of drug companies, which are some of the biggest financial donors to the GOP.

In March, the FDA warned Rx Depot, Inc., based in Lowell, Ark., that it has violated federal drug-importation laws and lied to customers that it is selling FDA-approved medications. [57] The company could be subject to seizure or court injunction if it does not cease its drug-importation practices, the FDA warned.

Two major drugmakers — AstraZeneca and Glaxo SmithKline — have reduced the availability of their products in Canada to dissuade Americans from purchasing them abroad at the lower prices. An estimated 1 million Americans buy medications from Canada via the Internet, according to AARP and the Canadian International Pharmacy Association.

Rep. Bernard Sanders, I-Vt., opposes the crackdown and has offered legislation to permit the reimportation of FDA-approved drugs from other countries. The congressman lists some Quebec pharmacists and physicians on his Web site to assist seniors crossing the border from Vermont to Canada to buy medications. During the Clinton administration, legislation permitting the reimportation of drugs from overseas passed Congress but was never implemented because then-HHS Secretary Donna Shalala, and now Secretary Thompson would not certify that such drugs are safe.

Despite McClellan's initiatives, no one expects the culture of the FDA to change anytime soon, largely because the agency relies heavily on industry user fees for its funding. According to a 2002 GAO report, the FDA received about $170 million in user fees from the pharmaceutical industry in 2002 — about 51 percent of the $332 million it spent reviewing drugs. The report linked the user fees to the higher percentage of drugs being withdrawn due to safety reasons and to expedited drug reviews, reinforcing questions raised by critics of the user-fee program.

The FDA insists there's no conflict of interest. "FDA has not compromised its traditionally high standards for safety and effectiveness," the agency said in a written response to the GAO. [58] Instead, the agency says the fees allow it to "bring access to new drugs fast or faster than anywhere in the world" while maintaining a thorough review process. "Along with supporting increased staff, drug-user fees help the FDA upgrade resources in information technology. [59]

The FDA insists it is not rushing drug approvals and emphasizes that only one in five drugs involved in clinical testing receives FDA approval. Agency officials cite Singulair, an asthma medication made by Merck, as an example of a blockbuster that took a long time to win approval. Merck began studying the drug in humans in 1992, but the FDA did not approve it until 1998. [60]

Meanwhile, some in Congress are concerned that some prescription drugs are being sold in the United States without FDA approval. In a recent letter to HHS Secretary Thompson, Rep. Waxman cited a *Wall Street Journal* report that many drugs that have never been approved by the FDA are being sold in the United States, and the agency has only a handful of people working toward getting them removed.

Waxman cited the case of the hormone-replacement therapy Estratest, which has been on the market since 1964 without FDA approval. "FDA explicitly rejected an application for approval of the drug in 1979 and has failed to act on an application that was resubmitted in 1981," the congressman wrote. Yet, Solvay, the drug's manufacturer, has repeatedly stated or implied that the medication had been approved, and apparently many health officials and even doctors that prescribe the drug "are unaware that the drug has never been approved," he wrote. [61]

An FDA official, speaking on condition on anonymity, says drugs on the market without FDA approval have been "grandfathered in," because the law governing permissible medications has changed. But recently, the FDA reopened its review of Estratest, out of concern that it might not be effective. The official conceded that the protracted review of Estratest, spanning several decades, fuels the perception that the agency is slow and mismanaged.

"It's enormously resource-intensive to take regulatory action to take a drug off the market. It's enormously complex to go to court one-by-one," he says. "We've prioritized the unapproved universe of drugs, and we've gone after drugs with safety concerns." [62]

Legislative Action

Drug prices will no doubt come under scrutiny as debate heats up in Congress over adding a prescription-drug benefit to the Medicare program, which provides health benefits to 40 million elderly and disabled Americans. In March, President Bush proposed a new Medicare drug benefit costing $400 billion over 10 years. Seniors switching from traditional Medicare to private health plans in the Medicare+Choice program would receive significant prescription-drug coverage.

Drug companies support Bush's approach because they'd have more bargaining power over prices if they can negotiate with private health plans instead of the entire Medicare program.

But critics say that seniors electing this option would have fewer choices of doctors because most of the participating plans are HMOs. And in some rural areas, Medicare+Choice is not available. Moreover, seniors remaining under traditional Medicare would see only 10 to 25 percent discounts on prescriptions, and would only receive substantial drug coverage after spending thousands of dollars out-of-pocket on health costs, Pollack of Families USA says.

Today, seven out of eight seniors are in Medicare, and the rest are in private health plans, he points out. "The Bush administration is trying to push people into these private plans and out of traditional Medicare.

"The industry is most worried that the Medicare program would have enormous bargaining clout — bargaining on behalf of 40 million beneficiaries — forcing it to moderate its pricing practices," Pollack continues. The issue is critical to drugmakers, he says, because seniors account for 42 percent of spending on prescription drugs.

Critics are also eyeing how much the benefit will cost beneficiaries, who will have to shell out money for co-payments, premiums and deductibles.

Bush's proposal was not particularly well received by Democrats, industry watchdogs or even some Republicans. Senate Majority Leader Bill Frist of Tennessee, a medical doctor, is expected to play a key role in crafting the legislation this session. Other key Senate players include Health Committee Chairman Judd Gregg, N.H., and Finance Committee Chairman Charles E. Grassley, Iowa — both Republicans — and Daschle. Grassley expects to have a draft Medicare bill ready by mid-June, and Sen. Frist plans to move it to the floor in the second half of June.[63]

OUTLOOK

Rise of Generics

Time may be on the side of generic-drug companies. By offering cheaper medications and driving down the prices of existing ones, generics are winning friends among lawmakers and major employers. Copycat drugs have grown from 19 percent of the marketplace in 1984 to at least 47 percent today — and some say it's as high as 51 percent.

On average, generics cost from one-third to two-thirds less than brand-name equivalents. "Over the next decade, a number of the most well-known brand-name pharmaceuticals will lose patent protection, theoretically allowing the introduction of more affordable generic versions of these blockbuster drugs," Kathleen D. Jaeger, president and CEO of the Generic Pharmaceutical Association told the House Energy and Commerce Subcommittee on Health last fall. "Within the next three years, 27 brand-name pharmaceuticals with annual sales of more than $37 billion should go off patent."

Generic companies also are becoming savvier about getting their products to market. An Indian drug company, Reddy's Laboratories, Ltd., entered the U.S. market with a so-called "branded generic" of Pfizer's blood-pressure drug Norvasc before Norvasc's patent had expired by successfully arguing in court that its medication didn't infringe on Pfizer's patent because it is made with different ingredients.[64]

But generics still face obstacles. The industry's growth is contingent on changing the 1984 Hatch-Waxman Act, which brand-name companies often use to block generics from competing. Sens. Charles E. Schumer, D-N.Y., and John McCain, R-Ariz., are championing legislation to close loopholes in the law, which could save Americans between $8 billion and $10 billion a year, according to the Congressional Budget Office.[65]

Last year, the McCain-Schumer bill — supported by consumer groups, insurers and major corporations seeking to save money on drug coverage offered by their company health plans — easily passed the then-Democrat-controlled Senate, 78-21. But it is now stalled in the GOP-controlled Congress.

Generic drugmakers support compromise language in McCain-Schumer that eliminates automatic delays on the entry of generic drugs into the marketplace, which occur when brand-name companies exploit a loophole in the Hatch-Waxman act by filing last-minute patents. Under the compromise, brand-name companies could seek remedies through the courts. The Bush administration would permit one automatic 30-month stay per drug but wants to ban successive stays. Pharmaceutical companies want no changes.

"We have the right to say, 'You've challenged the patent, we're going to defend the patent,' " PhRMA's Trewhitt says. He views the automatic stays as a balance against other sections of the law that favor generic companies. "They've done quite well with the incentives of the federal law," he says.

Jaeger noted in her testimony that the average number of patents granted for each blockbuster grew from two in 1984 to 10 in 2002. Meanwhile, the average price in 2001 of a prescription filled with a generic drug was $16.85, she said, but $72 for a brand-name drug.

The Generic Pharmaceutical Association maintains that just a 1 percent increase in the use of generics would save taxpayers $1.3 billion a year.

"The more competition that occurs among generics and brand-name drugs, the greater the likelihood that we'll see a moderation of drug pricing," says Pollack of Families USA.

At the same time, Pollack calls for greater transparency in brand-name drug pricing, noting that prices can vary significantly from one health provider, hospital or pharmacy to another. "It's a shell game today, and nobody knows what the next person is paying," he says.

NOTES

1. For background, see Sarah Glazer, "Treating Anxiety," *The CQ Researcher*, Feb. 8, 2002, pp. 97-120.
2. See "Generic Drug Entry: Prior to Patent Expiration," Federal Trade Commission, July 2002, p. i.
3. See Michael E. Gluck, "Federal Policies Affecting the Cost and Availability of New Pharmaceuticals," Kaiser Family Foundation, July 2002, p. 8.
4. See "Fortune 500: How the Industries Stack Up," *Fortune*, April 14, 2003, p. F-24.
5. See "Prescription Drug Trends" Fact Sheet 3057-02, Kaiser Family Foundation, March 2003.
6. "Peter Jennings Reporting — Bitter Medicine: Pills, Profit and the Public Health," ABC News, May 29, 2002.
7. For background see Richard L. Worsnop, "Reforming the FDA," *The CQ Researcher*, June 6, 1997, pp. 481-503.
8. See "Food and Drug Administration: Effect of User Fees on Drug Approval Times, Withdrawals, and Other Agency Activities," General Accounting Office, September 2002, p. 8.
9. See "Prescription Drug Trends: A Chartbook Update," Kaiser Family Foundation, November 2001, pp. 7-8.
10. See Arnold S. Relman and Marcia Angell, "America's Other Drug Problem," *The New Republic*, Dec. 16, 2002, p. 32.
11. See "No Recess From High Prescription Drug Costs Campaign," on AARP's Web site, www.aarp.org/rx.
12. See House Committee on Government Reform, Minority Staff, "Fact Sheet: Response to Drug Industry Claims on Prescription Drug Price Differences Between the United States and Other Countries," July 2002.
13. See Doug Bandow, "Policy Analysis: Demonizing Drugmakers — The Political Assault on the Pharmaceutical Industry," Cato Institute, May 8, 2003, pp. 1, 5.
14. Relman and Angell, *ibid.*, p. 32.
15. For background, see "Bitter Pill: The Rising Prices of Prescription Drugs for Older Americans" Families USA, June 2002.
16. Introduction, "Pharmaceutical Industry Profile 2003," Pharmaceutical Research and Manufacturers of America.
17. Bandow, *op. cit.*, pp. 8-9.
18. See Relman and Angell, *op. cit.*, p. 29.
19. See Families USA, "Profiting from Pain: Where Prescription Drug Dollars Go," July 2002, pp. 4-5.
20. *Ibid.*
21. Bandow, *op. cit.*, p. 1. For background on AIDS, see Adriel Bettelheim, "AIDS Update," *The CQ Researcher*, Dec. 4, 1998, pp. 1049-1072.
22. See Bandow, *op. cit.*, p. 31.
23. See "Understanding the Effects of Direct-to-Consumer Prescription Drug Advertising," Kaiser Family Foundation, November 2001, p. 1.
24. See "Prescription Drugs: FDA Oversight of Direct-to-Consumer Advertising Has Limitations," GAO, October 2002.
25. *Ibid.*, p. 30.
26. GAO, *op. cit.*
27. For background see http://www.newswire1.net/releases/Rodale/DTC_02/index_print.htm
28. Bandow, *op. cit.*
29. *Op. cit.*

30. *Ibid.*

31. See Susan Okie, "AMA Criticized for Letting Drug Firms Pay for Ethics Campaign," *The Washington Post*, Sept. 8, 2001, p. A3.

32. See Relman and Angell, *op. cit.*, p. 13.

33. See Leslie Wayne and Melody Petersen, "A Muscular Lobby Tries to Shape Nation's Bioterror Plan," *The New York Times*, Nov. 4, 2001, p. C1.

34. Center for Responsive Politics, www.opensecrets. org.

35. Relman and Angell, *op. cit.*, p. 39.

36. David Willman, "How a New Policy Led to Seven Deadly Drugs," *Los Angeles Times*, Dec. 20, 2000, pp. A6-A7.

37. Food and Drug Administration, www.fda.gov.

38. For background, see Julie Rovner, "Prescription Drug Prices," *The CQ Researcher*, July 17, 1992, pp. 597-620.

39. See Thomas Burton, "Why Cheap Drugs That Appear To Halt Fatal Sepsis Go Unused," *The Wall Street Journal*, May 17, 2002, p. A1.

40. See *2001 CQ Almanac*, "Patent Exclusivity Plan Extended," pp. 12-10 to 12-11.

41. See Brooke A. Masters, "Drug Company Unit May Face Indictment," *The Washington Post*, May 30, 2003, p. E1.

42. Melody Peterson, "Doctor Explains Why He Blew the Whistle," *The New York Times*, March 12, 2003, p. C1.

43. Quoted in press release posted at www.prescription accesslitigation.org, Feb. 4, 2003.

44. Quoted in Bob Edwards and Wade Goodwyn, National Public Radio, "Morning Edition," April 28, 2003.

45. *Ibid.*

46. *Ibid.*

47. See "Food and Drug Administration: Effect of User Fees on Drug Approval Times, Withdrawals, and Other Agency Activities," GAO-02-958, Sept. 17, 2002, p. 4.

48. For background see Adriel Bettelheim, "Drugmakers Under Siege," *The CQ Researcher*, Sept. 3, 1999, pp. 753-776.

49. See Denise Gellene, "Panel Unclear on Drug-Cancer Link," *Los Angeles Times*, March 5, 2003, Business Section, p. 3.

50. See Willman, *op. cit.*, p. A6.

51. See Alex Branson, "Trial Lawyers Are Now Focusing on Lawsuits Against Drugmakers," *The New York Times*, May 18, 2003, p. A1.

52. Bandow, *op. cit.*, pp. 33-34.

53. See Alex Berenson, "Trial Lawyers Are Now Focusing on Lawsuits Against Drugmakers," *The New York Times*, May 18, 2003, p. A1.

54. *Ibid.*

55. See Jim Hopkins, "Bayer Scores Crucial Victory in $560M Baycol Lawsuit," *USA Today*, March 19, 2003, p. 1B.

56. See "FDA Launches Initiative to Improve the Development and Availability of Innovative Medical Products," FDA news release, Jan. 31, 2003.

57. See Laura Neergaard, "FDA Begins Crackdown on Cheaper Drugs from Canada," The Associated Press, March 21, 2003.

58. See FDA, *op. cit.*, p. 8.

59. See Michelle Meadows, "The FDA's Drug Review Process: Ensuring Drugs are Safe and Effective," *FDA Consumer Magazine*, July-August, 2002.

60. *Ibid.*

61. See Chris Adams, "Unapproved Drugs Linger on the Market," *The Wall Street Journal*, March 20, 2003, p. A4.

62. See Richard L. Worsnop, "Reforming the FDA," *The CQ Researcher*, June 6, 1997, pp. 481-504.

63. See Steven Patrick and John Cochran, "GOP Leaders Set Medicare, Appropriations as Top Priorities for June," *CQ Today*, May 30, 2003.

64. See Gardiner Harris and Joanna Slater, "Bitter Pill: 'Branded Generics' Eat Into Drugmakers' Profits," *The Wall Street Journal*, April 17, 2003, p. A1.

65. See "Makers of Generic Drugs Find Potent Formula: Friends on Hill," *The Wall Street Journal*, July 29, 2002, p. A1.

BIBLIOGRAPHY

Books

Cohen, Jay S., *Overdose — The Case Against the Drug Companies: Prescription Drugs, Side Effects and Your Health*, Penguin USA, 2001.
A professor of medicine suggests warning labels on medications are incomplete and describes how drugmakers offer exotic weekend trips to entice doctors to prescribe their products.

Greider, Katharine, *The Big Fix: How the Pharmaceutical Industry Rips Off American Consumers,* PublicAffairs, 2003.
Journalist Greider writes that instead of offering innovation, drug companies seek to extend their product lines by peddling "me-too" drugs and fending off competitors.

Articles and Television News Reports

"Peter Jennings Reporting — Bitter Medicine: Pills, Profit and the Public Health," ABC News Special, May 5, 2002.
Jennings explores why drugs are so expensive and how the industry quietly maneuvers to block competition.

McGinley, Laurie, and Chris Adams, "Makers of Generic Drugs Find Potent Formula: Friends on Hill," *The Wall Street Journal,* July 29, 2002, p. 1.
Generic-drug companies are making advances in their lobbying efforts against the better-financed brand-name drug companies.

Relman, Arnold S., and Marcia Angell, "America's Other Drug Problem," *The New Republic,* Dec. 16, 2002, pp. 27-41.
Drug companies use cutthroat tactics to hike prices, block competitors and sell over-hyped drugs. The authors are both former editors of *The New England Journal of Medicine.* Relman taught at Harvard Medical School, where Angell lectures in social medicine.

Stephens, Joe, "The Body Hunters: As Drug Testing Spreads, Profits and Lives Hang in the Balance," *The Washington Post,* Dec. 17, 2000, p. A1.
The first of six articles on drug testing by pharmaceutical companies in developing countries explores allegations that people are coerced into participating in tests and given unsafe medications.

Willman, David, "How a New Policy Led to Seven Deadly Drugs," *Los Angeles Times,* Dec. 30, 2000, p. A1.
Drug reviews say scientists are discouraged from expressing safety concerns about drugs being tested.

Reports and Studies

Bandow, Douglas, "Policy Analysis — Demonizing Drugmakers: The Political Assault on the Pharmaceutical Industry," CATO Institute, May 8, 2003.
This comprehensive 55-page report presents the pharmaceutical industry viewpoint on a range of issues, including pricing, patent protection, Medicare reform and drug advertising. Author maintains that drug companies are treated as scapegoats by lawmakers and watchdogs.

"Bitter Pill: The Rising Prices of Prescription Drugs for Older Americans," Families USA, June 2002.
The advocacy group's survey of prices over a 10-year period documents dramatic increases in popular brand-name and generic medications.

"Generic Drug Entry Prior to Patent Extension: An FTC Study," Federal Trade Commission, July 2002.
A watershed government report documents anti-competitive actions by brand-name companies to block generic competitors and recommends moderate changes to the Hatch-Waxman act to address the alleged abuses.

Gluck, Michael E., "Federal Policies Affecting the Cost and Availability of Pharmaceuticals," Georgetown University Institute for Health Care Research and Policy, July 2002.
A report prepared for the Kaiser Family Foundation examines the factors that influence drug costs and pricing, such as research and development expenditures and tax credits.

"Pharmaceutical Industry Profile," Pharmaceutical Research and Manufacturers of America, 2003.
PhRMA's annual compendium provides the industry perspective on policy and regulatory issues facing drugmakers. Includes numerous charts and statistics.

"Prescription Drugs: FDA Oversight of Direct-to-Consumer Advertising Has Limitations," General Accounting Office, Oct. 2002.
The GAO review of pharmaceutical advertising to consumers finds lax regulation by the FDA and flagrant and repeat violations of FDA ad guidelines by drugmakers.

"A Primer: Generic Drugs, Patents and the Pharmaceutical Marketplace," National Institute for Health Care Management Research and Educational Foundation, summer 2002.
The foundation examines the complex laws governing pharmaceutical patents, with detailed discussion of the patent histories of certain drugs.

For More Information

AARP, 601 E St., N.W., Washington, DC 20049; (888) 687-2277; www.aarp.org. Advocacy group for persons over age 50.

Cato Institute, 1000 Massachusetts Ave., N.W., Washington, DC 20001-5403; (202) 842-0200; www.cato.org. Public policy organization that advocates limited government.

Center for Responsive Politics, 1101 14th St., N.W., Suite 1030, Washington DC 20005-5635; (202) 857-0044; www.opensecrets.org. Conducts research on campaign finance and related issues.

Common Cause, 1250 Connecticut Ave., N.W., Suite 600, Washington, DC 20036; (202) 628-3030; www.commoncause.org. Citizens' advocacy group.

Families USA, 1334 G St., N.W., Suite 300, Washington, DC 20005; (202) 628-3030; www.familiesusa.org.

Advocacy group focusing on health care and Social Security.

Generic Pharmaceutical Association, 2300 Clarendon Blvd., Suite 400, Arlington, VA 22201; (703) 647-2480; www.gphaonline.com.

Kaiser Family Foundation, 2400 Sand Hill Road, Menlo Park, CA 94025; (650) 854-9400; www.kff.org; Washington office, (202) 347-5270. An independent philanthropy focusing on health issues.

Pharmaceutical Research and Manufacturers of America (PhRMA), 1100 15th St., N.W., Suite 900, Washington, DC 20005; (202) 835-3400; www.phrma.org.

Public Citizen, Health Research Group, 1600 20th St., N.W., Washington, DC 20009; (202) 588-1000; www.citizen.org. Citizens' interest group.

5

Affirmative Action

Kenneth Jost

First-year engineering students at the University of Michigan–Ann Arbor gather during welcome week. A federal judge ruled in December 2000 that the school's race-based admissions system in 1995 was illegal but that a revised system adopted later was constitutional. The case is widely expected to reach the Supreme Court.

From *The CQ Researcher,*
September 19, 2003.
(Revised April 29, 2004.)

Jennifer Gratz wanted to go to the University of Michigan's flagship Ann Arbor campus as soon as she began thinking about college. "It's the best school in Michigan to go to," she explains. The white suburban teenager's dream turned to disappointment in April 1995, however, when the university told her that even though she was "well qualified," she had been rejected for one of the nearly 4,000 slots in the incoming freshman class.

Gratz was convinced something was wrong. "I knew that the University of Michigan was giving preference to minorities," she recalls. "If you give extra points for being of a particular race, then you're not giving applicants an equal opportunity."

Gratz went on to earn a degree from Michigan's less prestigious Dearborn campus and a job in San Diego. But she also became the lead plaintiff in a showdown legal battle in the long-simmering conflict over racial preferences in college admissions.

On the opposite side of Gratz's federal court lawsuit was Lee Bollinger, a staunch advocate of race-conscious admissions policies who served as president of the University of Michigan for five-and-a-half years before leaving in June 2002 to assume the presidency of Columbia University.

"Racial and ethnic diversity is one part of the core liberal educational goal," Bollinger says. "People have different educational experiences when they grow up as an African-American, Hispanic or white."

Gratz won a partial victory in December 2000, when a federal judge agreed that the university's admissions system in 1995 was illegal. The ruling came too late to help her, however, and Judge Patrick Duggan went on to rule that the revised system the university adopted in 1998 passed constitutional muster.

Some three months later, however, another federal judge ruled in a separate case that the admissions system used at the university's law school was illegal. Judge Bernard Friedman said the law school's admissions policies were "practically indistinguishable from a quota system."

The decision came in a suit filed by Barbara Grutter, who unsuccessfully sought admission to the law school in December 1996 while in her 40s after having raised a family and worked as a health care consultant. Grutter, who is white, blamed her rejection on minority preferences used by the law school.

The two cases — *Gratz v. Bollinger* and *Grutter v. Bollinger* — went on to be argued together before the federal appeals court in Cincinnati and then again before the U.S. Supreme Court. Then, in a dramatic day at the high court, the justices issued companion rulings on June 23, 2003, that upheld the law school's policies, but struck down the college's system.

The law school system satisfied constitutional standards, Justice Sandra Day O'Connor wrote in the 5-4 decision, because it was narrowly tailored to achieve the goal of attaining a diverse student body. Writing for a different 6-3 majority, however, Chief Justice William H. Rehnquist said the college's admissions system was unconstitutional because it awarded minority candidates a fixed numerical bonus without individualized consideration of the applicants' backgrounds and records.[1]

The rulings were aimed at resolving legal uncertainty stemming from the long time span — 23 years — since the Supreme Court's only previous full-scale ruling on race-based admissions policies: the famous *Bakke* decision. In that fractured ruling, *University of California Regents v. Bakke*, the high court in 1978 ruled that fixed racial quotas were illegal but allowed the use of race as one factor in college admissions.[2]

After Bakke, race-based admissions policies became widespread in U.S. higher education — "well accepted and entrenched," according to Sheldon Steinbach, general counsel of the pro-affirmative action American Council on Education.

Roger Clegg, general counsel of the Center for Equal Opportunity, which opposes racial preferences, agrees with Steinbach but from a different perspective. "Evidence is overwhelming that racial and ethnic discrimination occurs frequently in public college and university admissions," Clegg says.[3]

Higher-education organizations and traditional civil rights groups say racial admissions policies are essential to ensure racial and ethnic diversity at the nation's elite universities — including the most selective state schools, such as Michigan's Ann

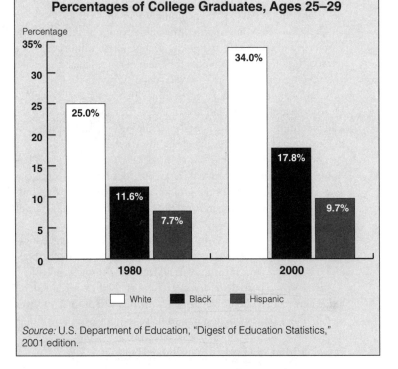

Despite Progress, Minorities Still Trail Whites

A larger percentage of young adult African-Americans and Hispanics have completed college today than 20 years ago. But college completion rates for African-Americans and Hispanics continue to be significantly lower than the rate for whites. Today, the national college completion rate — 30 percent — is more than triple the rate in 1950.

Percentages of College Graduates, Ages 25–29

Percentage

- 1980: White 25.0%, Black 11.6%, Hispanic 7.7%
- 2000: White 34.0%, Black 17.8%, Hispanic 9.7%

Legend: White, Black, Hispanic

Source: U.S. Department of Education, "Digest of Education Statistics," 2001 edition.

Arbor campus. "The overwhelming majority of students who apply to highly selective institutions are still white," says Theodore Shaw, director of the NAACP Legal Defense and Educational Fund, which represented minority students who intervened in the two Michigan cases. "If we are not conscious of selecting minority students, they're not going to be there."

Opponents, however, say racial preferences are wrong in terms of law and social policy. "It's immoral. It's illegal. It stigmatizes the beneficiary. It encourages hypocrisy. It lowers standards. It encourages the use of stereotypes," Clegg says. "There are all kinds of social costs, and we don't think the benefits outweigh those costs."

The race-based admissions policies now in use around the country have evolved gradually after the passage of federal civil rights legislation in the mid-1960s. By 1970, the phrase "affirmative action" had become common usage to describe efforts to increase the number of African-Americans (and, later, Hispanics) in U.S. workplaces and on college campuses.[4] Since then, the proportions of African-Americans and Hispanics on college campuses have increased, though they are still underrepresented in terms of their respective proportions in the U.S. population. (*See chart, p. 102.*)

Michigan's efforts ranged from uncontroversial minority-outreach programs to an admissions system that explicitly took an applicant's race or ethnicity into account in deciding whether to accept or reject the applicant. The system formerly used by the undergraduate College of Literature, Science and the Arts had separate grids for white and minority applicants. It was replaced by a system that used a numerical rating with a 20-point bonus (out of a total possible score of 150) for "underrepresented minorities" — African-Americans, Hispanics and Native Americans (but not Asian-Americans). The law school's system — devised in 1992 — was aimed at producing a minority enrollment of about 10 percent to 12 percent of the entering class.

Critics of racial preferences say they are not opposed to affirmative action. "Certainly there are some positive aspects to affirmative action," says Michael Rosman, attorney for the Center for Individual Rights in Washington, which represented the plaintiffs in the Michigan cases. Rossman says he approves of increased recruitment of minorities and reassessment by colleges of criteria for evaluating applicants. But, he adds, "To the extent that suggests that they have carte blanche to discriminate

between people on the basis of race, it's not a good thing."

Higher-education officials respond that they should have discretion to explicitly consider race — along with a host of other factors — to ensure a fully representative student body and provide the best learning environment for an increasingly multicultural nation and world. "Having a diverse student body contributes to the educational process and is necessary in the 21st-century global economy," Steinbach says.

As colleges and universities examine the impact of the Supreme Court's rulings in the University of Michigan cases, here are some of the major questions being debated:

Should colleges use race-based admissions policies to remedy discrimination against minorities?

The University of Michigan relies heavily on high school students' scores on standardized tests in evaluating applications — tests that have been widely criticized as biased against African-Americans and other minorities. It gives preferences to children of Michigan alumni — who are disproportionately white — as well as to applicants from "underrepresented" parts of the state, such as Michigan's predominantly white Upper Peninsula.

Even apart from the university's past record of racial segregation, those factors could be cited as evidence that Michigan's admissions policies were racially discriminatory because they had a "disparate impact" on minorities. And the Supreme Court, in *Bakke*, said that racial classifications were constitutional if they were used as a remedy for proven discrimination.

But Michigan did not defend its racial admissions policies on that basis. "Every public university has its share of decisions that we're now embarrassed by," Bollinger conceded. But the university defended its use of race — along with an array of other factors — only as a method of producing racial diversity, not as a way to remedy current or past discrimination.

Some civil rights advocates, however, insist that colleges and universities are still guilty of racially biased policies that warrant — even require — explicit racial preferences as corrective measures.

"Universities should use race-conscious admissions as a way of countering both past and ongoing ways in which the admission process continues to engage in practices that perpetuate racism or are unconsciously racist,"

Minority Enrollments Increased

African-Americans and Hispanics make up a larger percentage of the U.S. college population today than they did in 1976, but they are still underrepresented in comparison to their proportion of the total U.S. population. Hispanics comprise 12.5 percent of the population, African-Americans 12.3 percent.

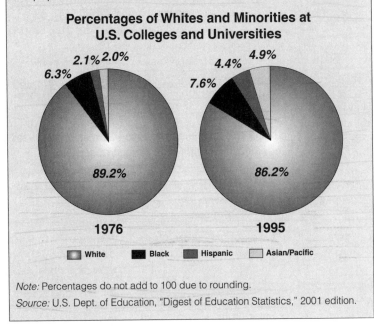

Percentages of Whites and Minorities at U.S. Colleges and Universities

1976: 89.2%, 6.3%, 2.1%, 2.0%
1995: 86.2%, 7.6%, 4.4%, 4.9%

White · Black · Hispanic · Asian/Pacific

Note: Percentages do not add to 100 due to rounding.
Source: U.S. Dept. of Education, "Digest of Education Statistics," 2001 edition.

says Charles Lawrence, a professor at Georgetown University Law Center in Washington.

Opponents of racial preferences, however, say colleges should be very wary about justifying such policies on the basis of past or current discrimination against minorities. "The Supreme Court has been pretty clear that you can't use the justification of past societal discrimination as a ground for a race-based admissions policy at an institution that did not itself discriminate," says Stephen Balch, president of the National Association of Scholars, a Princeton, N.J.-based group of academics opposed to racial preferences.

Balch defends alumni preferences, the most frequently mentioned example of an admissions policy that disadvantages minority applicants. "It's not at all unreasonable for colleges and universities to cultivate their alumni base," Balch says. In any event, he adds, "As student bodies change, the effect of that policy will change."

For his part, Rosman of the Center for Individual Rights says racial preferences are not justified even if colleges are wrong to grant alumni preferences or to rely so heavily on standardized test scores. "If you have criteria that discriminate and are not educationally justified, then the appropriate response is to get rid of those criteria, not to use 'two wrongs make a right,'" Rosman says.

Minority students intervened in both the undergraduate and law school suits to present evidence of discrimination by the university and to use that evidence to justify the racial admissions policies. In the undergraduate case, evidence showed that the university refused to desegregate fraternities and sororities until the 1960s, allowed white students to refuse to room with black students and did not hire its first black professor until 1967. The evidence also showed that black students reported continuing discrimination and racial hostility through the 1980s and into the '90s.

In his Dec. 13, 2000, ruling, Judge Duggan acknowledged the evidence but rejected it as a justification for the admissions policies. The racial segregation occurred too long ago to be a reason for current policies, Duggan said. He also rejected the minority students' argument that the racial impact of alumni preferences, standardized test scores and other admissions criteria justified preferences for minority applicants.

Judge Friedman rejected similar arguments in the final portion of his March 27, 2001, ruling in the law school case. "This is a social and political matter, which calls for social and political solutions," Friedman wrote. "The solution is not for the law school, or any other state institution, to prefer some applicants over others because of race."

Should colleges use race-based admissions policies to promote diversity in their student populations?

Michigan's high schools graduated some 100,000 students in 1999. Out of that number, only 327 African-

American students had a B-plus average and an SAT score above 1,000 — the kind of record needed to make them strong contenders for admission to the University of Michigan's Ann Arbor campus based on those factors alone.

University officials cited that stark statistic to underline the difficulty in admitting a racially diverse student body — and to justify their policy of giving minority applicants special consideration in the admissions process. Without the bonus for minority applicants, the number of African-American and Hispanic students "would drop dramatically" from the current level of about 13 percent of undergraduates to "somewhere around 5 percent," according to Elizabeth Barry, the university's associate vice president and deputy general counsel.

Opponents of racial preferences dismiss the warnings. "It's certainly not inevitable that the number of students from racial and ethnic minorities will decline" under a color-blind system, Rosman says. In any event, he says that diversity is "not a sufficiently powerful goal to discriminate and treat people differently on the basis of race."

The dispute between supporters and opponents of racial admissions policies turns in part on two somewhat rarefied issues. Supporters claim to have social-science evidence to show that racial and ethnic diversity produces quantifiable educational benefits for all students — evidence that opponents deride as dubious at best. *(See story, p. 112.)* The opposing camps also differ on the question of whether the *Bakke* decision allows colleges to use diversity as the kind of "compelling government interest" needed to satisfy the so-called strict-scrutiny standard of constitutional review. *(See story, p. 105.)*

Apart from those specialized disputes, opponents of racial preferences argue simply that they constitute a form of stereotyping and discrimination. "We don't believe that there is a black outlook or an Asian outlook or a white experience or a Hispanic experience," Clegg

---

Gratz v. Bollinger: Race and College Admissions

Jennifer Gratz, a white woman, sued the University of Michigan contending she was improperly denied admission because of race. The lawsuit is shaping up as a key battle in the long-simmering conflict over racial preferences in college admissions.

"I see benefits from different opinions, different thoughts on any number of subjects. But I don't think that's necessarily race coming through. I don't think like every other white person. . . . Your race doesn't mean that you're going to think this way or that way."

Jennifer Gratz, B.S., University of Michigan, Dearborn

"You get a better education and a better society in an environment where you are mixing with lots of different people — people from different parts of the country, people from different parts of the socioeconomic system, people from abroad, and people from different races and ethnicities."

Lee Bollinger, former president, University of Michigan

---

says. "Students are individuals, and they should be treated as individuals, not as fungible members of racial and ethnic groups."

Some critics — including a few African-Americans — also say racial preferences "stigmatize" the intended beneficiaries by creating the impression that they could not be successful without being given some advantage over whites. "There is no way that a young black at an Ivy League university is going to get credit for [doing well]," says Shelby Steele, a prominent black critic of racial preferences and a research fellow at the Hoover Institution at Stanford University. "There's no way that he's going to feel his achievements are his own."

Supporters of racial admission policies, however, say that race plays an independent and important role in American society that colleges are entitled to take into account. "It is reasonable for educational institutions to believe that race is not a proxy for something else," Bollinger says. "It is a defining experience in American life — and therefore an important one for this goal" of educational diversity.

White supporters of affirmative action generally deny or minimize any supposed stigmatization from race-conscious policies. Some blacks acknowledge some stigmatizing effects, but blame white racism rather than affirmative action. "The stigmatizing beliefs about people of color," Professor Lawrence writes, "have their origin not in affirmative action programs but in the cultural belief system of white supremacy."[5]

The two judges in the Michigan cases reached different conclusions on the diversity issue. In his ruling in the undergraduate case, Duggan agreed with the university's argument that a "racially and ethnically diverse student body produces significant education benefits, such that diversity, in the context of higher education, constitutes a compelling governmental interest under strict scrutiny."

Ruling in the law school case, Judge Friedman acknowledged that racial diversity may provide "educational and societal benefits," though he also called for drawing "a distinction . . . between viewpoint diversity and racial diversity." Based on his interpretation of *Bakke*, however, Friedman said these "important and laudable" benefits did not amount to a compelling interest sufficient to justify the law school's use of race in admissions decisions.

Should colleges adopt other policies to try to increase minority enrollment?

Texas and Florida have a different approach to ensuring a racial mix in their state university systems. Texas' "10 percent plan" — adopted in 1997 under then-Gov. George W. Bush — promises a spot in the state university to anyone who graduates in the top 10 percent of any high schools in the state. Florida's plan — adopted in 1999 under Gov. Jeb Bush, the president's brother — makes the same commitment to anyone in the top 20 percent.

The plans are drawing much attention and some favorable comment as an ostensibly race-neutral alternative to racial preferences. But major participants on both sides of the debate over racial admissions policies view the idea with skepticism.

"It's silly to suggest that all high schools are equal in terms of the quality of their student body," Clegg says. "And therefore it makes no sense to have an across-the-board rule that the top 10 percent of every high school is going to be admitted."

Both Clegg and Rosman also say that a 10 percent-type plan is dubious if it is adopted to circumvent a ban on explicit racial preferences. "Any neutral policy that is just a pretext for discrimination would have to survive strict scrutiny," Rosman says.

Supporters of race-based admissions are also unenthusiastic. "The only reason they work is because we have segregated high schools, segregated communities," Shaw says. "From a philosophical standpoint, I'd rather deal with race in a more honest and upfront way and make a more principled approach to these issues."

In the Michigan lawsuits, the university cited testimony from a prominent supporter of racial admissions policies in opposition to 10 percent-type plans. "Treating all applicants alike if they finished above a given high school class rank provides a spurious form of equality that is likely to damage the academic profile of the overall class of students admitted to selective institutions," said former Princeton University President William G. Bowen, later president of the Andrew W. Mellon Foundation in New York City.

Rosman looks more favorably on another alternative: giving preferences to applicants who come from disadvantaged socioeconomic backgrounds. "It's not a bad idea to take into account a person's ability to overcome obstacles," he says. "That's useful in assessing a person's qualifications."

In his testimony, however, Bowen also criticized that approach. Youngsters from poor black and Hispanic families are "much less likely" to excel in school than those from poor white families, Bowen said. On that basis, he predicted that a "class-based" rather than race-based admissions policy "would substantially reduce the minority enrollments at selective institutions."

For its part, the University of Michigan stressed that its system gave up to 20 points to an applicant based on socioeconomic disadvantage — the same number given to minority applicants. "We consider a number of factors in order to enroll a diverse student body," Barry said while the system was in use, "because race is not the only element that's important to diversity in education."

In their rulings, Duggan and Friedman both favorably noted a number of alternatives to race-based admissions policies. Friedman suggested the law school could have increased recruiting efforts or decreased the emphasis on

What Does *Bakke* Mean? Two Judges Disagree

The Supreme Court's 1978 decision to prohibit fixed racial quotas in colleges and universities but to allow the use of race as one factor in admissions was hailed by some people at the time as a Solomon-like compromise.

But the meaning of the high court's famous *Bakke* decision was sharply disputed. And the disagreement lay at the heart of conflicting rulings by two federal judges in Michigan on the legality of racial preferences used at the University of Michigan's flagship Ann Arbor campus.

In upholding the flexible race-based admissions system used by the undergraduate College of Literature, Science and the Arts in December 2000, Judge Patrick Duggan said *Bakke* means that colleges can evaluate white and minority applicants differently in order to enroll a racially and ethnically diverse student body.

But Judge Bernard Friedman rejected that widely held interpretation in his March 2001 decision striking down the law school's use of race in admissions. Friedman — like Duggan an appointee of President Ronald Reagan — said that racial and ethnic diversity did not qualify as a "compelling governmental interest" needed under the so-called strict scrutiny constitutional standard to justify a race-based government policy.

The differing interpretations stem from the Supreme Court's unusual 4-1-4 vote in the case, *University of California Regents v. Bakke*. Four of the justices found the quota system used by the UC-Davis Medical School — reserving 16 out of 100 seats for minorities — to be a violation of the federal civil rights law prohibiting racial discrimination in federally funded institutions. Four others — led by the liberal Justice William J. Brennan Jr. — voted to reject Alan Bakke's challenge to the system.

In the pivotal opinion, Justice Lewis F. Powell Jr. found the UC-Davis admissions system to be a violation of the constitutional requirement of equal protection but said race could be used as a "plus" factor in admissions decisions. The "attainment of a diverse student body," Powell wrote, "clearly is a constitutionally permissible goal for an institution of higher education."

Under Supreme Court case law, it takes a majority of the justices — five — to produce a "holding" that can serve as a precedent for future cases. In a fractured ruling, the court's holding is said to be the "narrowest" rationale endorsed by five justices. But Brennan's group did not explicitly address the question of diversity. Instead, they said that race-based admissions decisions were justified to remedy past discrimination — a proposition that Powell also endorsed.

Critics of racial preferences in recent years have argued that the Brennan group's silence on diversity means that they did not join Powell's reasoning. On that basis, these critics say, Powell's opinion cannot be viewed as a controlling precedent. They won an important victory when the federal appeals court in New Orleans adopted that reasoning in the so-called *Hopwood* case in 1996 striking down the University of Texas Law School's racial preferences.

In his ruling in the Michigan law school case, Friedman also agreed with this revisionist view of *Bakke*. "The diversity rationale articulated by Justice Powell is neither narrower nor broader than the remedial rationale articulated by the Brennan group," Friedman wrote. "They are completely different rationales, neither one of which is subsumed within the other."

But in the undergraduate case, Duggan followed the previous interpretation of *Bakke*. Brennan's "silence regarding the diversity interest in *Bakke* was not an implicit rejection of such an interest, but rather, an implicit approval of such an interest," Duggan wrote.

The two judges also differed on how to interpret later Supreme Court decisions. Duggan cited Brennan's 1990 majority opinion in a case upholding racial preferences in broadcasting — *Metro Broadcasting, Inc. v. Federal Communications Commission* — as supporting the use of diversity to justify racial policies. But Friedman said other recent rulings showed that the Supreme Court had become much more skeptical of racial policies than it had been in 1978. Among the decisions he cited was the 1995 ruling, *Adamant Constructors v. Pena* that overruled the *Metro Broadcasting* holding.

Reporters follow Alan Bakke on his first day at the University of California-Davis Medical School on Sept. 25, 1978. The Supreme Court ordered him admitted after ruling that the school violated his rights by maintaining a fixed quota for minority applicants.

AP Photo/Walt Zeboski

undergraduate grades and scores on the Law School Aptitude Test. He also said the school could have used a lottery for all qualified applicants or admitted some fixed number or percentage of top graduates from various colleges and universities. Friedman said the law school's "apparent failure to investigate alternative means for increasing minority enrollment" was one factor in rejecting the school's admissions policies.

For his part, Duggan noted the possibility of using race-neutral policies to increase minority enrollment when he rejected the minority students' critique of such policies as alumni preferences. "If the current selection criteria have a discriminatory impact on minority applicants," Duggan wrote, "it seems to this court that the narrowly tailored remedy would be to remove or redistribute such criteria to accommodate for socially and economically disadvantaged applicants of all races and ethnicities, not to add another suspect criteria [sic] to the list."

BACKGROUND

Unequal Opportunity

African-Americans and other racial and ethnic minority groups have been underrepresented on college campuses throughout U.S. history. The civil rights revolution has effectively dismantled most legal barriers to higher education for minorities. But the social and economic inequalities that persist between white Americans and racial and ethnic minority groups continue to make the goal of equal opportunity less than reality for many African-Americans and Hispanics.

The legal battles that ended mandatory racial segregation in the United States began with higher education nearly two decades before the Supreme Court's historic ruling in *Brown v. Board of Education*.[6] In the first of the rulings that ended the doctrine of "separate but equal," the court in 1938 ruled that Missouri violated a black law school applicant's equal protection rights by offering to pay his tuition to an out-of-state school rather than admit him to the state's all-white law school.

The court followed with a pair of rulings in 1950 that similarly found states guilty of violating black students' rights to equal higher education. Texas was ordered to admit a black student to the state's all-white law school rather than force him to attend an inferior all-black

school. And Oklahoma was found to have discriminated against a black student by admitting him to a previously all-white state university but denying him the opportunity to use all its facilities.

At the time of these decisions, whites had substantially greater educational opportunities than African-Americans. As of 1950, a majority of white Americans ages 25-29 — 56 percent — had completed high school, compared with only 24 percent of African-Americans. Eight percent of whites in that age group had completed college compared with fewer than 3 percent of blacks. Most of the African-American college graduates had attended all-black institutions: either private colleges established for blacks or racially segregated state universities.

The Supreme Court's 1954 decision in *Brown* to begin dismantling racial segregation in elementary and secondary education started to reduce the inequality in educational opportunities for whites and blacks, but changes were slow. It was not until 1970 that a majority of African-Americans ages 25-29 had attained high school degrees.

Changes at the nation's elite colleges and universities were even slower. In their book *The Shape of the River*, two former Ivy League presidents — Bowen and Derek Bok — say that as of 1960 "no selective college or university was making determined efforts to seek out and admit substantial numbers of African-American students." As of 1965, they report, African-Americans comprised only 4.8 percent of students on the nation's college campuses and fewer than 1 percent of students at select New England colleges.[7]

As part of the Civil Rights Act of 1964, Congress included provisions in Title IV to authorize the Justice Department to initiate racial-desegregation lawsuits against public schools and colleges and to require the U.S. Office of Education (now the Department of Education) to give technical assistance to school systems undergoing desegregation. A year later, President Lyndon B. Johnson delivered his famous commencement speech at historically black Howard University that laid the foundation for a more proactive approach to equalizing opportunities for African-Americans. "You do not take a person," Johnson said, "who, for years, has been hobbled by chains and liberate him, bring him up to the starting line of a race and then say, 'You are free to compete with all the others,' and still justly believe that you have been completely fair."[8]

Affirmative Action

Colleges began in the mid-1960s to make deliberate efforts to increase the number of minority students. Many universities instituted "affirmative action" programs that included targeted recruitment of minority applicants as well as explicit use of race as a factor in admissions policies. White students challenged the use of racial preferences, but the Supreme Court — in the *Bakke* decision in 1978 — gave colleges and universities a flashing green light to consider race as one factor in admissions policies aimed at ensuring a racially diverse student body.

The federal government encouraged universities to look to enrollment figures as the criterion for judging the success of their affirmative action policies. By requiring universities to report minority enrollment figures, the Nixon administration appeared to suggest that race-conscious admissions were "not only permissible but mandatory," according to Bowen and Bok. But universities were also motivated, they say, to remedy past racial discrimination, to educate minority leaders and to create diversity on campuses.

As early as 1966, Bowen and Bok report, Harvard Law School moved to increase the number of minority students by "admitting black applicants with test scores far below those of white classmates." As other law schools adopted the strategy, enrollment of African-Americans increased — from 1 percent of all law students in 1965 to 4.5 percent in 1975. Similar efforts produced a significant increase in black students in Ivy League colleges. The proportion of African-American students at Ivy League schools increased from 2.3 percent in 1967 to 6.7 percent in 1976, Bowen and Bok report.[9]

Critics, predominantly but not exclusively political conservatives, charged that the racial preferences amounted to "reverse discrimination" against white students and applicants. Some white students challenged the policies in court. The Supreme Court sought to resolve the issue in 1978 in a case brought by a California man, Alan Bakke, who had been denied admission to the University of California Medical School at Davis under a system that explicitly reserved 16 of 100 seats for minority applicants. The 4-1-4 decision fell short of a definitive resolution, though.

Justice Lewis F. Powell Jr. cast the decisive vote in the case. He joined four justices to reject Davis' fixed-quota approach and four others to allow use of race as one fac-

President Lyndon B. Johnson signs the Civil Rights Act on July 2, 1964. Race-based admissions policies now in use around the country evolved gradually from the landmark law.

tor in admissions decisions. In summarizing his opinion from the bench, Powell explained that it meant Bakke would be admitted to the medical school but that Davis was free to adopt a more "flexible program designed to achieve diversity" just like those "proved to be successful at many of our great universities."[10]

Civil rights advocates initially reacted with "consternation," according to Steinbach of the American Council on Education. Quickly, though, college officials and higher-education groups took up the invitation to devise programs that used race — in Powell's terms — as a "plus factor" without setting aside any seats specifically for minority applicants. The ruling, Steinbach says, "enabled institutions in a creative manner to legally provide for a diverse student body."

The Supreme Court avoided re-examining *Bakke* after 1978, but narrowed the scope of affirmative action in other areas. The court in 1986 ruled that government employers could not lay off senior white workers to make room for new minority hires, though it upheld affirmative action in hiring and promotions in two other decisions that year and another ruling in a sex-discrimination case a year later. As for government contracting, the court ruled in 1989 that state and local governments could not use racial preferences except to remedy past discrimination and extended that limitation to federal programs in 1995.[11]

All of the court's decisions were closely divided, but the conservative majority made clear their discomfort with race-specific policies. Indeed, as legal-affairs writer Lincoln Caplan notes, none of the five current conservatives — Chief Justice William H. Rehnquist and Associate Justices Sandra Day O'Connor, Antonin Scalia, Anthony M. Kennedy and Clarence Thomas — had ever voted to approve a race-based affirmative action program prior to the Michigan cases.[12]

Negative Reaction

A political and legal backlash against affirmative action emerged with full force in the 1990s — highlighted by moves in California to scrap race-conscious policies in the state's university system and a federal appeals court decision barring racial preferences in admissions in Texas and two neighboring states. But President Bill Clinton rebuffed calls to scrap federal affirmative action programs. And colleges continued to follow race-conscious admissions policies in the absence of a new Supreme Court pronouncement on the issue.

In the first of the moves against race-conscious admissions, the 5th U.S. Circuit Court of Appeals in New Orleans in March 1996 struck down the University of Texas Law School's system that used separate procedures for white and minority applicants with the goal of admitting a class with 5 percent African-American and 10 percent Mexican-American students.[13] The ruling in the *Hopwood* case unanimously rejected the university's attempt to justify the racial preferences on grounds of past discrimination. Two judges also rejected the university's diversity defense and directly contradicted the prevailing interpretation of *Bakke* that diversity amounted to a "compelling governmental interest" justifying race-based policies.[14]

The ruling specifically applied only to the three states in the 5th Circuit — Louisiana, Mississippi and Texas — but observers saw the decision as significant. "This is incredibly big," said John C. Jeffries Jr., a University of Virginia law professor and Justice Powell's biographer. "This could affect every public institution in America because all of them take racial diversity into account in admissions."[15]

Four months later, the University of California Board of Regents — policy-making body for the prestigious, 162,000-student state university system — narrowly voted to abolish racial and sexual preferences in admissions by fall 1997. The 14-10 vote approved a resolution submitted by a black businessman, Ward Connerly, and supported by the state's Republican governor, Pete Wilson. Connerly was also the driving force behind a voter initiative — Proposition 209 — to abolish racial preferences in state government employment and contracting as well as college and university admissions. Voters approved the measure, 54 percent to 46 percent, in November 1996.

In the face of opposition from UC President Richard Atkinson, the move to scrap racial preferences was delayed to admissions for the 1998-1999 academic year. In May 1998, the university released figures showing a modest overall decline in acceptances by non-Asian minorities to 15.2 percent for the coming year from 17.6 percent for the 1997-1998 school year. But the figures also showed a steep drop in the number of black and Hispanic students in the entering classes at the two most prestigious campuses — Berkeley and UCLA. At Berkeley, African-American and Hispanic acceptances fell to 10.5 percent from 21.9 percent for the previous year; at UCLA, the drop was to 14.1 percent from 21.8 percent.

The Supreme Court did nothing to counteract the legal shift away from racial preferences in education. It declined in 1995 to review a decision by the federal appeals court in Richmond, Va., that struck down a University of Maryland scholarship program reserved for African-American students. A year later, the justices refused to hear Texas' appeal of the *Hopwood* decision; and a year after that they also turned aside a challenge by labor and civil rights groups to Proposition 209. Instead, the high court concentrated on a series of rulings beginning in June 1993 that limited the use of race in congressional and legislative redistricting.[16] And in June 1995 the court issued a decision, *Adarand Constructors, Inc. v. Peña*, that limited the federal government's discretion to give minority-owned firms preferences in government contracting.[17]

With affirmative action under sharp attack, Bowen and Bok came out in 1998 with their book-length study of graduates of selective colleges that they said refuted many of the criticisms of race-based admissions. Using a

CHRONOLOGY

Before 1960 *Limited opportunities for minorities in private and public colleges and universities.*

1938 Supreme Court says Missouri violated Constitution by operating all-white law school but no school for blacks.

1950 Supreme Court says Texas violated Constitution by operating "inferior" law school for blacks.

1954 Supreme Court rules racial segregation in public elementary and secondary schools unconstitutional; ruling is extended to dismantle racially segregated colleges.

1960s–1980s *Civil rights era: higher education desegregated; affirmative action widely adopted, approved by Supreme Court if racial quotas not used.*

1964 Civil Rights Act bars discrimination by federally funded colleges.

1978 Supreme Court rules in *Bakke* that colleges and universities can consider race as one factor in admissions policies.

1980s Supreme Court leaves *Bakke* unchanged.

1990s *Opposition to race-based admissions policies grows.*

1995 President Clinton defends affirmative action; University of California ends use of race and sex in admissions.

1996 University of Texas law school's use of racial preferences in admissions ruled unconstitutional in *Hopwood* case; California voters approve Proposition 209 banning state-sponsored affirmative action in employment, contracting and admissions.

1997 Texas Gov. George W. Bush signs law guaranteeing admission to University of Texas to top 10 percent of graduates in state high schools.

1998 Washington state voters approve initiative barring racial preferences in state colleges and universities.

1999 Gov. Jeb Bush of Florida issues executive order banning racial preferences but granting admission to state colleges to top 20 percent of graduates in all state high schools.

2000s *Legal challenges to affirmative action continue.*

Dec. 4, 2000 University of Washington Law School's former admissions system — discontinued after Proposition 200 — is upheld by federal court.

Dec. 13, 2000 University of Michigan undergraduate admissions policies upheld by federal judge, though former system ruled illegal.

March 26, 2001 Supreme Court agrees to hear new appeal in *Adarand* case.

March 27, 2001 University of Michigan Law School admissions policies ruled unconstitutional by federal judge.

June 2001 Supreme Court declines to review conflicting rulings in *University of Washington*, *University of Texas* cases.

Aug. 27, 2001 Federal appeals court in Atlanta rules University of Georgia admissions system giving bonuses to all non-white applicants is unconstitutional.

May 2002 University of Michigan Law School admissions system upheld by federal appeals court in Cincinnati by 5-4 vote; court issues no ruling in challenge to admissions policies at Michigan's undergraduate college.

December 2002 Supreme Court agrees to take up challenges to admissions policies for undergraduates and law students at University of Michigan.

June 23, 2003 Supreme Court upholds, 5-4, use of race in admissions at University of Michigan Law School, but rules racial preferences in undergraduate admissions unconstitutional by 6-3 vote; in pivotal opinion, Justice Sandra Day O'Connor calls for racial preferences to end in 25 years.

pq ?

Minority Preferences: Will They Disappear in 25 Years?

We take the Law School at its word that it would "like nothing better than to find a race-neutral admissions formula" and will terminate its race-conscious admissions program as soon as practicable. . . . It has been 25 years since Justice Powell first approved the use of race to further an interest in student body diversity in the context of public higher education. Since that time, the number of minority applicants with high grades and test scores has indeed increased. . . . We expect that 25 years from now, the use of racial preferences will no longer be necessary to further the interest approved today."

Justice Sandra Day O'Connor, majority opinion,
Grutter v. Bollinger

"I agree with the Court's holding that racial discrimination in higher education admissions will be illegal in 25 years. . . For the immediate future, however, the majority has placed its *imprimatur* on a practice that can only weaken the principle of equality embodied in the Declaration of Independence and the Equal Protection Clause. . . . It has been nearly 140 years since . . . the Nation adopted the Fourteenth Amendment. Now we must wait another 25 years to see this principle of equality vindicated.

Justice Clarence Thomas, separate opinion,
Grutter v. Bollinger

"However strong the public's desire for improved education systems may be, . . . it remains the current reality that many minority students encounter markedly inadequate and unequal educational opportunities. Despite these inequalities, some minority students are able to meet the high threshold requirements set for admission to the country's finest undergraduate and graduate educational institutions. As lower school education in minority communities improves, an increase in the number of such students may be anticipated. From today's vantage point, one may hope, but not firmly forecast, that over the next generation's span, progress toward nondiscrimination and genuinely equal opportunity will make it safe to sunset affirmative action."

Justice Ruth Bader Ginsburg, separate opinion,
Grutter v. Bollinger

database of some 80,000 students who entered 28 elite colleges and universities in 1951, 1976 and 1989, the two former Ivy League presidents confirmed the increase in minority enrollment at the schools and the impact of racial preferences: More than half the black students admitted in 1976 and 1989 would not have been admitted under race-neutral policies, they said. But they said dropout rates among black students were low, satisfaction with their college experiences high and post-graduation accomplishments comparable with — or better than — white graduates.[18]

The Bowen-Bok book buttressed college and university officials in resisting calls to scrap racial preferences. While voters in Washington state moved to eliminate race-based admissions with an anti-affirmative action initiative in 1998, no other state university system followed the UC lead in voluntarily abolishing the use of race in weighing applications.

In Texas, then-Gov. George W. Bush sought to bolster minority enrollment in the UT system after *Hopwood* by proposing the 10 percent plan — guaranteeing admission to any graduating senior in the top 10 percent of his class. (Florida Gov. Jeb Bush followed suit with his 20 percent plan two years later.) Many schools — both public and private — re-examined their admissions policies after *Hopwood*. But, according to Steinbach, most of them "found that what they had was satisfactory."

Legal Battles

Critics of race-based admissions kept up their pressure on the issue by waging expensive, protracted legal battles in four states: Georgia, Michigan, Texas and Washington. The cases produced conflicting decisions. The conflict was starkest in the two University of Michigan cases, where two judges, both appointed in the 1980s by President Ronald Reagan, reached different results in evaluating the use of race at the undergraduate college and at the law school.

The controversy in Michigan began in a sense with the discontent of a longtime Ann Arbor faculty member, Carl Cohen.[19] A professor of philosophy and a "proud" member of the American Civil Liberties Union (ACLU), Cohen had been troubled by racial preferences since the 1970s. In 1995 he read a journal article that described admissions rates for black college applicants as higher nationally than those for white applicants. The article prompted Cohen to begin poking around to learn about Michigan's system.[20]

As Cohen tells the story, administrators stonewalled him until he used the state's freedom of information law to obtain the pertinent documents. He found that the admissions offices used a grid system that charted applicants based on high school grade point average on a horizontal axis and standardized test scores on a vertical axis — and that there were separate grids or different "action codes" (reject or admit) for white applicants and for minority applicants. "The racially discriminatory policies of the university are blatant," Cohen says today. "They are written in black and white by the university. It's just incredible."

Cohen wrote up his findings in a report that he presented later in the year at a meeting of the state chapter of the American Association of University Professors. The report also found its way to a Republican state legislator, Rep. Deborah Whyman, who conducted a hearing on the issue and later held a news conference to solicit unsuccessful applicants to challenge the university's admission system. They forwarded about 100 of the replies to the Center for Individual Rights, a conservative public-interest law firm already active in challenging racial preferences.

Gratz and a second unsuccessful white applicant — Patrick Hamacher — were chosen to be the named plaintiffs in a class-action suit filed in federal court in Detroit in October 1997. The center filed a second suit on behalf of Grutter against the law school's admission system in December 1997. Grutter thought she deserved admission based on her 3.8 undergraduate grade-point average 18 years earlier and a respectable score on the law school admission test (161, or 86th percentile nationally). After the rejection, she did not enroll elsewhere.

The cases proved to be long and expensive. By fall 2000, the university said it had spent $4.3 million

defending the two suits, not counting personnel costs; the center had spent $400,000, including salaries, and also received the equivalent of $1 million in pro bono legal services from a Minneapolis firm helping to litigate the suits. Among the key pieces of evidence was a long report by an Ann Arbor faculty member — psychology professor Patricia Gurin — concluding that diversity in enrollment has "far-reaching and significant benefits for all students, non-minorities and minorities alike." The center countered with a lengthy study issued under the auspices of the National Association of Scholars that analyzed the same data and found "no connection . . . between campus racial diversity and the supposed educational benefits."

In the meantime, the university revised its undergraduate admissions system, beginning with the entering class of 1999. The race-based grids and codes were replaced by a numerical system that assigned points to each applicant based on any of a number of characteristics. An applicant from an "underrepresented minority group" — African-Americans, Hispanics and Native Americans — was given 20 points. (One hundred points was typically required for admission, according to Cohen.) The same number was given to an applicant from a disadvantaged socioeconomic status, to a white student from a predominantly minority high school or to a scholarship athlete, according to university counsel Barry. The most important single factor, she added, was an applicant's high school grades.

Judge Duggan's Dec. 13, 2000, ruling in the undergraduate case sustained the plaintiffs' complaint against the system used when Gratz and Hamacher had been rejected. Duggan said that the "racially different grids and codes based solely upon an applicant's race" amounted to an "impermissible use of race." But Duggan said the revised system was on the right side of what he called "the thin line that divides the permissible and the impermissible."

Three months later, however, Judge Friedman on March 27, 2001, struck down the law school's admission system. Evidence showed that the school had used a "special admissions" program since 1992 aimed at a minority enrollment of 10 percent to 12 percent.

Friedman relied on a statistical analysis that showed an African-American applicant's relative odds of acceptance were up to 400 times as great as a white applicant's. Friedman rejected the use of diversity to justify the racial

Evidence of Diversity Benefits Disputed

The University of Michigan defended its race-based admissions policies not only with law but also with evidence of the educational benefits of having a racially mixed student body. But opponents of racial preferences dismissed the evidence as distorted and biased.

The largest of the studies introduced as evidence in the two federal court lawsuits over the university's undergraduate and law school admissions policies runs 850 pages. Written by Patricia Gurin, chairman of the Psychology Department, it contains detailed statistics derived from a national student database and surveys of Michigan students. Gurin contends that students "learn more and think in deeper, more complex ways in a diverse educational environment.[1]

In addition, Gurin says students "are more motivated and better able to participate in an increasingly heterogeneous and complex democracy." And students who had "diversity experiences" during college — such as taking courses in Afro-American studies — also had "the most cross-racial interactions" five years after leaving college.

The National Association of Scholars, which opposes racial preferences, released two lengthy critiques of Gurin's study after the trials of the two suits. The studies were included in a friend-of-the-court brief filed in the appeals of the rulings.[2]

In the major critique, Thomas E. Wood and Malcolm J. Sherman contend that the national student database actually shows "no relationship" between the proportion of minorities on campus and educational benefits. They also say that "diversity activities" had only a "trivial impact" on educational outcomes.

The university also included "expert reports" from William G. Bowen and Derek Bok, the two former Ivy League university presidents who co-authored the pro-affirmative action book *The Shape of the River*. Bowen and Bok repeat their conclusions from the 1998 book that black students admitted to the "highly selective" colleges and universities studied did "exceedingly well" after college in terms of graduate degrees, income and civic life.[3] About half of the blacks admitted to the schools would not have been admitted under race-neutral policies, Bowen and Bok say.

In their reports for the Michigan suits, Bowen and Bok briefly acknowledge that black students at the schools had lower grades and lower graduation rates than whites. In an early critique of the book, two well-known critics of racial preferences — Abigail and Stephan Thernstrom — call Bowen and Bok to task for glossing over the evidence of poor performance by black students. They note that the dropout rate for black students — about 20 percent — was three times higher than for whites and that black students' grades overall were at the 23rd percentile — that is, in the bottom quarter.[4]

The studies are the tip of a large iceberg of academic literature that has sought to examine the effects of diversity in colleges and universities. In one of the most recent of the studies to be published, a team of authors from Pennsylvania State University concluded that the evidence is "almost uniformly consistent" that students in a racially or ethnically diverse community or engaged in "diversity-related" activities "reap a wide array of positive educational benefits."[5] In their own study of students at seven engineering schools, the scholars found what they called "a small, if statistically significant, link between the level of racial/ethnic diversity in a classroom and students' reports of increases in their problem-solving and group skills."

University of Michigan student Agnes Aleobua speaks out against a court ruling in March 2001 that the law school's race-based admission policy is illegal.

AP Photo/Paul Sancya

---

[1] Gurin's report can be found on the university's Web site: www.umich.edu.

[2] Thomas E. Wood and Malcolm J. Sherman, "Is Campus Racial Diversity Correlated With Educational Benefits?", National Association of Scholars, April 4, 2001 (www.nas.org). Wood is executive director of the California Association of Scholars; Sherman is an associate professor of mathematics and statistics at the State University of New York in Albany.

[3] William G. Bowen and Derek Bok, *The Shape of the River: Long-Term Consequences of Considering Race in College and University Admissions,* 1998. Bowen is a former president of Princeton University, Bok a former president of Harvard University.

[4] Stephan Thernstrom and Abigail Thernstrom, "Reflections on The Shape of the River," *UCLA Law Review,* Vol. 45, No. 5 (June 1999), pp. 1583-1631. Stephan Thernstrom is a history professor at Harvard; his wife is a senior fellow at the Manhattan Institute and a member of the Massachusetts Board of Education.

[5] Patrick T. Terenzini et al., "Racial and Ethnic Diversity in the Classroom: Does It Promote Student Learning?", Journal of Higher Education (September/October 2001), pp. 509–531. Terenzini is a professor and senior scientist with the Center for the Study of Higher Education at Pennsylvania State University.

preferences, but in any event said the law school's system was not "narrowly tailored" because there was no time limit and there had been no consideration of alternative means of increasing minority enrollment.

The two Michigan cases took on added significance in June 2001 when the Supreme Court declined for a second time to hear Texas' appeal in the *Hopwood* case or to hear the plaintiffs' appeal of a ruling by the 9th U.S. Circuit Court of Appeals upholding a discontinued system of racial preferences at the University of Washington Law School. Then on Aug. 27, 2001, the 11th U.S. Circuit Court of Appeals issued a ruling striking down the University of Georgia's admissions system.[21]

The Sixth U.S. Circuit Court of Appeals decided to hear the two Michigan cases together in October 2001 before the full court instead of three-judge panels. Seven months later, the appeals court on May 14, 2002, issued a sharply divided, 5-4 decision upholding the law school admissions system. The majority said the school considered race along with other factors in an effort to admit enough minority students so that all students could enjoy "the educational benefits of an academically diverse student body." The dissenting judges maintained that the procedures were indistinguishable from a numerical quota.

The appeals court did not rule on the undergraduate case at the same time and issued no explanation for the omission. The Center for Individual Rights asked the Supreme Court to review the law school ruling and later — with the college case still undecided — asked the justices to bypass the appeals court and take jurisdiction of Gratz's case too. The university opposed reviewing the law school case, but agreed that if review was granted the two cases should be heard together.

The Court granted certiorari in both cases on December 2, 2002. By the time the cases came to be argued, they had attracted a record number of friend-of-the-court briefs: eighty-one in all, more than two-thirds

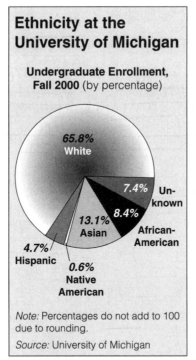

Ethnicity at the University of Michigan

Undergraduate Enrollment, Fall 2000 (by percentage)

- 65.8% White
- 7.4% Unknown
- 8.4% African-American
- 13.1% Asian
- 4.7% Hispanic
- 0.6% Native American

Note: Percentages do not add to 100 due to rounding.

Source: University of Michigan

of them supporting the university. Court watchers noted in particular briefs filed by a group of retired military officers stressing the importance of affirmative action in producing a racially diverse officer corps and a separate brief by the Michigan-based General Motors Corp. defending affirmative action as a means of a diverse workforce at supervisory and managerial levels. On the opposite side, the Bush administration urged the Court to hold procedures at both schools unconstitutional but did not call for prohibiting any consideration of race in admissions.

CURRENT SITUATION

Split Decisions?

The Supreme Court's rulings in the Michigan cases — issued together on June 23, 2003 — appeared at quick glance to be a compromise of sorts: upholding the law school policies while ruling the college's admissions system unconstitutional. On closer examination, though, affirmative action supporters stressed that the law school decision squarely held — and the undergraduate case acknowledged — that universities could use individualized race-conscious admissions procedures to promote the compelling government interest in diversity.

Writing for the majority in *Grutter*, Justice O'Connor said the law school's admissions policies satisfied the constitutional requirement that any government use of race be "narrowly tailored" to achieve a compelling interest — in this case, attaining a diverse student body. The law school, she wrote, "engages in a highly individualized, holistic review of each applicant's file, giving serious consideration to all the ways an applicant might contribute to a diverse educational environment."

In contrast to the undergraduate admissions procedures, O'Connor said, the law school "awards no mechanical, predetermined diversity 'bonuses' based on race or ethnicity." Under the law school program, an applicant's race or ethnicity was not "the defining feature" of his or her application, she wrote. And even though the law school explicitly sought a "critical mass" of minority admittees, O'Connor said that the admissions program "does not operate as a quota."

O'Connor ended her opinion, though, by suggesting that race-conscious admissions policies should not be permanent. Colleges and universities, she said, should include "sunset provisions" and "periodic reviews" to determine whether racial preferences are still needed to achieve student body diversity. Citing the twenty-five year period since *Bakke*, O'Connor concluded, "We expect that 25 years from now, the use of racial preferences will no longer be necessary to further the interest approved today." O'Connor's opinion — was joined by the court's four liberal-leaning justices: John Paul Stevens, David H. Souter, Ruth Bader Ginsburg and Stephen G. Breyer. The four dissenting justices — William H. Rehnquist, Antonin Scalia, Anthony M. Kennedy and Clarence Thomas — each wrote opinions explaining why they disagreed with the decision to uphold the law school's admissions program.

Writing for all four, Rehnquist said the procedures appeared to be "a carefully managed program designed to ensure proportionate representation of applicants from selected minority groups." Rehnquist also faulted the majority for what he called "unprecedented" deference to the law school's defense of its program. In a lone opinion, Kennedy also criticized the majority for what he called a "perfunctory" review of the program. But Kennedy explicitly agreed that racial diversity was a constitutionally legitimate goal in higher education.

In the longest of the dissents, Thomas strongly criticized affirmative action on both legal and practical grounds. Referring to diversity as "classroom aesthetics," Thomas said the majority made "no serious effort" to explain its educational benefits. In practice, he said, racial preferences provoked resentment among unsuccessful applicants while most blacks admitted under the policies were "tarred as undeserving." Thomas also warned the decision would produce further "controversy and litigation." Scalia joined Thomas's opinion and wrote a shorter dissent of his own.

Both Thomas and Scalia did note their agreement with the Court's suggestion that race-conscious admissions policies should be terminated in twenty-five years. From the other side, Ginsburg wrote a concurring opinion somewhat discounting the deadline. ". . . [O]ne may

hope, but not firmly forecast, that over the next generation's span, progress toward nondiscrimination and genuinely equal opportunity will make it safe to sunset affirmative action," she wrote. Breyer joined her opinion.

Writing for the majority in *Gratz*, Rehnquist said the program violated the Equal Protection Clause because its use of race was "not narrowly tailored to achieve the interest in educational diversity that [university officials] claim justifies their program." The automatic distribution of 20 points, he said, had the effect of making race the decisive factor "for virtually every minimally qualified underrepresented minority applicant."

Rehnquist rejected the college's argument that the volume of applications made it "impractical" to adopt the kind of individualized review of applications approved by the Court in the law school case. "The fact that the implementation of a program capable of providing individualized consideration might present administrative challenges does not render constitutional an otherwise problematic system," he wrote.

Rehnquist was joined by the other three dissenters from the law school case and O'Connor. In a concurring opinion, O'Connor said the undergraduate admissions system was "a nonindivdiualized, mechanical one" that did not provide for "a meaningful individualized review of applicants." Breyer concurred in the judgment; he said he concurred in O'Connor's opinion "except insofar as it joins that of the Court."

The dissenters objected on procedural and substantive grounds. Procedurally, Stevens and Souter said that Gratz and Hamacher had no standing to seek to enjoin the further use of the admissions policies because they had both graduated from different schools and were no longer seeking admission. On the merits, Souter and Ginsburg both said they would uphold the admissions program. In her opinion, Ginsburg said racial policies aimed at "inclusion" should be treated more favorably than policies aimed at "exclusion." Breyer said he joined that part of Ginsburg's opinion.

OUTLOOK

Reform or Status Quo?

The Supreme Court's decisions in the Michigan cases heartened supporters of affirmative action and disappointed opponents. For their part, university officials

Should colleges eliminate the use of race in admissions?

YES
Thomas E. Wood
Executive Director, California Association of Scholars, co-author of California Prop. 209

Written for The CQ Researcher, September 2001

Colleges should eliminate the use of race in admissions. One cannot prefer on the basis of race without discriminating against others on the basis of race. Treating people differently on the basis of their race violates the Constitution's guarantee of equal protection under the laws.

There is only one national database for higher education that is in a position to adequately address this question whether, or to what extent, campus racial diversity is a necessary component of educational excellence. So far, the American Council on Education/Higher Education Research Institute database has failed to find any connection between campus racial diversity and any of the 82 cognitive and non-cognitive outcome variables incorporated in the study.

Proponents claim that the abandonment of racial classifications will result in the resegregation of higher education. Since preferences have been used to increase the number of minorities in the past, their abandonment will lead in the near term to lower numbers for minorities (though only in the most elite institutions of higher education).

But the claim that abandoning the use of race in college admissions will lead to resegregation implies that all or virtually all minorities who are presently enrolled in the most elite institutions are there only because they have been given preferences, which is both untrue and demeaning. The claim also ignores the fact that the country was making significant progress toward diversity *before* the advent of racial preferences in university admissions in the mid-to-late 1970s.

This analysis is confirmed by the experience of Texas, California and Washington, which already have bans on racial classifications in university admissions. The experience in these states has been that while there is an initial decline when racial classifications are abandoned (though only in the most elite institutions), the underlying trend toward greater diversity resumes after the initial correction.

For some, of course, any regression from the numbers that are obtainable through the use of preferences is unacceptable. At its heart, this is the view that racial diversity is a value that trumps all others. But that is a view that has clearly been rejected by the courts, and for good reason. Diversity is an important public policy goal, but there is a right way and a wrong way to pursue it. Racial classifications are the wrong way.

NO
Angelo Ancheta
Director, Legal and Advocacy Programs, Civil Rights Project, Harvard Law School

Written for The CQ Researcher, September 2001

Affirmative action policies advance the tenet that colleges, like the workplace and our public institutions, should reflect the full character of American society. Race-conscious admissions policies not only promote the integration ideal first realized in *Brown v. Board of Education* but also help create educational environments that improve basic learning and better equip students for an increasingly diverse society.

The U.S. Supreme Court upheld race-conscious admissions over 20 years ago in *Regents of the University of California v. Bakke.* Yet, affirmative action opponents, armed with the rhetoric of quotas and tokenism for the unqualified, persist in trying to undermine *Bakke.* Educators know that quotas are illegal under *Bakke* and that granting admission to the unqualified serves no one's interest. Colleges have been highly circumspect, employing carefully crafted policies that consider all applicants competitively and that use race as only one of many factors in admissions decisions.

Nevertheless, recent litigation challenging affirmative action in Texas, Washington, Georgia and Michigan portends that the Supreme Court will soon revisit *Bakke.* But the case that promoting educational diversity is, in the language of the law, "a compelling governmental interest" and that race-conscious admissions policies can best serve that interest has only strengthened in recent years.

The latest findings show that student-body diversity significantly improves the quality of higher education. Studies at the University of Michigan have found that diverse learning environments can enhance students' critical-thinking skills, augment their understanding and tolerance of different opinions and groups, increase their motivation and participation in civic activities and better prepare them for living in a diverse society. Several studies support these findings and further show that interaction across races has positive effects on retention rates, satisfaction with college, self-confidence and leadership ability.

Without race-conscious admissions, the student-body diversity necessary to advance these educational outcomes would be lost. The declining enrollment of minority students at public universities that have abandoned affirmative action strongly suggests that the "color-blind" path is not the path to equal opportunity; nor is it the path to the highest-quality education.

Affirmative action policies reflect the reality that race has always shaped our educational institutions. Justice Blackmun's admonition in *Bakke* thus remains as vital as ever: "In order to get beyond racism, we must first take account of race. There is no other way."

across the country generally said the rulings would allow them to continue using racial preferences in admissions with only minor modifications if any.

Affirmative action supporters were beaming after announcement of the decisions. "This is a wonderful day," University of Michigan president Mary Sue Coleman told reporters on the Supreme Court plaza. The decisions, she said, provided "a green light to pursue diversity" and "a road map to get us there."

Liberal interest groups also praised the decisions. "The Court has reiterated America's commitment to affirmative action, and the nation is better off for it," said Vincent Warren, a staff attorney with the American Civil Liberties Union who worked on the cases. "They're not willing to turn the clock back," said Theodore Shaw of the NAACP Legal Defense and Educational Fund. "That's the message for the nation."

Conservative groups, which had generally expected a clear-cut victory in the cases, tried to conceal their disappointment by depicting the rulings as a partial win. Terrence Pell, president of the Center for Individual Rights, said the rulings would make it "more difficult" for universities to use race-based admissions procedures. Clint Bolick, vice president of the libertarian Institute for Justice, said the decisions "will leave the nation racially polarized."

Both Pell and Bolick also contended that the rulings did nothing to address racial gaps in elementary and secondary education. "Racial preferences in post-secondary education make us think that we are solving that problem when in fact it is growing," Bolick said. "For that reason, this decision is a tragedy for all Americans."

President Bush cautiously praised the decisions for recognizing "the value of diversity" while requiring universities to "engage in a serious, good faith consideration of workable race-neutral alternatives."

Coleman told reporters that the university would quickly revise its undergraduate admissions policies in line with the Court's ruling in time for the class entering the college in 2004. Officials representing other colleges and universities said the rulings cleared up legal confusion over the issues and predicted the decisions would lead to few changes.

The ruling "has the effect of defining current practices as constitutional," said Barmak Nassirian, associate executive director of the American Association of Collegiate Registrars and Admissions Officers. "There are very few institutions that would be negatively affected by the undergraduate decision."

But Pell warned universities not to use the rulings as a "fig leaf" to preserve the status quo. "Some schools are determined to continue to take race into account, and it's business as usual for them," Pell said. He said the center would monitor responses to the decisions and challenge any schools that used a "mechanistic" formula to favor minority candidates.

NOTES

1. For extensive information on both cases, including the texts of the two rulings and other legal documents, see the University of Michigan's Web site (www.umich.edu) or the Web site of the public-interest law firm representing the plaintiffs, the Center for Individual Rights (www.cir-usa.org).

2. The legal citation is 438 U.S. 265; Supreme Court decisions can be found on a number of Web sites, including the court's official site: www.supreme-courtus.gov. For background, see Kenneth Jost, "Rethinking Affirmative Action," *The CQ Researcher*, April 28, 1995, pp. 369-392.

3. See Robert Lerner and Althea K. Nagai, "Pervasive Preferences: Racial and Ethnic Discrimination in Undergraduate Admissions Across the Nation," Center for Equal Opportunity, Feb. 22, 2001 (www.ceo-usa.org).

4. For background, see David Masci, "Hispanic Americans' New Clout," *The CQ Researcher*, Sept. 18, 1998, pp. 809-832; David Masci, "The Black Middle Class," *The CQ Researcher*, Jan. 23, 1998, pp. 49-72; and Kenneth Jost, "Diversity in the Workplace," *The CQ Researcher*, Oct. 10, 1997, pp. 889-912.

5. Charles R. Lawrence III and Mari J. Matsuda, *We Won't Go Back: Making the Case for Affirmative Action* (1997), p. 127. Matsuda, Lawrence's wife, is also a professor at Georgetown law school.

6. For background, see Joan Biskupic and Elder Witt, *Guide to the U.S. Supreme Court* (3d ed.), 1997, pp. 362-363. The cases discussed are *Missouri ex rel. Gaines v. Canada*, 305 U.S. 337 (1938); *Sweatt v. Painter*, 339 U.S. 629 (1950); and *McLaurin v. Oklahoma State Regents for Higher Education*, 339 U.S. 637 (1950).

7. William G. Bowen and Derek Bok, *The Shape of the River: Long-Term Consequences of Considering Race in College and University Admissions* (1998), pp. 4-5. Bowen, a former president of Princeton University, is now president of the Andrew W. Mellon Foundation in New York City; Bok is a former president of Harvard University and now University Professor at the John. F. Kennedy School of Government at Harvard.

8. Reprinted in Gabriel J. Chin (ed.), *Affirmative Action and the Constitution: Affirmative Action Before Constitutional Law, 1964-1977*, Vol. 1 (1998), pp. 21-26.

9. Bowen and Bok, *op. cit.*, pp. 6-7.

10. Description of the announcement of the decision taken from Bernard Schwartz, *Behind* Bakke: *Affirmative Action and the Supreme Court* (1988), pp. 142-150.

11. The cases are *Wygant v. Jackson Bd. of Education*, 476 U.S. 267 (1986); *Johnson v. Transportation Agency of Santa Clara County*, 480 U.S. 646 (1987); *City of Richmond v. J.A. Croson Co.*, 488 U.S. 469 (1989); and *Adarand Constructors, Inc. v. Peña*, 575 U.S. 200 (1995).

12. Lincoln Caplan, *Up Against the Law: Affirmative Action and the Supreme Court* (1997), p. 16.

13. The case is *Hopwood v. Texas.* Some background on this and other cases in this section drawn from Girardeau A. Spann, *The Law of Affirmative Action: Twenty-Five Years of Supreme Court Decisions on Race and Remedies* (2000).

14. The legal citation is *Hopwood v. Texas*, 78 F.2d 932 (5th Cir. 1996). In a subsequent decision, the appeals court on Dec. 21, 2000, reaffirmed its legal holding, but upheld the lower court judge's finding that none of the four plaintiffs would have been admitted to the law school under a race-blind system. See *Hopwood v. Texas*, 236 F.2d 256 (5th Cir. 2000).

15. Quoted in Facts on File, March 28, 1996.

16. For background, see Jennifer Gavin, "Redistricting," *The CQ Researcher*, Feb. 16, 2001, pp. 113-128; Nadine Cahodas, "Electing Minorities," *The CQ Researcher*, Aug. 12, 1994, pp. 697-720.

17. The legal citation is 515 U.S. 200.

18. For a critique, see Stephan and Abigail Thernstrom, "Reflections on the Shape of the River," *UCLA Law Review*, Vol. 46, No. 5 (June 1999), pp. 1583-1631.

19. For a good overview, see Nicholas Lemann, "The Empathy Defense," *The New Yorker*, Dec. 18, 2000, pp. 46-51. See also Carl Cohen, "Race Preference and the Universities — A Final Reckoning," *Commentary*, September 2001, pp. 31-39.

20. "Vital Signs: The Statistics that Describe the Present and Suggest the Future of African Americans in Higher Education," *The Journal of Blacks in Higher Education*, No. 9 (autumn 1995), pp. 43-49.

21. The Washington case is *Smith v. University of Washington Law School*, 9th Circuit, Dec. 4, 2000; the Georgia case is *Johnson v. Board of Regents of the University of Georgia*, 11th Circuit, Aug. 27.

BIBLIOGRAPHY

Books

Bowen, **William G.**, **and Derek Bok,** *The Shape of the River: Long-Term Consequences of Considering Race in College and University Admissions,* **Princeton University Press, 1998.**

The book analyzes data on 80,000 students admitted to 28 selective private or public colleges and universities in 1951, 1976 and 1989 to examine the impact of race-based admissions on enrollment and to compare the educational and post-graduation experiences of white and minority students. Includes statistical tables as well as a nine-page list of references. Bowen, a former president of Princeton University, heads the Andrew W. Mellon Foundation; Bok is a former president of Harvard University and now a professor at Harvard's John F. Kennedy School of Government.

Caplan, Lincoln, *Up Against the Law: Affirmative Action and the Supreme Court,* **Twentieth Century Fund Press, 1997.**

The 60-page monograph provides an overview of the Supreme Court's affirmative action rulings with analysis written from a pro race-conscious policies perspective. Caplan, a longtime legal-affairs writer, is a senior writer in residence at Yale Law School.

Chin, Gabriel J. (ed.), *Affirmative Action and the Constitution: Affirmative Action Before Constitutional Law, 1964-1977* **(Vol. 1);** *The Supreme Court "Solves" the Affirmative Action Issue, 1978-1988* **(Vol. 2);**

Judicial Reaction to Affirmative Action, 1988-1997 **(Vol. 3), Garland Publishing, 1998.**
The three-volume compendium includes a variety of materials on affirmative action from President Lyndon B. Johnson's famous speech at Howard University in 1965 to President Bill Clinton's defense of affirmative action in 1995 as well as the full text of the federal appeals court decision in the 1995 Hopwood decision barring racial preferences at the University of Texas Law School. Chin, who wrote an introduction for each volume, is a professor at the University of Cincinnati College of Law.

Edley, Christopher Jr., *Not All Black and White: Affirmative Action, Race, and American Values,* **Hill & Wang, 1996.**
Edley, a Harvard Law School professor, recounts his role in overseeing the Clinton administration's review of affirmative action in 1995 as part of a broad look at the issue that ends with measured support for affirmative action "until the justification for it no longer exists."

Schwartz, Bernard, *Behind Bakke: Affirmative Action and the Supreme Court,* **New York University Press.**
Schwartz, a leading Supreme Court scholar until his death in 1997, was granted unusual access to the private papers of the justices for this detailed, behind-the-scenes account of the Bakke case from its origins through the justices' deliberations and final decision.

Spann, Girardeau A., *The Law of Affirmative Action: Twenty-Five Years of Supreme Court Decisions on Races and Remedies,* **New York University Press, 2000.**
The book includes summaries — concise and precise — of major Supreme Court decisions from *Bakke* in 1978 to *Adarand* in 1995 Spann is a professor at Georgetown University Law Center.

Steele, Shelby, *A Dream Deferred: The Second Betrayal of Black Freedom in America,* **HarperCollins, 1998.**
Steele, a prominent black critic of affirmative action and a research fellow at the Hoover Institution at Stanford University, argues in four essays that affirmative action represents an "extravagant" liberalism that "often betrayed America's best principles" in order to atone for white guilt over racial injustice.

Articles

Lawrence, Charles R. III, "Two Views of the River: A Critique of the Liberal Defense of Affirmative Action," *Columbia Law Review,* **Vol. 101, No. 4 (May 2001), pp. 928-975.**
Lawrence argues that liberals' "diversity" defense of affirmative action overlooks "more radical substantive" arguments based on "the need to remedy past discrimination, address present discriminatory practices, and reexamine traditional notions of merit and the role of universities in the reproduction of elites." Lawrence is a professor at Georgetown University Law Center.

PBS NewsHour, "Admitting for Diversity," Aug. 21, 2001 (www.pbs.org/newshour).
The report by correspondent Elizabeth Brackett features interviews with, among others, Barbara Grutter, the plaintiff in the lawsuit challenging the University of Michigan Law School's race-based admissions policies, and the law school's dean, Jeffrey Lehman.

Thernstrom, Stephan, and Abigail Thernstrom, "Reflections on The Shape of the River," *UCLA Law Review,* **Vol. 46, No. 5 (June 1999), pp. 1583-1.**
The Thernstroms contend that racial preferences constitute a "pernicious palliative" that deflect attention from real educational problems and conflict with the country's unrealized egalitarian dream. Stephan Thernstrom is a professor of history at Harvard University; his wife Abigail is a senior fellow at the Manhattan Institute and a member of the Massachusetts State Board of Education. An earlier version appeared in Commentary (February 1999).

For More Information

American Council on Education, 1 Dupont Circle, N.W., Suite 800, Washington, D.C. 20036; (202) 939-9300; www.acenet.edu. The council was the lead organization in a friend-of-the-court brief filed by 30 higher-education groups in support of the University of Michigan's race-conscious admissions policies.

Center for Equal Opportunity, 14 Pidgeon Hill Dr., Suite 500, Sterling, VA 20165; (703) 421-5443; www.ceousa.org. The center filed a friend-of-the-court brief in support of the plaintiffs challenging University of Michigan admissions policies.

Center for Individual Rights, 1233 20th St., N.W., Suite 300, Washington, D.C. 20036; (202) 833-8400; www. cir-usa.org. The public-interest law firm, founded in 1989, represents plaintiffs in the University of Michigan and other cases challenging race-conscious admission policies.

NAACP Legal Defense Fund, 99 Hudson St., 16th Floor, New York, N.Y. 10013; (212) 965-2200; www.naacpldf. org. The Legal Defense Fund, which traces its history to the NAACP's earliest civil rights litigation in the early 1900s, represents the minority student intervenors in the two suits contesting admission policies at the University of Michigan.

National Association of Scholars, 221 Witherspoon St., Second Floor, Princeton, N.J. 08542-3215; (609) 683-7878; www.nas.org. The organization studies and advocates on academic issues including race-based admissions policies.

6

Gay Marriage

Kenneth Jost

As a lawyer with Gay and Lesbian Advocates and Defenders (GLAD), Mary Bonauto sympathized with the couples who came to her for help. Many of their problems — health benefits that could not be shared, child-custody limits, tax penalties — grew out of the inability of same-sex couples to be legally married.

But throughout most of the 1990s, Bonauto fended off the gay-marriage issue as premature: Not yet, she would say, the time is not right. In 1998, however, she and other GLAD lawyers decided the time for action had come, and under a unique provision of Vermont's constitution they sued the state.

In a stunning decision in December 1999, the Vermont Supreme Court ordered the legislature to grant gay and lesbian couples the same legal benefits enjoyed by married heterosexuals. Over protests from social conservatives, the legislature created a new, marriage-like legal status for same-sex couples: "civil unions."[1]

Now Bonauto is hoping to go even further in Massachusetts. Hillary and Julie Goodridge and six other gay and lesbian couples represented by GLAD are anxiously awaiting a decision from the state's highest court in a suit — *Goodridge v. Massachusetts Department of Public Health* — that could make Massachusetts the first state to recognize gay marriage.

The Goodridges see nothing extraordinary about their legal plea. Instead, they find it more surprising that the law gives them no opportunity to formalize their relationship even though they have been together for 16 years and have been raising a daughter together for the last eight.

"We have a child. We own real estate together. We have wills. We have health-care proxies. But we have no legal relationship to

Massachusetts could become the first state to recognize gay marriage if the state's highest court rules in favor of Hillary and Julie Goodridge, here with their daughter Annie, and other gay couples. Gay-rights advocates say homosexuals need and deserve the same symbolic and practical benefits for their relationships enjoyed by heterosexuals. But religious groups and social conservatives say legal recognition for same-sex couples runs counter to historical tradition, moral order and the best interests of children and society at large.

From *The CQ Researcher,*
September 5, 2003.

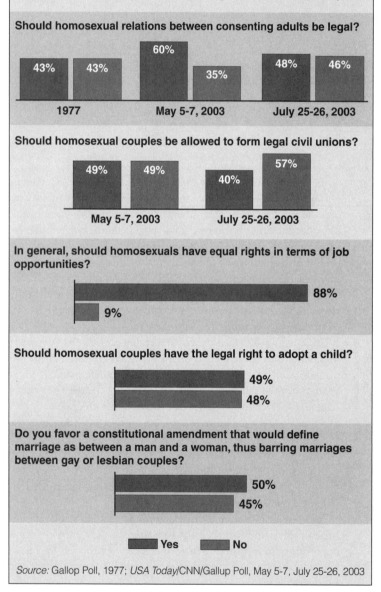

Support for Gay Relationships Drops

Americans' support for legal homosexual relations and gay civil unions rose steadily from the 1960s through the 1980s but declined measurably after the Supreme Court struck down a Texas anti-sodomy law on June 26. The ruling had been hailed as clearing the way for new gay civil rights, but recent polls appear to indicate a backlash against recognizing same-sex relationships.

Should homosexual relations between consenting adults be legal?

43% | 43% | 60% | 35% | 48% | 46%

1977　May 5-7, 2003　July 25-26, 2003

Should homosexual couples be allowed to form legal civil unions?

49% | 49% | 40% | 57%

May 5-7, 2003　July 25-26, 2003

In general, should homosexuals have equal rights in terms of job opportunities?

88%
9%

Should homosexual couples have the legal right to adopt a child?

49%
48%

Do you favor a constitutional amendment that would define marriage as between a man and a woman, thus barring marriages between gay or lesbian couples?

50%
45%

■ Yes ■ No

Source: Gallop Poll, 1977; *USA Today*/CNN/Gallup Poll, May 5-7, July 25-26, 2003

each other," Julie explains. "That's what we're trying to change with the marriage case."

Gay-rights advocates emphasize the distinction between legalizing civil marriage between same-sex couples and gaining religious recognition for gay marriages. "Every religion can decide for itself whether to perform or honor any marriage," says Evan Wolfson, a longtime gay-rights litigator, who is now executive director of the New York-based advocacy group Freedom to Marry. "But no religion should be able to dictate who gets a civil marriage license."

Even so, an array of religious and conservative advocacy groups strongly opposes legal recognition for same-sex couples, saying it runs counter to historical tradition, moral order and the best interests of children and society at large.

"We favor the tradition of a one-man, one-woman marriage," says Connie Mackey, vice president of the Family Research Council, a Washington-based Christian organization. "We reject the attempts of the gay community to foist its agenda on the general public."

"Marriage means the union of one man and one woman," says Ron Crews, president of the Massachusetts Family Institute, which filed a friend-of-the-court brief in the Massachusetts case. "It's a risky business for courts or legislatures to get into the business of changing the definition of a word."

"Only the relationship between a man and a woman has a natural association with the generation of new children," says Daniel Avila, an attorney with the Massachusetts Catholic Conference. "No other relationship has that potential."

Advocates of same-sex marriage counter that allowing gay men and lesbians to marry would strengthen their relationships and also provide concrete legal protections and economic benefits.

"Only marriage conveys the love and commitment that others automatically understand and respect," Bonauto says. "Only marriage provides a legal safety net protecting the couple's emotional bonds and their economic security."

"Civil marriage is a powerful and important affirmation of love, a source of social recognition and support, and the legal gateway to a vast array of protections, responsibilities and benefits, most of which cannot be replicated in any other way," Wolfson says.

Supporters also say legalizing same-sex marriage will help, not hurt, the increasing number of children being raised by gay or lesbian parents. "It means a great deal to the kids that their parents have all the support and acknowledgment that a family deserves," Wolfson says. (*See story, p. 132.*)

The seven couples who filed suit in Massachusetts have been together for periods ranging from three to more than 30 years. Four of the couples have children. (*See box, p. 126.*) In a news conference when the suit was filed in April 2001, several of the plaintiffs noted practical problems that they had encountered because they were not married. But the Goodridges also say they were prompted to join the suit by a surprising exchange with their then 5-year-old daughter Annie.

One night, after listening to the Beatles' song "All You Need Is Love," Hillary asked Annie if she knew any people who loved each other. Annie listed several of her mothers' married friends.

"What about Mommy and Ma?" Hillary asked, using the names she and Julie had taken for themselves before Annie's birth.

"If you loved each other," Annie replied, "you'd get married."

The Supreme Judicial Court of Massachusetts heard arguments in the case on March 4. The state attorney general's office urged the seven justices to reject the suit, saying the legislature had a rational basis — encouraging procreation and child rearing — for limiting marriage to heterosexual couples. Moreover, argued Assistant State Attorney General Judith Yogman, any change was up to the legislature, not the courts.

The court's unofficial deadline for a decision passed in mid-July, but Bonauto says she is not surprised that the justices are taking their time with the case. "This is an opinion that is being watched very carefully," she says. "The pressure here is tremendous."

The gay-marriage issue has simmered for decades but did not become a priority for gay-rights advocates till the 1990s. Before the Vermont case, state courts in Hawaii and Alaska issued preliminary rulings in favor of gay marriage, but the court moves were thwarted by state constitutional amendments.

In the meantime, however, the Netherlands and Belgium became the first and second countries to recognize same-sex marriage, both by parliamentary action. Then in June the Canadian government announced that it would bow to a ruling by Ontario's highest provincial court and prepare legislation to legalize marriage for same-sex couples throughout the country.

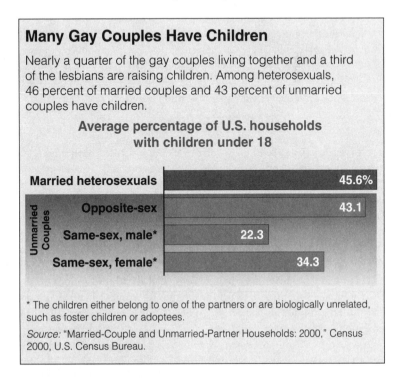

Many Gay Couples Have Children

Nearly a quarter of the gay couples living together and a third of the lesbians are raising children. Among heterosexuals, 46 percent of married couples and 43 percent of unmarried couples have children.

Average percentage of U.S. households with children under 18

Category		Percentage
Married heterosexuals		45.6%
Unmarried Couples	Opposite-sex	43.1
	Same-sex, male*	22.3
	Same-sex, female*	34.3

* The children either belong to one of the partners or are biologically unrelated, such as foster children or adoptees.

Source: "Married-Couple and Unmarried-Partner Households: 2000," Census 2000, U.S. Census Bureau.

Blessing Gay Marriage Widely Opposed in U.S.

Former Boston priest Jon Schum does not think of himself as a renegade, but he goes against the Roman Catholic Church's official teachings: He lives in a committed relationship with another man and performs commitment ceremonies for gay and lesbian couples.

Schum never sought out opportunities to officiate at same-sex ceremonies. But people who heard about him through Dignity, a gay Catholic organization, asked him to help them celebrate their unions "in the context of their Catholic traditions."

The half-dozen ceremonies Schum has performed over the past two years have had most of the trappings of a Catholic wedding, including scripture readings and exchanged vows and rings. He believes they are fully Catholic in substance as well. "The love between gay and lesbian persons is just as real, just as authentic, just as holy, just as sacramental, as the love between any married persons," Schum says.

The church hierarchy, however, strongly opposes any recognition for same-sex unions, either within the church or in law. "There are absolutely no grounds for considering homosexual unions to be in any way similar or even remotely analogous to God's plan for marriage and family," the Vatican said in a doctrinal statement on July 31. The statement said Catholic lawmakers have "a moral duty" to oppose any moves to recognize gay marriage.[1]

The U.S. Conference of Catholic Bishops had earlier issued a similar statement opposing "attempts to grant the legal status of marriage" to same-sex relationships. "No same-sex union can realize the full and unique potential which the marital relationship expresses," the conference's secretariat for family, laity, women and youth said in a June 3 policy statement.

The blessing of same-sex unions also is opposed by most other U.S. denominations, including Eastern Orthodoxy, the Southern Baptist Convention and other evangelical Protestant denominations, the Church of Jesus Christ of Latter-day Saints, the Orthodox and Conservative branches of Judaism, and Islam.[2]

The Episcopal Church U.S.A. officially recognized the blessing of same-sex unions at its August convention in Minneapolis but declined to establish a liturgy for those ceremonies. The compromise culminated a tumultuous convention dominated by a sharp debate over the eventual election of an openly gay priest, V. Gene Robinson, as bishop of New Hampshire.[3]

Among other mainline Protestant denominations, the United Methodist Church bans same-sex ceremonies while the Presbyterian Church U.S.A. allows clergy to officiate at same-sex rituals but specifies that such events differ from marriages. The Evangelical Lutheran Church plans a report on the issue in 2005.

The issue moved to the top of the U.S. political agenda following a landmark decision by the Supreme Court that invalidated state laws against gay sex. The June 26 ruling in *Lawrence v. Texas* said homosexuals have the right to engage in physically intimate conduct without government intervention.

The opinion did not deal directly with same-sex marriage. But Bonauto says the ruling supports the gay-marriage suit. "*Lawrence* confirmed what we had already been arguing — that if a right is fundamental for some, it's fundamental for all," she says. "There's not a gay exception in the Constitution."

A leading academic opponent of same-sex marriage says the *Lawrence* decision has mobilized partisans on both sides of the issue. "It has certainly energized the gay-rights movement," says Lynn Wardle, a professor at Brigham Young University Law School in Provo, Utah. "It's also going to energize the conservative, pro-family movement. So there are going to be political clashes."

Gay-marriage supporters hope — and opponents fear — that a ruling to recognize same-sex relationships in one state will have a cascading effect in other states. Opponents hope that so-called defense-of-marriage (DOMA) laws enacted by Congress and 37 states will allow individual states to refuse to recognize same-sex marriages granted elsewhere.

President Bush entered the debate on July 30 by saying his administration is looking at ways to "codify" the

Meanwhile, ministers in the predominantly gay Universal Fellowship of Metropolitan Community Churches have performed same-sex commitment ceremonies since 1968. The Unitarian Universalist Association and the United Church of Christ advocate tolerance for same-sex unions. Judaism's liberal Reform branch gives rabbis the option of presiding at gay commitment ceremonies.

Clergy members who perform same-sex ceremonies see their roles as part of their pastoral duties. "I consider myself a priest who is trying to live out his ministry in the best way possible," Schum says. "This is the work that I'm called to do."

Schum says he was "angry," but not surprised, by the Vatican statement on same-sex marriage. "The tone of the letter is cruel," he says. "It's uninformed. It's unjust. It just reflects the unwillingness of the hierarchy to have any kind of dialogue with gay and lesbian Catholics and to have any kind of dialogue about the new knowledge about homosexuality."

Marianne Duddy, former executive director of Dignity, has similar reactions to the Vatican statement today, five years after she was "married" to her partner by a Catholic priest. "I felt incredibly sad and incredibly attacked," says Duddy, a clinical social worker in Boston. "The Vatican is totally depersonalizing us."

The Vatican statement also opposed adoption by gay or lesbian persons, saying it "would actually mean doing violence to these children" because it would put them in unhealthy home environments. Duddy, who is in the process of adopting a foster daughter who has lived with her and her partner since early 2002, says that part of the statement was "especially hurtful."

U.S. Catholics appear divided on the issue. A survey by the Pew Forum on Religion in Public Life last spring found support for gay marriage among U.S. Catholics had increased to 38 percent from 27 percent in 1996.[4] The survey was conducted before the U.S. Supreme Court's decision striking down state anti-sodomy laws in late June. Other polls since that time have indicated a decline in public support for gay marriage.

Specifically, a *Washington Post* poll conducted in August just after the Episcopal Church's action found that a large majority of Americans — 60 percent — oppose church sanctions of homosexual relationships. In fact, nearly half of all church-going Americans said they would leave their churches if their minister blessed gay couples. Slightly fewer — 58 percent — opposed civil unions, which would grant gay partners some of the legal rights of married couples without the involvement of a religious institution.[5]

[1] "Considerations Regarding Proposals to Give Legal Recognition to Unions Between Homosexual Persons," July 31, 2003, www.vatican.va. For coverage, see Frank Bruni, "Vatican Exhorts Legislators to Reject Same-Sex Unions," *The New York Times*, Aug. 1, 2003, p. A1; Alan Cooperman and David von Drehle, "Vatican Instructs Legislators on Gays," *The Washington Post*, Aug. 1, 2003, p. A1.

[2] "Few U.S. Religions Bless Same-Sex Unions," The Associated Press, Aug. 7, 2003.

[3] For coverage, see Alan Cooperman, "Episcopal Church Ratifies Compromise on Gay Unions," *The Washington Post*, Aug. 8, 2003, p. A2; Monica Davey, "Episcopal Church Leaders Reject Proposal for Same-Sex Union Liturgy," *The New York Times*, Aug. 8, 2003, p. A20.

[4] Pew Forum on Religion and Public Life, "Religion and Politics: Contention and Consensus," July 24, 2003 (http://www.pewforum.org).

[5] Richard Morin and Alan Cooperman, "Majority Against Blessing Gay Unions," *The Washington Post*, Aug. 14, 2003, p. A1.

definition of marriage as one man, one woman. Some opponents of gay marriage say a constitutional amendment is needed, but acknowledge that it will be difficult to win the two-thirds majority in Congress and approval by three-fourths of the states to ratify an amendment.

For their part, all but two of the Democratic presidential candidates favor granting legal benefits to same-sex couples, but only three contenders — all of whom are low in the polls — favor gay marriage.[2]

Meanwhile, opinion polls indicate an apparent backlash on the issue in the weeks since the *Lawrence* decision. Support for civil unions had been increasing, but it dropped by 10 percentage points or more in polls conducted in May and July. (*See box, p. 122.*)

As the issue proceeds in the courts and elsewhere, here are some of the major questions being debated:

Would recognizing same-sex unions benefit gay men and lesbians?

Bill Flanigan and Robert Daniel, a gay couple in San Francisco, did all that they could to formalize their relationship. They registered as domestic partners, as permitted under a San Francisco ordinance, and Daniel executed a health-care proxy allowing Flanigan to make medical decisions relating to Daniel's treatment for AIDS.

The preparations were not enough, however, when a critically ill Daniel was admitted to the University of Maryland's Shock Trauma Center in Baltimore on

Oct. 16, 2000. Hospital personnel barred Flanigan from Daniel's room for four hours until Daniel's mother and sister arrived to give permission. By then, Daniel was unconscious, his eyes taped shut. He died with no chance for the two men to say goodbye.

Lawyers for Lambda Legal Defense and Education Fund, an advocacy group for gays, say the hospital's refusal shows that gay men and lesbians can gain the practical benefits that heterosexual couples take for granted only if they are allowed to legally marry. "We are a nation divided by discrimination in marriage," says attorney David Buckel. "Bill and Robert paid a terrible price for that discrimination."

Some opponents of same-sex marriage object to any legal steps to permit gay couples to enjoy marriage-like benefits. "What makes them different from other kinds of people who might want to get the same benefits of marriage?" asks Mackey of the Family Research Council. "Why special rights for this group of people?"

Other opponents, however, say they have no objections to gay couples enjoying some of the benefits of marriage as long as marriage itself is reserved for heterosexuals. "Much that they are asking to be done can be done without the radical redefinition of the word 'marriage,'" says Crews, of the Massachusetts Family Institute. "There are things that are already available for those who want to be in a relationship that doesn't qualify for marriage."

In fact, many gay and lesbian couples already structure their affairs jointly. They buy houses together, name each other in their wills and — in a few states — jointly adopt children. Domestic-partnership provisions recognized by some city and state governments and a growing number of private employers allow an employee to designate a gay or lesbian partner for health benefits.

Gay-marriage advocates, however, complain that homosexual couples cannot achieve these benefits without making special efforts. "It's time-consuming and complicated," says Mark Strasser, a professor at Capital University Law School in Columbus, Ohio. In addition, some of the rights and benefits of marriage simply cannot be achieved without changes in the law, such as spousal support in the event of a breakup or the confidentiality of marital communications.

"Access to health care, medical decision-making, inheritance, taxation, immigration — the list literally goes on and on," says Wolfson, of Freedom to Marry. "Gay people have the same needs for structure, support and responsibility that straight people do."

Meet the Massachusetts Plaintiffs

The seven gay couples who filed suit in Massachusetts seeking the right to marry have had long-term relationships ranging from three to 32 years. The suit — *Goodridge v. Massachusetts Department of Public Health* — could make Massachusetts the first state in the country to recognize gay marriage.

Julie and Hillary Goodridge
Julie, 45, investment adviser; Hillary, 46, grant administrator. Together, 16 years; commitment ceremony, 1995; one daughter, Annie, 8.

David Wilson and Robert Compton
David, 58, business executive; Rob, 53, dentist.
Together, three years; commitment ceremony, October 2000

Gloria Bailey and Linda Davies
Gloria, 62; Linda, 57; joint psychotherapy practice.
Together, 32 years

Richard Linnell and Gary Chalmers
Rich, 39, nurse; Gary, 37, school teacher.
Together, 14 years; one son, Paige, 10.

Maureen Brodoff and Ellen Wade
Maureen, 50, lawyer; Ellen, 54, lawyer, private practice.
Together, 20-plus years; one daughter, Kate, 14.

Gina Smith and Heidi Norton
Gina, 38, researcher; Heidi, 38, law program director, both with Center for Contemplative Mind in Society.
Together, 12 years; commitment ceremony, 1993; two sons: Avery, 6; Quinn, 3.

Ed Balmelli and Michael Horgan
Ed, 42, computer engineer; Michael, 43, computer systems administrator.
Together, seven years; civil union, Vermont, October 2000.

Source: Gay and Lesbian Advocates and Defenders (www.glad.org).

Gay couples also want the symbolic recognition of their relationships that only marriage can convey. "Marriage is an important vocabulary" in defining a relationship, Wolfson says.

Strasser says marriage constitutes "a public statement" as well as "an internal recognition" about a couple's commitment to each other.

Lawyers in the Massachusetts case stress both the practical and symbolic benefits of marriage for gay and lesbian couples. "Only 'marriage' conveys the love and commitment that others automatically understand and respect," GLAD attorney Bonauto says. "Only 'marriage' provides a legal safety net protecting the couple's emotional bonds and their economic security."

In its brief, the state acknowledges the policy arguments for affording same-sex couples some of the benefits accorded to married couples, but it says the issue is not for the courts to decide. The legislature is "best suited to decide whether, when and how to make such a basic and far-reaching change in Massachusetts law," the state's attorneys contend.

In the past, some gay-rights advocates have been opposed to or unenthusiastic about pushing for marriage rights, viewing the issue either as a low priority or as an undesirable assimilation to "straight" social norms. Today, the gay community appears to be largely unified on the issue and committed to making it a priority.

For his part, Brigham Young University's Wardle acknowledges that homosexual couples could benefit from legal recognition. But, "the benefits would be enjoyed by a very few, a very small group," he points out. "The costs would be borne by society as a whole."

Would recognizing same-sex unions hurt heterosexual marriage?

The United States has the highest divorce rate of any industrialized country, with somewhere between one-third and one-half of all marriages ending in a break-up. The number of opposite-sex couples living together without being married is also high: nearly 5.5 million households — 9.1 percent of all households in the United States.[3]

Opponents of same-sex marriage cite those figures as evidence that traditional marriage is in trouble. Legal recognition of gay and lesbian couples, they say, can only add to the pressures on an institution they consider vital to American society.

"Marriage is the most preferred institution in the law, and for good reason," Wardle says. "It contributes to a society in which rights, values and cultures are passed on, and liberties are protected. It is critical to our way of life."

Recognizing gay marriage "breaks down thousands of years of culture," adds the Family Research Council's Mackey. "It would have a very strange effect."

But proponents say recognizing same-sex unions would have no effect on heterosexual couples, while strengthening homosexual relationships.

"Same-sex couples are interested in the exact same thing that different-sex couples are interested in," Buckel says. "Any time you have people committing to being legally responsible for each other, that's good for communities."

"It's nonsense to say that gay couples taking on a commitment and building a life together takes anything away from anyone else," Wolfson says. "There is enough marriage to share. It's not as though gay couples are going to use up all the marriage licenses."

Opponents are most specific in warning about the potential effects on children from legalizing gay marriage. When pressed to list other possible consequences, Mackey says there might be pressure to bestow marriage-like benefits on other living arrangements. "If an aunt and a niece are living together, why would they not be privileged to the same tax laws?" Mackey asks.

Mackey also suggests that legalizing gay marriage might increase the divorce rate and the incidence of opposite-sex couples living together. "There would be no reason to marry at all," she says. Asked if recognizing gay marriage would promote homosexuality, Mackey replies, "Absolutely, yes."

In its brief in the *Goodridge* case, the Massachusetts attorney general's office acknowledges that public attitudes toward "non-traditional marriages" have changed since enactment of the state's marriage laws. The brief significantly avoids any specific criticisms of gay or lesbian relationships and makes no claim that recognizing same-sex unions would affect the behavior of heterosexual couples.

A coalition of conservative religious groups, however, argues in a friend-of-the-court brief that recognizing homosexual marriage "would institutionalize a radically different vision of sexual relationships." The groups, including the Massachusetts Catholic Conference and the National Association of Evangelicals, suggest that

Here are the seven gay couples that filed suit in Massachusetts seeking the right to marry; Julie and Hillary Goodridge are at far right. A ruling in the suit — *Goodridge v. Massachusetts Department of Public Health* — is expected at any time.

recognizing homosexual marriage would "teach that fundamentally the sexes do not need each other and can — perhaps ought to — live separately."

The plaintiffs' brief does not specifically address the potential effect on heterosexual couples, but an amicus brief filed by a group of 26 social and legal historians points out that court-mandated changes in marriage law — such as striking down anti-miscegenation (racial intermarriage) laws — are now widely accepted. Allowing same-sex couples to marry, the historians argue, "represents the logical next step in . . . reforming marriage to fit the evolving nature of committed intimate relationships and the rights of the individuals in those relationships."

Bonauto says flatly there would be no effect on heterosexual marriage if same-sex marriage is recognized. "Right now, gay and lesbian people are working side by side with non-gay people in the workplace," she says. "Gay and lesbian people are making commitments to each other, gay and lesbian parents are sending children to school. None of that will change with marriage."

"Gay and lesbian families are already part of the community," Bonauto continues. "We're talking about providing them with more legal protections. It's not going to be an issue in changing anyone else's life."

Wardle, however, maintains that the effect on society would be substantial — and detrimental. "You have to look at the children who would be raised in their homes. What message would be sent to society as a whole as to the equality of men and women? What message are we sending to children who are growing up in this society? What kind of message does society send about the value of this institution, about the value of the commitment to this institution?" he asks.

"Marriage is suffering already," Wardle adds. "Marriage and marriage-based families are already carrying a heavy load."

Are children helped or hurt by being raised in homosexual households?

Lawyers for the state of Vermont urged the state Supreme Court four years ago to uphold the ban on same-sex marriage primarily on the grounds that preserving traditional marriage was essential to "legitimize" children and provide for their security. The court rejected the argument.

Many gay couples already adopt children or give birth through assisted reproductive techniques, the justices said. Excluding same-sex couples from the legal protections of marriage, the Vermont court concluded, "exposes their children to the precise risks that the State argues the marriage laws are designed to secure against."

Advocates and opponents of same-sex marriage sharply disagree about the effects of raising children in homosexual households. Opponents insist that a traditional marriage is the best setting for raising children. "Every reputable social study done to date is that the optimal setting for child rearing is a married mom and dad in a home, not just two adults," says Crews, of the Massachusetts Family Institute.

In fact, some opponents of same-sex marriage even contend that being raised in a gay household harms children. "The homosexual lifestyle is inconsistent with the proper raising of children," writes Timothy Dailey, a former research associate with the Family Research Council. "Homosexual relationships are characteristically unstable and are fundamentally incapable of providing children the security they need."[4]

Supporters of same-sex marriage maintain that social-science studies, in fact, show that children raised in homosexual households do as well as children from heterosexual homes. (*See sidebar, p. 132*) "Gay people make fit and loving parents, and the children raised show happy, healthy lives," says Wolfson, of Freedom to Marry.

Legal recognition for gay couples, law Professor Strasser adds, would strengthen their ability to raise children. "This is a way of helping them cement those couples, so children can be raised well and can thrive," Strasser says. "This is a reason to recognize, not a reason not to recognize."

The debate turns in part on social-science evidence that is sharply disputed. Supporters of same-sex marriage say studies consistently show no significant differences between children raised in gay households and those raised by straight couples. Opponents of same-sex marriage say the studies are methodologically flawed and ideologically biased.

Two gay-friendly researchers have added to the debate recently by reinterpreting previous studies as showing that children raised in gay households are more tolerant of homosexual behavior than children from straight households. Researchers Judith Stacey of New York University and Timothy Biblarz of the University of Southern California in Los Angeles view that result favorably, but opponents of same-sex marriage claim the study substantiates their argument that gay parenting is bad for children.[5]

The Massachusetts attorney general's office cites the Stacey-Biblarz study — along with other research — to contend that evidence of the effect of homosexual parenting is "inconclusive." Despite changing sex roles, the state's lawyers argue, the legislature "could still rationally believe that a favorable setting for raising children is a two-parent family with one parent of each sex."

On the opposite side, a coalition of mental-health and social-welfare organizations told the state high court in a friend-of-the-court brief that it is "beyond scientific dispute" that children of gay and lesbian parents are "as well adjusted and psychologically healthy" as those of heterosexual parents.

Same-sex marriage advocates note that virtually all states permit — and many encourage — adoption of children by gay or lesbian parents because it helps relieve the burdens on overcrowded and underfunded state foster-care systems.

"This is a major difficulty for the state — how to deal with children who've been taken out of the home," Strasser says. "The notion that somehow the children would be better off in the system than having two loving, same-sex adults caring for them — it's an amazing argument to make."

Some opponents of same-sex marriage acknowledge the benefits of gay adoption but say it does not require broader legal recognition for gay couples. "If we redefine marriage, then it becomes very difficult for the state to distinguish on a legal basis a married couple and someone else wanting to adopt," says Avila, of the Massachusetts

Catholic Conference. "There may be very good reasons for maintaining the presumption in favor of a married couple."

Other opponents of same-sex marriage, however, are simply opposed to gay adoption. "We've got too many children in our foster-care and social-service systems," Crews says. "But you don't have to radically redefine marriage to tackle a problem of the needs of children."

BACKGROUND

'More Than Brothers'

Men have paired up with men and women with women throughout history and around the globe seeking companionship, support and — often — physical love. These same-sex relationships have enjoyed some measure of social acceptance. But in the West, religious and secular authorities have been virtually unanimous in condemning homosexual relationships at least since the Middle Ages.

Present-day advocates of gay marriage — notably, Yale law Professor William Eskridge in his book *The Case for Same-Sex Marriage* — find historical analogues dating back to the Biblical accounts of David and Jonathan and Ruth and Naomi.[6] Eskridge notes that same-sex relationships between men were common in ancient Greece — witness Plato's discourse on love in the dialogue *Symposium* — and that the Roman Emperor Nero had a formal wedding ceremony with his male lover Sporus.

"Same-sex marriages are a commonplace in human history," Eskridge writes, and have been "tolerated in most societies" except in the West.

Opponents of same-sex marriage view the history differently. They emphasize that the Bible condemns homosexuality: "Thou shalt not lie with mankind, as with womankind: it is abomination" (*Leviticus*, 18:22). Despite the acceptance of same-sex relationships in ancient Greece and Rome, they emphasize — as Eskridge acknowledges — that attitudes changed by the time of the late Roman Empire. Accounts of male-male couplings assumed a satirical tone, and an imperial decree in 342 A.D. prescribed execution for men who married other men.

The divergent views of history emerged dramatically with the publication of a controversial 1994 book,

Same-Sex Unions in Premodern Europe, by Yale historian John Boswell.[7] The first openly gay tenured professor at an Ivy League college, Boswell found evidence in some 60 liturgical manuscripts from the eighth through the 16th centuries to support his thesis that the medieval Catholic Church routinely sanctified same-sex unions.

Prayers for uniting "brothers" appeared in manuscripts alongside prayers for betrothals and marriages, Boswell reported. The ceremonies included rituals associated with marriage: the burning of candles, the placing of the two parties' hands on the Gospel, the joining of their right hands, crowning, a kiss and sometimes circling around the altar, according to Boswell. These rites "most likely signified a marriage in the eyes of most ordinary Christians," he concluded.[8]

Critics argued that Boswell — who died six months after the book's publication — exaggerated, misconstrued or misrepresented the ceremonies described in the liturgies. They contended that the ceremonies blessed fraternal adoptions or friendships, not physical relationships. "To try to make scripture condoning the homosexual lifestyle or somehow blessing it, it's just not there," says Crews, a Presbyterian minister.

In a sympathetic assessment on a gay-history Web site, Fordham University Professor Paul Halsall today calls Boswell's thesis "groundbreaking" but acknowledges criticisms from various experts, including some openly gay professors.

But James Brundage, a professor of law and history at the University of Kansas who specializes in the medieval period, says Boswell's thesis has few supporters today. "The academic historians no longer take that book all that seriously," he says.

Whatever acceptance same-sex relationships had enjoyed earlier, European religious and secular authorities adopted unambiguous opposition, according to Eskridge. Beginning in the 13th century, governments enacted the first laws prohibiting "crimes against nature," he writes, and prior ecclesiastical laws "came to be more stringently enforced."[9]

Despite the opposition, same-sex relationships survived in the modern West, both in Europe and in the United States. Homosexual subcultures have existed in many European cities since the 18th century and by the beginning of the 20th century in such U.S. cities as New York, Chicago, San Francisco and Washington.

CHRONOLOGY

1950s-1970s *U.S. gay-liberation movement emerges; gay marriage debated.*

1951 Publication of *The Homosexual in America*.

1969 Gay-liberation movement energized after two days of rioting, triggered by police raid on Stonewall Inn, a popular New York City gay bar; many early leaders are skeptical of or opposed to gay marriage.

1971 In first American appellate decision on same-sex marriage, Minnesota Supreme Court upholds refusal to issue marriage license for gay couple.

1979 First National Gay and Lesbian Civil Rights March draws estimated 100,000 people to Washington, D.C.

1980s *Gay rights advances, but social conservatives strengthen their opposition; AIDS becomes an epidemic.*

1984 Berkeley, Calif., becomes first city to provide domestic-partner benefits for gays and lesbians.

1986 U.S. Supreme Court upholds state laws prohibiting consensual homosexual sodomy.

1987 Sweden provides most legal benefits of marriage to cohabiting couples, including same-sex couples; similar laws enacted in Denmark (1989) and Norway (1993).

1990s *First U.S. court rulings to hint at recognition of same-sex unions provoke strong resistance from social conservatives.*

1993 Hawaii Supreme Court says state must justify its prohibition of same-sex marriages. . . . second gay-rights march on Washington draws crowd officially estimated at 300,000.

1994 Historian John Boswell publishes book claiming medieval Catholic Church routinely sanctified same-sex unions; thesis is widely publicized and criticized.

1996 U.S. Supreme Court on May 20 invalidates Colorado initiative barring anti-gay discrimination measures. . . . President Bill Clinton on Sept. 21 signs Defense of Marriage Act, denying federal recognition to same-sex marriages and buttressing similar refusals by states; 37 states enact similar laws by 2003. . . . Hawaii trial court on Dec. 2 rules ban on same-sex marriage is unconstitutional.

1998 Alaska trial judge on Feb. 27 issues preliminary ruling requiring state to justify same-sex marriage ban. . . . Alaska voters approve constitutional amendment on Nov. 3 prohibiting homosexual marriage; Hawaii voters approve amendment same day authorizing legislature to bar same-sex marriage.

1999 Vermont Supreme Court on Dec. 20 orders state to allow same-sex couples to enjoy legal benefits accorded to heterosexuals.

2000-Present *Gay-rights advocates and social conservatives continue to battle over same-sex unions.*

2000 California voters on March 7 approve Proposition 22 barring recognition of same-sex marriages. . . . Vermont Gov. Howard Dean on April 26 signs legislation creating "civil union" status for same-sex couples, effective July 1. . . . The Netherlands on Sept. 12 enacts first nationwide law officially recognizing same-sex marriage.

2001 Seven gay and lesbian couples file same-sex marriage suit in state court in Boston on April 11. Trial judge upholds ban on same-sex marriage on May 8, 2002.

2002 *New York Times* in September becomes most prominent newspaper to publish announcements of same-sex commitment ceremonies.

2003 Belgium recognizes same-sex marriage on Jan. 30. . . . Supreme Judicial Court of Massachusetts hears arguments March 4 in gay-marriage suit. . . . Ontario's high court on June 10 orders the province to immediately allow same-sex couples to marry. . . . U.S. Supreme Court on June 26 rules state laws banning gay sex unconstitutional. . . . Three Democratic candidates for president endorse gay marriage in July 15 forum before gay-rights group; six others favor granting legal benefits to same-sex couples. . . . President Bush says on July 30 he wants to "codify" definition of marriage as between one man, one woman.

Disputed Studies Give Gay Parents Good Marks

Mark Brown always wanted to have children, but his partner Bob Cesario liked the quiet privacy of a kid-free home. After more than 20 years together, however, the one-time college sweethearts finally decided a few years ago they were ready — as Mark puts it — "to get pregnant."

Now, with a 4-year-old daughter and infant son in their Los Angeles home, Mark goes to the office every day, while Bob's acting career is on hold as he devotes most of his time to parenting.

"He's the stay-at-home dad, the soccer mom," Mark says. "He's the primary caregiver while I'm out making a living."

Their children, Ella and Sander Brown, are among the estimated 1 million to 9 million youngsters being raised in the United States today by gay or lesbian parents — by either same-sex couples or single parents.[1] The number is almost certainly on the rise, as gay men and lesbians increasingly turn to adoption, co-parenting, surrogacy or assisted reproduction to bring children into their lives and homes.

Gay-advocacy groups are proud of the trend. "There are all sorts of kids being raised out there in wonderful homes headed by gay parents," says David Buckel, a staff attorney with Lambda Legal Defense and Education Fund in New York City.

Religious and social conservatives, however, view the development as a dangerous social experiment. "The traditional structure of one-man-one-woman marriage is clearly the best structure for raising children," says Connie Mackey, vice president for government affairs at the Washington-based Family Research Council.

But a range of child welfare, medical, and other professional groups agree with gay organizations that children who grow up in same-sex households fare as well overall as children raised by heterosexual parents. In the most comprehensive position paper on the issue, a task force of the American Academy of Pediatrics concludes, "No data have pointed to any risk to children of growing up in a family with one or more gay parents."[2]

The report, published in February 2002, catalogued some 20 published research papers studying gay and lesbian parents and their children. It concluded that there was "no systematic difference" between gay and non-gay parents in emotional health, parenting skills or attitudes toward parenting.

Most studies also indicate no substantial differences in emotional and social development or in gender identity and sexual orientation between children of gay parents and those of heterosexual parents. If anything, some studies suggest advantages for children raised by homosexual parents — such as greater tolerance of diversity or less aggressiveness than children raised by heterosexuals.

Critics generally claim the studies are flawed — because of poor design, small sample size or researchers' bias. The studies "are all gravely deficient," Robert Lerner and Althea Nagai, partners in a social-science research consulting firm, write in a paper posted on an anti-gay marriage Web site.[3]

However, one British study often cited by critics found that children raised by lesbians were slightly more likely to consider having a same-sex partner than children of single mothers. The study examined 27 households in each group and conducted follow-up interviews with 46 children from the two groups 14 years later.[4]

Lynn Wardle, a law professor at Brigham Young University in Provo, Utah, says the study proves children of homosexual parents are "more likely to experiment with homosexual behavior." He goes on to say that homosexuality among adolescents "is associated with" alcohol and drug abuse and multiple sexual partners. "Before we endorse [gay parenting], we ought to think very seriously about what life would be like for those children," Wardle says.

Ellen Perrin, the head of the pediatrics group's task force and a professor at New England Medical Center in Boston, says critics like Wardle ignore a second finding of the study: that the number of children who eventually identified themselves as homosexual was roughly equal in the two groups. She says it was "no surprise" that more children of lesbian parents were open to same-sex behavior because they had grown up with someone who had a same-sex partner.

One gay-friendly researcher, however, says she suspects that further studies may show that a "slightly higher minority" of children of homosexual parents turn out to be "not exclusively heterosexual" than children of straight parents. But Judith Stacey, a professor of sociology at New York University, adds, "The majority of gay people have straight parents, and the majority of gay parents have straight kids."

For his part, Brown scoffs at the notion that a parent's sexual orientation affects his or her child's. "Every gay person I know was raised by extremely heterosexual parents," Brown says. "I don't think it has any bearing whatsoever."

Stacey, along with a colleague at her former school, the University of Southern California, shifted the debate on gay parenting somewhat when they co-wrote a 2001 article claiming evidence of "beneficial effects" on children raised in homosexual households. She and Timothy Biblarz — who are both heterosexual — concluded in the paper that there was "suggestive evidence" of "modest and interesting" differences between children raised by gay parents and those raised by straight parents.[5]

Stacey says that many of those differences are likely to be advantages, not disadvantages, for the kids in gay households. She suspects the unconventional path to parenthood taken by gay men and lesbians is responsible for the differences. "Gay parenting is one of the most planned forms of parenting," Stacey says. "You don't have accidental kids, you don't have unplanned kids." Heterosexuals, Stacey adds, are much more likely to "wander backwards into parenting."

After more than 20 years together, Mark Brown, left, and his partner Bob Cesario are raising a 4-year-old daughter and an infant son. Bob, an actor, is the "stay at home dad," says Mark, who works full time.

children of parents who are gay or lesbian," Perrin says. "But there is also an awful lot that we don't know about the children of parents who are heterosexual."

Wardle agrees. "There are a few things we know that raise startling issues," he says. "There are also a lot of things we don't know because these [parenting arrangements] are so new."

Brown, a television writer and producer who is co-president of the Los Angeles gay fathers group the Pop Luck Club, believes most gay parents are "extremely conscientious, conscious and very loving." He adds, "Children thrive in a loving environment, whether that child has a single parent, a gay parent or a straight parent."

Brown and Cesario, both 48, took a somewhat conventional path to parenthood: adoption. They adopted Ella through an agency and 4-month-old Sander through a private placement. Both children are biracial: mixed black and white. Under an executive order signed by California Gov. Gray Davis in 1999, the two men adopted both children jointly. Gay or lesbian couples in most other states have to follow a two-step procedure, with adoption first by one of the partners and then a "second-parent adoption" by the other.

Adoption by gay or lesbian couples is prohibited by law in three states and generally not allowed by judges in several others. A constitutional challenge to Florida's statute, which prohibits adoption by gay or lesbian individuals or couples, is currently pending before the federal appeals court in Atlanta.[6] Mississippi's law prohibits adoption by gay or lesbian couples, but not individuals; Utah's prohibits adoption by any cohabiting couple.

Other homosexuals take more difficult paths to parenthood, parallel to routes chosen by infertile heterosexual parents. Some gay men "co-parent" with single lesbians or lesbian couples — often, with sperm provided by the man used to artificially inseminate the birth mother. Some women use sperm from anonymous donors for an otherwise natural birth. Some gay men provide sperm to a woman who serves as surrogate mother — so-called traditional surrogacy. And some men or women use so-called "gestational surrogacy" — where a woman's embryo is fertilized with a man's sperm and then implanted in a woman who carries the child to term.

Experts and advocates on both sides agree that further studies are needed about the effects of gay parenting on children. "There is an awful lot that we don't know about

As for marriage, Brown and Cesario have not given it much thought. "We joke sometimes that it would jinx us," Brown says. "Our relationship has worked so well that if we formalized it, we might get divorced."

Brown has had second thoughts, however, since the family returned from a niece's wedding in Boston in June. Ella enjoyed the wedding a lot, Brown says, and asked afterward whether he and Cesario were married. "Daddy and Poppa are married in our hearts and minds," Brown told her.

"I would love to get married," Brown says now. "It would be particularly joyous for us to get married in front of our children. If it were legal, I'd go out and get married tomorrow."

[1] Edward O. Laumann, "National Health and Social Life Survey, 1995," cited in American Academy of Pediatrics, "Technical Report: Coparent or Second-Parent Adoption by Same-Sex Parents," Vol. 109, No. 2 (February 2002), pp. 341-344.

[2] *Ibid.*, p. 344.

[3] Robert Lerner and Althea K. Nagai, "No Basis: What the Studies *Don't* Tell Us About Same-Sex Parenting," January 2001 (www.marriagewatch.org).

[4] S. Golombok, F. Tasker, C. Murray, "Children Raised in Fatherless Families From Infancy: Family Relationships and the Socioemotional Development of Children of Lesbian and Single Heterosexual Mothers," in *Journal of Child Psychology and Psychiatry*, Vol. 38 (1997), pp. 783-791.

[5] Judith Stacey and Timothy J. Biblarz, "(How) Does the Sexual Orientation of Parents Matter?" *American Sociological Review*, Vol. 66 (April 2001), pp. 159-183. Biblarz is an associate professor of sociology at USC.

[6] The case is *Lofton v. Kearney*, 01-16723-DD. The Florida law was upheld by a U.S. District Court Aug. 30, 2001; the case was argued before the 11th U.S. Circuit Court of Appeals in March.

Courtesy Mark Brown

Demonstrators in Chicago march in celebration of the U.S. Supreme Court's landmark June 26 ruling striking down a Texas law against gay sex. The ruling did not deal directly with same-sex marriage, but gay-rights advocates say it supports the gay-marriage suit pending in Massachusetts.

Typically, same-sex couples were discreet, but by the mid-20th century interest in openly partnering was increasing. By the 1960s, the early forerunners of today's gay-rights groups were debating marriage, and some couples were engaging in mock wedding ceremonies. As Eskridge concludes, however, "these 'marriages' enjoyed neither legal recognition nor the prospect of legal recognition."[10]

Coming Out

In the 1970s, gay and lesbian couples began trying to legally marry, but courts uniformly rebuffed their efforts through the 1980s. However, the issue was not a high priority within the growing gay-rights movement. Opinions were divided about the importance — or even the value — of marriage. Besides, gay-rights advocates had more pressing issues to pursue, such as job discrimination, anti-sodomy laws and AIDS.[11]

The debate within the gay and lesbian community dated to 1951, when the first major homosexual manifesto in the United States was published: *The Homosexual in America*, written by the pseudonymous Donald Webster Cory. In a chapter on relationships, Cory concluded that homosexuals should be allowed to marry. But he reached that view only after what Eskridge calls an "agonized" discussion citing self-hatred and promiscuity as impediments to stable relationships among gay men.

The nascent gay-liberation movement emerged energized and radicalized after a police raid on the Stonewall Inn, a popular Greenwich Village bar, touched off two days of rioting by homosexual activists in New York City in 1969. Marriage, however, was not a widely shared goal. Leaders of the Gay Liberation Front denounced it as "one of the most insidious and basic sustainers of the system" and family as "the microcosm of oppression." Marriage, in this view, stifled sexual freedom, oppressed women and propped up the capitalist system.

Demand for formalized relationships was nonetheless emerging among gay and lesbian couples by the late 1960s. The gay-welcoming Universal Fellowship of Metropolitan Community Churches began conducting ceremonies for same-sex couples in 1968. Gay and lesbian synagogues followed suit in the early '70s. In Minnesota, a gay couple — Richard John Baker and James Michael McConnell — were married in a religious ceremony in 1970 and then unsuccessfully applied for a state marriage license. They sued in state court, contending that the denial of the license was unconstitutional. In the first appellate decision in the United States on same-sex marriage, the Minnesota Supreme Court rejected their plea in 1971.[12]

Public officials and courts in other jurisdictions responded in kind, with only isolated exceptions. In 1975, the Boulder County (Colo.) clerk issued marriage licenses to at least six same-sex couples after receiving approval from the county district attorney. After public protests, the state attorney general ordered the practice stopped. In Washington, D.C., a city councilman introduced a proposal to legalize gay marriage but withdrew it after strong opposition from religious groups. Gay couples who took the issue to court ran into a stone wall. As Yale law Professor Eskridge notes, between 1971 and 1993 every judge to consider the issue ruled that same-sex couples had no statutory or constitutional right to marry.[13]

With divided opinion within the community and stout resistance without, gay-rights advocates put marriage on a back burner through the 1980s and concentrated on other issues — with some success. In 1981, Wisconsin became the first state to prohibit discrimination on the basis of sexual orientation in housing, employment or public accommodations. Many states repealed anti-sodomy laws used to prosecute homosexual behavior, though advocates of gay rights were disappointed by the U.S. Supreme Court's 1986 decision upholding the constitutionality of such measures.[14] Nonetheless, gay-rights advocates won a measure of recognition for same-sex couples by persuading some city and state governments — starting with Berkeley, Calif., in 1984 — to provide domestic-partner benefits to gays.

The debate over marriage within the gay community became more visible in 1989 after an extraordinary debate between two top officials of the Lambda Legal Defense and Education Fund published in a gay journal. Executive Director Thomas Stoddard argued that marriage was "the issue most likely to lead ultimately to a world free from discrimination against lesbians and gay men." Legal Director Paula Ettelbrick countered that marriage would force homosexuals "into the mainstream" and divert the movement's efforts at broader social reforms.[15]

Despite the ongoing debate, most gay men and lesbians responding to a mail-in survey in 1994 in *The Advocate*, a gay newsmagazine, wanted the option of getting married. Among gay men, 59 percent said they would want to marry another man if they could, and another 26 percent said they might. In a similar survey of lesbians in 1995, seven of 10 respondents said they would marry if legally permitted.[16]

Defending Marriage

Efforts to win legal recognition for same-sex unions intensified during the 1990s — spurred by favorable court rulings in Hawaii and Alaska and by an apparent increase in monogamy among gay and lesbian couples. Despite growing social acceptance of homosexuality, however, the new trend in the courts provoked a forceful backlash. The Hawaii and Alaska rulings were effectively nullified by state constitutional amendments, while Congress and two-thirds of the states passed laws aimed at barring recognition of same-sex marriage. However, at decade's end, Vermont had became the first state to grant

same-sex couples marriage-like benefits in a newly created status: civil unions.

The Hawaii case began with a suit filed in 1991 in state court by three homosexual couples seeking to invalidate the statutory exclusion of same-sex marriage on either state or federal constitutional grounds.[17] A trial judge rejected the suit, but the Hawaii Supreme Court gave the plaintiffs a precedent-setting interim victory in May 1993. The court ruled that the same-sex marriage ban amounted to discrimination on the basis of sex and could be upheld under Hawaii's constitution only if the state could show a "compelling" government interest to justify it.[18]

When the case was back in the trial court, the state defended the same-sex marriage ban on the ground that gay and lesbian couples would not be sufficiently good parents. Rejecting the argument, the judge ruled the same-sex marriage ban unconstitutional in December 1996 but stayed the decision pending appeal. While the appeal was pending, opponents of same-sex marriage won voter ratification of a constitutional amendment in November 1998 authorizing the legislature to limit marriage to heterosexual couples. In 1999, the state Supreme Court interpreted the amendment to retroactively validate the same-sex marriage ban — eliminating any need for legislative action.[19]

A similar suit filed by a gay couple in Alaska started along a comparable course but was cut short by a constitutional amendment at an earlier stage. The judge in the case gave the plaintiffs a preliminary victory in February 1998 by ruling that the state had to justify denying them their "fundamental" right to choose a partner.[20] The state appealed to Alaska's Supreme Court, but within the year the legislature approved and voters ratified a constitutional amendment defining marriage as a union between one man and one woman.

The Hawaii case raised fears among opponents that a final ruling for the plaintiffs could force the other 49 states to recognize gay marriages sanctioned there. As the suit moved toward trial, Congress moved quickly — in an election year — to enact federal legislation aimed at thwarting any state court rulings in favor of gay marriage. The Defense of Marriage Act (DOMA) — passed overwhelmingly by both houses and signed into law by President Bill Clinton on Sept. 21, 1996 — declared that states were not obligated to recognize any same-sex marriages that might be legally sanctioned in other states. It

Lifting the Lid on Gay Domestic Violence

Like many of Stephen's rages, it comes on unexpectedly. One minute, he is preparing dinner, "chatting and bopping around." The next, he is livid, furious that his lover, Patrick, has cut the carrots wrong.

"Look at these!" he shouts. "These are no good! With one swipe of his hand, the carrots are off the cutting board and onto the floor.

Seconds later, he is pummeling Patrick in the head, the face, the chest. Terrified, Patrick runs to the bedroom.

So begins *Men Who Beat the Men Who Love Them*, Patrick Letellier and David Island's account of same-sex domestic abuse.[1]

The 1991 book was the first to address the taboo topic of same-sex partner abuse, a problem that had been largely overlooked by the domestic-violence movement. Letellier and Island raised the then-radical notion that domestic abuse is as prevalent in gay couples as it is among straight couples, affecting an estimated 500,000 gay men nationwide.

"Domestic violence [is] the third-largest health problem facing gay men today," they wrote.[2]

While research into domestic violence among homosexuals is still in its infancy and often anecdotal, at least one large-scale scientific study corroborates the authors' claim.[3] It surveyed 2,881 gay men from four cities and found that two in five respondents had experienced domestic violence. Other smaller studies suggest that domestic violence may occur in an even greater number of lesbian relationships.[4] By comparison, domestic violence occurs in 25 to 33 percent of straight relationships.[5]

Despite these findings, many straight people doubt there is much same-sex domestic violence. Most people are socialized to see men as dominant and women as passive and cannot picture men as victims and women as batterers, researchers say.

Claire Renzetti, a sociology professor at Saint Joseph's College in Philadelphia, says that when she speaks about the topic in public, people "act really surprised, or almost find it humorous, like it's one more oddity."

Gays and lesbians themselves often are reluctant to discuss homosexual abuse. Lesbian women may be unwilling to shatter a "utopic vision of a peaceful, women-centered world," and gay men may want to maintain the illusion that they are somehow more evolved than the paternalistic, dominant society they live in, explains Sandra E. Lundy, a Boston lawyer and author of a 1993 *New England Law Review* article about homosexual abuse.[6]

Others feel so threatened by societal homophobia that they don't want to acknowledge internal problems. "When you're always focused on the violence from without, seeing it from within can be very scary," says Melissa Bates, a victim advocate with the Violence Recovery Program at Fenway Community Health in Boston.

The gay community may also be suppressing the problem out of fear that statistics on same-sex domestic violence will be exploited to derail gay marriage, says Rachel Baum, associate director of the New York City-based National Coalition of Anti-Violence Programs, which compiles statistics on abuse. "People don't want to give ammunition to antis who would say our relationships are sick and wrong," she says.

Victim advocates say the silence surrounding same-sex abuse, coupled with a lack of role models for healthy same-

also defined marriage and spouse in heterosexual terms for federal law, thus precluding homosexual couples from filing joint tax returns or obtaining any spousal benefits under Social Security or other federal programs.[21]

Some state legislatures had already approved comparable laws before Congress acted; more followed suit over the next few years. By the end of 2000, more than 30 states had so-called "mini-DOMAs" on the books. The list included three measures approved by voters in 2000: a ballot initiative adopted in March in California and constitutional amendments ratified in November in Nebraska and Nevada. All of the laws specifically defined marriage as the union of one man and one woman. Some appeared simply to bar same-sex marriage by the state's own residents; most went further and barred recognition of same-sex marriages sanctioned in other states, too.

Meanwhile, however, three homosexual couples in Vermont had won a landmark victory from the state's Supreme Court. In a nearly unanimous decision in December 1999, the court said that the state had to grant same-sex couples "the common benefits and protections that flow from marriage under Vermont law." The court left it up to the state legislature whether to legalize marriage — as the lone dissenting justice argued — or to

sex relationships, empowers batterers and makes it harder for victims to recognize that they are in abusive relationships.

"Batterers will try to define reality for their partners," says Beth Leventhal, executive director and founder of The Network/La Red, a Boston organization serving battered lesbians. "If it is the victim's first relationship after coming out, they will tell them, 'This is how we do things.' "

Even for those who decide to come forward, help is scant or non-existent. While a handful of hotlines and counseling programs have cropped up in major cities over the last 20 years, huge swaths of rural America remain without any services. "Victims can be a long way from resources in terms of mountain ranges, snow, you name it," says Denise de Percin, executive director of the Colorado Anti-Violence Program, which serves the entire state.

Battered-women's shelters are geared toward heterosexuals and may either refuse to serve lesbians or fail to screen applicants, enabling batterers to infiltrate the system.

Gay men and transgender individuals have even fewer shelter options, mostly limited to short-term emergency housing at hotels.

Only a handful of cities have treatment programs for batterers, forcing many to seek help at 12-step programs, anger-management classes and couples counseling. Meanwhile, treatment of same-sex violence by police forces varies dramatically. While some police forces are trained to handle same-sex domestic-violence calls, others have a hard time distinguishing victim from aggressor.[7]

Some officers "make judgments based on who the bigger partner is, or who the more butch or masculine partner is," Bates says. "Sometimes, even the victim is arrested." In cases where the victim fights back, law enforcement may label the violence "mutual abuse," assuming that it is a fight between equals.

Victims encounter even more inconsistencies in the courts. In some states, domestic-violence law applies only to heterosexual couples; in others, judges may issue mutual restraining orders.

Laws that prevent same-sex couples from adopting also work against victims. When the biological parent is the batterer, he or she can threaten that if the victim leaves he or she will never see the child again.[8]

Facing the prospect of institutional "re-victimization" by the police and courts, many victims choose not to come forward.

Shawna Virago, director of the domestic-violence survivor program at Community United Against Violence in San Francisco, says education about domestic abuse in general is the solution.

"It's a national epidemic of violence, and it's not being addressed," Virago says.

— Kelly Field

---

[1] David Island and Patrick Letellier, *Men Who Beat the Men Who Love Them* (1991), p. 1.

[2] *Ibid.*

[3] Gregory L. Greenwood, *et al.*, "Battering Victimization Among a Probability-Based Sample of Men Who Have Sex With Men," *American Journal of Public Health*, December 2002, pp. 1964-1969.

[4] Gwat-Yong Lie and S. Gentlewarrier, "Intimate Violence in Lesbian Relationships: Discussion of Survey Findings and Practice Implications," *Journal of Social Service Research*, 1991, p. 146.

[5] National Coalition Against Domestic Violence.

[6] Sandra E. Lundy, "Abuse That Dare Not Speak Its Name: Assisting Victims of Lesbian and Gay Domestic Violence in Boston," *New England Law Review*, winter 1993.

[7] National Coalition of Anti-Violence Programs, "Lesbian, Gay, Bisexual and Transgender Domestic Violence in 2002," July 2003, p. 17.

[8] Beth Leventhal and Sandra E. Lundy, eds., *Same Sex Domestic Violence* (1999), p. 21.

---

create some form of "parallel 'domestic-partnership' system."[22] With no room to maneuver, the legislature in April 2000 approved a bill creating a "civil union" status for homosexuals; then-Democratic Gov. Howard Dean signed it into law, to take effect on July 1.

'Marriage Equality'

Vermont's civil-union law was less than a year old when seven gay and lesbian couples filed a new suit seeking to legalize gay marriage in neighboring Massachusetts. *Goodridge v. Massachusetts Department of Public Health* became a major showdown on the issue, with a total of 26 friend-of-the-court briefs filed on both sides before the state's highest court heard arguments in March 2003.

Meanwhile, same-sex marriage was advancing in other countries — first in the Netherlands in September 2000 and then in Belgium and Canada in 2003. In addition, gay-marriage advocates say the U.S. Supreme Court's June 26 decision striking down state anti-sodomy laws laid the groundwork for broader legal equality for homosexuals in the United States.

The seven Massachusetts plaintiff couples stressed the practical problems resulting from being unable to marry.[23] Hillary Goodridge recalled that even with a legal document known as a health-care proxy she had difficulty visiting her partner Julie in the hospital when Julie had a difficult childbirth. Teacher Richard Linnell noted that his health insurance covered the child he jointly adopted with his partner, Gary Chalmers, but he had to pay extra for Chalmers. Gloria Bailey and Linda Davies said that as they considered retirement, they realized that they would face taxes that married couples would not have to pay in selling their home or their joint psychotherapy practice.

"Unequal treatment is inconsistent with the Constitution," Jennifer Levi, a GLAD attorney, said at an April 2001 news conference announcing the suit. "All these couples seek is equality."

Acting Gov. Jane Swift responded by restating her opposition to same-sex marriage. "I think that marriage and the recognition of marriage is an important institution in our commonwealth and in our country and should be for heterosexual couples," said Swift, a Republican.

In his 26-page opinion rejecting the suit a year later, Judge Thomas Connolly relied on what he called the "centuries-old" definition of marriage and the "central" role of procreation in marriage. "Recognizing that procreation is marriage's central purpose, it is rational for the legislature to limit marriage to opposite-sex couples who, theoretically, are capable of procreation," Connolly wrote. The judge said the plaintiffs should direct the plea to the legislature, not the courts.[24]

European countries, in fact, were dealing with the issue legislatively rather than judicially. Three Scandinavian countries had passed laws several years earlier granting legal benefits to same-sex couples: Sweden in 1987, Norway in 1989 and Denmark in 1993. The Netherlands went further in September 2000, legalizing marriage between persons of the same sex. The measure passed the Dutch parliament 109-33 after drawing opposition only from a few small Christian parties. Belgium, predominantly Catholic, followed suit in January 2003, but only after a more protracted parliamentary debate.

Justices on Massachusetts' high court actively questioned lawyers for both sides when the *Goodridge* case was before them on March 4.[25] "Why do you think that this is an issue that we should decide?" Justice Roderick Ireland asked Bonauto, representing the couples. Justice Martha Sosman asked whether a ruling for the couples would lead to recognizing polygamy.

But one justice noted the seeming paradox in allowing same-sex couples to adopt children, but not to marry each other. "Are those ideas somewhat at odds?" Justice John Greaney asked Judith Yogman, the assistant state attorney general handling the case. Some observers saw the questioning as encouraging for the plaintiffs, but others cautioned against making predictions.

While the Massachusetts justices deliberated the case, the Canadian government took steps to become the third Western country to officially recognize same-sex marriage. Prime Minister Jean Chretien announced on June 17 that his government would prepare legislation to recognize gay marriage — a week after Ontario's highest court ordered immediate recognition of same-sex marriage in Canada's most populous provinces.[26] Provincial courts in British Columbia and Quebec had also backed gay marriage in earlier rulings.

The U.S. Supreme Court's 6-3 decision striking down anti-sodomy laws gave gay-marriage advocates further encouragement. Justice Anthony M. Kennedy's opinion for the majority noted that the case did not involve "whether the government must give formal recognition to any relationship that homosexual persons seek to enter."

In dissent, however, Justice Antonin Scalia said the June 26 ruling left laws limiting marriage to opposite-sex couples on "pretty shaky grounds." *Newsweek's* cover story on the decision framed the issue dramatically: "Is Gay Marriage Next?"[27]

CURRENT SITUATION

Making Commitments

Deb Price and Joyce Murdoch have been a committed couple since 1985, but the two Washington, D.C., journalists feel like newlyweds since they were married in Toronto on June 27.

"Tears welled up in my eyes as I realized that after 18 years together, Joyce and I were being legally wed," Price, a reporter for *The Detroit News*, writes in her syndicated gay-lifestyle column. She says she and Murdoch "have been dizzy" adjusting to their new status as "spouses."[28]

"Both of us were really shocked at how moving it felt, how we had this feeling of being brought back into this institution that goes back thousands of years," says Murdoch, managing editor for politics at the weekly magazine *National Journal.* "It was this wonderful new page."

AT ISSUE

Should gay marriage be legally recognized?

YES — Mary Bonauto
Civil Rights Project Director, Gay and Lesbian Advocates and Defenders (GLAD)

Excerpted from The Glad Web Site, Aug. 15, 2003

Marriage is a major building block for strong families and communities. Weddings are an opportunity for friends, family and neighbors to come together to recognize a couple's lifelong commitment to one another. This occasion strengthens a couple's bond and marks their inclusion as a family into the communities of which they are a part.

But marriage is much more than that. First, it is a unique relationship — synonymous with "family" — so that if you are "married," no one would dare challenge a person's right to be by his or her spouse's side. The word itself is one of the protections. Second, it is a gateway to hundreds of legal protections established by the state and over 1,000 by the federal government. Married couples can take for granted rights of hospital visitation, security for their children and rights of inheritance.

While gay and lesbian families can protect themselves in limited ways by creating wills, health-care proxies and co-parent adoptions, this does not come close to emulating the automatic protections and peace of mind that marriage confers. People cannot contract their way into changing pension laws, survivorship rights, worker's-compensation dependency protection or the tax system, to name just a few.

Marriage is also a social institution of the highest importance, the ultimate expression of love and commitment. While it remains exclusive to opposite-sex couples, gay men and lesbians will continue to fall short of the status of full citizenship, marking them and their children with a stamp of inferiority. Denying the security that marriage can bring only serves to weaken gay and lesbian families and the communities of which they are a part.

Far from undermining marriage, the struggle for full equality for gay and lesbian couples is an acknowledgement of the importance marriage has in society and the power it has over all our lives. Increasing access to marriage for adults in committed relationships will strengthen the institution, not weaken it. Marriage will not be destroyed by allowing same-sex couples to marry, just as it was not destroyed by women's equality within marriage or the repeal of interracial marriage bans.

In seeking the freedom to marry, gay and lesbian couples simply ask that their relationships be given the same respect under law accorded to others, so that they may obtain the security and protection their families need.

NO — Ron Crews
President, Massachusetts Family Institute

Written for The CQ Researcher, August 2003

The push for legalizing homosexual "marriage" is based on at least three myths: that same-sex sexual behavior is genetic and unchangeable, that homosexual relationships are just like marriage between a man and a woman and that children raised by same-sex couples do just as well as those with a married mother and father. None of these myths is true.

The definition of marriage is based on the fact that all human beings from conception have, in every cell of their bodies, either XX chromosomes if they are female or XY chromosomes if they are male. Even a sex-change operation and hormone treatments cannot change those chromosomes.

These permanent distinctions make for a permanent definition of what it means to be married. This has been the legal, social, historical and theological definition of marriage throughout the ages.

On the other hand, sexual orientation, or same-sex attraction, can and does change. Jeffrey Satinover, psychiatrist and author of *Homosexuality and the Politics of Truth,* states that a major study, conducted for U.S. agencies tracking the AIDS epidemic found that 75 percent of boys who at age 16 think they are homosexual become permanently heterosexual by age 25 without any intervention. Furthermore, the average lifespan of those who practice homosexual sex is reduced by approximately 20 years, often leaving children orphaned.

Same-sex couples may look in some respects like a married couple, but they are missing the essential element. They may have children; but an orphanage has children. That does not make it a marriage. They may have long-term committed relationships. Parents and children, brothers and sisters and friends have long-term committed relationships. That does not make a marriage. Only the union of a woman and a man, with immutable XX and XY chromosomes in every cell of their bodies, representing the two halves of the human race, can make a marriage and produce the next generation.

That next generation needs a mother and a father. Every reputable social science study done to date has affirmed that children do best, by whatever measure is used, when they have a married mom and dad. Deliberately depriving a child of a mother or father is cruel and unfair.

Do people with same-sex attraction deserve to be treated with dignity? Absolutely! Do we need to change the definition of marriage to please them? Absolutely not!

Price and Murdoch are among the hundreds of U.S. couples who have crossed into Canada to be married since Ontario's provincial court ruled in favor of same-sex marriage on June 10. Canada beckons not only because it is geographically close but also because it imposes no citizenship or residency requirement — unlike the other countries to recognize same-sex marriage, the Netherlands and Belgium.

The sudden surge of cross-border gay marriages is only one sign of the increasing visibility of same-sex couples throughout the United States. More than 200 U.S. newspapers — most prominently, *The New York Times* — now publish same-sex couples' announcements of commitment ceremonies.[29] *Bride's* magazine, the leading mass-circulation bridal magazine, has a one-page news story about same-sex unions in its current issue.[30]

Getty Images/Douglas McFadd

Karen Ahlers and Michelle Blair walk down the aisle after exchanging symbolic marriage vows at First Parish Church of Framingham, Mass., on Aug. 2. Gay-rights advocates say religious groups can decide for themselves whether to perform marriages but shouldn't have a say in whether civil marriages are legalized. Episcopal Church leaders in early August gave U.S. dioceses the option of blessing same-sex unions.

Recognition of same-sex couples by the mainstream media has been dramatically mirrored on network TV. This year's Tony Awards featured two winning male gay-partner song writers sharing a celebratory kiss. And this summer's new reality show "Boy Meets Boy" follows high-profile gay-oriented shows like the over-the-top "Will and Grace" and the new make-over show "Queer Eye for the Straight Guy," in which five gay men transform clueless straight men into cool guys.

For its part, the U.S. Census Bureau reported in March that it found 594,000 same-sex couples living together in its 2000 population count — a threefold increase over the number recorded in 1990.[31] The number — almost equally divided between gay and lesbian couples — represents about 1 percent of households nationwide.

Demographers and other experts on gay issues say that the actual number is almost certainly higher. The reported increase since 1990 is attributed in large part to an increased willingness of same-sex couples to disclose their status.

"Many gay and lesbian couples felt more comfortable acknowledging their relationship to the government [in 2000] than they did in 1990," says Gary Gates, a research associate at the Urban Institute, a liberal-leaning research organization in Washington. "That results from the increasing acceptance of same-sex couples in our society."

About one-third of the lesbian couples (34.3 percent) and one-fourth of the gay couples (22.3 percent) have children in their households, according to Census data. The comparable figure is 45.6 percent for married-couple households and 43.1 percent for unmarried opposite-sex couples.

The Census data also showed an increase in the number of unmarried opposite-sex couples — from 3.2 million in 1990 to 5.5 million in 2000. Social conservatives found the statistics distressing.

"It's a continuing trend that has been growing," Allan Carlson, a fellow at the Family Research Council, told *The New York Times*. "It's not a healthy thing. The commitments that go with cohabitation are not as firm or strong as marriage." [32]

Gates says other Census data indicate that same-sex couples are in between unmarried opposite-sex couples and married couples on other measures of social stability. Two-thirds of same-sex couples own their homes — compared to 43 percent of unmarried opposite-sex couples and 81 percent of married couples. Slightly over one-third (38 percent) of same-sex couples live in the same households as five years ago — compared to 18 percent for unmarried opposite-sex couples and 58 percent of married couples.

"I find it fascinating that even in the absence of marriage, gay and lesbian couples exhibit traits that have fairly high measures of stability," Gates says. "At the same time, there are many rights and privileges associated with marriage that same-sex couples don't have. Over the lifetime, it's much more difficult to be a same-sex couple than a married couple."

After 12 years together, Martin Grochala and Fred Reuland have been through those problems: the difficulties of being open about their relationship, the fear of rejection by friends or family and the extra steps that a gay couple has to take to maintain a household and protect their lives and property. When the Chicago couple observed a commitment ceremony in July, however, the friend they selected to preside urged them to view those difficulties as a cause for celebration rather than regret.

"Yes, there are challenges," Grochala says today. "But rather than saying woe are us, he told us those challenges are wonderful opportunities to be the best persons we can be."

Debating Marriage

Gay-rights advocates are broadening and intensifying their push for same-sex marriage while waiting for what many expect to be a favorable ruling from the Massachusetts high court. Opponents, in turn, are stepping up their efforts to thwart any state court rulings to sanction same-sex relationships through federal legislation or a constitutional amendment, if necessary.

Opinion polls indicate a decline in support for same-sex relationships since the Supreme Court's June decision in the Texas anti-sodomy case. Anti-gay groups say the shift amounts to a backlash against gay marriage and other parts of what they call the gay agenda. Gay-rights advocates depict the shift as a short-term dip and cite the

Ten States Have Laws on Adoption by Gays

Although laws in only 10 states specifically allow gay and lesbian couples to adopt kids, 96 percent of all U.S. counties have at least one same-sex couple raising children under 18.

States Allowing Adoption by Gay Couples	
California	Pennsylvania
Connecticut	Massachusetts
Illinois	Vermont
New Jersey	Washington
New York	Wisconsin

Source: Urban Institute, May 30, 2003

majority support for same-sex marriage among young people as an indication of the long-term trend of public opinion on the issue.

Gay-rights groups are working to mobilize support for same-sex marriage from like-minded organizations and individuals outside the gay and lesbian community. Lambda Legal, for example, is gathering endorsements from a wide variety of religious and civil-liberties organizations, political figures and celebrities from entertainment, business and other professions. "As with any civil-rights movement, there is a need to reach out to allies, particularly non-gay allies," Freedom to Marry's Wolfson explains.

In the largest effort for mass support, Human Rights Campaign, the gay political-action organization, is using a Web site (www.millionformarriage.org) to seek 1 million signatures on a petition supporting gay marriage. As of early September, the site claimed more than 155,000 signatures.

On the opposite side, socially conservative groups are stepping up their media and outreach efforts on the issue. "The gay community has forced the agenda," says Mackey of the Family Research Council, "so people are now having to respond."

As one example, the Traditional Values Coalition, a conservative Christian group, says it is sending out 1.5 million mailings a month to conservative voters to enlist support for a constitutional amendment to bar same-sex marriage. "I call this the defining moment for American Christianity," the Rev. Lou Sheldon, founder of the group, told *The Washington Post.* "What is at stake is no less than the doctrine of creation."[33]

Opponents are focusing in part on a possible amendment to the U.S. Constitution to block any state from recognizing same-sex marriage or from being required to recognize a same-sex marriage granted in any other state. Three days after the Supreme Court decision in the gay-sex case, Senate Majority Leader Bill Frist, R-Tenn., told a television interviewer that he "absolutely" supported a constitutional amendment to bar gay marriage. In

Gay-Marriage Issue Poses Political Risks

The gay-marriage issue poses risks for both Republicans and Democrats in next year's presidential election. Some conservatives, like former presidential candidate Gary Bauer — now president of the conservative American Values group — say it will be a defining "values" issue for voters.

President Bush will no doubt by pressured to elaborate on his marriage-is-between-a-man-and-a-woman position. In doing so, he'll have to keep the Christian right wing of his party happy without alienating moderate GOP and independent voters favoring individual privacy over government intrusiveness.

"I can't imagine the White House being AWOL on that debate and just repeating, 'We believe marriage is between a man and a woman,'" Bauer says. "You've got to put a policy on the table to implement the values of your supporters. Otherwise, why would your supporters continue to be engaged in your coalition?"[1]

Meanwhile, Vice President Dick Cheney's wife Lynn — a conservative stalwart — calls the idea that government has any business in people's bedrooms "a stretch."[2] Cheney's daughter is gay, as is Democratic presidential candidate Richard Gephardt's. Both are actively campaigning for their fathers.

Still another branch of the GOP, the gay Log Cabin Republicans, may also push Bush to take a stand. "The Bush administration is going to have to decide to go on record" embracing gays "as part of the American family and the Republican Party," said Patrick Guerriero, the former Melrose, Mass., mayor who now heads the group.

Democratic candidates also have been reluctant to endorse gay marriage. At a July forum sponsored by Human Rights Campaign, all nine Democratic presidential candidates endorsed same-sex partnership benefits, but none of the major candidates has embraced gay marriage.

The gay-marriage issue could affect Democrats' performance in the Midwest, the southern Border States, rural areas and among over-50 Americans — all key demographic segments where support for gay rights is weaker than among urban, coastal and younger voters.

---

[1] Quoted in Susan Page, "Gay Rights Tough to Sharpen into Political 'Wedge Issue,'" *USA Today*, July 28 2003, p. A10.

[2] Frank Rich, "Gay Kiss: Business As Usual," *The New York Times*, June 22, 2003.

August, however, Frist said the issue was not on the Senate's agenda for the rest of the year.[34]

For his part, President Bush told a news conference on July 30 that he favors legally limiting marriage to heterosexual couples. "I believe marriage is between a man and a woman, and I believe we ought to codify that one way or the other, and we have lawyers looking at the best way to do that," Bush said.

A proposed amendment introduced by Rep. Marilyn Musgrave, R-Colo., would define marriage only as "a union of a man and a woman." It would then stipulate that the U.S. Constitution, state constitutions or state or federal laws cannot be construed to require that "marital status or the legal incidents thereof be conferred upon unmarried couples or groups."

Some opponents of gay marriage are not convinced a constitutional amendment is necessary. "We would favor defense-of-marriage acts in every state and if necessary a constitutional amendment," Mackey says. Others think Musgrave's amendment may not go far enough. "We want to see an amendment that would prevent civil unions and domestic partnership, one that would prevent the legal recognition of same-sex partnerships no matter what you call it," says Sandy Rios, president of Concerned Women of America.

Gay-marriage supporters, on the other hand, say the amendment goes too far by effectively prohibiting any marriage-like arrangements between same-sex partners. The amendment "limits all the indicia of marriage," including rights of inheritance, child support or health-care decision making, according to Vincent Samar, who teaches a course on sexual orientation and the law at Chicago's Kent College of Law. Samar calls the amendment "dangerous."[35]

To be ratified, a constitutional amendment must be approved by two-thirds majorities in both houses of Congress and then by legislatures in three-fourths (38) of the states. Supporters acknowledge ratification faces an uphill battle. But a recent opinion poll indicates majority support for either a law or constitutional amendment to ban gay marriage.

The poll, conducted for The Associated Press by International Communications Research, reported that 52 percent of respondents favored and 41 percent opposed a law to ban gay marriage. A constitutional amendment to define marriage as one man and one woman was supported by 54 percent of respondents and opposed by 42 percent. The poll also found a majority — 53 percent — opposed to laws allowing gays or lesbians to form a civil union with marriage-like benefits.

OUTLOOK

Brave New World?

In his argument for recognizing same-sex marriage in the mid-1990s, Yale law Professor Eskridge predicted the move would bring about significant changes in the gay community and in society at large. Same-sex marriage, he wrote, "civilizes gays" — by fostering commitment, reducing promiscuity and promoting integration into the larger culture. It also "civilizes America," Eskridge said, by replacing homophobic "group hatred" with the kind of "group acceptance and cooperation" that is a source of American strength and pride.

Opponents of same-sex marriage envision significant change, too — but not for the better. Invoking the image of novelist Aldous Huxley's negative utopia, lawyers with the Marriage Watch Project at Catholic University, say in their amicus brief in the *Goodridge* case that the "proposed 'brave new world' of marriage" would necessarily lead to legalizing incest and polygamy [and] leave "moral restraints . . . consigned to the ash heap."

Advocates of same-sex marriage today dispute the dire predictions from opponents but also minimize, to some extent, the likely changes for the gay community or society at large. "Gay married couples will pay their taxes, enroll their kids in school and fight over who takes out the garbage just like other married couples, and it will do nothing to undermine anyone else's marriage and family," says Wolfson of Freedom to Marry.

For the moment, however, acceptance of gay marriage seems to be receding, according to the three polls conducted for national news organizations since the Supreme Court's *Lawrence* decision in late June. The AP poll, the most recent of the three, indicates likely trouble for any political candidate who takes up the issue. Close to half of those surveyed said they would be less likely to support a presidential candidate who backs civil unions (44 percent) or gay marriage (49 percent), while only around 10 percent said they would be more likely.

A dose of political reality is also deflating the euphoria within the gay community about the moves toward same-sex marriage in Canada. The government's planned legislation to legalize same-sex marriage nationwide faces uncertain prospects for passage, according to news accounts. Some members of Canada's Parliament are suggesting the issue be put before the voters in a national referendum. Polls indicate Canadians are almost equally divided on the subject.

Gay-marriage advocates in the United States play down the recent poll numbers as a momentary dip. With suits advancing in Arizona and New Jersey and the Massachusetts case still awaiting decision, they profess confidence that a breakthrough is imminent.[36] "Within a year, we will see gay couples legally married in the United States," Wolfson says, "and Americans will accept that."

Opponents denounce the courts' role on the issue. "The only way the gay agenda is moved forward is from runaway courts," says Mackey of the Family Research Council. "We think that's a very serious problem when the courts take on something that they shouldn't."

For his part, gay-marriage opponent Wardle, of Brigham Young University, says he is resigned to unfavorable rulings from some state courts: "It will mean that gay relationships recognized in one state will not be recognized in some other states."

However, Wardle and gay-marriage advocate Strasser at Capital University Law School both believe the Supreme Court is unlikely to endorse same-sex marriage any time soon.

Individual state legislatures, however, could decide to provide marriage-like benefits to homosexual couples even without court action. The California legislature is on the verge of approving a bill to give registered domestic partners — including gay and lesbian couples — an array of benefits, including the ability to ask for child support and alimony and the right to health coverage under a partner's plan. The bill, approved by the state Senate on Aug. 28 and awaiting final approval of amendments by the Assembly, would also give domestic partners the same privilege for marital confidentiality enjoyed by heterosexuals. Democratic Gov. Gray Davis supports the bill and has promised to sign it when it reaches his desk.[37]

With no definitive resolution on the issue on the horizon, both sides appear to be preparing for a long struggle. Opponents believe public opinion is on their side and will ultimately prevail. "In spite of what you're seeing in pop culture and in the media, in the absence of anything pushing back on the gay agenda, in spite of that silence except from groups like ours, Americans seem to be resonating with what we believe to be true," says Rios of Concerned Women of America.

"If the masses of the people decide they're going to have to take this on, marriage will be codified as one man, one woman."

Gay-marriage supporters, however, note that other civil-rights movements have struggled long and hard to win over public opinion. "Our civil-rights movement will be on the same type of slow-but-sure march toward equality in marriage," says Lambda Legal Defense attorney Buckel.

"The outcome is inevitable," he continues. "It's about family. Anybody who has a family knows how far they will go to get the protections that family needs."

NOTES

1. For general background, see the following *CQ Researcher* reports: Kenneth Jost, "Gay Rights Update," April 14, 2000, pp. 305-328; Richard L. Worsnop, "Gay Rights," March 5, 1993, pp. 193-216; Charles S. Clark, "Marriage and Divorce," May 10, 1996, pp. 409-432.

2. Darryl Fears, "3 Support Same-Sex Marriage; Democrats Appear At Rights Forum," *The Washington Post*, July 16, 2003, p. A8.

3. U.S. Census Bureau, "Married-Couple and Unmarried-Partner Households: 2000," *Census 2000 Special Reports*, February 2003, pp. 1-13.

4. Timothy J. Dailey, "Homosexual Parenting: Placing Children at Risk," Family Research Council, Oct. 30, 2001.

5. Judith Stacey and Timothy J. Biblarz, "(How) Does the Sexual Orientation of Parents Matter?" *American Sociological Review*, Vol. 66 (April 2001), pp. 159-183.

6. Background drawn from William N. Eskridge Jr., *The Case for Same-Sex Marriage: From Sexual Liberty to Civilized Commitment* (1996), pp. 15-50. The chapter can also be found at "People with a History: An Online Guide to Lesbian, Gay, Bisexual, and Trans History," a Web site maintained by Fordham University Professor Paul Halsall (www.fordham.edu/halsall/pwh).

7. John Boswell, *Same-Sex Unions in Premodern Europe* (1994). For representative reviews, see Marina Warner, "More Than Friendship," *The New York Times Book Review*, Aug. 28, 1994, p. 7; Wendy Doniger, "Making Brothers," *Los Angeles Times Book Review*, July 31, 1994, p. 1; and Camille Paglia, "Plighting Their Troth," *Book World* (*The Washington Post*), July 17, 1994, p. X1. For a compendium of sources, see "People with a History," *op. cit.*

8. Boswell, *op. cit.*, p. 191.

9. Eskridge, *op. cit.*, p. 35.

10. *Ibid.*, p. 44.

11. Background drawn from Eskridge, *op. cit.*, pp. 51-86.

12. The case is *Baker v. Nelson*, 191 N.W.2d 185 (Minn. 1971).

13. Eskridge, *op. cit.*, p. 56. The cases from eight states are listed in footnote 28, at pp. 232-233.

14. The case is *Bowers v. Hardwick*, 478 U.S. 186 (1986).

15. The debate, originally published in *OUT/LOOK, National Lesbian and Gay Quarterly* (fall 1989), is reprinted in Suzanne Sherman (ed.), *Lesbian and Gay Marriage: Private Commitments, Public Ceremonies* (1992), pp. 13-26. Stoddard died in 1997; Ettelbrick, currently family policy director of the National Gay and Lesbian Task Force, is now more supportive of efforts to win legal recognition of same-sex relationships.

16. Janet Levin, "Sexual Relations: The 1994 Advocate Survey of Sexuality and Relationships: The Men," *The Advocate*, Aug. 23, 1994, pp. 32-33; Janet Levin, "Lesbian Sex Survey: The 1995 Advocate Survey of Sexuality and Relationships: The Women," *The Advocate*, Aug. 22, 1995, pp. 26-27.

17. For background on the lead plaintiffs, Ninia Baehr and Genora Dancel, see Eskridge, *op. cit.*, pp. 1-4.

18. The decision is *Baehr v. Lewin*, 852 P.2d 44 (Hawaii 1993).

19. The decision is *Baehr v. Miike*. The Hawaii Supreme Court decision, not officially published, can be found at 1999 *LEXIS* 391.

20. The decision is *Brause v. Bureau of Vital Statistics*, 1998 WL 88743 (Alaska Super.).

21. See *1996 CQ Almanac*, pp. 5-26 — 5-29.

22. The case is *Baker v. State*, 744 A.2d 864 (Vt. 1999).

23. For coverage, see Trudy Tynan, "Gay couples sue over right to marry in Massachusetts," The Associated Press, April 11, 2001; Yvonne Abraham, "Gays Seek Right to Marry," *The Boston Globe*, April 12, 2001, p. A1; Linda Bock, "Gays Seek OK for Marriage," *The* (Worcester) *Telegram and Gazette*, April 12, 2001, p. A1.

24. For coverage, see Kathleen Burge, "Judge Dismisses Same-Sex Marriage Suit," *The Boston Globe*, May 9, 2002, p. B6.

25. For coverage, see Kathleen Burge, "SJC Peppers Lawyers on Same-Sex Marriage," *The Boston Globe*, March 5, 2003, p. A1.

26. The case is *Halpern v. Canada* (A.G.), C39172 (Court of Appeal for Ontario, June 10, 2003). http://www.ontariocourts.on.ca/decisions/2003/june/halpernC39172.htm.

27 Evan Thomas, "The War Over Gay Marriage," *Newsweek*, July 7, 2003, pp. 38-45.

28. Deb Price, "Gay Newlyweds Embrace Canadian Marriage," *The Detroit News*, July 7, 2003.

29. Three states have no newspapers that publish same-sex couples' announcements: Mississippi, Oklahoma and South Dakota. For a complete list, see the Gay and Lesbian Alliance Against Defamation's Web Site: www.glaad.org.

30. David Toussaint, "Outward Bound," *Bride's*, September-October 2003, p. 346.

31. U.S. Census Bureau, *op. cit.*

32. Quoted in Christopher Marquis, "Total of Unmarried Couples Surged in 2000 U.S. Census," *The New York Times*, March 13, 2003, p. A22.

33. Quoted in Evelyn Nieves, "Family Values Groups Gear Up for Battle Over Gay Marriage," *The Washington Post*, Aug. 17, 2003, p. A6.

34. See Bill Swindell and John Cochran, "Gay Marriage Debate Holds Land Mines for Both Parties," *CQ Today*, Aug. 1, 2003.

35. Appearance on PBS "NewsHour with Jim Lehrer," July 31, 2003.

36. The New Jersey case is *Lewis v. Harris*, L-00-4233-02 (Hudson County Superior Court), filed June 26, 2002. The Arizona case is *Standhardt vs. Superior Court*, 1 CA-SA-03-0150, argued before the Arizona Court of Appeal on Aug. 19, 2003.

37. See Carl Ingram, "Domestic Partners Bill OKd," *Los Angeles Times*, Aug. 29, 2003, p. B1.

BIBLIOGRAPHY

Books

Boswell, John, *Same-Sex Unions in Premodern Europe*, **Villard, 1994.**
Presents highly controversial thesis by the late, openly gay Yale historian that the medieval Catholic Church routinely conducted ceremonies solemnizing "same-sex unions" between men. Heavily annotated; includes texts of manuscripts, translated. Draws on author's earlier work, *Christianity, Social Tolerance, and Homosexuality: Gay People in Western Europe from the Beginning of the Christian Era to the Fourteenth Century* (University of Chicago Press, 1980).

Eskridge, William N., *The Case for Same-Sex Marriage: From Sexual Liberty to Civilized Commitment*, **Free Press, 1996.**
A professor at Yale Law School strongly argues for legal recognition of same-sex marriage. Chapters cover history of same-sex marriage, debate within gay and lesbian community, mainstream objections to same-sex marriage, and constitutional arguments for recognition. Includes notes, list of court cases and 20-page list of references.

Lewin, Ellen, *Recognizing Ourselves: Ceremonies of Gay and Lesbian Commitment*, **Columbia University Press, 1998.**
A professor of anthropology and women's studies at the University of Iowa provides a comprehensive account of gay and lesbian commitment ceremonies in the United States, including the author's own. Includes notes and 10 pages of references. For an older collection of vignettes of gay and lesbian couples, see Suzanne Sherman (ed.), *Lesbian and Gay Marriage: Private Commitments, Public Ceremonies* (Temple University Press, 1992).

Strasser, Mark, *On Same-Sex Marriage, Civil Unions, and the Rule of Law: Constitutional Interpretation at the Crossroads*, **Praeger, 2002.**
A professor at Capital University Law School, Columbus, Ohio, argues for recognition of same-sex marriage with analysis of legal developments from Hawaii Supreme Court ruling through enactment of Vermont "civil union" legislation. Includes notes, list of court cases and bibliography. For earlier titles, see *The Challenge of Same-Sex Marriage: Federalist Principles and Constitutional Protections* (Praeger, 1999); and *Legally Wed: Same-Sex*

Marriage and the Constitution (Cornell University Press, 1997).

Wardle, Lynn D., Mark Strasser, William C. Duncan and David Orgon Coolidge (eds.), *Marriage and Same-Sex Unions: A Debate,* **Praeger, 2003.**
Carefully balanced essays by some 20 contributors on historical, philosophical and constitutional views of same-sex marriage. Includes two-page table of cases. Wardle and Strasser are identified under their individual titles. Duncan is assistant director of the Marriage Law Project, Columbus School of Law, Catholic University of America; Coolidge was the project's director before his death in 2002.

Articles

Bumiller, Elisabeth, "Why America Has Gay Marriage Jitters," *The New York Times,* **Aug. 10, 2003, Sec. 4, p. 1.**
Analyzes public opinion on gay marriage after polls registered drop in popular support.

Thomas, Evan, "The War Over Gay Marriage," *Newsweek,* **July 7, 2003, pp. 38-45.**
Journalistic analysis of gay-marriage issue immediately following U.S. Supreme Court's decision striking down state anti-sodomy laws.

Wardle, Lynn D., "A Critical Analysis of Constitutional Claims for Same-Sex Marriage," *Brigham Young University Law Review,* **Vol. 1996, No. 1, pp. 1-101.**
Comprehensively criticizes arguments for recognizing same-sex marriage; also notes "imbalance" in legal literature on the issue. Wardle is a professor at Brigham Young University's J. Ruben Clark School of Law. For a more recent article, see "'Multiply and Replenish': Considering Same-Sex Marriage in Light of State Interests in Marital Procreation," *Harvard Journal of Law and Public Policy,* Vol. 24, No. 3 (summer 2001), pp. 771-814.

Reports and Studies

American Academy of Pediatrics, "Technical Report: Coparent or Second-Parent Adoption by Same-Sex Parents," Vol. 109, No. 2 (February 2002), pp. 341-344.
Task force of pediatricians' group examines some 20 studies to conclude that children raised by gay or lesbian parents fare as well as children raised in heterosexual households.

Cahill, Sean, Mitra Ellen and Sarah Tobias, "Family Policy: Issues Affecting Gay, Lesbian, Bisexual and Transgender Families," National Gay and Lesbian Task Force Policy Institute, 2002.
Comprehensively catalogs from an advocacy perspective laws and policies affecting gay and lesbian individuals and families.

Lerner, Robert, and Althea K. Nagai, "No Basis: What the Studies Don't Tell Us About Same-Sex Parenting," January 2001 (www.marriagewatch.org).
Critique by two social scientists of studies purporting to show that children raised by gay or lesbian parents fare as well as those raised in heterosexual households.

For More Information

Concerned Women for America, 1015 15th St., N.W., Suite 1100, Washington, DC 20005; (202) 488-7000; www.cwfa.org. Conservative advocacy group opposed to gay marriage and other parts of what it calls the "homosexual agenda."

Family Research Council, 801 G St., N.W., Washington, DC 20001; (202) 393-2100; www.frc.org. Nationwide pro-family group opposed to gay marriage.

Freedom to Marry, 116 West 23rd St, Suite 500, New York, NY 10011; (212) 851-8418; www.freedomtomarry.org. Gay-marriage advocacy group seeks to mobilize supporters outside gay-lesbian community.

Gay and Lesbian Advocates and Defenders, 30 Winter St., Suite 800, Boston, MA 02108; (617) 426-1350; www.glad.org. Regional gay-rights organization representing plaintiffs in Massachusetts gay-marriage case.

Lambda Legal Defense and Education Fund, Inc., 120 Wall St., Suite 1500, New York, NY 10005-3904; (212) 809-8585; www.lambdalegal.org. National gay-rights organization representing plaintiffs in New Jersey gay-marriage case.

Massachusetts Family Institute, 381 Elliot St., Newton, MA 02464; (617) 928-0800; www.mafamily.org. Pro-family organization, founded in 1991, opposed to gay marriage.

7

Race in America

Alan Greenblatt

Benny Robinson hugs his daughter Jada after he and other African-Americans in Tulia, Texas, were released from prison in June. Some three-dozen residents — mainly blacks — were convicted of drug charges based on the now-discredited testimony of a racist policeman. Although African-Americans have made economic, political and social progress over the last four decades, such incidents periodically erupt, shattering Americans' complacency about race.

From *The CQ Researcher*, July 11, 2003.

When Joe Moore got out of jail in June, the 60-year-old hog farmer told reporters, "I just want to go home, look at TV and stay out of trouble." After her release, Kizzie White, 26, hugged her two children and said, "I'm going to be the best mother I can to them."[1]

Moore and White were among the more than three-dozen, mostly black residents of the West Texas town of Tulia convicted of drug crimes four years ago solely on the now-discredited testimony of an undercover police officer widely labeled as a racist.

Many white Americans believe that race no longer matters in America, now that public schools have been integrated, blacks can vote and race-based job and housing discrimination are illegal. Yet racial incidents like Tulia continue to erupt, periodically shattering Americans' complacency about race and signaling to many observers that racist sentiments still linger in some psyches.

Often the eruptions spill into the streets — usually in response to allegedly racist police actions — such as the riots that broke out in Cincinnati in April 2001 or in Benton Harbor, Mich., this past June.

Lately, some of the incidents — particularly in the South — appear to represent a longing by some for the pre-1960s era of segregation. In Georgia this spring, white high-school students held a prom at which African-American students pointedly were excluded — a year after the school's first integrated prom. That followed the downfall last fall of Sen. Trent Lott of Mississippi, who was forced to resign as majority leader after saying America would have been better off if then-Gov. Strom Thurmond of South Carolina had won the presidency in 1948, when he was an ardent segregationist.

White Students Are the Most Isolated

The average white student in the United States attends a school made up of 80 percent whites. Similarly, most black students attend schools in which the majority of their fellow students are the same race as themselves. Asians are the most integrated in American schools.

Racial Composition of Schools Attended by the Average . . .

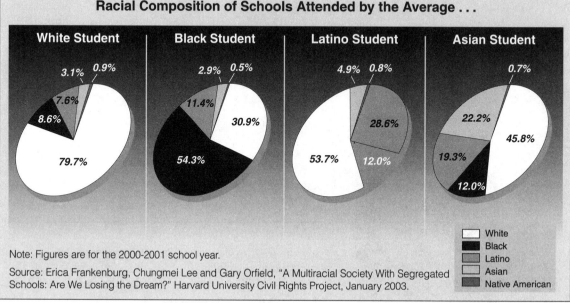

Note: Figures are for the 2000-2001 school year.

Source: Erica Frankenburg, Chungmei Lee and Gary Orfield, "A Multiracial Society With Segregated Schools: Are We Losing the Dream?" Harvard University Civil Rights Project, January 2003.

And some of the racially tinged incidents have been particularly conscience-searing: the murder of James Byrd Jr., chained behind a truck in Jasper, Texas, and dragged to death; the broomstick sodomizing of Haitian immigrant Abner Louima and the shooting of unarmed African immigrant Amadou Diallo by New York policemen; the beating in Los Angeles of Rodney King.

Such cases bring into dramatic focus the often diametrically opposing ways in which whites and blacks view race relations in America, especially when the criminal-justice system is involved. Many whites saw the acquittal of O.J. Simpson in the murder of his ex-wife Nicole Simpson and her friend Ron Goldman as a miscarriage of justice, while blacks generally viewed it as a triumph over racist police tactics. Similarly, blacks in Tulia celebrated the release of their fellow citizens as righting a racial injustice while whites continued to question the prisoners' innocence.

And even the Supreme Court's landmark approval recently of the University of Michigan's use of affirmative action in law-school admissions was viewed differently by some blacks and whites (*see pp.* 158, 170).

But many Americans — whites as well as blacks — say the nation's racial problems go beyond racial preferences and the criminal-justice system. They say discrimination still exists despite civil-rights laws, undercutting blacks educationally and economically. Although African-Americans have made economic, political and social progress over the last four decades, by several objective measures they are trailing whites:

- Median income among black men is only 73 percent as high as that of white men, and only 84 percent for black women compared with white women.[2]
- Blacks are 60 percent less likely than whites to receive access to sophisticated medical treatments such as coronary angioplasty and bypass surgery.[3]

- Minorities are far more likely to pay higher, "predatory" mortgage rates than whites.[4]
- A majority of black students score below the basic level in five out of seven subject areas on the National Assessment of Educational Progress (NAEP) tests, compared to only about 20 percent of white students.[5]
- One in five black men spends part of his life in prison — seven times the rate for whites.[6] Blacks are 13 percent of the U.S. population, but make up more than 40 percent of the prisoners on Death Row.[7]

Meanwhile, some social critics warn that Latinos and Arabs increasingly experience discrimination in the United States. Latinos, expected to become the nation's largest minority group in the next few years, struggle with levels of poverty and education similar to those of blacks. And Arabs and civil-liberties advocates say the nation's war on terrorism subjects Middle Easterners to widespread harassment. (*See sidebar, p. 170.*)

Some social scientists say that civil-rights laws are working and that blacks' lack of achievement is often due to lack of hard work and criminal behavior, not racism. Moreover, they point to progress in a number of areas, including the recent decision by New Jersey to stop racial profiling by its state troopers.

Gary Orfield, co-director of the Harvard Civil Rights Project, says the racial divide still appears to be widest in public education. Despite decades of court-ordered school integration, more than one in six black children attends a school comprised of 99-100 percent minority students; by comparison, less than 1 percent of white public-school students attend such schools.

Many observers have expected the Republican Party to adopt a more conciliatory stance toward blacks, who overwhelmingly favor Democrats in elections for all levels of office. Indeed, a day after 12 of the Tulia defen-

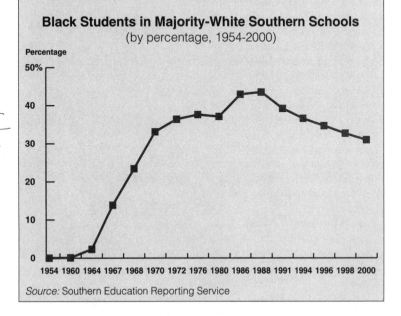

Re-Segregation Increasing in Southern Schools

By 1988 — after decades of court-ordered desegregation — the South had become the country's most integrated region, with 43.5 percent of black students attending majority-white schools. But by 2000 the percentage had dropped to 31 percent, following the abandonment of busing and other school-desegregation efforts in the 1990s.

Black Students in Majority-White Southern Schools
(by percentage, 1954-2000)

Source: Southern Education Reporting Service

dants were released from prison, the Bush administration barred federal officers from using race or ethnicity as a factor in conducting investigations (except in cases involving terrorism or national security).[8]

But some African-American leaders question the Bush administration's commitment to fighting racism. "Bush represents anathema to our struggle for social justice," says civil-rights activist Jesse Jackson. "He would not permit [Secretary of State Colin] Powell to go to the U.N. conference on racism in South Africa; he has sought to stock the courts with anti-civil rights judges; he is anti-affirmative action. . . . We are simply on different teams."[9]

Less than a month after Lott stepped down, President Bush spoke out against the University of Michigan's use of racial preferences.

Bush's supporters, however, say he has appointed as many women and minorities to top government jobs as Bill Clinton, whose administration was the most racially diverse in history. "The president is very committed to

Are Blacks Losing Political Clout?

Even at age 100, Sen. Strom Thurmond, R-S.C., was a lightning rod for debates about racism. In Washington, powerful Mississippi Sen. Trent Lott lost his job as majority leader last year for waxing nostalgic for segregation at a 100th birthday party for Thurmond, who died recently. Lott told the celebration he wished the centenarian had won the presidency back in 1948, when he ran as a segregationist.

And in South Carolina this spring, GOP state legislators angered some of their Democratic colleagues by including several pictures of a young Thurmond in the state legislative manual. "Nobody could dispute the fact that Strom Thurmond was probably the No. 1 racist Dixiecrat of the day," says state Sen. Robert Ford.

Former Sen. Carol Moseley Braun, D-Ill., one of only two blacks ever elected to the U.S. Senate in modern times, is seeking the Democratic presidential nomination.

Ford, an African-American and veteran of the civil-rights movement, believes Thurmond sincerely tempered his views on race later in his career. Still, Ford took to the Senate floor to express his dismay over the pictures of a younger, unreconstructed Thurmond in the manual.

Several Republican legislators said Ford was making a big deal out of nothing, or, worse, that he was unnecessarily criticizing a man revered as an icon throughout South Carolina. "They don't want to hear any-thing negative about Strom Thurmond," Ford says. "They are living in another world."

In fact, whites in the state literally do live in a different world. Because of redistricting maneuvers, South Carolina blacks live in predominantly black political districts. Conversely, most districts are so dominated by whites that politicians rep-

diversity of thought, of professional background, of geography, ethnicity and gender," said Clay Johnson, who coordinated appointments for Bush. By March 2001, he noted, 27 percent of Bush's selections were women, and 20 to 25 percent were minorities.[10]

Like many conservatives, Bush believes that the interests of blacks, as well as whites, are best served by race-neutral policies. "As we work to address the wrong of racial prejudice, we must not use means that create another wrong, and thus perpetuate our divisions," he said.

Indeed, Heather Mac Donald, a senior fellow at the Manhattan Institute, says "the white establishment is doing everything it can to hire as many black employees

as it can. If you are a black high-school student who graduates with modest SATs today, you're going to have colleges beating down your door to try and persuade you to come."

But David Wellman, a white professor of community studies at the University of California, Santa Cruz, sees an opposite reality. "Race not only matters, but whites have an advantage because blacks have a disadvantage," says Wellman, co-author of the forthcoming book *Whitewashing Race*. "That's the dirty little secret that nobody wants to talk about anymore.

"Everyone wants to believe that racism has been essentially solved through legislation," he insists.

resenting those districts have no practical incentives to consider the needs or historical sensitivities of African-Americans. This political segregation encourages both black and white politicians to pick fights over racially charged matters — such as disputes about pictures of Thurmond or whether to allow the Confederate flag to fly over state buildings — because they get high-profile coverage back home.

"On both sides of the aisle, they log onto largely symbolic issues," says Dick Harpootlian, who recently stepped down as chairman of the South Carolina Democratic Party.

"If you want to get re-elected and you're black, you don't want to talk to white voters," Harpootlian says. "If you're white and running for re-election, you don't want to talk to blacks. We've institutionalized this idea that race predominates over any other interest."

The Voting Rights Act of 1982 encouraged some blacks to join with Republicans to create majority-black districts after the 1980 and 1990 censuses — mostly in the South. The deal allowed African-Americans to create districts that would likely elect blacks. For Republicans, concentrating black voters into a relatively few districts weakened Democratic candidates' chances in neighboring districts.

Partly as a result, there are about 600 black state legislators in the United States today — twice as many as there were in 1970. But now that Democrats are losing power in the South, black legislators in the South are in the dubious position of becoming more important in a national party that has become less powerful.

"African-Americans now have a seat at the table but no plate, no forks and nothing to eat," Harpootlian says. "African-Americans have no influence in our legislature now — zero, nada, none."

Although today there are more black elected officials at all levels of government than in earlier years, the trend appears to have peaked, at least for now. Over the last 40 years, only one African-American has been elected governor — L. Douglas Wilder of Virginia — and only two blacks have been elected to the U.S. Senate — Edward W. Brooke, R-Mass., and Carol Moseley Braun, D-Ill.

Blacks have enjoyed the most real political power at the city level — but even that power is receding. New York, Los Angeles, Chicago, Denver, Oakland, Cleveland, St. Louis, Baltimore, Seattle, Minneapolis, Dallas and numerous other cities had black mayors during the 1980s and '90s but have white mayors today.

University of Maryland political scientist Ronald Walters says that as increasing numbers of blacks moved out of the center cities, whites have gained the upper hand because they vote in greater numbers. "It's sort of a cycle of expectations that didn't pan out," Walters says. "There was a lot of euphoria around the first generation of black mayors and what they could accomplish."

But just as blacks were taking the reins of power, Walters points out, urban populations began declining, and aid to cities began drying up. "The irony was that they couldn't accomplish a whole hell of a lot. The whole conservative movement at the state and national level robbed them of the ability to do much."

"Unfortunately, when you look at the evidence in terms of education, crime and welfare, it's just shocking how important race continues to be."

Some scholars argue that, absent overt discrimination, blacks must share much of the blame if their circumstances are not equal to whites. "The grip of the Cult of Victimology encourages the black American from birth to fixate upon remnants of racism and resolutely downplay all signs of its demise," writes John McWhorter, a professor at the University of California, Berkeley.[11]

Faith Mitchell, deputy director of the National Research Council's Division on Behavioral and Social Sciences, acknowledges that her fellow African-Americans have made much progress — but only to a point. "Yes, you have a growing black middle class," she says, "but it's still disproportionately small relative to the rest of the black population. The lower class is growing faster."[12]

As blacks and whites examine race relations in the United States, here are some of the questions they are asking:

Is discrimination still a problem in the United States?

In 1988, when a residential treatment center opened in Indianapolis for convicted child molesters, neighbors

Most Inmates Are Black, Hispanic

Minorities represented nearly two-thirds of the 1.8 million American men over age 18 in local jails and state or federal prisons in 2002.

Men in U.S. Jails and Prisons
(as of June 30, 2002)

		Percentage of Inmate Total	Percentage of Race in U.S. Population
White	630,700	34.0%	75.0%
Black	818,900	44.0	13.0
Hispanic	342,500	18.5	12.0
Total	**1,848,700**		

Note: American Indians, Alaska Natives, Asians, Native Hawaiians and other Pacific Islanders are included in the total.

Source: U.S. Department of Justice, Bureau of Justice Statistics, "Prison and Jail Inmates at Midyear 2002," April 2003.

just as widespread as ever," says Jared Taylor, editor of *American Renaissance* magazine, who has been described as a white nationalist. "Even if few people acknowledge it, people prefer the company of people like themselves, and race is an important ingredient. Given the chance, they spend their time in homogeneous groups. It is part of human nature."

Taylor's sentiments are echoed by Carol Swain, a black professor of law and political science at Vanderbilt University. "Clearly, discrimination exists, and in very subtle ways," she says, but it is "human nature for people to favor their own group." Indeed, many "black separatists" argue that African-Americans can achieve more by running their own businesses in their own communities, rather than seeking opportunities among whites.

"I would prefer to see more integration," says Bob Zelnick, chairman of the Boston University journalism department and a member of the conservative Citizens' Initiative on Race and Ethnicity. "But I don't think it's a mark of failure if people prefer to live among their own kind. There's some lingering discrimination [in the United States], but I think the determined middle-class or upper-middle-class minority family that seeks to live in a white neighborhood can do so."

Zelnick is "not overly concerned" about segregated patterns of residential living, but only "so long as you have real opportunity for African-Americans to get access to educational opportunity and institutions of higher learning, and as long as you have access to employment opportunities after college or high school."

But others are quick to point out that educational opportunities are not, in fact, allocated evenly to all races. They cite a recent decision in which the New York Court of Appeals found that the city's longstanding system of providing less money to inner-city schools than to wealthier suburban schools violates the state Constitution because it deprives students of an equal education. The court gave the state 13 months to change the funding formulas that provide less money for urban students — a common practice in American school districts.[14]

accepted it with little comment. But three years later, when it was converted into a facility for homeless veterans — half of them black — neighborhood whites vandalized a car and burned a cross.

"An all-white cadre of child molesters was evidently acceptable," wrote Randall Kennedy, a black Harvard law-school professor, "but the presence of blacks made a racially integrated group of homeless veterans intolerable!"[13]

The Indianapolis case was unusually overt, says Leonard Steinhorn, an American University professor and co-author of the book *By the Color of Our Skin: The Illusion of Integration and the Reality of Race.* Most opposition to racial integration is much more subtle, he says. "Today, a black person moves in and most white people accept it, or even like it," Steinhorn says. "But one or two families get nervous and move out. More blacks may move in, because they see that the first blacks have been accepted. Then a couple more whites say we better move.

"It's a slow and gradual phenomenon, not the spontaneous, overnight reaction we saw in the past," Steinhorn explains. Even if the African-Americans share the same socioeconomic footing as the whites, most whites will not stay in a neighborhood once it becomes more than 10 to 15 percent black, he says.

But some observers argue that segregation today is more a matter of choice than of bigotry. "White flight is

Meanwhile, Harvard history Professor Stephan Thernstrom says studies show residential segregation has been declining since the 1960s. "[Segregation] is now at the lowest level since 1920," he says. Real estate agents and home sellers are more interested in closing the deal than engaging in discrimination. If residential segregation exists, he says, it's largely a matter of choice.

But some racial separation may not be by mutual choice. A recent Urban Institute analysis of home-loan applications in Chicago and Los Angeles found that information was withheld from blacks and Hispanics in "statistically significant patterns of unequal treatment" that "systematically favor whites."[15] In another study, African-American women had access to about half as many rental properties as white males because of disparities in the information the women received.[16]

Meanwhile, Southern public schools are "re-segregating." According to researchers at the Harvard Civil Rights Project, the proportion of black students in majority-white Southern schools has reached its lowest level since 1968.[17] (*See graph, p. 151.*)

Moreover, American University's Steinhorn says, many forms of de facto discrimination still are practiced today, such as requiring black job applicants — but not whites — to take writing tests; department store security guards following blacks more closely than whites; and drug stores failing to carry African-American hair-care products to discourage their patronage.

"It doesn't have to be legalized, high-profile segregation to be meaningful," Steinhorn says. "This is the stuff of life. If it's death by a thousand cuts, that's as powerful as being told you have to sit at the back of the bus."

Predatory Lending on the Rise

The number of subprime home-mortgage loans — or loans with high interest rates, exorbitant fees and harmful terms — has skyrocketed in recent years. The increase in these so-called predatory loans has been most dramatic in minority communities, particularly among Latinos. At the same time, the number of prime, or lower-rate, loans decreased for blacks but increased for whites and Latinos. Subprime loans are intended for people who are unable to obtain a conventional prime loan at the standard bank rate. The loans have higher interest rates to compensate for the potentially greater risk that these borrowers represent, but Fannie Mae (Federal National Mortgage Association) estimates that as many as half of all subprime borrowers could have qualified for a lower-cost mortgage. Elderly homeowners, communities of color, and low-income neighborhoods are the most severely affected by such practices. Subprime loans represented 9 percent of all conventional home-purchase loans in the U.S. in 2001.

Increases in Subprime and Prime Lending, 1995-2001

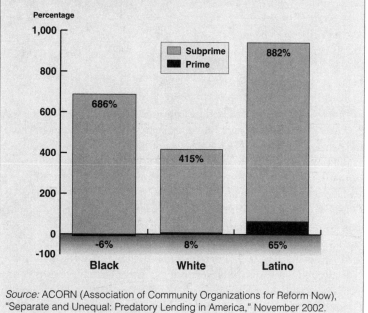

Source: ACORN (Association of Community Organizations for Reform Now), "Separate and Unequal: Predatory Lending in America," November 2002.

Are blacks still economically disadvantaged due to racism?

Nearly everyone agrees that blacks, generally, are far better off financially than they were 40 years ago. But blacks still hold a fraction of whites' accumulated assets. For instance, the proportion of blacks that own their own homes has doubled since 1940, but it is still about a third below the rate for whites.[18]

Are these financial disparities between the races due to racism or to socioeconomic factors and differences in education levels? Steinhorn and others say the persistent separation of the races has negative financial consequences for blacks. Segregation, for instance, can prevent blacks from having access to the social networks that can lead to good jobs. Some economists also argue that urban blacks suffer from "spatial mismatch" — unequal access to suburban jobs located near white residential areas. High crime rates also hamper black wealth creation.

"Crime depresses the property values in cities and neighborhoods that blacks tend to live in," says George R. La Noue, a political scientist at the University of Maryland, Baltimore County.

Much of the racial disparity in wealth is the result of the historical legacy of segregation, according to Steinhorn and others. Black families simply have not had time to accrue wealth to match the generations of inherited property and other assets enjoyed by whites. Blacks also have a harder time investing in major assets, such as real estate.

"There is no question that minorities are less likely than whites to obtain mortgage financing and that, if successful, they receive less generous loan amounts and terms," concluded a 1999 Urban Institute study.[19]

Education is perhaps the biggest factor affecting black incomes. Blacks consistently trail behind whites on standardized tests, and people who achieve higher test scores usually can command higher salaries.

But the University of California's McWhorter says the disparity in education levels can't be attributed solely to racism. "A cultural trait is the driving factor in depressing black scholarly performance," he writes. "A wariness of books and learning for learning's sake as [being] 'white' has become ingrained in black American culture."[20]

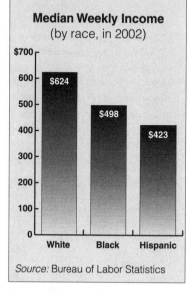

Whites Earn the Most

The average white worker made $126 a week more than the average black worker in 2002, and $201 a week more than the average Hispanic.

Median Weekly Income
(by race, in 2002)

White: $624
Black: $498
Hispanic: $423

Source: Bureau of Labor Statistics

Harvard's Thernstrom, co-author of a forthcoming book on racial disparities in education, *No Excuses: Closing the Racial Gap in Learning*, says the education gap largely explains the income gap. Too many studies unfairly compare income levels for blacks and whites who have completed the same level of education, he argues. But blacks score more poorly on standardized tests than whites at the same grade level, indicating that they are not receiving the same level of instruction.

"When you measure educational achievement — not by the time you've spent under a school roof, but by what you know — the disparity in racial income mostly disappears," he says. "People of different races with equal levels of cognitive skills have earned about the same amount of money in our society for the past 25 years. Even if employers aren't discriminating at all on the basis of race, they are paying higher-skilled workers more."

Thernstrom believes that blacks' poor test scores are not so much due to racism but to flaws in K-12 public education in general. He says concentrating efforts on improving schools would aid education in general while also aiding blacks and other minorities.

"In a society committed to equal opportunity, we still have a racially identifiable group of educational have-nots — young African-Americans and Latinos," write Thernstrom and his wife and co-author, Abigail Thernstrom, a senior fellow at the Manhattan Institute and a member of the U.S. Civil Rights Commission. "They place some blame on members of these groups for failing to place an emphasis on education and for a cultural work ethic that sometimes equates achievement with "acting white or selling out."

But the Thernstroms place heavier blame on schools for failing to adapt to group cultural differences and for not demanding high standards from their students. "Plenty of white and Asian kids are also being short-changed," they write, "but it is the black and Hispanic [statistics] that suggest appalling indifference."[21]

Many people on the other side, however, citing the recent New York appeals court decision, point out that American school-funding policies — which unlike any other industrialized country are based on property values — are clearly lopsided against poorer school districts, which often are made up primarily of blacks, Latinos and other minorities.

However, William E. Spriggs, executive director of the National Urban League's Institute for Opportunity and Equality, says even highly educated blacks suffer higher unemployment rates than whites. "Year after year, the unemployment rate for [black] college graduates has continued to climb," Spriggs says, "whereas for whites, it's been fairly stable."

But the disparities don't end there, adds Spriggs, a former president of the black National Economics Association. Blacks with the same skills as whites earn 10 to 20 percent less, he says. "Every hour at work, to make 80 cents on somebody else's dollar is a huge disadvantage," he says. "You can't start the race 20 percent behind."

William Rodgers, an economics professor at the College of William and Mary in Williamsburg, Va., and former chief economist at the Department of Labor in the Clinton administration, agrees that economic disparities cannot be explained entirely by differences in education. "Even if they come in with skills and education like their white counterparts, minorities are still experiencing labor-market discrimination," he says, with blacks receiving fewer callbacks and job offers.

The University of Maryland's La Noue admits that racism and discrimination persist, but he says other factors — such as limited educational opportunities — also can affect members of all races. Thus he opposes trying to alleviate income disparities through racial quotas or special race-based programs, because he says they are unfair to whites with limited opportunities.

For the same reason, La Noue opposes government programs that set aside a certain percentage of contracts for minority-owned companies. "Too often in this area, we created race-based solutions that are not really congruent with the problems we're trying to solve, and based on gross generalizations that all people of one race are privileged and all people of another race are disadvantaged," he says.

Demonstrators reflect both sides of the affirmative-action debate following the Supreme Court's June 23 ruling supporting the University of Michigan's use of race as a factor in admissions.

Is the criminal-justice system racially biased?

Black comedian Richard Pryor used to joke about going to court seeking justice in America. "And that's exactly what I saw," he said. "Just us."

Indeed, blacks comprise 13 percent of the country's population but more than 40 percent of the U.S. prison population, according to the Washington-based Sentencing Project. A black male born in 1991 stands a 29 percent chance of spending time in prison, compared with 4 percent for white males. In 1995, one in three black men between the ages of 20 and 29 was either in prison, on probation or on parole.[22]

Many African-Americans argue that more blacks are in jail because police and prosecutors target blacks. Many blacks say they have been pulled over for the "crime" of "driving while black." "Nothing has poi-

Few Changes Seen in Racial Admissions Plans

College and university officials expect few changes in admissions practices following the Supreme Court's qualified approval of affirmative action. But opponents of affirmative action vow to continue their fight in court and elsewhere.

Most undergraduate and graduate schools with race-conscious admissions policies use an individualized application process akin to the University of Michigan Law School's system approved by the high court on June 23, education officials and experts say. They add that only a few schools award all minority applicants a fixed, quantitative bonus similar to the point system used at Michigan's undergraduate college, which the court found unconstitutional.

The court's ruling "has the effect of defining current practices as constitutional," says Barmak Nassirian, associate executive director of the American Association of Collegiate Registrars and Admissions Officers. "There are very few institutions that would be negatively affected by the undergraduate decision."

The head of the conservative public-interest law firm that represented unsuccessful white applicants to Michigan, however, says the court's action will make it more difficult for universities to use racial preferences by precluding the mechanistic formulae that he believes are common. Terence Pell, president of the Washington-based Center for Individual Rights, warns universities not to use the rulings as a "fig leaf" to preserve the status quo.

"Some schools are determined to continue to take race into account, and it's business as usual for them," Pell said after the court's decisions. The center plans to monitor responses to the decisions, Pell said, and challenge any schools claiming to review applicants individually but still using a "mechanistic" formula to favor minority candidates.[1]

Immediately after the rulings, Michigan President Mary Sue Coleman greeted reporters at the Supreme Court with a broad smile. "This is a wonderful day," she said, adding that the undergraduate college would be able to change its system to comply with the court's decision by the fall.[2]

The court's 6-3 ruling in the undergraduate case — *Gratz v. Bollinger* — faulted the College of Literature, Science and the Arts for awarding minority applicants a fixed bonus of 20 points out of a maximum score of 150, with 100 points needed to qualify for admission. By contrast, the 5-4 majority in the law-school case — *Grutter v. Bollinger* — found that the admissions process used by the law school was constitutional because officers considered race or ethnicity as only one factor in trying to achieve a "critical mass" of minority candidates needed for a diverse student body.

Nassirian says the rulings will speed a movement already under way among colleges and universities toward what admissions officers call "full-folder review" of applicants. "Most applicants want to be treated fairly," he says, "and

soned race relations more," writes Harvard's Kennedy, "than racially discriminatory policing, pursuant to which blacks are watched, questioned and detained more than others."[23]

Lawsuits challenging the constitutionality of racial profiling have led to settlements in California, Maryland and other states, many of which have revised their policies for stopping motorists.[24] In March, New Jersey became the first state to ban profiling.[25] And in June, President Bush banned racial profiling at the federal level — except in cases involving terrorism and national security.

But the Manhattan Institute's Mac Donald, author of *Are Cops Racist?* says police don't target blacks because of race. "It's not racism that sends police departments into black neighborhoods," she says. "It's crime."

Merely comparing numbers of stops and arrests with raw census data is an exercise in false logic, she argues. "The way the anti-police activists are spinning numbers is very clever," Mac Donald says. Comparing arrest records for blacks and whites is just as spurious as complaining that too few senior citizens are arrested, despite the fact that they don't commit as many violent crimes as younger people, she says.

Complaints about profiling, Mac Donald warns, can make police officers wary of going after black offenders, for fear of exceeding their allowable quota of African-American arrests. In Cincinnati, where police changed their tactics after blacks rioted in 2001, arrests dropped by 30 percent in 2002, but homicides reached a 15-year high, she notes.[26]

they don't want to be eliminated on the basis of two or three data elements."

But Bradford Wilson, executive director of the National Association of Scholars, in Princeton, N.J., notes that the undergraduate college defended its fixed-bonus system on the grounds that individualized review was impossible given its large volume of applications. "I just don't see how it's possible to do what the Supreme Court called meaningful, individualized review without having a virtual army of [undergraduate] admissions officers reviewing applicants," says Wilson, whose group opposed both Michigan admissions procedures.

The court's rulings came after a period of retrenchment on affirmative action in some states, including three with big public-university systems: Texas, California and Florida. Texas had to suspend racial preferences in admissions after a March 1996 federal appeals-court decision in a suit against the University of Texas Law School.[3] California voters approved an initiative in November 1996, Proposition 209, which barred consideration of race or national origin in admissions. And in February 2000, Gov. Jeb Bush, R-Fla., adopted a so-called "One Florida" program that similarly ended the use of race in admissions at state universities.

In Texas, Larry Faulkner, president of the university's Austin campus, said the school would resume some form of racial admissions policies for the class entering in fall 2004.[4] University of California President Richard Atkinson, however, said the school would continue to comply with the state's initiative barring race-based admis-

sions. In Florida, Bush also reaffirmed the policy against considering race in university admissions.

All three states also adopted so-called percentage plans for state universities to admit any high-school graduate with a class rank above a fixed cutoff point — the top 10 percent, for example, in Texas. In a brief opposing the Michigan admissions policies, the Bush administration endorsed the ostensibly race-neutral alternative to racial preferences. Percentage plans are designed to create diversity by ensuring representation from all schools, including those that are predominantly black or Hispanic.

But in her majority opinion in the Michigan law-school case, Justice Sandra Day O'Connor said such approaches "may preclude" individualized assessment of applicants and prevent universities from achieving diversity in other respects besides race.

— *Kenneth Jost*

[1] Quoted in Diana J. Schemo, "Group Vows to Monitor Academia's Responses," *The New York Times*, June 24, 2003, p. A22. For other statements and materials, see the center's Web site: www.cir.org.

[2] For the text of a letter on the ruling that Coleman sent to the university community and other materials, see the university's Web site: http://www.umich.edu/~urel/admissions/.

[3] The case is *Hopwood v. University of Texas Law School*, 78 F.3d 392.(5th Cir. 1996). The ruling, which the U.S. Supreme Court declined to review, also covered the states of Louisiana and Mississippi.

[4] Reaction from the three states is compiled in Jeffrey Selingo, "Decisions May Prompt Return of Race-Conscious Admissions at Some Colleges," *The Chronicle of Higher Education*, July 4, 2003, p. S5.

In a widely cited study, Michael Tonry, director of the University of Cambridge's Institute of Criminology, maintains that more blacks are locked up because they commit more "imprisonable crimes."[27]

Perhaps more poignantly, Jesse Jackson once said, "There is nothing more painful for me at this stage in my life than to walk down the street and hear footsteps and start to think about robbery and see it's somebody white and feel relieved." [28]

Still, some critics say when blacks do commit crimes, they can't get a fair shake from the criminal-justice system. Although even critics of the system admit that data is scarce comparing how blacks and whites are sentenced for committing the same crimes, the University of California's Wellman cites studies in Georgia and New

York that show racial differences in the prison terms imposed for similar offenses.

Members of the Congressional Black Caucus — including Rep. John Conyers, D-Mich., the ranking Democrat on the Judiciary Committee — often complain that sentencing guidelines are much harsher for crack cocaine, predominantly used and sold by blacks, than for powder cocaine, used primarily by whites. But critics of that argument note the Black Caucus pushed hard for tough laws against crack precisely because it is a scourge in predominantly black communities.[29]

But the biggest disparities result because of where police concentrate their enforcement efforts, says Marc Mauer, assistant director of the Sentencing Project. "Drug use and abuse cuts across race and class lines, but drug-law enforcement is primarily located in the inner cities," Mauer says. Moreover, he points out, white suburban teenagers caught with drugs might be sent to treatment programs instead of being prosecuted, but similar treatment isn't offered to blacks: "In a low-income community, those resources aren't provided to the same extent, so [drug possession] is much more likely to be defined as a criminal-justice problem."

Critics of the criminal-justice system also argue that street crimes are prosecuted more harshly than white-collar crimes, which primarily are committed by whites. But that's because tax fraud and securities abuse are less of a societal concern than armed robbery, says Harvard sociologist Christopher Jencks. "Given a choice, almost everyone would rather be robbed by a computer than at gunpoint," he writes.[30]

Racial disparities also exist in the use of the death penalty, according to a recent Maryland study. It found that blacks who murdered whites were far more likely to face the death penalty than either white killers or blacks who killed other blacks.[31] A court-appointed committee in Pennsylvania announced in March that the state should halt executions pending a study of racial bias.[32] Several other states have commissioned studies to determine whether the death penalty is applied more often or unfairly to blacks.

"Generally, discrimination based on the race of the defendant has tremendously declined," says David Baldus, a University of Iowa law professor who has studied racial bias in the death penalty. "But discrimination based on the race of victim has continued."

BACKGROUND

Road to Emancipation

By 1619, the first African slaves had been brought to Virginia, and by the 1640s slavery was well-established, mostly in the Southern colonies. Between 1680 and 1750, the colonies' blacks — who were virtually all slaves — grew from just under 5 percent of the population to more than 20 percent.[33] As slavery grew, so did the repressiveness of racial laws governing non-slaves. In the early 18th century, free blacks endured higher taxes and more severe criminal punishments than white colonials, with several Southern states denying them suffrage.

However, whites turned to blacks for support in their war against the British during the American Revolution. In part, this was a natural outgrowth of the egalitarian ideals that had become the rallying call for the Americans — even though the Continental Congress had struck anti-slavery language from Thomas Jefferson's draft of the Declaration of Independence.

"How is it that we hear the loudest yelps for liberty among the drivers of Negroes?" mocked British author Samuel Johnson.[34]

But British commanders had promised freedom to any slave who fought on their side, so the Americans matched the offer. By 1775, George Washington, who had originally opposed recruiting black soldiers, wrote: "Success will depend on which side can arm the Negroes the faster."[35]

By war's end, most colonies and the Continental Congress were enlisting blacks, with the understanding that freedom would be their reward for fighting. Thousands served as soldiers and laborers, while thousands more took advantage of the confusion of war to flee from white masters in the South.

But the promises of freedom turned out, in many cases, to be empty ones. After the war, most of the New England states banned slavery, but the Southern states, of course, continued the practice.

Many of the economic gains made by blacks during the war were short-lived, and their political and legal status soon slipped as well. The Fugitive Slave Law of 1793 pledged the aid of federal courts in returning escaped slaves to their masters. With fear of slave revolts growing, abolitionism never took root in the South, and by the early 19th century several Northern states had disenfranchised free blacks.

A number of frontier states barred not just slaves but all blacks, purely out of racial hatred, as contemporary debates made clear. Then a new Fugitive Slave Act in 1850 expanded the role of the federal government in the search for escaped slaves.

Life for freed blacks was tenuous, indeed, a situation made abundantly clear by the Supreme Court's 1857 *Dred Scott* decision. The infamous ruling determined that runaway slaves like Scott remained the property of their masters, even after they had escaped to free states. The court also said persons of African descent could never become citizens with the right to sue, and overturned bans on slavery in the frontier territories.

In early 1861, Congress approved a constitutional amendment protecting the institution of slavery, but it

CHRONOLOGY

1940s–1950s *World War II and its aftermath presage big changes for African-Americans as the migration north intensifies and the civil-rights movement takes off.*

1941 World War II causes an immediate shortage of industrial labor at home, increasing the migration of Southern African-Americans to Northern urban areas.

1947 Jackie Robinson joins the Brooklyn Dodgers, becoming the first black to play Major League Baseball.

July 26, 1948 President Harry S Truman ends racial segregation in the armed forces.

1954 The Supreme Court's landmark *Brown v. Board of Education* ruling overturns the previous "separate but equal" policy in public education.

1955 Rosa Parks refuses to give up her seat on a city bus to a white man, sparking the Montgomery, Ala., bus boycott. The Rev. Dr. Martin Luther King Jr. emerges as a civil-rights leader.

1960s *The civil-rights movement prompts Congress to enact legislation aimed at ending discrimination.*

1961 President John F. Kennedy uses the term "affirmative action" for the first time, ordering federal contractors to give preferential treatment to minorities in hiring.

1963 Dr. King gives his stirring "I Have a Dream" speech at the Lincoln Memorial in Washington.

1964 The Civil Rights Act prohibits job discrimination based on race, sex or national origin.

1965 President Lyndon B. Johnson signs the Voting Rights Act. In September he orders federal contractors to actively recruit minorities.

1968 Dr. King is assassinated, touching off race riots in many U.S. cities.

1970s–1980s *New policies like affirmative action are adopted, prompting a backlash among whites.*

1970 President Richard M. Nixon requires contractors to set goals for minority employment.

1978 In *University of California Regents v. Bakke*, the Supreme Court rules that universities can use race as a factor in admissions, but may not impose quotas.

1980 Affirmative-action foe Ronald Reagan is elected to the presidency. The Justice Department begins attacking racial quotas.

1990s–2000s *As affirmative action is challenged in the courts, racist-tinged incidents continue to shock the nation.*

1991 Black motorist Rodney King is kicked and beaten by white Los Angeles police officers; their acquittal in 1992 touches off major rioting. Eventually they are convicted of civil-rights violations.

1993 Supreme Court rules in *Shaw v. Reno* that race cannot be used as the "predominant" factor in drawing political districts.

1996 Voters in California approve Proposition 209 outlawing the use of race or gender preferences at all state government institutions.

1998 Three white men in Jasper, Texas, drag black James Byrd Jr. to death behind their pickup truck. Two are sentenced to death; a third is sentenced to life in prison.

2002 Sen. Trent Lott says the country would have been better off if then-segregationist Gov. Strom Thurmond had been elected president in 1948; after outcry, Lott steps down as Senate majority leader.

Jan. 15, 2003 President Bush announces that his administration sides with affirmative-action opponents against University of Michigan admissions policies.

June 2003 Supreme Court upholds the University of Michigan's qualified use of race as a factor in admissions. . . . Blacks riot in Benton Harbor, Mich., to protest allegedly racist police tactics.

The N-Word and Other Racist Symbols

If you want to rile up black folk," says jazz singer Rene Marie of Atlanta, Ga., "wave the Confederate flag, sing 'Dixie' or say 'nigger.' "

Marie notes that the words to "Dixie" are not objectionable in and of themselves. But they hold negative connotations for her fellow African-Americans because it was the South's Civil War anthem and was sometimes sung by white Southerners in reaction to the civil-rights movement. Marie wants to reclaim "Dixie" to protest her feelings of being excluded from mainstream Southern culture even though she was born in the region. "That song talks about longing for the South. Well, a majority of black people are from the South — they should be able to express those feelings, too."

Marie's emotionally vulnerable version, though, speaks to different memories of the Old South. On stage, she segues from "Dixie" into "Strange Fruit," the graphic song about lynching made famous by jazz singer Billie Holiday. But with its pounding rhythm and wrenching cries, Marie's rendition is more aggressive than Holiday's.

Marie remembers being nervous about how audiences would respond to the medley, particularly black listeners. Now, when she starts "Dixie," her fans applaud. Still, the combined effect of the two songs is harrowing, an angry reminder of the uglier legacies of the South.

Some black performers and other African-Americans have sought to reconfigure the meaning of "nigger," which Los Angeles prosecutor Christopher Darden famously called the "filthiest, dirtiest, nastiest word in the English language" during the O.J. Simpson murder trial. It has been "a familiar and influential insult" at least since the 1830s,

writes Harvard University Professor Randall Kennedy in his recent book about the hateful word.[1]

Today, many blacks use the term to mean "friend" or simply to signify a black person.[2] "When we call each other 'nigger,' it means no harm," says the rap star and actor Ice Cube. "But if a white person uses it, it's something different, it's a racist word."[3]

Black comedian Chris Rock jokes about the differences between black people and "niggers," yet follows that up with a story in which he punches a white fan for repeating the same material. For blacks, whites using the word are offering an insulting reminder that they are perceived as inferior, a caste at a level to which whites can never sink. (Sen. Robert C. Byrd, D-W. Va., who as a young man belonged to the Ku Klux Klan, had to apologize for twice referring to "white niggers" during a Fox TV appearance in 2001.)

Over the past year, local governments from Baltimore to San Jose have passed resolutions denouncing the use of the word.[4] Indeed, it remains such a potent insult that some white people claim not to be racist just because they refrain from saying it. A mobster who referred to blacks as "spades," "shines" and "coons" insisted to author Studs Terkel that he was nonetheless not a racist. "Did you ever hear me say 'nigger'? Never!"[5]

Whites and blacks also remain in conflict over the Confederate flag. For African-Americans, the "stars and bars" are a reminder not only of the South's fight to preserve slavery but also its resistance to desegregation. Some states returned to waving Confederate flags, or added aspects of it to their official state flags, during the

was never ratified by the requisite three-quarters of the states. The measure apparently was designed to allay Southerners' fears that the 1860 election of President Lincoln — who had advocated banning slavery in the territories — threatened slavery in the South. Unconvinced, 11 Southern states seceded from the Union, beginning in 1861. The country was soon at war.

Rise of 'Jim Crow'

On Jan. 1, 1863, Lincoln issued his Emancipation Proclamation, freeing all slaves in the territories and Border States. Although Lincoln had not wanted to

make slavery the central issue of the conflict between the North and the South, the Confederacy still focused on it. Even before issuing the proclamation, Lincoln — like Washington — recognized that putting blacks to use as soldiers had become "a military necessity."

After the North's victory, Congress passed the 13th, 14th and 15th amendments to the Constitution, which vacated the *Dred Scott* decision and gave blacks citizenship and the vote. Southern states wishing to rejoin the Union had to ratify the amendments.

After an anti-abolitionist assassinated Lincoln in 1865, his successors were reluctant to advocate further civil rights

1950s and '60s to symbolize their defiance of civil-rights pressures.

Since 1999, the National Association for the Advancement of Colored People (NAACP) has organized economic boycotts of states that fly the Confederate flag. South Carolina has since taken the flag down from its Capitol, while Mississippi voters opted to keep it flying. In Georgia, Republican Gov. Sonny Perdue was elected last fall largely on his pledge to let voters decide whether to restore the Confederate cross to the state flag.[6]

Many Southern whites argue that the Confederate flag, which some Southerners call the "battle flag," is not meant to be racist, but represents their heritage and is an expression of pride.

"Actually, in the South the battle flag is so ubiquitous it doesn't have a single meaning," says William Rolen, Southern-heritage defense coordinator for the Council of Conservative Citizens in Tennessee. Not only is the emblem found on countless bumper stickers, but Confederate flag T-shirts marketed to children are million-

Liaison/Erik S. Lesser

Georgia voters will decide in March whether to restore the traditional Confederate battle symbol (shown above in the 1956 flag) to the state flag.

sellers. But dozens of Southern school districts have banned them.[7]

"It's just totally inconceivable that any other group that stood for something so vile and was defeated would be given this place of honor," says William Spriggs, executive director of the National Urban League's Institute for Opportunity and Equality, referring to Southern capitals that fly the flag. "One could not imagine that the mayor of Paris would fly a Nazi flag because the Germans ruled France for part of World War II."

---

[1] Randall Kennedy, *Nigger: The Strange Career of a Troublesome Word* (2002), p. 4.

[2] Clarence Page, "A Word That Wounds — If We Let It," *Chicago Tribune*, Oct. 12, 1997, p. 25.

[3] Quoted in Kennedy, *op. cit.*, p. 41.

[4] Sarah Lubman, "Black Activists in S.J. Mount Campaign to Eliminate Slur," *San Jose Mercury News*, Jan. 28, 2003, p. A1.

[5] Studs Terkel, *Race: How Blacks and Whites Think and Feel About the American Obsession* (1992), p. 5.

[6] See "Phew," *The Economist*, May 3, 2003, p. 33.

[7] "Dixie Chic," *People*, March 10, 2003, p. 100.

---

for blacks, and the Supreme Court did little to encourage enforcement of the civil-rights laws that existed.

In fact, emboldened by court interpretations that elevated states' rights above those of blacks, Southern states passed a series of so-called Jim Crow laws stripping blacks of stature and legal protections. Named after a minstrel character, the legislation was carefully written in race-neutral language to pass constitutional muster. Most infamously, the Supreme Court in 1896 upheld segregation laws, ruling in *Plessy v. Ferguson* that "separate but equal" accommodations did not intrinsically benefit one race over another.

Oklahoma soon required "separate but equal" telephone booths. New Orleans kept black and white prostitutes segregated. Florida and North Carolina made it illegal for whites to read textbooks that had been used by blacks.[36] Meanwhile, throughout the first half of the 20th century, Southern schools for blacks received only a fraction of what was spent to educate whites. As Mississippi Gov. James K. Vardaman put it in 1909, "Money spent today for the maintenance of public school for Negroes is robbery of the white man, and a waste upon the Negro."[37]

In many places, blacks were systematically deprived of the right to vote, and between the post-Civil War

Reconstruction period and the turn of the century their turnout dropped 90 percent or more in some Southern states. The Supreme Court, increasingly influenced by Justice (and ex-klansman) Edward White, was deaf to the loudest complaints about voting-rights abuses.

Some Southern leaders even bragged about the region's concerted efforts to marginalize — and even eliminate — blacks. "We have done our level best," said Ben Tillman of the South Carolina Constitutional Convention. "We have scratched our heads to find out how we could eliminate the last one of them. We stuffed ballot boxes. We shot them. We are not ashamed."[38]

By the turn of the century, lynchings were more common in some years than legal executions. In a recent history of lynching, author Philip Dray notes that more than 3,400 blacks were lynched between 1882 and 1944. "Is it possible for white America to really understand blacks' distrust of the legal system, their fears of racial profiling and the police, without understanding how cheap a black life was for so long a time in our nation's history?" Dray asks.[39]

Blacks began to move north searching for better jobs and more political opportunity. Racial tensions during the economic upheaval that followed World War I led to riots in 1919 in about two-dozen Northern cities. But whites were unable to drive the blacks out, despite dozens of fire-bombings of black homes.

Instead, beginning in the 1920s, whites left the cities in droves, a phenomenon called "white flight." Jobs often followed the whites to the suburbs. By 1940, 80 percent of the country's urban blacks lived in segregated neighborhoods, compared to less than a third in 1860.[40] Meanwhile, none of the five Deep South states — home to 40 percent of the nation's black population — had even a single black policeman.[41]

Civil-Rights Era

As in the Revolutionary and Civil wars, the pressures of World War II helped move desegregation forward. In 1941, as thousands of African-Americans were planning to march on Washington to protest hiring discrimination in the defense industries, President Franklin D. Roosevelt signed an executive order barring such discrimination and creating a Fair Employment Practices Committee (FEPC) to investigate such complaints. (Although the planned march

The Rev. Dr. Martin Luther King Jr. delivered his stirring "I Have a Dream" address during the March on Washington in August 1963. The assassination of the civil-rights leader five years later touched off race riots in many cities.

was canceled, the idea was to re-emerge in 1963, providing the occasion for civil-rights leader Martin Luther King Jr.'s celebrated "I Have a Dream" speech.)

Meanwhile, Southern blacks continued migrating by the millions to Northern cities in search of factory jobs; more than 3 million African-Americans moved north between 1940 and 1960.[42]

In 1948, President Harry S Truman — bowing to pressure from blacks, whom he needed for political support, and his personal revulsion at how some black veterans were physically attacked when they returned home from the war — signed an executive order desegregating the armed services. His action, coupled with a strong civil-rights plank in the Democratic Party's presidential platform that year, prompted many Southerners to walk out of the Democratic convention to protest the party's new commitment to civil-rights. South Carolina Gov. Strom Thurmond then ran for president as the nominee of the States' Rights Party, better known as the Dixiecrats, as an opponent of integration. Thurmond carried four Southern states.

On May 17, 1954, in the landmark *Brown v. Board of Education* decision, the U.S. Supreme Court unanimously declared that separate educational facilities are "inherently unequal" and thus violate the Constitution's 14th Amendment, which guarantees all citizens "equal protection under the law." The court ordered schools to be desegregated "with all deliberate speed." But the South was recalcitrant. Several years after the decision, less than 2 percent of Southern black students attended integrated schools.[43]

But if Southern whites were defiant, so, increasingly, were Southern blacks. In 1955 in Montgomery, Ala., Rosa Parks refused to give up her bus seat to a white man. Her arrest sparked a bus boycott led by King, which eventually prompted a Supreme Court decision banning segregation on buses.

Other blacks pressed their demands for equal rights through lunch-counter sit-ins, marches and "freedom rides." They were met with violence, as were orders to desegregate schools. In 1957 President Dwight D. Eisenhower federalized the Arkansas National Guard to force the entry of nine black students into Little Rock's Central High School. Five years later, President John F. Kennedy made the same decision in response to white violence when James Meredith became the first black to enroll in the University of Mississippi.

On June 11, 1963, after a confrontation over Gov. George Wallace's refusal to allow black students to register at the University of Alabama, Kennedy announced in a televised address that he would push Congress to pass a civil-rights bill that had been languishing for years. As was often the case during the 1960s, Kennedy couched the importance of the bill in terms of improving America's image abroad — an important strategic consideration during the Cold War.

Five months later Kennedy was assassinated, and President Lyndon B. Johnson vowed that passing the civil-rights bill would be a fitting memorial. Johnson eventually outlasted the filibuster — the obstructionist tactic typically employed by Southern senators — against such bills.[44] The Senate voted to close debate and passed the most important piece of civil-rights legislation in the nation's history — the Civil Rights Act of 1964 — outlawing discrimination in employment and public accommodations.[45]

However, King and others continued a series of nonviolent protests in the South, including a 1965 march from Selma to Montgomery, Ala., to protest state and local discrimination against blacks seeking the right to vote. They were met by state troopers wielding cattle prods, nightsticks and rubber hoses wrapped in barbed wire.

In response, Johnson proposed a law to "strike down restrictions to voting in all elections — federal, state and local — which have been used to deny Negroes the right to vote." The Voting Rights Act, cleared by Congress in 1965, outlawed literacy tests and similar qualification devices used to keep blacks off the rolls. Johnson signed the bill in full knowledge that it might weaken his party in the South.

That same year, Johnson ordered federal contractors to take "affirmative action to ensure that [black] applicants are employed." He had declared earlier, "You do not take a person who, for years, has been hobbled by chains and liberate him, bring him up to the starting line in a race and then say, 'you are free to compete with all the others.' "[46]

After King was assassinated in 1968, blacks rioted in 125 cities, mostly in the North. Within days, Congress passed an open-housing law — the Fair Housing Act — which had previously languished, but included no enforcement provisions.[47]

A Dream Deferred?

The Johnson administration proved to be the high-water mark for civil-rights legislation, although new versions of the Civil and Voting Rights acts have since been passed.

By the 1970s, de jure (legal) segregation was finished, voting rights for blacks were secure for the first time in U.S. history and economic improvements for many blacks had become irreversible. By 1970, 22 percent of black men and 36 percent of black women were holding white-collar jobs — four to six times the percentages, respectively, in 1940.

But some of the laws had little or no enforcement power. The rigor with which anti-discrimination laws were enforced would vary from one administration to the next. Meanwhile, the focus of anti-discrimination efforts broadened to include women, Hispanics, Native Americans and the young. (The voting age was lowered from 21 to 18 in 1970 as part of a Voting Rights Act extension.)

One of the major controversies between the races during the 1970s concerned the attempt to force integration by busing children out of their home neighborhoods in order to balance schools' racial demographics. Some of the stiffest resistance occurred in the North, notably in Boston, where a photograph of a white crowd holding a black man and attempting to impale him with an American flag won a Pulitzer Prize. The focus of numerous court challenges, busing has since been discontinued.

Since the 1970s, Johnson's prediction about Southern whites bolting the Democratic Party has largely

Fostering Integration on Campus and Beyond

Irini Bekhit was born in Egypt, but she feels right at home at the New Jersey Institute of Technology (NJIT) in Newark. When her fellow students socialize, some separate along racial or ethnic lines, but Bekhit says most students are working so hard they don't have time for the racial rivalries that mark many other campuses. Even many of the fraternities are racially mixed. "Everyone here is so different, it becomes a non-issue," Bekhit says. "You get used to it just from walking around."

U.S. News & World Report magazine ranked NJIT the eighth-most-diverse doctorate-granting campus in the nation.[1] The school is 20 percent Asian, 9 percent black, 9 percent Hispanic and 18 percent foreign-born. Dean of Students Jack Gentul says the school has fewer racial problems than New York University — which has the country's largest proportion of international students — where he ran diversity programs for 15 years.

The U.S. armed services, desegregated by President Harry S Truman in 1948, are generally considered a strong example of successful integration.

"The degree of integration here is much greater, and I don't know why," he admits. "I would certainly get another Ph.D. if I could explain it well. I wish I could bottle it."

Most successfully integrated institutions work hard to create and maintain an inclusive atmosphere. The armed services, desegregated by President Harry S Truman in 1948, are often touted as an exceptionally strong example of integration — and one of the rare places in American life where whites routinely take orders from blacks.

"There are aspects of military culture that were conducive to change despite massive resistance," says Sherie Merson, co-author of a study of military integration. Those aspects include the military's culture of meritocracy; its sense of shared purpose, to which individuals subordinate their individual identities; and its command-and-control structure, which can impose programs over the objections of those individuals.

come true. President Richard M. Nixon, a Republican, initially opposed the 1970 Voting Rights extension, responding to pressure from Southerners objecting to aspects of the law that applied only to their region. In the face of a growing political backlash against race-based preferential treatment in education or employment, the once solidly Democratic South has turned to a modern Republican Party that favors color-blind policies of equal opportunity for all. Beginning in 1968, working-class whites began to abandon the Democrats in presidential politics, and the party would go on to lose four out of the next five presidential contests.

Republicans aggressively encouraged the exodus of disaffected white voters from the Democratic Party. In 1980, GOP presidential nominee Ronald Reagan was accusing "strapping young bucks" and Cadillac-driving "welfare queens" of abusing the welfare system. "If you happen to belong to an ethnic group not recognized by the federal government as entitled to special treatment, you are the victim of reverse discrimination," he said.[48]

Reagan slashed funding for federal equal-protection agencies, but his administration was unable to limit affirmative-action programs. Meanwhile, in 1996, a federal court ruled that the University of Texas law school could not use affirmative action to create a diverse student body. That same year, California voters barred the state from using race as a factor in employment, contracts or university admissions. Black freshman enrollment dropped throughout the University of California system, but has since recovered except at the flagship Berkeley campus.[49]

Even many African-Americans worry that affirmative-action programs have primarily helped the most affluent

Moreover, the Department of Defense diligently runs racial-awareness programs to keep biases from coloring decisions. "What really makes the difference is the training we give. It helps officers realize they have to treat each person fairly and with respect, and they don't allow any embedded biases to cause them to treat one person better than another," says Capt. Robert Watts, commander of the Defense Equal Opportunity Management Institute.

Weldon Latham, who runs the corporate-diversity practice at Holland & Knight, one of the nation's biggest and most diverse law firms, says that although blacks are still underrepresented in corporate America, many big companies have taken major strides toward integrating their work forces. "The enlightened CEOs get it — and get it for the right reason, the same reason they get everything else — the bottom line," Latham says.

America's shifting demographics and the ever-increasing pursuit of markets overseas have made it advantageous for companies to have staffs that match, to some extent, the profile of their customers, he points out.

Yet even organizations that strive to recruit blacks find that racial disparities can slip back into their midst. Blacks have never been as well represented in the military officer corps as among enlisted personnel, and even their share of the enlisted ranks has been slipping in recent years as the job market has improved.

Affluent Shaker Heights, Ohio, is often touted for having bucked the trend toward residential segregation that is pronounced in the Cleveland area. The city has long devoted about a half-million dollars annually to providing low-interest loans to people willing to buy houses in neighborhoods where their race is underrepresented. "Shaker Heights has been as aggressive as any place in trying to address the issue," says Ronald Ferguson, who teaches at Harvard University's Kennedy School of Government and is senior research associate at Harvard's Weiner Center for Social Policy. "It's trying to maintain racial and, to a lesser degree, socioeconomic diversity."

Yet city officials say their vaunted loan program has found fewer takers of late, largely because interest rates are so low generally. As a result, locals worry about the re-segregation of many blocks. They are especially concerned that white parents have begun pulling their children from the public schools.

NJIT's Gentul finds it heartening to know that in little pockets effort at racial integration and understanding can work. But Harry Holzer, a labor economist at Georgetown University, finds himself discouraged by the fact that such situations are difficult to replicate, or sustain. "You can end your career with a broken heart," he says, "because there are great model programs here or there, and you try to re-create them or bring them up to scale, and they fail."

---

[1] "Step 2: Choose the Right School," *U.S. News & World Report,* Sept. 13, 2002, p. 45.

blacks instead of the neediest. And the policy has not lowered poverty rates among African-Americans: Since 1970, the overall poverty rate for blacks has not budged, dragged down by ever-burgeoning numbers of households headed by single women.[50]

Persistent Poverty

Both liberal and conservative writers blame persistent poverty on high rates of unwed pregnancy, particularly among teenagers. But while liberals generally blamed the pregnancies on poverty, conservatives blamed what they felt were wrong-headed welfare policies that rewarded out-of-wedlock births, perpetuating cycles of poverty from generation to generation. In 1996, Congress changed the welfare law to limit the lifespan of benefits and require recipients, including mothers, to work.

Republicans claim that the new law has done more to lift black families out of poverty than any of the Johnson-era Great Society programs.[51]

Despite persistent poverty, a black middle class has arisen, primarily the result of public and nonprofit-sector employment, with middle-class blacks disproportionately entering jobs in government, the postal service, teaching and social work. In 2000, African-Americans made up 35 percent of the nation's postal clerks and 25 percent of the social workers, but only 5 percent of the lawyers and engineers and 4 percent of the dentists.[52] Yet, even critics of affirmative action agree that it helped accelerate, albeit slowly, the entry of African-Americans into the professional class.

In 1990, concerned that a series of Supreme Court rulings had weakened employment-discrimination law,

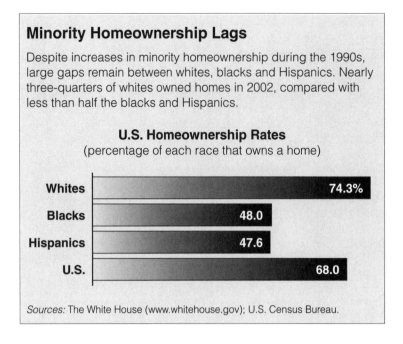

Minority Homeownership Lags

Despite increases in minority homeownership during the 1990s, large gaps remain between whites, blacks and Hispanics. Nearly three-quarters of whites owned homes in 2002, compared with less than half the blacks and Hispanics.

U.S. Homeownership Rates
(percentage of each race that owns a home)

Whites	74.3%
Blacks	48.0
Hispanics	47.6
U.S.	68.0

Sources: The White House (www.whitehouse.gov); U.S. Census Bureau.

Congress passed a tough, new Civil Rights Act to counteract the decisions. After lengthy negotiations and a major fight over the appointment of African-American Clarence Thomas to the Supreme Court, an initially reluctant President George Bush signed the new law in 1991.[53] The law expanded the anti-discrimination law to cover women and the disabled, as well as racial groups, and boosted the power of the Equal Employment Opportunity Commission (EEOC).

The Supreme Court was heavily involved in racial politics during the 1990s as well. The Justice Department had interpreted the 1982 Voting Rights Act to mean that, whenever possible, legislative districts with a high likelihood of electing blacks or other minorities should be drawn. After the redistricting cycle of the early 1990s, this led to large increases in the numbers of African-Americans elected to Congress and state legislatures.

However, the Supreme Court took exception to the Justice Department's earlier interpretation. In cases involving majority-minority congressional districts, the court ruled in the 1990s that such districts violated the 14th Amendment rights of white voters and said race could not be used as a "predominant" factor in drawing legislative districts.[54] In another voting-rights controversy, the U.S. Civil Rights Commission investigated

hundreds of complaints stemming from the 2000 presidential election alleging racial discrimination in Florida and elsewhere.

Meanwhile, the age-old debate continues about the harmful effects the legacy of slavery might be having on today's African-Americans. Since 1989, Rep. Conyers repeatedly has introduced legislation calling for reparations — payments to the descendants of slaves — sparking controversy in the states and on college campuses.[55]

With racial discrimination outlawed by the federal government, the political goals of blacks seeking to improve their standing in society became less clear. An age-old split widened between African-Americans who favored confrontation or reparations and those who favored individual improvement. As a result, many observers argue that black conservatives have "sold out"; others say civil-rights activists continue to be pessimistic about race relations to serve their own cause.

In essence, the "double-consciousness" for black Americans that the celebrated civil-rights leader and author W.E.B. Du Bois wrote about a century ago — "to be both a Negro and an American, without being cursed and spit upon by his fellows, without having the doors of opportunity closed roughly in his face" — continues today.[56]

CURRENT SITUATION

Affirmative-Action Ruling

The Supreme Court's June 23 decisions involving two University of Michigan admissions policies turned on the question of whether racial preferences are discriminatory toward other groups, such as whites.

By a 5-4 vote in *Grutter v. Bollinger*, the court granted continuing legal favor to the law school's practice of affirmative action. The case centered on a challenge to the law school's policy of using race as a "plus factor" in accepting students. The court found that using race as one factor among many in determining individual admissions was acceptable.

But in *Gratz v. Bollinger*, by a 6-3 vote, the justices found unconstitutional the undergraduate school's practice of granting 20 points, on a 150-point scale, to blacks and Latinos just because of their race. Quantifying race as a universal value, the court said, was unacceptable.

"In order to cultivate a set of leaders with legitimacy in the eyes of the citizenry," wrote Justice Sandra Day O'Connor in the majority opinion in *Grutter*, "it is necessary that the path to leadership be visibly open to talented and qualified individuals of every race and ethnicity." The law school engages in a "highly individualized, holistic review of each applicant's file," she wrote, in which race counts as a factor but is not used in a "mechanical way." For that reason, O'Connor explained, the policy was in keeping with a 1978 court ruling on affirmative action that permits using race as a "plus factor."

The court's ruling that decisions can be made based on race as long as they are not done in a purely quantitative manner struck some observers as hazy. But the biggest complaints were lodged by those who thought the court had given credence to the notion that members of some races should be granted advantages that are not enjoyed by all.

"Racial classifications in the United States have a long and ugly history," wrote U.S. Civil Rights Commissioner Thernstrom. "Racial subordination was all about double standards, with different entitlements depending on your racial identity. Nevertheless, the highest court in the land has now embraced them. It is a bleak day in American constitutional law."[57]

Affirmative-action supporters, however, echoed O'Connor's assertion that creating a diverse leadership class through more racially balanced admissions to top universities was a societal good worth preserving. For them, the court's decision was a cheering answer to a long series of attacks on affirmative action, including state-ballot initiatives banning the practice in California and elsewhere.

"A diverse and racially integrated campus benefits all students and ultimately, all of America," says Marc Morial, president of the National Urban League. "The court clearly upheld the argument that the government has a compelling interest in promoting diversity in education and the workplace."

Thus, the notion of helping members of minority groups, such as blacks and Latinos, through some formal process rather than relying on "color-blind" admissions and hiring policies, is, legally, here to stay. However, O'Connor also expressed the hope that race-based admissions policies would no longer be necessary in 25 years.

Advocates of such policies point to public universities in California, Florida and Texas that have devised new formulas for continued minority enrollment after dumping affirmative action. Admission is either guaranteed to the top students from each high school, including those where students are predominantly minorities, or they seek out low-income students, who are disproportionately black or Latino. The university systems have maintained or even increased their minority enrollments, except at their flagship campuses.[58]

The cases in many ways demonstrate the shifting political dynamics when race is at issue. When the court considered affirmative-action policies in *University of California Regents v. Bakke* in 1978, hardly any corporations engaged in the issue. In the Michigan case this time, however, a group of five-dozen *Fortune* 500 companies filed an *amicus* brief with the court, arguing that diverse campuses better prepare future workers for a global economy, especially in a country whose demographic trends suggest that whites no longer will account for a majority of the population by 2050.

Three days after the Michigan ruling, the Supreme Court used a Georgia case, *Georgia v. Ashcroft*, to signal a new direction in the ways blacks and other minorities can be represented politically. For the past 20 years, Justice Department officials have interpreted the Voting Rights Act to mean that whenever a legislative district could be created with a majority of minority voters, such districts should be created. Majority-minority districts have led to more black and Latino representation in both Congress and state legislatures over the past dozen years.

But some blacks and Democrats argued that majority-minority districts actually weaken political representation for blacks: By "packing" most black voters within racially separate districts, politicians from neighboring "bleached" (all-white) districts have no natural incentive to represent black interests. The state of Georgia created a map of state Senate districts that broke up some majority-black districts, in favor of creating more districts in which blacks could compete politically.

Anti-Arab Sentiment on the Rise $\rho \varphi^?$

For Yashar Zendehdel, an Iranian student at the University of Colorado, confusion over the number of academic credits he listed on his immigration paperwork led to a harrowing 26 hours in a federal jail. He was eventually cleared of any wrongdoing, but remains furious that he was treated like a criminal.[1]

"I couldn't believe it," Zendehdel said. "It was awful. I have never been to jail before. Government officials are wasting American people's tax money, my time, their time."[2]

"Discrimination against Arab-Americans and those perceived to be Arab-American has been a much bigger problem" since the Sept. 11, 2001, terrorist attacks by 19 Arab Muslims, says Laila Al-Qatami, of the American-Arab Anti-Discrimination Committee. "We've seen a lot more discrimination and hate-crime cases and a greater variety of cases."

In 2001, the FBI recorded 481 attacks against Middle Easterners, Muslims and Sikhs, compared with 28 attacks reported the previous year.[3] Job-discrimination complaints from Muslims roughly doubled after Sept. 11, from 542 in 2001 to 1,157 in 2002, according to the U.S. Equal Employment Opportunity Commission.[4]

And despite President Bush's declaration that Islam is a "religion of peace," some prominent politicians and religious leaders have made inflammatory remarks about Islam and Muslims. The Rev. Franklin Graham, son of the Rev. Billy Graham, called Islam "a very evil and wicked religion." Jerry Vines, former president of the Southern Baptist Convention, denounced the Islamic prophet Muhammad as a "demon-possessed pedophile."[5]

And Rep. John Cooksey, R-La., recommended that airline personnel selectively question Arab passengers. "If I see someone who comes in that's got a diaper on his head and a fan belt wrapped around the diaper on his head, that guy needs to be pulled over," Cooksey told a Louisiana radio interviewer.[6]

Moreover, some of the government's post-9/11 anti-terrorism programs have exacerbated Arabs' feelings of persecution and discrimination. The FBI began monitoring American mosques and encouraging thousands of Arab-Americans to undergo voluntary interviews. Many were arrested when they showed up. Recently, the FBI interviewed 5,000 Iraqis in the U.S. in an attempt to pre-empt terrorism related to the war in Iraq.[7]

The new National Security Entry-Exit Registration System (NSEERS) — created by Attorney General John Ashcroft under a congressional mandate — required tens of thousands of mostly Arab and Muslim men living in the United States to be fingerprinted by the government during so-called special-registration sweeps.[8]

The program also has begun registering foreigners at U.S. borders who meet government criteria as potential threats or persons of interest. So far, the programs have documented visitors from 155 countries, says Jorge Martinez, a Justice Department spokesman.

In some instances, large Arab turnouts at registration locations have overloaded officials and forced them to detain hundreds of people until they could be fully documented, complains James Zogby, president of the Washington-based Arab American Institute.

It's now widely believed that black politicians can win office in districts where blacks make up less than a majority of the electorate. Giving blacks a real opportunity, rather than an assured win, is good enough to protect their interests in the current racial climate, according to Swain of Vanderbilt Law School and other black scholars.

The Justice Department opposed Georgia's map, but the high court upheld the plan, 6-3. Writing for the majority, Justice O'Connor wrote that "various studies have suggested that the most effective way to maximize minority voting strength may be to create" districts "where minority voters may not

be able to elect a candidate of choice but [can] play a substantial, if not decisive, role in the electoral process."

Bush Administration

Many people predicted that after Lott lost his Senate leadership post for pro-segregationist remarks, the Republicans might show an increased interest in '60s-style civil-rights legislation. That has not been the case. With the momentum for race-specific programs slowing, the Congressional Black Caucus and African-American advocates have begun focusing on seeking equal treatment under laws and programs that apply to

"If you take all these pieces and you put them together, it produces a lot of fear in the Arab-American community," adds Al-Qatami.

Others say the registration programs are tantamount to racial profiling, a practice recently banned by the Bush administration. "The NSEERS program and special registration was a disaster," Zogby says, "and it clearly targeted Muslims and Arabs."

But the Justice Department insists registration programs only targeted people from countries that sponsor terrorism or harbor Al-Qaeda members. "The registration programs have absolutely nothing to do with race or religion," Martinez says. "People from certain countries were registered because they presented a higher national-security threat, and it's just coincidence that those countries happen to be a majority Arab and Muslim."

Others doubt the efficacy of registration programs. "So far, registration programs haven't netted much," Al-Qatami says. "If we just focus on certain ethnic or racial characteristics, we're going to miss other people who also commit crimes and terrorism," such as Richard Reid — the British Al-Qaeda sympathizer convicted of trying to destroy an airliner with a shoe bomb.

Government officials counter that national security trumps concerns over racial profiling. "When it relates to a national-security investigation, efforts to identify terrorists may include factors like race and ethnicity," Martinez says.

On a more positive note, law enforcement has won praise for prosecuting backlash crimes against Arab-Americans. Martinez notes the Justice Department has investigated more than 500 alleged backlash crimes, and 13 have been prosecuted successfully.

"Clearly, after Sept. 11 there was a directive that the government would take backlash crimes against Arab-Americans and Muslims seriously in an effort to stem hate crimes," Zogby says.

To strengthen ties with the Arab community, the FBI recently established an Arab-American Advisory Committee in Washington similar to committees in several other cities.[9] "Both law enforcement and the Arab-American community believe that a community-policing situation was the ideal way to break down the barriers of mistrust," says Zogby, a member of the D.C. advisory committee. "We've been able to do some good stuff together."

Others are more cautious. "Some positive things have come out of the experience," Al-Qatami says, "but we still have a long way to go."

— *Benton Ives-Halperin*

---

[1] Eric Hoover, "Closing the Gates: A Student Under Suspicion," *The Chronicle of Higher Education*, April 11, 2003, p. 12.

[2] Maria Bondes, "Foreign Students to Leave U. Colorado?" *Colorado Daily*, Jan. 7, 2003.

[3] Darryl Fears, "Hate Crimes Against Arabs Surge, FBI Finds," *The Washington Post*, Nov. 26, 2002, p. A2.

[4] Equal Employment Opportunity Commission fact sheet, June 11, 2003.

[5] Laurie Goodstein, "Seeing Islam as 'Evil' Faith, Evangelicals Seek Converts," *The New York Times*, May 27, 2003, p. A1.

[6] "National Briefing South: Louisiana: Apology From Congressman," *The New York Times*, Sept. 21, 2001, p. A16.

[7] "Under Suspicion," *The Economist*, March 29, 2003.

[8] Patrick J. McDonell, "Nearly 24,000 Foreign Men Register in U.S," *Los Angeles Times*, Jan. 19, 2003, p. A22.

[9] Alan Lengel and Caryle Murphy, "FBI, Arab Community Join Forces With Panel," *The Washington Post*, March 29, 2003, p. B1.

---

all Americans, advocating increased funding for domestic priorities like education and health. Meanwhile, Republicans continue to argue that race-neutral, market-based proposals will work better than further government intrusions into private-sector practices.

President Bush opposes race-specific government-aid programs. Afterschool programs that get federal aid are often in minority neighborhoods, because they are targeted at poor districts. In his fiscal 2004 budget, Bush proposed cutting federal grants to afterschool programs by 40 percent, to $600 million. It appears that Congress will fund the grants at last year's level of $1

billion, but that is still well below the $1.75 billion authorized by Bush's No Child Left Behind education-reform law.

In response to the Supreme Court's affirmative-action decisions and O'Connor's comments about the need for affirmative action fading after 25 years, Bush said he was glad that the court shared his vision of a color-blind America.

On June 17, Bush announced a new policy designed to severely curtail racial profiling by federal law-enforcement officers. Agents running auto-theft or drug investigations, for instance, cannot stop black or Latino motorists based on the "generalized assumption" that

Should colleges be allowed to use race as a factor in admissions?

YES — David W. DeBruin
Attorney, Jenner & Block

Excerpted from a Brief filed in the U.S. Supreme Court, *Grutter v. Bollinger,* Feb. 18, 2003.

Diversity in higher education is a compelling government interest not only because of its positive effects on the educational environment itself, but also because of the crucial role diversity in higher education plays in preparing students to be the leaders this country needs in business, law and all other pursuits that affect the public interest. . . .

[B]y enriching students' education with a variety of perspectives, experiences and ideas, a university with a diverse student body equips all of its students with the skills and understanding necessary to succeed in any profession. Those skills include the ability to understand, learn from, and work and build consensus with individuals from different backgrounds and cultures. . . .

There are several reasons for the importance of maintaining diversity in higher education. First, a diverse group of individuals educated in a cross-cultural environment has the ability to facilitate unique and creative approaches to problem-solving arising from the integration of different perspectives.

Second, such individuals are better able to develop products and services that appeal to a variety of consumers and to market offerings in ways that appeal to those consumers. Third, a racially diverse group of managers with cross-cultural experience is better able to work with business partners, employees and clientele in the United States and around the world. Fourth, individuals who have been educated in a diverse setting are likely to contribute to a positive work environment, by decreasing incidents of discrimination and stereotyping.

Overall, an educational environment that ensures participation by diverse people, viewpoints and ideas will help produce the most talented workforce. The thrust of the government's position is that it is permissible to take affirmative steps to ensure educational diversity — a goal that itself includes consideration of race. The United States defends particular admissions programs it prefers in Texas, Florida and California explicitly on the ground that those programs allegedly continue to produce, at least in raw numbers, the same racial and ethnic diversity in enrollment.

Institutions of higher learning must be allowed to prepare students to thrive in an increasingly diverse environment. The best way to do this is to ensure that students learn in an environment of diversity, including racial and cultural diversity. Accordingly, institutions of higher learning should be able to use "competitive consideration of race and ethnic origin" in pursuit of a diverse student body.

NO — George W. Bush
President of the United States

Excerpted from remarks made on Jan. 15, 2003

Our Constitution makes it clear that people of all races must be treated equally under the law. Yet we know that our society has not fully achieved that ideal. Racial prejudice is a reality in America. It hurts many of our citizens. As a nation, as a government, as individuals, we must be vigilant in responding to prejudice wherever we find it. Yet, as we work to address the wrong of racial prejudice, we must not use means that create another wrong, and thus perpetuate our divisions.

America is a diverse country, racially, economically and ethnically. And our institutions of higher education should reflect our diversity. A college education should teach respect and understanding and goodwill. And these values are strengthened when students live and learn with people from many backgrounds. Yet quota systems that use race to include or exclude people from higher education and the opportunities it offers are divisive, unfair and impossible to square with the Constitution. . . .

The University of Michigan has established an admissions process based on race. At the undergraduate level, African-American students and some Hispanic students and Native American students receive 20 points out of a maximum of 150, not because of any academic achievement or life experience, but solely because they are African-American, Hispanic or Native American. To put this in perspective, a perfect SAT score is worth only 12 points in the Michigan system. Students who accumulate 100 points are generally admitted, so those 20 points awarded solely based on race are often the decisive factor.

At the law school, some minority students are admitted to meet percentage targets while other applicants with higher grades and better scores are passed over. This means that students are being selected or rejected based primarily on the color of their skin. The motivation for such an admissions policy may be very good, but its result is discrimination, and that discrimination is wrong.

Some states are using innovative ways to diversify their student bodies. Recent history has proven that diversity can be achieved without using quotas. Systems in California and Florida and Texas have proven that by guaranteeing admissions to the top students from high schools throughout the state, including low-income neighborhoods, colleges can attain broad racial diversity. In these states, race-neutral admissions policies have resulted in levels of minority attendance for incoming students that are close to, and in some instances slightly surpass, those under the old race-based approach.

Is the Confederate flag a racist symbol?

YES
Sanford Cloud, Jr.
President and CEO, National Conference for Community and Justice

Excerpted from the NCCJ Web Site, dated 2002

Historically, the Confederate flag was a symbol during the Civil War of the Confederate States of America, which defended the rights of individual states that maintained their economy through slave labor. Although the Civil War ended 138 years ago, the battle over the legacy of slavery, segregation and civil rights continues.

Through the years, the Confederate flag has taken on additional negative connotations because it was used as a symbol of resistance during the civil-rights movement and is currently a prominent symbol of active white-supremacist groups. This is not to say that all individuals who bear the Confederate flag are racist. However, the symbolic meaning of the flag is that of white domination and Southern pride.

Some people assert that the Confederate flag is a symbol of their heritage; however, for many people of color and religious minorities across the United States and other communities around the world, it represents hatred, bigotry, racism, and anti-Semitism. This symbol is a very powerful nonverbal communication tool that, according to the Anti-Defamation League (ADL), generates deep meaning, intent and significance in a compact, immediately recognizable form. Members of racist organizations often use the symbol along with more specific images associated with their groups. Independent racists can avoid association with a specific group, and perhaps prosecution of that group by law enforcement, by opting for more universal racist symbols.

The National Conference for Community and Justice (NCCJ) maintains that the Confederate flag is a visible, confrontational racist symbol that represents racial oppression, segregation and slavery. As noted by Kweisi Mfume, president and CEO of the National Association for the Advancement of Colored People, "The [Confederate] flag is representative of an era that epitomized everything that was wrong and inhumane in this country and should be stripped of any sovereignty context and placed into a historical context." NCCJ concurs with this sentiment and calls for the removal of the Confederate flag from all public properties with allowances for its usage in appropriate historical and educational contexts.

All people of goodwill need to recognize that the Confederate flag . . . is an attack on the freedoms of our nation. Similarly, racism has no boundaries, and this issue cannot be confined to the Southern states. NCCJ therefore calls on all residents of the United States to actively oppose the usage of the Confederate flag and denounce it as a visible public statement that is offensive in nature.

NO
William Rolen
Director and Southern Heritage Defense Coordinator, Council of Conservative Citizens

Written for The CQ Researcher, May 2003

For thirty years, the 1956 Georgia flag flew peacefully over every public building in the state. Not many people seemed disturbed by the large Confederate portion of the flag, which was put there in 1956 to honor the Southern soldiers who had fought and died defending Georgia against the atrocities of Gen. Sherman.

Then in 1991, the NAACP national convention passed a resolution condemning the Confederate flag as racist. From that year on, the Confederate flag and other Confederate icons have been subjected to relentless vitriolic wrath. One by one, Confederate flags have been removed, banned or desecrated simply because threats from the NAACP terrify the political status quo in virtually every Southern state.

The problem with the Confederate flag does not involve illicit connections with the klan or any other "guilt by association" flummery. The NAACP took aim at the Confederate flag because the emblem is revered by most Southerners. Confederate flag decals stick on every type of vehicle from trucks to tricycles. Confederate-flag clothing, from Dixie Outfitter T-shirts to G.R.I.T.S. (Girls Raised In The South) swimsuits are ordinary sights. The images of celebrities like Elvis and Hank Williams are superimposed on Confederate flags sold at truck stops and souvenir shops. Only a very jaundiced eye sees racism lurking behind every Southern-cross belt buckle and bandana worn on race day at Talledega.

Certainly, the Confederate flag honors the Southern soldier and the memory of generals Lee, Jackson, and Beauregard. More significantly, the Confederate flag represents the continuum of Southern experience. Does the flag have a racial dimension? Yes, but the racial connotations are no more negative than the FUBU (For Us, By Us) clothing that is designed, marketed and intended only for blacks.

The Confederate flag is not an aggressive symbol. No one is trying to hoist the Confederate colors over the Capitol of Vermont, nor are Confederate flag ski jackets a fashion statement on the slopes of Aspen. The Confederate flag is largely a regional phenomenon, and one of multiple interpretations. The NAACP, however, allows for only one, narrow viewpoint.

The time has come to honor and respect the Confederate flag for all the sacrifices Southerners have made over the last 20 years to display the symbol with honor, dignity and pride. And a word of caution to the NAACP: The harder you try to pull it down, the higher it will fly.

Getty Images/Scott Olson

Getty Images/Mike Simons

Police Tactics Spark Riots

The racially tinged incidents that periodically break out across the country are often provoked by outrage in the black community over police tactics that are seen by many African-Americans as heavy-handed and racist. At least five homes were torched and up to 15 people injured during a riot in Benton Harbor, Mich., in mid-June following the death of a black motorcyclist during a police chase (top). Police arrest a demonstrator during a protest march outside Cincinnati in June 2001 (bottom). The march followed riots sparked by the fatal shooting of an unarmed black man by a white policeman.

search. The new policy also exempts national-security cases in "narrow" circumstances. Immigration officers, for example, can continue to require registration by visitors from Middle Eastern countries thought to foster terrorism.

Skeptics, though, wonder whether cash-strapped states and the federal government will pick up a larger tab for funding anti-poverty programs and other measures that apply not only to blacks but also to a much-expanded pool of disadvantaged citizens of all races.

At a recent forum, Stephen Goldsmith, a special adviser to the president, said, "There is now a broad consensus that a work-based benefit system is where we want to be." But he acknowledged that even if there is consensus about work being the best way to help low-income Americans, there isn't agreement about how much money to provide for such a system.[59]

As Congress prepares to consider its latest reauthorization of the welfare-reform law, black and Latino activists are concerned that states are not properly monitoring civil rights in the law's assistance programs. They want Congress to beef up enforcement, claiming that African-American and Hispanic women have not been given support services equal to members of other races.

Similarly, as Congress prepares to reauthorize the Workforce Investment Act of 1998, which consolidated dozens of job-training programs into block grants to the states, members of the Congressional Black Caucus are concerned that the law's data-collection requirements make it harder to determine whether African-Americans are being discriminated against.

members of those racial or ethnic groups are more likely to commit such crimes.

If a specific description identifies a suspect as black, however, the agents can target blacks as part of their

Some black advocates claim that blacks, Asians and Hispanics are being steered toward less-useful training — into areas such as résumé writing — rather than more potentially lucrative occupational job training.

Action in the States

California, Maryland and New Jersey have recently revised their racial-profiling policies in an effort to discourage bias among their troopers. Mac Donald, at the Manhattan Institute, argues that the increasing number of states and cities requiring police to record interactions with civilians on the basis of race will have a "chilling effect . . . on legitimate police work," as police officers avoid "all but the most mandatory and cursory interactions with potential minority suspects."[60] Nevertheless, about 20 other states are either setting up commissions to study racial profiling or considering legislation to curb the practice.

Meanwhile, as part of the ongoing debate about whether the descendants of slaves should receive reparations, several states also are considering establishing commissions to determine the effects of slavery on contemporary African-Americans.

In some states, the most pressing racial issues are largely symbolic. In his successful campaign for governor of Georgia last year, Republican Sonny Perdue promised voters a referendum on restoring a Confederate emblem to the state flag that had been removed in 2001.

California voters next year will vote on the "Racial Privacy Initiative," which would prohibit state and local agencies, such as schools and the Department of Motor Vehicles, from asking people about their racial identities or including voluntary racial check-off boxes on their forms. The goal is to end policies of racial classification that serve to separate people into different categories.

Critics worry that blocking racial-data collection will make it harder to track civil-rights abuses and may also hamper medical research. The initiative's main sponsor is conservative activist Ward Connerly, who also sponsored California's 1996 initiative ending state affirmative-action programs.

OUTLOOK

Lingering Problems?

The nation's historic blend of European colonialists, displaced Native Americans, African slaves and immigrants from around the world has made for an often-volatile racial mix. Given current predictions that by 2050 no racial group will comprise a majority of the population, racial relations are expected to evolve in complex ways.

Optimists believe that the demographic changes, along with the changes in social norms that make open discrimination against blacks taboo, will eventually lead to a society that is less divided and concerned about race. "It may be no accident," says Harvard's Thernstrom, "that the first state to bar racial preferences by constitutional amendment, California, is also the state with the most complex racial mix."

But even some optimists say racism will remain potent for a long time. "Hopefully, we've set in motion enough positive activities where we do ultimately get to a color-blind society," says Weldon Latham, corporate-diversity director at the giant Holland & Knight law firm. "But it's many decades from now."

Similarly, while University of California, Berkeley psychologist Jack Glaser sees racism declining, "Sadly, I can't imagine that it will ever go away," he says. "People are pretty hard-wired to see things in categories. You can put people into very arbitrary groups, and they know it's arbitrary, but they will still show favor to members of their group."

During his recent tenure as president of the American Bar Association (ABA), Oklahoma City attorney William G. Paul made diversity his top priority because, he said, his profession is 92.5 percent white. He has been heartened by the scholarship fund the ABA established and by data showing that blacks and other minorities are better represented in law schools than they are, as yet, in the legal profession itself.

"I didn't find anyone voicing any opposition," recalls Paul, who is white. Yet he admits that habits and the status quo are so ingrained that achieving equality even in his high-profile profession is "going to require a multi-decade effort."

Indeed, the most pessimistic observers of race relations predict that there could yet be a new backlash against blacks and minorities, mirroring the historic setbacks blacks faced following the Revolutionary and Civil wars. "I don't really think the white population is going to lose its powers or prestige because its numbers are going down," says *Two Nations* author Andrew Hacker.

Even without ill will or conscious discrimination, recent history suggests that institutions long dominated by whites will continue to be dominated by whites, with few exceptions. "If you assume attitudes and expectations are institutionalized," says Mitchell, of the National Research Council, "time won't make a difference."

NOTES

1. Lee Hockstader, "For Tulia 12, 'It Feels So Good,'" *The Washington Post*, June 17, 2003, p. A1.

2. Andrew Hacker, *Two Nations: Black & White, Separate, Hostile, Unequal* (3rd ed. 2003, originally published 1992), p. 111.

3. Sheryl Gay Stolberg, "Cultural Issues Pose Obstacles in Cancer Fight," *The New York Times*, March 14, 1998, p. A1.

4. Margery Austin Turner and Felicity Skidmore, ed., "Mortgage Lending Discrimination: A Review of Existing Evidence," The Urban Institute, June 1999, p. 1.

5. Stephan Thernstrom and Abigail Thernstrom, *America in Black and White: One Nation, Indivisible* (1997), p. 222. See "The Nation's Report Card," National Assessment of Educational Progress, National Center for Education Statistics. http://nces.ed.gov/nationsreportcard/.

6. Hacker, *op. cit.*, p. 222.

7. Thernstrom and Thernstrom, *op. cit.*, p. 274.

8. Eric Lichtblau, "Bush Issues Racial Profiling Ban But Exempts Security Inquiries," *The New York Times*, June 18, 2003, p. A1.

9. Quoted in Bettijane Levine, "Harry Belafonte won't retreat from slavery remarks," *Chicago Tribune*, Oct. 23, 2002, p. 1.

10. See Ellen Nakashima and Al Kamen, "Bush Official Hails Diversity," *The Washington Post*, March 31, 2001, p. A10.

11. John McWhorter, *Losing the Race: Self-Sabotage in Black America* (2000).

12. For background, see David Masci, "The Black Middle Class," *The CQ Researcher*, Jan. 23, 1998, pp. 49-72.

13. Randall Kennedy, *Nigger: The Strange Career of a Troublesome Word* (2002), p. 27.

14. See Greg Winter, "State Underfinancing Damages City Schools, New York Court Finds," *The New York Times*, June 27, 2003, p. A1. For background on school funding issues, see Kathy Koch, "Reforming School Funding," *The CQ Researcher*, Dec. 10, 1999, pp. 1041-1064.

15. Office of Policy Research and Development, "All Other Things Being Equal: A Paired Testing Study of Mortgage Lending Institutions," U.S. Department of Housing and Urban Development, April 2002, p. 10, http://www.huduser.org/Publications/PDF/aotbe.pdf.

16. Douglas S. Massey and Garvey Lundy, "Use of Black English and Racial Discrimination in Urban Housing Markets: New Methods and Findings," *Urban Affairs Review 36* (2001): 470-96.

17. Erica Frankenburg, Chungmei Lee and Gary Orfield, "A Multiracial Society With Segregated Schools: Are We Losing the Dream?" Harvard University Civil Rights Project, January 2003, p. 28, http://www.civilrightsproject.harvard.edu/research/reseg03/AreWeLosingtheDream.pdf.

18. Thernstrom and Thernstrom, *op. cit.*, p. 199.

19. Turner and Skidmore, *op. cit.*

20. McWhorter, *op. cit.*

21. Thernstrom and Thernstrom, *op. cit.*

22. Mark Mauer, "The Crisis of the Young African-American Male and the Criminal Justice System," testimony submitted to the U.S. Commission on Civil Rights, April 15-16, 1999.

23. Randall Kennedy, *Race, Crime, and the Law* (1997), p. x.

24. For background, see Kenneth Jost, "Policing the Police," *The CQ Researcher*, March 17, 2000, pp. 209-240.

25. David Kocieniewski, "New Jersey Adopts Ban on Racial Profiling," *The New York Times*, March 14, 2003, p. B5.

26. The Associated Press, "Cincinnati Police Want Community Pact Ended," *The Washington Post*, April 30, 2003, p. A8.

27. Michael Tonry, *Malign Neglect: Race, Crime, and Punishment in America* (1995), p. 79.

28. Quoted in Kennedy 1997, p. 15. See Clarence Page, "Message to Jackson: The Word Is Crime, Not Black Criminals," *Chicago Tribune*, Jan. 5, 1994, p. 15.

29. See Kennedy 1997, pp. 370 ff.

30. Quoted in Kennedy 1997, p. 14.

31. Adam Liptak, "Death Penalty Found More Likely If Victim Is White," *The New York Times*, Jan. 8, 2003, p. A12.

32. Henry Weinstein, "Panel Urges Halt to Executions in Pa.," *Los Angeles Times*, March 5, 2003, p. 15.

33. Philip A. Klinkner with Rogers M. Smith, *The Unsteady March: The Rise and Decline of Racial Equality in America* (1999), p. 12.

34. Quoted in Philip S. Foner, *From Africa to the Emergence of the Cotton Kingdom* (1975), p. 303.

35. Quoted in Klinkner and Smith, *op. cit.*, p. 18.

36. Lerone Bennett, Jr., *Before the Mayflower: A History of Black America* (5th ed., 1984; originally published 1962), p. 257.

37. Quoted in Thernstrom and Thernstrom, *op. cit.*

38. Quoted in Bennett, *op. cit.*

39. Philip Dray, *At the Hands of Persons Unknown: The Lynching of Black America* (2002), p. iii.

40. Klinkner and Smith, *op. cit.*

41. Thernstrom and Thernstrom, *op. cit.*

42. *Ibid.*, p. 79.

43. Gerald N. Rosenberg, *The Hollow Hope: Can Courts Bring About Social Change?* (1991), p. 50.

44. Thurmond had led a record-breaking filibuster of 24 hours and 18 minutes against the Civil Rights Bill of 1957.

45. *Congress and the Nation*, Vol. 1, p. 1635.

46. *Congress and the Nation*, Vol. 2, p. 356.

47. Niel J. Smelser, William Julius Wilson and Faith Mitchell, eds., *America Becoming: Racial Trends and Their Consequences, Vol. 1* (2001), p. 321.

48. Quoted in Klinkner and Smith, *op. cit.*

49. Carol Pogash, "Berkeley Makes Its Pitch to Top Minority Students," *Los Angeles Times*, April 20, 2003, Part 2, p. A6.

50. Thernstrom and Thernstrom, *op. cit.*

51. For background, see Sarah Glazer, "Welfare Reform," *The CQ Researcher*, Aug. 3, 2001, pp. 601-632.

52. Hacker, *op. cit.*, p. 130.

53. *Congress and the Nation*, Vol. VIII, p. 757.

54. For background see Jennifer Gavin, "Redistricting," *The CQ Researcher*, Feb. 16, 2001, pp. 113-128.

55. For background, see David Masci, "Reparations Movement," *The CQ Researcher*, June 22, 2001, pp. 529-552.

56. W.E.B. Du Bois, *The Souls of Black Folk* (1933).

57. Abigail Thernstrom, "Court Rulings Add Insult to Injury," *Los Angeles Times*, June 29, 2003, p. M1.

58. Mitchell Landsberg, Peter Y. Hong and Rebecca Trounson, " 'Race-Neutral' University Admissions in Spotlight," *Los Angeles Times*, Jan. 17, 2003, p. 1.

59. Quoted in David Callahan and Tamara Draut, "Broken Bargain: Why Bush May Be Destroying A Hard-Won Consensus on Helping the Poor," *The Boston Globe*, May 11, 2003, p. H1.

60. Heather Mac Donald, "A 'Profiling' Pall on the Terror War," *The Washington Post*, May 5, 2003, p. A21.

BIBLIOGRAPHY

Books

Correspondents of *The New York Times*, *How Race Is Lived in America*, Times Books, 2001.
A collection of the *Times'* Pulitzer Prize-winning series of reporting about how issues of race still affect American society.

Hacker, Andrew, *Two Nations: Black & White, Separate, Hostile, Unequal*, 3rd ed. 2003 (originally published 1992).
A political scientist finds race to be an "obdurate" problem, portraying an America in which blacks and whites are still separate and unequal, with illustrations drawn largely from census figures.

Kennedy, Randall, *Nigger: The Strange Career of a Troublesome Word*, Pantheon, 2002.
A Harvard Law School professor examines the history and usage of "the paradigmatic slur" and what it expresses about racial enmities.

Kennedy, Randall, *Race, Crime, and the Law*, Pantheon, 1997.
The Harvard law professor analyzes issues at the intersection of race and the criminal-justice system, including anti-drug laws, the death penalty and jury selection.

Klinkner, Philip A., with Rogers M. Smith, *The Unsteady March: The Rise and Decline of Racial Equality in America*, University of Chicago Press, 1999.
The authors survey African-American rights from Colonial times to the late 1990s and conclude that each period of advancement for blacks has been followed by a lengthy backlash. Klinkner teaches government at Hamilton College; Smith teaches race and politics at Yale University.

McWhorter, John, *Losing the Race: Self-Sabotage in Black America*, Free Press, 2000.
A linguistics professor at the University of California,Berkeley argues that African-Americans cling to a "Cult of Victimology" that keeps them fixated on racism at the expense of making improvements in their own lives.

Patterson, Orlando, *The Ordeal of Integration: Progress and Resentment in America's "Racial" Crisis*, Civitas/Counterpoint, 1997.
A Harvard sociologist examines the state of progress among Afro-Americans and the impact various ideologies have on public policy.

Smelser, Neil J., William Julius Wilson and Faith Mitchell, eds., *America Becoming: Racial Trends and Their Consequences, Vols. I and II*, National Academy Press, 2001.
Essays from a National Research Council conference on race cover trends in housing, labor, income, justice and other issues.

Steinhorn, Leonard, and Barbara Diggs-Brown, *By the Color of Our Skin: The Illusion of Integration and the Reality of Race*, Dutton, 1999.
Two American University professors — one white, one black — conclude that America has not successfully integrated.

Thernstrom, Stephan, and Abigail Thernstrom, *America in Black and White: One Nation Indivisible*, Simon & Schuster, 1997.
The authors trace the history of U.S. race relations and political, social and economic trends since the civil-rights movement. They argue that race-neutral policies are a better cure for society's ills than race-conscious ones.

Stephan Thernstrom teaches history at Harvard; Abigail Thernstrom is a senior fellow at the Manhattan Institute.

Reports and Studies

Frankenburg, Erika, Chungmei Lee and Gary Orfield, "A Multiracial Society With Segregated Schools: Are We Losing the Dream?" *Civil Rights Project*, January 2003; http://www.civilrights project.harvard.edu/research/reseg03/AreWeLosing theDream.pdf.
Harvard researchers find that schools are re-segregating, with most whites attending predominantly white schools and many blacks and Hispanics attending "apartheid schools" with almost entirely minority student bodies.

Office of Policy Research and Development, *All Other Things Being Equal: A Paired Testing Study of Mortgage Lending Institutions, U.S. Department of Housing and Urban Development*, http://www. huduser.org/Publications/PDF/aotbe.pdf, April 2002.
The report concludes that blacks and Hispanics often receive less favorable treatment than whites when applying for mortgages.

Rawlston, Valerie A., and William E. Spriggs, "Pay Equity 2000: Are We There Yet?" National Urban League Institute for Opportunity and Equality, April 2001; http://www.nul.org/departments/inst_opp_ equality/word/reports_statistics/pay_equity_report. doc.
A study of federal contractors finds that women and minorities make about 73 cents for every dollar earned by non-Hispanic white men, in large part due to differences in the types of work they do. White men are still paid more, however, for doing the same jobs.

For More Information

American Civil Rights Institute, P.O. Box 188350, Sacramento, CA 95818; (916) 444-2278; www.acri.org. A group dedicated to educating the public about programs that promote race and gender preferences.

Center for Equal Opportunity, 14 Pidgeon Hill Dr., Suite 500, Sterling, VA 20165; (703) 421-5443; www.ceousa.org. A think tank promoting color-blind policies.

Center for Individual Rights, 1233 20th St., N.W., Suite 300, Washington, DC 20036; (202) 833-8400; www.cir-usa.org. A public-interest law firm that has challenged affirmative-action policies.

Center for New Black Leadership, 815 15th St., N.W., Suite 930, Washington, DC 20002; (202) 546-9505. An advocacy organization supporting policies that "enhance the ability of individuals and communities to develop market-oriented, community-based" solutions to economic and social problems.

The Civil Rights Project, 125 Mt. Auburn St., 3rd Floor, Cambridge, MA 02138; (617) 496-6367; www.civilrights project.harvard.edu. A Harvard-affiliated think tank.

Joint Center for Political and Economic Studies, 1090 Vermont Ave., N.W., Suite 1100 Washington, DC 20005-4928; (202) 789-3500; www.jointcenter.org. Founded to train black elected officials, it studies issues of importance to black Americans.

Leadership Conference on Civil Rights, 1629 K St., N.W., 10th Floor, Washington, DC 20006; (202) 466-3311; www.civilrights.org. A coalition of 180 national organizations promoting civil-rights legislation and policy.

The Manhattan Institute, 52 Vanderbilt Ave., 2nd Floor, New York, NY 10017; (212) 599-7000; www.manhattan-institute.org. A think tank that fosters "greater economic choice and individual responsibility."

National Association for the Advancement of Colored People, 8 W. 26th St., Baltimore, MD 21218; (410) 366-3300; www.naacp.org. Century-old organization committed to improving the civil rights of African-Americans and other minorities.

National Conference for Community and Justice, 475 Park Ave. South, 19th Floor, New York, NY 10016; (212) 545-1300; www.nccj.org. Formerly the National Conference of Christians and Jews, it fights bias and racism in America.

National Urban League, 120 Wall St., 8th Floor, New York, NY, 10005; (212) 558-5300; www.nul.org. Consortium of community-based organizations that promotes access to education, economic activity and civil rights among African-Americans.

Southern Poverty Law Center, 400 Washington Ave., Montgomery, AL 36104; (334) 956-8200; www.splcenter.org/splc.html. A group that fights discrimination through educational programs, litigation and its maintenance of the Civil Rights Memorial.

U.S. Commission on Civil Rights, 624 Ninth St., N.W., Washington, DC 20425; (202) 376-7700; www.usccr.gov. Government agency that investigates complaints about discrimination.

8

Abortion Debates

Kenneth Jost

Getty Images

Anti-abortion militant James Kopp faces up to life in prison after being found guilty on March 18 of second-degree murder in the 1998 shooting of Barnett Slepian, a Buffalo, N.Y., doctor who carried out abortions. Violence directed against abortion providers and clinics has ebbed over the past few years, but legislative and judicial fights between anti-abortion and abortion-rights groups continue unabated 30 years after the Supreme Court's landmark *Roe v. Wade* decision establishing a constitutional right to abortion.

From *The CQ Researcher,* March 21, 2003.

rmed with prayer book, rosary and anti-abortion literature, Christine Walsh takes up her post on a chilly Saturday morning recently outside a Planned Parenthood clinic within sight of the White House. As women approach, the teenage college student rushes to their side and tries with soft-spoken insistence to dissuade them from having an abortion.

Invariably, the women quickly turn away and are shepherded inside by volunteer "escorts" from the Washington Area Clinic Task Force. Wearing orange vests, they lock arms to block Walsh or her fellow "sidewalk counselors" from going farther once the patients reach the clinic's grounds.

Thirty years after the Supreme Court's landmark *Roe v. Wade* decision allowing abortions, the abortion wars continue — in Congress and state legislatures, in the courts and outside women's clinics across the country.

The sidewalk confrontations are usually orderly, but the potential for violence lurks in the background. The clinic has bullet-resistant windows and a 600-pound steel door; doctors often wear bulletproof vests.[1]

The number of protesters and clinic escorts grows on special occasions — notably, every Jan. 22, the anniversary of the *Roe* decision. Sometimes, the two sides get into shoving matches. "It's like a war zone," Walsh comments as two motorcycle police officers set up watch across the street in case of a disturbance.

Walsh says she simply wants prospective patients to "take a step back" and think about their choices. "They're killing children here," she explains, "and we're here trying to offer alternatives."

Rebecca Fox, 24, the leader of a team of 10 escorts, says the "anti-choice harassers," as she calls them, never succeed. In four years, she says, she has never seen a sidewalk change-of-mind. "The women know what their choices are," Fox says, "and they've made their decision."

The arguments are no less fervent for being well worn.[2] Abortion-rights advocates praise *Roe v. Wade* as a landmark guarantee of what they call a woman's "right to choose." Anti-abortion groups bitterly assail the 1973 ruling and defend what they call the "right to life" of the "unborn child." Public opinion polls generally favor a woman's right to choose an abortion but also favor certain restrictions on that right, many of which have been enacted at the state and federal levels in recent years. (*For state laws, see chart, p. 188; public opinion polls, p. 185.*)

Today, with Congress and the White House in Republican hands, anti-abortion groups see their best chance in more than a decade of winning federal passage of parts of their agenda. The GOP has been closely aligned with anti-abortion forces since 1980, when the party platform first supported a "right-to-life" constitutional amendment.

"We're in better shape as pro-lifers than we have been in a while," says Connie Mackey, vice president for government affairs at the Family Research Council, a Christian-oriented family-advocacy group. Republican control "should give us a leg up that we haven't had in a while."

"Abortion rights are in great peril," says Elizabeth Cavendish, legislative director for the newly named NARAL Pro-Choice America — formerly, the National Abortion Rights Action League. "We're likely to see a renewed assault on a woman's right to choose."

At the top of the right-to-life agenda is a bill to ban so-called partial-birth abortions — in which a fetus is brought partly outside a woman's body before being aborted, usually after 20 weeks gestation. "This is closer to infanticide than it is to abortion," Sen. Rick Santorum, R-Pa., told a March 10 news conference, three days before the Senate voted 64-33 to ban the procedure.

The bill is expected to win easy House approval and be signed into law by President Bush, but still faces legal hurdles. The Supreme Court in 2000 struck down a Nebraska ban on the procedure, but supporters of the measure say it was rewritten to meet the court's objections.[3]

But abortion-rights groups say the new bill suffers from the same constitutional defects cited in the Supreme Court's Nebraska decision. "Make no mistake," says NARAL President Kate Michelman, "this bill goes directly to the heart of a woman's constitutional right to choose."

Anti-abortion groups are pushing three other bills to regulate abortion practices in the United States. The measures would:

• Make it a federal crime to help a minor cross state lines to get an abortion without parental notification or consent;

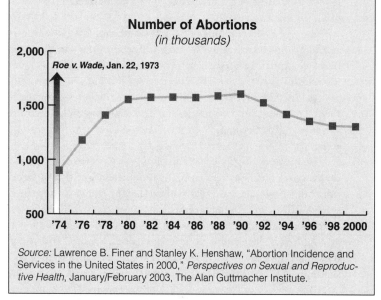

Number of Abortions Has Been Dropping

The number of abortions performed in the United States each year increased through the 1970s, leveled off in the 1980s and has been falling since 1990. The decline is attributed to a decline in sexual activity by adolescents and increased use of contraceptives, including the "morning-after" pill. Anti-abortion groups also note a public-opinion shift against abortion except under limited circumstances.

Number of Abortions
(in thousands)

Roe v. Wade, Jan. 22, 1973

Source: Lawrence B. Finer and Stanley K. Henshaw, "Abortion Incidence and Services in the United States in 2000," *Perspectives on Sexual and Reproductive Health*, January/February 2003, The Alan Guttmacher Institute.

- Allow hospitals and doctors to refuse to perform, and health insurers to refuse to cover, abortions without risking loss of federal funding; and
- Make it a federal crime to injure or kill a fetus during the commission of any one of a specified list of other violent offenses.

Anti-abortion groups will also continue to try to block any international aid for groups that promote abortion. And they have strongly backed legislation to ban any form of human cloning — a measure the House approved, 241-155, on Feb. 27.

Some of the bills were approved previously in the House, where anti-abortion groups have held narrow but secure majorities for several years. But they stalled in the Democratic-controlled Senate. Now — as evidenced by the Senate's March 13 ban on partial-birth abortions — the Republican-controlled Senate is expected to be more hospitable to anti-abortion measures, even though it is still considered more abortion-rights-minded than the House.

Most important, anti-abortion groups believe they have a strong and reliable ally in President Bush. On his first workday in office, he reinstated a Reagan-era ban on U.S. funding of overseas groups that promote abortions. He has also appointed well-known abortion foes to key agency positions dealing with abortion policy, and his administration has instituted a laundry list of what abortion-rights advocates call "anti-choice" executive orders, regulatory policies and legal briefs championed by anti-abortion groups.

"On every pro-life legislative measure [the administration] has been effectively involved," says Douglas Johnson, director of federal legislation for the National Right to Life Committee (NRLC). "And on matters of administrative discretion, they have come down on the side of a culture of life."

In addition, Bush has nominated conservatives to federal judgeships — some of them openly critical of abortion rights — and endorsed anti-abortion measures in Congress, including the partial-birth abortion ban. Pro-choice groups are also bracing for a full-scale confrontation over a Bush Supreme Court appointee if one or more vacancies arise — as many political and legal observers expect to happen as early as this summer.

"It's very possible that President Bush will have the opportunity to reshape the court," Cavendish says. If one of the "pro-choice" justices is replaced, she says, the court could end up approving some "draconian" restrictions on abortion, including a revised partial-birth abortion ban. With two new appointments, she warns, the court might formally overrule *Roe*.

The political situation is mixed in the states, although anti-abortion groups appear to have the upper hand. NARAL estimates that 335 anti-choice measures have been enacted by state legislatures since 1995. Moreover, the NRLC claimed "critical gains" in state legislative races in the November 2002 elections. "We're in a better position than we were last year," said Mary Balch, NRLC's director of state legislation.[4]

In its annual state-by-state report, NARAL counts 23 states with anti-abortion majorities in both houses, but claims the number of "pro-choice" governors increased from 15 to 22 after the November elections.[5] Cavendish predicts that at least 12 and as many as 17 states might ban abortion altogether if the Supreme Court overturns *Roe* and gives states discretion to regulate abortions with minimal constitutional constraints.

As the abortion debates continue, here are some of the major questions at issue:

Should *Roe v. Wade* be overturned?

As he was completing his opinion for the Supreme Court in *Roe v. Wade*, Justice Harry A. Blackmun cautioned his colleagues that the decision "will probably result in the Court's being severely criticized."[6] Thirty years later, the ruling indeed remains controversial: praised by abortion-rights advocates, bitterly opposed by anti-abortion groups and held in some disrepute among legal scholars.

Anti-abortion groups want to overturn the decision, even though they have failed to nullify the ruling by constitutional amendment or to persuade the high court to overrule the decision itself. "It's been an enormous tragedy," says Johnson of the National Right to Life Committee.

For their part, abortion-rights groups say *Roe* has survived only in a weakened state — and could be overruled if President Bush gets the chance to name one or more new justices to the Supreme Court. "*Roe* is in jeopardy," says NARAL's Cavendish.

Criticisms of *Roe* stem not only from its outcome but also from the structure of the opinion. Legal critics have long said Blackmun based his opinion more on medical policy than constitutional law. They also contend that the decision's trimester approach — allowing unregulated

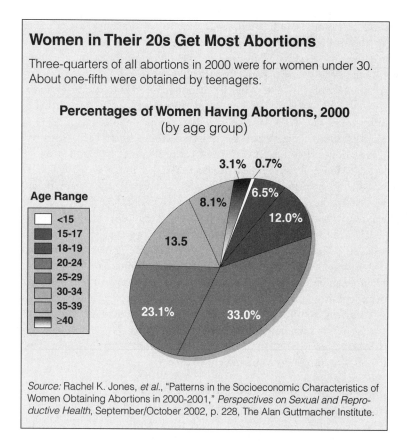

Women in Their 20s Get Most Abortions

Three-quarters of all abortions in 2000 were for women under 30. About one-fifth were obtained by teenagers.

Percentages of Women Having Abortions, 2000
(by age group)

3.1% 0.7%

6.5%

12.0%

8.1%

13.5

23.1%   33.0%

Age Range

- ☐ <15
- ■ 15-17
- ■ 18-19
- ■ 20-24
- ☐ 25-29
- ☐ 30-34
- ☐ 35-39
- ■ ≥40

Source: Rachel K. Jones, *et al.*, "Patterns in the Socioeconomic Characteristics of Women Obtaining Abortions in 2000-2001," *Perspectives on Sexual and Reproductive Health*, September/October 2002, p. 228, The Alan Guttmacher Institute.

abortion during the first three months of pregnancy, some regulations up to the point of fetal viability and a near-ban except to save the life of the mother during the final trimester — amounts to what Johnson calls "the apex of judicial legislation."

"There is consensus within the legal academy, whether one is pro-life or pro-abortion, whether one is liberal or conservative, that *Roe* had no grounding in the Constitution or in constitutional jurisprudence," says Douglas Kmiec, dean of the Columbus School of Law at the Catholic University of America in Washington, D.C.

"That's just not true," counters Louis Michael Seidman, a constitutional-law expert at the Georgetown University Law Center in Washington. "If you did a survey of constitutional-law professors, I'd be pretty confident that a majority think *Roe* was correctly decided."

Seidman acknowledges the criticism of the trimester approach, but says such line-drawing is common in constitutional decisions. "To give meaning to constitutional rights, it's sometimes necessary for justices to draw what

may seem like arbitrary lines," he says. "You have to draw them someplace."

In a showdown case two decades after the 1973 decision, the Supreme Court reaffirmed what three of the justices — Sandra Day O'Connor, Anthony M. Kennedy and David H. Souter — called, in an unusual joint opinion, *Roe's* "essential holding." Their ruling in *Planned Parenthood v. Casey* rebuffed repeated calls from the Justice Department under Presidents Ronald Reagan and George Bush to overturn *Roe*. But the decision also appeared to discard the trimester approach and to allow states to regulate abortion unless the laws imposed an "undue burden" on women's rights.[7]

The three justices sought to strengthen the constitutional basis of the ruling by explicitly tying the abortion right to the "liberty interest" protected by the 14th Amendment's Due Process Clause. They also defended the decision not to overrule *Roe*, in part on the legal doctrine of *"stare decisis"* — Latin for let the decision stand.

Johnson calls that part of the decision especially unjustifiable. "They didn't try to defend the constitutional analysis," Johnson says. "They just said, 'That's what we did. If we changed it now, people would be upset.' "

Some critics also fault the *Roe* court for taking the issue out of the hands of state legislatures — several of which were moving in the early 1970s to liberalize abortion laws. Today, though, Johnson says most Americans support more restrictions on abortion than are allowed under the Supreme Court's decisions.

"There is a great gulf between the policy that is supported by the majority of Americans and the regime that has been imposed by judicial decree," Johnson says.

Abortion-rights advocates, however, note that polls show most Americans agree that the abortion decision should rest with women rather than the government. In any event, they say women's reproductive freedom should not be subject to the legislative process. "It would be a terrible thing for women to have to lobby for their liberty state by state, year by year, and legislature by legislature," Cavendish says.

Indeed, abortion-rights advocates say the court itself has already undermined *Roe*. "It's already been eroded by cases like *Casey*," Cavendish says.

Johnson disagrees. "The notion that *Casey* was a rollback of *Roe* is pure fiction," he says.

As for a direct overruling of *Roe*, anti-abortion groups are hopeful and abortion-rights groups fearful. But experts on both sides of the issue discount the likelihood.

"It's just not going to happen," says Ronald Rotunda, a conservative professor at George Mason University Law School in Fairfax, Va., outside Washington. "It's just like asking whether we should change the speed of light."

Seidman agrees: "In my lifetime, *Roe* will not be overruled."

Should Congress ban so-called "partial-birth" abortions?

Anti-abortion groups describe the procedure in stark terms: a late-stage fetus is brought through the woman's dilated cervix feet first; then — because the head is too big to pass through — the skull is pierced, the contents suctioned out and the skull finally crushed or collapsed. "A partial-birth abortion brutally and painfully takes the life of a human baby who is inches away from being born alive," the NRLC's Johnson says.

Abortion-rights groups bristle at the terminology, which they call medically inaccurate and politically inflammatory. In fact, the medical term is "dilation and extraction" — shortened to "D&X" — or, alternatively, an "intact D&E" for "dilation and evacuation."

The opposing groups also disagree over the frequency of the procedure. Abortion-rights advocates generally depict the procedure as relatively rare and used only

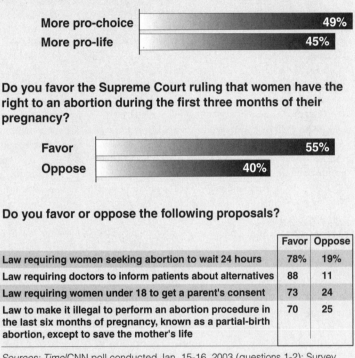

Public Favors Abortion Rights

More Americans favor a woman's right to have an abortion than oppose it. But a majority of Americans also approve of placing some restrictions on abortions.

Would you describe yourself as being more pro-choice — supporting a woman's right to have an abortion — or more pro-life — protecting the rights of the unborn children?

More pro-choice	49%
More pro-life	45%

Do you favor the Supreme Court ruling that women have the right to an abortion during the first three months of their pregnancy?

Favor	55%
Oppose	40%

Do you favor or oppose the following proposals?

	Favor	Oppose
Law requiring women seeking abortion to wait 24 hours	78%	19%
Law requiring doctors to inform patients about alternatives	88	11
Law requiring women under 18 to get a parent's consent	73	24
Law to make it illegal to perform an abortion procedure in the last six months of pregnancy, known as a partial-birth abortion, except to save the mother's life	70	25

Sources: Time/CNN poll conducted Jan. 15-16, 2003 (questions 1-2); Survey Research Center, University of California-Berkeley, fall 2002 (questions 3-6).

when medically necessary. Anti-abortion groups insist the procedure is more common than acknowledged and never medically justifiable.

Public opinion polls that use the term partial-birth abortion indicate substantial public support for banning the procedure: 70 percent in the most recent Gallup survey in January.[8] When a state law banning the procedure reached the Supreme Court, however, the justices voted 5-4 to strike it down on the ground that the statute interfered with women's abortion rights.

The court's 2000 decision in *Stenberg v. Carhart* said the Nebraska law was defective because it could be con-

Anti-Abortion Tactics Test Free-Speech Limits

The Web site opened by a militant anti-abortion group in January 1997 sent a chilling message. The site listed the names of some 200 physicians identified as "abortionists." Some of the names were grayed out. "Wounded," the home page explained. Other names had a horizontal strikethrough — for "fatality."

Among the doctors named on the site were four Oregon physicians who also had been pictured two years earlier on a Wild West-style poster released by the American Coalition of Life Activists. The poster bore the headline "Guilty" and identified the 13 physicians shown as "baby butchers."

At a time when abortion clinic violence was at a peak, the Oregon doctors viewed the Web site and poster as threats on their lives. Along with taking security precautions, the physicians also filed a federal court suit hoping to take down the postings and collect damages from the groups and individuals responsible.

A jury in Oregon awarded $107 million to the four doctors and two women's clinics that joined as plaintiffs. A federal appeals court upheld the award in May 2002, but dissenting judges in the 6-5 decision strongly argued that the anti-abortion messages were constitutionally protected speech.[1]

Now, the anti-abortion groups' appeal is presenting the Supreme Court with another in a series of difficult cases testing the limits of free speech in the context of anti-abortion activities that entail violence or disruption, actual or threatened. The Bush administration also appears to be struggling with the case. The court asked the Justice Department's solicitor general's office to submit a brief on the case in mid-December, but as of mid-March nothing had been filed. The justices would normally wait for the government's brief before deciding whether to hear the appeal.

The closely watched case comes against the backdrop of a decade of abortion-related violence that included shootings, bombings, arson and clinic blockades. At least seven people have been killed: three physicians, two clinic employees, a clinic escort and an off-duty police officer who died in a Birmingham, Ala., clinic bombing in 1998.[2]

James Kopp, the defendant in the most recent of the shootings, went on trial in Buffalo, N.Y., on March 17. Kopp has admitted shooting Barnet Slepian at his home in Amherst, N.Y., in 1998, but claimed he meant only to wound the doctor. Kopp was convicted of second-degree murder on March 18; he faces a minimum prison term of 15 years and a maximum of 25 years to life.

strued to apply to the more common D&E procedure, where the fetus is dismembered while still in utero. The court also held that the law failed to include a constitutionally required exemption to permit the procedure necessary to protect the woman's health.[9]

Now, anti-abortion groups are celebrating the March 13 Senate passage of a measure banning the procedure nationwide. Family Research Council President Ken Connor said the Senate's action would help "put an end to this unnecessary and grisly procedure which has taken the lives of thousands of partially born children and hurt so many women."

Abortion-rights groups assailed the bill as unnecessary, ill-advised and constitutionally flawed. "It's pretty much flagrantly unconstitutional," says NARAL's Cavendish. She contends that anti-abortion groups are pushing the proposal in the hope that by the time the issue reaches the

Supreme Court again, there will be one or more new justices who will vote for a different outcome.

The Nebraska law defined a partial-birth abortion as a procedure performed after "delivering into the vagina a living unborn child, or a substantial portion thereof." To narrow the definition, the new bill pending in Congress prohibits an abortion in which "the entire fetal head" or "any part of the fetal trunk past the navel" is "outside the mother."

Johnson says the new phrasing meets the Supreme Court's objection that the Nebraska law covered commonly used techniques. "By no stretch of the imagination could it be subject to that construction," he says.

Abortion-rights advocates, including abortion providers, disagree. "The law is not what they say it is," says Vicki Saporta, president of the National Abortion Federation (NAF), an organization of abortion clinics and

Violence and disruption have been ebbing for the past three years. For 2002, the National Abortion Federation (NAF), which represents abortion clinics, counted 265 incidents of "violence," but almost all were in the least serious categories of trespassing, vandalism or stalking. The federation listed one arson and one "invasion" for the year. It also counted four clinic blockades, with no arrests.

NAF President Vicki Saporta attributes the decline in violence to federal law enforcement. She notes that former Attorney General Janet Reno put Kopp and another anti-abortion fugitive — Eric Rudolph — on the FBI's "Ten Most Wanted" list. Kopp was arrested in France and extradited to the U.S. Rudolph, charged in the Birmingham bombing, is still at large.

Operation Rescue, once the largest of the militant anti-abortion groups, is now bankrupt and defunct; none of the existing groups matches its size or visibility. Major anti-abortion organizations routinely condemn violence. The National Right to Life Committee says it prohibits any violence or illegal activity by its members. Still, Saporta says she fears trials such as Kopp's give militant organizations "the chance to recruit the next assassin."

The Supreme Court has bolstered clinics' legal efforts against violence with a series of divided rulings over the past decade.[3] Three rulings in 1994, 1997 and 2000 allow court injunctions or state laws to establish "buffer zones" requiring protesters to keep some minimum distance from clinic entrances or clinic personnel and patients as they enter or leave the premises. Dissenting justices in each of the decisions argued the rulings infringed on free speech.

A separate ruling in 1994 allowed women's clinics to sue demonstrators for damages under the federal anti-racketeering law commonly known as RICO. Under that ruling, women's clinics later won a $250,000 verdict in the case, but the Supreme Court on Feb. 26 threw out the award. The court ruled, 8-1, that the demonstrators' conduct did not amount to extortion for purposes of the racketeering law.[4]

---

[1] *Planned Parenthood v. American Coalition of Life Activists*, 290 F.3d 1058 (CA9 2002). Plaintiffs included Robert Crist, James Hern, Elizabeth Newhall and James Newhall; defendants included two organizations — American Coalition of Life Activists and Advocates for Life Ministries — and 15 individuals. For coverage, see Henry Weinstein, "Abortion Foes Are Ruled a Threat," *Los Angeles Times*, May 17, 2002, p. B1.

[2] Summary information on the cases can be found on the National Abortion Federation's Web site: www.naf.org.

[3] For a summary, see Claire Cushman (ed.), *Supreme Court Decisions and Women's Rights* (2001), pp. 204-206.

[4] The case is *Scheidler v. National Organization for Women, Inc.*

physicians. "It's a pre-viability ban, with a definition so vague as to encompass more than one procedure," she says.

The new bill seeks to meet the Supreme Court's insistence on a health exception with a series of "congressional findings" that the procedure is "never medically indicated to preserve the health of the mother," is "unrecognized as a valid procedure by the mainstream medical community" and "poses additional health risks for the mother."

"The court has recognized in the past that Congress has a fact-finding role of its own that's entitled to deference," Johnson says.

But Saporta calls the findings "nonsense," with "no basis in scientific medical evidence."

Congress put the issue on hold immediately following the Supreme Court's 2000 decision, but the House again passed a ban in 2002. With the Democrats in control of the Senate, however, then-Majority Leader Tom Daschle of South Dakota blocked consideration of the measure.

The major legislative fight in the Senate turned on failed amendments sponsored by Democratic senators who wanted to add a health exception to the bill. A health exception "would ban no abortions at all," argued Sandy Rios, president of the Concerned Women for America, a conservative policy group.

NARAL's Cavendish countered that the proponents' refusal to agree to a health exception "just reveals that they really want to shackle doctors and have the government inserted squarely into medical decision-making."

Whatever happens in Congress, both sides expect the issue to be settled again in the courts — eventually, at the Supreme Court. Catholic University's Kmiec, a leading constitutional scholar on the anti-abortion side, doubts the bill will be upheld. "Not unless the Supreme Court changes its mind," he says.

The more explicit definition of the procedure "may convince five justices," he says, "especially if there's a new justice looking at it for the first time." But the law will be struck down, he predicts, if it does not allow the procedure when necessary to protect the woman's health. "I don't think you get around the health exception," Kmiec concludes.

Should Congress and the states enact additional restrictions on abortion?

State legislatures have adopted hundreds of laws regulating or limiting abortions in recent years. One type of anti-abortion law — requiring parental notification or consent before an abortion can be performed on a minor — has been adopted by at least 20 states, and 15 others are considering similar measures.

But anti-abortion groups say Planned Parenthood and other abortion-rights organizations help teenagers get around these laws by referring them to women's clinics in states without parental-involvement statutes.

To counteract the practice, anti-abortion groups are urging Congress to make it a federal crime punishable by up to a year in prison for anyone other than a parent to transport a minor from a parental-consent state to a non-parental-involvement state in order to obtain an abortion. Abortion-rights groups strongly oppose the bill, saying it would endanger girls in dysfunctional families and expose relatives, such as aunts or grandmothers, to prosecution.

Twice approved by the House, the proposal is one of several abortion-related measures sought by anti-abortion groups, girded with greater confidence now that Republicans also control the Senate.

Most States Limit Abortion Rights

Forty-three states required parents to be notified before an abortion is performed on a minor child in 2002, and more than 30 states had informed-consent, TRAP laws or measures banning "partial-birth" abortion or other procedures.

Selected State Abortion Rates and Limits, 2002
(x = state has such a law)

States	Rate (per 1,000 women)	Informed Consent	Parental Notification	Waiting Period	Abortion Methods Banned*	TRAP Laws**
Alabama	14.3	x	x	x	x	x
Alaska	11.7	x	x		x	x
Arizona	16.5		x		x	x
Arkansas	9.8	x	x	x	x	x
California	31.2	x	x			x
Colorado	15.9	x				
Connecticut	21.1	x			x	
Delaware	31.3	x	x	x		
Dist. of Columbia	68.1					
Florida	31.9	x	x		x	x
Georgia	16.9		x		x	x
Hawaii	22.2					x
Idaho	7.0	x	x	x	x	x
Illinois	23.2		x		x	x
Indiana	9.4	x	x	x	x	x
Iowa	9.8		x		x	x
Kansas	21.4	x	x	x	x	
Kentucky	5.3	x	x	x	x	x

Continued ——————→

* Includes partial-birth abortions and certain other procedures.

** So-called TRAP (targeted regulations of abortion providers) laws govern what an abortion doctor must do before performing an abortion, such as requiring a woman to first undergo an ultrasound procedure.

Sources: "Who Decides: A State-by-State Review of Abortion and Reproductive Rights, 2003," NARAL, pp. iii-xxv; rates are from Lawrence B. Finer and Stanley K. Henshaw, "Abortion Incidence and Services In the United States in 2000," *Perspectives on Sexual and Reproductive Health,* January/February 2003, The Alan Guttmacher Institute.

Meanwhile, state legislatures are engaged in pitched battles over other abortion measures. NARAL Pro-Choice America counts 23 states as considering either informed-consent measures — which require that women be given certain information about fetal development and the procedure itself before an abortion can be performed — or bills requiring that a woman wait at least 24 hours before an abortion. Nine states are considering measures to ban most or all abortions.

Selected State Abortion Limits, 2002
(x = state has such a law)

States	Rate (per 1,000 women)	Informed Consent	Parental Notification	Waiting Period	Abortion Methods Banned*	TRAP Laws**
Louisiana	13.0	x	x	x	x	x
Maine	9.9	x	x			
Maryland	29.0		x			
Massachusetts	21.4	x	x	x		x
Michigan	21.6	x	x	x	x	x
Minnesota	13.5	x	x			x
Mississippi	6.0	x	x	x	x	x
Missouri	6.6	x	x		x	x
Montana	13.5	x	x	x	x	
Nebraska	11.6	x	x	x	x	x
Nevada	32.2	x	x		x	
New Hampshire	11.2					
New Jersey	36.3		x		x	x
New Mexico	14.7		x		x	
New York	39.1					x
North Carolina	21.0	x				x
North Dakota	9.9	x	x	x	x	x
Ohio	16.5	x	x	x	x	x
Oklahoma	10.1		x		x	x
Oregon	23.5					
Pennsylvania	14.3	x	x	x		x
Rhode Island	24.1	x	x		x	x
South Carolina	9.3	x	x	x	x	x
South Dakota	5.5	x	x	x	x	x
Tennessee	15.2	x	x	x	x	x
Texas	18.8		x			x
Utah	6.6	x	x	x	x	x
Vermont	12.7					
Virginia	18.1	x	x	x	x	x
Washington	20.2					
West Virginia	6.8		x		x	
Wisconsin	9.6	x	x	x	x	x
Wyoming	1.0		x			
		31	43	22	31	35

Both sides in the debate agree the restrictions already on the books have reduced the number of abortions. "The states that have passed pro-life legislation have had a significant impact on their abortion rates, birth rates and the number of abortions generally," says the NRLC's Balch. "They've all gone down."

Abortion-rights groups point in particular to waiting-period laws, which in some states require a woman to make two trips to a clinic before undergoing an abortion.

One study suggested such laws reduced the number of abortions by 10 percent or more in two states: Mississippi and Utah.[10] "It definitely has an impact," says Erica Smock, legislative counsel for the Center for Reproductive Rights, a national litigation center based in New York City. "It increases burdens for women who already face obstacles."

Anti-abortion groups say the proposed federal Child Custody Protection Act will strengthen state parental-involvement laws by making it illegal to take a minor to another state for an abortion if state law requires parental-involvement in a minor's abortion. "Parental-notification laws are being systemically evaded by organized activity," Johnson says. "Elements of the abortion industry set up systems for shunting girls across state lines to get abortions without notifying their parents."

Abortion-rights groups say young women with abusive or unsupportive parents need to be able to turn to other relatives or other "trusted adults" in the event of an unwanted pregnancy. "This bill would endanger young women and isolate them when confronted with a crisis pregnancy," says NARAL's Cavendish. "The government cannot force healthy family communication where it doesn't already exist."

Among other bills pending in Congress, the Unborn Victims of Violence Act would make harming or killing a fetus a federal crime if the injury or death resulted from any one of 68 existing federal offenses, whether or not the assailant knew the woman was pregnant or intended to harm the fetus. Many states already have such laws.

Abortion-rights advocates say such laws are unnecessary. "The crime is on the pregnant woman who loses a wanted fetus or a wanted embryo," Cavendish says. She says the bill is "part of a strategy to undermine the foundations of *Roe* by weaving throughout the law a fabric of fetal personhood or embryonic personhood."

Anti-abortion groups say the bill simply recognizes that crimes that result in injury or death to a fetus have "two victims, not one." And Johnson denies any intention of using the bill to undercut *Roe*. "Pro-abortion groups try to enforce a policy that the unborn child must be invisible," he says. "Most Americans, whatever their views on abortion, don't think of it that way."

A so-called right-to-refuse bill — passed by the House in September 2002 — is designed to prevent health-care providers with religious or moral objections to abortion from being forced to perform the procedure. Supporters say it merely clarifies a "conscience clause" inserted into federal public-health law after the 1973 *Roe* decision. But opponents say the bill expands existing law by allowing hospitals, as well as health insurers, to prevent physicians or others from performing abortions or providing referrals to abortion counseling.

The child custody, right-to-refuse and fetal-protection bills all passed the House during the past (107th) Congress but failed to come to a vote in the Democratic-controlled Senate. Today, even with Republican control, the Senate is still regarded as a difficult hurdle for anti-abortion groups. Johnson counts 53 senators — a majority — on the record in support of *Roe v. Wade*. Nonetheless, he says, "some of those senators will support specific pro-life legislation."

BACKGROUND

Road to *Roe*

Abortion laws — adopted by nearly all the states by the end of the 19th century — came under strong attack from a reform movement beginning in the 1950s. It was slowly gaining ground when the U.S. Supreme Court in 1973 dramatically invalidated all existing abortion laws with its landmark decision in *Roe v. Wade*. The ruling triggered a bitter fight between opposing forces now in its fourth decade.

The common law that the United States carried over from the Colonial period generally permitted abortion until "quickening," or the first movement of the fetus.[11] Connecticut became the first state to pass an abortion statute with an 1821 law prohibiting the inducement of abortion through dangerous poisons. By 1900, almost all

the states had passed anti-abortion laws, largely in response to urgings from doctors. The laws typically permitted abortions when necessary in a doctor's opinion to preserve the life of the woman.

The laws remained on the books through the mid-20th century, but enforcement was uneven at most. Middle- and upper-class women often found ways to circumvent the laws by finding doctors willing to certify the procedure as medically necessary. Low-income women resorted to illegal abortions performed figuratively, if not literally, in the back alleys of metropolitan areas, often by people with little, if any, formal medical training. As of the late 1960s, the number of illegal abortions performed annually in the United States was variously estimated at between 200,000 and 1.2 million. In 1965, an estimated 200 women died from botched abortions, some of them crudely self-administered.[12]

The abortion-reform movement of the 1950s and '60s drew from the work of family-planning groups such as Planned Parenthood, anti-poverty organizations and the nascent women's-liberation movement. The movement gained ground despite strong opposition from the Roman Catholic Church and public ambivalence about what were then termed "elective" abortions.

Colorado in 1967 became the first state to liberalize its abortion law; by 1970, a dozen states had passed laws generally legalizing abortion in cases of rape, incest or to protect a woman's health or life. Then, in early 1970, New York dramatically became the first of four states to pass a "repeal law," virtually eliminating any barriers to abortion.

Reformers also had challenged abortion laws in courts, but with little success at first. In 1971, however, the justices agreed to hear challenges to laws in two states: Texas' 1857 ban on abortions except to save the woman's life and Georgia's 1968 "reform" statute allowing abortions if approved by a hospital committee after examination by two physicians other than the woman's personal doctor. The plaintiffs sued under the pseudonyms Jane Roe and Mary Doe, but years later identified themselves as Norma Jane McCorvey and Sandra Race Cano. Both women gave birth in 1970 after they were unable to obtain abortions in their states.

The Supreme Court struggled with the case, hearing arguments twice: once in December 1971 and then again in October 1972 after Justice Blackmun's initial draft of a decision failed to satisfy colleagues. Blackmun's second

CHRONOLOGY

Before 1970 *Most states enact laws in 19th century generally prohibiting abortions; movement to reform or repeal statutes forms in 1950s, advances slowly through 1960s.*

1970s *Abortion-reform movement gains in state legislatures, then wins constitutional ruling from U.S. Supreme Court; decision spawns "right-to-life" movement.*

1970 New York and three other states pass abortion "repeal laws."

1973 Supreme Court's *Roe v. Wade* decision establishes a woman's qualified constitutional right to abortion during most of pregnancy; "right-to-life" groups seek to limit or overturn ruling.

1977 Supreme Court allows states to deny abortion funding under Medicaid; three years later, court similarly upholds Hyde amendment barring use of federal funds for abortion for poor women.

1980s *Presidents Reagan and Bush support anti-abortion initiatives; Supreme Court, in conservative shift, upholds some abortion regulations.*

1983 Parental consent for abortion for minors upheld by Supreme Court if law allows "judicial-bypass" procedure; court invalidates "informed consent" and waiting-period provisions.

1984 Reagan adopts "Mexico City" policy to bar U.S. funds to groups that promote abortion overseas.

1989 Missouri abortion law upheld by Supreme Court in 5-4 vote; four justices criticize *Roe*, one short of majority.

1990s *Supreme Court reaffirms Roe's "essential holding," with modification; President Clinton adopts abortion-rights stands on several issues.*

1991 Supreme Court upholds rule barring abortion counseling at federally funded family-planning clinics.

1992 Three-justice plurality provides key votes for Supreme Court to reaffirm *Roe* while giving states leeway to regulate abortion unless laws impose "undue burden" on women's rights; ruling upholds most provisions of Pennsylvania law, including waiting period and informed consent.

1993 President Clinton reverses several Reagan-era anti-abortion policies on *Roe's* 20th anniversary. . . . First killing of doctor who performs abortions.

1994 Congress approves Freedom of Access to Clinic Entrances Act to establish criminal and civil penalties for use of force to intimidate abortion-clinic staff, patients.

1996, 1997 Clinton vetoes bills passed by Congress to ban "partial-birth abortions."

2000-Present *President Bush supports anti-abortion initiatives in Congress, controlled by Republicans after midterm elections.*

2000 Supreme Court on June 28 strikes down Nebraska statute banning "partial-birth" abortions. . . . Food and Drug Administration in September approves the "abortion pill" RU-486. . . . Texas Gov. George W. Bush soft-pedals anti-abortion views during presidential campaign, wins disputed election.

2001 President Bush re-establishes "global gag rule" on his first workday, barring federal funds for international organizations that promote abortions; draws fire from abortion-rights groups on judicial nominations.

2002 Bush signs Born-Alive Infants Protection Act on Aug. 5. . . . Health and Human Services regulation approved Sept. 27 allows states to define fetus as "unborn child" for purposes of prenatal care under federal health-insurance program.

2003 *Roe's* 30th anniversary marked by demonstrations by both sides. . . . Partial-birth abortion ban approved by Senate March 12, with House expected to follow and send to Bush to become law subject to certain court test.

draft — strengthened by a summer's worth of research at the Mayo Clinic in Minnesota — eventually won concurrence from six other justices, including Chief Justice Warren Burger. Blackmun relied heavily on medical history, but based the decision on a "personal-liberty interest" protected under either the Ninth Amendment's "unenumerated rights" provision or the 14th Amendment's Due Process Clause. In a short dissent, then-Associate Justice William H. Rehnquist said the court's "conscious weighing of competing factors" was "far more appropriate to a legislative judgment than a judicial one."

From *Roe* to *Casey*

Anti-abortion forces responded to *Roe v. Wade* first with protests and then with well-organized campaigns that failed to overturn the decision but won enactment of a host of restrictive state and federal laws. Over the next two decades, the Supreme Court struck down some of the restrictions but upheld others. The court rejected pleas during the 1980s to reconsider the *Roe* decision, but significantly modified the ruling with its 1992 decision in *Casey* fortifying the states' discretion to regulate abortion procedures.[13]

The court fights played out against a political backdrop that became increasingly polarized over time. At the national level, President Ronald Reagan decisively aligned the Republican Party with the anti-abortion movement by such steps as prohibiting abortion counseling at federally funded family-planning clinics (the so-called "gag rule"), cutting off federal funds for international family-planning organizations promoting abortions (the "Mexico City policy") and barring the importation of the so-called abortion pill RU-486.

The first President George Bush continued the policies in his four years in the White House. Both Reagan and Bush also appeared to be choosing federal judges — including Supreme Court justices — likely to be skeptical at best of expanding abortion rights. As the GOP stance hardened, the Democratic Party equally committed itself to supporting abortion rights and opposing legislated restrictions or judicial efforts to overturn *Roe*.

Along with political organizing and lobbying, some elements of the anti-abortion movement turned to civil disobedience and violence. The National Abortion Federation counted some 161 incidents of arson or bombings against abortion clinics from 1977-1992.

There were more than 100 clinic blockades each year in 1988 and 1989, resulting in more than 10,000 arrests per year. Most ominous were death threats and actual killings. Anti-abortion activists killed five people in 1993 and 1994: a physician at a Pensacola, Fla., clinic in March 1993; a second physician and a volunteer escort outside another Pensacola clinic in July 1994; and receptionists at separate Brookline, Mass., clinics on Dec. 30, 1994.[14]

The Supreme Court, meanwhile, gave anti-abortion forces major victories with decisions in 1977 and 1980 that permitted first the states and then the federal government to deny abortion funding under the Medicaid program for the indigent. Through the 1980s, the so-called Hyde amendment — named after Rep. Henry J. Hyde, R-Ill. — barred federal funding of abortions except to save the life of the woman. The court, on the other hand, struck down provisions requiring spousal consent, waiting periods or informed consent before an abortion could be performed.

After some wavering, the court in 1990 ruled that states could require parental notification for a minor to obtain an abortion, but only with a judicial procedure to bypass the requirement under certain circumstances. The court in 1991 also upheld the "gag rule" on family-planning clinics.

By the end of the 1980s, Reagan had appeared to shift the high court in a conservative direction with four appointments: Rehnquist's elevation to chief justice in 1986 and the selection of Justices O'Connor in 1981, Antonin Scalia in 1986 and Kennedy in 1987. The shift encouraged anti-abortion groups to view a challenge to a Missouri abortion law as a vehicle for overturning *Roe*. In fact, the court in 1989 upheld the law by a 5-4 vote, with four of the justices explicitly criticizing *Roe*: Rehnquist, Scalia, Kennedy and Byron R. White. But O'Connor declined to reconsider *Roe* and instead upheld the Missouri law because it did not create what she had described in previous opinions as an "undue burden" on a woman's right to an abortion.

The first President Bush appeared to shift the court further to the right with his appointments of Justice Souter in 1990 and Clarence Thomas in 1991. A new showdown came in a case challenging a Pennsylvania law that required a waiting period, informed consent and spousal consent — provisions seemingly barred by previous decisions. The Bush administration defended the law and expressly urged the court to overturn *Roe*. In an unusual move, however, three of the Republican-appointed justices — O'Connor, Kennedy and Souter — filed a pivotal joint opinion that reaffirmed what they called *Roe's* "essential holding" but nonetheless upheld all of the Pennsylvania law except the spousal consent portion, arguing that the measure met O'Connor's "undue burden" test.

Blackmun praised the three for "personal courage" while lamenting the apparent narrowing of *Roe*. From the opposite side, four justices — including Thomas — said abortion regulations should be permitted if "rationally related to a legitimate state interest."

Abortion-Rights Gains

The election of Democrat Clinton as president in 1992 brought an abortion-rights supporter to the White House for the first time in 12 years. Clinton reversed several Reagan-Bush abortion policies, supported abortion-rights measures in Congress and — perhaps most significantly — fortified the Supreme Court's abortion-rights bloc with his appointments of Justices Ruth Bader Ginsburg and Stephen G. Breyer. Those appointments helped produce a pivotal victory for abortion-rights forces with the court's 5-4 decision in 2000 striking down a state ban on "partial-birth abortions."[15]

Clinton cheered abortion-rights groups by changing three Reagan-Bush policies on his second day in office: Jan. 22, 1993 — the 20th anniversary of *Roe*. By executive order, Clinton ended enforcement of the "gag rule" on family-planning clinics and overturned the Mexico City policy on aid to international family-planning organizations. He also lifted a ban on abortions at overseas military facilities and directed the Department of Health and Human Services (HHS) to study whether to allow the importation of RU-486.

With Democratic majorities in the House and the Senate, Clinton also won enactment in 1994 of a law aimed at countering blockades of women's clinics. The Freedom of Access to Clinic Entrances Act — dubbed FACE — provided criminal and civil penalties for anyone using force or the threat of force against clinic workers or patients. In addition, Congress eased the Hyde amendment by allowing federal funding for abortions in cases of rape, incest or to protect the life of the mother. Abortion-rights supporters also won House and Senate committee approval of the "Freedom of Choice Act," aimed at writing the *Roe* decision into federal law. Neither bill was brought up for a floor vote, however, and anti-abortion forces gained the upper hand when Republicans won control of the House in the 1994 elections.

Ginsburg, a pioneer in women's-rights litigation before her appointment to the federal bench in 1980, and Breyer, a one-time aide to abortion-rights supporter Sen. Edward M. Kennedy, D-Mass., have both supported abortion rights after their appointments to the high court in 1993 and 1994, respectively. For several years, however, the court dealt with abortion issues only tangentially. In two decisions in 1994, the court ruled that judges could restrict anti-abortion demonstrations by setting up "buffer zones" around abortion-clinic entrances and that abortion clinics or patients could sue anti-abortion protesters for damages under the federal anti-racketeering law. Dissenting justices said the rulings limited anti-abortion groups' free-speech rights.

Beginning in 1995, anti-abortion groups were lobbying for laws to ban the procedure that they provocatively termed "partial-birth abortion." A federal ban won

Abortion Rates Higher for Low-Income Women

Abortion rates have been increasing dramatically among low-income women while declining among wealthier women.

Woman's Economic Status	Abortion Rate (No. of abortions per 1,000 women)	
	1994	2000
Income below poverty level	36	44
Income up to twice poverty level	31	38
Income two to three times poverty level	25	21
Income more than triple poverty level	16	10

Source: Rachel K. Jones, *et al.*, "Patterns in the Socioeconomic Characteristics of Women Obtaining Abortions in 2000-2001," *Perspectives on Sexual and Reproductive Health*, September/October 2002, pp. 226-235, The Alan Guttmacher Institute.

approval in the GOP-controlled House and the Democratic-controlled Senate in 1996, but Clinton vetoed the measure in a White House ceremony on April 10, attended by several women who insisted the procedure had saved their lives and their future ability to bear children. A second legislative push also ended with a veto in 1997. Anti-abortion groups were more successful with state legislatures; by the end of the decade, some 30 states had banned the procedure.

A challenge to one of those state laws — Nebraska's — reached the high court in 2000. In an opinion by Breyer, the court ruled that the measure created "an undue burden on a woman's right to make an abortion decision." First, he said, the law could be construed to prohibit the commonly done dilation and extraction (D&E) procedure. In addition, Breyer said, the law conflicted with *Roe* and subsequent cases because it did not include an exception for the procedure if necessary to protect the woman's health. In a pivotal concurring opinion, O'Connor suggested a more carefully drawn statute might pass constitutional muster. For the dissenters, Thomas likened the procedure to "infanticide."[16]

As the presidential campaign unfolded later that year, the Supreme Court's composition became a proxy for the opposing views of Republican George W. Bush and Democrat Al Gore.[17] Bush said he would appoint future justices in the mold of the court's strongest abortion opponents: Thomas and Scalia. Gore countered by pledging his support for abortion rights and warning of a likely reversal of *Roe v. Wade* if Bush made good on his pledge.

The two candidates staked out contrasting positions on other abortion issues, including partial-birth abortions and RU-486, but they also appeared to play down the issue to avoid alienating swing voters. For his part, Bush said he supported a constitutional amendment to ban abortions, but cautioned that it would not be adopted "until a lot of people change their minds."

Anti-Abortion Advances

During his first two years in office, President Bush has cheered anti-abortion groups with an array of policy moves and appointments. Anti-abortion bills won approval in the Republican-controlled House but stalled in the Senate after the Democrats gained control in May 2001. The GOP's recapture of the Senate in the 2002 midterm congressional elections improved the chances for

the anti-abortion agenda, including the ban on partial-birth abortions. But abortion-rights advocates vowed to continue opposing the bills — and immediately to challenge the partial-birth abortion measure if it became law.

Bush touched off fierce fights before his inauguration by naming determined abortion opponents to two key Cabinet posts: John Ashcroft, a former Missouri governor who had been defeated for re-election to the Senate, as attorney general; and Wisconsin Gov. Tommy G. Thompson as HHS secretary. Then two days after his inauguration, Bush marked *Roe's* 28th anniversary by sending greetings to the annual "March for Life" and, more tangibly, by reinstating the Mexico City policy of barring U.S. funds to international family-planning organizations that promote abortion.

Abortion-rights supporters had no leverage to try to block the reinstated funding policy. They tried hard but failed to block Ashcroft's confirmation. In his confirmation hearings, however, Democratic senators secured Ashcroft's promise to enforce federal laws protecting abortion rights — including the access-to-clinic-entrances act. He also said he would not try to overturn *Roe v. Wade*. Despite the concessions, anti-abortion groups hailed the Senate's 58-42 vote to confirm him on Feb. 1. Thompson had won easier confirmation earlier, after initial opposition to the nomination failed to harden.

Abortion politics also shaped the reaction to Bush's judicial nominations, including his first batch of 11 nominees for federal appeals courts, announced on May 9, 2001.[18] Abortion-rights groups criticized several of the nominees for taking anti-abortion stands as academics, lawyers or judges. Under Democratic control, the Senate held up many of Bush's nominees in 2001 and 2002, including the most controversial. Priscilla R. Owen, a Texas Supreme Court justice chosen for the federal appeals court in New Orleans, failed to win approval by the Judiciary Committee last September after being criticized for arguing in a dissenting opinion for a restrictive interpretation of the state's parental-notification law. (Owen is expected to be approved by the committee, now under Republican control, in the next two weeks.)

As Bush began his second year in office, he renewed his anti-abortion credentials with a more detailed message to the annual "March for Life" on Jan. 22. In an eight-paragraph statement read by telephone, Bush promised his administration would oppose partial-birth abortion and public financing of abortions and support teen abstinence, crisis-pregnancy centers and parental consent and notification laws. He also vowed to support "a comprehensive and effective ban on all forms of human cloning."[19] Some abortion opponents believe cloning human embryos to extract the cells for biomedical research is the equivalent of murder.

The administration also won praise the same month from anti-abortion groups — and strong opposition from abortion-rights organizations — with a proposed rule to define a fetus as a child eligible for government-subsidized health care under the Children's Health Insurance Program. Congress created the program in 1997 to benefit children in near-poverty families ineligible for Medicaid. Thompson said the proposed rule would allow states to increase insurance coverage for pre-natal care and delivery. But abortion-rights advocates said the proposal was really a backdoor attempt to establish a legal precedent for recognizing the fetus as a person; they called for simply adding pregnant women to the program's coverage.

The debate continued through the administrative rule-making process. Nearly 7,800 comments were received on the proposed rule before Thompson gave final approval on Sept. 27 for the regulation to go into effect 30 days later.[20] The fight then shifted to the states. Abortion-rights advocates said they would urge states to reject the option and instead ask HHS for permission to include pregnant women in the program. Two states had already taken that approach: New Jersey and Rhode Island.

In the meantime, Bush had signed into law a bill sought by anti-abortion groups to guarantee legal protection to babies born alive at any state of development. The Born-Alive Infants Protection Act defined a child as born alive if he or she has been expelled from the mother; is breathing; and has a beating heart, a pulsating umbilical cord or muscle movement, even if the expulsion occurred during an abortion. The bill included a disclaimer that it was not intended to infringe on abortion rights. Abortion-rights supporters in Congress called the measure unnecessary but did not oppose it. Bush signed the measure on Aug. 5, saying that it would give legal rights to "every infant born alive — including an infant who survives an abortion procedure."

As midterm elections approached, the House on Sept. 25 passed by a comfortable 229-189 margin the right-to-refuse bill, exempting health-care providers with religious or moral objections from being forced to perform abor-

tions. But the anti-abortion agenda remained blocked in the Democratic-controlled Senate. The GOP gains in the midterm elections immediately buoyed the anti-abortion forces, who counted eight of the 10 newly elected senators as "pro-life." Three of those took seats previously held by Democrats who had supported abortion rights. The election results helped clear one logjam when the Senate shifted to GOP control, with the early swearing in of two of the new Republicans. The move allowed confirmation of one of Bush's judicial nominees: Michael McConnell, a conservative law professor named to the federal appeals court in Denver, who had been opposed by abortion-rights groups because of writings critical of *Roe*.

On the 30th anniversary of the decision, Bush again spoke to the anti-abortion march by telephone.[21] "You and I share a commitment to building a culture of life in America," the president said, "and we are making progress."

The crowd numbered in the tens of thousands, leading abortion-rights groups to sound urgent alarms. "Pro-choice America has to wake up," NARAL's Cavendish declared.

CURRENT SITUATION

'Abortion-Pill' Controversy

For more than a decade, American women waited to learn whether a new drug developed in Europe — the so-called abortion pill — would be approved for use in the United States. Finally, in August 2000, the Food and Drug Administration (FDA) gave the official green light for doctors who wanted to prescribe the drug, known most commonly as RU-486.[22]

Some observers speculated that use of the drug — now called mifepristone — could defuse the abortion controversy. But today RU-486 remains a source of contention between the opposing camps. Anti-abortion groups call it unsafe and are asking the FDA to rescind its approval, while abortion-rights groups are actively promoting what they prefer to call the "early-option pill."

The dispute underscores the chasm that continues to separate the opposing camps in the abortion debate on virtually every issue relating to women's reproductive health. Occasional efforts to find common ground appear to make little headway, as the rhetoric remains hot and accusatory. Anti-abortion groups call their opponents "the abortion industry" or more provocatively "baby killers," while abortion-rights organizations label their adversaries not just "anti-choice" but sometimes "anti-woman."

Whatever its political impact, RU-486 appeals to abortion-rights advocates as an additional and, at first blush, more convenient option for women to terminate unwanted pregnancies. Two years after FDA approval, the drug had been used to complete more than 100,000 abortions in the United States, according to Danco Laboratories, the New York-based company that markets the drug here.[23] The Alan Guttmacher Institute — a nonprofit research center affiliated with Planned Parenthood — estimates that pill-induced, or medical, abortions comprised about 6 percent of all abortions in the first half of 2001, the most recent period covered in its survey.

Abortion providers insist RU-486 is both safe and effective. "This has been a very acceptable method for women," says the National Abortion Federation's Saporta. Medical abortion can be completed earlier than surgical procedures — an important advantage, Saporta says. "Earlier abortion by any method is safer," she explains.

Anti-abortion groups, however, say RU-486 can cause hemorrhaging, or even death, and its approval was the result of political pressure in the last year of the Clinton administration. "The evidence would seem to show that it is not safe for the woman and obviously not safe for the baby," says Wendy Wright, senior policy director for Concerned Women for America (CWFA). The Christian-oriented organization petitioned the FDA in August 2002 to rescind its approval of RU-486 because of safety complaints and alleged procedural flaws in the approval process.

The National Abortion Federation is working on a response to correct what it calls the "medical misinformation" in CWFA's petition. "There isn't any question that mifepristone is safe and effective," says Saporta. "We don't believe the FDA will change its approval."

Anti-abortion groups emphasize — and an NAF fact sheet acknowledges — that use of RU-486 is not so simple as some news coverage might suggest. The drug works by blocking the body's production of progesterone, a hormone crucial to the early progress of pregnancy. The treatment requires at least two visits to a clinic or medical office, can take anywhere from three days to three to four weeks and fails about 5 percent of the time — necessitating a surgical procedure. Anti-abortion groups also say that a pill-induced abortion has a greater emotional impact on the woman because she is likely to see the aborted fetus when it is expelled.

For abortion-rights advocates, on the other hand, RU-486 helps to circumvent the persistent problem of limited availability of abortion providers. "Access is probably the biggest problem facing women who choose to have an abortion," Saporta says. The number of abortion providers has declined by more than one-third since 1982, according to the Guttmacher Institute. More than one-third of American women live in a county without an abortion provider.[24]

Doctors today often are not trained in how to perform an abortion. Fewer than half of the obstetrics-gynecology residency programs require or even offer abortion training, Saporta says. To remedy the problem, NAF and other abortion-rights groups are calling for laws — like an executive order issued by New York City Mayor Michael Bloomberg in April 2002 — to require abortion training in residency programs at public hospitals. Anti-abortion groups say such requirements run afoul of existing federal law that prohibits discrimination against any health-care entity for refusing to provide abortion training.

In another fight, opposing camps have squared off on the question of whether women who have abortions have a heightened risk of developing breast cancer. Although most cancer experts doubt any link, the National Cancer Institute — part of the National Institutes of Health within the HHS Department — acceded to lobbying from anti-abortion lawmakers last summer and changed its Web site to describe the research on the subject as "inconsistent."[25]

Abortion-rights groups strongly criticized the revision. The institute responded by convening a closed-door conference on the issue in February that ended by reverting to the previous position. In a conference summary posted on its Web site, the institute now states flatly: "Induced abortion is not associated with increased breast cancer risk."

Legislative Battles

Anti-abortion groups are exulting in the Senate's quick approval of legislation to ban so-called partial-birth abortions and predicting easy passage in the House in April en route to being signed into law by President Bush. Meanwhile, other parts of the anti-abortion groups' agenda are progressing in Congress and in some state legislatures.

Should Congress ban so-called partial-birth abortions?

YES
Rep. Christopher H. Smith, R-N.J.
Chairman, Bipartisan Congressional Pro-life Caucus

Written for The CQ Researcher, March 2003

A society is measured by how well — or poorly — it treats the most vulnerable in its midst, and partial-birth abortion, like all abortions, is horrific violence against women and children.

Justice Clarence Thomas accurately described the procedure in his *Stenberg v. Carhart* (2000) dissent: "After dilating the cervix, the physician will grab the fetus by its feet and pull the fetal body out of the uterus into the vaginal cavity. At this stage of development, the head is the largest part of the body. . . . the head will be held inside the uterus by the woman's cervix. While the fetus is stuck in this position, dangling partly out of the woman's body, and just a few inches from a completed birth, the physician uses an instrument such as a pair of scissors to tear or perforate the skull. The physician will then either crush the skull or will use a vacuum to remove the brain and other intracranial contents from the fetal skull, collapse the fetus' head, and pull the fetus from the uterus."

Most partial-birth abortions are committed between the 20th and 26th week of pregnancy. At this stage, a prematurely delivered infant is usually born alive. These are babies who are extremely sensitive to pain — whether inside the womb, fully born or anywhere in-between.

An overwhelming majority of Americans are outraged that this procedure is legal in our country. A January Gallup Poll found that 70 percent favored and 25 percent opposed "a law that would make it illegal to perform a specific abortion procedure conducted in the last six months of pregnancy known as 'partial birth abortion,' except in cases necessary to save the life of the mother."

In a January speech, President Bush agreed: "Partial-birth abortion is an abhorrent procedure that offends human dignity."

I have written two torture-victims relief laws and many other pieces of human-rights legislation including a law to stop exploitation of women by sex traffickers. Partial-birth abortion is torture of baby girls and boys, and I am ashamed of my colleagues who stand on the House floor to defend it.

Abortion methods are violence against children. There is absolutely nothing compassionate or benign about dousing a baby with superconcentrated salt solutions or lethal injections or hacking them to pieces with surgical knives, and there is absolutely nothing compassionate or caring about sucking a baby's brains out.

NO
Rep. Louise Slaughter, D-N.Y.
Co-Chair, Pro-Choice Caucus

Written for The CQ Researcher, March 2003

I do solemnly swear that I will support and defend the Constitution of the United States against all enemies, foreign and domestic. . . ." Before taking office, Members of Congress pledge these words to uphold the Constitution. Yet, again this year, anti-choice legislators introduce legislation that disregards the Constitution and the precious rights it guarantees.

The right to privacy as recognized in *Roe v. Wade* and reaffirmed in *Planned Parenthood v. Casey* is a fundamental American value. Opponents of a woman's right to choose have failed in their efforts to eliminate this constitutionally protected right, so they have changed tactics. Their strategy now is to whittle away at a woman's right to choose until all that remains are hollow guarantees in a faded court opinion.

The legislative centerpiece of this strategy is misleadingly titled Partial Birth Abortion Ban Act of 2003. Three years after the Supreme Court addressed this issue in the landmark *Stenberg v. Carhart* decision overturning Nebraska's prohibition of so-called "partial-birth" abortions, opponents of reproductive freedom want to force through Congress legislation that contains the same serious constitutional flaws as the Nebraska ban.

The court ruled that the Nebraska law was unconstitutional because it did not provide an exception to protect a woman's health. Further, it ruled that the law was an undue burden on women's rights to privacy, because the vague description of partial-birth abortions covered multiple procedures, including the most common form of second trimester abortion.

The legislation's authors could have drafted a bill that complies with constitutional standards, yet they have not done so. This bill does NOT include an exception for the health of the woman, and it does NOT prohibit a specific abortion procedure.

Congress should not invade the doctor-patient relationship. These intensely personal choices must be made by women, their doctors and their families — not by politicians. We should praise doctors who care for women faced with this difficult decision, not make them federal criminals. This legislation is an attack on the power of the Supreme Court, the Constitution and women's health and dignity.

Forcing members of Congress year after year to consider a bill that is clearly unconstitutional is a waste of taxpayers' money. Instead of continually reintroducing unconstitutional legislation, proponents of this measure should put their energies and resources into promoting women's health by improving access to contraception and supporting comprehensive family-planning programs.

Seeking Common Ground

Cristina Page and Amanda Peterman are both thirty-something college graduates and self-described feminists with a common interest in promoting women's health and family welfare. Since they first met a little over two years ago, they have become fast friends. They happen to disagree, however, on one major issue: abortion.

Page works as program director for the New York affiliate of NARAL Pro-Choice America, while Peterman serves as life media director for Right to Life of Michigan. Nonetheless, Page and Peterman marked the 30th anniversary of *Roe v. Wade* in January with a jointly bylined op-ed article in *The New York Times* calling for the opposing camps in the abortion debate to find common ground on such issues as pregnancy prevention, high-quality child care and "family friendly" workplace policies.

"If the pro-choice and pro-life movements work together to support legislation to expand the social safety net for low-income mothers, and to lobby for more family-friendly policies for working parents, their power would be formidable," Page and Peterman wrote. "But sadly, they are issues that often get lost in the larger debate."[1]

Since they met on the eve of the 2000 election, Page and Peterman have traveled together and talked at length. Page took Peterman to an abortion clinic in Pittsburgh to try to dispel the image of counselors rushing women to have the procedure. For her part, Page says she better appreciates that many people in the right-to-life movement are turned off by violence and harsh rhetoric.

Together, Page and Peterman are now working to raise money for a new organization to collaborate on what Page calls "the surprising number of important issues on which we agree."

The project is both ambitious and delicate. Page says her abortion-rights colleagues have been supportive for the most part, but Peterman bowed out of a scheduled interview in March because of what she called "stuff inside my ranks. It's a very slow process to educate both sides," Peterman said apologetically.

"There's a lot of distrust, there's been a lot of violence," Page says. "We can retrace the disagreements, but that's what we've been doing for 30 years."

---

[1] Cristina Page and Amanda Peterman, "The Right to Agree," *The New York Times*, Jan. 22, 2003, p. A21.

The Senate's March 13 ban on partial-birth abortions came after two days of debate and unsuccessful efforts by opponents to soften the measure. With some Democratic votes, the Republican majority rejected by margins of more than 20 votes each of two Democratic-sponsored amendments to add a health exception to the bill.

Abortion-rights advocates scored a symbolic victory with a 52-46 vote on March 12 adding a "sense of the Senate" amendment in support of *Roe v. Wade*, but the language is certain to be rejected by the House and stripped out in conference. More substantively, abortion-rights advocates suffered a narrow loss on March 11 with a failed amendment to require health insurance plans to provide coverage for birth control pills. The measure was approved, 49-47, but under Senate rules needed 60 votes to overcome a point of order because it would have raised federal spending.

On final passage, 16 Democrats joined 48 of the chamber's 51 Republicans in voting for the ban. Democrats voting aye included Minority Leader Daschle. The three GOP "no" votes came from moderate New Englanders: Lincoln Chafee of Rhode Island and Maine's Olympia J. Snowe and Susan Collins. Sen. James M. Jeffords, I-Vt., also voted no. The three non-voting senators were all Democrats, including two declared presidential candidates — John Kerry of Massachusetts and John Edwards of North Carolina — and Delaware's Joseph Biden, Jr.

President Bush issued a statement commending the Senate for voting to outlaw what he called "an abhorrent procedure that offends human dignity."

Opponents continued to insist, however, that the bill will not survive a court test. "Anti-choice senators simply ignored Supreme Court precedent," said NARAL's Michelman, referring to the 2000 decision striking down Nebraska's partial-birth ban. But the NRLC's Johnson noted that four justices had voted to uphold the Nebraska law and voiced hope for a different outcome when a case testing the federal law reaches the high court.

Meanwhile, anti-abortion groups are also advancing a variety of restrictive bills in state legislatures around the country. But the only major bills to win final legislative approval by mid-March were a package of measures in Virginia that faced a possible veto from the state's Democratic governor, Mark Warner. Abortion-rights groups, however, are having some success with bills designed to reduce the need for abortions by easing women's access to emergency contraception — so-called morning-after bills.

The bills approved by the Virginia legislature include a new ban on so-called "partial-birth infanticide" to replace the state's previous law that was invalidated following the Supreme Court's decision in the Nebraska case. The bill prohibits "any deliberate act that is intended to kill a human infant (or that does kill an infant) who has been born alive but who has not been completely extracted or expelled from its mother." A second measure would require a minor to obtain the consent from one parent before an abortion; current state law only requires notice.

Warner says he may veto the measures, which he calls "a frontal assault on a woman's right to choose." But both bills originally passed with veto-proof majorities; the legislature is to return on April 1 to consider any gubernatorial vetoes. Opponents vow to challenge the partial-birth abortion bill in court if it does become law.[26]

Some of the other bills gaining in state legislatures are examples of what abortion-rights groups call "TRAP laws" — for "targeted regulation of abortion providers." A Kansas House committee has approved a bill setting safety standards for abortion clinics; opponents say the bill is unnecessary and designed to impose unaffordable costs.[27]

Some other bills are largely symbolic. A Georgia lawmaker is proposing to require a judge to issue a death warrant before an abortion can proceed. In South Carolina, a legislator has a bill to erect a six-foot statue of a fetus outside the statehouse as a memorial to "unborn children who have given their lives because of legal abortion."

For their part, abortion-rights advocates won legislative approval in two states — Hawaii and New Mexico — requiring hospitals to inform sexual-assault survivors about emergency contraception. Hawaii also passed a bill to allow women to obtain emergency contraception from pharmacists without an individual prescription from a physician; similar proposals were pending in other states, including New York, Oregon and Texas.

OUTLOOK

Unabated Conflict

The abortion wars show no signs of abating.

The dueling press releases issued after the Senate passed the partial-birth abortion bill carried forward the harsh debates from the Senate floor. The NRLC accused opponents of "extremism in defense of abortion," while NARAL said the bill took "direct aim at a woman's right to choose."

The bill's ultimate fate rests with the courts — most likely, the Supreme Court itself. The justices have shied away from abortion disputes since their 2000 decision striking down the Nebraska ban. In February, for example, the court declined to hear a women's-clinic challenge to an Indiana waiting-period law upheld by the federal appeals court in Chicago. The justices are likely to feel obliged to take up a case testing a new federal law, but any legal challenge will take more than a year to reach them.

By then, the court may have one or more new justices, but its tilt on abortion issues depends on who retires. The court's three oldest members are Rehnquist, 78, who opposes abortion rights; and Justices John Paul Stevens, 82, a strong abortion-rights supporter, and O'Connor, nearly 73, who helped preserve *Roe v. Wade* in 1992 but has voted to uphold most state restrictions on abortion.

Rehnquist's retirement would not give President Bush the chance to shift the court's balance toward the anti-abortion side; Stevens' or O'Connor's departure might. Any vacancy, however, will result in a likely confirmation fight between liberals and conservatives in the narrowly divided Senate.

The opposing abortion-related groups are both using a fight over one of Bush's judicial nominees as a rehearsal of sorts for a potential Supreme Court fight. Anti-abortion groups are strongly supporting and abortion-rights organizations strenuously opposing confirmation for Miguel Estrada, a Washington lawyer and former assistant U.S. solicitor general, to the federal appeals court in Washington. Republicans say they have sufficient votes — 54 — to approve the nomination, but they have been unable to muster the 60 votes needed to overcome a Democratic filibuster.

Legislatively, anti-abortion lawmakers enjoy the upper hand on Capitol Hill, but they still face significant hurdles. As the new Congress convened, NARAL estimated that it had only prevailed in 25 out of 148 votes on reproductive rights issues since 1996. With the newly strengthened GOP hold in Congress, abortion-rights advocates already have been on the losing end of two major votes — the House's ban on human cloning in February and the Senate's partial-birth abortion ban in March. Abortion-rights advocates are likely to face more rough sledding over the next two years.

Meanwhile, the debates continue not only in legislative chambers but also on the sidewalks outside women's clinics, where abortion-rights advocates appear determined but beleaguered. "I don't think *Roe v. Wade* will be overturned," clinic escort Fox says. "But it's going to continue to be broken down until we only have a right to abortion under very limited parameters."

For her part, "sidewalk counselor" Walsh is equally determined and seemingly more hopeful of eventual victory in the fight against *Roe v. Wade*. "With the way our society is, our government is, it would take a miracle" to overturn *Roe*, Walsh says. "But God does do miracles. The most effective thing we can do is pray. So with God's grace, one day it will happen."

NOTES

1. For background, see Charles S. Clark, "Abortion Clinic Protests," *The CQ Researcher*, April 7, 1995, pp. 297-320.

2. For background, see Sarah Glazer, "Roe v. Wade at 25," *The CQ Researcher*, Nov. 28, 1997, pp. 1033-1056.

3. See *1996 CQ Almanac*, pp. 6-42 to 6-45; *1997 CQ Almanac*, pp. 6-12 to 6-18.

4. Mary Balch, "Pro-Lifers Celebrate Gains in State Legislative Elections," *NRLC News*, December 2002 (www.nrlc.org/news/2002).

5. NARAL Pro-Choice America Foundation, "Who Decides? A State-by-State Review of Abortion and Reproductive Rights," January 2003 (www.naral.org/mediaresources/publications.html).

6. "Memorandum to the Conference," Nov. 21, 1972, cited in Barbara Hinkson Craig and David M. O'Brien, *Abortion and American Politics* (1993), p. 21.

7. *Planned Parenthood of Southeastern Pennsylvania v. Casey*, 505 U.S. 833 (1992). For accounts of the case, see David J. Garrow, *Liberty and Sexuality: The Right to Privacy and the Making of Roe v. Wade* (1998),

pp. 681-701; N.E.H. Hull and Peter Charles Hoffer, *Roe v. Wade: The Abortion Rights Controversy in American History* (2001), pp. 249-258.

8. *Time*/CNN/Gallup Poll conducted Jan. 15-16, 2003, among 1,010 adult Americans age 18 or older.

9. *Stenberg v. Carhart*, 505 U.S. 833 (2000).

10. The studies are discussed in a recent federal appeals court decision upholding Indiana's waiting-period law. See *A Woman's Choice-East Side Women's Clinic v. Newman*, 7th U.S. Circuit Court of Appeals, 01-2107, Sept. 16, 2002.

11. For historical background, see Hull and Hoffer, *op. cit.*, pp. 11-88; James C. Mohr, *Abortion in America: The Origins and Evolution of National Policy, 1800-1900* (1978).

12. The Alan Guttmacher Institute, "Trends in Abortion in the United States, 1973-2000," January 2003.

13. For a compact summary of Supreme Court decisions from *Roe* through the partial-birth abortion decision in *Stenberg v. Carhart* (2000), see "Abortion" in Claire Cushman (ed.), *Supreme Court Decisions and Women's Rights* (2001), pp. 188-206.

14. See Dallas A. Blanchard, *The Anti-Abortion Movement and the Rise of the Religious Right: From Polite to Fiery Protest* (1994), pp. 53-60; Garrow, *op. cit.*, p. 705.

15. For summaries, see *Congress and the Nation, Vol. IX, 1993-1996* (1998), pp. 536-541, 563-565; *Congress and the Nation*, Vol. X, 1997-2000 (2002), pp. 455-459, 472-475.

16. For an account, see Kenneth Jost, *Supreme Court Yearbook 1999-2000* (2000), pp. 34-41.

17. Account drawn from Mary Leonard, "Both Candidates Keep Quiet on Abortion," *The Boston Globe*, Nov. 1, 2000, p. A23.

18. For background, see Kenneth Jost, "Judges and Politics," *The CQ Researcher*, July 27, 2001, pp. 577-600.

19. The complete text can be found on *National Right to Life News*, February 2002 (www.nrlc.org/news).

20. See Robert Pear, "Bush Rule Makes Fetuses Eligible for Health Benefits," *The New York Times*, Sept. 28, 2002, p. A13; Laura Meckler, " 'Unborn Child' Coverage Rule Set," The Associated Press, Sept. 29, 2002.

21. See Robin Toner, "At a Distance, Bush Joins Abortion Protest," *The New York Times*, Jan. 23, 2003, p. A16.

22. Some background drawn from interest-group Web sites: National Abortion Federation (www.naf.org); National Right to Life Committee (www.nrlc.org). For a journalistic account, see Sharon Bernstein, "Persistence Brought Abortion Pill to U.S.," *Los Angeles Times*, Nov. 5, 2000, p. A1.
23. Marc Kaufman, "Abortion Pill Sales Rising, Firm Says," *The Washington Post*, Sept. 25, 2002, p. A3.
24. Stanley K. Henshaw and Lawrence B. Finer, "The Accessibility of Abortion Services in the United States, 2001," *Perspectives on Sexual and Reproductive Health*, Vol. 35, No. 1 (January/February 2003), pp. 15-24 (www.agi-usa.org/journals).
25. See Daniel Costello, "An Enduring Debate: Cancer and Abortion," *Los Angeles Times*, March 10, 2003.
26. Warner quoted in Warren Fiske, "Now, the Vetoes," *The* (Norfolk) *Virginian-Pilot*, Feb. 28, 2003, p. A1. See also Tammie Smith, "Lawmakers Focus on Abortion," *The* (Richmond) *Times-Dispatch*, Feb. 23, 2003, p. A11.
27. See David Crary, "Abortion Foes Step Up Efforts Nationally," The Associated Press, March 11, 2003.

BIBLIOGRAPHY

Books

Blanchard, Dallas A., *The Anti-Abortion Movement and the Rise of the Religious Right: From Polite to Fiery Protest*, Twayne Publishers, 1994.
Critically examines the movement from *Roe* through *Casey* (1992). Blanchard is professor emeritus at the University of West Florida. Lists major anti-abortion publications and organizations.

Cook, Elizabeth Adell, Ted G. Jelen and Clyde Wilcox, *Between Two Absolutes: Public Opinion and the Politics of Abortion*, Westview Press, 1992.
Detailed analyses of public opinion on abortion with extensive statistical information over 20-year period. Cook is now an editor at the *American Political Science Review*; Jelen teaches at the University of Nevada-Las Vegas, and Wilcox at Georgetown University. Jelen is also editor or co-editor of *Abortion Politics in the United States and Canada* (with Marthe A. Chandler), Praeger, 1994; *Perspectives on the Politics of Abortion*, Praeger, 1995.

Craig, Barbara Hinkson, and David M. O'Brien, *Abortion and American Politics*, Chatham House, 1993.
Analyzes the politics of the abortion issue from *Roe* through *Casey*. Craig is a professor emerita at Wesleyan University, O'Brien teaches at the University of Virginia. Includes major statutes and case index.

Garrow, David J., *Liberty and Sexuality: The Right to Privacy and the Making of Roe v. Wade*, Macmillan, 1994 [updated edition, University of California Press, 1998].
Definitive history of Supreme Court decisions on reproductive rights. Historian Garrow, an abortion-rights advocate, is a professor at Emory Law School. Includes voluminous notes, 30-page bibliography.

Gorney, Cynthia, *Articles of Faith: A Frontline History of the Abortion Wars*, Simon & Schuster, 1998.
Details the personalities and issues in the "abortion wars" by focusing on one of the most contentious battleground states: Missouri. Gorney is associate dean at the University of California's Graduate School of Journalism in Berkeley. Includes long source list.

Hull, N.E.H., and Peter Charles Hoffer, *Roe v. Wade: The Abortion Rights Controversy in American History*, University Press of Kansas, 2001.
Compactly traces history of abortion law from 19th-century state laws through *Casey*. Hull teaches at Rutgers University, Hoffer at the University of Georgia. Includes lengthy chronology and bibliographical essay.

Tribe, Laurence H., *Abortion: The Clash of Absolutes*, W.W. Norton, 1990.
The prominent Harvard Law School professor, an abortion-rights advocate, tries to look at the issue anew. In a 1992 edition, Tribe describes the *Casey* decision as watering down *Roe* by permitting states new powers to restrict abortion.

Articles

Savage, David, "As Roe vs. Wade Turns 30, Ruling's Future Is Unsure," *Los Angeles Times*, Jan. 21, 2003, p. A1.

Analyzes possible impact on abortion-rights ruling if President Bush gets to fill one or more Supreme Court vacancies.

Tumulty, Karen, and Viveca Novak, "Under the Radar," *Time*, Jan. 27, 2003, pp. 38-41.
Examines the White House strategy to undercut abortion rights legalized by *Roe v. Wade*.

Zernike, Kate, "Thirty Years After Abortion Ruling, New Trends but the Old Debate," *The New York Times*, Jan. 20, 2003, p. A1.
Discusses views on abortion among women, activists and others against backdrop of decline in abortion rate to lowest level since 1974. Package includes sidebar by same reporter: "An Abortion Doctor's View."

Reports and Studies

Finer, Lawrence B., and Stanley K. Henshaw, "Abortion Incidence and Services in the United States in 2000," *Perspectives on Sexual and Reproductive Health* (January/February 2003) (www.agi-usa.org/journals).

Documents a decline in U.S. abortions; a second article in the issue details information about abortion providers: Stanley K. Henshaw and Lawrence B. Finer, "The Accessibility of Abortion Services in the United States, 2001." The authors are researchers at the Alan Guttmacher Institute, a research center affiliated with Planned Parenthood but accepted as reliable by both sides in abortion debates.

NARAL Pro-Choice America, "Who Decides? A State-by-State Review of Abortion and Reproductive Rights," January 2003 (www.naral.org/mediaresources/publications/2003).
The advocacy group's 12th compendium of state abortion laws details what it calls the "further erosion" of *Roe v. Wade*.

National Right to Life Committee, "NRL News," monthly series (www.nrlc.org/news).
The anti-abortion group's monthly newsletter provides up-to-date information and perspective on legislative and legal developments.

For More Information

Alan Guttmacher Institute, 120 Wall St., 21st Floor, New York, NY 10005; (212) 248-1111; www.agi-usa.org. Nonprofit research center on reproductive issues; "special affiliate" of Planned Parenthood Federation.

Center for Reproductive Rights, 120 Wall St., New York, NY 10005; (917) 637-3600; www.crlp.org.

Concerned Women for America, 1015 15th St., N.W., Suite 1100, Washington, DC 20005; (202) 488-7000; www.cwfa.org. Opposes abortion.

Family Research Council, 801 G St., N.W., Washington, DC 20001; (202) 393-2100; www.frc.org. Opposes abortion.

NARAL Pro-Choice America, 1156 15th St., N.W., Suite 700, Washington, DC 20005; (202) 973-3000; www.naral.org.

National Abortion Federation. 1755 Massachusetts Ave., N.W., Suite 600, Washington, DC 20036; (202) 667-5881; www.prochoice.org. Represents abortion clinics.

National Right to Life Committee, 512 10th St., N.W., Washington, DC 20004-2293; (202) 626-8800; www.nrlc.org.

9

SUV Debate

Mary H. Cooper

The three-ton, $117,000 Hummer H2 counts actor Arnold Schwarzenegger among its biggest fans. SUVs like the Hummer are seen as the ultimate escape vehicle and safe commuter car but also despised as gas-guzzling polluters that threaten their own occupants and everyone else on the road. But there's no disputing their popularity: SUVs account for 25 percent of all new-car sales.

S tan Bishop got so upset about the controversy surrounding his wife's car that he started up a Web site to defend her purchase. Bishop's wife drives a $117,000 Hummer H1, a civilian knockoff of the military Humvee.

"She'd been talking about one for two years, and that's what she wants to drive," says Bishop, an Atlanta developer. "She bought it because she thinks it's cool, it's top of the food chain, it's big and it's strong and she likes it."

The H1 is indeed big and strong. Equipped with a 195-horsepower, V8 diesel engine, the three-ton behemoth can ford a stream two-and-a-half-feet deep and conquer the most rugged terrain. It's also 15 feet long and wider than any passenger vehicle on the road. Humvees are great for Army patrols. But does a suburban mom need one to fetch a quart of milk?

That's not the point, say Hummer drivers. "We live in America," says David Harris, Hummer sales manager at Moore Cadillac Hummer, in the Northern Virginia suburbs of Washington, D.C. "Are we not allowed to choose what we drive?"

Harris says his customers don't blink at the H1's price tag — the cheaper H2 goes for around $50,000 — for a variety of reasons. "A lot of soccer moms are willing to pay the cost for that added protection," he says. "The extremists want to get out into the woods, and not many other SUVs can do that without expensive modifications. And then there are the wealthy guys who just want a new toy."

Sport-utility vehicles are, perhaps, the quintessential icon of the 1990s. Extolled as the ultimate escape vehicle and safe commuter car, they also are despised by critics as gas-guzzling, turnover-prone polluters that, contrary to widespread belief — are not safer than

From *The CQ Researcher,*
May 16, 2003.

cars. Indeed, critics say, SUVs threaten the lives of both their own occupants and everyone else on the road.

"To buy a Hummer, you'd have to have an ego as big as the car," says Joan B. Claybrook, president of Public Citizen, a nonprofit safety-advocacy group. But the Hummer is only the most blatant expression of the "wasteful" and "dangerous" excess she and other critics attach to all SUVs.

A growing anti-SUV backlash has united an unlikely coalition against the big vehicles. The activists include such disparate forces as columnist and socialite Arianna Huffington, whose television ads blame SUVs for increasing U.S. dependence on Middle Eastern oil; religious leaders, whose "What Would Jesus Drive?" campaign makes fuel efficiency a moral issue; and environmental and safety activists, who plaster tickets and bumper stickers on SUVs "charging" owners with endangering lives and befouling the planet.[1]

The recent invasion of oil-rich Iraq — which some critics said was motivated by America's dependence on foreign oil — helped turn SUVs into a moral issue for some. "America needs a line of cars that can get us to work in the morning without sending us to war in the afternoon," Huffington said in launching her latest TV ad, on May 7. "It's time to make sure our military and economic strength are never held captive to the politics of petroleum. We need cars and trucks that meet our transportation and safety needs without sacrificing our freedom, security or prosperity."[2]

The anti-SUV campaign is unprecedented in American society, pitting as it does advocates of one consumer item against another. "When was the last time that you saw people almost come to blows over the Apple vs. the PC, or the cell phone vs. the regular old telephone?" asks Daniel Becker, director of the Sierra Club's global warming and energy program.[3] "There is a level of divisiveness about SUVs and the selfishness that some people attribute to their drivers that causes enormous friction in our society."

Several key attributes set sport-utility vehicles apart from traditional sedans and coupes. Most noticeably, they're taller and boxier. Because they typically are built on a pickup-truck chassis, with higher clearance between the road and the undercarriage, SUVs are higher than cars. The higher center of gravity also explains the often choppy ride and truck-like feel of a typical SUV, despite the addition of such creature comforts as power accessories, leather seats and advanced sound systems usually associated with sedans.

Moreover, like minivans, SUVs are categorized by the government as light trucks, so they are held to less stringent fuel-efficiency and safety standards than cars.[4] Since they are heavier than most cars, SUVs generally get much poorer gas mileage. In fact, the largest SUVs are so heavy they don't fall under federal fuel-economy standards at all. The Hummer, for example, gets only around 10 miles per gallon. The average car gets 27.5 miles per gallon.[5]

SUVs have been around for decades, but until the early 1990s they appealed mostly to outdoor enthusiasts who wanted the four-wheel drive capability typically offered in SUVs to access remote destinations. But after Ford Motor Co. introduced its popular Explorer in 1991, sales of SUVs skyrocketed, from less than a million a year to 3 million in 2002. In the past decade, SUVs — along with minivans — have essentially replaced the station wagon as the suburban car of choice in America. Today, there are 73 different models of SUVs, and they account for 25 percent of all new-car sales.[6]

"The SUV has evolved from a very spartan, unrefined, not accessorized, primarily two-door configuration with almost exclusively four-wheel drive to the point where today's SUVs in many households are the family car," says George Pipas, Ford's manager of sales analysis. "And they come in all sizes, from quite small vehicles all the way to the very large SUVs."

It's the largest SUVs — which account for only about 5 percent of new-vehicle sales — that have become "the poster children for the SUV controversy," Pipas notes.

Many drivers of the larger SUVs say they like the vehicle's massive size and high profile because it gives them better visibility over traffic and more safety. "We have two children, and my wife wants them wrapped up in an envelope of safety," says Bishop of the family Hummer. "We don't speed, we don't take chances and we don't get tickets. We just motor around and pick up our kids from school like everybody else. It's just that she's driving a little bit bigger car than anybody else."

But critics say the safety advantages of SUVs are illusory. In fact, the very attributes that SUV owners think make them safer — their heavier weight and higher center of gravity — make them more dangerous in certain circumstances. The higher profile makes them more likely to roll over, endangering their occupants. The

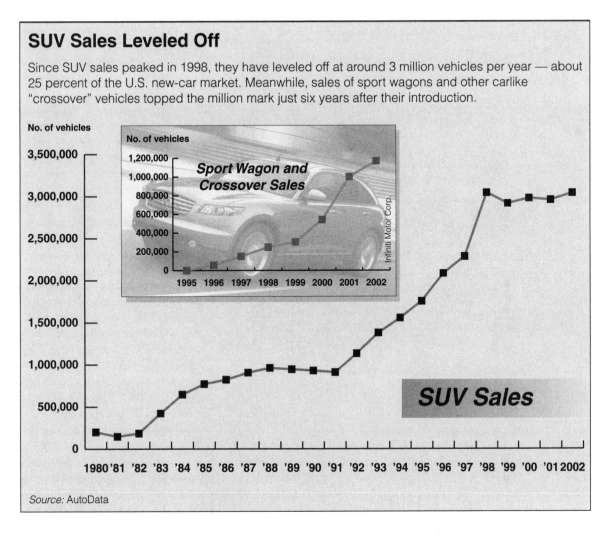

SUV Sales Leveled Off

Since SUV sales peaked in 1998, they have leveled off at around 3 million vehicles per year — about 25 percent of the U.S. new-car market. Meanwhile, sales of sport wagons and other carlike "crossover" vehicles topped the million mark just six years after their introduction.

Source: AutoData

SUV's greater size and weight also put passenger-car occupants at a disadvantage in case of collision.

It is the illusion of greater safety for the SUV's occupants that galls many critics, who see SUV drivers as selfish bullies willing to put their own personal safety above that of their fellow drivers. "One of the things they taught us in driver's ed. was to look ahead so we could anticipate what's going on in traffic several cars ahead," says Becker. "Well, if you're stuck behind an SUV, you can't see several cars ahead."

There is also the intimidation factor, he says. "It's literally designed into the SUV, with its growling front end, which is clearly designed to intimidate," he says. Indeed, one of the Hummer's latest ad campaigns touts the vehicle as a way women can "threaten men in a whole new way."[7]

SUVs do look different from their light-truck cousin, the minivan. "Minivan ads tend to emphasize themes like protection, togetherness and helping others," writes Keith Bradsher, a former *New York Times* Detroit bureau chief and author of *The High and Mighty*, a new book about the rise of SUVs. "SUV ads celebrate a more individualistic, sybaritic and even sometimes epicurean vision of life."

Like many critics, Bradsher attributes the SUV's explosive popularity in part to a cynical calculation by the auto industry.[8] "In marketing SUVs, automakers also try to capitalize on motorists' fear of crime or violence. In the process, the manufacturers have subtly raised the stakes in the highway arms race by making it appear unsafe to drive anything but an SUV."[9]

SUV Rollover Deaths Increased Most

The biggest increase in vehicle rollover deaths from 2001 to 2002 — nearly 10 percent — occurred among occupants of SUVs. The number who died in car crashes increased by only 4.3 percent, while deaths in vans dropped 11 percent. Overall, the number of people killed in rollover accidents in the one-year period jumped nearly 5 percent nationwide.

Percent Change in Rollover Deaths
(By vehicle type, 2001 to 2002)

Type of vehicle	Deaths in 2001	Deaths in 2002	Percent change
SUV	2,142	2,353	9.9%
Pickup truck	2,643	2,819	6.7
Passenger car	4,549	4,746	4.3
Van	784	695	-11.4
Total killed*	10,130	10,626	4.9%

* Includes occupants of all light trucks

Source: National Highway Traffic Safety Administration

Indeed, SUV advocates say drivers of smaller vehicles are irresponsibly endangering the lives of their loved ones. And they insist that SUVs meet a legitimate need. "The public has a need for vehicles beyond what even large sedans can offer," says Ron Defore, spokesman for the Sport Utility Vehicle Owners Association. "SUVs let you carry four or five passengers safely when the in-laws are in town or when you're picking up the soccer team. Many Americans do their own home improvements, so on weekends they're hauling mulch and lumber, things you just can't do very easily in most sedans. That's why SUVs have become so popular."

As long as consumers continue to buy SUVs, the controversy will likely continue to rage. As many Americans go shopping for a new vehicle to take on the road this summer, these are some of the questions they may wish to consider:

Are SUVs more dangerous than cars?

In the late 1990s, a spate of fatal accidents involving Ford Explorers equipped with defective Firestone tires revealed the vehicles' propensity to roll over. The accidents focused intense scrutiny on the widely held perception that SUVs are safer than cars because they are heavier. Automakers often reinforced that perception in congressional testimony, arguing that they could not make SUVs more fuel-efficient because that would require a decrease in vehicle weight, making them more dangerous.[10]

"SUVs are among the safest vehicles on the road and have contributed dramatically to the decline in the nation's fatality rate over the last decade," General Motors said recently.[11]

However, as the Ford scandal revealed, most mid-size SUVs have a much narrower and somewhat taller profile, making them more prone to roll over in a blowout, or when the driver takes a corner too fast.

Critics claim deceptive advertising campaigns continue to draw consumers to the perceived safety advantages of SUVs. "The auto industry has duplicitously created a false impression that you're safer in an SUV because you're surrounded by so much steel," says Becker of the Sierra Club. "The reality is that you are no safer than in a car because of the design flaws built into SUVs that make them just as dangerous to their occupants as they are to the occupants of the vehicles they hit. These vehicles have a higher center of mass, and they drive like trucks. They are unforgiving, and people roll over at a fairly alarming rate."

In fact, the National Highway Traffic Safety Administration (NHTSA) reported in April that between 2001 and 2002 total traffic fatalities increased by 1.7 percent nationwide — to 42,850 — but that SUV rollover deaths jumped almost 10 percent.[12] Jeffrey W. Runge, an emergency-room physician who now heads the agency, said that since SUVs and other light trucks account for an increasing portion of total passenger-vehicle sales, "Deaths and injuries in rollover crashes will become a greater safety problem unless something changes."[13]

Runge shocked automakers in January when he told them he would never allow his daughter to drive an SUV that flunked his agency's rollover tests, even "if it was the last one on Earth."[14]

Defenders of SUVs concede they are more prone to roll over than cars but still offer greater protection for their occupants than cars do. "It's true that SUVs have a higher center of gravity and therefore a higher propensity to roll over," says Defore of the SUV Owners Association. "But when you get into your car today, if you're going to be in a crash, you don't know what kind of crash you're going to be in."

The best measure of a vehicle's safety, Defore says, is the overall fatality rate of its occupants. "The largest of the SUVs have the lowest fatality rate of all," he says. According to association figures, rollovers account for only 2.5 percent of crashes, and SUVs are more protective of their occupants in rear and side collisions, which make up the other 97.5 percent of crashes.[15]

"What the critics do is very cleverly point you to rollovers, but rollovers are very rare events," Defore says. "When you look at the overall risk, the largest of the SUVs come out the best."

But critics point out that while rollovers may account for less than 3 percent of accidents, they cause 30 percent of vehicular deaths.[16]

In addition, they cite two recent studies — including one by the industry itself — that have cast doubt on the bigger-is-safer assumption. The first study, conducted jointly by scientists at the University of Michigan and the Lawrence Berkeley National Laboratory, found that SUV drivers are not necessarily safer than those in smaller cars.

"On average, [SUVs] are as risky as the average mid-size or large car," the study concluded, "and no safer than many of the most popular compact and subcompact models." The report was the first to analyze both the risk to SUV drivers and to drivers of other vehicles on the road — which the authors called combined risk. "If combined risk is considered," the report said, "most cars are safer than the average SUV."[17]

"We need to move away from the idea that bigger and heavier vehicles are automatically safer," said Marc Ross, a University of Michigan physicist. "Quality is a bigger predictor of safety than weight."[18]

Responding to the study, Priya Prasad, a senior technical fellow for safety at Ford Motor Co., insisted that in all Ford's studies, "Heavier is better, especially when you get into two-way accidents."[19]

A week later, the Alliance of Automobile Manufacturers released figures conceding for the first time that

One person died and four were injured in Indianapolis when a Chevrolet Trailblazer hit a Volkswagen Beetle head-on. SUVs are held to weaker safety standards than passenger cars, but automakers have voluntarily begun taking steps to make SUVs safer, including reducing their rollover tendency.

SUV occupants are 3.5 percent more likely to die in crashes than sedan occupants. The automakers' analysis found that while SUV occupants were less likely to die in front-end, side and rear-end collisions than passenger-car occupants, they are nearly three times more likely to be killed in rollovers.

The alliance's vice president for safety, Robert Strassburger, said, "At a minimum, SUVs are as safe as automobiles." He noted that 72 percent of those killed in SUV rollovers were not wearing their seat belts.

Safety advocates said the alliance's Feb. 25 press briefing marked the first time automakers have acknowledged that SUVs overall are not as safe as cars. "They are recognizing that there are safety issues that are unique to SUVs," said Brian O'Neill, president of the Insurance Institute for Highway Safety (IIHS).[20]

In addition to the rollover danger, Becker says, SUVs are more dangerous to their own occupants because they use a solid-steel beam that extends from bumper to bumper to make the vehicle strong enough to sustain heavy off-road use. "When that vehicle hits something else, the beam doesn't absorb the impact of the crash and dissipate it over the vehicle like a car, which crumples and dissipates the force of the impact around the occupants," he says. "If a Ford Expedition SUV and a subcompact GM Saturn hit the same bridge abutment at the same speed, the occupants of the Saturn will come out better in that crash than the occupants of the Expedition because the Saturn has crashworthiness built into it, and the Expedition does not."

SUVs Fall Through Safety Loopholes

Sport-utility vehicles (SUVs) are not only held to less-stringent fuel-economy and pollution regulations than cars, they also enjoy far less stringent federal scrutiny when it comes to safety.

"When the safety, fuel-economy and emissions laws were originally passed in the 1960s and '70s, it was unimagined that SUVs and other light trucks would become nearly half of all new vehicles sold," said Joan B. Claybrook, president of Public Citizen, a safety-advocacy group. "Most safety standards and emissions rules are more than 30 years old, and relentless industry lobbying has killed off interim attempts to update them or pass badly needed new ones on rollover or vehicle crash compatibility."[1]

The gap in safety regulations for SUVs became apparent in the late 1990s, when 271 people died and more than 700 were injured in rollover accidents involving Ford Explorers fitted with defective Firestone tires. In the scandal that followed, nearly 20 million tires were recalled, and Congress passed the 2000 Transportation Recall Enhancement, Accountability and Documentation (TREAD) Act.

The new law required vehicle and equipment manufacturers to promptly report potential safety defects to the National Highway Traffic Safety Administration (NHTSA), increased penalties for safety violations and imposed criminal penalties for misleading the government about dangerous defects.

But the new law did not mandate that the government establish minimum rollover standards for SUVs — which safety experts have advocated for years — even though nearly 13,000 people died in SUV rollover accidents between 1994 and 2001, according to Claybrook. Instead, the TREAD law only required that by November 2002 NHTSA begin rating new cars on their propensity to roll over. While the agency already rates vehicles for their rollover propensity in a single-car crash, it has yet to comply with the TREAD Act's requirement to assess vehicles' rollover risks under emergency steering maneuvers in the absence of a crash. NHTSA Administrator Jeffrey W. Runge recently said the agency would finalize such a test "in the near future."[2]

But critics say it really doesn't matter, because the propensity ratings will be meaningless without a minimum standard by which to judge them. "Congress should require crash protections that will protect occupants in rollovers," Claybrook said. "Rollovers are primarily dangerous due to poor vehicle design. Safety belts and seat structures are not made to keep occupants in place during a crash, and vehicle roofs are so flimsy they crush into occupants' heads and spines, inflicting very serious injuries."

Despite the lack of a federal standard, most automakers voluntarily began taking steps to reduce the rollover tendency of SUVs. They lowered the center of gravity of some models and introduced new "crossover" SUVs — such as the Subaru Forester and the Lexus RX 300. Built on a car

In addition to endangering their own occupants, say critics, SUVs threaten smaller vehicles. Drivers of passenger cars can't see around SUVs to observe traffic ahead, and cars are likely to incur greater damage in collisions with the heavier, taller vehicles. (See "At Issue," p. 219.)

According to studies by the IIHS, a passenger car is at a significant disadvantage in a collision with an SUV, especially if hit from the side. In a side crash, according to a 1998 IIHS "crash-incompatibility" study, the car's occupants are 25 times more likely to die than the SUV's occupants.[21]

"The theory that I'm going to protect myself and my family even if it costs other people's lives has been the operative incentive for the design of these vehicles, and that's just wrong," NHTSA's Runge said. "That's not compassionate conservatism."[22]

During his Jan. 14 speech to automakers, Runge told automakers that he had appointed a NHTSA panel to consider new safety regulations for SUVs and challenged the industry to solve the problems of rollovers and disproportionate crash damage to smaller vehicles.

Faced with the threat of new regulations, the automakers alliance quietly signaled that they are willing to work with Runge to make SUVs less lethal. In a Feb. 13 letter to Runge, they pledged to work with the IIHS to develop short- and long-term measures to deal with SUV safety hazards.[23]

Indeed, some manufacturers already have begun making voluntary changes. Ford and GM have lowered bumper heights or the center of gravity on some models to reduce the risk of rollover and bumper override.

chassis and designed to resemble SUVs, crossovers blend the attributes of cars and SUVs and are held to the same safety regulations as cars.

With their higher bumpers and heavier weight, sport-utility vehicles also pose a major safety hazard to lower-riding vehicles. According to NHTSA, although SUVs and other light trucks represent 36 percent of all registered vehicles, they are involved in about half of all fatal two-vehicle crashes with passenger cars. Over 80 percent of the fatalities from such accidents are to occupants of passenger cars. Moreover, the Insurance Institute for Highway Safety has found that when an SUV collides with a car, occupant deaths in the car are about 50 percent more likely in side impacts than in frontal impacts.

Automakers have taken steps in recent years to improve their SUVs' safety records and reduce crash incompatibility with passenger cars. Ford, for example, now installs side airbags that protect the head and chest areas of occupants in its Escape and Excursion models. Ford Excursions now include "Blocker Beams" that lower the point of impact with a car in a frontal collision, helping prevent the SUV from riding over the car.

"The automotive industry in general, and Ford in particular, will continue to build vehicles with the utility and safety that our customers require," said Susan M. Cischke, Ford vice president for environmental and safety engineering.[3]

Nevertheless, Claybrook lists several other safety loopholes enjoyed by SUVs, including:

- **Side-impact protection:** SUVs heavier than 6,000 lbs. are held to a weaker standard than cars.

- **Roof strength:** SUVs over 6,000 lbs. need not meet any crash-protection standard for roof strength.
- **Child-restraint anchors:** Unlike cars, the biggest SUVs (above 8,500 lbs. carrying weight) are not required to provide anchorage systems to accommodate child restraints.
- **Brake lights:** Unlike cars, SUVs are not required to provide a center, high-mounted brake light.

Meanwhile, the Explorer continues to outsell all other SUVs, even though hundreds of lawsuits against both Ford and Bridgestone/Firestone are still pending. So far, all cases have been settled before going to a jury, and the U.S. Supreme Court handed the companies a victory in January by refusing to hear a case on whether Explorer owners qualified for class-action status.[4]

But Ford and Bridgestone/Firestone are not out of the woods on the rollover issue. In February, federal prosecutors in southern Illinois subpoenaed documents from both companies in a possible criminal investigation of tire failures.[5]

---

[1] Claybrook testified Feb. 26, 2003, before the Senate Commerce, Science and Transportation Committee.

[2] Runge testified Feb. 26, 2003, before the Senate Commerce, Science and Transportation Committee.

[3] Cischke testified Feb. 26, 2003, before the Senate Commerce, Science and Transportation Committee.

[4] See Davis Lazarus, "Greed Takes Class out of Class Action," *The San Francisco Chronicle*, Jan. 17, 2003.

[5] United Press International, "UPI News Update," Feb. 28, 2003.

Others have introduced new "crossover" SUVs. Built on a car chassis and designed to resemble SUVs, crossovers look like SUVs but are subject to most of the same safety regulations as cars.

"Crossovers are much more humane, both for their occupants and other people on the road," says Claybrook of Public Citizen. "They're easier to see around, they have shorter stopping distances and they're not as high up as SUVs."

Yet SUV advocates like Defore — who calls SUV critics like Claybrook "social nannies" — dismisses the compatibility issue. "There has always been a disparity in size of vehicles, and I hope there always will be," he says. "You're always going to have a wide variety of needs, from 18-wheelers to dump trucks to municipal buses to small compact cars."

Other SUV advocates blame the compatibility problem on small-car owners themselves. "By choosing to buy a smaller vehicle because they want to save a few hundred dollars a year, [small car owners] put their families in jeopardy," says Atlanta developer Bishop. "That is a personal choice."

But David M. Nemtzow, president of the Alliance to Save Energy, responds: If all car drivers were to trade in their small cars for SUVs, "We'd end up with a kind of arms race, where you trade in your small car for something bigger, and the other guy gets an SUV that's bigger still."

Should SUVs be held to stricter fuel-economy standards?

When Arab oil producers imposed an embargo on exports to the United States in 1973, skyrocketing oil

Toyota SUVs Are Most Fuel-Efficient

The Japanese-made Toyota Rav4 sport-utility vehicle gets twice the mileage of the least-efficient SUVs.

Fuel Efficiency of 2003 SUVs and Vans
(by city and highway mpg)

Make/Model Drive train/Engine/Transmission	MPG City	MPG Hwy
Most-Efficient		
Sport-Utility Vehicles		
Toyota Rav4, 2WD, 4 cyl, Manual	25	31
Toyota Rav4, 2WD, 4 cyl, Automatic	24	29
Minivans		
Chrysler Voyager/Town & Cntry, 2WD, 4 cyl, Automatic	21	27
Dodge Caravan, 2WD, 4 cyl, Automatic	21	27
Passenger Vans		
Chevrolet Astro 2WD, 6 cyl, Automatic	16	20
GMC Safari 2WD, 6 cyl, Automatic	16	20
Least-Efficient		
Sport-Utility Vehicles		
Cadillac Escalade, AWD, 8 cyl, Automatic	12	16
GMC K1500 Yukon, AWD, 8 cyl, Automatic	12	16
Land Rover Discovery Series II, 4WD, 8 cyl, Automatic	12	16
Minivans		
Kia Sedona, 6 cyl, Automatic	15	20
Passenger Vans		
Chevrolet H1500 Express, AWD 8 cyl, Automatic	13	17
Ford E150 Club Wagon, RWD 8 cyl, Automatic	13	17
GMC H1500 Savana, AWD, 8 cyl, Automatic	13	17

Source: Environmental Protection Agency

At the time, light trucks were a relatively small segment of the auto market, mostly pickups and cargo vans used by farmers and small-business owners for work-related transportation. So Congress set a more lenient mileage standard for these vehicles — currently 20.7 miles per gallon, as opposed to the 27.5 mpg required of passenger cars. The looser standard has continued to apply to minivans and SUVs — essentially modified pickup trucks — even as they became best-selling alternatives to passenger cars. Light trucks also are exempt from the "gas-guzzler tax," a separate levy imposed on the sale of new cars whose fuel economy falls below 22.5 mpg.

Nemtzow, of the Alliance to Save Energy, recalls that when the CAFE standards went into effect, then-Chrysler Corp. Chairman Lee Iacocca lamented that within a decade everyone in America would be driving a subcompact Ford Pinto, one of the few cars that met the standard at that time.

"That was duplicitous," Nemtzow says. "It's a time-honored tradition for auto industry lobbyists to always undersell their own engineers. The lobbyists say it can't be done, it's fabulously expensive; then if they're forced to do it, the engineers always come through and figure out inexpensive ways to make cars more fuel-efficient. Luckily, American ingenuity is more successful than American lobbying."

prices plunged the country into its first energy crisis. Congress responded in 1975 with a flurry of energy regulations, including Corporate Average Fuel Economy (CAFE) standards requiring automakers to improve fuel efficiency in new cars. Automakers were allowed to continue manufacturing gas-guzzlers, but they had to make enough fuel-efficient models to keep their overall mileage within the required federal limits.[24]

Indeed, the Big Three Detroit automakers — General Motors, Ford and Chrysler — made rapid gains in fuel efficiency during the 1970s by reducing vehicle size and weight. Then they implemented more innovative technological changes during the 1980s, such as radial tires, aerodynamic body design and four-cylinder engines, which enabled them to meet the CAFE standards and improve performance.

"The technology revolution has been very helpful for fuel efficiency as well as environmental performance because cars now are much better at taking the available gasoline and combusting it accurately in the cylinder using sensors and control technology," Nemtzow says. "As a result, they waste less gas and emit less unburned hydrocarbon."

But critics of fuel-economy regulations trace the phenomenal popularity of SUVs to the standards themselves. "As CAFE standards rose for cars, it became increasingly difficult for vehicle manufacturers to satisfy the demand of many Americans who wanted the utility of larger and more powerful vehicles," says the SUV Owners Association's Defore, a former official at NHTSA, which administers the standards. "Thirty years ago, those needs were met by the station wagon, which was built on a passenger-car platform. But it just became too difficult for the manufacturers to keep building them in any great number and still comply with CAFE standards." To fill the need for utility vehicles, automakers started making minivans and SUVs, built on truck platforms. "SUVs, minivans and pickups are the last remaining vehicles that can meet those needs," Defore says.

But industry critics say the SUV was less a response to pent-up consumer demand for bigger vehicles than the product of a cynical effort to cut production costs by sidestepping federal fuel and safety regulations. "The American manufacturers discovered, and have taught the Japanese manufacturers, that you can make a lot of money — $8,000 to $20,000 per vehicle — by creating a gas-guzzling behemoth that poses safety threats to its own occupants and others, consumes prodigious amounts of gas and pollutes too much," says the Sierra Club's Becker.

The critics say Detroit created demand for SUVs by aggressively marketing what were essentially inexpensive trucks as "safer," high-end cars. "SUVs are basically gussied-up pickup trucks, and most have never been comprehensively redesigned to be safely used as passenger vehicles," said Claybrook of Public Citizen. "In the SUV, the industry found and developed a broad market that allowed it to rake in cash while taking every step to avoid spending money to fix the unstable and threatening vehicle that resulted."[25]

In 1996, automakers repeated their earlier arguments against proposals to tighten CAFE standards, this time covering SUVs. Under pressure from the automakers, Congress actually prohibited NHTSA from even studying the possibility of raising the CAFE standards.

Lawmakers later lifted the ban and required the agency to issue a new, tighter standard for the 2004 model year of SUVs, vans and other light trucks. In July 2001 the National Academy of Sciences released a long-awaited review of fuel-economy standards stating that existing technology allowed for fuel-efficiency improvements in SUVs. However, industry representatives put a different spin on the report, claiming that it proved their argument that it would not be feasible to improve SUV fuel efficiency.[26] NHTSA announced last year that it would maintain the current light-truck standard of 20.7 mpg through 2004, saying it would be too hard for the industry to make the needed improvements by the deadline.

Responding to complaints that the 2004 standard was too lenient, the U.S. Department of Transportation (DOT) announced on April 1 that it was raising the CAFE standard for SUVs and other light trucks. Automakers will now have to increase light-truck mileage by a total of 1.5 mpg to 22.2 mpg during the 2005-'07 model years.

However, the new standard seems unlikely to end the debate. "The administration thought it could take the fuel-economy issue off the table forever by making a minuscule improvement in fuel-economy standards," Becker says. "Fortunately, no one bought their argument that they've dealt with this issue by calling for a 1.5 mpg improvement. The reality is that we could save 3 million barrels of oil a day if our cars, SUVs and other trucks averaged 40 mpg — and we have the technology right now to do that."

Indeed, former Ford CEO Jacques Nasser promised in July 2000 that his company would reduce fuel consumption in its new SUVs by 25 percent by 2005. Though his successor, William Clay Ford Jr., recently recanted that promise, Ford still plans to introduce next summer a hybrid version of its small Escape SUV that will get 40 mpg.[27] Hybrid vehicles run on a combination of gas and electricity.

"Beyond a shadow of a doubt, automakers are perfectly capable of building SUVs with greater mileage," said Rep. Sherwood Boehlert, R-NY. "In fact, they crow about it every place but Washington, D.C. GM and Ford have both announced plans to bring out an SUV that gets 40 miles per gallon in the next model year. What we're told is impossible on the House floor turns out to be perfectly possible on the auto-assembly floor."

Boehlert concedes that the 1.5-mile-per-gallon change is better than nothing. "The administration should be congratulated for at least acknowledging the need to improve fuel economy," he said. "But the 1.5 mile per gallon increase over three years sought by the administration is minuscule — far less than what is needed, and far less than what is possible."[28]

Boehlert and Rep. Edward J. Markey, D-Mass., have sponsored a measure that would eliminate the fuel-economy disparity between cars and light trucks and require automakers to achieve an average of 30 mpg across their product lines by 2010. "The automakers can decide whether they want to reach these levels by improving the mileage of cars or SUVs or both," Boehlert said. "It does not set a specific standard for SUVs."

On April 11, the House defeated the Boehlert-Markey proposal, 268-162. The same fate may await another effort, by Sens. Dianne Feinstein, D-Calif., and Olympia J. Snowe, R-Maine, to require SUVs to meet the same fuel standards as cars by 2011.[29]

It appears unlikely, in fact, that Congress will require additional changes to CAFE standards so soon after the administration's regulatory action on SUVs, a fact that some supporters of stricter regulations now concede. "Improvements in fuel-economy standards have worked before," Becker says. "They will likely work again if either Detroit will stop fighting it or the Congress will stop listening to Detroit's siren song."

Do Americans have a moral duty to conserve energy?

Hostility toward SUV drivers also stems from their use of more gasoline than many other vehicles on the road. SUVs get less than 18 mpg, compared to 22.5 mpg for the average passenger car.[30] Because Americans import more than half the oil they consume, higher fuel consumption means greater dependence on foreign oil, as well as more carbon-dioxide emissions, considered a primary cause of global warming. The United States is the world's largest emitter of carbon dioxide — a third of which comes from burning transportation fuels.[31]

Environmentalists say these statistics alone constitute a moral indictment against the use of SUVs for most personal transportation.

"The United States uses 25 percent of the world's oil, and we sit on 3 percent of the world's known reserves,"

says the Sierra Club's Becker. "Being dependent on others for the natural resources that we don't have when we use a disproportionate share of those resources causes problems for the United States. I believe the war we just fought in Iraq had something to do with oil. A bunch of U.S. soldiers just died, and a bunch of Iraqis died, too, in part because we needed to secure oil for SUVs."

Becker's group estimates that switching from an average car to a 13-mpg SUV for one year would waste more energy than leaving your refrigerator door open for six years.[32] "Making cars go further on a gallon of gas is the biggest, single step we can take to curb our oil dependence and cut global-warming pollution," Becker says.

Some religious leaders echo the call for improved fuel economy and cleaner-running engines. "The cars that we buy represent probably the single, largest expenditure with ecological impact that most of us will make," says Paul Gorman, director of the National Religious Partnership for the Environment. "People should learn a little about why this represents a moral choice."

Last November, the Partnership spearheaded the widely publicized "What Would Jesus Drive?" campaign to encourage people to consider the environmental impact of their car-purchasing decisions. Though Gorman denies that the campaign was intended to vilify SUVs or any other specific vehicle type, heeding its call would undoubtedly result in fewer SUV sales in favor of more fuel-efficient cars. "Our goal is not to become another environmental advocate," Gorman says, "but to bring issues of environmental sustainability and justice to the heart of religious life. Caring for God's creation has got to be central to every tradition that cares about God."

SUV advocate Bishop says Americans are unlikely to shun big vehicles on moral or religious grounds alone. "America is a car-centric society, and you can't mandate that a person drive a car that's too small," he says. "Can we continue to improve safety? Yes. Can we improve fuel economy? Absolutely. But you're not going to get Americans into physically smaller vehicles on the basis of a perception of whether there's a hole in the ozone layer or whether we have an insufficient amount of oil."

In the past, energy conservation has figured high on the list of efforts expected of patriotic Americans. During the energy crises of the 1970s, President Jimmy Carter called conservation "the moral equivalent of war." Later administrations also placed conservation and environmental protection high on their policy agendas.

C H R O N O L O G Y

1930s-1960s *Early SUVs draw limited numbers of outdoors enthusiasts.*

1935 General Motors Corp. introduces the Suburban Carryall, an eight-passenger vehicle combining a passenger-car body with a light-truck chassis.

1946 Responding to heavy post-war demand, Willys-Overland introduces a civilian version of the four-wheel drive Jeep.

1956 Congress authorizes construction of the Interstate Highway System. Detroit automakers indulge Americans' passion for cars with powerful, V8-driven behemoths.

1966 The National Traffic and Motor Vehicle Safety Act and Highway Safety Act establish federal safety standards for cars and tires — including padded dashboards, outside mirrors and impact-absorbing steering columns — and require states to establish highway-safety programs or lose highway-construction funds.

1970s *Energy crises spark regulations to curb fuel consumption.*

1970 Congress creates the National Highway Traffic Safety Administration (NHTSA) to administer auto-safety regulations and set new ones to address design flaws that pose an "unreasonable risk" to public safety.

Oct. 29, 1973 Arab oil producers impose an embargo on exports to the United States, hiking oil prices and plunging the country into its first energy crisis.

1975 As part of the 1975 Energy Policy and Conservation Act, Congress authorizes Corporate Average Fuel Economy (CAFE) standards requiring automakers to improve fuel efficiency in new cars. Light trucks, used mainly by farmers and small-business owners, are held to less-stringent standards.

1980s *Regulation-driven technological changes improve auto mileage and safety.*

1984 Chrysler Corp.'s minivan quickly displaces the station wagon as the Baby Boom generation's standard family car.

1900s *SUVs are among the nation's most popular passenger vehicles.*

1991 Ford Motor Co. introduces the Explorer, which becomes the best-selling SUV.

1996 Under pressure from automakers, Congress prohibits NHTSA from even studying the possibility of raising CAFE standards.

February 1999 Ford introduces its largest SUV to date, the four-ton, "super-duty" Excursion. The Sierra Club blasts Ford for producing a "sport-utility vehicle that guzzles enough gas to make Saddam Hussein smile."

2000s *A string of rollover crashes highlights SUV safety flaws.*

Aug. 9, 2000 Defective Firestone tires are implicated in dozens of Explorer rollover accidents; Firestone recalls 17.9 million tires.

Nov. 1, 2000 President Bill Clinton signs the Transportation Recall Enhancement, Accountability and Documentation (TREAD) Act aimed at forcing auto companies and their suppliers to more promptly recall defective products. It also mandates that within two years NHTSA test new cars for rollover propensity.

2001 SUVs, minivans and pickup trucks capture 52 percent of total vehicle sales.

February 2003 Federal prosecutors in southern Illinois subpoena documents from Bridgestone/Firestone and Ford in a possible criminal investigation of tire failures.

April 2003 NHTSA reports that 42,850 people died in traffic accidents in 2002, the most since 1990. Most of the increase in fatalities was in pickup trucks, SUVs and vans; SUV rollover deaths were almost 10 percent higher than in 2001.

SUV Rates Pollution 'Loopholes'

Environmentalists have long complained that sport-utility vehicles (SUVs) pollute more than passenger cars, largely because they are held to weaker mileage and emissions standards.

Defined as "light trucks," most SUVs are held to less stringent fuel-economy standards than cars: currently 20.7 miles per gallon (mpg), compared with 27.5 mpg required for cars under the Corporate Average Fuel Economy (CAFE) standards passed in 1975 to curb gasoline consumption.

The higher a vehicle's gas mileage, the less carbon dioxide it emits as a byproduct of the fuel-combustion process. The United States is by far the world's biggest emitter of carbon dioxide — the main "greenhouse" gas believed responsible for global warming — and almost a third of America's carbon dioxide emissions come from cars and trucks.

Bowing to pressure from the public and environmentalists, the Bush administration recently tightened CAFE standards for light trucks, including the majority of SUVs, by 1.5 mpg — to 22.2 mpg by 2007. But even with the new standard, most SUVs, pickups and minivans will continue to consume more gasoline than automobiles.

"The auto companies have been using the loophole that allows SUVs and other trucks to guzzle more gas and pollute more," says Daniel Becker, director of the Sierra Club's Global Warming and Energy Program. The really big SUVs — like General Motors' Hummer series, the Ford Excursion and Lincoln Navigator — don't have to meet any fuel-economy standards at all because they're classified as medium-duty trucks, a category that once consisted almost exclusively of commercial haulers. "By using the loophole, the auto industry has increased our gas guzzling, increased our dependence on OPEC [Organization of Petroleum Exporting Countries] and increased the emissions spewing from these vehicles," Becker says.

In referring to emissions, Becker and other environmental advocates include carbon dioxide, because of its

The Mercedes G500 and other big SUVs don't have to meet fuel-economy standards because they're classified as medium-duty trucks.

Courtesy Daimler Chrysler

impact on global climate, as well as the traditional tailpipe pollutants that cause urban smog and ground-level ozone. But SUV advocates reject that definition, saying carbon dioxide is not an officially designated pollutant like nitrogen oxides and sulfur dioxide, which are regulated under the 1970 Clean Air Act.

"The Environmental Protection Agency (EPA) does not classify carbon dioxide as a pollutant," says Ron Defore, a spokesman for the Sport Utility Vehicle Owners Association and a former official at the National Highway Traffic Safety Administration (NHTSA). "As for the so-called loophole in the [Clean Air Act] emissions standard, EPA has already promulgated rules that are going to require all vehicles in the light-truck category to meet the same strict emissions standards as passenger cars. So end of story."

Defore was referring to a Clean Air Act "loophole" that allowed light trucks — because they were used chiefly as farm and commercial vehicles at the time — to meet less stringent tailpipe emissions standards than cars. All vans and most SUVs and pickups were allowed to emit up to 47 percent more carbon monoxide and 175 percent more nitrogen oxides than passenger cars.

But in November 1998, in order to meet its overall Clean Air Act goals, California ruled that all light trucks would have to meet the same emissions standards as cars no later than the 2004 model year. On Feb. 10, 2000, the EPA followed California's lead and required that all light trucks and passenger cars — as well as medium-duty SUVs and passenger vans — meet the same emissions standards by the 2009 model year, which will arrive in showrooms in 2008.[1]

But that doesn't close the emissions loophole for SUVs on the road today.

---

[1] See Brent D. Yacobucci, "Sport Utility Vehicles, Mini-Vans, and Light Trucks: An Overview of Fuel Economy and Emissions Standards," *CRS Report for Congress*, Congressional Research Service, Feb. 28, 2003.

But SUV buyers have received little discouragement from President Bush. The administration's energy policy, laid out in 2001, focuses more on increasing domestic oil drilling, including in Alaska's Arctic National Wildlife Refuge (ANWR) and other protected lands, than on reducing fuel consumption. Bush also renounced the Kyoto Protocol, an international agreement to curb emissions of carbon dioxide and other greenhouse gases contributing to global warming.[33] And critics say the administration's recent tightening of fuel-efficiency standards for SUVs will have little impact on fuel consumption or auto emissions.

"Many Americans just don't want to think they're trashing the environment," says Nemtzow of the Alliance to Save Energy. In his view, it is to this group that Bush is appealing with his new SUV fuel-economy standard, as well as a recent tightening of diesel-emission standards for off-road vehicles and the administration's recent call for a $1.2 billion program to develop non-polluting hydrogen cars by 2020.[34] "These actions show the Bush administration's new thinking as they look forward to 2004. They recognize they won't be able to persuade those Americans who want them to lead on the environment, but they're trying to reach out to Middle-American swing voters by saying we're not so bad on the environment."

But SUV advocates say the administration's approach is in tune with Americans' views on energy and environmental issues. "Nobody wants to be anti-environment," says Defore of the SUV Owners Association. "But when it comes to the most expensive consumer product that most people buy, second to a house, people act a lot differently. Many people are willing to pay extra for safety advantages, but when it comes to environmental advantages — which are more societal and less personal — the majority are not willing to pay much, if anything, for that."

BACKGROUND

Station-Wagon Era

Sport-utility vehicles trace their ancestry back to 1935, when, in the midst of the Great Depression, General Motors (GM) introduced the Chevrolet Suburban Carryall. The eight-passenger vehicle lacked four-wheel drive, but like SUVs it combined a passenger-car body with a light-truck chassis. The next year, GM used the same combination to produce the first station wagon with a body made entirely of steel instead of wood.

The first car with off-road capabilities typical of modern SUVs was the classic, open-sided Jeep used in World War II.[35] Willys-Overland churned out more than 700,000 of the small, versatile workhorses during the war. Ford also produced Jeeps under license for the military.

After the war, farmers and sportsmen snapped up decommissioned Jeeps for their off-road capability and inexpensive upkeep. They were in such great demand that Willys introduced a nearly identical, four-wheel-drive "civilian Jeep" in 1946. The original Jeep's appeal proved so enduring that an updated but visually similar model, the Wrangler, continues to sell.

Willys produced the first SUV forerunner in 1949, with the Jeep All-Steel Station Wagon, equipped with four-wheel drive. Farmers, ranchers and sportsmen were the main consumers of both the civilian Jeep and the new wagon, which remained popular through the early 1950s. Britain's Land Rover, a similarly rugged, off-road vehicle used extensively in Africa, was no match in the U.S. market for the Jeep.

Development of Jeep station wagons continued apace during a post-war economic boom in the late 1950s and '60s that enabled more and more Americans to buy vehicles of all types. But the biggest focus in automotive design was on passenger sedans suited for travel on the country's expanding roadway network. With seemingly unlimited gasoline supplies, Americans' love affair with the car blossomed, and Detroit indulged their passion with powerful, V8-driven behemoths with dramatic tailfins, three-tone paint jobs and convertible tops. Comfort and convenience were the order of the day, as automatic transmissions gradually replaced the standard gearshift, and air-conditioning, power steering and power brakes became popular options.

The station wagon was Detroit's answer to the post-war Baby Boom, with its burgeoning families. The elongated version of a standard passenger car, with a large, windowed, rear storage area accessed by a separate door, the wagon became the family car of the 1950s. By decade's end, one in every six vehicles made in Detroit was a station wagon.

Compact Cars

During the 1960s, small, zippy, sports cars made by foreign automakers like MG, Triumph and Alfa Romeo began to claim a small share of the U.S. market. With rising incomes, more and more American households opted for a second car, often a smaller model made by Japan's Datsun (now Nissan) and Toyota, as well as European Volkswagens, Renaults and Saabs.

Detroit, which continued to account for 90 percent of U.S. auto sales, followed suit with "compact" cars such as the Ford Falcon and Chevrolet Corvair (1960). Toward the end of the 1960s, as the first Baby Boomers reached driving age, Detroit turned out "muscle cars" like the Dodge Charger and sporty models like the popular Ford Mustang (1964).

Throughout the 1950s and '60s, utility vehicles continued to serve a limited but growing niche in the auto market. In 1956, Chevrolet equipped the Suburban with four-wheel drive, producing the first model of what would become its later SUV prototype. Farm-equipment maker International Harvester introduced the Travelall, a four-wheel-drive passenger vehicle, and a smaller model, the Scout. Jeep came out with a similar vehicle, the Wagoneer, in 1962. Toyota, then an obscure Japanese manufacturer, sent its first Land Cruiser SUVs to the United States. Ford entered the SUV market in 1966 with the Bronco, a two-door passenger vehicle mounted on a full-size pickup chassis. Three years later, GM followed with the similarly built Chevrolet Blazer and GMC Jimmy.

In the 1960s, concern arose about the number of cars, which doubled from 49 million in 1950 to 102 million in 1968. Congress passed the Clean Air Act in 1963 to improve air quality and reduce auto-induced urban smog. Later amendments required automakers to reduce exhaust emissions, starting with 1968 models.

Deaths from auto accidents also rose, from 35,000 in 1950 to 55,000 in 1968. Although Swedish automaker Volvo had first introduced three-point safety belts as early as 1959, U.S. automakers resisted installing anything more than lap belts, despite mounting highway deaths and injuries.

In 1965, consumer advocate Ralph Nader's scathing criticism of the industry's safety record, *Unsafe at Any Speed*, called for safer cars. Congress responded with the National Traffic and Motor Vehicle Safety Act and the Highway Safety Act, signed in 1966 by President Lyndon B. Johnson. The laws established federal safety standards for cars and tires and required states to set up

highway safety programs or lose part of their federal highway-construction funds. The newly created DOT administered the programs.[36] By 1968, automakers were required to install front seat lap-and-shoulder safety belts in all new cars.

Energy Crunch

The age of the large passenger vehicle abruptly ended after the 1973 Arab oil embargo.[37] The national energy policy that emerged from the resulting gas shortage — embodied in the 1975 Energy Policy and Conservation Act — required automakers to improve fuel efficiency. Manufacturers were required to meet a companywide average threshold on all new cars of 18 mpg by 1978, 20 mpg by 1980 and 27.5 mpg by 1985.[38]

But the CAFE standards contained a loophole that would prove critical to the later development of SUVs. Congress set more lenient mileage standards for "light trucks," a special category of vehicles that included pickups (and later vans and sport-utility vehicles) weighing 8,500 pounds or less. Average light-truck mileage, originally mandated at 17.5 mpg for 1982, gradually rose to 20.7 mpg in 1996.[39]

While automakers could continue selling the popular station wagons, SUV precursors and other gas-guzzlers, they also were required to produce more fuel-efficient vehicles in order to meet their fleetwide average. Japanese and European automakers specializing in small, energy-efficient cars — like Toyota, Honda and Volkswagen — quickly stepped in to meet America's sudden demand for more economical vehicles. Detroit responded with subcompacts like the AMC Gremlin, Chevrolet Vega and Ford Pinto, but they were no match for the foreign competition. By 1980, Japanese manufacturers had captured 20 percent of the U.S. auto market.

Detroit soon gained a reputation for producing inferior vehicles, especially after a sensational 1980 trial confirmed that a design flaw caused the gas tank of the subcompact Ford Pinto to explode when rear-ended.

Meanwhile, in an effort to improve fuel efficiency and reduce highway deaths, Congress in 1973 enacted a nationwide speed limit of 55 mpg. And in 1975 and 1976, lawmakers tightened emission standards for passenger vehicles. Automakers responded with new technology, including catalytic converters to capture pollutants released during fuel combustion.

Enter the SUV

By the 1980s, new sources of oil had been discovered in the North Sea and Africa, contributing to a decline in worldwide oil and gasoline prices. Interest in SUVs — albeit smaller and lighter models — resumed. In 1983, GM introduced the Chevy S-10 Blazer and GMC S-15 Jimmy, relatively compact SUVs powered by four-cylinder and six-cylinder engines instead of the V8s of earlier models. Ford followed with another "compact" SUV, the Bronco II.

In 1984, Jeep came out with smaller versions of its 1960s-era Cherokee and Wagoneer. Like modern SUVs, the Jeep models were marketed as peppier, sportier alternatives to the station wagon.

Building on their reputation as makers of superior-quality, energy-efficient compacts, Japanese carmakers made further inroads into the U.S. auto market in the 1980s with truck-based models of their own, including the Mitsubishi Montero (1982), Isuzu Trooper (1984), Nissan Pathfinder (1987) and Toyota 4Runner (1985).

Detroit continued to market station wagons, but the 1980s saw a revolution in family-car design. Ford, tarnished by the Pinto controversy, made a speedy comeback in 1986 with the Ford Taurus and Mercury Sable. The aerodynamic, jellybean shape of the midsize cars and wagons marked a departure from the boxy profiles typical of earlier models; it also improved fuel efficiency by cutting down on wind resistance. Consumers turned the Taurus into a best-seller for several years, even as Japanese brands captured 30 percent of total U.S. vehicle sales.

Chrysler Corp., which had been saved from bankruptcy in 1979 by a federal loan bailout, also scored a major success in the 1980s family-car market. Chrysler's bulbous, new Dodge Caravan minivan, introduced in 1984, became a favorite among Baby Boomers, many of whom jettisoned their parents' stodgy wagons. The carpooling, Baby-Boomer "soccer mom" behind the wheel of a minivan became a ubiquitous symbol of the times.

The 1990s booming economy boosted the SUV from a niche product to an industry standard. Buoyed by a bullish stock market, declining interest rates, low unemployment and low gasoline prices, American consumers discarded their concerns about fuel economy (the 55-mph speed limit was repealed in 1995) and sought vehicles reflecting their optimism. SUVs fit the bill.

Ford's hugely popular Explorer led the way. Introduced in 1991, it combined the lure of the outdoors

Ford says its 2004 Hybrid SUV Escape will get 40 mpg. Hybrids run on a combination of gas and electricity.

through its rugged, truck-like appearance with power windows and locks, leather seats, advanced sound systems and other passenger-car refinements. The Explorer's four-wheel drive capability made it appealing not only to outdoor enthusiasts but also to suburban wannabes anxious to shed their domesticated wagons and minivans. With Explorers dominating the best-seller charts for both cars and trucks, the SUV as hip commuter car was born.

Reflecting the Explorer's phenomenal popularity, sales figures rose from 187,000 units in 1982 to 900,000 in 1992, the year after the Explorer appeared. For the rest of the 1990s, SUVs continued to be the industry's fastest-growing segment. To satisfy a broader range of consumers, carmakers in the mid-1990s began introducing a variety of smaller, car-based models, combining all-wheel drive and the SUV look with carlike handling and comfort, such as Toyota's RAV4 and Highlander, the Honda CR-V and the Subaru Forester.

Luxury SUVs also made their entrance with the unveiling of the Lexus RX 300. Continued low fuel prices helped boost sales of the biggest SUVs, such as the Chevy Suburban and its new competitor, the Ford Expedition. By 2000, SUV sales reached a record 3.3 million vehicles; by 2001, SUVs, minivans and pickups captured 52 percent of total vehicle sales.

CURRENT SITUATION

Anti-SUV Backlash

As SUV sales have mounted, America's streetscape has changed. A decade ago, a typical line of suburban traffic consisted of traditional passenger cars of approximately the same height. Today, the passenger car is often in the minority; SUVs ranging from the small Subaru Forester to the massive Hummer H1 make up about half the vehicles on the road.

The rise of a backlash among non-SUV drivers was only a matter of time. Frustrated by what they saw as aggressive, intimidating behavior by SUV drivers who cut them off and barred their visibility, angry sedan drivers began filling the traffic columns of newspapers around the country.

Then, as automakers introduced ever-larger models, environmental groups stepped up their criticism of SUVs as gas-guzzling polluters. In February 1999, when Ford introduced its largest model to date, the four-ton, "super-duty" Excursion, the Sierra Club awarded the automaker with its "Exxon Valdez Award" for producing a "a rolling monument to environmental destruction."[40]

It wasn't long before activists began taking matters into their own hands. In 2000, Robert Lind of San Francisco launched an anti-SUV Web site — changingtheclimate.com — and began posting bumper stickers on SUVs that read, "I'm Changing the Climate! Ask Me How."[41] Others left fake traffic citations on SUV windshields chiding owners for polluting the environment. Reports of vandalism against SUVs, including slashed tires and broken windshields, also mounted.[42]

Last fall, the anti-SUV backlash gained national attention after Huffington launched the Detroit Project, a full-blown anti-SUV campaign complete with a Web site and television ads excoriating SUV buyers. Some of the ads were modeled on anti-drug commercials charging marijuana users with funding terrorists who profit from the illegal drug trade. One Huffington ad pictures masked, armed men in the desert and warns, "These are the terrorists who get money from those countries every time George fills up his SUV. Oil money supports some terrible things. What kind of mileage does your SUV get?"[43]

Huffington's campaign rankled SUV owners.[44] "Excuse me, Arianna, I didn't realize that black smoke billowing out the back of your Lear jet doesn't pollute the environment," Atlanta developer Bishop scoffs. "You're flying from rally to rally on your private jet, and that kind of fuel consumption doesn't seem to irritate you, but Middle Americans driving their little SUVs really tick you off!"

Last Nov. 20, Christian and Jewish religious leaders belonging to the Interfaith Climate and Energy Campaign went to Detroit to ask automakers to produce cleaner, more fuel-efficient vehicles. GM responded with a statement affirming consumers' right to pick the car of their choice: "GM embraces a strong ethic of environmental and social responsibility. Ultimately, this issue is rooted in vehicle choice, and GM respects the rights of all people to make those choices."

The Evangelical Environmental Network also launched its controversial "What Would Jesus Drive?" campaign, which sparked a heated response from conservative religious leaders such as Jerry Falwell, who staunchly defended the right to drive an SUV.

"I believe that global warming is a myth," Falwell said. "Therefore, I have no conscience problems at all, and I'm going to buy a Suburban next time." Falwell also chided his fellow evangelicals involved in the campaign. "If you spent as much time winning people to Christ and building soul-winning churches and sending missionaries around the world as you're worrying about God being unable to take care of his creation, we would get a lot more done. I urge everyone to go out and buy an SUV today."[45]

Still the King

Recent sales figures suggest that many Americans share Falwell's sentiments. Although the overall market for new vehicles is slow — with April sales 6.1 percent below last year at this time — SUVs continue to pull consumers into the auto showrooms. Honda, for example, saw sales of its SUVs, pickups and minivans soar by 55 percent over last year, even as its passenger-car sales fell by half.

Indeed, current trends suggest that the anti-SUV backlash has largely fallen on deaf ears. The hottest-selling SUVs today are the very behemoths that are the targets of the strongest criticism. Ford enjoyed record sales of its big Lincoln Navigator in April, while sales of Cadillac's comparable Escalade were up 18.6 percent.[46]

Ford analyst Pipas attributes the enduring popularity of SUVs to the same demographic phenomenon that made the muscle cars, station wagons and minivans such hot sellers in earlier decades, the 65-million-strong Baby Boom generation. "Throughout the 1990s, most of the growth in the SUV segment was in traditional, truck-based models," he says. "There's an element of toughness to them that appeals to the Baby Boomers. In the 1990s,

Are SUVs a safety threat to occupants of other vehicles?

YES
Joan B. Claybrook
President, Public Citizen

From Testimony Before Senate Commerce, Science And Transportation Committee, Feb. 26, 2003

The criticism of SUVs is richly deserved. SUVs are basically gussied-up pickup trucks, and most have never been comprehensively redesigned to be safely used as passenger vehicles. In a crash, the high bumper, stiff frame and steel-panel construction of SUVs override crash protections of other vehicles. Due to their cut-rate safety design, SUVs often fail to adequately absorb crash energy or to crumple, as they should, so they ram into other motorists and shock their own occupants' bodies. . . . Overall, SUVs are less safe on average for their occupants than large or midsize cars, yet they inflict far greater costs in both lives and money for the dangers they inflict on other motorists.

The SUV is a bad bargain for society and a nightmare for American roads. The switch from midsize and large passenger cars to SUVs has endangered millions of Americans, without any recognizable benefits. One former NHTSA [National Highway Traffic Safety Administration] administrator estimated in 1997 that the aggressive design of light trucks (a category including SUVs, pickup trucks, vans and minivans) has killed 2,000 additional people needlessly each year. Yet automakers continue to exploit special-interest exemptions and safety loopholes, while creating consumer demand and shaping consumer choice with a multibillion-dollar marketing campaign because SUVs bring in maximum dollars for minimal effort. . . .

Manufacturers have known for decades about the tendency of SUVs to roll over, and about the damage incurred when the vehicles' weak roof crushes in on the heads and spines of motorists. . . . They've also unblinkingly faced the carnage inflicted on other motorists from high SUV bumpers and menacing front grilles, building ever-more heavy and terrible SUVs over time and continuing to market them militaristically, such as the ads calling the Lincoln Navigator an "urban assault vehicle. . . ."

Although many Americans purchase SUVs because they believe that they will safely transport their families, the truth is that SUVs are among the most dangerous vehicles on the road. They are no more safe for their drivers than many passenger cars and are much more dangerous for other drivers who share the highway, making them a net social loss for society. Yet this cycle is perpetuated by industry-spread myths that heavier vehicles are safer per se, so consumers believe that they must continue to "supersize" their own vehicle in order to remain safe. The self-reinforcing nature of this growing highway arms race makes the notion that SUVs are safe for their occupants one of the more harmful myths of our time.

NO
Susan M. Cischke
Vice President, Environmental And Safety Engineering, Ford Motor Co.

From Testimony Before Senate Commerce, Science And Transportation Committee, Feb. 26, 2003

Cars, as well as motorcycles and bicycles, have always shared the road with large commercial trucks, buses, cargo vans and pickup trucks. Historically, size differences among vehicles were more pronounced in the 1970s than they are today.

While the vehicle fleet in the U.S. is changing to include more and more light trucks and vans . . . the number of vehicle miles traveled has continued to increase, [but] the total number of crash fatalities has stayed relatively constant.

Ford continues to be a leader in researching the factors that contribute to crash safety and compatibility, including weight, geometry and stiffness and in translating that research into enhancements to vehicle design. Ford is working with NHTSA [National Highway Transportation Safety Administration] to assess whether vehicle compatibility can be predicted by measuring average height of force, to evaluate not just "bumper alignment" but also the load path that would transmit force by the striking vehicle. By aligning the load path, it is possible to reduce harm to the struck vehicle. . . .

Ford has been working to improve the safety of cars in collisions with SUVs by adding structure and lowering rail heights of SUVs. For example, in the 2003 Expedition and Navigator, the bumper beam is attached directly to the front of the frame rail, instead of being bracketed to the top. This allows the rails to more directly engage a struck object and manages the crash forces more efficiently. For example, the Expedition bumper beam and rail are compatible with the height of the bumper on a Ford Taurus or Mercury Sable. Also, the frame of the 2003 Explorer and Mountaineer was lowered to be more compatible with other vehicles on the road.

In addition, Ford introduced on the 2000 Excursion Ford's BlockerBeam that offers front-bumper underside protection for crash compatibility with smaller vehicles. The BlockerBeam lowers the point of engagement for a frontal impact with an SUV to the same level as a Taurus. This helps prevent the SUV from riding over the passenger car, and transfers crash forces to engineered crumple zones on both the striking and the struck vehicles, where they can be best managed.

The automotive industry in general, and Ford in particular, will continue to build vehicles with the utility and safety that our customers require. Nevertheless, we view vehicle safety as a partnership, and where vehicle design ends, customer responsibility begins.

Comparing David and Goliath

The Toyota Prius, a compact hybrid, gets nearly four-times better gas mileage than the GMC Yukon, which is four feet longer and weighs twice as much.

Comparing the Toyota Prius and GMC Yukon

	Toyota Prius	GMC Yukon
Base Price (suggested retail)	$20,450	$35,552
Mileage rating: city/hwy/combined	52/45/48	12/16/14
Weight	2,765 lbs.	5,839 lbs.
Height	57.6"	75.7"
Width	66.7"	78.8"
Length (inches)	169.6"	219.3"
Seating capacity	5	9
CO_2 production (tons)*	36	124

* Over the vehicle's 124,000-mile lifetime

Source: Sierra Club

they had mature households, with adolescent children, they were pretty affluent after benefiting from the stock market's go-go years, and they led very active lifestyles. The SUV ideally suited that go-anywhere, do-anything approach to life."

But most of these boomers are buying an adventure-seeking image that few will put into practice. "Only a little over half of all SUVs are four-wheel drive, and while some people do take them hunting and boating, less than one-fifth of the people who drive them actually go off-road," Pipas says.

"You can get an interesting view of Americana at a Home Depot parking lot on a Saturday morning," Pipas adds. "It will be filled with pickups and SUVs because, while a Ford Taurus or a Toyota Camry may be appropriate for bringing home a can of paint, they aren't particularly well suited for bringing home plywood, flats of flowers and other kinds of landscaping materials."

Energy Prices

A spike in gasoline prices earlier this year also failed to dampen Americans' enthusiasm for SUVs. Due in part to a cutoff in oil exports from Venezuela during an oil-industry strike and fears that Iraq would destroy its oilfields during

the recent war to oust Saddam Hussein, prices peaked at $1.76 a gallon on March 21, up from $1.45 a year earlier. But sales of fuel-guzzling SUVs were seemingly unaffected.

That doesn't surprise analysts. Unlike the 1970s, when high gas prices resulted from a true shortage of oil, prompting consumers to trade their gas-guzzlers for smaller cars, no one predicts a permanent oil shortage today. Though the 11-member Organization of Petroleum Exporting Countries (OPEC) tries to keep oil prices stable through production quotas, it controls only about a third of the world's oil production, and thus cannot interrupt oil supplies to the United States; non-members such as Canada, Russia and Britain ensure a plentiful supply to the United States. "In the 1970s, there was no fuel, and people were totally panicked," says Claybrook of Public Citizen. "Today it's just a matter of price, and because SUV owners are wealthy, they will pay more than $2 a gallon. It will have to go to $5 before it will change their behavior."

As a result, many consumers ignore gas prices when car shopping today. "There was a 50 percent increase in gas prices several years ago, and it made not one whit of difference in people's driving patterns or car-purchasing patterns," says Becker of the Sierra Club. "People will pay whatever they need to pay for gas. They may drive an extra two miles to go to the cheaper pump and save 25 cents, but they aren't going to buy a different kind of vehicle or drive less because prices go up 50 cents a gallon."

The rising price of new cars, including SUVs, also helps explain why consumers ignore gas prices. Many SUVs cost upward of $30,000, and the most expensive more than $50,000. "The price of gas only accounts for about 10 percent of annual operating costs," says Pipas. "Once you've decided to spend whatever it is you're going to spend on a vehicle, it really doesn't make too much difference whether the price of gas is a buck or two-fifty."

OUTLOOK

New Kid on the Block

There are signs that consumers' love affair with SUVs, at least with the biggest models, may be cooling. Citing poor sales, Ford will discontinue its jumbo-sized Excursion in 2004. Even the Hummer — the only GM model that doesn't need financing incentives to lure buyers — may be in for a bumpy ride. According to a recent customer-satisfaction survey, the new Hummer H2 ranked last among 36 brands.[47]

Surprisingly, the biggest complaint about the $50,000 H2 was its poor gas mileage. Apparently Hummer buyers were surprised that their 6,400 lb., six-liter V8 truck got less than 10 mpg. As gas prices inched toward the $2 mark during the Iraq war, they were hit with sticker shock when it came time to fill the 32-gallon tank.

Gas mileage rarely figures among car buyers' top complaints, presumably because fuel-efficiency information stickers are required on most new cars. But because the Hummer and other big SUVs are classified as commercial vehicles, the manufacturers don't have to post that information. GM reportedly is considering voluntarily putting mileage stickers on its Hummers anyway to avoid future complaints.[48]

It's too soon to write off mega-SUVs as a relic of the booming 1990s, however. Last year alone, Americans bought more than 787,000 large SUVs, including Hummers, Chevy Tahoes and Ford Expeditions.[49] But the best-selling SUVs continue to be the midsize models, such as the ever-popular Explorer, Trailblazer and Grand Cherokee, which accounted for almost two-thirds of the 3 million truck-based SUVs sold in 2002.

SUV advocates cite these figures in dismissing critics' complaints. "People are moving away from the really big SUVs," says Defore of the SUV Owners Association. "Even over the past five years, the predominance of SUV sales is not in the behemoths, but rather in the small to midsize SUVs. So what's the problem? It's not like it's an epidemic or something."

Indeed, the spring auto shows in Detroit and New York City featured several so-called crossover vehicles designed to appeal to a broader swath of consumers by incorporating some of the design features more commonly found in cars into slightly downsized SUV pro-files. In addition to the usual safety and fuel-efficiency advantages incorporated into cars, many crossovers offer safety features that go beyond federal requirements. The popular Lexus RX series, for example, contains an air-suspension system that automatically lowers the vehicle's height at high speeds, reducing rollover risk. The new Volvo XC90 SUV features a stability-control system designed to detect an impending rollover and help the driver maintain control, as well as head-protection airbags for occupants in all three rows of seats.[50]

Once again, it appears that Baby Boomers are driving automotive-design trends. The oldest boomers reach 57 this year, and while they aren't quite ready to give up the adventurous self-image that draws them to SUVs, many are looking for a little more comfort and additional safety.

"We at Ford still see SUVs outperforming other segments in the coming year, but over the next decade most of the growth is going to come from crossover SUVs," Pipas says. Environmentalists may welcome the trend because crossovers — which technically are classified as cars rather than light trucks — are smaller, consume less gas and pollute less than traditional SUVs. "But the popularity of crossovers has little to do with the environment or fuel consumption," Pipas says. "These Baby Boomers are seeking vehicles that suit their needs.

"The SUV was unquestionably the vehicle of the 1990s," Pipas continues. "When we look back, we'll find that the crossover SUV is going to be the vehicle of the 21st century."

NOTES

1. For background, see Mary H. Cooper, "Energy and the Environment," *The CQ Researcher*, March 3, 2000, pp. 161-184.
2. Huffington launched her latest TV ad on May 7, 2003, www.detroitproject.com.
3. For background, see Mary H. Cooper, "Global Warming Update," *The CQ Researcher*, Nov. 1, 1996, pp. 961-984; Mary H. Cooper, "Global Warming Treaty," *The CQ Researcher*, Jan. 26, 2001, pp. 41-64.
4. Kathy Koch, "Truck Safety," *The CQ Researcher*, March 12, 1999, pp. 209-232.
5. See Warren Brown, "It's Rugged, and They're Cross," *The Washington Post*, April 24, 2003, p. G7.

6. Autodata Corp.

7. See www.hummer.com.

8. For background, see David Masci, "Auto Industry's Future," *The CQ Researcher*, Jan. 21, 2000, pp. 17-40.

9. Keith Bradsher, *High and Mighty: SUVs: The World's Most Dangerous Vehicles and How They Got That Way* (2002), pp. 110-111.

10. For background, see Brian Hansen, "Auto Safety," *The CQ Researcher*, Oct. 26, 2001, pp. 873-896.

11. Ricardo Alonso-Zaldivar, "Automaker Data Say SUVs Are Riskier," *Los Angeles Times*, Feb. 26, 2003, p. A1.

12. NHTSA, April, 2003 statistics. Also, see Greg Schneider, "Deadly Driving Trend Alters Safety Focus; Fatalities Turn Attention to SUVs, Crash-Avoidance Technology," *The Washington Post*, May 3, 2003.

13. Testifying April 3, 2003, before the House Appropriations Subcommittee on Transportation and Treasury.

14. From comments before an automotive group in Detroit, Jan. 14, 2003. See Cindy Skrzycki, "Regulator Assails Safety of SUVs," *The Washington Post*, Jan. 16, 2003.

15. Insurance Institute for Highway Safety, "Status Report," Feb. 14, 1998.

16. Quoted in Myron Levin, "Study Questions Safety of SUVs," *Los Angeles Times*, Feb. 18, 2003, p. A1.

17. Marc Ross and Tom Wenzel, "An Analysis of Traffic Deaths by Vehicle Type and Model," Lawrence Berkeley Laboratory/University of Michigan, with funding from the Department of Energy, March 2002.

18. Quoted in Levin, *op. cit.*

19. *Ibid.*

20. Alonso-Zaldivar, *op. cit.*

21. Insurance Institute, *op. cit.*

22. Quoted in Danny Hakim, "A Regulator Takes Aim At Hazards of S.U.V.'s," *The New York Times*, Dec. 22, 2002, p. C1.

23. Levin, *op. cit.*

24. For background, see Mary H. Cooper, "Energy Security," *The CQ Researcher*, Feb. 1, 2002, pp. 73-96.

25. From testimony before the Senate Commerce, Science and Transportation Committee, Feb. 26, 2003.

26. National Academy of Sciences, "Effectiveness and Impact of Corporate Average Fuel Economy Standards," July 31, 2001. For the industry response, see Alliance of Automobile Manufacturers, "NAS Report Confirms Need for Reform of CAFE Program," July 30, 2001.

27. See Danny Hakim, "Ford Backs Off Efficiency Pledge for Its S.U.V.'s," *The New York Times*, April 18, 2003, p. C1.

28. From a statement to the House floor, April 10, 2003.

29. Richard Simon, "House Stalls Bid to Increase Fuel Standards for SUVs," *Los Angeles Times*, April 11, 2003, p. 38.

30. As of 2001. See Energy Information Administration, *Monthly Energy Review*, March 2003, p. 17.

31. See Cooper, "Global Warming Treaty," *op. cit.*

32. See "Driving Up the Heat: SUVs and Global Warming," www.sierraclub.org.

33. See Mary H. Cooper, "Transatlantic Tensions," *The CQ Researcher*, July 13, 2001, pp. 553-576.

34. Bush announced the fuel-cell initiative during his State of the Union speech, Jan. 28, 2003. The off-road diesel rule, which would curb particulate-matter emissions, was announced by the Environmental Protection Agency on April 16, 2003.

35. Information in this section is based on "SUV Heritage: From Carryalls to Crossovers," www.cars.com; and "Looking Back: Special 50th Anniversary Section," *Consumer Reports*, April 2003, pp. 21-26.

36. For background on early legislation on auto safety, see Congressional Quarterly, *Congress and the Nation: Volume II, 1965-1968*, (1969).

37. For background, see Mary H. Cooper, "Energy Policy," *The CQ Researcher*, May 25, 2001, pp. 441-464.

38. The standard was tightened to 26 mpg from 1986-88, but loosened to 26.5 mpg in 1989 and restored in 1990 to 27.5 mpg, where it has remained ever since.

39. For more information on CAFE standards, see www.fueleconomy.gov. See also Robert Bamberger, "Automobile and Light Truck Fuel Economy: The CAFE Standards," Congressional Research Service, March 12, 2003.

40. Sierra Club, "Sierra Club Awards Ford Motor Company the 'Exxon Valdez Environmental Achievement Award,' " Feb. 25, 1999, www.sierraclub.org.

41. See Ann Grimes, "SUV-Driver Alert: Steer Clear of This Guy at Cocktail Parties," *The Wall Street Journal*, Oct. 13, 2000, p. B1.

42. "Madison Police Suspect Environmentalists Slashed SUV Tires," The Associated Press, April 23, 2003.

43. The ads can be seen at www.detroitproject.com.

44. See, for example, Woody Hochswender, "Did My Car Join Al Qaeda?" *The New York Times*, Feb. 16, 2003, p. D11.

45. Speaking on CNN, "Inside Politics," Nov. 20, 2002.

46. See Danny Hakim, "Auto Sales Dropped 6.1 percent During April," *The New York Times*, May 2, 2003, p. C1.

47. J.D. Power and Associates,

48. See Danny Hakim, "Whether a Hummer or a Hybrid, The Big Complaint Is Fuel Use," *The New York Times*, May 7, 2003, p. C1.

49. Sales statistics from Autodata Corp., Woodcliff Lake, N.J.

50. See *Consumer Reports, op. cit.*

BIBLIOGRAPHY

Books

Bradsher, Keith, *High and Mighty: SUVs — The World's Most Dangerous Vehicles and How They Got That Way,* **Public Affairs, 2002.**
A former Detroit bureau chief for *The New York Times* traces the auto industry's successful marketing strategy for SUVs, which are cheaper to build than cars because of loopholes in federal fuel and safety regulations.

Penenberg, Adam, *Tragic Indifference: One Man's Battle with the Auto Industry Over the Dangers of SUVs,* **HarperBusiness, 2003.**
A business reporter chronicles the legal battles that have ensued from a spate of SUV rollover accidents in the late 1990s involving the Ford Explorer equipped with defective Firestone tires. Scheduled for publication in October.

Articles

"Annual Auto Issue," *Consumer Reports,* **April 2003.**
A respected annual review of the current auto lineup provides safety, customer-satisfaction, resale and fuel-economy data for 2003 models as well as a history of auto trends and regulations over the past half-century.

"Roadroller," *The Economist,* **Jan. 16, 2003.**
The belief among SUV owners that their vehicles are safer than cars is "nonsense," in light of government statistics showing that SUV rollover accidents are responsible for a third of all highway deaths.

Brown, Stuart F., "Dude, Where's My Hybrid?" *Fortune,* **April 28, 2003, p. 112.**
Cars with hybrid engines, which run on a combination of gasoline and electricity, have sold out in the United States, but analysts question whether Americans will demand enough of them to ensure their future viability.

Hakim, Danny, "Whether a Hummer or a Hybrid, The Big Complaint Is Fuel Use," *The New York Times,* **May 7, 2003, p. C1.**
A recent customer-satisfaction survey placed the giant Hummer at the bottom of the list — with its roughly 10 mpg mileage the biggest complaint.

Mateja, Jim, "System Makes Volvo SUV Anti-Roll Model," *Chicago Tribune,* **March 27, 2003, p. CARS 1.**
Volvo has taken the lead in voluntarily installing new technology to reduce the safety threat SUVs pose to their occupants and those of other cars on the road.

Salkever, Alex, "Where High-Tech Cars Still Sputter," *Business Week Online,* **May 1, 2003.**
While Ford Motor Co. plans to introduce a new version of its popular hybrid SUV, the Escape, it has backed away from an earlier pledge to boost the fuel efficiency of all its SUVs by 25 percent by 2005.

Reports and Studies

Bamberger, Robert, "Automobile and Light Truck Fuel Economy: The CAFE Standards," *Issue Brief for Congress,* **Congressional Research Service, March 12, 2003.**
The author reviews the history and current status of fuel-efficiency standards in place since 1975 and how they differ for passenger cars and SUVs.

Insurance Institute for Highway Safety, "Special Issue: Incompatibility of Vehicles in Crashes, Status Report," April 26, 2003.
The study focuses on the crash incompatibility of passenger cars and SUVs and the safety risks posed by SUVs to occupants of smaller, lower-profile vehicles.

Insurance Institute for Highway Safety, "Status Report," Feb. 14, 1998.
This early study on crash incompatibility between SUVs and cars concluded that the occupants of cars struck in the side by pickups or SUVs are more than 25 times more likely to die than the occupants of the striking vehicle.

National Academy of Sciences, "Effectiveness and Impact of Corporate Average Fuel Economy Standards," July 31, 2001.
Although fuel-economy standards have helped reduce U.S. dependence on imported oil and lowered emissions of carbon dioxide, tightening the standards for SUVs and light trucks would make the regulations more effective.

Ross, Marc, and Tom Wenzel, "An Analysis of Traffic Deaths by Vehicle Type and Model," American Council for an Energy-Efficient Economy, March 2002.
Ross, a University of Michigan physicist, and Wenzel, a researcher at the Lawrence Berkeley National Laboratory, conclude that most cars are safer than most SUVs.

Yacobucci, Brent D., "Sport Utility Vehicles, Mini-Vans, and Light Trucks: An Overview of Fuel Economy and Emissions Standards," *CRS Report for Congress*, Congressional Research Service, Feb. 28, 2003.
This brief summarizes the latest developments related to SUVs, which are held to more lenient emission and fuel-economy standards than passenger cars.

For More Information

Alliance to Save Energy, 1200 18th St., N.W., Suite 900, Washington, DC 20036; (202) 857-0666; www.ase.org. Monitors energy legislation and provides information on energy conservation.

Insurance Institute for Highway Safety, 1005 North Glebe Road, Suite 800, Arlington, VA 22201; (703) 247-1500; www.hwysafety.org. An independent research organization funded by auto insurers.

National Religious Partnership for the Environment, 49 South Pleasant St., Suite 301, Amherst, MA 01002; (413) 253-1515; www.nrpe.org. A coalition of faith groups that launched the "What Would Jesus Drive?" campaign to spur consumers to drive fuel-efficient vehicles.

Public Citizen, 1600 20th St., N.W., Washington, DC 20009; (202) 588-1000; www.citizen.org. A consumer-advocacy organization founded by Ralph Nader that calls for more stringent safety standards for SUVs.

Sierra Club, 408 C St., N.E., Washington, DC 20002; (202) 547-1141; www.sierraclub.org. An environmental organization that provides information about the impact of fuel-inefficient vehicles on global warming.

Sport Utility Vehicle Owners of America, P.O. Box 34076, Washington, DC 20043; (877) 447-8862; www.suvoa.com.

10

Air Pollution Conflict

Mary H. Cooper

President Bush promotes his proposed changes to the landmark Clean Air Act at a power plant in Monroe, Mich., on Sept. 15. One of the changes would relax a rule requiring older power plants to install modern pollution-control technology when they modernize. Plant operators say the change will make it easier to reduce harmful emissions. But environmentalists contend they will merely reverse improvements in air quality made over the past three decades.

From *The CQ Researcher*, November 14, 2003.

An enthusiastic crowd of utility workers and executives recently greeted President Bush at the Detroit Edison power plant in Monroe, Mich. The president had traveled to the aging utility on Sept. 15 to promote two initiatives he said would improve the nation's air quality and ease industry anti-pollution requirements at the same time.

"Regulations intended to enhance air quality made it really difficult for companies to do that which is necessary — to not only produce more energy, but to do it in a cleaner way," Bush told his cheering audience. "It makes sense to change these regulations. It makes sense for the workplace environment. It makes sense for the protection of the air."

Critics of the administration's environmental policies dismissed the president's claims. "The backdrop of President Bush's latest environmental photo-op — the dirtiest power plant in Michigan — says it all," remarked Sen. Joseph I. Lieberman, D-Conn., one of nine contenders for the Democratic presidential nomination. "Under Bush's policies, this antiquated, coal-burning plant will get a free pass to keep pumping smoke and soot into the air with impunity."

"Plants like it give our kids asthma, taint our fish with mercury and cause the premature death of thousands of Americans a year," Lieberman continued. "Rather than praise polluters, our president should demand they clean up their act."[1]

In the weeks since his Michigan speech, Bush has provided more relief to polluting industries and more ammunition to clean-air advocates. On Oct 27, the Environmental Protection Agency (EPA) finalized a Bush rule change that would no longer force polluting

Revised Pollution Rules Benefit 17,700 Plants

Beginning Dec. 31, the Bush administration will ease the "New Source Review" provision of the Clean Air Act requiring the most polluting industrial facilities — mainly refineries and old, coal-fired power plants — to install "scrubbers" if equipment upgrades result in higher emissions. More than 17,700 plants will be affected.

Plants Affected by Revised "New Source Review" Rules

Source: SaveTheCleanAirAct.org

coal-fired plants and oil refineries to install smokestack filters known as "scrubbers" when they modernize their facilities. On Nov. 5, the EPA confirmed that because of the rule change it would likely drop more than 50 investigations into violations of anti-pollution rules, a move that prompted several smog-ridden states to threaten lawsuits of their own (*see p. 240*).

Bush's proposals would make sweeping changes to the 1970 Clean Air Act and its subsequent amendments. The landmark environmental statute authorized the EPA to enforce health-based limits on emissions of six major air pollutants from the smokestacks of industrial plants and the tailpipes of cars, trucks and buses.

By forcing automakers, utilities and other industries to install pollution-control technology, such as tailpipe catalytic converters and scrubbers, the Clean Air Act has significantly reduced air pollution over the past three decades, even as industrial production has increased and the number of vehicles on the roads has mushroomed. The law has virtually eliminated toxic lead and cut emissions of sulfur dioxide and carbon monoxide by more than a third, the EPA says. (*See graph, p. 227.*)

Despite these improvements, however, air pollution continues to sicken millions of Americans, causing or aggravating heart disease, asthma and other respiratory ailments, especially in children and the elderly. The problems are most severe in cities where auto emissions combine with industrial pollutants to make it hard to breathe on hot, summer days. (*See box, p. 233.*)

While acknowledging that the law has helped reduce pollution, many U.S. industries complain that clean-air regulations are too costly and hamper economic growth. "We've had a major increase in electricity use, even as emissions have come down substantially," says Dan Riedinger, spokesman for the Edison Electric Institute, the utilities' main lobbying group. "[But] as the different regulatory programs pile up over time, and our CEOs try to plan their business strategies — and a major part of that always is how to deal with environmental controls — there's a lot of uncertainty."

Bush's new initiatives would address the utility industry's concerns in several ways. First, they would replace the Clean Air Act's rules governing factories and utilities with a single program covering sulfur dioxide, which causes acid rain and contributes to smog; nitrogen oxides, which are major components of smog; and mercury, a toxic heavy metal that poisons fish and sickens humans who eat them. Coal-fired electric power plants and oil refineries are major sources of all three pollutants.[2]

Bush's proposal, known as the "Clear Skies" initiative, would replace traditional regulations requiring companies to limit their emissions of these pollutants at each plant with a market-based approach called "cap-and-trade." This approach would allow companies that install costly scrubbers and reduce their emissions well below the legal limits to sell pollution "credits" to companies whose emissions exceed their limits.

The president claims his approach would reduce emissions by 70 percent over 10 years, or 35 million tons more than the current Clean Air Act. But critics say the measure would cause 21 million tons more pollution than current law would allow.[3]

"Clear Skies doesn't go far enough, fast enough," says Conrad Schneider, advocacy director of the Clean Air Task Force, a Boston environmental organization. "On the other hand, in exchange for delivering weak, slow cleanup, it offers complete regulatory relief to the affected power sector."

Bush's second policy shift on air quality, which takes effect in December, required no congressional action because it was accomplished through an administrative change in EPA rules.

The provision is known as the New Source Review rule because it requires a review when a plant adds new generating equipment that could raise emissions. (*See p. 234.*) It exempted older plants from rigorous pollution caps because it was assumed the plants would soon be junked in favor of more efficient, less-polluting generators fueled by natural gas.

But the plants weren't junked. Hundreds of coal-fired power plants have continued operating by exploiting another part of the New Source Review provision that allows older plants to avoid meeting new-plant emissions standards so long as they do not make major upgrades to the older equipment. During the Clinton administration, the Justice Department sued 51 coal-fired plants for violating the law by upgrading their equipment while claiming the improvements were only routine maintenance.

The new rule would allow plants to modernize without installing scrubbers as long as the improvements cost less than 20 percent of the plant's total value and do not increase emissions. Utility industry representatives welcome the change as a long overdue correction of a flawed program.

"In terms of its environmental impact, New Source Review is one of the biggest red herrings and biggest

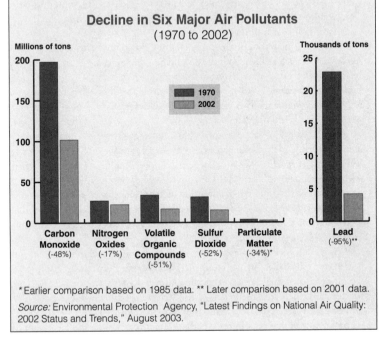

Clean Air Act Reduced Pollutants

Six major air pollutants have declined since the Clean Air Act was passed in 1970. Carbon monoxide — emitted by cars, buses and trucks — still accounts for the bulk of the nation's air pollution.

Decline in Six Major Air Pollutants
(1970 to 2002)

Legend: 1970, 2002

Carbon Monoxide (-48%), Nitrogen Oxides (-17%), Volatile Organic Compounds (-51%), Sulfur Dioxide (-52%), Particulate Matter (-34%)*, Lead (-95%)**

* Earlier comparison based on 1985 data. ** Later comparison based on 2001 data.

Source: Environmental Protection Agency, "Latest Findings on National Air Quality: 2002 Status and Trends," August 2003.

public relations coups by environmentalist groups of the past decade," Riedinger says. Because utilities are subject to the Clean Air Act's emissions standards, he says, "even if the New Source Review rule were wiped off the books, those emissions caps are still in place. Nothing in the New Source Review program changes that."

But environmental advocates reject Riedinger's claim, suggesting the place Bush chose to promote his policy confirms the administration's willingness to buckle under industry pressure. "The Monroe plant is the eighth-dirtiest plant in the country and emits more sulfur dioxide than some entire states," says John Walke, director of clean-air programs at the New York-based Natural Resources Defense Council (NRDC). "The president's effective repeal of the New Source Review program would allow this plant to increase its pollution by over 30 percent. It's really astonishing — and cynical — that he went there because it highlights just how dangerous these policies are."

Hot Washington Welcome for New EPA Chief

Critics of President Bush's environmental policies gave Utah Gov. Michael O. Leavitt, Bush's nominee to head the EPA, a blistering welcome to Washington last month.

"Governor, the record of the Environmental Protection Agency under the president is abysmal," said Sen. James M. Jeffords, I-Vt., during Senate committee hearings on Leavitt's nomination. "We have watched the administration roll back environmental laws and regulations day after day, week after week, month after month."[1]

After 10 years as governor, Leavitt left a mixed environmental record. Widely admired as an effective administrator, he had convinced fellow Western governors to join Utah in a plan to reduce regional haze. But be-cause Leavitt, a Republican, also had a record of advancing industry interests — including a controversial plan to open millions of protected acres to development — environmental advocates greeted his nomination with skepticism.

Leavitt defended his environmental record during the heated committee meeting. "I passionately believe that this nation deserves to have a clean and safe and healthy environment," Leavitt told the panel. "I also believe that the United States can increase the velocity of our environmental progress, and that we can do it without compromising our competitive position economically in the world."

"With confidence, I would hold up Utah's environmental record to that of any other state in the Union," said Sen. Orrin G. Hatch, R-Utah. "Michael Leavitt has brought about a 41 percent increase in spending on environmental protection. And that's after adjusting for inflation."[2]

But Leavitt's nomination in August was widely seen as the latest indication of a two-year shift in Bush's environmental policy. When he appointed moderate Gov. Christine Todd Whitman, R-N.J., to head the EPA in 2001, environmentalists hoped the appointment signaled the new president would continue some of the Clinton administration's policies.

As governor, Whitman had advanced a mix of market-based incentives and enforcement of regulations to improve environmental quality in her heavily industrialized state. But as EPA administrator she oversaw several policy shifts that were at odds with her earlier support of clean-air measures. On her watch, the administration rejected the Kyoto Protocol and earlier promises to regulate carbon dioxide and other greenhouse gases implicated in global warming; devised an energy policy that relies heavily on accelerated use of polluting fossil fuels; and weakened a program aimed at reducing emissions from old, coal-fired power plants.

Whitman remained a team player to the last. When the administration released a controversial status report on the environment that ignored the threat of global warming, she defended the document, calling it a "baseline" of data for future reference. "This is about what we know today and what that tells us," she said.

Bush also has shifted federal air-quality policy involving global warming. The president reversed a campaign promise to add carbon dioxide to the list of pollutants regulated by the Clean Air Act. Industrial emissions of carbon dioxide are thought to be the main cause of a potentially disastrous warming of Earth's atmosphere.

Concern about global warming prompted the United States and more than 150 other nations in 1997 to sign the Kyoto Protocol requiring global reductions in carbon emissions. But just weeks into his presidency, Bush disavowed the treaty and reneged on his pledge to regulate carbon emissions.[4]

Meanwhile, Vice President Dick Cheney chaired an energy-policy task force that helped draft sweeping legislation, pending before Congress, which would greatly expand domestic production of fossil fuels, the main source of carbon emissions.

Dismayed by Bush's reversal on global warming, Lieberman and Sen. John McCain, R-Ariz., introduced legislation limiting carbon emissions, but the Republican-controlled Senate rejected the measure by a relatively slim 55-43 margin on Oct. 30.

"I want to assure my colleagues we will be back," Lieberman said after the vote, predicting a global-warming bill would eventually pass.[5]

As lawmakers take up the Clear Skies initiative, alternative proposals to improve air quality and the energy bill, these are some of the issues they will consider:

"We didn't want to project" what might happen in the future.[3]

But on June 27, 2003, just four days after the report's release, Whitman resigned amid rumors of her growing frustration with the administration's refusal to regulate greenhouse gases and enforce the Clean Air Act.

Bush's choice of Leavitt to head EPA prompted six Democratic lawmakers, including three presidential candidates and Sen. Hillary Rodham Clinton, D-N.Y., to threaten to block Senate confirmation of the nomination to protest administration policies. At issue were the administration's efforts to relax key provisions of the Clean Air Act and its failure to warn the public about dangerous air pollution caused by the collapse of the World Trade Center following the terrorist attacks of Sept. 11, 2001.[4]

But the threatened challenge to Leavitt's nomination collapsed after the administration promised lawmakers that it

Gerry Images/Mark Wilson

New EPA Administrator Michael O. Leavitt

would step up its investigation into the Trade Center findings.[5] On Oct. 28, after two months of debate, the Senate confirmed Leavitt as EPA administrator, 88-8. He was sworn in Nov. 6.

Even Jeffords emphasized that the vote demonstrated support for the person, not the policies. "This vote," he said, "should not be seen as an endorsement of the Bush administration's environmental policies but a vote in support of a fine and honorable man who has an extremely difficult job ahead."[6]

---

[1] Testimony before the Senate Environment and Public Works Committee, Sept. 23, 2003.

[2] *Ibid.*

[3] See Guy Gugliotta, "EPA Issues Environmental Overview," *The Washington Post*, June 24, 2003, p. A19.

[4] The three Democratic presidential contenders who challenged Leavitt's nomination are Sens. John Edwards, N.C., John F. Kerry, Mass., and Joseph I. Lieberman, Conn.

[5] See Eric Pianin, "Senate Confirms Leavitt as EPA Chief," *The Washington Post*, Oct. 29, 2003, p. A23.

[6] From an Oct. 28, 2003, statement.

Do environmental regulations hinder rather than encourage improvements in air quality?

Since its passage in 1970, U.S. industries have complained that the costs of complying with the Clean Air Act outweigh the benefits produced.

Auto-industry representatives predicted that regulations requiring them to install catalytic converters on new vehicles to reduce tailpipe emissions would bankrupt the industry. Instead, the rules spawned a surge in technological advances that quickly lowered both the cost of pollution-control equipment and the amount of tailpipe emissions.

Indeed, all parties agree that the Clean Air Act is among the most cost-effective regulatory efforts currently

on the books. The White House Office of Management and Budget recently concluded that over the past 10 years, 107 major federal regulations produced $146 billion-$230 billion worth of benefits, while costing only $36 billion-$42 billion. (*See graph, p. 231.*)

"The majority of the quantified benefits are attributable to a handful of clean-air rules issued by EPA pursuant to the 1990 amendments to the Clean Air Act," the mandatory report to Congress concluded.[6]

Power company spokesmen concede the act reduced total emissions over the years, but they say further improvements will require changes to the traditional "command-and-control" approach to anti-pollution efforts. The old approach, they say, discourages industries from expanding output because any modernization of a plant triggers rules that scrubbers be installed if the changes result in higher pollution levels. They support the administration's Clear Skies initiative, which would replace emissions limits on individual plants with a "cap-and-trade" mechanism allowing companies to buy and sell pollution credits. That market-based approach would remove some of the uncertainties implicit in the current law, they say.

"We know that our emissions will keep coming down, as they have in the past," says Riedinger of the Edison Electric Institute. "Our concern is the uncertainty about what will be the most cost-effective way to control emissions in the future." Successive amendments have added new programs to the Clean Air Act, including rules to reduce acid rain, regional haze, transport of ozone-forming pollutants and other provisions.

"All these new regulations, piled on top of the old ones, add up to well over a dozen individual Clean Air Act requirements on power generators alone," Riedinger says. "Over the years, this pancaking of regulatory requirements has made it hard to plan ahead."

But industry critics say uncertainty about the future is a poor excuse for egregious violations of the New Source Review provision, which applies primarily to coal-fired power plants and oil refineries. "If you want to know whether a proposed upgrade to your plant would trigger New Source Review, all you have to do is ask for a formal opinion," says Schneider of the Clean Air Task Force. "EPA will then provide you with a letter letting you know whether it would trigger New Source Review. The companies that have been cited for violation of the New Source Review didn't ask. They just sought forgiveness [later]."

Planning concerns aside, industry insists the old rules discourage executives from installing new technology to curb emissions. "Previous interpretations of the New Source Review program created perverse disincentives to environmentally friendly projects," says Jeffrey Marks, director of air quality for the National Association of Manufacturers (NAM). "Industrial facilities prevented from undertaking maintenance projects will rapidly deteriorate in reliability and productivity — increasing fuel consumption, reducing energy efficiency and increasing air pollution and greenhouse-gas emissions."[7]

Electric-utility industry spokesmen concur. "The less flexible and less clear the New Source Review policy is, the greater impediment it is to improving efficiency at power plants and industrial facilities," says Scott H. Segal, of the Electric Reliability Coordinating Council. Electric utilities thus welcome the administration's new rule relaxing the provision, which Segal calls "an attempt to address the unintended consequence of removing the incentive for technological improvement." The new rule's greater clarity will improve environmental performance of utilities, he predicts.

But environmental advocates say the rule change will do just the opposite by deferring the replacement of coal-fired power plants with cleaner-burning facilities. "There are a handful of companies heavily invested in old coal plants, which are economically very competitive because they're not controlled," says Eric Schaeffer, a former chief of EPA's civil enforcement division who now directs the Rockefeller Family Fund's Environmental Integrity Project. If they were held to the same pollution standards as the rest of the utility industry, he says, many would be forced to close.

"But that's not a public policy problem, as far as I'm concerned," he says. "As a society, we don't have a vested interest in 1950-era boilers. At some point they need to get out of the way and make room for a new generation of power plants."

Do air-quality rules undermine the electricity grid's reliability?

On Aug. 14, some 50 million people in eight Eastern states and two Canadian provinces suddenly lost electrical power. The biggest outage in U.S. history cost an estimated $6 billion in lost revenues. Experts generally agree that communication flaws within the electrical grid in Ohio and surrounding states played a role in the cascading blackout, but a joint U.S.-Canadian investigative body has yet to identify the precise cause.[8] The final report is due to be released later this month.[9]

Meanwhile, critics of current air-quality regulations suggest that the rules themselves may have contributed to the grid's failure. "Lights went out last month," Bush said during his Sept. 15 speech at the Detroit Edison plant. "We've got an issue with our electricity grid, and we need to modernize it. . . . Power plants are discouraged from doing routine maintenance because of government regulations. And by routine maintenance, I mean replacing worn-out boiler tubes or boiler fans [that] make the plant less reliable, less efficient and not as environmentally friendly as it should be."

Economy Grew Despite Pollution Regulations

Since passage of the Clean Air Act in 1970, air pollutants have dropped by almost half while economic output, energy consumption and auto usage have grown.

U.S. Growth vs. Emission Trends
(1970-2002)

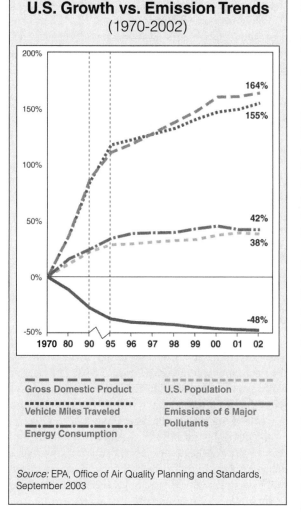

Gross Domestic Product
U.S. Population
Vehicle Miles Traveled
Emissions of 6 Major Pollutants
Energy Consumption

Source: EPA, Office of Air Quality Planning and Standards, September 2003

transmission system and failures in the electric generation system," Segal says. "Transmission-related problems and generation-related problems are irresistibly linked."

During a blackout, he explains, all affected generators are taken offline to ensure they aren't damaged by the outage, and then they are slowly brought back online. If maintenance cannot be performed on the generating facilities, the chances are much greater that something will go wrong while taking the facilities offline or bringing them back online, he says.

"In responding to blackouts like the one in August, we have to maintain our generating facilities," Segal says. "And to maintain our generating facilities, we've got to make sure the New Source Review program doesn't discourage people from doing maintenance activities."

But to many environmentalists, the connection between regulations and grid reliability is marginal, at best. "This was not a situation in which there were not enough generators to get power to people," says Schneider of the Clean Air Task Force. "It was a failure of the grid of some type." Schneider recalls that the outage occurred during a cool spell, when several generators were idle because of low electricity demand. "So there's no cause-and-effect relationship."

The outage prompted lawmakers to include several provisions aimed at preventing future blackouts in the massive energy bill pending before a House-Senate conference committee. And while some say the recent deregulation of electricity markets has undermined grid reliability, lawmakers are divided over whether they should now require utilities to participate in regional transmission organizations in order to control access to power grids, rather than continuing to allow participation to remain voluntary.[10]

But some environmental advocates say the grid would be less vulnerable to blackouts if the administration promoted greater use of renewable-energy sources and more efficient appliances. One such proposal, put forth by Sen. James M. Jeffords, I-Vt., would fund state energy-efficiency programs and require utilities to adopt programs to reduce electricity consumption.

Should carbon dioxide be regulated under the Clean Air Act?

For more than 15 years, the Intergovernmental Panel on Climate Change (IPCC), a group of more than 1,000 scientists from around the world, has warned that global

While Bush stopped short of blaming environmental regulations for the blackout, some industry spokesmen draw a more direct connection between the two. "In any blackout there are two components — failures in the

warming poses a potentially disastrous threat to the environment.* The panel's findings prompted the United States and more than 150 other nations to sign the 1997 Kyoto Protocol calling for a reduction in carbon emissions, which the panel said are emitted primarily by the burning of fossil fuels. Failure to act, the panel warned, would cause polar ice caps and glaciers to melt, coastal regions to flood, disruptions in agriculture and the spread of malaria and other insect-borne diseases.

The United States, with less than 5 percent of the world's population, produces a quarter of global carbon emissions. The protocol mandated that by 2010 the United States cut its carbon emissions by 7 percent below 1990 levels. The United States signed the protocol, but President Bill Clinton never submitted it to the Senate for ratification because of opposition to the mandatory carbon reductions, which the business community said would spell economic disaster.

Shortly after entering the White House, President Bush formally renounced the protocol and retracted his campaign promise to regulate vehicular and industrial carbon dioxide emissions.

In February 2002, Bush offered an alternative approach to curbing greenhouse gas emissions. Instead of mandatory caps, he called on U.S. industries to voluntarily reduce their carbon emissions by 18 percent over the next 10 years. The EPA launched Climate Leaders, a voluntary industry-government partnership in which participating companies would work with the EPA to measure their carbon emissions and set reduction goals. As of August, about 40 companies had joined the program, according to the EPA.

Any hope that the United States would become a leader in combating global warming through mandatory caps died on Aug. 28, when the EPA declared that it had no authority to regulate carbon dioxide emissions. The announcement came in response to a petition filed by environmental groups asking the agency to regulate vehicular carbon dioxide emissions.

"We cannot try to use the Clean Air Act to regulate for climate change purposes because the act was not designed or intended for that purpose," said EPA Assistant Administrator Jeff Holmstead.[11]

U.S. manufacturers, a leading source of carbon emissions, applauded the EPA's action. "The EPA has never found carbon dioxide to be a 'pollutant' as defined under the Clean Air Act," says Marks of the NAM. "Other emissions, such as sulfur dioxide and nitrogen oxides, have been found to create some harm to public health, welfare or the environment. Carbon emissions have shown no such finding."

Like some other industry advocates, Marks says concerns about global warming are misplaced. "Current science does not support the 'sky-is-falling' climate-change rhetoric of various groups," he says.

Reflecting that view, Sen. James M. Inhofe, R-Okla., chairman of the Senate Environment and Public Works Committee, welcomed the Senate's rejection, 55-43, of the McCain-Lieberman bill, calling instead for mandatory caps on emissions of carbon dioxide and other greenhouse gases.

"A majority of the Senate today told the American people that mandatory carbon dioxide reductions are unacceptable, and rightly so," he said after the vote. "The science underlying this bill has been repudiated, the economic costs are far too high, and the environmental benefits are nonexistent."[12] At an earlier hearing, Inhofe had dismissed global warming as "maybe the greatest hoax ever perpetrated on the American people."[13]

But many environmentalists say that denial of the widely accepted evidence that global warming threatens Earth's climate stems from political, not scientific interests. "There is a fairly active right-wing constituency that is working to debunk global warming," says Schaeffer of the Environmental Integrity Project. "That view doesn't have scientific support. The overwhelming majority of scientists think that global warming is a problem and that something needs to be done about it."

In 2001, a National Research Council report tried to remove some of the doubts raised by the climate-change debate in the United States.† "Global warming could well have serious adverse societal and ecological impacts by the end of this century," the authors warned. In fact, they said, the IPCC's projections — which U.S. critics reject as alarmist — may actually understate the global

---

* The IPCC was established by the World Meteorological Organization and the United Nations Environment Program in 1988. The IPCC does not carry out research nor monitor climate-related data. It bases its assessment mainly on peer-reviewed and published scientific/technical literature.

† The council is part of the nonprofit National Academies of Science, which Congress created to provide expert advice on science policy.

threat. "Even in the more conservative scenarios, the models project temperatures and sea levels that continue to increase well beyond the end of this century, suggesting that assessments examining only the next 100 years may well underestimate the magnitude of the eventual impacts."[14]

But industry representatives say even if they accepted the need to curb greenhouse-gas emissions, treating carbon dioxide as a regulated air pollutant because of its climatic impact would make the scope of the Clean Air Act too broad. "If anything that has a potential climatic effect could be regulated under the Clean Air Act, there is virtually no human activity that wouldn't be regulated by the act," says utility-industry advocate Segal. Manufacturing, farming and other human activities release various climate-altering gases like methane and water vapor, he points out, making those activities equally valid candidates for regulation.

"Those other gases don't tap into the popular concern as much as carbon dioxide does, but they are there, and they are extremely valid in terms of the calculus of what causes global warming," he says.

Environmentalists reject Segal's argument, and a coalition of states and environmental groups is suing the EPA over its August decision that it lacks the authority to regulate carbon emissions.

"The Clean Air Act says explicitly that EPA has the authority to regulate any air pollutant that affects health or welfare, and welfare is explicitly defined to include effects on climate," says David Bookbinder, Washington legal director of the Sierra Club. "The administration has gone from saying climate change is not a problem to saying climate change is a problem but it's too late. Now they're saying we can't do anything about it because we have no authority to do anything about it."

"It strikes us as odd that the administration is reading the Clean Air Act in a way to strip it of all authority to

---

Smoggiest U.S. Cities

California cities dominate the list of the 10 smoggiest metropolitan areas in America, according to the American Lung Association. The ratings are based on how often cities' air quality reached unhealthy levels of ozone pollution, according to Environmental Protection Agency data.

1. Los Angeles-Riverside-Orange County, Calif.
2. Fresno, Calif.
3. Bakersfield, Calif.
4. Visalia-Tulare-Porterfield, Calif.
5. Houston-Galveston-Brazoria, Texas
6. Sacramento-Yolo, Calif.
7. Merced, Calif.
8. Atlanta, Ga.
9. Knoxville, Tenn.
10. Charlotte-Gastonia-Rock Hill, N.C.

Source: "State of the Air, 2003," American Lung Association

---

address what many people consider the most pressing environmental threat on the face of the planet."

BACKGROUND

Clean Air Act

The post-World War II economic boom sparked a rise in industrial output, employment and personal income in the United States. It also spread a pall of air pollutants from factory smokestacks and automobile tailpipes that shrouded many of the nation's cities — and even pristine national parks — in smog.[15]

Air pollution threatened more than Americans' quality of life. In October 1948, 20 people died and more than 7,000 were sickened when deadly smog covered the Pennsylvania coal town of Donora. The Donora disaster marked the birth of the clean-air movement in the United States and prompted Congress to pass the first air-quality law in 1955. That year, the U.S. Public Health Service had begun studying the effects of air pollution on human health and found it contributed to chronic lung ailments such as asthma, especially in children and the elderly. The findings prompted Congress to pass the first Clean Air Act in 1963. The law funded research into air pollution's impact and authorized federal, state and local governments to regulate pollutant emissions.

In 1965, lawmakers authorized the Department of Health, Education and Welfare (HEW, the predecessor of today's Department of Health and Human Services) to set the first auto-emissions standards. The rules, which took effect in the 1968 model year, applied to the smog-producing hydrocarbons and carbon monoxide emitted by gasoline engines.

However, few states took on the role of regulating emissions assigned them by the 1963 law, so Congress passed the 1967 Air Quality Act. It authorized HEW to create metropolitan air-quality regions and establish federal pollution standards for the states if they failed to act. By 1970, despite the threat of federal clean-air standards being imposed on them, no state had issued standards for any air pollutant.

To prevent the flight of polluting industries from regulated to unregulated jurisdictions, President Richard M. Nixon (1969-74) proposed "national ambient air-quality standards" (NAAQS) for harmful pollutants. Congress then amended the Air Quality Act, requiring states to devise plans to implement the uniform nationwide standards.

While most states failed to embrace the call to protect air quality, U.S. industry reacted quickly. Automakers denounced the 1968 tailpipe standards as unfair, technologically unfeasible and prohibitively expensive. The industry was especially upset that the Clean Air Act allowed states to set stricter air-quality standards than those set by the federal government.

For example, in an effort to reduce smog in Los Angeles, the nation's most heavily polluted region, California had already adopted auto-emission and fuel standards exceeding the federal specifications.

In the late 1960s, however, public pressure to clean up the environment was mounting faster than industry resistance to regulations. By April 1970, when the first Earth Day was organized, the public was demanding new policies to combat all forms of pollution. Lawmakers responded over the next several years with a series of landmark laws — an updated Clean Air Act, the National Environmental Policy Act, the Clean Water Act and the Endangered Species Act — that formed the basis for national environmental policy.

The Clean Air Act of 1970 — the nation's first major environmental legislation — aimed to bring all areas of the country into compliance with a new set of national air-quality standards. Once the fledgling EPA issued the standards, the states were given nine months to formulate plans for meeting them. "Stationary sources" of air pollution — such as factories, power plants and refineries — had five years to comply with the state plans, plus a two-year grace period if needed.

"Mobile sources" of air pollution — cars, trucks and other modes of transportation — also had five years to meet emissions standards for hydrocarbons and carbon monoxide. They had until 1976 to comply with a new standard for nitrogen oxides (known as NOx), toxic products of fossil-fuel combustion that form ground-level ozone, or smog. To ensure compliance with the new standards, states were required to establish periodic auto inspections.

New Source Review

In 1977, Congress amended the Clean Air Act to include the New Source Review program. Most of the electric-power plants in operation at the time were coal-fired. Many were several decades old and were expected to be replaced soon with more efficient generators fueled by natural gas. To ease the regulatory burden on the older plants, Congress "grandfathered," or exempted, them from the pollution-control standards required of newer plants.

But coal-fired power plants produced more than 90 percent of the utility industry's emissions of sulfur dioxide, nitrogen oxides and mercury. To prevent abuses of the exemption, lawmakers devised the New Source Review provision, requiring grandfathered power plants that made any major modifications to install the best available pollution-control technology.

The 1970 law authorized the EPA to seek injunctions to enforce its mandates and permitted citizens to sue both the agency — for failure to enforce the standards — and polluters for violating them. But the enforcement terms were not enough to ensure timely compliance, and Congress extended the law's original deadlines several times during the 1970s.

Despite the delays, by 1980 the Clean Air Act had already begun to improve U.S. air quality. The law had been expanded over the years to cover six major "criteria" air pollutants considered as threats to human health and the environment — carbon monoxide, lead, nitrogen dioxide, ozone, particulate matter and sulfur dioxide.

To meet the new regulations, industries installed smokestack scrubbers and auto manufacturers installed catalytic converters in new-car exhaust systems to curb carbon monoxide emissions. They were less effective in reducing emissions of nitrogen oxides, however, and smog levels remained high.

Indeed, over the next decade the rapid improvements in air quality made in the 1970s began to slow. Bowing to industry opposition to strict air-quality standards, the administration of President Ronald Reagan (1981-89) oversaw a relaxation of auto-emission standards and enforcement of regulations for factories and power plants.

CHRONOLOGY

1950s-1960s *Congress acts to combat worsening air pollution.*

1955 Congress authorizes the first federal program to study and remedy air pollution, produced mainly by coal-fired plants and vehicle exhaust.

1963 Lawmakers pass the first Clean Air Act, funding research and authorizing states and localities to issue regulations to curb pollutants.

1967 Air Quality Act authorizes the federal government to regulate pollution if the states fail to do so. The first auto emission standards take effect.

1970s-1980s *Growing environmental movement leads to landmark environmental-protection laws.*

December 1970 A sweeping, new Clean Air Act authorizes the government to set air-quality standards for six major pollutants and requires the states to implement them.

1977 Congress amends the Clean Air Act to include the New Source Review program. To ease the regulatory burden on older, coal-fired power plants, the rule exempts them from the pollution-control standards required of newer plants as long as they only perform "routine maintenance" on their equipment.

Sept. 16, 1987 The United States and 23 other countries sign the Montreal Protocol on Substances That Deplete the Ozone Layer, to halt industrial emissions of chlorofluorocarbons (CFCs) and other chemicals that erode the protective stratospheric ozone layer.

1990s *Clinton administration supports clean-air initiatives.*

1990 Amendments to Clean Air Act strengthen the EPA's enforcement authority and introduce market-based incentives to encourage greater industry compliance.

1995 EPA's Ozone Transport Rule aims to reduce the interstate transport of pollutants among 19 Eastern

states and Washington, D.C., by requiring coal-fired plants and other upwind polluters to curb emissions.

1997 Kyoto Protocol calls for mandatory cuts in emissions of "greenhouse gases" thought to cause global warming; U.S. and more than 150 other nations sign the treaty.

Nov. 3, 1999 Justice Department charges dozens of power plants with violating the Clean Air Act's New Source Review provision by not installing pollution-reduction technology when they modernized.

2000s *Bush administration backtracks on clean-air protections.*

Sept. 29, 2000 Then-Gov. George W. Bush, R-Texas, calls for mandatory cuts in industrial emissions during his campaign for the presidency.

March 13, 2001 Bush drops carbon dioxide from the list of pollutants he promised to regulate.

Jan.15, 2002 Justice Department announces that Clinton-era lawsuits to enforce the New Source Review program are based on a proper interpretation of the law.

Feb. 14, 2002 President Bush predicts his "Clear Skies" initiative will lead to a 70 percent reduction in industrial emissions of three major pollutants over 10 years.

Dec. 31, 2002 EPA proposes relaxing New Source Review rules to exempt many coal-fired plants.

Aug 7, 2003 A federal judge in Ohio rules that FirstEnergy's Ohio Edison Co. violated the Clean Air Act by upgrading seven coal-fired plants without installing anti-pollution "scrubbers."

Oct. 30, 2003 Senate rejects a proposal by Sens. John McCain, R-Ariz., and Joseph I. Lieberman, D-Conn., limiting carbon emissions.

Nov. 5, 2003 EPA announces it will likely drop investigations of power plants suspected of violating the Clean Air Act in anticipation of changes in New Source Review rules. Attorneys general of several Northeastern states announce they will pursue the investigations and litigation on their own.

How Electricity Generation Pollutes the Air

Americans tend to take electricity for granted — as the August 2003 blackout reminded some 50 million residents of the Northeast and southern Canada.

"People expect the lights to go on," says Dan Riedinger, spokesman for the Edison Electric Institute, the main utility-industry lobby. "When they flip a switch, they don't want to have to think about it."

But while flipping a switch may seem innocuous enough, Americans' dependence on electrical power has a negative impact on the air they breathe. Fuels used to generate power in the United States are among the biggest contributors to urban smog, soot and acid rain. The sulfur dioxide, nitrogen oxides and particulate matter emitted by many of the nation's 3,170 electric utilities contribute to asthma and other respiratory illnesses, especially in children and the elderly. Utilities also emit mercury, a nerve-damaging, toxic heavy metal that can seep into the nation's waterways and poison fish. Eating the contaminated fish can cause neurological problems in adults and damage the nervous systems of developing fetuses in pregnant women.

About 70 percent of the electricity generated in America comes from the burning of fossil fuels — chiefly coal, petroleum and natural gas. The dirtiest fuel of all is coal, which emits sulfur dioxide, nitrogen oxides and mercury and is used in about 500 older generators that produce more than half of the power in the United States. Most of these coal-fired plants are in the Midwest and a few Southern states, but prevailing winds carry their air pollutants to the heavily populated East Coast.

Coal has always played a leading role in America's electricity generation. But until the mid-1970s, oil was the fuel of choice for many utilities. After 1973, however, when the Organization of Petroleum Exporting Countries (OPEC) embargoed oil exports to the United States, petroleum prices skyrocketed, making cheap, domestically produced coal a more attractive fuel alternative. Today, only a handful of utilities, mostly in the Northeast, burn oil — which now accounts for just 3 percent of total electricity output.

Natural gas has become an attractive, albeit more expensive, alternative for newer utilities and now accounts for 10 percent of all electricity. Although it can't be stockpiled like oil and coal to ensure a steady fuel supply, gas emits much less pollution, making it easier for utilities to comply with Clean Air Act regulations.

Other fuels emit less smokestack pollution than fossil fuels, but some of them pose other threats. A fifth of all electricity in the United States comes from nuclear power plants. While they emit little more than water vapor under normal operations, a malfunctioning nuclear plant could release deadly radioactivity.

Another 10 percent of U.S. power comes from hydro-electric dams, mostly in the West. While dams emit few air pollutants, they disrupt natural river flows and sometimes destroy the habitats of endangered aquatic species. And thus far, utilities have shunned renewable-energy sources — such as biomass, wind power and geothermal power — because they are not as cost-effective as conventional sources. Today, renewable energy sources account for less than 1 percent of U.S. electricity.

1990 Amendments

Acting on proposals by President George H.W. Bush (1989-93), Congress expanded the Clean Air Act to encompass a wider range of air pollutants and introduce innovative, market-based incentives to encourage polluters to reduce some harmful emissions. Bush signed the new Clean Air Act Amendments on Nov. 15, 1990.

After 20 years, the Clean Air Act had measurably improved air quality. New cars, for example, emitted less than half the pollutants of 1960s models. But the rapid increase in the number of cars on the road and — with ever-expanding suburbs — the total miles driven nearly wiped out these advances, especially in many urban areas that continued to endure unhealthy levels of smog.

The 1990 amendments established tighter pollution standards for cars and trucks, limited the sulfur content of diesel fuel and required cleaner-burning, "reformulated" gasoline to be sold in cities with heavy ozone pollution.

The new measures also expanded from seven to 189 the number of toxic pollutants regulated by the act. The

Utilities are unlikely to abandon coal, even when they upgrade their facilities to make them more efficient, because coal is uniquely suited to power generation. "It's a very reliable fuel, people have a lot of experience using it, and we've got lots of supply," says Eric Schaeffer, director of the Rockefeller Family Fund's Environmental Integrity Project. "So coal will continue to have a big role."

Of course, the utility industry isn't solely responsible for the nation's persistent air-pollution problems. Oil refineries, chemical producers and other industries also dirty the air, even though total air pollution has improved since the Clean Air Act took effect in 1970. And cars, trucks and buses emit 71 percent of the nation's pollutants, especially those that contribute to ground-level ozone.

The rapid increase in the number of vehicles on the road over the past three decades has prevented a significant reduction in vehicular pollution, despite the development of technology to cut tailpipe emissions. SUVs, which account for a quarter of new-car sales, are held to more lenient fuel-efficiency standards than cars, and because they consume more fuel than most cars, they also emit more pollutants.[1]

Thus, efforts to develop less-polluting vehicles have yet to have a measurable impact on tailpipe emissions. Pollution-

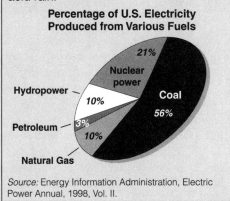

Coal Fuels Most Electric Utilities

More than half of the electricity generated in America is produced from burning coal, a major cause of urban smog, soot and acid rain.

Percentage of U.S. Electricity Produced from Various Fuels

Nuclear power 21%
Coal 56%
Hydropower 10%
Petroleum 3%
Natural Gas 10%

Source: Energy Information Administration, Electric Power Annual, 1998, Vol. II.

free electric cars, introduced to Southern California in 1997 to comply with the state's stringent air-quality standards, failed to capture consumer interest, and automakers have stopped making them.[2] They are focusing instead on building more hybrid cars, which run on a combination of gasoline and electricity. Hybrids emit fewer pollutants than standard, gasoline-powered vehicles and are selling out in many U.S. markets.[3] The ultimate non-polluting vehicle, powered by a hydrogen fuel cell, is still the focus of federally supported research.

"Detroit has done a lot to reduce emissions from individual vehicles, but there are a lot more of them, and more miles are being driven each year," Riedinger says. "There's no question that we in the utility industry have to do our share to curb emissions, but the localities and regions are then going to have to take some additional steps to figure out what else is preventing us from reaching attainment of clean-air standards."

---

[1] For background, see Mary H. Cooper, "SUV Debate," *The CQ Researcher*, May 16, 2003, pp. 449-472.

[2] See Greg Schneider, "The Electric-Car Slide," *The Washington Post*, Oct. 22, 2003, p. E1.

[3] See Cheryl Jensen, "Coming Soon to the Market: A Bumper Crop of Hybrid Cars," *The New York Times*, Aug. 24, 2003, p. A17.

new pollutants, which included carcinogens and chemicals that can cause genetic mutations in developing fetuses, were believed to cause up to 3,000 cancer deaths each year.[16] The amendments required EPA to issue standards to be met by major sources of toxic air pollution, primarily chemical plants, steel mills and petroleum refineries.

The 1990 amendments also expanded regulations for sulfur dioxide, previously regulated as one of the pollutants implicated in urban smog. Formed when

coal and other sulfur-containing fossil fuels are burned, sulfur dioxide readily dissolves in atmospheric water vapor to form acid and falls to Earth in the form of acid precipitation.

More than half the sulfur dioxide emitted in the United States comes from coal-burning electric-power plants, primarily located in the Midwest and the South. Prevailing winds blow contaminated clouds into the Eastern United States and southern Canada, where acid rain has defoliated forests and crops. Over the decades, acid rain also has altered the chemistry of the region's lakes and streams, killing millions of fish and acres of aquatic vegetation.

The Clean Air Act amendments set up an acid rain program that offered incentives to polluting industries to curb their sulfur-dioxide emissions. Companies that reduced their emissions below the target level earned "emissions credits," which could be sold to companies whose emissions exceeded permissible levels. The trading system proved a popular alternative to the traditional regulatory approach: applying universal standards to each source of pollution.

Lawmakers used the traditional regulatory approach, however, to tackle a potentially deadlier environmental threat — a widening hole in the stratospheric ozone layer. Unlike ground-level ozone, or smog, naturally occurring stratospheric ozone forms a layer 10-25 miles above Earth's surface that blocks much of the sun's harmful ultraviolet radiation. After scientists discovered a rapidly expanding hole in that protective ozone layer in the 1970s, health experts warned that exposure to sunlight could damage crops and animals and cause a rise in deadly skin cancer in humans.

The ozone hole, it was discovered, had been caused by industrial emissions of chlorofluorocarbons (CFCs) and halons, chemicals used as refrigerants, solvents and aerosol propellants. On Sept. 16, 1987, the United States and 23 other countries, plus the European Community, signed the Montreal Protocol on Substances That Deplete the Ozone Layer, administered by the U.N. Environment Program (UNEP).

To enable the United States — by far the biggest producer of ozone-depleting chemicals — to comply with the treaty, U.S. manufacturers had to find alternatives to the ozone-depleting substances. Since then, 132 countries have ratified the Montreal Protocol, considered one of the most successful international environmental-protection agreements in force.[17]

Clinton Initiatives

By the mid-1990s, coal-fired utilities were among the country's leading sources of air pollution, accounting for 24 percent of nitrogen oxides, 62 percent of sulfur dioxide, 31 percent of carbon dioxide and a third of the mercury emitted from all U.S. sources.[18] During the Clinton administration, the EPA initiated several enforcement actions, primarily against utilities the agency charged had

modernized coal-fired plants without installing pollution-control technology, in violation of the Clean Air Act's New Source Review provision.

In 1995, a dozen East Coast states petitioned the EPA for help, charging that nitrogen oxide emissions from upwind Midwestern and Southern utilities prevented them from attaining federal ozone standards. Later that year, the agency issued its Ozone Transport Rule, which required upwind polluters to curb their emissions in order to reduce the interstate transport of nitrogen oxides and other pollutants into 19 Eastern states and Washington, D.C. And in 1996, the EPA began investigating utility compliance with the New Source Review provision.

Taken together, these actions focused federal efforts to control ozone depletion and acid rain in the Eastern United States on emissions from the electric-utility industry, mostly in the Midwest and South.

Meanwhile, the industry struck back with a series of lawsuits challenging the New Source Review program. In 1988, the Wisconsin Electric Power Co. (WEPCO) sued the EPA; questioning the agency's finding that WEPCO's plant modifications amounted to more than "routine maintenance" and thus smokestack scrubbers needed to be installed to prevent an increase in emissions.

In 1990, the 7th U.S. Circuit Court of Appeals ruled in *WEPCO v. Reilly* that the EPA had not accurately determined the increase in emissions resulting from the utility's plant changes. But the court agreed with the agency's finding that the utility had undertaken a massive overhaul that went beyond routine maintenance.

Armed with the ruling, the Justice Department filed lawsuits in November 1999 on behalf of the EPA against seven other utilities it alleged had violated the New Source Review provision at 51 power plants. A separate administrative order was filed against the Tennessee Valley Authority (TVA) alleging the nation's largest public electric utility had violated the New Source Review provision at its 11 coal-fired plants as well.

Several of the cases have since been settled, including a February 2000 agreement with Tampa Electric Co. to reduce nitrogen oxide and sulfur dioxide emissions by 85 percent by switching to natural gas and improving pollution controls. Similar settlement agreements were reached later that year with Virginia Electric and Power Co. (now Dominion Virginia Power) and Cinergy Corp. of Cincinnati.[19]

CURRENT SITUATION

Improved Quality

Both sides in the controversy over air-pollution policy acknowledge the Clean Air Act has dramatically improved the nation's air quality. Since 1970, emissions of the six "criteria" air pollutants regulated under the law have fallen by 48 percent while economic output rose 164 percent and energy consumption increased 42 percent.[20]

Since 1980, the utility industry has cut emissions of nitrogen oxides by 30 percent and total emissions of air pollutants by 40 percent, the Edison Electric Institute's Riedinger says. "From 1980 to 2001, sulfur dioxide emissions from power plants dropped 38 percent at the same time that electricity generation increased by 72 percent," he says. "So over time, the Clean Air Act worked very well."

The acid rain program — one of the most effective air-pollution control measures — set the stage for a market in pollution credits and helped sulfur-dioxide-emitting industries improve their pollution-control technology.[21]

Thanks to near-100 percent industry compliance, "the acid rain program is well on the way to achieving its goal of a 50 percent reduction from 1980 sulfur dioxide emissions," says the EPA.

But gaps exist in the nation's progress toward cleaner air. After dropping in the 1980s, smog levels stalled between 1993 and 2002, according to the EPA, despite continued efforts to improve urban air quality. Part of the problem can be traced to the increasingly popular SUVs and other big cars and trucks Americans drive, which burn more fuel and emit more pollutants than the smaller models that dominated the market in the 1980s.[22] Suburban sprawl and inadequate public transportation means drivers are spending more time behind the wheel, further adding to tailpipe emissions.[23]

Smog levels in several Eastern cities also can be traced to power plants in the Midwest and South. As many as 600 plants are 30-50 years old and emit up to 10 times the pollutants of modern plants. Indeed, according to the Sierra Club Clean Air Program, coal-fired power plants account for 96 percent of the sulfur dioxide, 93 percent of the nitrogen oxides, 88 percent of the carbon dioxide and 99 percent of the mercury emitted by the entire electric utility industry.[24] East Coast smog levels are attributed to a combination of both transported nitrogen oxides and tailpipe emissions.

Recent research suggests that ozone triggers health problems in vulnerable individuals at even lower levels than currently reflected in the law. Children with severe asthma, for example, have been found to suffer from shortness of breath and coughing — even when air quality is listed as "good" by EPA standards.[25]

Smog also reduces visibility in many rural areas, such as Great Smoky Mountains National Park on the North Carolina-Tennessee border, and other areas long noted for their pristine beauty. Particulate matter, or soot, from coal-fired power plants lacking scrubbers is largely to blame for the haze that covers many Eastern areas.

Not all air pollution is visible, of course. Like sulfur dioxide, which causes acid rain, the toxic heavy metal mercury, which causes severe nerve damage — mixes with water vapor and falls with rain and snow into rivers and oceans, where it poisons fish and those who consume them. More than 60,000 children are born each year with a risk of nervous-system damage from mercury exposure in the womb, according to the Environmental Integrity Project.[26]

Bush's Agenda

The new president moved quickly to set the tone for his administration's air-quality policy. In March 2001, barely two months into his term, Bush withdrew U.S. support for the Kyoto Protocol. Then he rescinded his campaign pledge to regulate carbon dioxide emissions, saying such regulations would hurt the economy.[27]

"The administration does not believe the government should impose mandatory carbon dioxide emissions reductions on power plants at a time when the cost of energy is soaring in this nation," explained EPA Administrator Christine Todd Whitman. "I agree with the president that we must be very careful not to take actions that could harm consumers."[28]

A year later, on Feb. 14, 2002, Bush introduced his Clear Skies initiative. Citing the success of the market-based acid rain program, he proposed replacing the existing regulatory approach embodied in the Clean Air Act with the cap-and-trade program for sulfur dioxide, nitrogen oxides and mercury. By encouraging rather than forcing power plants to install modern anti-pollution technology, Bush said, Clear Skies would cut emissions of all three pollutants by about 70 percent by 2018.

"This legislation will constitute the most significant step America has ever taken — has ever taken — to cut power plant emissions that contribute to urban smog, acid rain and numerous health problems for our citizens," Bush said.[29]

Then, in a low-profile statement issued while Bush was out of the country, an EPA assistant administrator announced on Nov. 22, 2002, that the administration planned to revise the controversial New Source Review program.[30] The agency said the new rules would raise the amount of pollution allowed from entire facilities (rather than limiting emissions from individual pieces of equipment) and would exempt plants that had installed modern pollution controls from further improvements for 10 years — even if their emissions exceeded the allowable cap. The changes also included a more lenient definition of "routine maintenance" for older plants — allowing them to replace existing equipment without having to install new pollution controls.

On Oct. 27 — the day the new rule was finalized — 12 smog-plagued Eastern and Midwestern states and more than 20 cities sued the EPA, charging that the new rule is both illegal and harmful to regional air quality.

"Our powerful, bipartisan court challenge says to this administration: 'No, you cannot repeal the federal Clean Air Act by dictatorial edict,'" said Connecticut Attorney General Richard Blumenthal. "'Your attempted rollback grants a presidential pardon to power plant polluters who have defied the law year after year.' The rollback is probably the worst, single environmental decision by any administration ever. It leaves the administration without even a fig leaf of credibility on environmental issues."[31]

However, many environmental advocates welcomed another Bush rule change announced in spring 2003. The change is expected to reduce by 95 percent the emissions of pollutants from off-road, diesel-powered engines, a major source of soot and other pollutants that have been

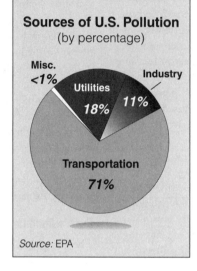

Vehicles Cause Most Air Pollution

More than 70 percent of the 158 million tons of air pollution produced in the United States each year comes from cars, trucks and other vehicles.

Sources of U.S. Pollution
(by percentage)

Misc. <1%
Utilities 18%
Industry 11%
Transportation 71%

Source: EPA

linked to cancer and respiratory disease. The change would bring this class of engines, including bulldozers and tractors, under the same, more stringent standards adopted for trucks and buses under a Clinton-era rule.

Once the low-sulfur diesel fuel needed to comply with the new rules becomes available — production is due to begin in 2007 — the combined rules are expected to greatly reduce nitrogen oxide and soot emissions from diesel engines, preventing an estimated 8,300 premature deaths and 23,000 cases of bronchitis each year.[32]

But the new rules would exempt stationary diesel engines, such as those used for backup generators and compressors for oil and gas wells. Fearing that the administration's support for accelerated domestic oil and gas drilling would increase the number of diesels operating throughout the West, several environmental organizations have asked the EPA to add stationary diesel engines to the new requirements.[33]

Meanwhile, the administration's approach to global warming continues to draw criticism from environmentalists. The 2002 edition of the EPA's annual air-pollution report deleted sections included in earlier reports on U.S. emissions of carbon dioxide and other greenhouse gases.[34]

Former Vice President Al Gore charged that the EPA, in a July 2003 document, had replaced scientific data on global warming with passages prepared by oil-industry analysts. "The White House ordered its own EPA to strip important scientific information about the dangers of global warming out of a public report," Gore charged. "Instead, the White House substituted information that was partly paid for by the American Petroleum Institute."[35]

Gore voiced the growing concern among administration critics that industry was effectively setting environmental policy: "The administration has developed a

Will the president's new policies improve air quality?

YES   President George W. Bush

From Remarks at Detroit Edison Monroe Power Plant,
Monroe, Mich., Sept. 15, 2003

We're in the process of fixing what they call New Source Review regulations. . . . The old regulations . . . undermined our goals for protecting the environment and growing the economy. The old regulations on the books made it difficult to either protect the environment or grow the economy. Therefore, I wanted to get rid of them. I'm interested in job creation and clean air, and I believe we can do both.

One of the things we've got to do is encourage companies to invest in new technologies, convince utilities to modernize their equipment, so that they can produce more energy and pollute less. In other words, as technologies come on, we want to encourage companies to make investment in those technologies.

Yet old regulations, the ones we're changing, actually discourage companies from even making routine repairs and replacing old equipment. That's the reality. Regulations intended to enhance air quality made it really difficult for companies to do that which is necessary to not only produce more energy but to do it in a cleaner way.

Power plants and companies wanted to make one change they could afford. The regulators could come in and order them to change everything, making every change a massive, multi-year battle. That's the reality here at Monroe plant. The people who are trying to modernize this plant and do their job on behalf of the people of Michigan found out that the regulations were so complex that they could be interpreted any different way. And that's what happened. And when you have complex regulations that are open for interpretation, guess what happens? The lawyers come in. And then you have litigation, and then things grind to a standstill.

So a lot of planners and people who were charged with providing electricity and to protect the air decided not to do anything. They didn't want to have to fight through the bureaucracy or fight through the endless lawsuits. And when that happens, fewer power plants are upgraded; they become old and tired — which means people start losing their jobs; which means our economy is not robust so people can find work if they're looking for work; which means in some cases, energy costs are higher than they should be. . . .

There is a lot of debate about the change of New Source Review. It makes sense to change these regulations. It makes sense for the workplace environment; it makes sense for the protection of our air. Not only do I believe that, but union leaders believe that, manufacturers believe that, the utilities believe that, a bipartisan coalition in Congress believes it. . . .

NO   Rep. Earl Blumenauer, D-Ore.

From a House Floor Speech, Sept. 16, 2003

The administration's habit of using misleading language is at its worst with the environment. Their Clear Skies Initiative will actually permit dirtier air. Relaxation of the New Source Review rules will inhibit the intent of the Clean Air Act, which 30 years ago gave a reprieve to the dirtiest coal-fired plants. . . . The New Source Review rules were designed so that when plants modernize, new anti-pollution technology must be put in place. Instead, [they] have kept these aging dinosaurs in use because, simply, they make more money. . . .

Because of the prevailing winds, the pollution is not just in the vicinity of the plant or in the state that allows it to operate. The effects are concentrated, particularly in the New England states. And attorneys general in New York, New Jersey and Pennsylvania, as well as some Midwestern states like Wisconsin and Illinois are lining up to challenge this rule in court.

Yesterday the president was in Michigan to promote his Clear Skies Initiative, but he had the audacity to appear at one of the nation's dirtiest power plants, in Monroe, which is responsible, we are told, for approximately 300 premature deaths each year. . . .

The president attempted to point to this as a jobs-creation issue, but local labor leaders pointed out that when the Monroe plant owner, Detroit Edison, found out that the New Source Review rules were going to be relaxed, they promptly stopped their efforts to install pollution controls required by law and fired 800 union workers who had been installing them. . . .

The pending energy bill should be an opportunity to rectify these problems with cleaner air, reducing the dependence on foreign oil and maybe even protecting the power grid recently proven vulnerable. Instead, we currently have a grab bag of incentives for special interests that shortchanges efficiency, continues reliance on expensive imported foreign oil and delays the day of reckoning for electrical power to clean the air and [for] a more fuel-efficient auto industry.

It is not too late for the administration and the Congress to deal meaningfully with two or three of these items. It is not just protecting the environment and the health of our citizens; it is a matter of long-term economic stability and security at a time when we have almost 140,000 American troops in and around Iraq, in no small measure to secure Middle East oil.

The Bush administration should be straight with the American public about the economic, environmental and security consequences. Rather than a misleading photo-op, we should work for the meaningful environmental progress that America deserves.

highly effective propaganda machine to imbed in the public mind mythologies that grow out of the one central doctrine that all of the special interests agree on, which — in its purest form — is that government is very bad and should be done away with as much as possible — except the parts of it that redirect money through big contracts to industries that have won their way into the inner circle."

After Bush reneged on his promise to regulate greenhouse gases, at least half of the states stepped into the void by enacting caps on carbon emissions, creating registries to track emissions or forcing utilities to diversify their fuels beyond coal.

California has passed the nation's first law mandating curbs on tailpipe emissions of carbon dioxide, which Republican Gov.-elect Arnold Schwarzenegger has pledged to uphold. On the other hand, six states — Alabama, Illinois, Kentucky, Oklahoma, West Virginia and Wyoming — have barred mandatory reductions of greenhouse gases.[36]

In addition to taking the initiative at the state level, 12 states recently joined 14 environmental groups and two cities in a legal effort to force the federal government's hand. The lawsuit, filed Oct. 23, came as an appeal of the EPA's decision to reject an earlier petition seeking to have the agency regulate greenhouse gas emissions from new motor vehicles.[37]

But industry spokesmen argue that the administration's air-quality initiatives, while an improvement over current policy, fall short of their goals. The main focus of their concern continues to be the New Source Review program, despite the administration's relaxation of the standards.

"Are we 100 percent satisfied with everything that was done with these rules?" asks utility industry advocate Segal. "No. We view it as a step in the right direction that was long overdue."

OUTLOOK

Legal Battles

While the Bush administration is altering air-quality regulations through administrative changes, and Congress is considering Bush's Clear Skies proposal and other legislative measures, several pending lawsuits against the Clean Air Act could significantly alter federal policy.

Of the eight lawsuits brought against 51 power plants in 1999 for alleged New Source Review violations, several have been settled out of court. Prosecutors won the government's first litigated case on Aug. 7, when a federal judge in Ohio ruled that FirstEnergy Corp.'s Ohio Edison Co. had illegally upgraded seven coal-fired plants without installing scrubbers.[38]

Another case, involving Dynegy Midwest Generation, Inc., has recently come under intense scrutiny. On Sept. 5, government prosecutors filed a brief with the U.S. District Court for the Southern District of Illinois notifying the court that the administration had changed the New Source Review rules that are the subject of the lawsuit. The brief noted that the rule changes are "prospective only" and insisted that they should have no impact on the case, which is based on the current, more stringent rule.[39]

But critics charge the Justice Department has jeopardized its own case against the utility with the filing. "While the new rule may be prospective, the Justice Department brief has taken away one of the primary arguments in the existing cases," says former EPA enforcement chief Schaeffer. "If you're a lawyer for the government, you always want to argue that the law's requirements are as plain as the nose on your face. By filing that brief, the Justice Department is now arguing that the law is vague and is down to asking the court to accept its interpretation of what amounts to a vague law. Calling the rule change prospective and claiming it won't affect the case is just disingenuous, and they know better."

> **Many lawmakers, including some Republicans, predict that Congress will eventually accept regulations on carbon emissions to address the threat of global warming.**

Schaeffer's prediction proved accurate on Nov. 5, when the EPA announced it would suspend its investigations of 50 power plants suspected of violating the current rule, almost two months before the revised rule is to take effect. The agency also announced that it was considering dropping 13 additional cases that it had already referred to the Justice Department for legal action.[40]

The utility industry, which had long opposed the New Source Review program, welcomed the change. "The new regulations largely reaffirm the government's historic position that the activities for which a number of facilities were sued should be allowed or even encouraged," says Riedinger of the Edison Electric Institute.

In any case, Riedinger says, despite its notoriety, the New Source Review program is a minor component of the Clean Air Act whose weakening will have no adverse impact on pollution levels. "Ten and 20 years from now, you'll see that our emissions will keep coming down," he says. "By no stretch of the imagination are the regulatory changes going to slow air-quality progress."

But environmentalists and officials in states with downwind pollution from many of the plants under investigation expressed outrage at the move. "In 1999, my office formed a partnership with the federal government to reduce air pollution from power plants," said New York Attorney General Eliot Spitzer. "That effort is now at risk because of the EPA's decision . . . to abandon a series of important Clean Air Act cases."[41]

Spitzer called on the agency to hand over its enforcement files to state agencies so they could proceed with the suits. "A federal-state partnership is the best way to enforce air quality laws," he said. "But if the federal government refuses to act to protect citizens, the states must be provided with appropriate information so that they can step forward to do so."

The U.S. Supreme Court is expected to rule early next year on another case that some judicial experts say illustrates a disturbing trend affecting many areas of environmental law. In 2001, the Engine Manufacturers Association, which represents makers of diesel engines, sued California's South Coast Air Quality Management District, challenging the agency's authority to require bus companies and other fleet owners to meet stricter pollution standards than those set by the federal government — a right specifically accorded the states by the Clean Air Act.

Some judicial activists say the lawsuit is just one of a broader assault on federal environmental statutes that conservative legal groups have been advancing in recent years based on constitutional arguments.

"This is part of a more conservative, anti-government trend in the country that is there for everybody to see," says Leslie Carothers, president of the Environmental Law Institute, a research group in New York City. "We have been stewards of a set of laws that have worked very well and that have widespread support. We don't take kindly to seeing advocates come in with these new federalism arguments intended to get courts to undermine those laws by narrowing their reach. And that's what's happening in some of these cases."

Legislative Prospects

Bush has yet to prod Congress to pass his Clear Skies proposal as freestanding legislation. As the measure has languished, lawmakers have introduced several tougher proposals to amend the Clean Air Act.

The Clean Power Act, introduced in 2001 by Sen. Jeffords, would require all power plants, including those exempted under the New Source Review program, to meet the most recent pollution control standards. The measure would allow companies to use emissions trading to meet pollution targets, as long as the trade does not cause higher overall emissions.

The 2003 Clean Air Planning Act — introduced by Sen. Thomas R. Carper, D-Del., and cosponsored by Sens. Lincoln Chafee, R-R.I., John B. Breaux, D-La., and Max Baucus, D-Mont. — attempts to find a middle ground between Clear Skies and the Jeffords bill. Like companion legislation introduced in the House, it would cut power plant emissions of sulfur dioxide, nitrogen oxides and mercury by 80 percent by 2013 while holding carbon dioxide to 2001 levels. The bill also includes a cap-and-trade provision to give power plants flexibility to comply.

Supporters of Clear Skies greeted the Oct. 28 defeat of the McCain-Lieberman proposal to limit U.S. carbon emissions as a chance to reintroduce the president's bill with a major new concession to the utility industry.

"Now that the Senate has rejected economically harmful restrictions on carbon dioxide emissions, it's time to pass the president's Clear Skies initiative, which will provide real public health and environmental benefits to the American people," said Sen. Inhofe, who, with

Sen. George Voinovich, R-Ohio, had introduced the original bill last May.

The new version, introduced on Nov. 10, would allow power plants to emit more toxic mercury than the original Bush proposal. "The Senate made it clear in a bipartisan vote last week that it won't support legislation that cripples businesses and costs American jobs in the name of the environment," Voinovich said.[42]

But the defeat of McCain-Lieberman was not an unqualified victory for opponents of regulating greenhouse gas emissions. Many lawmakers, including some Republicans, voted in favor of the bill, leading some analysts to predict that Congress will eventually accept regulations on carbon emissions to address the threat of global warming.

"Over the next 10 to 15 years, it is imaginable that the United States might engage in some sort of mandatory carbon dioxide control regime," says Schneider of the Clean Air Task Force.

NOTES

1. From a press release, Sept. 15, 2003.

2. For background, see Mary H. Cooper, "Energy and the Environment," *The CQ Researcher*, March 3, 2000, pp. 161-184.

3. "The Bush Administration Air Pollution Plan," Natural Resources Defense Council.

4. For background, see Mary H. Cooper, "Global Warming Treaty," *The CQ Researcher*, Jan. 26, 2001, pp. 41-64.

5. See Eric Pianin, "Senate Rejects Mandatory Cap on Greenhouse Gas Emissions," *The Washington Post*, Oct. 31, 2003, p. A4.

6. Office of Management and Budget, Office of Information and Regulatory Affairs, "Informing Regulatory Decisions: 2003 Report to Congress on the Costs and Benefits of Federal Regulations and Unfunded Mandates on State, Local, and Tribal Entities," October 2003.

7. Marks responded in writing to queries for this report.

8. See Mary Ethridge, Jim Mackinnon and Ed Meyer, "Powerless: Flawed Monitoring System Vulnerable to Blackouts," *Akron Beacon Journal*, Sept. 28, 2003, p. 1A.

9. For more information on the August blackout, see the Office of Electric Transmission and Distribution, Department of Energy, at www.electricity.doe.gov/2003_blackout.htm.

10. See Samuel Goldreich, "Final Deal on Omnibus Energy Bill Hinging on Electricity Regulation," *CQ Weekly*, Sept. 27, 2003, pp. 2352-2353. For background on electricity markets, see Adriel Bettelheim, "Utility Deregulation," *The CQ Researcher*, Jan. 14, 2000, pp. 1-16.

11. Environmental Protection Agency, "EPA Denies Petition to Regulate Greenhouse Gas Emissions from Motor Vehicles," Aug. 28, 2003.

12. Pianin, *op. cit.*

13. Testimony before the Senate Environment and Public Works Committee, Sept. 23, 2003.

14. National Research Council, Climate Change *Science: An Analysis of Some Key Questions* (2001), p. 4.

15. For background, see Mary H. Cooper, "New Air Quality Standards," *The CQ Researcher*, March 7, 1997, pp. 193-216.

16. Environmental Protection Agency, "The Clean Air Act Amendments of 1990," www.epa.gov/oar/caa/overview.txt.

17. For more information, see the United Nations Environment Program, unep.org/ozone.

18. See Larry B. Parker and John E. Blodgett, "Air Quality and Electricity: Initiatives to Increase Pollution Controls," CRS Report for Congress, Congressional Research Service, Oct. 25, 2003.

19. *Ibid.*

20. Environmental Protection Agency, "Latest Findings on National Air Quality: 2002 Status and Trends," August 2003.

21. Environmental Protection Agency, "Air Quality Improving According to 2002 Trends Report and Acid Rain Data," press release, Sept. 15, 2003.

22. For background, see Mary H. Cooper, "SUV Debate," *The CQ Researcher*, May 16, 2003, pp. 449-472.

23. For background, see Mary H. Cooper, "Saving Open Spaces," *The CQ Researcher*, Nov. 5, 1999, pp. 953-976.

24. Sierra Club Clean Air Program, "Power Plant Facts," 2002, www.savethecleanairact.org.

25. Janneane Gent *et al.*, "Association of Low-Level Ozone and Fine Particles With Respiratory Symptoms in Children With Asthma," *Journal of the American Medical Association*, Oct. 8, 2003, pp. 1859-1867.

26. Environmental Integrity Project, "Power Plant Emissions and Your Health: Frequently Asked Questions."

27. For background, see Mary. H. Cooper, "Bush and the Environment," *The CQ Researcher*, Oct. 25, 2002, pp. 865-888.

28. Whitman addressed the administration's climate-change policy on March 16, 2001.

29. Bush announced his proposal on Feb. 14, 2002, in a speech at the National Oceanic and Atmospheric Administration in Silver Spring, Md.

30. See Matthew L. Wald, "E.P.A. Says It Will Change Rules Governing Industrial Pollution," *The New York Times*, Nov. 23, 2002, p. A1.

31. From a statement, Oct. 27, 2003.

32. Environmental Protection Agency, "Fuel Suppliers Prepared to Meet Future Low-Sulfur Diesel Requirements," Oct. 29, 2003.

33. See Theo Stein, "Eco-Group Threatens Lawsuit over Diesel Fumes," *USA Today*, Aug. 15, 2003, p. 17A.

34. EPA, "Latest Findings," *op. cit.*

35. From a speech at New York University, Aug. 7, 2003.

36. See Marc Sandalow and Zachary Coile, "Tough Choices on D.C. Junket; Schwarzenegger Must Decide Whose Side He's On," *San Francisco Chronicle*, Oct. 26, 2003, p. A1.

37. See Brian Stempeck, "Climate Change: Twelve States Appeal EPA Decision on GHG Emissions," *Greenwire*, Oct. 23, 2003.

38. See Eric Pianin, "EPA Rule Revisions Roil U.S. Case Against Power Plant," *The Washington Post*, Oct. 6, 2003, p. A8.

39. *United States of America v. Illinois Power Company and Dynegy Midwest Generation*, "Plaintiff's Reply to Defendants' Proposed Findings of Fact and Conclusions of Law (Liability Phase)," filed Sept. 5, 2003, p. 3.

40. See Christopher Drew and Richard A. Oppel Jr., "Lawyers at E.P.A. Say It Will Drop Pollution Cases," *The New York Times*, Nov. 6, 2003, p. A1.

41. From a statement, Nov. 6, 2003.

42. "Inhofe, Voinovich Introduce Revised Clear Skies Legislation," Senate Environment and Public Works Committee, epw.senate.gov, Nov. 10, 2003.

BIBLIOGRAPHY

Books

Freese, Barbara, *Coal: A Human History*, Perseus Publishing, 2003.
The most abundant fossil fuel produced in the U.S. comes at a high cost in human life from air pollution.

Weart, Spencer R., *The Discovery of Global Warming*, Harvard University Press, 2003.
Evidence that greenhouse gases are changing the climate has won widespread recognition only in recent decades.

Articles

Anselmo, Joseph C., "Energy Overhaul: Not Much Difference After a Decade," *CQ Weekly*, Nov. 8, 2003, p. 2750.
The administration's energy plan, drawn up by an industry-dominated task force headed by Vice President Dick Cheney, emphasizes increased domestic production of coal, oil and natural gas.

Easterbrook, Gregg, "Air Condition: Bush, Pollution and Hysteria," *The New Republic*, July 1, 2002.
The author criticizes Democrats and environmentalists for overstating the importance of the Clean Air Act's New Source Review provision.

Kolbert, Elizabeth, "Clouding the Air," *The New Yorker*, Sept. 29, 2003, p. 37.
President Bush's call for approval of his Clear Skies bill outside a Michigan power plant known for its high pollution levels constituted the latest assault on the 30-year federal campaign to improve air quality.

Krugman, Paul, "Every Breath You Take," *The New York Times*, Nov. 26, 2002, p. A27.
The Bush administration's New Source Review revisions suggest "the beginning of a new era of environmental degradation."

Whitman, Christine Todd, "Greens Just Keep Singing the Blues," *The Washington Post*, June 28, 2003, p. A25.
A day after resigning as EPA administrator Whitman defended the Bush administration's environmental record.

Reports and Studies

Paltsev, Sergey, *et al.*, "Emissions Trading to Reduce Greenhouse Gas Emissions in the United States: The McCain-Lieberman Proposal," MIT Joint Program on the Science and Policy of Global Change, June 2003.
The report analyzes the cap-and-trade provisions of the proposed 2003 Climate Stewardship Act and estimates regulating carbon emissions could cost between $20 and $350 per household by 2020.

Clean Air Task Force, "Unfinished Business: Why the Acid Rain Problem Is Not Solved," October 2001.
Although an innovative program has reduced acid rain, defoliated trees and lifeless rivers still trouble the Northeast.

Environmental Integrity Project, "Reform or Rollback? How EPA's Changes to New Source Review Affect Air Pollution in 12 States," July 28, 2003.
An environmental group reports the proposal to relax the New Source Review program would allow emissions to increase by almost 1.6 million tons in 12 states.

Environmental Protection Agency, "Draft Report on the Environment 2003," June 23, 2003.
The last major report issued before Christine Todd Whitman resigned as EPA administrator left out all mention of global warming and estimated major pollutants had declined by 25 percent since 1970.

Environmental Protection Agency, "Initial Results of Updated Clear Skies Analysis," July 2, 2003.
The administration's proposal to alter the Clean Air Act would provide "substantial benefits to the public at a reasonable cost," the agency reports.

Environmental Protection Agency, "Latest Findings on National Air Quality: 2002 Status and Trends," August 2003.
The EPA revised its June estimate (see above) of pollution reductions since passage of the Clean Air Act, from 25 percent to 48 percent.

Environmental Protection Agency, "The Plain English Guide to the Clean Air Act," (www.epa.gov).
This undated Web document provides a useful overview of the Clean Air Act's history as well as the health impact of air pollution.

U.S. Department of Justice, Environment and Natural Resources Division, "Fiscal Year 2002 Summary of Litigation Accomplishments."
A summary of the alleged civil and criminal violations of the Clean Air Act pursued by Justice Department lawyers on behalf of the EPA.

World Health Organization, "Climate Change and Human Health — Risks and Responses," 2003.
The U.N. health agency warns of "major, and largely unfamiliar" impacts of global warming on human health.

For More Information

Clean Air Task Force, 77 Summer St., 8th Floor, Boston, MA 02110; (617) 292-0234; www.catf.us. A nonprofit organization dedicated to restoring healthy environments through research, education and advocacy.

Edison Electric Institute, 701 Pennsylvania Ave., N.W., Washington, DC 20004-62696; (202) 508-5024; www.eei.org. The main trade association for shareholder-owned electric companies.

Electric Reliability Coordinating Council, www.electricreliability.org. A coalition of utilities and other industries created to oppose EPA enforcement of New Source Review rules.

Energy Information Administration, 1000 Independence Ave. S.W., Washington, DC 20585; (202) 586-8800; www.eia.doe.gov. An Energy Department branch that provides data on energy sources and consumption.

Environmental Integrity Project, 919 18th St., N.W., Suite 975, Washington, DC 20006; (202) 296-8800; www.environmentalintegrity.org. A nonpartisan organization established in 2002 to advocate for more effective enforcement of environmental laws.

Intergovernmental Panel on Climate Change (IPCC), World Meteorological Organization, 7bis Avenue de la Paix, C.P. 2300, CH- 1211 Geneva 2, Switzerland; +41-22-730-8208; www.ipcc.ch. The U.N. group assesses data on global warming.

National Association of Manufacturers, 1331 Pennsylvania Ave., N.W, Washington, DC 20004-1790; (202) 637-3000; www.nam.org. The NAM supports the administration's proposed changes to the Clean Air Act.

Natural Resources Defense Council, 40 West 20th St., New York, NY 10011; (212) 727-2700; www.nrdc.org. The environmental advocacy group opposes changes to the Clean Air Act.

Sierra Club, 85 Second St., 2nd Floor, San Francisco, CA 94105; (415) 977-5500; www.sierraclub.org. The environmental organization is a party to suits seeking to force compliance with the Clean Air Act.

U.S. Environmental Protection Agency (EPA), Ariel Rios Bldg., 1200 Pennsylvania Ave., N.W., Washington, DC 20460; (202) 272-0167; www.epa.gov. An independent agency that enforces the Clean Air Act and other federal environmental laws.

11

Civil Liberties Debates

Kenneth Jost

Terrorism suspect José Padilla, a U.S. citizen, has been held incommunicado for 16 months in a Navy brig in Charleston, S.C., as an "enemy combatant." He has not been charged with a crime but has had no access to lawyers or family members. Critics of the Bush administration's war on terrorism say such detentions violate civil and constitutional rights.

From *The CQ Researcher*, October 24, 2003.

Top government officials trumpeted the arrest of José Padilla in May 2002 as a major coup in the war on terrorism. The one-time Chicago gang member and convert to Islam allegedly conspired with a leader of the al Qaeda terrorist network to build and detonate a radioactive bomb in the United States, possibly Washington, D.C.

"We have significantly disrupted a potential plot," Attorney General John Ashcroft told a news briefing on June 10. Padilla, a U.S. citizen, had been arrested on May 8 as he arrived in Chicago — carrying $10,000 in cash — after a flight from Pakistan via Egypt and Switzerland.

More than a year later, however, Padilla, also known as Abdullah al-Muhajir, embodies what many critics of the Bush administration view as the dark side of the war on terrorism: a disregard for civil and constitutional rights.

Padilla has been held incommunicado in a Navy brig in Charleston, S.C., under an order signed by President Bush as commander-in-chief designating him as an "enemy combatant" — in effect, as a captured enemy soldier. Padilla has not been charged with a crime, but for the past 16 months he has had no access to lawyers or family members: no visits, no telephone calls, no letters.

"It's not justice. It's the absence of justice," said Donna Newman, one of two New York City lawyers representing Padilla. "It's a void of rights. It's a black hole."[1]

Newman and co-counsel Andrew Patel have been fighting since June 2002 to win Padilla's release from military custody through a habeas corpus action. They won a partial victory in December 2002

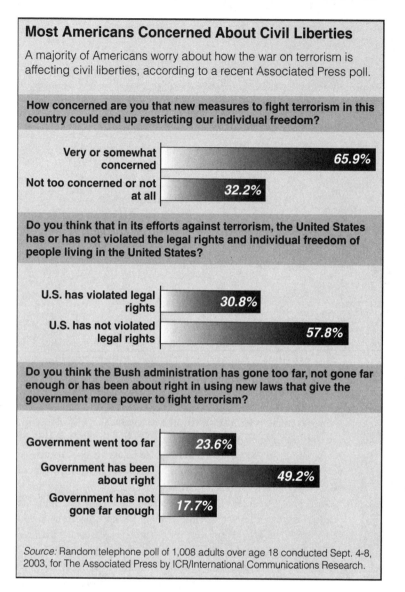

Most Americans Concerned About Civil Liberties

A majority of Americans worry about how the war on terrorism is affecting civil liberties, according to a recent Associated Press poll.

How concerned are you that new measures to fight terrorism in this country could end up restricting our individual freedom?

Very or somewhat concerned — **65.9%**

Not too concerned or not at all — **32.2%**

Do you think that in its efforts against terrorism, the United States has or has not violated the legal rights and individual freedom of people living in the United States?

U.S. has violated legal rights — **30.8%**

U.S. has not violated legal rights — **57.8%**

Do you think the Bush administration has gone too far, not gone far enough or has been about right in using new laws that give the government more power to fight terrorism?

Government went too far — **23.6%**

Government has been about right — **49.2%**

Government has not gone far enough — **17.7%**

Source: Random telephone poll of 1,008 adults over age 18 conducted Sept. 4-8, 2003, for The Associated Press by ICR/International Communications Research.

"critically compromising the military's efforts to obtain vital intelligence." The case — *Padilla v. Rumsfeld* — is now set for argument before the 2nd U.S. Court of Appeals in New York on Nov. 17.

Padilla's detention is only one of a long list of government moves since the Sept. 11, 2001, terrorist attacks that critics say are compromising the individual rights — of both citizens and foreigners — protected by the U.S. Constitution:

- The government rounded up more than 750 Arab residents, the so-called 9/11 detainees, and refused to release their names. It held many of them for weeks or months and deported hundreds after secret immigration hearings — all without charging any in connection with the attacks.

- Congress passed and Bush signed a sweeping law — the USA Patriot Act — enlarging the government's powers to conduct electronic surveillance or obtain personal records not only in terrorism cases but also in other criminal investigations.[2]

- The Justice Department broadened the FBI's discretion to conduct surveillance on domestic organizations, even as the Patriot Act made it easier for the CIA to share information with the FBI or other domestic law enforcement agencies.

- Some 660 foreigners captured in Afghanistan as "enemy combatants" are being held at Guantanamo Naval Base in Cuba without charges, access to lawyers or any form of judicial review, while the government plans military trials critics say will provide few procedural rights. Two cases challenging the detentions are pending before the U.S. Supreme Court.

- Besides Padilla, two other men are being held incommunicado at the Charleston brig as "enemy

when U.S. District Judge Michael Mukasey ordered the government to allow Padilla to meet with one or both of the lawyers.

Padilla's right to contest his detention "will be destroyed utterly if he is not allowed to consult with counsel," Mukasey, chief federal judge for the Southern District of New York, wrote in a 102-page opinion.

However, the government balked at even that limited step. In an appeal, the Justice Department contends that allowing enemy combatants access to lawyers would risk

combatants"; one of them is a U.S. citizen: Yasser Hamdi, captured in Afghanistan while fighting for the Taliban regime. His case is now pending before the Supreme Court.*

U.S. officials insist the moves are both effective and constitutional. "We are winning the war on terror," Ashcroft said in a series of speeches in August and September aimed at rebutting criticism of the administration's tactics.

"We are safer" today than before Sept. 11, Assistant Attorney General Daniel Bryant remarked, "without having sacrificed any of our constitutional liberties and traditions."[3]

Civil liberties advocates disagree on both counts. "Since Sept. 11, there has been a steady assault on many fundamental liberties in the name of fighting terrorism but in ways that have nothing at all to do with catching terrorists," says Kate Martin, executive director of the Center for National Security Studies in Washington.

"I worry that in the name of fighting terrorism we haven't done some of the things that could be effective and, instead, are doing some things that will do much more harm than good," says Elliot Mincberg, vice president and legal director of People for the American Way.[4]

Independent legal experts have mixed views about the impact the administration's anti-terrorism tactics have had on civil liberties. Some, like Stuart Taylor, a veteran legal-affairs writer and columnist for *National Journal,* says the civil libertarians' warnings are "at best shrill and overblown and at worst flat-out false."

Other experts, however, lambaste the administration's broad claims that it can act unilaterally in secret and without normal judicial review. "They cut out the courts, they cut out defense counsel, they cut out the press, they cut out the public generally," says Stuart Schulhofer, a professor at New York University Law School and author of a report on the issues for the Century Foundation. "This is not a good prescription for effective government."[5]

So far, legal challenges to the administration's actions have proved fruitless. Suits by civil liberties advocates

failed to open the secret immigration hearings for the 9/11 detainees or even to force the administration to identify those being held. (*See sidebar, p. 252.*) A federal appeals court upheld the government's incommunicado detention of Hamdi earlier this year. In his ruling in the Padilla case, Mukasey also upheld the government's power to hold enemy combatants but reserved a limited role for courts to review the basis for the detentions.

Somewhat surprisingly, Congress has proven to be a bit more responsive to civil liberties concerns. With a measure of bipartisan support, Congress derailed proposals for a national identification card, killed a plan to ask the general public to report suspicious activities and stymied another plan for scanning computer databases to try to identify suspected terrorists.

"When we think about the greatest civil liberties victories since 9/11, most have come from Congress," says Jeffrey Rosen, an associate professor at George Washington University Law School in Washington and legal-affairs editor for *The New Republic.*

Many previous episodes have tested Americans' support for civil liberties in the face of security threats, both domestic and international. Political dissidents were subjected to surveillance, investigation and, in some cases, prosecution during and after both of the 20th century's world wars, much of the Cold War and the domestic upheavals of the 1960s and '70s. Ethnic Germans were harassed during World War I, while 110,000 persons of Japanese ancestry — most of them U.S. citizens — were forced into internment camps during World War II.

The government's roundup of Muslims and Arabs strikes many critics as a repetition of episodes now widely acknowledged as shameful. "We've targeted the liberties of foreign nationals, and especially Arabs and Muslims," says David Cole, a professor at Georgetown University Law Center in Washington.[6]

Most observers, however, say any infringements on civil liberties in the current war on terrorism are less severe than those of the past. "We [may] come to regret some of the laws and technologies established after Sept. 11," Rosen says. "But I don't think any of them compare to the excesses committed after the previous wars."

The administration and its supporters counter all of the criticisms with one overarching fact: the absence of any repeat of a 9/11-type terrorist incident. "Another major victory is that we've gone two-plus years, and it hasn't happened again," says Paul Rosenzweig, senior legal research

---

* The third person being held as an enemy combatant in the brig in Charleston is Ali Saleh Kahlah al-Marri, a Qatari who lived in Peoria, Ill. Prosecutors said he had more than 1,000 credit-cards in files on his laptop computer along with oaths to protect al Qaeda leader Osama bin Laden, photos of the 9/11 attacks and files detailing weaponry and dangerous chemicals.

fellow at the Heritage Foundation and an adjunct professor at George Mason University Law School in Fairfax, Va. "We can be pretty darn happy that the Golden Gate Bridge is still standing, Mount Rushmore is still there, the Arch in St. Louis hasn't been bombed."

Critics, however, are less inclined to credit the administration with having prevented any new terrorist attacks. "It is as if I say I have an elephant gun in my office and there are no elephants in my office, therefore the gun has been successful," said Laura Murphy, Washington office director for the American Civil Liberties Union (ACLU). "We cannot protect the American people by military might and increased law enforcement powers alone."[7]

As the country struggles with liberty and security issues, here are some of the major questions being debated:

Are parts of the Patriot Act unconstitutional?

Congress wasted little time after the 9/11 attacks in overwhelmingly approving new law enforcement powers in the fight against terrorism when it passed the Patriot Act in October 2001. Less than two years later, however, a solid bipartisan majority in the House of Representatives voted to bar funding for one of the act's provisions broadening the government's power to conduct so-called "sneak and peek" searches with delayed notification to the subjects of the investigations.

"This is the first of a whole group of assaults we are going to launch on the Patriot Act," said Rep. C. L. "Butch" Otter, R-Idaho, before the House voted 309-118 to approve the prohibition as part of the Justice Department appropriations bill. "It was built in a day,"

Inspector General Criticizes 9/11 Detentions

After the Sept. 11, 2001, terrorist attacks, federal agents searching for terrorists in the United States arrested hundreds of foreign nationals — mostly Arab and Muslim men.

In New York City, an Egyptian cabdriver with an expired visa was arrested carrying pictures of the World Trade Center. He was held for five months and then released.

In Louisville, 40 Mauritanians were detained because one of them was rumored to be taking flying lessons. Four were charged with overstaying their visas and held in jail for more than a month.[1]

Most of the detainees were jailed for months in federal detention centers on immigration violations but were never charged with crimes. Immigration violators are not automatically granted legal counsel, so many detainees had trouble retaining lawyers. Secret hearings determined their fate, and because the government refused to disclose their whereabouts, frantic relatives struggled to find them.

The government also detained terrorism suspects on minor criminal violations. Two Somali men were stopped in Texas for carrying a fake ID and a pocketknife one-quarter inch longer than legal. They were released the next day.[2]

The Department of Justice (DoJ) claimed the detentions were vital to national security. "Taking suspected terrorists in violation of the law off the streets and keeping them locked up is our clear strategy to prevent terrorism within our borders," Attorney General John Ashcroft said six weeks after 9/11.[3]

But a report on the detention of 762 illegal aliens by the DoJ's inspector general in the 11 months following Sept. 11 sharply criticized Justice Department tactics.

The report found "significant problems in the way the detainees were handled." Some were beaten while incarcerated. In other instances, the government violated immigration policy by failing to promptly tell the detainees why they were being held.[4]

"People were denied access to lawyers; they were beaten up in jail and held in abusively harsh conditions when they weren't ever even charged with a crime," says Kate Martin, director of the Center for National Security Studies.

In fact, none of the detainees were ever charged with crimes related to Sept. 11, writes Georgetown University law Professor David Cole in a new book about civil liberties and terrorism, and only two or three proved to have any terrorism ties, such as donating money to organizations with links to terrorists.[5]

According to the inspector general, the government cast too wide a net. "The FBI should have taken more care to distinguish between aliens whom it actually suspected of having a connection to terrorism from those aliens who, while possibly guilty of violating federal immigration law, had no connection to terrorism but simply were encountered in connection with an investigative lead," the report said.

The report also criticized the government's "hold until clear" policy, which kept immigrants behind bars longer

Otter continued. "We're going to have to tear it down piece by piece."[8]

Bush administration officials appeared likely to win support in the Senate for stripping out the provision and hinted at a presidential veto if it stayed in the bill. But the legislative maneuver highlights the growing controversy around many of the Patriot Act's provisions for expanded law enforcement powers.

Critics contend a number of the act's provisions — including the sneak-and-peek provision, Section 213 — broaden the government's powers so much as to violate the Fourth Amendment's restrictions on law enforcement searches and surveillance. (*See box, p. 261.*) "The Patriot Act went too far, too fast in taking away basic checks and balances on government surveillance and other law enforcement powers," says Timothy Edgar, legislative counsel in the ACLU's Washington office.[9]

The administration insists that the provisions enlarge law enforcement powers only marginally and fully satisfy constitutional standards. "We must be better equipped to strike hard blows against terrorism," Bryant says. "At the same time, however, the Justice Department is committed to honoring and strengthening constitutional liberty so that we will not strike foul blows."[10]

Besides the sneak-and-peek provision, one other section of the law has been the principal target of opponents: Section 215, which makes it easier for the government to obtain personal records held by so-called "third parties" without notice to the subject of the search. The section has been dubbed the "angry librarian" provision because it

---

than necessary because overworked FBI agents often took months to clear detainees of any terrorism ties.

"The government's use of immigration laws as a pretext for holding people indefinitely turned out to be a terrible policy for civil liberties," says Timothy Edgar, legislative counsel for the American Civil Liberties Union (ACLU). "Immigration law is not the detention of aliens statute; it's the statute that allows the government to remove people from the country." Normally, immigration detainees are held for a day or two, not months, Edgar adds.

The inspector general's report outlined 21 recommendations for improving immigration detentions, including streamlining the FBI clearance process, clarifying the rights of detainees and improving jail conditions.

The Justice Department said it was implementing some of the recommendations.[6] But Barbara Comstock, a DoJ spokeswoman, said, "We make no apologies for finding every legal way possible to protect the American public from further terrorist attacks."[7]

Last month, the inspector general said the Justice Department was addressing many of its concerns but that "significant work remains before the recommendations are fully implemented."

Some legal experts say the government has a right to detain immigrants suspected of being terrorists. "The inspector general did not find any actual rights violations, nor did he question the legal authority of the government to detain people. He just questioned the way the detentions were carried out," says Heather Mac Donald, a fellow at the conservative Manhattan Institute, a think tank.

Mac Donald also says that national-security issues trump concerns over civil rights: "The government was doing what was perfectly appropriate to protect the security of the country, which is its paramount duty, and without which, nothing else matters."

A leading architect of the administration's anti-terrorism policies, however, now acknowledges the government overstepped its bounds. "The [inspector general's] report was a very dramatic wake-up call," says Viet Dinh, the author of the USA Patriot Act who served as assistant attorney general under Ashcroft for two years until returning to Georgetown University Law Center in Washington as a professor in summer 2003. "The Department of Justice rightly said, 'We regret the mistakes, and we are taking steps to rectify them.'"

— Benton Ives-Halperin

[1] Human Rights Watch, *Presumption of Guilt*, August 2002, pp. 13-14.

[2] *Ibid.*

[3] National Public Radio, "Weekend All Things Considered," Oct. 27, 2001.

[4] U.S. Department of Justice, Office of Inspector General, "The September 11 Detainees: A Review of the Treatment of Aliens Held on Immigration Charges in Connection With the Investigation of the September 11 Attacks," April 29, 2003. www.usdoj.gov/oig

[5] David Cole, *Enemy Aliens* (2003), p. 22.

[6] Richard B. Schmitt and Richard A. Serrano, "U.S. Finds Abuses of 9/11 Detainees," *Los Angeles Times*, June 3, 2003, p. A1.

[7] Eric Lichtblau, "Ashcroft Defends Detentions as Immigrants Recount Toll," *The New York Times*, June 4, 2003, p. A23.

could be used to obtain records of a person's library borrowings. But it also applies to a person's financial or medical records — or, in the act's terms, "any tangible thing." The provision allows the government to obtain the records by certifying to a special, secret federal court that the investigation is terrorism-related. And it provides for no notice to the person whose records are being sought and prohibits anyone holding the records from divulging the government's request for them.

The provision "violates the Fourth Amendment because it allows the government to obtain a vast array of personal records about any person in the United States without first establishing probable cause that the target has done anything wrong," says Ann Beeson, an ACLU lawyer. She is representing six Arab-American and Islamic organizations in a federal court suit in Detroit challenging the constitutionality of the provision.[11]

"These charges are nonsense," writes Heather Mac Donald, a senior fellow with the Manhattan Institute, a New York City-based conservative think tank. "Critics of Section 215 deliberately ignore the fact that any request for items under the section requires judicial approval."[12]

Beeson says the provision also violates the First and Fourth Amendments by "gagging" anyone from talking about the search and barring notice to the target. But Mac Donald says those restrictions are "crucial for the Justice Department's war-making function."

Justice Department officials say the provision changes existing law only slightly because the government already had the power to obtain personal records through a grand jury subpoena. Some independent experts agree at least in part. "Critics have certainly distorted [Section 215] in suggesting that it completely changes the legal landscape," Rosen says.

Beeson points out, however, that the new law allows the federal secret court to use a lower standard of evidence to approve a records search than is generally required by grand juries. Moreover, she notes, the secrecy surrounding the records searches — notably the gag rule — is new legal landscape.

Rosen acknowledges that the act makes "troubling" changes in previous practices — most significantly by imposing the gag rule. "That degree of opacity is something the government hasn't sought before," he says. "It seems hard to justify."

Ashcroft announced in September that the government, in fact, has never used the new section. "We're relieved that it hasn't been used," Beeson says, "but we don't have any reason to believe the attorney general won't start using it tomorrow."

Should Congress give the government additional powers in anti-terrorism cases?

On the eve of the second anniversary of the 9/11 attacks President Bush called for new legislation to strengthen the government's hand against terrorists. In Sept. 10 remarks to the FBI Training Academy in Quantico, Va., Bush asked for legislation to deny bail to suspected terrorists and broaden the death penalty for terrorism-related offenses.

Most controversially, the president said the government should be able to obtain records in terrorism investigations with "administrative subpoenas" issued by federal law enforcement agencies rather than judicial subpoenas issued by courts.

Bush pointed out that administrative subpoenas are used in "a wide range of criminal and civil matters," including health-care fraud. "If we can use these subpoenas to catch crooked doctors," Bush said, "the Congress should allow law enforcement officials to use them in catching terrorists."[13]

Bush's proposal was more limited than a draft bill circulated by the Justice Department in early January 2003 but later disavowed. That 120-page proposal included provisions to bar the release of information about persons detained in terrorism investigations, create a DNA database on suspected terrorists and allow the government to strip someone of U.S. citizenship for supporting a terrorist organization.[14]

Despite the limited agenda, Bush's proposal drew fire from civil libertarians and skepticism even from leading Republicans on Capitol Hill. Anthony Romero, the ACLU's executive director, said in a press release that it was "unfortunate" that Bush had used the 9/11 anniversary to "continue to endorse the increasingly anti-civil liberties policies" of the Justice Department. Meanwhile, Senate Judiciary Committee Chairman Orrin Hatch, R-Utah, said it was unlikely that any proposals would be enacted this year.[15]

Administrative subpoenas are already used in some federal law enforcement contexts, but typically in regulatory-type cases where government attorneys consider civil penalties as well as criminal prosecutions. Assistant Attorney General Bryant says allowing their use in terrorism investigations would save government the time and trouble of finding a judge to authorize the subpoena.

"It comes down to a question of speed," Bryant says. "If we're going to prevent a terrorist episode, speed is of the essence."

Advocates on the left and the right say the administration has not made the case for the change. "Where is the need to not have a little bit of independent check by the judicial branch?" says Mincberg of People for the American Way. "That independent check is very important."

The Heritage Foundation's Rosenzweig is also unenthusiastic. "Administrative subpoenas are rare in situations where the tools available to the government are exclusively criminal in nature," he says. "Before accepting this proposed change, I would want more data and more information as to their actual practical necessity."

But columnist Taylor goes even further than the administration proposals, calling for a "systematic reassessment" of civil liberties rules that limit the government's powers to investigate terrorism and hold suspected terrorists. Writing in *The Brookings Review* in January 2003, Taylor specifically proposed easing the rules on search warrants in terrorism cases and permitting "coercive" interrogation or "preventive detention" of suspected terrorists if necessary to prevent a terrorist attack.[16]

Of the three proposals, preventive detention appears to be the one most likely to draw serious consideration. Taylor argued that the administration already is effectively exercising a preventive-detention power by holding suspected terrorists as "enemy combatants" or as "material witnesses" under existing federal law. He noted that civil liberties groups had accused the administration of misusing the material-witness statute and argued that a carefully drawn preventive-detention law could provide greater protection for individual liberties than existing practices.

Mincberg agrees — up to a point. "I support the idea . . . so that the president and Congress can debate it and make a conscious decision as to whether it's appropriate," he says. "We may well decide that it's not appropriate, but the advantage is that it brings the issue out in the open."

Rosenzweig is openly supportive. "Instead of using existing laws on an ad hoc and inappropriate basis, we would have a law more suitably targeted to those very few situations where it would be appropriate," he says. "Great Britain has such a law, and it hasn't diminished the level of civil liberties there."

AFP Photo/Peter Muhly

U.S. Army MPs take a terrorist suspect detained at the U.S. Naval Base in Guantanamo Bay, Cuba, to an interrogation facility.

Taylor's proposal would allow what he called a "preventive search or wiretap" of anyone whom the government has reasonable grounds to suspect of preparing or helping others prepare for a terrorist attack. On interrogation, he says law enforcement agents should be allowed to use "psychological coercion short of torture or brutality" if necessary to prevent a terrorist attack — even if the statements might be inadmissible in a criminal prosecution.

Rosenzweig endorses both suggestions. "If we have more significant needs than criminal punishment, we can forgo the criminal punishment for purposes of saving a million lives," he says.

Mincberg disagrees, particularly about coercive interrogation. "Once you allow what is explicitly considered coercive, the line between that and physical and mental torture is an awfully thin line," he says.

Is the administration misusing the power to detain "enemy combatants"?

The Bush administration has strongly defended its treatment of the 660 foreigners captured in Afghanistan and

POW vs. enemy combatant

held since early 2002 as "enemy combatants" at the U.S. naval base at Guantanamo Bay, Cuba. But, departing from its usual practice of confidentiality, inspectors from the International Committee of the Red Cross (ICRC) have strongly criticized the legal basis for and the mental-health effects of the protracted detentions.

"U.S. authorities have placed the internees in Guantanamo beyond the law," the ICRC said in a report dated Aug. 25 but first publicized in October. "This means that, after more than 18 months of captivity, the internees still have no idea about their fate, and no means of recourse through any legal mechanism."[17]

White House spokesman Scott McClellan rejected the ICRC criticism. "I remind you these are enemy combatants that are being detained at Guantanamo Bay," he said in a regular news briefing. "They are treated humanely." At the same time, Maj. Gen. Geoffrey Miller, the commander of the Army task force that runs the detention center, defended the prolonged captivity.

"We don't want the enemy combatants here to stay one day longer than is necessary," Miller told *The New York Times.* He added, however, that questioning of the detainees was "producing intelligence of enormous value" but necessarily took time.

Despite the White House brush-off, the Red Cross' unusual public statement adds to the growing chorus of complaints about the administration's use of its power to hold "enemy combatants," both at Guantanamo Bay and within the United States. Even some of the administration's supporters have criticized the decision to hold two U.S. citizens as enemy combatants within the United States and to deny them access to families or lawyers or direct review by the courts. And several major human rights groups have criticized the uncertain legal status of the detainees held at Guantanamo.

"The situation increasingly looks like a case of indefinite detention, which is something the United States condemns when it takes place in other countries," says Tom Malinowski, Washington advocacy director for Human Rights Watch.

The Guantanamo detainees include alleged Taliban and al Qaeda fighters. Miller has said all of the detainees are terrorists or terrorism supporters and may be held until the war on terrorism is over. The administration refuses to classify the detainees as prisoners of war, but nevertheless claims they are being treated in accord with the Geneva Conventions.[18]

Malinowski acknowledges the United States acted legally in the original captures, but claims the Taliban fighters were entitled to prisoner-of-war status and thus should have been repatriated to Afghanistan unless they are to be tried for war crimes. The Heritage Foundation's Rosenzweig disagrees.

He says most, if not all, of the detainees, including the Taliban captives, were "clearly unlawful combatants" under the rules of war that require, for example, soldiers to be in uniform. "They were fighting illegally, and are therefore not entitled to the protections of the Geneva Convention."

Even so, Rosenzweig says the administration should process the detainees faster. "As a matter of American policy we should be working toward sorting them appropriately so that those who are potentially innocent or pose no dangers can be released," he says.

The administration has even less support for its decision to hold U.S. citizens Hamdi and Padilla as enemy combatants. Civil liberties advocates and independent legal experts have criticized the moves in the strongest of terms, and vocal support for the administration is minimal.

People for the American Way, for example, says the moves are evidence of "the administration's unilateral form of justice." NYU Law Professor Schulhofer calls the administration's actions "utterly unjustified." Columnist Taylor calls the incommunicado detentions "outrageous." And even Rosenzweig voices doubts. "I'm troubled by the idea that an American citizen in prison on American soil doesn't have access to a lawyer," he says.

Defending the administration, Mac Donald of the Manhattan Institute describes Padilla's as a "hard case." She says the Constitution gives Padilla the right to a lawyer only if he is being criminally prosecuted, but notes that Judge Mukasey appointed two attorneys to represent him in a habeas corpus action.

More broadly, Mac Donald argues that allowing attorneys to meet with Padilla would interfere with the government's ability to interrogate him about al Qaeda operations. "What if Padilla were about to crack and give up his superiors just before a lawyer began consulting with him?" Mac Donald writes. "The opportunity to pierce al Qaeda's structure could be lost forever."

But Schulhofer strongly disagrees. "There is nothing more central to civil liberties than the power of the executive branch to detain citizens," he says. "The whole history of habeas corpus going back to the 13th century has been a fight over this exact point: whether the executive can arrest people and throw them into jail without ever having to answer to the courts."

BACKGROUND

Wartime Fears

Civil liberties have been compromised repeatedly in the past when the country was at war or in fear of attack from without or from subversion within. In historical hindsight, the government's actions during many of those episodes have come to be widely, though not universally, regarded as mistakes.[19]

Less than a decade after ratification of the Bill of Rights, Congress in 1798 approved a package of laws — the Alien and Sedition Acts — ostensibly aimed at preventing attack or subversion from Napoleonic France. The Alien Act, which was never enforced, authorized the president to deport any non-citizen he deemed dangerous without any judicial review. The Sedition Act — which outlawed criticism of the government, Congress or the president — became notorious because it was largely used against President John Adams' political opponents.

Both laws expired after two years, and President Thomas Jefferson pardoned all those convicted under the Sedition Act. As Georgetown's Cole notes, however, Congress also passed a law still on the books — the Enemy Alien Act — authorizing the president to detain or expel any citizen of a country with which the United States is at war. The Supreme Court upheld the law as recently as 1948.[20]

During the Civil War, President Abraham Lincoln on eight separate occasions suspended the writ of habeas corpus — the centuries-old judicial procedure by which prisoners may challenge the legality of their detention. Lincoln acted so the government could deal with rebel sympathizers and anti-draft rioters. The broadest order, issued in September 1862, suspended habeas corpus nationwide. The military used this authority to imprison as many as 38,000 civilians. In one case, Chief Justice Roger Taney ruled that Lincoln had exceeded his authority, but the president ignored the ruling. A year after war's end — and Lincoln's assassination — the Supreme Court held that the president has no power to unilaterally suspend habeas corpus, even in time of war, if ordinary civil courts are functioning.[21]

After the United States entered World War I in 1917, Congress passed a law, the Espionage Act, which made it a crime to cause insubordination or disloyalty within the military or to advocate resistance to the draft. The Sedition Act, passed in 1918, was aimed more broadly at anarchist or communist dissent. It prohibited "any disloyal, profane, scurrilous, or abusive language" regarding the form of the U.S. government, the Constitution or the flag. More than 2,000 persons were prosecuted under one or the other of the laws. The Supreme Court reviewed only a handful of the convictions, upholding all of them typically by unanimous votes.[22]

The crackdown on dissent continued after the war. A series of terrorist mail-bombs that began in April 1919 prompted Attorney General A. Mitchell Palmer to launch a series of raids that resulted over the next two years in the arrest of an estimated 4,000 to 10,000 aliens for suspected communist views. Hundreds were deported as a result of the so-called "Palmer Raids." More would have been arrested but for the opposition to the mass arrests by Labor Secretary Louis Post, then in charge of immigration matters.[23]

In the most notorious wartime infringement of civil liberties, more than 110,000 people — mostly Americans of Japanese descent — were removed from their homes and interned in concentration camps during World War II. The forced removals resulted from an executive order that President Franklin D. Roosevelt issued on Feb. 19, 1942 — two-and-a-half months after the Japanese bombing of Pearl Harbor. Citing fears of Japanese attacks along the West Coast, Executive Order 9066 authorized the Army to designate "strategic areas" from which all persons of Japanese ancestry would be excluded. The Army also issued a curfew for anyone of Japanese descent.

In successive decisions, the Supreme Court upheld both the curfew and the relocations in 1943 and 1944.[24] In 1988 — more than 40 years later — Congress passed a law formally apologizing to and providing reparations for Japanese-Americans interned during the war.[25]

In his book detailing the events of the Civil War and the two world wars, Chief Justice William H. Rehnquist concludes that it is "neither desirable nor . . . remotely likely that civil liberty will occupy as favored a position in wartime as it does in peacetime."[26]

But Geoffrey Stone, a professor and former dean at the University of Chicago Law School, viewed the history less favorably in a speech to the Supreme Court

Historical Society. "In time of war or national emergency," Stone said, "we respond too harshly in our restriction of civil liberties, and then, later, when it is too late, we regret our behavior."[27]

Cold War Scares

Civil liberties were again tested — this time for a protracted period — during the decades-long Cold War against global communism and the domestic upheavals occasioned by the civil rights and anti-war movements of the 1960s and '70s. Congress and the states passed an array of laws aimed at limiting the rights of communists or other "subversives." Some were eventually struck down as infringing on political and free-speech rights. The FBI and the CIA conducted surreptitious surveillance and infiltrated civil-rights and anti-war groups, and when the activities were exposed, Congress and presidents of both parties acted to prevent similar abuses in the future.[28]

The anti-subversive laws included the so-called Smith Act — Title I of the Alien Registration Act of 1940 — which made it a crime to advocate the overthrow of the government by force or violence or to belong to a group dedicated to that purpose. A decade later, the McCarran Act — formally, the Internal Security Act of 1950 — required communist or so-called communist-front organizations to register with the government and disclose their membership lists. Members of registered groups were barred from holding federal jobs. Many states also passed laws barring communists or suspected subversives from holding various jobs — notably, as teachers.

Meanwhile, congressional investigations by the House Un-American Activities Committee (HUAC) and a Senate subcommittee headed by Sen. Joseph R. McCarthy, R-Wis., pressured federal agencies to ferret out and fire suspected subversives. Congressional probes also drove movie studios and television networks to "blacklist" current and former Communist Party members and others with leftist political views from jobs in the entertainment industry.

The anti-communist investigations — viewed as "witch-hunts" by critics — eventually petered out, but only after grievous harm to the lives and reputations of the people caught up in the probes. In 1954 the Senate censured McCarthy for his tactics; in the 1960s HUAC shifted its focus to civil rights and anti-war groups before being renamed and then abolished in 1975.

The Supreme Court's response was "mixed and evolved over time," according to Professor Stone. The court during the early 1950s upheld both the Smith and the McCarran acts as well as laws barring communists from the bar, the ballot or public employment. In the late 1950s and the '60s, however, the court issued rulings that restricted the scope of the Smith Act, limited legislative investigations of individuals based on political views and narrowed governmental discretion to bar public employment on the basis of political beliefs or association.[29]

The FBI's targeting of civil rights and anti-war groups in the 1960s utilized the same kinds of surveillance, infiltration and disruption that the agency, under its longtime director J. Edgar Hoover, had first used against subversive organizations in the 1950s. Under the bureaucratic acronym COINTELPRO, FBI agents monitored and sometimes infiltrated dissident groups, compiled political-intelligence files on more than 500,000 Americans and worked to discredit and disrupt organizations the agency deemed to be subversive. Among the most notorious episodes was the FBI's wiretapping of the Rev. Dr. Martin Luther King Jr. over a period of several years.

Meanwhile, the CIA — limited by its 1947 charter to foreign intelligence activities — also joined in clandestine surveillance of domestic groups. Operation CHAOS, launched in 1967, eventually compiled files on 13,000 people, including 7,000 U.S. citizens, and 1,000 domestic organizations. Investigations encompassed an array of questionable tactics, some of them arguably illegal, including wiretaps, burglaries, opening of mail and inspection of income tax records.

The FBI and CIA abuses were exposed first in news stories and then thoroughly documented in the mid-1970s by two congressional committees and a blue-ribbon commission appointed by President Gerald Ford and headed by Vice President Nelson Rockefeller. Reforms followed. Ford issued an executive order in 1976 reiterating the bar on CIA involvement in domestic intelligence-gathering and barring information-sharing with law enforcement agencies, including the FBI. Ford's attorney general, Edward Levi, issued guidelines aimed at narrowing the FBI's discretion in surveillance and intelligence-gathering of political groups — guidelines reinforced under President Jimmy Carter's attorney general, Griffin Bell. And Congress in 1978 approved the Foreign Intelligence Surveillance Act which required a warrant for all but one category of foreign intelligence surveillances conducted within the U.S.

CHRONOLOGY

Before 1945 *Civil liberties restricted during times of war and threats of war.*

1798 Fearing war with France, Federalist-controlled Congress passes Alien and Sedition Acts targeting foreigners, political opponents.

Civil War President Lincoln suspends right of habeas corpus, allowing military trials of rebel sympathizers, draft resisters; Supreme Court rules Lincoln went beyond constitutional powers.

World War I Espionage Act bars draft resistance; Sedition Act prohibits "disloyal" language; more than 2,000 prosecutions under one or the other law; Supreme Court upholds laws.

World War II Japanese-Americans interned in concentration camps; Supreme Court upholds government actions.

1946-1990 *Civil liberties tested during Cold War and civil rights and anti-war movements.*

1950s Federal and state laws and congressional investigations target communists, "subversives"; Supreme Court upholds laws at first.

1960s FBI and CIA infiltrate and disrupt civil rights, anti-war groups.

1970s CIA barred from domestic intelligence-gathering; FBI curbed in investigations of domestic political groups; Foreign Intelligence Surveillance Act of 1978 permits but limits wiretaps within U.S.

1990s *Terrorism tied to Islamic fundamentalist group al Qaeda strikes U.S. soil.*

1993 Bomb at World Trade Center kills six.

1996 Antiterrorism and Effective Death Penalty Act, signed in April. . . . Truck bomb at U.S. barracks in Saudi Arabia claims 19.

1998 Twelve Americans among 224 killed in bombings at U.S. embassies in Kenya, Tanzania.

2000 Suicide bombers kill 17 seamen aboard USS *Cole* in Yemen.

2001-Present *Terrorist attacks lead to new anti-terrorism powers for government.*

Sept. 11, 2001 Al Qaeda operatives crash hijacked airliners into World Trade Center, Pentagon and Pennsylvania field. . . . Hundreds of Musliims are detained on immigration charges.

October 2001 U.S. leads invasion of Afghanistan to topple Taliban regime for harboring al Qaeda network. . . . USA Patriot Act provides new anti-terrorism tools.

November-December 2001 Taliban regime falls in Afghanistan; hundreds of Taliban, al Qaeda fighters later brought to Guantanamo Naval Base in Cuba.

April-May 2002 Yaser Esam Hamdi, U.S. citizen captured as Taliban soldier, challenges his detention as "enemy combatant."

May-June 2002 José Padilla, accused May 8 of plotting to detonate radioactive bomb; designated as "enemy combatant" in early June and transferred to military brig.

December 2002 Federal judge in New York City rules government must allow Padilla access to lawyers; government's appeal to be argued on Nov. 17 before federal court.

Spring-Summer 2003 Federal appeals court in Washington in March rejects challenge by families of Guantanamo detainees. . . . Justice Department watchdog group blasts treatment of 9/11 detainees in June, but appeals court blocks release of names. . . . Federal appeals court in Richmond, Va., says Hamdi not entitled to lawyer.

July 2003 House bars "sneak and peek" search warrants under Patriot Act; Senate unlikely to follow suit.

August 2003 Attorney General Ashcroft launches public relations offensive to defend Patriot Act after criticism grows.

October 2003 Supreme Court opens new term, facing petitions on 9/11 detainees, Guantanamo internees, Hamdi.

The reforms quieted the controversy, but the new focus on terrorism has caused a re-examination. Kate Martin of the Center for National Security Studies says the changes have served the country well. "There's certainly much more awareness of Fourth Amendment privacy and First Amendment speech and religion being protected," she says.

But Richard Morgan, a professor of political science at Bowdoin College in Brunswick, Maine, and author of a book on the issues, says the changes went too far. "We really did overcorrect in the late 1970s," Morgan says. "We built firewalls between domestic and foreign intelligence which cost us grievously."

Terror Attacks

New threats to U.S. security at home and abroad emerged in the 1980s and '90s in the form of terrorism — both international and domestic. Nothing prepared the country, however, for the horrific attacks of Sept. 11, 2001, that left nearly 3,000 people dead and the entire country in grief and shock. President Bush declared war on global terrorism, and Congress passed the Patriot Act to strengthen the government's hand against terrorist organizations. Civil libertarians' warnings about the moves found little support at first, but drew more attention as the government tested the reach of the new powers.[30]

The earliest of the terrorist incidents directed against the United States occurred overseas. An elderly American, Leon Klinghoffer, was thrown overboard during the hijacking of an Italian cruise liner by Palestinian terrorists in October 1985. More than 270 persons were killed when a bomb planted by Libyan intelligence agents caused Pan American Flight 103 to crash in Scotland in December 1988.

International terrorism arrived on domestic soil in February 1993 when a bomb exploded beneath New York City's World Trade Center, killing six and injuring more than 1,000. The perpetrators were Islamic fundamentalists later linked to al Qaeda. International terrorists were initially blamed when a powerful truck bomb destroyed a federal office building in Oklahoma City in April 1995, killing 168 people. The deed was, instead, masterminded by a domestic terrorist: Timothy McVeigh, an Army veteran turned anti-government zealot.

Congress responded to the growing threat of terrorism in 1996 by passing the Antiterrorism and Effective Death Penalty Act, a complex statute that combined several mod-

est anti-terrorism provisions with major restrictions on the use of federal habeas corpus in state death penalty cases. Among other provisions, the law allowed the government to block fund-raising by terrorist organizations and to deny visas to foreigners who belonged to such groups.[31]

Calls for stronger action later in the decade went largely unheeded, even after two attacks on U.S. facilities abroad. A truck bomb exploded outside a U.S. military barracks in Saudi Arabia in June 1996, killing 19 Americans. Two years later, bombs damaged U.S. embassies in Kenya and Tanzania on the same day — Aug. 7, 1998 — killing 224 persons, including 12 Americans. In a third incident, 17 U.S. seamen were killed when the USS *Cole* was severely damaged in an explosion in October 2000 while refueling in Aden, Yemen. All three bombings are now linked to al Qaeda.

The previously unimaginable quantum of death and destruction wrought by the carefully coordinated airline hijackings of Sept. 11, 2001, destroyed any trace of complacency about terrorism within the United States. President Bush rallied the nation and the world to a war against global terrorism in general and specifically against Osama bin Laden's al Qaeda network and the Taliban government in Afghanistan that provided him safe haven. Domestically, Bush proposed and Congress passed within six weeks an omnibus bill — 342 pages long — aimed at strengthening law enforcement powers to prevent terrorist incidents and prosecute and punish suspected terrorists. The Patriot Act raised penalties for terrorism-related offenses, created new anti-money laundering procedures aimed at drying up funding for foreign terrorist groups and gave immigration officials new powers to detain or deport suspected foreign terrorists.[32]

Along with the immigration provisions, the search-and-surveillance powers were the focus of most of the debate in Congress. The final bill included some Justice Department requests — such as roving wiretaps — that Congress had previously turned aside. In a compromise, the bill also included a "sunset" clause terminating some of the new search-and-surveillance powers in 2005 unless reauthorized by Congress. Two major provisions, however, are not subject to the sunset clause: the expanded authority for the government to use sneak-and-peek search warrants and to obtain business and other records held by third parties.

In the two years since enactment, sentiment about the law has shifted both on Capitol Hill and among the public at large. Discontent with the sneak-and-peek and

Key Provisions of the Patriot Act

The sweeping 2001 law known as the USA Patriot Act expands the search-and-surveillance powers of federal law enforcement agents in anti-terrorism and other investigations. Several provisions amend the Foreign Intelligence Surveillance Act (FISA) — the 1978 law that created a special, secret court for authorizing searches and surveillance in foreign-intelligence investigations.[1] Here are major provisions of the act:

Roving wiretaps (Section 206) — Allows the FISA court to authorize wiretaps or intercepts on any phone or computer that may be used by the target of an investigation if the target's actions "may have the effect of thwarting . . . identification"; previously, only a specific computer or phone could be tapped.

"Sneak and peek" searches (Section 213) — Permits delayed notice of execution of search warrant in any criminal investigation if immediate notification "may have an adverse result"; the warrant must provide for notice to the target "within a reasonable time," but the period may be extended by court "for good cause shown."

Pen registers; "trap and trace" (Section 214) — Sets a minimal standard allowing government to obtain an order from the FISA court to trace outgoing telephone calls (pen registers) or incoming calls ("trap and trace") if "relevant to protect an ongoing investigation of international terrorism or clandestine intelligence activities." Previously, the minimal standard — less than the general "probable cause" requirement — applied only in foreign intelligence investigations.

"Angry librarians" provision (Section 215) — Allows FBI to apply to the FISA court for order requiring libraries, booksellers and other businesses to produce "any tangible things (including books, records, papers, documents, and other items)" for an "authorized investigation . . . to protect against international terrorism or clandestine intelligence activities"; "no person" may disclose that the FBI has sought or obtained items under this section. Previously, FISA authorized such orders only "for purposes of conducting foreign intelligence" and required target to be "linked to foreign espionage."

Internet surveillance (Section 216) — Permits government to monitor "the processing and transmitting of wire or electronic communications" — specifically, by obtaining information about "dialing, routing, addressing or signaling," but not "the contents" of any communication; allows any court to issue such order if information likely to be obtained "is relevant to an ongoing criminal investigation" — that is, not solely for anti-terrorism investigations. Previous law had no explicit provision for Internet surveillance.

Business records (Section 218) — Allows physical searches, wiretaps and subpoenas of business records as authorized in proceeding before FISA court if foreign intelligence-gathering is a "significant purpose" (rather than "the purpose" under original law).

Nationwide wiretaps (Section 220) — Allows single federal court to issue nationwide search warrant for electronic evidence. Previously, a court could authorize searches only within its geographic district.

Sources: Congressional Research Service; Dahlia Litwick and Julia Turner, "A Guide to the Patriot Act," *Slate,* Sept. 8-11, 2003 (www.msn.com).

[1] The title of the law is an acronym for Uniting and Strengthening America by Providing Appropriate Tools Required to Intercept and Obstruct Terrorism (USA PATRIOT) Act of 2001, Pub. L. No. 107-56, 115 Stat. 272 (Oct. 26, 2001).

---

records search provisions boiled up this summer as Congress considered the Justice Department appropriations measure. On July 22 the House attached a rider to the bill barring use of any funds for sneak-and-peek warrants; the 309 members voting for the amendment included almost all of the chamber's Democrats (195); nearly half of the Republicans (113) and the lone independent, Bernard Sanders of Vermont. Sanders had a similar amendment to bar funding for any records searches under the law, but a procedural dispute blocked consideration.[33]

Meanwhile, popular discontent with the law was increasing, fueled by civil libertarians' critiques of the search-and-surveillance powers. By early October 2003, the ACLU was claiming that 194 communities in 34 states had adopted resolutions that criticized parts of the act. The Justice Department discounted the resolutions, but the actions helped prompt Ashcroft to launch his recent unusual public relations offensive to defend the law.

In the first of his speeches defending the law — an Aug. 19 address to the conservative American Enterprise Institute think tank — Ashcroft said the act "gave law

Critics Denounce Military Tribunals

On Nov. 12, 2001 — two months and a day after the terrorist attacks on New York and the Pentagon — President Bush ordered the use of secret military tribunals to try suspected terrorists captured in Afghanistan and elsewhere during the war on terrorism. Legal experts and human-rights activists immediately denounced the tribunals as unfair and unconstitutional.[1]

Almost two years later, 660 prisoners from 42 countries have been detained by U.S. and allied forces and are being held — virtually incommunicado — at the military's high-security Camp Delta prison in Guantanamo Bay, Cuba. Though none have been formally charged, six detainees — including two Britons and an Australian — could be tried at Guantanamo soon.

"We want to take the time and make sure it's done right," says Maj. John Smith of the Defense Department's Office of Military Commissions, adding that the military is "working expeditiously" to bring the six to trial.

But Defense Secretary Donald Rumsfeld has suggested that most of the inmates could be held without trial for the duration of the war on terrorism. "Our interest is not in trying them and letting them out," he said in September. "Our interest is in . . . keeping them off the streets."[2]

To date, the military has released 68 detainees to their home countries. Most were sent to Afghanistan and freed, but four were transferred to Saudi Arabia for detention there.[3] Smith says the released prisoners were no longer a threat and possessed no untapped intelligence.

Meanwhile, lawyers for several of the remaining detainees are seeking an explanation for why they are being held. They maintain that the prisoners are entitled to a status hearing under international law and the Geneva Convention.

"Due process goes where we go. That's what democracy means," said Barbara Olshansky, assistant legal director for the Center for Constitutional Rights in New York, which is representing two Britons and two Australians who have filed writs of habeas corpus.

Two federal courts have dismissed their petitions, ruling with the administration that the detainees have no legal rights since they are being held in Cuban territory. The case has been appealed to the Supreme Court. In October, a group of former judges, diplomats and prisoners of war filed several friend-of-the-court briefs on behalf of the detainees.[4]

Military-tribunal procedures have been criticized by human-rights activists for concentrating too much power in the executive branch. Activists say they allow the Defense Department to serve as prosecutor, defense lawyer, judge, jury and final arbiter of appeals.[5]

The tribunals also allow the military, in the interest of homeland security, to suspend procedural rights, such as denying detainees and their civilian lawyers access to evidence being used in the trial; barring civilian lawyers from

enforcement improved tools to prevent terrorism in the age of high technology" and "began to tear down the walls" between law enforcement and intelligence agencies. "We have used these tools to provide the security that ensures liberty," Ashcroft said.

CURRENT SITUATION

Legal Challenges

As the head of a resettlement services center for Middle Eastern refugees, Mary Lieberman did not pay much attention to the Patriot Act as Congress was approving the anti-terrorism law in October 2001. But she got a crash course on the law in November 2002, when the FBI delivered a subpoena under the act's controversial Section 215 demanding personal files on all of the center's current and past Iraqi-born clients.

"I don't want a terrorist to destroy this country any more than anyone else," says Lieberman, who serves as executive director of Bridge Refugee and Sponsorship Services in Knoxville, Tenn. But the "broad-brush" subpoena struck her as an invasion of privacy for the 40 or so Iraqi refugees that the center had helped over the past decade. "The far greater red flag for me is the violation of their civil liberties," she explains.

The center eventually negotiated with the FBI to provide names and addresses of its clients but no further information. But Lieberman was still discontented enough to agree readily when the ACLU asked the center to join a federal lawsuit challenging the constitutionality of the act's provision broadening the government's

proceedings on "sensitive" matters; and banning civilian lawyers from discussing the case.

Such rules are even more restrictive than those imposed on Japanese and Nazi leaders at the war-crimes trials after World War II, said Don Rehkoph, co-chair of the Military Law Committee of the National Association of Criminal Defense Lawyers (NACDL). The NACDL has said it would be "unethical" to represent a client under the current rules.[6]

The American Bar Association has called on the administration and Congress to revise the regulations to allow civilian lawyers to more actively participate in the trials.[7]

But administration officials insist that the courts can provide a "full and fair" hearing of the evidence and urge skeptics to wait and see. They say they're unlikely to overhaul the regulations, though they could fine-tune them. "It's very easy to be critical of the process when you haven't seen it in action," Maj. Smith says, noting that such legal tenets as presumption of innocence and the right to remain silent will apply in the tribunals. "It will look very much like a standard courtroom proceeding."

"There is clear authority under international law to set up and try people under the military tribunals," says John Norton Moore, a law professor at the University of Virginia and chairman of the national and international security section of the conservative Federalist Society. "There is very solid ground for the administration to be utilizing tribunals for combatants when they have violated a number of fundamental principles of international law. Indeed, I think it's the preferred method of proceeding. It protects national security. Moreover, domestic criminal litigation is not geared for war-fighting settings."

Meanwhile, human-rights activists and veterans' groups worry that U.S. policy will be used to justify other unlawful detentions abroad. Already, the de facto law minister of Malaysia has argued that its imprisonment of 70 alleged Islamic militants without trial is "just like the process in Guantanamo."[8]

And activists warn that it could "create a free license for tyranny in Africa" as well.[9] "We've exported a situation where the rule of law doesn't apply," Olshansky says.

— *Kelly Field*

[1] American Bar Association, "Task Force on Treatment of Enemy Combatants," Aug. 12, 2003, p. 1.

[2] Matt Kelley, "U.S. Defense Chief Says Trials are Likely But Most Will Remain in Detention for War's Duration," The Associated Press, Sept. 11. 2003.

[3] Neil A. Lewis, "Red Cross Criticizes Indefinite Detention in Guantanamo Bay", *The New York Times*, Oct. 10, 2003, p. A1.

[4] Jennifer C. Kerr, "Court Urged to Review Guantanamo Appeals," The Associated Press, Oct. 9, 2003.

[5] American Bar Association, *op. cit.*, p. 2.

[6] The Associated Press, "U.S. May Ease Tribunal Rules," *Newsday*, Aug. 14, 2003, p. A18.

[7] "Injustice in Guantanamo," *The New York Times*, Aug. 22, 2003, p. A22.

[8] Sean Yoong, "Malaysia Slams Criticism of Security Law Allowing Detention Without Trial," The Associated Press, Sept. 9, 2003.

[9] Shehu Sani, "U.S. Actions Send a Bad Signal to Africa," *International Herald Tribune*, Sept. 15, 2003, p. 6.

power to obtain third-party records in foreign intelligence or anti-terrorism investigations.

The suit — filed on behalf of the center and five organizations representing Arab- or Muslim-Americans — is one of several legal challenges to the administration's anti-terrorism tactics, including three now pending before the Supreme Court. The Justice Department is vigorously defending the administration's actions in all of the cases and so far has prevailed in all but one. In the only exception, a federal judge in New York City ordered the government to allow accused "dirty bomb" suspect Padilla access to a lawyer to challenge his detention as an "enemy combatant."

The government's appeal — scheduled for argument before the U.S. Court of Appeals for the Second Circuit on Nov. 17 — is shaping up as a pivotal showdown between the administration and a broad array of legal and civil liberties groups from across the ideological spectrum.[34] Friend-of-the-court briefs supporting Padilla's right to counsel have been filed by civil liberties groups ranging from the Cato Institute and Rutherford Institute on the political right to People for the American Way and the ACLU on the left. The American Bar Association also urged the appeals court to uphold the December 2002 order by Judge Mukasey in New York demanding that the government allow Padilla to meet with his lawyers.

In its appeal, the U.S. argues the Supreme Court upheld the president's power as commander-in-chief to detain enemy combatants captured on U.S. soil in a World War II decision — *Ex parte Qirin* (1942) — involving captured German saboteurs. The government contends the same principle applies in the war against terrorism even if the "enemy combatant" is a U.S. citizen and not a uniformed soldier for a recognized government.

The brief goes on to argue that Padilla has no right to counsel under either the U.S. Constitution or the Geneva Convention, which established internationally recognized rules for waging war. "The laws of war recognize no right of access to counsel for persons detained as enemy combatants," the brief states.

In their brief for Padilla, attorneys Newman and Patel argue that because he is a U.S. citizen and not a uniformed soldier for a foreign government he cannot be held as an enemy combatant. They contend that under the Constitution's Due Process Clause Padilla is entitled to "plenary review" of the basis for his detention. And they argue that denying him access to counsel "has effectively blocked Padilla's ability to present a defense" to the accusations against him.

The appeals court decision is likely to be several months away. Legal observers say the losing side is all but certain to appeal to the Supreme Court. The high court already has been asked to review a decision in a similar case that upheld the government's authority to deny a U.S. citizen held as an enemy combatant access to lawyers.

The detainee in that case, Hamdi, was captured in Afghanistan and later found to have been born in Louisiana. In a January 2003 ruling, a three-judge panel of the U.S. Court of Appeals for the Fourth Circuit overturned a lower court decision that would have allowed Hamdi to challenge his detention. The full appeals court voted 8-4 on July 9 to let the panel's decision stand.[35] Hamdi's lawyers have asked the high court to review the decision. The government's response is due on Nov. 3.

The Supreme Court has two other terrorism-related legal challenges before it. In companion cases, relatives of Guantanamo detainees are challenging the government's decision to hold them without judicial review on constitutional and international law grounds. The U.S. Court of Appeals for the District of Columbia Circuit ruled in March 2003 that the detainees had no access to American courts because they were not being held on U.S. soil.[36]

In the other challenge, a coalition of groups led by the Center for National Security Studies is pressing a Freedom of Information Act (FOIA) request for the names of the immigrants rounded up in the U.S. immediately after 9/11. In a 2-1 decision, the D.C. Circuit ruled in June 2003 that the government did not have to disclose the information because of a "law enforcement" exemption in the FOIA law.[37]

The government won one other important ruling that, for procedural reasons, will not get to the Supreme Court. In its first-ever appellate case, the three-judge Foreign Intelligence Surveillance Court of Review in November 2002 upheld the Justice Department's position that the Patriot Act authorizes sharing of foreign intelligence surveillance information with domestic law enforcement agencies. The 48-page ruling reversed a May 2002 decision by the seven judges who serve as trial courts for foreign intelligence wiretaps. That ruling had imposed restrictions on the government's surveillance and information-sharing procedures.[38]

Political Debates

The Bush administration's anti-terrorism tactics are drawing increased criticism from members of Congress, seemingly dooming any likelihood of new legislation to expand law enforcement powers. But Republicans and even many Democratic lawmakers continue to express support for most of the provisions of the Patriot Act, suggesting that any wholesale rollback of the law is also unlikely.

The mixed views were apparent as the Senate Judiciary Committee opened the first of a planned series of oversight hearings on the administration's anti-terrorism prosecutions and investigations. Chairman Orrin Hatch, R-Utah, opened the Oct. 21 hearing by casting doubt on what he called the "rhetoric, confusion, and distortion" surrounding the administration's domestic counterterrorism program. But Sen. Edward M. Kennedy, D-Mass., accused the administration of "extreme measures which may well threaten basic freedoms more than they prevent acts of terrorism."

Democrats aimed their strongest criticisms at the detentions of U.S. citizens as enemy combatants, the post-9/11 roundup of aliens and the detention of foreign enemy combatants at Guantanamo Naval Base in Cuba. On the Patriot Act itself, some Democrats said provisions of the law went too far, citing the expanded authority for "sneak and peek" search warrants and business records searches. Other Democrats, however, discounted the criticisms. Sen. Joseph R. Biden Jr. of Delaware, a former Judiciary Committee chairman, called criticism of the law "incorrect and overblown."

Justice Department officials appearing as witnesses at the hearing also rejected criticisms of the law. "The vari-

Is the government misusing the USA Patriot Act?

YES
Timothy Edgar
Legislative Counsel,
American Civil Liberties Union

Written for The CQ Researcher, October 2003

Inevitable abuse — by this administration or the next — is why the opposition to Patriot Act powers can't easily be pigeonholed with traditional labels. Groups like the American Conservative Union and the Free Congress Foundation fear a partisan Democrat could misuse its powers to investigate gun rights or anti-abortion activists.

Members of Congress feared the Patriot Act was really just a prosecutor's wish list, not limited to terrorism. They were right. In touting Patriot Act "successes," the government has often pointed to garden-variety cases such as drugs and fraud. Congress agreed to the Patriot Act, despite misgivings, because Attorney General John Ashcroft said it was vitally needed to prevent terrorism. But the ink was not yet dry on the act when the Department of Justice (DoJ) began training agents to use their new powers in ordinary criminal cases.

In June 2003, DoJ's own inspector general found serious flaws in the government's treatment of hundreds of people detained after 9/11. Many detainees languished incommunicado for months until they were finally cleared. The effect of the policy was to evade the safeguards incorporated in the never-used detention provision of the Patriot Act — a painstaking compromise hammered out after Congress rejected the administration's call for indefinite detention without judicial review.

Responding to librarians' concerns that the Patriot Act could be used to monitor the records of Americans' reading habits, Ashcroft declassified all the records orders issued under one part of the act — which turned out to be zero. He sidestepped whether other Patriot Act powers are being used to monitor Americans. The American Civil Liberties Union (ACLU) has obtained pages of blacked-out lists of these orders under the Freedom of Information Act. What types of records? Unfortunately, that remains classified.

The American public is skeptical of the Patriot Act. More than 180 local governments have urged a rollback of its expansive powers. And, in a recent poll, more than two-thirds of the respondents agreed that, whether or not civil liberties have been abused already, the government's overbroad powers will be abused at some point.

The Patriot Act contains many appropriate provisions, like those that provide more security along the Northern border and encourage hiring translators in national security positions. However, some of its expansive powers tempt federal agents to operate outside the bounds of our democratic traditions.

To keep America safe and free, some parts of the Patriot Act must be narrowed.

NO

Paul Rosenzweig
Senior Fellow, Heritage Foundation
Adjunct Professor of Law,
George Mason University

Written for The CQ Researcher, October 2003

How ironic that the war on terrorism — meant to ensure our safety — itself inspires fear in some Americans. But those fears are born largely of confusion: Critics of the Patriot Act constantly confuse potential abuse with actual abuse.

For example, one "icon" of alleged abuse — Section 215 of the act — has turned out to be nothing of the sort. For months, librarians complained that Section 215 allows the government to get the library reading lists of political opponents. From the beginning, this criticism was overwrought, at best.

It ignored the fact that library records already could be (and often had been) subpoenaed — without prior judicial approval — by grand juries investigating offenses such as organized crime and white-collar crime. It also ignored the fact that Section 215 orders are subject to prior judicial approval under a probable-cause standard already ruled constitutional by the Supreme Court.

Most instructive, though, is the simple truth that the government has never exercised its Section 215 power — not once in two years. Critics have confused the theoretical possibility of abuse with actual wrongdoing — a confusion that doesn't help the discussion.

To be sure, the possibility of abuse calls for great vigilance. But oversight, not prohibition, is the answer to potential abuse. So long as we keep an eye on law-enforcement activity, so long as the federal courts remain open and so long as the debate about governmental conduct remains vibrant, the risk of excessive encroachment on fundamental liberties is remote.

Critics of the Patriot Act err in exalting the protection of liberty as an absolute value. That vision reflects an incomplete understanding of why Americans formed a civil society. As Thomas Powers, author of *Intelligence Wars: American Secret History From Hitler to Al-Qaeda*, recently wrote: "In a liberal republic, liberty presupposes security; the point of security is liberty."

Thus, government has a dual obligation: to protect civil safety and to preserve civil liberty. That goal can be achieved, but we must recognize that security need not be traded off for liberty in equal measure.

Maintaining "balance" between freedom and security is not a zero-sum game. Policy-makers must respect and defend our Constitutional liberties when they act, but they also cannot fail to act when we face a serious threat from a foreign enemy.

Showdown With a Terrorist

The federal government is in a high-stakes legal showdown with Zacarias Moussaoui, the only person so far to be criminally prosecuted in connection with the 9/11 terrorist attacks.[1]

The dispute threatens to block the government from seeking the death penalty against the burly, French-born Moroccan and member of the al Qaeda terrorist organization. But it could also lead the government to take the case from federal court to a military tribunal — where Moussaoui would have fewer procedural rights than in a normal criminal prosecution.

The impasse stems from the refusal by U.S. prosecutors to comply with a federal judge's orders that Moussaoui be allowed to interview three al Qaeda prisoners to try to support his defense that he did not play a part in planning the 9/11 hijackings.

Under the Sixth Amendment, a criminal defendant is generally entitled to present witnesses in his behalf and to interview potential witnesses before trial. But U.S. Attorney Paul McNulty Jr., the lead prosecutor, says Moussaoui is "an avowed terrorist" who should not be allowed to meet with "terrorist confederates."

U.S. District Judge Leonie Brinkema, who sits in Alexandria, Va., rejected the government's positions in an order first issued in January 2003 and reaffirmed in September. When the government defied the order, Brinkema scheduled a hearing on what penalty to impose.

Moussaoui — who is representing himself — asked that the case be dismissed. In an unusual legal maneuver, the government also filed a motion to have the case dismissed — a move aimed at getting an immediate appeal. Brinkema responded with a ruling on Oct. 2 that barred the government from introducing evidence tying Moussaoui to the 9/11 attacks — the only charges that could warrant the death penalty.

"It would simply be unfair to require Moussaoui to defend against such prejudicial accusations while being denied the ability to present testimony from witnesses who could assist him in contradicting those accusations," Brinkema ruled.

The government has appealed the ruling to the Fourth U.S. Circuit Court of Appeals, in Richmond, Va. Appellate arguments are scheduled for Dec. 3.

The government alleges Moussaoui was supposed to be the 20th hijacker. He entered the U.S. in February 2001 and enrolled at a flight school in Norman, Okla. After washing out, he enrolled in a school in Eagan, Minn., where he used flight simulators designed to train commercial pilots. His instructors became suspicious and called the FBI, which arrested Moussaoui on Aug. 17 on immigration charges.

At the time of his arrest, FBI agents applied to the Department of Justice for permission to go to court for a special warrant to examine the contents of Moussaoui's computer but were turned down.

AFP Photo

Zacarias Moussaoui, a French national of Moroccan descent arrested in Minnesota, was supposed to be the 20th hijacker on Sept. 11, the government alleges.

---

[1] Account drawn from Associated Press dispatches, September-October 2003.

ous misperceptions that have been perpetuated about the Patriot Act are disturbing and simply wrong," said Christopher Wray, assistant attorney general for the criminal division. Echoing Attorney General Ashcroft's speeches in defense of the law, Wray pointed out that the law required judicial approval for records searches and delayed notification search warrants. He also noted that no library borrowing records have been sought under the law, but said that such information could be useful in some cases in identifying and thwarting suspected terrorists.

Civil liberties concerns were raised as Congress was working on the Patriot Act in September and October 2001 and had some effect. Some lawmakers, for example, voiced support for a national identification card to help shield against foreign terrorists, but the proposal fell by the wayside in the face of criticism from civil libertarians.

A year later, then-House Majority Leader Dick Armey, R-Texas, helped kill a plan that Ashcroft pushed to create a nationwide program to collect reports of suspicious activity from people who work in a community, such as postal employees or utility repair personnel. The proposed Terrorist Information and Prevention Systems — dubbed Operation TIPS — would have set up a central hotline to call to file such reports. Civil libertarians on the left and the right said the government should not encourage mass snooping by non-law enforcement personnel. Armey insisted the plan be dropped as a condition of allowing legislation authorizing the new Department of Homeland Security to move through the House.[39]

Congress balked again in early 2003 at a controversial Defense Department proposal to scan computer databases to try to detect possible terrorist activities. The so-called "Total Information Awareness" program would have used state-of-the-art computer technology to spot patterns of suspicious behavior. Electronic privacy advocates and lawmakers from both parties criticized the proposal as government surveillance with Orwellian overtones. A provision barring use of any funds for the proposal for the time being was inserted into an omnibus appropriations bill approved in February 2003.[40]

OUTLOOK

Liberty and Security?

Judging by the names of their respective Web sites, the Justice Department and the American Civil Liberties

Union apparently agree on one point in the debate over the administration's anti-terrorism tactics: Liberty and security are not mutually exclusive. The Justice Department named its special site on the war on terror www.lifeandliberty.gov; the ACLU calls its site www.safeandfree.org.

The American people, however, disagree. In a recent poll, two-thirds of those responding said they are concerned that anti-terrorism measures could result in restricting individual freedom. So far, however, most people — 58 percent — believe the government has not violated legal rights, and a near majority — 49 percent — believe the administration has been "about right" in using new laws to fight terrorism.[41]

Attorney General Ashcroft and other administration officials stoutly maintain that no rights have been infringed and none are in jeopardy. "These reforms have been rooted in constitutionally tried and true, court-tested regimes," says Assistant Attorney General Bryant.

Civil liberties groups counter that individual rights have already suffered and will suffer more if the administration does not change course. The Justice Department and other federal agencies "have impeded some of the most basic freedoms enjoyed in this country," People for the American Way says.[42]

The administration also claims that its tactics are paying off in terms of successful criminal prosecutions. In his Sept. 10 speech, Bush said that more than 260 "suspected terrorists" have been charged in U.S. courts and that more than 140 had already been convicted. Bush also said the government had "shut down phony charities that serve as terrorist fronts" and "thwarted" terrorists in half a dozen locations around the country, including Buffalo, N.Y., and Portland, Ore.

Bush's statistics are subject to doubt, however. The General Accounting Office, the congressional watchdog agency, reported in January that nearly half of the terrorism-related convictions claimed by federal prosecutors in 2002 were "misclassified."[43]

Some of the successful criminal prosecutions have also been questioned on civil liberties grounds. Attorneys for John Walker Lindh, the California man who pleaded guilty in July 2002 to aiding the Taliban, had earlier charged the FBI with interrogating him under inhumane conditions.[44] The government may have used the threat of military trials to help win guilty pleas in 2003 from six defendants charged with being members of an al Qaeda cell in Lackawanna, N.Y., outside Buffalo.[45] Civil liberties advocates also criticize the government's acknowledged decision to use Patriot Act powers in non-terrorism-related cases.[46]

On the other hand, federal prosecutors in the recent "Portland Seven" cases — which yielded guilty pleas by six defendants to plotting to aid the Taliban — cited evidence from monitored conversations that the Patriot Act was helping to dry up financial support for terrorist groups. The plea agreements "would have been more difficult to achieve, were it not for the legal tools provided by the USA Patriot Act," Ashcroft told a news conference as the last of the guilty pleas were being entered on Oct. 16.[47]

One major question mark among advocates and experts is the Supreme Court's likely attitude toward the terrorism-related case to come before the justices. Some civil liberties advocates hope the justices will be skeptical. "I do think the Supreme Court is very sensitive to its legacy and very reluctant to get itself in the position again of deferring blindly to the government during war and regretting it 20 years later," says Steven Shapiro, the ACLU's national legal director.

John Norton Moore, a University of Virginia law professor and chairman of the national and international security section of the conservative Federalist Society, predicts the court will uphold the government's actions in some of the pending cases. But he also says he expects the court to be "vigilant" in guarding against excesses. "It is precisely the role of the court to provide that kind of balancing and assessment," he says.

For their part, liberal expert Schulhofer and conservative Rosenzweig both agree that the presumed tradeoff between liberty and security is neither inevitable nor desirable. "I don't think it's a zero-sum game," Rosenzweig says. "I think we can do both."

"There's absolutely no reasons to think that you have to give up some liberty to buy some additional security," Schulhofer says. "And even if you can buy some security by giving up some liberty, it's by no means clear that giving up the liberty is the best way to buy that security." The debate, Schulhofer adds, "is distracting people from some of the issues that should be more salient."

NOTES

1. Quoted in Thomas Adcock, "Defense of 'Enemy Combatant' Turns Solo's Life Upside Down," *American Lawyer Media*, Aug. 29, 2003.

2. The title of the law is an acronym for Uniting and Strengthening America by Providing Appropriate Tools Required to Intercept and Obstruct Terrorism (USA PATRIOT) Act of 2001.

3. Ashcroft's speeches can be found at www.usdoj.gov; Bryant's remarks were before a panel discussion sponsored by the Washington Legal Foundation, Sept. 25, 2003.

4. See Center for National Security Studies, "Aftermath of September 11," www.cnss.gwu.edu; People for the American Way, "Two Years After 9/11: Ashcroft's Assault on the Constitution," Sept. 9, 2003 (www.pfaw.org).

5. See Stephen J. Schulhofer, "The Enemy Within: Intelligence Gathering, Law Enforcement, and Civil Liberties in the Wake of September 11," The Century Foundation, Sept. 5, 2002 (www.tcf.org).

6. See David Cole, *Enemy Aliens: Double Standards and Constitutional Freedoms in the War on Terrorism* (2003).

7. Appearance on PBS' "The NewsHour with Jim Lehrer," Aug. 19, 2003 (www.pbs.org/newshour).

8. See Jennifer A. Dlouhy, "House Moves to Eliminate Search-and-Seizure Provision of Anti-Terrorism Law," *CQ Weekly*, July 26, 2003, p. 1905 (www.cq.com).

9. The ACLU site includes the text of the act and various analyses and commentaries (www.safeandfree.org).

10. For the text of the act, analysis and commentary, see this Justice Department Web site: www.lifeandliberty.gov.

11. The case is *Muslim Community Association of Ann Arbor v. Ashcroft*, 03-72913 filed in U.S. District Court for the Eastern District of Michigan, July 2003. Other plaintiff organizations are American-Arab Anti-Discrimination Committee; Arab Community Center for Economic and Social Services; Bridge Refugee and Sponsorship Services; Council on American-Islamic Relations; and Islamic Center of Portland (Ore.).

12. Heather Mac Donald, "Straight Talk on Homeland Security," *City Journal*, Vol. 13, No. 3 (July 2003), pp. 28-41 (www.manhattan-institute.org).

13. See "Weekly Compilation of Presidential Documents," Sept. 15, 2003, pp. 1190-1195.

14. The draft proposal is posted on at www.publicintegrity.org.

15. See Keith Perine, "Legislators Hesitant to Expand Law Enforcement Authority as Comity Wanes on the Hill," *CQ Weekly*, Sept. 13, 2003, p. 2231.

16. Stuart Taylor Jr., "Rights, Liberties, and Security: Recalibrating the Balance after September 11," *The Brookings Review*, winter 2003, pp. 25-31.

17. International Committee of the Red Cross, "Guantanamo Bay: Overview of the ICRC's work for internees," Aug. 8, 2003 (www.icrc.org/eng).

18. For background on the POW debate, see David Masci, "Ethics of War," *The CQ Researcher*, Dec. 13, 2002, pp. 1013-1032.

19. Background drawn in part from David Cole, *op. cit.*; Peter Irons, *Justice at War* (1983); William H. Rehnquist, *All the Laws but One: Civil Liberties in Wartime* (1998). See also Geoffrey Stone, "Civil Liberties in Wartime," *Journal of Supreme Court History*, Vol. 28, No. 3 (December 2003), pp. 215-251.

20. Cole, *op. cit.*, pp. 91-92. The Supreme Court decision is *Ludecke v. Watkins* (1948).

21. Taney's decision, issued as circuit justice for Maryland, is *Ex parte Merryman* (1861); the full court's postwar decision is *Ex parte Milligan* (1866).

22. See, e.g., *Schenck v. United States* (1919). The court's only decision with a dissent was *Abrams v. United States* (1920).

23. See Cole, *op. cit.*, pp. 119-129.

24. The cases are *Hirabayashi v. United States* (1943) (curfew) and *Korematsu v. United States* (1944) (relocations).

25. For background, see David Masci, "Reparations Movement," *The CQ Researcher*, June 22, 2001, pp. 529-552.

26. Rehnquist, *op. cit.*, pp. 224-225.

27. Stone, *op. cit.*

28. Background on the intelligence agency controversies drawn from Morton H. Halperin *et al.*, *The Lawless State: The Crimes of the U.S. Intelligence Agencies* (1976); and Richard Morgan, *Domestic Intelligence: Monitoring Dissent in America* (1980).

29. See Stone, *op. cit.* Two of the major decisions are *Dennis v. United States* (1951) and *Yates v. United States* (1957).

30. Background drawn in part from the following *CQ Researcher* reports: Mary H. Cooper, "Combating Terrorism," July 21, 1995, pp. 633-656; David Masci and Kenneth Jost, "War on Terrorism," Oct. 12, 2001, pp. 817-840; David Masci and Patrick Marshall, "Civil Liberties in Wartime," Dec. 14, 2001, pp. 1017-1040.

31. See *1996 CQ Almanac*, "President Signs Anti-Terrorism Bill," pp. 5-18 to 5-25.

32. *2001 CQ Almanac*, pp. 14-3 to 14-13.

33. Dlouhy, *op. cit.*

34. The case is *Padilla v. Rumsfeld*, 03-2235.

35. The full court's decision is *Hamdi v. Rumsfeld*, 337 F.3d 335 (4th Cir. 2003). The petition for certiorari was filed with the Supreme Court on Oct. 1 (03-6696).

36. The decision is *Rasul v. Bush*, 321 F.3d 1134 (D.C. Cir. 2003). The petitions for certiorari in the companion cases, *Rasul v. Bush* and *Al Odah v. United States*, were filed with the Supreme Court on Sept. 2 (03-334, 03-343).

37. The decision is *Center for National Security Studies v. Department of Justice*, 331 F.3d 918 (D.C. Cir. 2003). The petition for certiorari was filed with the Supreme Court on Sept. 29 (03-472).

38. The case is *In re Sealed Case No. 02-001* (D.C. Cir 2003), issued Nov. 18, 2002.

39. See Jackie Koszczuk, "Ashcroft Drawing Criticism From Both Sides of the Aisle," *CQ Weekly*, Sept. 7, 2002, p. 2286.

40. Jonathan Riehl, "Lawmakers Likely to Limit New High-Tech Eavesdropping," *CQ Weekly*, Feb. 15, 2003, p. 406.

41. *Rasul v. Bush, op. cit.*

42. People for the American Way, *op. cit.*

43. U.S. General Accounting Office, "Justice Department: Better Management Oversight and Internal Controls Needed to Ensure Accuracy of Terrorism-Related Statistics," GAO-03-266, January 2003. See Mark Fazlollah and Peter Nicholas, "U.S. Overstates Arrests in Terrorism," *The Philadelphia Inquirer*, Dec. 16, 2001, p. A1.

44. Lindh pleaded guilty on July 15, 2002, to two felony counts and was sentenced to 20 years in prison. For a detailed, somewhat critical examination of the case, see Jane Mayer, "Annals of Justice: Lost in the Jihad," *The New Yorker*, May 10, 2003.

45. For a critical examination of the case, see Matthew Purdy and Lowell Bergman, "Unclear Danger: Inside the Lackawanna Terror Case," *The New York Times*, Oct. 12, 2003, p. A1.

46. See Eric Lichtblau, "U.S. Uses Terror Law to Pursue Crimes From Drugs to Swindling," *The New York Times*, Sept. 28, 2003, p. A1.

47. See Blaine Harden and Dan Eggen, "Duo Pleads Guilty to Conspiracy Against U.S.," *The Washington Post*, Oct. 17, 2003, p. A3.

BIBLIOGRAPHY

Books

Cole, David, *Enemy Aliens: Double Standards and Constitutional Freedoms in the War on Terrorism*, The New Press, 2003.
A Georgetown University law professor argues that anti-terrorism measures aimed at aliens are unconstitutional and counterproductive, and pave the way for infringement of citizens' rights. Includes detailed notes.

Hentoff, Nat, *The War on the Bill of Rights — and the Gathering Resistance*, Seven Stories Press, 2003.
The longtime *Village Voice* columnist strongly criticizes — on civil liberties grounds — various governmental activities in the war on terrorism. Hentoff's syndicated column is called "Sweet Land of Liberty."

Irons, Peter, *Justice at War*, University of California Press, 1983.
The director of the Earl Warren Bill of Rights Project at the University of California, San Diego, chronicles the wartime internment of Japanese-Americans and the court cases challenging the action. A 1993 edition discusses the government's subsequent decision to apologize for the internment and pay reparations.

Morgan, Richard E., *Domestic Intelligence: Monitoring Dissent in America*, University of Texas Press, 1980.
A professor of law and government at Bowdoin College succinctly reviews the domestic-intelligence abuses revealed in the 1970s and the reforms later adopted to prevent future abuses. Includes detailed notes. For a more argumentative account, see Morton H. Halperin, *et al*, *The Lawless State: The Crimes of the U.S. Intelligence Agencies* (Penguin, 1976).

Rehnquist, William H., *All the Laws but One: Civil Liberties in Wartime*, Knopf, 1998.
The chief justice of the United States details the history of President Lincoln's suspension of habeas corpus during the Civil War and recounts more briefly the civil liberties disputes during World War I and World War II. Includes reference notes and a five-page bibliography.

Rosen, Jeffrey, *The Naked Crowd: Reclaiming Security and Freedom in an Anxious Age*, Random House, January 2004.
An associate law professor at George Washington University and legal-affairs editor of *The New Republic* examines the effect on security and liberty of new technologies for surveillance and "data-mining." Includes reference notes.

Articles

Lithwick, Dahlia, and Julia Turner, "A Guide to the Patriot Act," *Slate*, Sept. 8-11, 2003 (www.slate.msn.com).
The four-part series provides a detailed and balanced examination of the law's major provisions.

Mac Donald, Heather, "Straight Talk on Homeland Security," *City Journal*, Vol. 13, No. 3 (July 2003), pp. 28-41 (www.manhattan-institute.org).
A senior fellow at the conservative Manhattan Institute defends the government's actions in the war on terrorism, calling criticisms "false and dangerous."

Stone, Geoffrey, "Civil Liberties in Wartime," *Journal of Supreme Court History*, Vol. 28, No. 3 (December 2003), pp. 215-251.
A former dean of the University of Chicago Law School surveys civil liberties conflicts in U.S. history from the Alien and Sedition Acts through the Cold War.

Taylor, Stuart, Jr., "Rights, Liberties, and Security: Recalibrating the Balance after September 11," *The Brookings Review*, Vol. 21, No. 1 (winter 2003), pp. 25-31 (www.brookings.org).
A *National Journal* columnist and *Newsweek* contributing editor calls for re-examining civil liberties rules limiting surveillance and detention because of "the threat of unprecedented carnage at the hands of modern terrorists."

Reports and Studies

Olshansky, Barbara, "Secret Trials: Military Tribunals and the Threat to Democracy," Seven Stories Press, 2002.

The 80-page report by the assistant legal director of the Center for Constitutional Rights sharply criticizes the Bush administration's creation of special military tribunals to try non-citizens suspected of terrorism.

People for the American Way, "Two Years After 9/11: Ashcroft's Assault on the Constitution," Sept. 9, 2003 (www.pfaw.org).
A detailed report by the liberal civil rights group says the government's actions in the war on terrorism have had a "devastating" impact on basic rights.

Schulhofer, Stephen J., "The Enemy Within: Intelligence Gathering, Law Enforcement, and Civil Liberties in the Wake of September 11," The Century Foundation, Sept. 5, 2002 (www.tcf.org).
A New York University law professor says individual freedoms have been "sacrificed" in the war on terrorism while concerns about effectiveness have been "neglected."

For More Information

American Civil Liberties Union, 125 Broad St., 18th floor; New York, N.Y. 10004; (212) 549-2500; 122 Maryland Ave., N.E., Washington, DC 20002; (202) 544-1681; www.aclu.org.

Center for National Security Studies, 1120 19th St., N.W., 8th Floor, Washington, DC 20036; (202) 721-5650; cnss.org.

Century Foundation, 41 East 70th St., New York, NY 10021; (212) 535-4441; www.tcf.org.

Federalist Society, 1015 18th St., N.W., Suite 425, Washington, DC 20036; (202) 822-8138; www.fed-soc.org.

Heritage Foundation, 214 Massachusetts Ave., N.E., Washington DC 20002-4999; (202) 546-4400; www.heritage.org.

People for the American Way, 2000 M St., N.W., Suite 400, Washington, DC 20036; (202) 467-4999; www.pfaw.org/pfaw/general.

12

School Desegregation

Kenneth Jost

Getty Images/Mario Villafuerte

Fifty years after the Supreme Court handed down its historic *Brown v. Board of Education* decision declaring racial segregation in public schools unconstitutional, most black and Latino students attend predominantly minority schools. At Birdwell Elementary in Tyler, Texas, 60 percent of the students are Hispanic.

From *The CQ Researcher*, April 23, 2004.

Civil rights advocates consider Louisville-Jefferson County, Ky., a model of desegregation — but don't tell that to David McFarland.

McFarland says the county's claimed success in racial mixing comes at the expense of his children's education. In his view, Stephen and Daniel were denied admission to the school of their choice simply because they are white. "Diversity should not be used as an excuse for discrimination," he says.

The county's 19 traditional schools — with their reputation for good discipline, structured teaching and parental involvement — are so popular that they cannot accommodate all the students who want to attend. So students are assigned to schools by lottery.

To keep enrollments at each school within racial guidelines, a separate list of African-American applicants is maintained. The county's voluntary "managed-choice" program — which replaced a court-ordered desegregation plan in 2000 — is designed to prevent any school from having fewer than 15 percent or more than 50 percent African-American students.

The program works. In a countywide system where African-Americans comprise about one-third of the 96,000 students, only one school has a majority-black enrollment.

Jefferson County was one of the first school systems in the country to begin integrating after the U.S. Supreme Court handed down its historic *Brown v. Board of Education* decision declaring racial segregation in schools unconstitutional.[1]

Today, as the 50th anniversary of the May 17, 1954, ruling approaches, Jefferson County stands in stark contrast to the ethnic and racial patterns in most other school districts. Across the coun-

Minority School Districts Receive Less Funding

School districts with high enrollments of minority or low-income students typically receive fewer funds compared to districts with more white or wealthier students. In 11 states, the funding gap between white and minority school districts is more than $1,000 per pupil.

Per-Pupil Funding Gaps Between Districts with High and Low Minority Enrollments

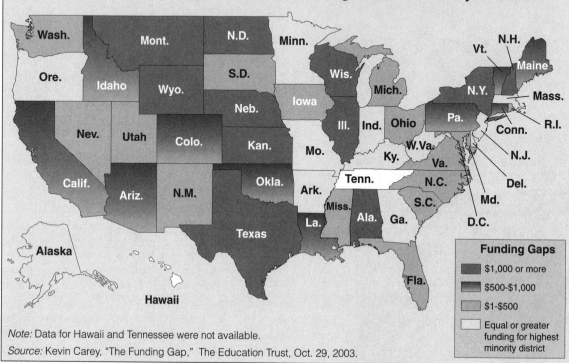

Funding Gaps
- $1,000 or more
- $500-$1,000
- $1-$500
- Equal or greater funding for highest minority district

Note: Data for Hawaii and Tennessee were not available.

Source: Kevin Carey, "The Funding Gap," The Education Trust, Oct. 29, 2003.

try today, most black students attend majority-black schools, and an even larger percentage of Latino students attend majority-Latino schools — evidence of what civil rights advocates call resegregation.

In Louisville, McFarland and three other families sued in federal court to bar the school system from using race in any student assignments.[2] "It can't be fair to discriminate against a white male because he's a white male," says Ted Gordon, the plaintiffs' attorney. "That can't be fair in anybody's book."

School administrators, however, say a ruling for McFarland would effectively bring back racial segregation in Louisville. "We would be back to majority-white suburban schools and majority-black inner-city schools," says Byron Leet, lead attorney for the school system. "That would not be in the best interest of young people

in the community, who have benefited greatly from attending desegregated schools."

The case is being closely watched at a time when school desegregation litigation nationwide is dormant, but parents in some areas are asking courts to block administrators from continuing to use race to promote integration.

"If the court decides that the sensitive way that Louisville has gone about trying to achieve integration is not acceptable, then I worry that there may be little or no way to reap the benefits of integration for our primary and secondary schools," says Chinh Quang Le, assistant counsel for the NAACP Legal Defense and Educational Fund, which filed a friend of the court brief on the side of the Louisville school system. The fund directed the court challenges against racial segregation that produced the *Brown* decision and remains the principal litigation center in school desegregation cases.

Today's pattern of school desegregation litigation underscores the changes in the nation's schools — and in the nation's attitudes toward race — since the *Brown* decision.[3] While the ruling is universally hailed, its promise is widely recognized as unfulfilled and its implications for educational policies today vigorously debated.

"*Brown v. Board of Education* is one of the signal legal events of our time," says Education Secretary Rod Paige, who himself attended racially segregated schools through college in his native Mississippi. But the ruling did not eliminate all the vestiges of segregation, Paige quickly adds. "If the goal was equality in education — to level the educational playing field for all children, especially children of color — we've yet to achieve that," he says.

"We have an unfulfilled promise of *Brown*," says Julie Underwood, general counsel for the National School Boards Association, which once resisted and now strongly supports desegregation. "If the civil rights people were actually seeking fully integrated public schools, we have not reached that point."

Civil rights advocates acknowledge that *Brown* fundamentally transformed American schools — and America itself. "Both whites and blacks have been in far more integrated settings than anyone would have imagined before *Brown*," says Gary Orfield, a professor at Harvard's Graduate School of Education and director of the Harvard Civil Rights Project.

But Orfield and other desegregation advocates also maintain that the hard-won progress of the post-*Brown* era has not merely stalled but is now being reversed. "We've been going backward almost every place in the country since the 1990s," Orfield says.

A coterie of educational conservatives from academia and various advocacy groups challenge both this view of present-day conditions and policies for the future. While praising the *Brown* decision, they argue that today's racial separation is not the result of law or policy and that race-conscious assignments violate *Brown*'s central meaning.

Brown "stands for the principles of integration and color-blindness," says Curt Levey, director of legal and public affairs for the Washington-based Center for Individual Rights.

"It's unfortunate that in the past few decades we have abandoned those principles in favor of racial preferences," Levey says. "It's just another form of discrimination." The center has represented plaintiffs challenging affirmative action in higher education and, in one case from Minneapolis, racial guidelines in public schools.

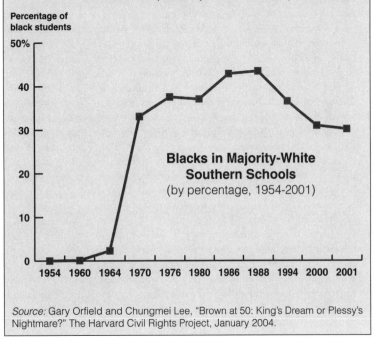

School-Integration Trend Reversing

The Supreme Court's landmark 1954 *Brown v. Board of Education* ruling declared racial segregation in public schools unconstitutional. But after more than three decades, the desegation trend in U.S. schools reversed after 1988 — particularly in the South. Then a series of Supreme Court decisions between 1991 and 1995 eased the pressure on school districts to continue desegregation efforts. Today U.S. classrooms are almost as segregated as they were in the late 1960s, and some experts say the trend is likely to continue.

Percentage of black students

Blacks in Majority-White Southern Schools (by percentage, 1954-2001)

1954 1960 1964 1970 1976 1980 1986 1988 1994 2000 2001

Source: Gary Orfield and Chungmei Lee, "Brown at 50: King's Dream or Plessy's Nightmare?" The Harvard Civil Rights Project, January 2004.

Latinos' Unheralded Struggles for Equal Education

When school board officials in Lemon Grove, Calif., became concerned in 1930 that Mexican-American students were slowing down the Anglo pupils, they hit upon a simple solution: build a new school solely for the Mexican-Americans.

To the board's surprise, however, Mexican-Americans in the small border community protested, deriding the new facility as a "barn." And — more than two decades before the Supreme Court declared racial segregation in public schools unconstitutional — they won a lower-court order forcing the school board to dismantle the plans for a dual system of education.[1]

The Lemon Grove incident is one of many efforts by Latinos to fight for educational equity well before the Supreme Court's landmark 1954 decision in *Brown v. Board of Education.* The history of those efforts, however, has gone largely untold. "These cases are not taught, even in law school," says Margaret Montoya, a professor at the University of New Mexico School of Law.

Today, Latinos continue to receive far less attention in school desegregation debates than African-Americans even though Latinos now comprise the nation's largest ethnic minority, and Latino students are somewhat more likely than blacks to be in ethnically identifiable schools.

"We don't see an equal commitment on the part of educational equity for Latinos," says James Ferg-Cadima, legislative staff attorney for the Mexican American Legal Defense and Educational Fund (MALDEF) in Washington.

The Lemon Grove ruling was never appealed and had no further impact in California. Chicano families won a similar ruling from a lower court in Texas around the same time. It, too, did nothing to undo the advancing segregation of Mexican-American students in that state.[2]

In 1946, however, a federal appeals court in California ruled in favor of Mexican-American parents contesting school segregation in four districts in Orange County, south of Los Angeles. Ferg-Cadima says the case "could have been a precursor to *Brown v. Board of Education,*" but the school districts decided not to appeal. The ruling did lead to a law in 1947, however, that barred school segregation in the state. The act was signed by then-Gov. Earl Warren, who later became chief justice and author of the *Brown* decision.[3]

Perversely, Mexican-American families prevailed in some of their early legal efforts on the grounds that they were white and could not be segregated as black students were. "We have not been treated as a white subgroup, and we don't think of ourselves as a white subgroup," Montoya

"Most of our schools became substantially racially balanced," says David J. Armor, a professor at George Mason University School of Public Policy in Fairfax, Va., and the leading academic critic of mandatory integration. Armor acknowledges that there's been "some resegregation of schools" but attributes the trend to changes in ethnic and racial residential patterns and the higher percentages of blacks and Latinos in public schools.

The debate over desegregation is waged against the disheartening persistence of large gaps in learning and achievement between whites, blacks and Latinos. "The magnitude of the gap is simply appalling," says Abigail Thernstrom, a senior scholar at the Manhattan Institute and co-author with her husband Stephan Thernstrom of a book on the subject.[4]

"A typical black student is graduating from high school with junior high school skills," Thernstrom says, citing figures from the National Assessment of Educational Progress (NAEP) — informally known as "the nation's report card." Hispanics, she says, "are doing only a tad better."

Traditional civil rights advocates acknowledge the gap, but they say that closing the gap requires more thoroughgoing desegregation and better funding for schools with large numbers of minority or low-income students. But educational conservatives discount those solutions, calling instead for changing "school culture" by improving discipline, teaching and student behavior.

One path to those changes, conservatives say, is "school choice" — vouchers that help students pay for

says. "But when the litigation was being developed, that seemed to be a reasonable way of trying to get kids educational rights." One consequence, Montoya adds, has been "to drive a wedge between Latinos and African-Americans."

The Supreme Court recognized Latinos as a separate group for desegregation purposes only in 1973 in a case from Denver.[4] By that time, however, the justices were about to pull back on school-desegregation remedies. "About the time we could have profited from *Brown* and used it ourselves, the protection starts crumbling," Ferg-Cadima says. Latinos have been the principal beneficiaries, however, of the Supreme Court's unanimous 1974 decision that school districts must make sure that non-English-speaking students are given language skills needed to profit from school attendance.[5]

Language is among the educational barriers distinctive to Latino students. Another, Ferg-Cadima says, is the migratory status of many Latino families, especially in agricultural areas in California, Texas and the Southwest.

Today, most Latino students attend majority-Latino schools in every region of the country, according to The Harvard Civil Rights Project.[6] As with African-American students, ethnic isolation for Latinos increased through the 1990s. The most intense segregation is found in the Northeast, where 45 percent of Hispanic students attend schools that are 90 to 100 percent Hispanic.

As for educational achievement, Latinos lag far behind white students and only slightly ahead of African-Americans. The average Latino student scored around the 25th percentile in both reading and mathematics in the 1999 National Assessment of Educational Performance — the so-called nation's report card.[7]

"The one lesson from *Brown* for all minority communities is that educational equity must be battled for on all fronts — it's something that has to be sought out," Ferg-Cadima says. "The schoolhouse gate isn't always open for our kids, so we have to fight for schools to be open and conducive to learning for all students."

---

[1] Robert R. Alvarez Jr., "The Lemon Grove Incident: The Nation's First Successful Desegregation Court Case," *The Journal of San Diego History*, Vol. 32, No. 2 (spring 1986). Alvarez is the son of the lead plaintiff in the case, *Alvarez v. Board of Trustees of the Lemon Grove School District.*

[2] See "Project Report: De Jure Segregation of Chicanos in Texas Schools," *Harvard Civil Rights-Civil Liberties Law Review*, Vol. 7, No. 2 (March 1972), pp. 307-391. The authors are Jorge C. Rangel and Carlos M. Alcala.

[3] See Vicki L. Ruiz, "'We Always Tell Our Children They Are Americans': *Méndez v. Westminster* and the California Road to *Brown v. Board of Education*," *The College Board Review*, No. 200 (fall 2003), pp. 20-27. See also Charles Wollenberg, *All Deliberate Speed: Segregation and Exclusion in California Schools, 1855-1975* (1976), pp. 108-135.

[4] The case is *Keyes v. Denver School District No. 1*, 413 U.S. 921 (1973).

[5] The case, brought by non-English-speaking Chinese students in San Francisco, is *Lau v. Nichols*, 414 U.S. 563 (1974).

[6] Gary Orfield and Chungmei Lee, "Brown at 50: King's Dream or Plessy's Nightmare?," Harvard Civil Rights Project, January 2004, p. 21.

[7] Cited in Abigail Thernstrom and Stephan Thernstrom, *No Excuses: Closing the Racial Gap in Learning* (2001), pp. 19-20.

private school tuition and charter schools that operate with freedom from traditional regulations. Traditional civil rights groups generally oppose vouchers and voice some doubts about charter schools, saying they drain support from public schools and risk further resegregation of minority students.

The policy debates underscore the shared view that *Brown* — despite its iconic status — has not proved a complete success. "You have to say it was a partial failure," says James Patterson, a professor emeritus of history at Brown University and author of a new account of the ruling and its impact.

Theodore Shaw, director of the Legal Defense Fund, agrees: "*Brown* changed everything and yet did not change everything."

As the nation prepares to unite in celebrating *Brown*, here are some of the issues that divide Americans 50 years later:

Is racial imbalance in schools increasing due to court actions?

North Carolina's Charlotte-Mecklenburg County school system in 1971 became the first in the country to operate under a court-ordered desegregation plan using wide-scale busing to achieve racial balance in school populations. Under the plan, African-Americans comprised between 30 percent and 40 percent of the students at most of the schools through the 1970s and '80s.[5]

With public support for desegregation weakening, however, the school system shifted in the 1990s to vol-

Three high school students in Clinton, Tenn., peacefully register their feelings about their school becoming the first in Tennessee to integrate, on Aug. 27, 1956. Many other protests were violent.

untary measures to maintain racial balance — chiefly by attracting white students to majority-black schools by turning them into magnet schools. Then, at the end of the decade, white families successfully sued the school system, forcing it to dismantle the busing plan altogether.[6]

The result, combined with increasing percentages of African-American and Hispanic students in the system, has been a growing concentration of minorities in many schools. Today, more than one-third of the county's 148 schools have at least 80 percent non-white enrollment.

Civil rights advocates say Charlotte is one of many school systems where political and legal developments have contributed to a trend toward resegregation. "The federal court required Charlotte to resegregate," says Harvard's Orfield, "and they are resegregating — fast."

Critics of mandatory integration, however, say today's concentration of non-white students, particularly in urban school systems, largely reflects residential demographics. Nationwide, whites comprise only about 60 percent of students in public schools, compared to 80 percent in the late 1960s. In Charlotte today, 43 percent of the system's 114,000 students are black, and only 42 percent white.

"It's wrong to say that schools are segregated or becoming resegregated," says Abigail Thernstrom, a former member of the Massachusetts Board of Education.

"Cities are becoming more heavily minority. There's nothing we can do about that. You can't helicopter kids in to get more white kids in the schools."

Orfield acknowledges that the increase in non-white enrollment poses "an obstacle" to racial mixing. But he and other desegregation advocates blame resegregation primarily on the courts, including the Supreme Court.

The percentage of black students attending majority-black schools was declining nationwide through the 1980s, Harvard Civil Rights Project reports show, but it increased during the 1990s — just as the Supreme Court was signaling to federal courts that they could ease desegregation orders. "The only basic thing that's changed since [the 1980s] is the Supreme Court of the United States," Orfield maintains.[7]

"This is a demographic process," responds Armor, "and has little to do with what the courts are doing in the desegregation area."

Education Secretary Paige also argues that court rulings are not responsible for the increasing racial isolation of blacks or Latinos. "It's not our impression that these patterns are the result of current legal practices," he says. "Ethnic communities cluster together because of a lot of different factors. Some of these factors include preferences; some are economic."

The Harvard civil rights report found that during the 1990s the trend toward integration was reversed, and the percentage of black students attending majority-black schools increased throughout the country. The percentage of Latino students attending majority-minority schools also increased in every region. Latinos are more likely than African-Americans to be in a racially or ethnically identifiable school, the report shows.

Educational conservatives, however, claim that Orfield presents a misleading picture by focusing exclusively on minority pupils' exposure to white students and not on white students' exposure to blacks and Latinos. "There are fewer white children who have no non-white classmates," says Stephan Thernstrom. "More and more white children have minority classmates."

More broadly, conservatives insist that talk of resegregation ignores the changes wrought by *Brown*. "There is no public school today that is segregated in the way that schools were routinely segregated before *Brown v. Board of Education*," says Roger Clegg, vice president and general counsel of the Center for Equal Opportunity, which opposes racial preferences. "Racial balance in a school that reflects the neighborhood is not segregation in the sense that we had segregation before *Brown*."

Shaw, of the Legal Defense Fund, counters that segregation never was eliminated completely and is increasing today. "The legal fiction is that we've severed the link between present-day segregation and our past segregated and discriminatory actions," Shaw says. "The truth is that the effects of decades and decades of segregation and discrimination were to segregate housing and to segregate other aspects of life.

"The busing remedies didn't eliminate the effects of that discrimination; they neutralized them," Shaw continues. "Once you get rid of the desegregation plans, those effects become operative once again."

Shaw and Orfield both say school boards should be allowed to consider race and ethnicity in pupil-assignment plans in order to promote integration. But educational conservatives oppose policies to deliberately increase racial mixing.

"I like racially mixed schools better than racially homogeneous schools," Abigail Thernstrom says. "But I do not want computer printouts that say you have no choice as to where to send your kids."

Minority Students Are Now More Isolated

The 1954 *Brown* ruling led to widespread school integration, but today, due to resegregation, an overwhelming percentage of African-American and Latino students attend schools with predominantly non-white student bodies. Segregation has increased nationwide since 1991, when the Supreme Court began to relax pressure on school districts to integrate.

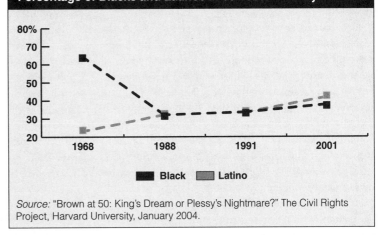

Source: "Brown at 50: King's Dream or Plessy's Nightmare?" The Civil Rights Project, Harvard University, January 2004.

Do minorities suffer educationally because of racial isolation?

Black and Latino youngsters lag significantly behind whites (and Asian-Americans) on every significant measure of academic achievement. The "racial gap" in learning deeply troubles advocates and experts on both sides of the desegregation debate.

Traditional civil rights advocates largely blame racial isolation for the lagging performance of blacks and Latinos. There is "a very systematic relation" between

segregation and the learning gap, Orfield says. "No one has ever made separate schools equal in American history on any scale."

Some critics of mandatory integration, however, see no solid evidence that racially mixed classrooms significantly benefit learning. "There is absolutely no reason to assume that because schools are heavily Hispanic or black that these children can't learn, that they have to sit next to whites or Asians in order to learn," Abigail Thernstrom says.

The social-science evidence on the issue is voluminous but less than clear-cut. In his review of the literature, George Mason University's Armor concludes that racial composition "by itself" has "no significant effect on black achievement." When combined with other educational improvements, he says, desegregation has improved black achievement "to a limited but significant degree."[8]

Desegregation advocates strongly disagree with this minimalist view. Orfield says the effect of desegregation on achievement is "significant, but not transformative." But he adds that desegregation has a "huge" effect on "life chances," such as graduating from high school, going to college and "being able to live in an interracial world as an adult."[9]

In an examination of data from Charlotte-Mecklenburg schools, Roslyn Mickelson, a professor of sociology at the University of North Carolina in Charlotte, found that black and white students both had higher average scores on standardized tests if they had been in racially integrated schools. "There is a small but significant effect on test scores that cumulates over time," she says.[10]

Orfield and other desegregation advocates say the achievement gap for minority students results in part from underfunding of schools with high percentages of black or Latino students. "The resources aren't equivalent because those are often schools that have a badge of poverty," says Underwood of the school boards association. "So they have fewer resources." U.S. schools traditionally have received most of their funding from property taxes, so schools in wealthier neighborhoods usually had more resources than schools in districts with lower property values.[11]

Armor and the Thernstroms instead blame the racial gap primarily on social and cultural factors. "There are very strong correlations between single-parent households, low birth-weight and performance in school," says Abigail Thernstrom. Armor lists single-parent households as one of 10 "risk factors" for low academic achievement. Some of the others include poverty, limited education of parents, the size of the family and the age of the mother at pregnancy.[12]

The most incendiary aspect of the issue, perhaps, concerns the claim that some black students disdain academic achievement for fear of being accused by their peers of "acting white." The thesis is most often associated with the work of the late John Ogbu, an African-American professor of anthropology at the University of California, Berkeley, who died in 2003. Ogbu first aired the theory in a co-authored article about Washington, D.C., high school students in 1986 and repeated similar views in a book about students in the affluent Cleveland suburb of Shaker Heights.[13]

Education Secretary Paige subscribes to the theory based not only on Ogbu's research but also on his own experience as school superintendent in Houston. "I had a chance to see examples where some kids were not putting their best efforts into this in an effort to keep status among some of their peers," Paige says. "It exists."

Armor, however, discounts the theory, noting that the educational gap for African-Americans can be found at the earliest grades. Abigail Thernstrom also says the evidence is "not very good." She places greater blame on schools' failure to instill educational ambitions in minority youngsters. "Schools are delivering a wrong message — that this is a racist society, and there's a limit to how far you can go," she says.

But the Legal Defense Fund's Shaw says there is evidence of an "acting white" syndrome and says the issue needs more discussion among African-Americans. But he adds that some of the debate over the educational gap for black students has "the lurking sense of racial inferiority."

"If people come to this issue in good faith and they want to focus on the causes, the first thing they have to recognize is that there's still massive inequality," Shaw says. "By the time you get to high school, African-American students have had a completely different experience from white students. Let's not blame the victim. Let's fix the problem."

Would "school choice" policies help reduce the racial gap in educational achievement for African-Americans and Latinos?

President Bush touts school vouchers, not integration, as the best way to help disadvantaged students get a better education. "When we find children trapped in schools that will not change, parents must be given another viable option," Bush told students and teachers at Archbishop Carroll High School in Washington on Feb. 13, 2004. The president used the appearance to plug a new law he had just signed to award vouchers to some 1,700 District of Columbia students per year to help pay tuition at private schools.[14]

Educational conservatives say "school choice" programs such as vouchers or charter schools will help improve schools by promoting innovation and overcoming resistance to change from public school administrators and teachers. Education Secretary Paige claims particular support for school choice among African-American families.

"My reading of the polls shows that African-American parents support choice, vouchers, strongly," Paige says. "The parents are supporters because the parents want the best education for the child."

The public school establishment strongly opposes vouchers, saying they would drain needed money from public schools. Underwood, the school boards association lawyer, says vouchers also "threaten any kind of diversity agenda that a school district may have." Private schools, she says, "can choose to discriminate. They can choose not to serve students with special needs or students who are poor or of a particular culture or ethnicity."

Local voucher programs are already operating in Milwaukee and Cleveland; Florida has a statewide program pushed by Gov. Jeb Bush, the president's brother. The programs are targeted to middle- and low-income families, but are small-scale because of limited funding. "Vouchers are going to be a sideshow for American education," Orfield says.

Charter schools — which operate under public auspices but free from some generally applicable regulations — are more widespread.[15] Some 2,700 charter schools were operating as of the 2002-2003 academic year. Many of them were established by black families and educators to serve the educational needs of African-American students. But Orfield and other desegregation advocates are skeptical that they will be better for black pupils than public schools.

"There is no evidence that charter schools are better than average," Orfield says, "and our studies show that they're more segregated than public schools."

Abigail Thernstrom counters that vouchers and charter schools "have the potential" to improve education for minority youngsters. "They have the potential for one very simple reason," she says. "They are out from under the constraints that make for such mediocre education in so many public schools."

Armor, however, sees no necessary benefit for minority youngsters from school choice programs. "I don't see

personally why vouchers or charters would have any automatic impact on school quality," Armor says. "It might or might not. There's nothing intrinsic about charters that says those teachers are going to have a better subject mastery" than teachers at regular schools. As for vouchers, Armor says they "can also be used to go to a school that doesn't have better programs" than regular public schools.

Public-education groups cite underfunding as a major barrier to improving education for minority youngsters. Nationwide, schools with the highest minority or low-income enrollments receive $1,000 less per student than schools with the lowest minority or poverty enrollments, according to a report by the Education Trust, a Washington advocacy group. (*See map, p. 274*)

"There is definitely a relationship between the amount of funding a district gets and academic performance," says Kevin Carey, a senior policy analyst with the group. "There are important issues besides money: organization, expectations for students, curricula, the way teachers are compensated. But money matters, too."

"We need to pay attention to sending resources where resources are needed," Underwood says, "so students with high educational needs get the resources they need to learn, so you really aren't leaving any child behind."

But Paige and other educational conservatives discount the importance of funding. "I don't accept that the achievement gap is a function of funding issues," Paige says. "It is a factor, but it is not *the* factor. The more important factors are those factors embedded in the No Child Left Behind Act: accountability, flexibility and parental choice — and teaching methods that work."

Orfield, however, says the No Child Left Behind Act has produced "confusion and frustration" for local school districts with scant evidence of help for minority pupils.[16] And the Legal Defense Fund's Shaw insists that school choice proposals could help only some minority students while leaving most of them behind.

"Most African-American students, like most students, are going to remain in public schools," Shaw says. "The promise of *Brown* isn't going to be realized by focusing on those few students who can escape from public schools. If we don't talk about fixing public education, then I think we betray not only *Brown* but also the fundamental notion of what public education is all about."

BACKGROUND

Long, Hard Road

The Supreme Court's celebrated decision in *Brown v. Board of Education* marks neither the beginning nor the end of the campaign for equal education for black Americans. It was only a turning point in a struggle with roots in the 19th century that now extends into the 21st.[17]

Black youngsters received no education in the antebellum South and little schooling in the decades immediately after the abolition of slavery. Where blacks did go to school, they were segregated from whites in most (though not all) parts of the country, by law or custom. Some legal challenges to the practice in the 19th century succeeded, but the Supreme Court thwarted any broad attack on segregation with its 1896 decision in *Plessy v. Ferguson* upholding "separate but equal" in public transportation.

The NAACP — founded in 1909 — won its first victory against racial segregation in education in 1935, with a state court ruling to admit a black student to the University of Maryland's law school. Four years later, one of the winning lawyers, Thurgood Marshall, was named to head a separate organization: the NAACP Legal Defense and Educational Fund, Inc. The Inc. Fund — as it was then known — won important victories from the Supreme Court with two unanimous decisions in 1950 striking down segregationist practices in graduate education at state universities in Oklahoma and Texas.[18]

Meanwhile, Marshall had been helping organize local campaigns against segregation in elementary and secondary education in four Southern and Border States. The four cases, which were consolidated in the *Brown* decision, differed in their facts and in their legal histories: Black schools in Clarendon County, S.C., were mostly ramshackle shanties; those in Topeka, Kansas, were more nearly comparable to schools for whites. The federal judge in the Prince Edward County, Va., case found "no hurt or harm to either race" in dual school systems; the state judge in the Delaware case declared that state-imposed segregation "adversely affected" education for blacks. The federal judge in Topeka also had agreed that separate schools were harmful for blacks but abided by Supreme Court precedent in rejecting any relief for the plaintiffs.

The four cases were argued before the Supreme Court twice — first in December 1952 and then again in December 1953. The justices were divided after the first argument. Five or six justices appeared inclined to declare segregation unconstitutional, according to later reconstructions of the deliberations.[19] But Chief Justice Fred M. Vinson hesitated to press for a final decision and accepted the suggestion of Justice Felix Frankfurter to ask for a reargument.

Vinson's death in September 1953 paved the way for the appointment of Chief Justice Earl Warren, who as governor of California had signed a law abolishing racial segregation in that state's public schools.[20] Warren used his considerable political skills to forge the unanimous decision on May 17, 1954, which buried the "separate but equal" doctrine, at least in public education. "Separate educational facilities," Warren wrote near the end of the 13-page opinion, "are inherently unequal."

A year later, the justices rejected both Marshall's plea to order immediate desegregation and a federal recommendation that a specific timetable for desegregation be established. Instead, the court in *Brown II* ruled that the four school districts be required to admit pupils on a racially non-discriminatory basis "with all deliberate speed."[21]

Public opinion polls indicated a narrow majority of Americans favored the ruling, but the court's gradualist approach allowed the formation of what became massive resistance. More than 100 members of Congress signed the "Southern Manifesto" in 1956 vowing to use "all lawful means" to reverse the ruling. Most school districts dragged their feet, while even token integration efforts brought forth scattered bombings and violence and more widespread intimidation and harassment. In the most dramatic instance, President Dwight D. Eisenhower had to call out National Guardsmen in September 1957 to maintain order at Central High School in Little Rock, Ark., after nine black students were enrolled. As of 1964, only 2 percent of black students in the South were attending majority-white schools.

Facing resistance both active and passive, the Supreme Court left local federal courts largely on their own for nearly a decade. In 1964, however, Congress included provisions in the landmark Civil Rights Act that authorized the federal government to file school desegregation suits and to withhold funds from school districts that failed to desegregate. Four years later, the

C H R O N O L O G Y

Before 1950 *Racial segregation takes root in public schools — by law in the South, by custom elsewhere; NAACP begins challenging "separate but equal" doctrine in the 1930s.*

1950s-1960s *Supreme Court outlaws racial segregation; ruling provokes massive resistance in South.*

1950 Supreme Court bars racial segregation in public graduate education.

1954 Supreme Court rules racial segregation in public elementary and secondary schools unconstitutional on May 17, 1954 (*Brown I*).

1955 Court says schools must be desegregated "with all deliberate speed" (*Brown II*).

1957 President Dwight D. Eisenhower calls out Arkansas National Guard to maintain order when Little Rock's Central High School is integrated.

1964 Civil Rights Act authorizes federal government to bring school-desegregation suits and to withhold funds from schools that fail to desegregate.

1968 Impatient with limited desegregation, Supreme Court says school districts must dismantle dual school systems "now."

1970s-1980s *Desegregation advances, but busing triggers battles in many cities.*

1971 Supreme Court upholds use of busing as desegregation tool.

1973 Supreme Court orders Denver to desegregate, making it the first non-Southern city ordered to integrate.

1974 Supreme Court bars federal courts from ordering cross-district busing to achieve desegregation . . . Start of busing in Boston provokes fierce opposition.

1975 Coleman report blames white-flight from urban public schools on court-ordered busing; desegregation advocates disagree.

Late 1980s Integration peaks, with most African-American students still attending predominantly black schools in each of five regions across country.

1990s *Many school systems freed from court supervision; race-conscious assignments challenged as "reverse discrimination."*

1998, 1999 Federal courts strike racial preferences used for Boston Latin School, "magnet" schools in two Washington, D.C., suburban districts.

1991 Supreme Court allows judges to lift court orders if segregation has been eliminated to all "practicable" extent.

1995 Supreme Court says judges in desegregation cases should try to end supervision of school systems.

2000-Present *Brown's promise hailed, impact debated.*

2001 President Bush wins passage of No Child Left Behind Act, providing penalties for school districts that fail to improve students' overall scores on standardized tests. . . . Federal court in September lifts desegregation decree for Charlotte-Mecklenburg schools in North Carolina.

2003 Supreme Court upholds affirmative action for colleges and universities. . . . Federal judge in December hears challenge to racial guidelines for Louisville-Jefferson County Schools; federal appeals court in same month considers suit to bar use of race as "tiebreaker" in pupil assignments in Seattle.

2004 *Brown* decision widely celebrated as 50th anniversary approaches; civil rights advocates decry "resegregation," while others say emphasis on racial balance is divisive and unproductive. . . . Federal appeals court to hear challenge in June to racial-balance transfer policy for Lynn, Mass., schools.

Success Asian-American Style

"Uncivilized, unclean and filthy beyond all conception . . . they know not the virtues of honesty, integrity or good faith," fulminated Horace Greeley, the 19th-century abolitionist and social reformer, describing Chinese immigrants.[1]

But the numbers today tell a different story. By any measure, Asian-Americans have been phenomenally successful academically. As a result, the concentration of Asian students in top American schools is wildly disproportionate to their ratio in the U.S. population.

For example, Asians make up approximately 70 percent of San Francisco's most prestigious public school, Lowell High, with Chinese-Americans alone constituting over 50 percent, although Chinese make up only 31.3 percent of the school district.

The excellent scholastic record of Asian students dates back at least to the 1930s, when California teachers wrote of "ideal" Japanese students who could serve as an example to other students. Their delinquency rate was one-third that of whites.

Today, although Asians make up only 3.8 percent of the U.S. population, Asian-Americans accounted for 27 percent of the freshman class at the Massachusetts Institute of Technology in the 2000-2001 school year, 25 percent at Stanford, 24 percent at the California Institute of Technology and 17 percent at Harvard; Asians were a phenomenal 40 percent of the freshmen at the University of California, Berkeley, in 1999. One in five American medical students is Asian.[2] Similarly, between 10 and 20 percent of the students at the nation's premier law schools are Asian.

The achievement gap between whites and Asians is greater than the gap between blacks and whites, by some measures. In 2001, 54 percent of Asian-Americans between ages 25 and 29 had at least a bachelor's degree, compared with 34 percent of whites and 18 percent of blacks.

Academics have long disputed the reasons for Asians' stellar performance. The controversial 1994 book, *The Bell Curve*, held that Asians did better because they were inherently more intelligent than others. But numerous academics attacked Richard J. Herrnstein and Charles Murray's methodology and racial conclusions. Some studies show that Asians, particularly Chinese, consistently score higher on IQ tests than other groups.[3] But there is increasing evidence that racial differences are minimal.[4]

Another explanation attributes the relative success of Asians in America to the socioeconomic and educational status of the Asian immigrants who were allowed to enter the United States. In 1965, immigration reforms allotted immigrant visas preferentially to people with needed skills. Many came from India or China with advanced degrees in medicine or technology.

The parents' educational and occupational attainments "far exceed the average for native-born Americans," according to Stephen L. Klineberg, a Rice University sociology professor studying Houston-area demographics.[5] With such parents, the children seem primed for success, but critics of socioeconomic explanations point out that even though many early Asian immigrants were mainly laborers and peasants, they still performed exceptionally well in school.

Most of those early Asian-Americans, mainly Chinese, lived in California, where school segregation developed quickly. By 1863, "Negroes, Mongolians and Indians" were prohibited from attending schools with white children.[6] Statewide restrictions were soon amended so non-white children could attend public schools with whites where no separate schools existed; in areas with fewer Chinese immigrants, they often attended schools with whites. San Francisco responded by building a separate school for Chinese children in 1885.

In 1906, Japanese and Koreans also were ordered to attend the so-called Oriental School in San Francisco, although the Japanese resisted, and by 1929 the vast majority of Japanese children attended integrated schools.[7] The courts and legislature ended legal segregation in California schools in 1947.

However, Chinese immigrants in California have staunchly opposed integration proposals that required their children to be bused out of local neighborhoods. "One time, in the 1960s and '70s, when integration of schools was the big issue, I almost got lynched in Chinatown by Chinese-Americans for supporting integration," said Ling-chi Wang, a professor of ethnic studies at Berkeley and veteran civil rights advocate.[8] More recently, Chinese-American parents successfully challenged a San Francisco school-integration plan, arguing that their children were losing out due to racial quotas at magnet schools.[9]

Today, regardless of their parents' income level or education, Asian students perform better academically than other groups, though their performance does improve as parental education and income increase. The persistent performance gap, even accounting for socioeconomic factors, leads to a third explanation for Asians' success: the great emphasis put on education by Asian parents, higher academic expectations and the attitude that successful achievement is simply a question of hard work.

For instance, a study by Temple University's Laurence Steinberg of 20,000 Wisconsin and California students found that Asian-American students felt any grade below A- would anger their parents; for whites the anger threshold was B-, for blacks and Latinos a C-. And research shows that more than 50 percent of Asian-American high school seniors spend an hour or more per night on homework, compared to 30 percent of Latinos and less than 25 percent of whites.[10]

Education experts often blame the gap between how white children and new immigrants perform educationally on the language barriers faced by the immigrants. But evidence suggests that newly arrived Asians learn English faster than Latinos, thus breaking down those barriers faster. For instance, 1990 Census data showed that 90 to 95 percent of third-generation Asian-American children spoke only English at home, compared to only 64 percent of Mexican-Americans.[11]

But Asian immigrants are not a monolithic "model minority." Asians who arrive already speaking English, such as Filipinos or Indians, fare better educationally and economically. The poverty rate among Filipino immigrants — who come from a country with a 95 percent literacy rate — is only 6.3 percent, compared with 37.8 percent among the Hmong — a mostly uneducated ethnic group from Southeast Asia.

In Sacramento, where Hmong comprise about 8 percent of public school students, they are the lowest-performing group, according to Suanna Gilman-Ponce, director of the

Asians were segregated from whites in California schools at the end of the 19th century. In 1885, San Francisco built a separate school for Chinese children.

school district's multilingual education department.[12] For example, only 3 percent of the Hmong had a bachelor's degree, according to the 1990 census, compared with 24 percent of the nation as a whole.

But there is progress: Among the 25-to-34 age group, the first Hmong generation to grow up in the United States, 13.5 percent had degrees. And of the Vietnamese, many of whom also arrived as refugees, 26.9 percent had a college degree; the national average is 27.5 percent.

— Kenneth Lukas

[1] Quoted in Andrew Gyory, *Closing the Gate* (1998), p. 17.

[2] Abigail Thernstrom and Stephan Thernstrom, *No Excuses: Closing the Racial Gap in Learning* (2003), p. 85.

[3] Jeff Wise, "Are Asians Smarter?" *Time International*, Sept. 11, 1995, p. 60.

[4] Natalie Angier, "Do Races Differ? Not Really, Genes Show," *The New York Times*, Aug. 22, 2000, p. F1 and Steve Olson, "The Genetic Archaeology of Race," *The Atlantic Monthly*, April 2, 2001, p. 69.

[5] Quoted in Mike Snyder, "Survey: Area Asians Have Head Start," *The Houston Chronicle*, Oct. 1, 2002, p. A1.

[6] For background on Asians in California, see Charles Wollenberg, *All Deliberate Speed: Segregation and Exclusion in California Schools, 1855-1975* (1976).

[7] Bill Hosokawa, *Nisei: The Quiet Americans* (2002), pp. 85-89.

[8] Quoted in Sam McManis, "Activist Fights for Asian Americans at U.S. Labs," *San Francisco Chronicle*, March 27, 2002, p. A1.

[9] David J. Hoff, "San Francisco Assignment Rules Anger Parents," *Education Week*, June 4, 2003, p. 9. See also "All Things Considered," National Public Radio, Aug. 10, 2002, and April 5, 2004.

[10] Thernstrom, *op. cit.*, p. 94.

[11] *Ibid.*, pp. 111-113.

[12] Quoted in Erika Chavez, "Hmong Cry for Help Has Been Heard," *Sacramento Bee*, May 28, 2002, p. B1.

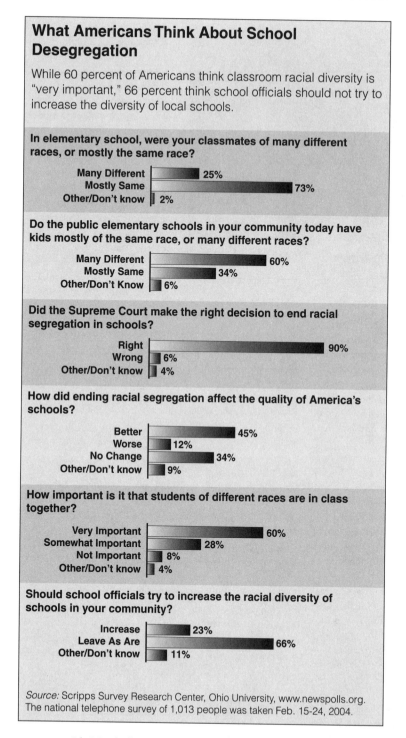

What Americans Think About School Desegregation

While 60 percent of Americans think classroom racial diversity is "very important," 66 percent think school officials should not try to increase the diversity of local schools.

In elementary school, were your classmates of many different races, or mostly the same race?

Many Different — 25%
Mostly Same — 73%
Other/Don't know — 2%

Do the public elementary schools in your community today have kids mostly of the same race, or many different races?

Many Different — 60%
Mostly Same — 34%
Other/Don't Know — 6%

Did the Supreme Court make the right decision to end racial segregation in schools?

Right — 90%
Wrong — 6%
Other/Don't know — 4%

How did ending racial segregation affect the quality of America's schools?

Better — 45%
Worse — 12%
No Change — 34%
Other/Don't know — 9%

How important is it that students of different races are in class together?

Very Important — 60%
Somewhat Important — 28%
Not Important — 8%
Other/Don't know — 4%

Should school officials try to increase the racial diversity of schools in your community?

Increase — 23%
Leave As Are — 66%
Other/Don't know — 11%

Source: Scripps Survey Research Center, Ohio University, www.newspolls.org. The national telephone survey of 1,013 people was taken Feb. 15-24, 2004.

offered by a rural Virginia school board and declared that school districts had to develop plans to dismantle dual systems "root and branch" — and to do it "now."

Given patterns of residential segregation, many plans devised by federal judges inevitably involved busing — typically, transporting black students to schools in predominantly white areas. Many white parents objected, but the court — under a new chief justice, Warren Burger — unanimously ruled in the *Charlotte-Mecklenburg* case in 1971 that courts had discretion to order busing as part of a desegregation plan.

Bumps in the Road

In the 1970s and '80s, desegregation advanced generally in the South and in most of the rest of the country. But the use of busing as a principal tool for racial mixing provoked fierce protests in some cities and widespread opposition from officials and the public at large. Meanwhile, Latino enrollment in public schools began to increase dramatically — and so, too, did the percentage of Latino students attending predominantly Latino schools.

The busing issue dominated the headlines and the policy debates in the 1970s, obscuring the less dramatic evidence of changes in public schools, especially in the South. From 1968 to 1988, the percentage of black students attending predominantly minority schools fell sharply in the South — from more than 80 percent to around 55 percent — and declined significantly in every other region except the Northeast.[22]

court — with Marshall now serving as the first African-American justice — announced that its patience was at an end. The justices rejected a "freedom of choice" plan

As historian Patterson notes, most of the heavily black schools in the South were more nearly comparable to white schools by the end of the 1980s, salaries for black teachers were more nearly equal to those for whites and teaching staffs were integrated.

Public education in the South, he concludes, "had been revolutionized" — thanks to pressure from the then-Department of Health, Education and Welfare and rulings from federal courts.[23]

For many Americans, however, desegregation came to be understood only as court-ordered transportation of students out of their neighborhoods to distant schools of uncertain character and quality. The polarizing issue erupted most dramatically in ostensibly liberal Boston, where a federal judge ordered racial mixing between heavily white South Boston and predominantly black Roxbury. Patterson notes that on the first day of the plan in September 1974, only 10 of the 525 white students assigned to Roxbury High School showed up, while buses carrying 56 black pupils bound for South Boston High School were stoned.[24]

Busing had few vocal supporters. President Gerald Ford, a Republican, complained that busing "brought fear to black students and white students." President Jimmy Carter, a Democrat, was lukewarm toward the practice. Sociologist James Coleman — who authored an influential report in 1968 documenting the educational achievement gap for African-American students — added respectability to the anti-busing critique with a report in 1975 blaming "white flight" from central-city schools on court-ordered busing and calling instead for voluntary desegregation.[25]

Civil rights supporters countered that opponents were exaggerating the costs and disruption of court-ordered busing when their real objection was to racial mixing altogether. They also sharply disputed Coleman's "white flight" theory, insisting that the movement of whites to the suburbs — and the resulting concentration of African-Americans in inner cities — stemmed from social and economic trends dating from the 1950s unrelated to school desegregation.

The Supreme Court itself acknowledged the logistical problems of busing in some of its decisions, but the justices couched their emerging disagreements on desegregation in legalistic terms. In 1973, the court established a critical distinction between "de jure" segregation — ordered by law — and "de facto" segregation resulting only from residential segregation. The ruling allowed a lower court to enforce a desegregation plan, but only on the grounds that the school district had intentionally drawn zones to separate black and white pupils. (The rul-

Pioneering civil rights attorney Thurgood Marshall, shown here in 1957, successfully argued the landmark *Brown v. Board of Education* case before the U.S. Supreme Court. President Lyndon B. Johnson appointed Marshall to the high court in 1967.

ing also recognized Hispanic students as an identifiable class for desegregation purposes.) In a partial dissent, Justice Lewis F. Powell Jr. criticized the distinction between "de facto" and "de jure" segregation, saying any racial separation of students was constitutionally suspect.

A year later, the court dealt integration advocates a more serious setback in a 5-4 ruling that barred transportation of students across school-district lines to achieve desegregation. The ruling struck down a desegregation plan for the heavily black Detroit school district and the predominantly white schools in surrounding Wayne County suburbs. For the majority, Chief Justice Burger said school district lines "could not be casually ignored." In dissent, Marshall called the ruling "a large step backwards."

Three years later, the court dealt another blow to desegregation advocates by ruling — in a case from Pasadena, Calif. — that a school district was not respon-

Police escort school buses carrying African-American students into South Boston in 1974, implementing a court-ordered busing plan to integrate schools.

sible for resegregation of students once it had adopted a racially neutral attendance plan.

The rulings combined with political opposition and socioeconomic trends to stall further increases in racial mixing of students by the end of the 1980s. The percentage of black students attending predominantly minority schools increased after 1988 in the South and West and after 1991 in the Northeast, Midwest and Border States. The Supreme Court, under the leadership of conservative Chief Justice William H. Rehnquist, then eased the pressure on school districts to continue desegregation efforts with three more decisions between 1991 and 1995.

The rulings — in cases from Oklahoma City; suburban DeKalb County, Ga.; and Kansas City — effectively told federal judges to ease judicial supervision once legally enforced segregation had been eliminated to the extent practicable. For the majority, Rehnquist wrote in the Kansas City case that federal judges should remember that their purpose was not only to remedy past violations but also to return schools to the control of local and state authorities.

Reversing Directions?

By the mid-1990s, traditional civil rights advocates were strongly criticizing what they termed the resegregation of African-American and Latino students. Critics of mandatory integration replied that legal segregation and its effects had been largely eliminated and that apparent racial and ethnic separation reflected residential neighborhoods and the growing proportion of African-American and Latino students in public schools.

As federal courts backed away from desegregation suits, white students brought — and in a few cases won — so-called reverse-discrimination suits contesting use of race in school-assignment plans. Meanwhile, some civil rights supporters shifted direction by bringing school-funding cases in state courts.

School-desegregation litigation all but petered out during the 1990s. Nearly 700 cases remain technically alive nationwide, but a law professor's examination of the period 1992-2002 found only 53 suits in active litigation.[26] Professor Wendy Parker of the University of Cincinnati College of Law also showed that school districts had succeeded in every instance but one when they asked for so-called unitary status — in order to get out from under further judicial supervision of desegregation decrees — even if enrollments continued to reflect racial imbalance.

In addition, Parker said judges were somewhat lax in requiring racial balance of teaching staffs and that any racial imbalance in teaching assignments invariably mirrored a school's racial composition: Schools with a disproportionate number of black teachers were predominantly black, those with disproportionate numbers of white teachers were predominantly white.

Meanwhile, a few federal courts were curbing school districts' discretion to consider race in assigning students to elite or so-called magnet schools. In 1998, the 1st U.S. Circuit Court of Appeals had ruled against the use of "flexible race/ethnicity guidelines" for filling about half of the places each year at the elite Boston Latin School. The court said the Boston School Committee had failed to show that the policy either promoted diversity or helped remedy vestiges of past discrimination.[27]

The next year, another federal appeals court ruled in favor of white students' claims that school boards in two suburban Washington, D.C., school districts — Montgomery County, Md., and Arlington, Va. — violated the Constitution's Equal Protection Clause by considering race in magnet-school placements. In both rulings, the 4th U.S. Circuit Court of Appeals said the use of race was not narrowly tailored to achieve the goal of diversity. The Supreme Court refused to hear the school districts' appeals.[28]

With federal courts seemingly uninterested in desegregation initiatives, civil rights groups put more resources into school-funding challenges before state legislatures or courts.[29] The various efforts, pushed in some 40 states, generally aimed at narrowing or eliminating financial disparities between well-to-do and less-well-off school districts. Funding-equity advocates succeeded in part in several states — sometimes through court order, sometimes by legislative changes spurred by actual or threatened litigation.

The initiatives helped cause a shift in education-funding sources away from the historic primary reliance on local property taxes. Today, just over half of local education funding comes from state rather than local revenues, according to Carey, of the Education Trust. Nonetheless, school districts with high minority or low-income enrollments still receive fewer funds compared to districts with more white or wealthier students.

The limited progress on funding issues gave civil rights advocates only slight consolation for the evidence of increasing racial imbalance in public schools. By 2001, at least two-thirds of black students and at least half of Latino students nationwide were enrolled in predominantly minority schools. Significantly, the Northeast is more segregated: More than half of black students (51 percent) and nearly half of Latino students (44 percent) attended intensely segregated schools with 90 to 100 percent minority enrollment. "We've been going backward almost every place in the country since the 1990s," Harvard's Orfield says.

Critics of mandatory integration, however, viewed the figures differently. They emphasized that white students' exposure to African-American and Latino students has continued to increase. In any event, they say, residential patterns, city-suburban boundary lines and the increasing percentages of African-American and Latino students in overall enrollment make it impractical to achieve greater racial mixing in many school districts.

"The proportion of minorities in large districts is growing," says George Mason's Armor. "When it crosses 50 percent, whatever your racial-assignment plan, you're going to have minority schools."

For his part, President Bush has pushed education reform aimed in part at helping low-income students but without adopting traditional civil rights goals or rhetoric. "American children must not be left in persistently dan-gerous or failing schools," Bush declared as he unveiled — on Jan. 23, 2001, his second full day in office — what eventually became the No Child Left Behind Act. Approved by Congress in May 2001, the law prescribes student testing to measure academic progress among public school students and provides financial penalties for school districts that fail to improve student performance.

Education Secretary Paige says the law seeks to continue the effort to improve educational opportunities for all students started by *Brown v. Board of Education.* The law passed with broad bipartisan support. By 2004, however, many Democrats were accusing the administration of failing to provide funding to support needed changes, while many school administrators were criticizing implementation of the law as excessively rigid and cumbersome.

CURRENT SITUATION

Race-Counting

Schools in Lynn, Mass., were facing a multifaceted crisis in the 1980s, with crumbling buildings, tattered textbooks, widespread racial strife and rapid white flight. To regain public confidence, the school board in 1989 adopted a plan combining neighborhood-school assignments with a transfer policy that included only one major restriction: No child could transfer from one school to another if the move would increase racial imbalance at either of the schools involved.

The Lynn school board credits the plan with stabilizing enrollment, easing race relations and helping lift academic performance throughout the 15,000-student system. But lawyers for parents whose children were denied transfers under the plan are asking a federal appeals court to rule that the policy amounts to illegal racial discrimination.

"They're denying school assignments based on the color of the kid who's asking for the assignment," says Michael Williams, a lawyer with the Boston-based Citizens for the Preservation of Constitutional Rights.

The case — expected to be argued in September 2004 before the 1st U.S. Circuit Court of Appeals in Boston — is one of several nationwide where school boards with voluntary integration plans are facing legal actions aimed at eliminating any use of race in student assignments. Attorneys for the school boards are vigorously defending race-conscious policies.

'We've Yet to Achieve' Equality of Education

Secretary of Education Rod Paige was interviewed on March 24, 2004, in his Washington office by Associate Editor Kenneth Jost. Here are verbatim excerpts from that interview.

On his experience attending racially segregated schools:

"The fact that [white students] had a gym was a big deal. They played basketball on the inside. They had a big gym with lights and stuff on the inside. We played basketball on the outside with a clay court. We played up until the time that you couldn't see the hoop any more. . . . I wanted to take band, but there was no music. I wanted to play football, but there was no football team [until senior year]. . . . The concept of separate but equal is not at all academic for me. It is very personal. And even today . . . I don't know what I missed."

On the impact of the Brown v. Board of Education decision:

"Was the goal to take 'separate but equal' away . . . ? The answer would be [yes], in a very strong and striking way. If the goal was equality education, to level the educational playing field for all children, especially children of color, the answer is we've yet to achieve that."

On the resegregation of black and Latino students:

"Ethnic communities cluster together because of a lot of different factors. Some of these factors include preferences; some are economic. So our goal should be now to provide a quality education for a child no matter where they are in this system."

On efforts to promote racial balance in schools:

"If anybody is in a segregated school based on unfairness, then, yes, they should work against that. But . . . we don't want to get integration confused with educational excellence. We want to provide educational excellence to kids no matter what their location is [or] the ethnic makeup of their community."

On the use of race in pupil assignments:

"A person should not be disadvantaged because of the color of their skin. Nor should that person be advantaged because of the color of their skin. . . . That's the principle I would apply to any set of circumstances."

On "equal" opportunities for African-American and Latino students:

"I've got to come down on the side that there's a large amount of lower expectations for minority kids. . . . If there

"You cannot ignore race and expect that the issue will not be present in your school system," says Richard Cole, senior counsel for civil rights in the Massachusetts attorney general's office, who is defending the Lynn plan. "The only way is to take steps to bring kids of different racial groups together."

Meanwhile, the federal appeals court for Washington state is considering a challenge to the Seattle School District's use of race as one of several factors — a so-called "tiebreaker" — in determining assignments to oversubscribed schools. The 9th Circuit appeals court heard arguments on Dec. 14, 2003, in a three-year-old suit by the predominantly white Parents Involved in Community Schools claiming that the policy violates equal-protection guarantees.[30]

Opposing experts and advocates in the desegregation debate are also closely watching the Louisville case, where U.S. District Judge John Heyburn II is expected to rule by the end of the school year on Jefferson County's racial guidelines for pupil assignments. And in another case, a conservative public-interest law firm is in California state court claiming that a statewide initiative barring racial preferences prevents the Berkeley school system from asking for racial information from students and families or using the information for assignment purposes.[31]

Schools in Lynn, a gritty former mill town 10 miles north of Boston, were in "dire straits" in the 1980s before adoption of the integration plan, according to Cole. Attendance was down; violence and racial conflict were up. White students — who comprised more than 80 percent of the enrollment as of 1977 — were fleeing the schools at the rate of 5 percent a year. There was also evidence that white students were being allowed to trans-are lower expectations for a child, then the answer to your question has to be that there is not a fair opportunity."

On causes of the "racial gap" in learning:

"There are three drivers. One is the quality of instructional circumstances. . . . The second is the quantity of it . . . And the third one is student engagement. Learning is an active activity between the teacher and the student. So the student does have some responsibility here in terms of student engagement."

On underfunding of minority and low-income schools:

"I don't accept that the achievement gap is a function of funding issues. I think it

Secretary of Education Rod Paige

U.S. Dept. of Education

is a factor, but it is not *the* factor. . . . The more important factors are those embedded in the No Child Left Behind Act: accountability, flexibility and parental choice — and teaching methods that work."

On school choice proposals — vouchers and charter schools:

"My reading of the polls show[s] that African-American parents support choice, vouchers, strongly. . . . The parents are supporters because [they] want the best education for the child. . . . Enforcing monopolistic tendencies on schools is a detriment to schools. The people who force these monopolistic tendencies on schools deny schools the opportunity to innovate, create and reach their potential."

fer out of predominantly black schools in violation of the district's stated rules.

The school board adopted a multipronged strategy to try to stem white flight and improve schools for white and minority youngsters alike, Cole says. A neighborhood-school assignment plan was combined with the construction of new schools, including magnet schools, using funds under a state law to aid racial-balance programs. Cole says attendance rates and achievement levels are up, discipline problems down and enrollment stabilized. The district's students are 58 percent minority, 42 percent white.

The citizens' group, which had earlier filed a suit that forced Boston to drop its use of busing for desegregation, sued Lynn schools in August 1999. Williams acknowledges the school system's past problems and more recent progress. But he says all of the improvements resulted

from "race-neutral stuff that could have happened if the plan had not included a racial element."

U.S. District Judge Nancy Gertner rejected the group's suit in a 156-page ruling in December 2003. "The Lynn plan does not entail coercive assignments or forced busing; nor does it prefer one race over another," said Gertner, who was appointed by President Bill Clinton. "The message it conveys to the students is that our society is heterogeneous, that racial harmony matters — a message that cannot be conveyed meaningfully in segregated schools."[32]

Legal Defense Fund Director Shaw calls the legal challenges to voluntary desegregation plans "Orwellian." "Our adversaries have this perverted sense of the law and the Constitution that holds mere race consciousness — even if it's in support of desegregation — as discriminatory," he says.

Should the federal government do more to promote racial and ethnic diversity in public schools?

YES
Gary Orfield
*Director, The Harvard Civil Rights Project
Co-author, "Brown at 50: King's Dream or
Plessy's Nightmare?"*

Written for The CQ Researcher, April 2004

The federal government has taken no significant, positive initiatives toward desegregation or even toward serious research on multiracial schools since the Carter administration.

In fact, Presidents Richard M. Nixon, Gerald Ford, Ronald Reagan and both George Bushes were generally opposed to urban desegregation and named like-minded appointees to run the major federal civil rights and education agencies. Attorney General John Ashcroft, for example, fought desegregation orders in St. Louis and Kansas City, and Reagan Supreme Court appointee Chief Justice William H. Rehnquist has consistently opposed urban desegregation.

Between 1965 and 1970, federal leadership played a decisive role in ending educational apartheid in the South and transforming it into the nation's most desegregated region. Southern schools were the most integrated for more than three decades, during which time black achievement, graduation and college attendance increased, and educational gaps began to close. But those schools now are seriously resegregating.

President Nixon largely ended enforcement of the 1964 Civil Rights Act in schools and intentionally stirred up national division over busing as part of his "Southern strategy." Then, in two separate 5-4 decisions in 1973 and 1974, four Nixon justices helped block school-finance equalization and desegregation across city-suburban lines. The federal government never enforced the Supreme Court's 1973 decision recognizing Latinos' right to desegregation. And in the 1990s the Rehnquist court thrice ended desegregation orders, effectively producing resegregation. Nearly 90 percent of the heavily segregated minority schools produced by this process have high rates of poverty and educational inequality.

Federal policy could help reverse the resegregation trend. First, leaders must make the compelling case that desegregation, properly implemented, is valuable for all students, preparing them to live and work in a multiracial society. Second, judicial vacancies and civil rights enforcement agencies should be staffed with progressives. Third, the desegregation-aid program could be revived to help suburbs experiencing racial change without preparation or resources.

In addition, serious research needs to be done on resegregation. Educational choice programs should forbid transfers that increase segregation and reward those that diminish it. And magnet school programs should be expanded. Finally, fair-housing enforcement should be greatly increased and policies adopted to help stabilize desegregated neighborhoods.

NO
David J. Armor
*Professor of Public Policy, School of Public
Policy, George Mason University*

Written for The CQ Researcher, April 2004

To answer this question, we must ask three related questions. First, do legal constraints prevent the promotion of diversity in public schools? The answer is yes. The Supreme Court has provided a legal framework for using race in public policy, and the justices recently clarified that framework in two cases involving college admissions in Michigan. Racial diversity can be a compelling government purpose, but policies must be narrowly tailored to reflect the use of race or ethnicity as only one factor, not the predominant factor, in the policy.

Applying this framework to public schools, race could not be used as the primary basis for assigning students to schools (as in old-fashioned busing plans), unless a school district was remedying illegal segregation. The use of race might be justified for controlling enrollment in a voluntary magnet school on the grounds that students should be allowed to choose racially diverse programs, but even this limited use of race is being challenged in the courts. The Supreme Court has yet to rule on diversity for K-12 public schools.

Second, does diversity bring clear social and educational benefits to public school children? Diversity unquestionably has social value, since it allows children from different backgrounds to learn about other cultures and how to work together. However, it is hard to find social outcomes that have consistently benefited from desegregation. For example, race relations have sometimes worsened after desegregation programs, particularly if they involved mandatory busing. Moreover, the formal educational value of diversity has not been proven, since large-scale school-desegregation programs have not reduced the racial gap in academic achievement.

The third question we must ask is what kind of promotion, if any, might be appropriate for the federal government? Federal agencies have an important but limited role in policies for K-12 public schools. They conduct research, sponsor special programs, conduct assessment and recently adopted policies to raise academic standards and accountability under the No Child Left Behind Act. Given the legal constraints on diversity programs and the uncertain educational benefits of diversity in K-12 schools, I do not think promoting diversity should be a high priority at this time.

However, since there is still a debate over the educational benefits of racial diversity programs, it would be appropriate for the federal government to sponsor research to help resolve this important issue.

But Clegg of the Center for Equal Opportunity says schools should not assign students on the basis of race or ethnicity. "The social benefits to achieving a predetermined racial or ethnic mix are very small compared to the social costs of institutionalized racial and ethnic discrimination," he says.

Race-Mixing?

Some two-dozen Washington, D.C., high school students gathered on a school day in late February for a "dialogue" with the president of the American Bar Association and the city's mayor about *Brown v. Board of Education.* Dennis Archer, a former mayor of Detroit, is black — as is Washington's mayor, Anthony Williams. And so, too, are all but three of Woodson High School's 700 students.

The students — chosen from an advanced-placement U.S. history course — listen respectfully as Archer and Williams relate the story of the *Brown* case and the implementation of the ruling over the ensuing 50 years. The students' questions, however, make clear that they feel little impact from the ruling in their daily lives.

"Why is there such a small percentage of white students in D.C. schools?" Danyelle Johnson asks. Wesley Young echoes the comment: "I feel that to make it better we should be like Wilson [High School] and have different races in schools," he says, referring to a well-regarded integrated school in a predominantly white neighborhood.

"It's really hard for me to make [*Brown*] relevant to them," assistant principal Phyllis Anderson remarks afterward, "because they've been in an all-black environment all their lives, and their parents before them."

With 84 percent of its 65,000 public school students black, another 10 percent Hispanic and only 5 percent white, Washington provides an extreme, but not unrepresentative, example of the situation in central-city school districts throughout the country. Nationwide, central-city black students typically attend schools with 87 percent minority enrollment, according to the Harvard Civil Rights Project. For Latinos, the figure is 86 percent. This "severe segregation" results from residential segregation and the "fragmentation" of large metropolitan regions into separate school districts, the project's most recent survey explains.[33]

The Supreme Court's 1974 ruling barring court-ordered interdistrict desegregation plans virtually elimi-

Stanton Elementary School, in Stanton, Ky., reflects the current status of school integration in most of the nation. Most public schools are as segregated today as they were in 1969. During the 2000-2001 school year, for instance, only 30 non-white students were enrolled in the 2,500-student Stanton school district.

nated the possibility of racial mixing between inner cities and suburbs except in countywide systems like those in Louisville-Jefferson County and Charlotte-Mecklenburg County. The court's ruling in the Kansas City desegregation case in 1995 also limited federal judges' power to order costly improvements for central-city schools in an effort to attract white students from the suburbs.

Over the past decade or so, middle-class blacks and Latinos have themselves migrated to the suburbs, but because of residential segregation the movement has not fundamentally changed the pattern of racial isolation in the schools, according to the Harvard report. Even in the suburbs of large metropolitan areas, the typical black student attends a school that is 65 percent minority, the typical Latino a school that is 69 percent minority.[34]

Federal courts, meanwhile, have been freeing dozens of school districts from judicial supervision by declaring the segregated systems dismantled and granting the districts "unitary status." In an examination of 35 such districts, the Harvard study found that black students' exposure to whites had fallen in all but four — typically, by at least 10 percent. "Desegregation is declining rapidly in places the federal courts no longer hold accountable," the report concludes.[35]

The Legal Defense Fund's Shaw says the trends result from judicial solicitude for school districts that once practiced segregation. "If a snapshot reveals a desegregated district," he says, "the court can grant judicial absolution, and the district can return to a segregated status."

The Manhattan Institute's Abigail Thernstrom counters that the focus on racial mixing is beside the point. "Teach the kids instead of worrying about the racial composition of the school," she says. "Otherwise, we're chasing demographic rainbows. Cities aren't going to get whiter. And they're not going to get more middle-class."

OUTLOOK

Mixed Records

Fifty years after the Supreme Court declared the end of racial segregation, the four communities involved in the historic cases present mixed records on the degree of progress in bringing black and white children together in public schools.[36]

Topeka — home of Oliver Brown and his daughter Linda, then in elementary school — achieved "substantial levels of integration" while under a court-ordered desegregation plan, according to the Harvard Civil Rights Project. But integration has receded slightly since the system was declared unitary and judicial supervision was ended in 1999.

As of 2001, black students in Topeka were in schools with 51 percent white enrollment — down from 59 percent in 1991. Just outside the city limits, however, better-off suburban school districts have predominantly white enrollments. "The city was then, as it is now, physically and emotionally segregated," Ronald Griffin, a black professor at Washburn University Law School in Topeka, remarked at a symposium in 2002. "That has not changed."[37]

The Delaware case "led to the merger and full desegregation of all students" in Wilmington and adjoining suburban districts, the Harvard report says. The federal court lifted judicial supervision in 1996, but Wilmington and the entire state remain as some of the most integrated school systems in the country, according to the report.

The two Southern communities involved in the four cases present a sharp contrast. Prince Edward County, Va., resisted integration to the point of closing all public

schools from 1959 until the Supreme Court ordered them reopened in 1964. Today, however, the school system has an integration level "far above the national average" and student achievement in line with other Virginia districts, despite a predominantly black enrollment, according to the Harvard report.

In Clarendon County, S.C., however, School District Number One in tiny Summertown has only 60 white students among a total enrollment of 1,100. Other white students attend a private academy set up at the start of desegregation in 1969. When an *Education Week* reporter recently asked Jonathan Henry — a great-great-grandson of one of the plaintiffs — about his interactions with white students, Henry seemed "bewildered. . . . He really doesn't know any."[38]

The legacy of the *Brown* cases is "mixed," according to historian Patterson. "It seems in the early 2000s to be somewhat more complicated, somewhat more mixed than anybody in the 1970s could have imagined."

"We are miles ahead because of *Brown*," Education Secretary Paige says. "But we have yet to achieve" the goal of equal educational opportunities for all students.

Whatever has or has not been accomplished in the past, the nation's changing demographics appear to be combining with law and educational policy to push ethnic and racial mixing to the side in favor of an increased emphasis on academic performance. Schools "are going to be more racially identifiable," the Legal Defense Fund's Shaw says. "I don't see any public policy right now that's going to turn that around."

Critics of mandatory integration applaud the change. "At the end of the day, what you want to ask is, 'Are the kids getting an education?'," Abigail Thernstrom says. "The right question is what are kids learning, not whom are they sitting next to."

The emphasis on academic performance makes the challenges for schools and education policy-makers all the more difficult, however, not less. "The black kid who arrives at school as a 5- or 6-year old is already way, way behind, and it just gets worse as they go on," historian Patterson says. "There's only so much the schools can do."

Latino youngsters enter school with many of the same socioeconomic deficits, often combined with limited English proficiency. In any event, the debates about educational policy have yet to catch up with the fact that

Latinos are now the nation's largest minority group.[39] "We don't see an equal commitment on the part of educational equity for Latinos," says James Ferg-Cadima, an attorney for the Mexican American Legal Defense and Educational Fund.

"It's a major challenge for all of us to work together collegially to make sure that our children get the education they deserve," ABA President Archer says. "We're going to have to do a lot more to make sure all of our children in public schools — or wherever they are — graduate with a good education and can be competitive in a global economy."

NOTES

1. The decision is *Brown v. Board of Education of Topeka*, 347 U.S. 483 (1954). The ruling came in four consolidated cases from Topeka; Clarendon County, S.C.; Prince Edward County, Va.; and Wilmington-Kent County, Del. In a companion case, the court also ruled racial segregation in the District of Columbia unconstitutional: *Bolling v. Sharpe*, 347 U.S. 497 (1954).

2. The case is *McFarland v. Jefferson County Public Schools*, 3:02CV-620-H. For coverage, see Chris Kenning, "School Desegregation Plan on Trial," *The* (Louisville) *Courier-Journal*, Dec. 8, 2003, p. 1A, and subsequent daily stories by Kenning, Dec. 9-13. McFarland's quote is from his in-court testimony.

3. For background, see Kenneth Jost, "Rethinking School Integration," *The CQ Researcher*, Oct. 18, 1996, pp. 913-936.

4. Abigail Thernstrom and Stephan Thernstrom, *No More Excuses: Closing the Racial Gap in Learning* (2003). For a statistical overview, see pp. 11-23.

5. Some background drawn from Roslyn Arlin Mickelson, "The Academic Consequences of Desegregation and Segregation: Evidence From the Charlotte-Mecklenburg Schools," *North Carolina Law Review*, Vol. 81, No. 4 (May 2003), pp. 1513-1562.

6. The decision is *Belk v. Charlotte-Mecklenburg Board of Education*, 269 F.3d 305 (4th Cir. 2001). For coverage, see Celeste Smith and Jennifer Wing Rothacker, "Court Rules That Schools Unitary," *The Charlotte Observer*, Sept. 22, 2001, p. 1A.

7. See Gary Orfield and Chungmei Lee, "*Brown* at 50: King's Dream or *Plessy's* Nightmare," The Civil Rights Project, Harvard University, January 2004.

8. David J. Armor, "Desegregation and Academic Achievement," in Christine H. Rossell *et al.*, *School Desegregation in the 21st Century* (2001), pp. 183-184.

9. See Orfield and Lee, *op. cit.*, pp. 22-26.

10. Mickelson, *op. cit.*, pp. 1543ff.

11. For background, see Kathy Koch, "Reforming School Funding," *The CQ Researcher*, Dec. 10, 1999, pp. 1041-1064.

12. See David J. Armor, *Maximizing Intelligence* (2003).

13. See John Ogbu, *Black Students in an Affluent Suburb: A Study of Academic Disengagement* (2003).

14. Quoted in Justin Blum, "Bush Praises D.C. Voucher Plan," *The Washington Post*, Feb. 14, 2004, p. B2. For background, see Kenneth Jost, "School Vouchers Showdown," *The CQ Researcher*, Feb. 15, 2002, pp. 121-144.

15. For background, see Charles S. Clark, "Charter Schools," *The CQ Researcher*, Dec. 20, 2002, pp. 1033-1056.

16. See Gary Orfield *et al.*, "No Child Left Behind: A Federal-, State- and District-Level Look at the First Year," The Civil Rights Project, Harvard University, Feb. 6, 2004.

17. For a recent, compact history, see James T. Patterson, Brown v. Board of Education: A *Civil Rights Milestone and Its Troubled Legacy*, 2001. The definitive history — Richard Kluger, *Simple Justice: The History of* Brown v. Board of Education *and Black America's Struggle for Equality* — was republished in April 2004, with a new preface and final chapter by the author.

18. The decisions are *Sweatt v. Painter*, 339 U.S. 629, and *McLaurin v. Oklahoma State Regents for Higher Education*, 339 U.S. 637. Sweatt required Texas to admit a black student to its main law school even though a "black" law school was available; McLaurin ruled that the University of Oklahoma could not deny a black student use of all its facilities, including the library, lunchroom and classrooms.

19. For a recent reconstruction of the deliberations, see National Public Radio, "All Things Considered," Dec. 9, 2003.

20. See Charles Wollenberg, *All Deliberate Speed: Segregation and Exclusion in California Schools, 1855-1975* (1976), p. 108.
21. The case is *Brown v. Board of Education of Topeka*, 349 U.S. 294 (1955).
22. "*Brown at 50*," Harvard Civil Rights Project, *op. cit.*, Appendix: Figure 5.
23. Patterson, *op. cit.*, p. 186.
24. *Ibid.*, p. 173.
25. James S. Coleman, Sara D. Kelly and John A. Moore, *Trends in School Segregation, 1968-1973*, The Urban Institute, 1975. The earlier report is James S. Coleman, *et al.*, *Equality of Educational Opportunity*, U.S. Department of Health, Education and Welfare, 1966.
26. Wendy Parker, "The Decline of Judicial Decision-making: School Desegregation and District Court Judges," *North Carolina Law Review*, Vol. 81, No. 4 (May 2003), pp. 1623-1658.
27. The case is *Wessmann v. Gittens*, 160 F.3d 790 (1st Cir. 1998).
28. The decisions are *Tuttle v. Arlington County School Board*, 195 F.3d 698 (4th Cir. 1999) and *Eisenberg v. Montgomery County Public Schools*, 197 F.3d 123 (4th Cir. 1999).
29. See Koch, *op. cit.*
30. The case is *Parents Involved in Community Schools v. Seattle School District No. 1*. For coverage, see Sarah Linn, "Appeals Judges Told of Schools' Racial Tiebreaker," The Associated Press, Dec. 16, 2003.
31. The case is *Avila v. Berkeley Unified School District*, filed in Alameda County Superior Court. For coverage, see Angela Hill, "Suit Accuses District of Racial Bias," *The Oakland Tribune*, Aug. 9, 2003.
32. The decision is *Comfort v. Lynn Schools Committee*, 283 F Supp, 2d 328 (D.Mass. 2003). For coverage, see Thanassis Cambanis, "Judge OK's Use of Race in School Assigning," *The Boston Globe*, June 7, 2003, p. A1.
33. Orfield and Lee, *op. cit.*, p. 34.
34. *Ibid.*
35. *Ibid.*, pp. 35-39.
36. *Ibid.*, pp. 11-13, 39 (Table 21).
37. Quoted in Vincent Brydon, "Panel: Segregation Still Exists in U.S. Schools," *The Topeka Capital-Journal*, Oct. 26, 2002. The Topeka district has a Web site section devoted to the *Brown* case (www.topeka.k12.ks.us).
38. Alan Richard, "Stuck in Time," *Education Week*, Jan. 21, 2004.
39. For background, see David Masci, "Latinos' Future," *The CQ Researcher*, Oct. 17, 2003, pp. 869-892.

BIBLIOGRAPHY

Books

Armor, David J., *Forced Justice: School Desegregation and the Law,* **Oxford University Press, 1995.**
A professor of public policy at George Mason University offers a strong critique of mandatory desegregation. Includes table of cases and seven-page bibliography.

Cushman, Clare, and Melvin I. Urofsky (eds.), *Black, White and* **Brown***: The School Desegregation Case in Retrospect,* **Supreme Court Historical Society/CQ Press, 2004.**
This collection of essays by various contributors — including the lawyer who represented Kansas in defending racial segregation in *Brown* — provides an historical overview of the famous case, from a variety of perspectives.

Klarman, Michael J., *From Jim Crow to Civil Rights: The Supreme Court and the Struggle for Racial Equality,* **Oxford University Press, 2004.**
A law professor at the University of Virginia offers a broad reinterpretation of racial issues, from the establishment of segregation through the *Brown* decision and passage of the Civil Rights Act of 1964. Includes extensive notes and a 46-page bibliography.

Kluger, Richard, *Simple Justice: The History of* **Brown v. Board of Education** *and Black America's Struggle for Equality,* **Vintage, 2004.**
A former journalist and book publisher has written a definitive history of the four school-desegregation suits decided in *Brown v. Board of Education.* Originally published by Knopf in 1976, the book has been reissued with a new chapter by the author.

Ogletree, Charles J., Jr., *All Deliberate Speed: Reflections on the First Half Century of* **Brown v. Board of Education,** **Norton, 2004.**
A well-known African-American professor at Harvard Law School offers a critical examination of the unfulfilled promise of the *Brown* decision. Includes notes, case list.

Patterson, James T., Brown v. Board of Education: *A Civil Rights Milestone and Its Troubled Legacy*, **Oxford University Press, 2001.**
A professor emeritus of history at Brown University provides a new compact history of *Brown* and its impact.

Rossell, Christine H., David J. Armor and Herbert J. Walberg (eds.), *School Desegregation in the 21st Century*, **Praeger, 2001.**
Various academics examine the history and current issues involving desegregation. Rossell is a professor of political science at Boston University, Armor a professor of public policy at George Mason University and Walberg a professor emeritus of education and psychology at the University of Illinois, Chicago. Includes chapter notes, references.

Thernstrom, Abigail, and Stephan Thernstrom, *No Excuses: Closing the Racial Gap in Learning*, **Simon & Schuster, 2003.**
An academic-scholar couple provides a strongly argued case for adopting educational reforms, including school choice, instead of racial mixing to reduce the learning gap for African-American and Latino pupils. Abigail Thernstrom is a senior scholar at the Manhattan Institute; Stephan Thernstrom is a professor of history at Harvard. Includes detailed notes.

Articles

Cohen, Adam, "The Supreme Struggle," *Education Life Supplement, The New York Times*, **Jan. 18, 2004, p. 22.**
A *Times* editorial writer offers an overview of the 1954 *Brown* decision and its impact.

Henderson, Cheryl Brown, "*Brown v. Board of Education* **at Fifty: A Personal Perspective,"** *The College Board Review*, **No. 200 (fall 2003), pp. 7-11.**
The daughter of Oliver Brown, first-named of the 13 plaintiffs in *Brown v. Board of Education of Topeka*, provides a personal reflection on the landmark case. Henderson is executive director of the Brown Foundation for Educational Equity, Excellence and Research in Topeka (www.brownvboard.org).

Hendrie, Caroline, "In U.S. Schools, Race Still Counts," *Education Week*, **Jan. 21, 2004.**
This broad survey of racial issues in public schools was the first of a five-part series marking the 50th anniversary of *Brown*. Other articles appeared on Feb. 18 (Charlotte-Mecklenburg County, N.C.), March 10 (Chicago; Latinos), April 14 (Arlington, Va., challenges of integration), with a final story scheduled for May 19 (parental choice).

Reports and Studies

Orfield, Gary, and Chungmei Lee, "*Brown* **at 50: King's Dream or** *Plessy's* **Nightmare?" The Civil Rights Project, Harvard University, January 2004.**
The project's most recent analysis of school-enrollment figures finds that racial separation is increasing among African-American and Latino students.

For More Information

Center for Equal Opportunity, 14 Pidgeon Hill Dr., Suite 500, Sterling, VA 20165; (703) 421-5443; www.ceousa. org. Opposes the expansion of racial preferences in education, employment and voting.

Center for Individual Rights, 1233 20th St., N.W., Suite 300, Washington, DC 20036; (202) 833-8400; www. cir-usa.org. A nonprofit, public-interest law firm that opposes racial preferences.

Harvard Civil Rights Project, 125 Mt. Auburn St., 3rd floor, Cambridge, MA 02138; (617) 496-6367; www.civilrightsproject.harvard.edu. A leading civil rights advocacy and research organization.

Mexican American Legal Defense and Educational Fund, 1717 K St., N.W. Suite 311, Washington, DC 20036; (202) 293-2828; www.maldef.org. Founded in 1968 in San Antonio, MALDEF is the leading non-profit Latino litigation, advocacy and educational outreach organization.

NAACP Legal Defense and Educational Fund, Inc., 99 Hudson St., 16th floor, New York, NY 10013; (212) 965-2200; www.naacpldf.org. The fund's nearly two-dozen attorneys litigate on education, economic access, affirmative action and criminal justice issues on behalf of African-Americans and others.

National School Boards Association, 1680 Duke St., Alexandria, VA 22314; (703) 838-6722; www.nsba.org. The association strongly supports school desegregation.

13

Media Ownership

David Hatch

Protesters in Los Angeles urge the Federal Communications Commission not to ease media-ownership rules. But on June 2, the FCC voted to allow media corporations to own dramatically more news outlets in any one city. Critics say fewer media conglomerates means fewer choices for consumers. But industry executives say consolidation enables them to stay competitive and provide more selections.

From *The CQ Researcher*,
October 10, 2003.

M ajor TV networks pulled out all the stops competing for the first televised interview with Pfc. Jessica Lynch after her dramatic rescue during the Iraq war. Big-name anchors called her on the phone, and sent her personalized trinkets, autographed books and photos.

But CBS News offered more than souvenirs. Tapping the synergies of its powerful parent company, Viacom — whose sprawling media empire includes publishing giant Simon & Schuster and MTV — CBS dangled book deals and music specials before the waifish soldier from West Virginia.[1]

After originally defending its efforts, the network conceded it overstepped the boundaries of journalistic ethics. Acknowledging the critics who think media companies are too consolidated and powerful, CBS Chairman and CEO Leslie Moonves blamed the aggressive wooing of Lynch on Viacom's sheer size and web of interconnected businesses.

"As these companies become more and more vertically integrated, you know, sometimes you do go over the line," he said.[2] In the end, ABC snared the first TV interview with Lynch, scheduled for Nov. 11 with Diane Sawyer.

Long gone are the days when media companies were one-horse enterprises specializing only in broadcasting or publishing. Today they are multifaceted conglomerates with stakes in everything from television, radio, movies, newspapers and books to the Internet, theme parks, billboards and concert promotion.[3]

Five media powerhouses now control up to 80 percent of America's prime-time TV programming: AOL Time Warner (CNN, WB, HBO); Disney (ABC, ESPN); General Electric (NBC, CNBC,

MSNBC); News Corp. (Fox, Fox News) and Viacom (CBS, MTV, UPN).[4]

But Federal Communications Commission (FCC) Chairman Michael K. Powell pointed out in a recent *New York Times* op-ed column that the five mega-companies actually own only 25 percent of today's more than 300 broadcast, satellite and cable channels. "But because of their popularity, 80 percent of the viewing audience chooses to watch them," Powell wrote. "Do we really want government to regulate what is popular?"[5]

Meanwhile, one company, Clear Channel Communications Inc., dominates radio, owning more than 1,200 stations — about 970 more than its closest competitor. Clear Channel is also the largest concert promoter in the world.[6]

Critics note that the number of TV-station owners in the United States has declined from 540 to 360 in the past 25 years, while daily-newspaper ownership has plummeted from 860 owners to 300.[7]

"You're running close to a monopoly or oligopoly situation, there's no question about that," says Michael Copps, a Democratic FCC commissioner and staunch opponent of the panel's recent move to loosen media-ownership rules. "It's about the ability of a very small number of companies to control [the content of] our media. To dictate what the entertainment is going to be, to dictate what the civic dialogue is going to be, to dictate that we'll no longer have as much [local news] and diversity as we had before. So it goes to the fundamentals of our democratic life as a country."

While the number of media competitors may be declining, the amount of diversity of content and technologies is not. Today there are six com-

mercial broadcast networks — double the number from a few decades ago — three 24-hour news networks, cable and satellite television, the Internet and a growing number of alternative-media choices, such as low-power FM, satellite radio and Internet "blogs," or Web logs written by

Inside Big Media

Media conglomerates today own holdings in broadcast, cable, Internet, music, book, video and movie companies. Here is a look at two of the biggest media corporations.*

Time Warner (formerly AOL/Time Warner) Revenue: $41 billion Selected holdings:	Viacom Revenue: $24.6 billion Selected holdings:
Broadcasting	**Broadcasting**
The WB Television Network	CBS
Cable	39 television stations
Cinemax	Infinity Broadcasting
CNN	(180 radio stations)
Comedy Central	King World Productions
Court TV	Paramount Television
HBO	Spelling Television
Time Warner Cable	UPN
Turner Broadcasting System	Viacom Productions
Internet	**Cable**
America Online	BET
Mapquest	CMT
Moviefone	MTV
Netscape	Nickelodeon
Film	Sundance Channel
Castle Rock Entertainment	Showtime
Hanna-Barbera Cartoons	The Movie Channel
New Line Cinema	VH1
Warner Brothers Pictures	**Film**
Music	Paramount Home Entertainment
Atlantic Recording	United Cinemas International
Elektra Entertainment	**Video**
Warner Brothers Records	Blockbuster
Publishing	**Publishing**
Little, Brown & Co.	Simon & Schuster
Time	
People	
Sports Illustrated	
Fortune	

* Holdings of other media firms are on the Center for Digital Democracy's Web site: www.democraticmedia.org/issues/mediaownership/industryData.php.

Source: "The B&C 25 Media Groups," Broadcasting & Cable, May 12, 2003.

everyday citizens. (*See sidebar, p. 310.*) Consumers today have "an overwhelming amount of choice," says NBC lobbyist Bob Okun.

Indeed, the three major networks that dominated prime-time TV for decades have ceded huge chunks of the market to cable and satellite competitors. As of June 2002, more than 85 percent of Americans subscribed to cable, satellite and other pay-TV services.[8] "The competition is real from cable," Okun says. "They put on edgier programming."

To fight back, three broadcast TV networks now operate their own studios so they can produce more content themselves, keep tighter control over the creative process and avoid bidding wars over hit shows. Critics say network ownership of studios has forced many independent producers out of business and left those remaining at the mercy of big media. As a result, they say, the broadcast networks are churning out lowbrow, cookie-cutter programming because independent voices have been locked out. Program diversity, creativity and localism — or attention to local needs or tastes — suffer when too few companies control much of what we see, read and hear, the critics say.

But industry executives say consolidation enables them to grow quickly so they can stay competitive. Mergers also create new opportunities for cross-promotion, content repackaging and elimination of redundant offerings, freeing up resources for other areas.

In response to marketplace changes, Republican Chairman Powell in June shepherded through the commission a sweeping relaxation of the FCC's media-ownership rules by a narrow 3-2 vote along party lines, with the two Democratic commissioners opposed.

Among other things, the commission increased the audience reach of network-owned TV stations, permitting them to reach 45 percent of households, up from 35 percent. It also lifted the ban on a single company owning both a broadcast station and a newspaper in the same market — combinations that until recently were only permitted on a limited basis. In sum, the new rules could allow one company — in a single market — to own three TV stations, one newspaper, eight radio outlets and a cable system. And TV-newspaper mergers would be permissible in about 200 markets, affecting 98 percent of the U.S. population.[9]

The new rules triggered an unexpectedly strong backlash from lawmakers, academics and advocacy groups

concerned that media control would fall into too few hands. The rhetoric on both sides has been harsh. Critics insist the new regulations could threaten democracy, while supporters warn that without them, free TV could eventually disappear, as more content migrates to pay TV.

Proponents of the FCC's action point out that network broadcasters today are facing more competition than ever before. "In 1979, the vast majority of households had six or fewer local television stations to choose from, three of which were typically affiliated with a broadcast network," the FCC said in a report accompanying its June decision.[10] Today the average U.S. household receives seven broadcast television networks and an average of 102 channels per home, it said.

But critics say the plethora of media choices can be deceptive. A consumer who watches CNN, subscribes to *Time* and *Fortune* and surfs AOL may think he's consulting several independent sources, but in fact, all are part of media giant AOL *Time* Warner (which recently decided to drop AOL from its name). "You may be hearing many different voices, yes, but they are from the same ventriloquist," said Sen. Byron Dorgan, a North Dakota Democrat.[11]

Because roughly 15 percent of Americans rely on free broadcast TV as their only source of television, a bipartisan coalition of lawmakers is trying to overturn key portions of the new FCC regulations, which a federal court on Sept. 4 barred from taking effect, pending further judicial review.

Meanwhile, the controversy has prompted Congress to re-evaluate whether media deregulation, a trend that has accelerated since Congress enacted the Telecommunications Act of 1996, has met its goal of fostering more competition.[12]

The firestorm has tainted the image of Chairman Powell, who is under attack from influential lawmakers on both sides of the political aisle. The son of Secretary of State Colin L. Powell, he had been a darling of Washington lawmakers for much of his tenure.

Although cable and satellite television sometimes trigger scrutiny into how much market power they exercise, mergers involving broadcasters are of special concern, because they use the public airwaves and are licensed to serve the "public interest."

Commissioner Copps says public-interest requirements have been relaxed over the years and that license renewals are now largely pro forma. In theory, he says, TV

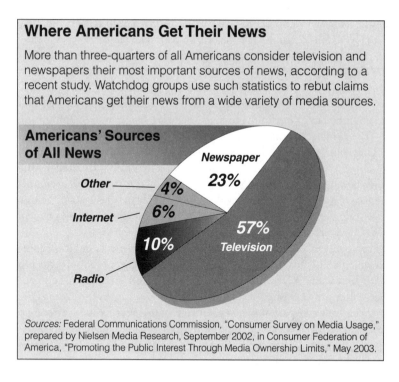

Where Americans Get Their News

More than three-quarters of all Americans consider television and newspapers their most important sources of news, according to a recent study. Watchdog groups use such statistics to rebut claims that Americans get their news from a wide variety of media sources.

Americans' Sources of All News

- Newspaper **23%**
- Television **57%**
- Radio **10%**
- Internet **6%**
- Other **4%**

Sources: Federal Communications Commission, "Consumer Survey on Media Usage," prepared by Nielsen Media Research, September 2002, in Consumer Federation of America, "Promoting the Public Interest Through Media Ownership Limits," May 2003.

General owns both *The Tampa Tribune* and the local NBC affiliate WFLA-TV.* They share a state-of-the-art newsroom, where they sometimes swap story ideas and collaborate on projects. Writers for the paper have appeared on WFLA shows, and some of WFLA's reports make it into the *Tribune.*

Proponents of the Tampa experiment said combining the newsrooms would effectively double the resources available to reporters, producing more in-depth journalism. But Robert Haiman, president emeritus of the Poynter Institute journalism school and former editor of the competing *St. Petersburg Times*, hasn't seen that result.** "Where are the huge investigative stories that run simultaneously in the newspaper and on the TV station?" he asked. "I'm not seeing incredible feats of journalism," he said. "I see those promotional connections, but I don't see a great leap."[14]

But others think Tampa's arrangement benefits the marketplace. "It has given power to both sides," says Barbara Cochran, president of the Radio-Television News Directors Association (RTNDA). The newspaper gets exposure to a broader audience with a younger demographic, and the television station has access to the paper's vast reporting staff, she notes, but "they still make very independent decisions."

Does the cross-ownership stifle competition? No, she says, because other voices remain. "You still have competition" in the Tampa television market, she says.

Gauging whether the media is too concentrated boils down to perspective. "Large media companies have become larger, but so has the entire sector," wrote telecom visionary Eli Noam in the *Financial Times.*[15] Industry supporters emphasize that none of the Big Four

and radio stations are supposed to put the public interest ahead of profit, but in reality, that is not always the case. To deflect congressional pressure, Powell launched a new effort in August to promote more localism.

In addition to concerns about content diversity, some critics worry about the ethnic diversity of media owners. Minorities own only 4.2 percent of the nation's TV and radio stations, according to the Minority Media and Telecommunications Council (MMTC), a civil-rights advocacy group. Viewed another way, minorities control 1.3 percent of the value of the nation's broadcast assets, which MMTC Executive Director David Honig calls "a national disgrace."

Meanwhile, a July survey detected a drop in minority employment at local television stations from 20.6 percent to 18.1 percent between 2002 and 2003, and from 8 percent to 6.5 percent at local radio stations.[13]

As Washington politicos debate how the media should be regulated, here are some issues being discussed:

Is the U.S. media industry too consolidated?

In Tampa, Fla., media consolidation is an everyday reality. Thanks to a waiver of the FCC ban on cross-ownership of local newspapers and TV stations, Media

---

* The FCC removed the ban in June, but it remains in effect while lawmakers and the courts decide its fate.

** The nonprofit Poynter Institute owns both the *St. Petersburg Times* and Congressional Quarterly Inc., the parent company of CQ Press, publisher of *The CQ Researcher.*

broadcast networks owns more than 3 percent of the nation's TV stations. Of the 1,340 commercial TV stations in the United States as of March 31, 2003, CBS owned only 2.9 percent, Fox owned 2.8 percent, NBC owned 2.2 percent and ABC owned 0.8 percent.[16]

And while the broadcast networks controlled 90 percent of the audience 25 years ago, today they control less than 50 percent.[17] The networks say the decline is due to the growth of cable, which — because it's a pay service — has fewer content restrictions and thus can offer racier and more violent programming. The major broadcasters insist they're at another disadvantage to cable: It has two revenue streams — advertising and subscriptions — while broadcasters have only advertising.

"You need somehow to create additional forms of revenue," NBC's Okun says, adding that skyrocketing costs for sports, movies, hit TV shows and other marquee programming have forced the networks to consolidate.

But media watchdogs say it's unfair for broadcasters to complain they are losing ground to cable, since broadcasters have migrated most of their channels to cable and satellite for distribution.[18]

Some critics also fear that the news divisions of huge media conglomerates feel pressure to go soft on corporate parents' wrongdoings. "I don't see the problem, frankly. Views are not being suppressed," said Time Inc. CEO Ann Moore, noting that *Fortune* has had tough coverage of its parent company.[19]

Public Broadcasting Service (PBS) President and CEO Pat Mitchell complains that companies often justify consolidation by promising that more resources will be available to invest in news and information-gathering, but they rarely deliver. "The American public seems less informed than ever about almost everything," she says.

That may come as a surprise to FCC Chairman Powell, who cites the emergence of all-news networks and the plethora of local TV newscasts as examples of a robust media environment.

"That's not diversity of news," responds Marvin Kalb, a senior fellow at Harvard University's Joan Shorenstein Center on the Press, Politics and Public Policy. "That's just multiplicity of news." When TV stations air local newscasts throughout the day they often repeat the same stories, and competing stations usually offer similar coverage, he says. Real diversity would occur if local stations offered a broader range of stories with more depth, he argues.

In fact, a recent study of local TV found that smaller station groups produce better-quality news than network-owned-and-operated stations (O&Os), which have far more resources.[20]

Meanwhile, even though there are many more news outlets today, "There's a lot less news being presented to the American people," says Kalb, a former CBS and NBC News reporter.

Nevertheless, the major broadcast networks remain the first place Americans turn for news, especially during times of tragedy, Kalb says. But the networks, assuming the public is getting its hard news from the 24-hour news stations like CNN, are offering less and less hard news. "They feel that you've already got the news elsewhere, so why bother," Kalb says. "But not everybody watches CNN all day. In fact, probably most of us don't watch it at all."

Did the FCC loosen its media-ownership rules too much?

It's not often that the National Rifle Association (NRA) and the National Organization for Women (NOW) agree on an issue. But their opposition to the FCC's historic June 2 decision easing its media-ownership restrictions put them in the same camp. Such diverse alliances are spelling trouble for the Republican-led FCC. A broad coalition of regulators, lawmakers and advocacy groups argues the commission's action threatens consumers, media diversity and democracy.

Ironically, some of the most outspoken critics have come from Powell's own party. "The FCC made a mistake," said Republican Sen. Trent Lott of Mississippi. "With too much concentration, companies no longer have to be competitive with rates or product," he said. "This is a question of fairness and access for both small media organizations and media consumers."[21]

On the other side of the political aisle, the comments have been all but apocalyptic. "Let me be blunt: I believe the recent changes to the FCC's media-ownership rules are a disaster for smaller and new entrants [into the media business]," said Democratic FCC Commissioner Jonathan Adelstein.[22]

"The homogenization of radio is a grim predictor of the ravages of deregulation," Sen. Russell D. Feingold, D-Wis., said in a Sept. 16 floor speech.

Former CBS News anchor Walter Cronkite, who lobbied against the rule changes, warned, "The gathering of

Radio Giant Clear Channel Riles Critics

When a freight train derailed in Minot, N.D, last year, releasing toxic fumes into the air, radio station KCJB-AM didn't answer when police phoned to request public alerts.

Critics of media consolidation say no one responded because the station — one of six outlets in Minot owned by Clear Channel Communications — was running on computers after the company consolidated local operations and slashed personnel.[1] But Andrew Levin, senior vice president for government affairs at Clear Channel, says personnel were on hand and blamed Minot police for not knowing how to operate emergency equipment that automatically prompts on-air alerts.

Tiny Minot, it turns out, was the wrong place for Clear Channel to have such problems because North Dakota Democrat Byron Dorgan sits on the powerful Senate panel that oversees the radio industry. The lawmaker wasn't pleased and is now seeking to clamp down on the looser ownership rules passed by the Federal Communications Commission (FCC) on June 2. He often cites the Minot case as a reason why he opposes further deregulation of television, newspapers and other mass media.

To its critics, Clear Channel provides a sobering lesson on the pitfalls of media mergers. Bolstered by the 1996 Telecommunications Act's deregulation of radio, it grew from 40 stations in 1996 to 1,220 today to become the dominant industry player, with 103 million listeners nationwide and revenue of $3.2 billion annually.[2] It is also the world's largest concert promoter and one of the nation's largest display-advertising companies, with about 770,000 billboards.[3] Coupled with its nearest competitor, Viacom-owned Infinity Broadcasting, the companies control 42 percent of the U.S. radio market and command 45 percent of the revenue.[4]

Detractors say Clear Channel's homogenized playlists make radio sound the same from coast to coast and that its use of "voice-tracking" — programming local radio stations with deejays and announcers in distant cities — undermines localism. "Only about 9 percent of all our programming is voice-tracked," Levin says, adding that the practice enables small communities to enjoy otherwise unaffordable talent. "We think that folks like it."

Noting that Clear Channel owns less than 12 percent of U.S. radio stations, CEO John Hogan said, "I don't see any

way possible to conclude that this is a consolidated industry or that Clear Channel has any real dominance inside that industry." Prior to 1996, he noted, up to 60 percent of radio stations were losing money, and many were in danger of going dark. He said Clear Channel should be heralded as an American success story and that the company helped rejuvenate radio.[5]

Clear Channel says it has increased format diversity in many markets, such as Los Angeles, where it owns stations ranging from nostalgia to Spanish hip-hop.[6] But the watchdog Future of Music Coalition (FMC) found hundreds of redundant radio formats nationwide with songs overlapping up to 76 percent of the time. Some stations altered format names without changing playlists.[7]

"Just because it's a [distinct] format doesn't mean that it's diverse," says FMC Executive Director Jenny Toomey. "The public realizes radio has homogenized since the '96 Act passed."

"Radio consolidation has contributed to a 34 percent decline in the number of owners, a 90 percent rise in the cost of advertising, a rise in indecent broadcasts and the replacement of local news and community programming with voice-tracking and syndicated hollering that ill-serves the public interest," railed Sen. Ernest Hollings, D-S.C., at a January hearing.[8]

Eric Boehlert, a *Salon* journalist who writes extensively about radio, told National Public Radio, "You can't have a hit without being on Clear Channel stations. You can't have a career without being on Clear Channel stations. So all of a sudden you have a company that is essentially dictating what gets heard on the radio." That was unheard of before the '96 act, he said.[9]

Don Henley, one of several musicians who accuse Clear Channel of heavy-handed, monopolistic practices, told lawmakers this year: "Artists can no longer stand for the exorbitant radio-promotion costs, nor can we tolerate the overt or covert threats posed by companies owning radio stations, venues and [advertising] agencies."[10]

A just-released report from the watchdog Center for Public Integrity finds that small and medium-sized radio markets have higher levels of radio concentration than large ones. Clear Channel, the report finds, is the main owner in 20 of the top 25 most-concentrated markets.[11]

Fueling the controversy surrounding the San Antonio, Texas-based company are its close ties to Republicans. CEO Lowry Mays is a friend of President Bush and contributes heavily to GOP causes. Tom Hicks, a Clear Channel board member, purchased the Texas Rangers baseball team from Bush and his associates. The company has made a star of conservative radio host Rush Limbaugh, whose show airs on 180 Clear Channel talk-radio channels. Others are concerned that Clear Channel could unduly influence a combined Hispanic Broadcasting Corp. (HBC) and Univision Communications, which recently won FCC approval to merge. Clear Channel is HBC's largest shareholder.[12]

Meanwhile, Rep. Howard Berman, D-Calif., worries that Clear Channel has "punished" Britney Spears and other artists who bypassed its concert-promotion service by burying radio ads for their concerts and denying airplay to their songs.[13] Competitors allege that Clear Channel secretly purchases radio stations — using front groups and shell companies — and "warehouses" them if there is public opposition to the company's expansion in the hope that regulatory limits will later be lifted.[14]

In September, the watchdog Alliance for Better Campaigns accused Clear Channel and Infinity of limiting the sale of radio ads to candidates in California's gubernatorial recall election. The alliance suggested the companies may be withholding ad space for more lucrative commercial clients.[15]

Clear Channel has strongly denied all of these charges, saying it is the target of criticism because it's the market leader.[16]

The National Association of Broadcasters (NAB) emphasizes there are nearly 4,000 separate owners of 13,000 local radio stations in the U.S. today. "The Hollywood movie studios, the record companies, direct-broadcast satellite, cable systems, newspapers — even the Internet — all have more of their revenue share concentrated among the top 10 owners than does radio," NAB President and CEO Eddie Fritts told lawmakers this year. "Spanish-language formats have increased by over 80 percent in the last decade, and other ethnicities are well represented on the dial."[17]

To some, Clear Channel is a harbinger of television's future. "We're already going that way under the old rules," complains Democratic FCC Commissioner Michael Copps, who already sees signs of the "Clear Channelization" of TV.

"I don't think anybody in the Congress really anticipated the extent of consolidation that has ensued from the 1996 act."

But even Copps sees upsides to concentration, such as the "economies and efficiencies" that have allowed some stations to operate more profitably and avoid going under, depriving listeners of service.[18] Nevertheless, he opposes the FCC's new media-ownership policies.

Clear Channel is now in Washington's crosshairs. Although the FCC loosened ownership rules for newspapers and television stations on June 2, it limited the number of radio stations that operators can own in certain markets. The FCC wanted to grandfather in existing non-compliant stations, but Sen. John McCain, R-Ariz., offered legislation to force the divestiture of such properties, including roughly 100 Clear Channel stations.

Meanwhile, the Justice Department is investigating whether Clear Channel requires musicians to sign with its concert-promotion division to get airplay, and whether it wields too much power in Southern California.[19]

---

[1] Marc Fisher, "Sounds Familiar for a Reason," *The Washington Post*, May 18, 2003, p. B1.

[2] From statement by Sen. Ernest Hollings, D-S.C., on radio consolidation before Senate Commerce Committee, Jan. 30, 2003.

[3] Eric Boehlert, "Habla usted Clear Channel?" *Salon.com*, April 24, 2003.

[4] See "Radio Deregulation: Has it Served Citizens and Musicians," Future of Music Coalition, www.futureofmusic.org, Nov. 18, 2002, p. 3.

[5] From NPR's "Fresh Air," July 23, 2003.

[6] NPR, *op. cit.*

[7] Future of Music Coalition, *op. cit.*, pp. 42-52.

[8] Hollings, *op. cit.*

[9] NPR, *op. cit.*

[10] From testimony before Senate Commerce Committee hearing on radio consolidation, Jan. 30, 2003.

[11] See "Big Radio Rules in Small Markets: A few behemoths dominate medium-sized cities throughout the U.S," www.openairwaves.org/telecom, released Oct. 1, 2003.

[12] Boehlert, *op. cit.*

[13] See Rep. Howard Berman, D-Calif., letter to U.S. Attorney General John Ashcroft, found at www.house.gov/berman/, Jan. 22, 2002.

[14] Eric Boehlert, "Washington Tunes In," *Salon.com*, March 27, 2002.

[15] See press release, Sept. 3, 2003.

[16] See "Issue Update," www.clearchannel.com, June 2, 2003.

[17] From testimony before Senate Commerce Committee, Jan. 30, 2003.

[18] Copps was speaking at the University of Southern California Media Consolidation Forum in Los Angeles, April 28, 2003, p. 7.

[19] Bill McConnell, "DoJ Investigates Clear Channel on Two Fronts," *Broadcasting & Cable*, www.broadcastingandcable.com, July 25, 2003.

more and more outlets under one owner clearly can be an impediment to a free and independent press."[23]

But proponents of the deregulation are equally ardent: "It has been said that the rules will allow one company to dominate all media in a community," said GOP Sen. George Allen of Virginia. "It is simply not true . . . If you look at the availability of information and programming, consumers have an unprecedented abundance of choices."[24]

Kenneth Ferree, chief of the FCC's Media Bureau, emphasizing that the agency had to work within parameters set by the courts, says, "I would have gotten rid of the national [network-TV ownership] cap entirely. I'm still doubtful that it can be defended in court, but we tried."

NBC lobbyist Okun says the new rules are "incremental" at best, and that big is not always bad. For instance, he says, increasing the national-audience reach of network-owned TV stations from 35 percent of households to 45 percent would merely "let us own a few more stations in large markets."

The commission lifted the cap after heavy lobbying from the Big Four networks, three of which are at — or above — the 35 percent limit due to waivers while the restriction is in limbo. Raising the cap would let the networks purchase more TV stations and reach more viewers. Fox owned-and-operated TV stations (O&Os, for short) reach 37 percent of U.S. households. CBS-owned stations reach 40 percent. NBC is at 34 percent and ABC, at 24 percent, has more acquisition leeway.[25]

The FCC also lifted its blanket ban on one company owning both a newspaper and broadcast station in a market, permitting the combinations in markets with at least four TV stations. Before, the combinations were allowed only if they were grandfathered in after being banned in the 1970s or with an FCC waiver to help a struggling outlet.

For the first time, the FCC permitted triopolies — single ownership of three TV stations in a market — in large metropolitan areas. But it retained its ban on the Big Four broadcast networks merging with each other.

Democratic Commissioner Copps also complains that the new ownership rules do not factor in the transition of broadcasters to digital. Noting that TV stations will be able to offer multiple digital TV channels in their markets, he asks rhetorically, "Doesn't that change the competitive landscape somehow?"

In fact, the FCC's Republican majority concluded that easing restrictions on common ownership of TV sta-

tions in local markets would "spur" the transition to digital because small-market stations face difficulties raising money to convert their facilities.[26]

Copps thinks the FCC should have more carefully considered the effect on advertisers, particularly small businesses that rely on local broadcast ads, and children, who are increasingly exposed to indecent TV images.[27] Some surveys indicate up to 70 percent of Americans think television is inappropriate for children, and 85 percent think it encourages youngsters to engage in sexual activity or commit violence, he says.

"We have no statutory charge to protect advertisers," Ferree says. "That's not what we do. We protect viewers and listeners." He says the agency determined the rules would not cause more indecency.

Copps says the FCC also failed to consider the impact on minorities, in terms of ownership and employment opportunities and diversity of views. Ferree notes the FCC is trying to address minority concerns through a separate advisory committee.

"Any further relaxation in the ownership rules is bad for our industry," says Jim Winston, executive director of the National Association of Black-owned Broadcasters, noting a 20 percent decline in minority-owned TV and radio stations since 1996, when the industry was deregulated. Many African-American broadcasters were forced to sell to bigger players that undercut them on ad rates and had more financial leverage. "Minorities have historically had difficulty raising capital," he says.

But NBC's Okun counters that existing media-ownership restrictions undermine diversity more than consolidation does. His network would like to increase the footprint of Telemundo, its Spanish-language broadcast network, but the network is "severely constrained" from doing so under current ownership rules.

Should Congress reimpose rules limiting television networks' ownership of programming?

Hollywood producer Dick Wolf stood to reap a windfall from NBC — an estimated $1.6 billion over three years — if the network renewed his series "Law & Order" and its spin-offs, "Special Victims Unit" and "Criminal Intent." But all that changed when NBC announced plans to buy Universal Television, a studio that has a partnership with Wolf.

Now, observers say, Universal has essentially switched sides in the negotiations and no longer has an incentive to help Wolf get the best deal from NBC. Victoria Riskin, president of the Writers Guild of America, West, said Wolf will still do well. "I'm more worried about what kind of leverage the Dick Wolfs of the future will have," she said. NBC executives insist the merger with Universal would create more programming opportunities for Wolf.[28]

For more than two decades, the FCC imposed so-called financial interest and syndication rules — commonly known as fin-syn — on TV broadcasters, curbing their ownership stakes in programming. The rules were intended to protect independent producers and promote program diversity. But as the media universe began to expand, the FCC removed some of its fin-syn rules in 1991 and eliminated them entirely in 1995.

The networks opposed fin-syn for financial reasons. Since they were assuming risk by putting up money on the front-end to help cover production costs, they wanted a slice of the lucrative back-end, or revenue from syndication. "It's the ability to generate content in a cost-effective way," says Okun, explaining why the networks have sought to combine with studios.

Critics blame fin-syn's repeal for ushering in an era of "vertical integration," in which the TV networks increasingly produce shows in-house, and for driving most independent producers out of business. The result, they say, is lowbrow, homogenized content that takes few creative chances.

The networks, however, argue that fin-syn is unnecessary. "There's more production going on today in this country than there ever has been, by a factor of 10 or 20," said NBC Chairman Bob Wright. "American consumers have never had video benefits like they have today."[29]

Testifying before the Senate Commerce Committee earlier this year, Rupert Murdoch, chairman of News Corp., which owns the Fox broadcast network, said, "If anyone comes to us with a show that can get us an audience, we'll be the first to buy."[30]

But Jonathan Rintels, president and executive director of the Center for the Creative Community, an advocacy group for independent producers, says it's time to bring fin-syn back. "The market has completely changed. It's gotten re-concentrated," he says. "Of the 40 new series airing on the four major broadcast networks in the 2002 season, 77.5 percent are owned in whole or part by the same four networks — an increase of over 37 percent in just one year — and up from only 12.5 percent in 1990," the group said in FCC comments.[31]

"The harm to the public is that they don't see the best work that can be put on television," Rintels says.

When veteran producer Norman Lear, for example, developed the now-classic sitcom "All in the Family" for ABC, the network balked at the controversial dialogue — mainly from bigoted paterfamilias "Archie Bunker" — so he took it to CBS, where it became a huge hit. Nowadays, networks lock producers into contracts that bar them from taking their ideas to competitors, Rintels says.

Other groups fighting to restore fin-syn include the Coalition for Program Diversity, whose members include Sony Pictures Television, the Screen Actors Guild, the Directors Guild and Carsey-Werner-Mandabach, a big independent-production company; and the Caucus for Television Producers, Writers & Directors.

As part of its June announcement, the FCC rejected the idea of restoring fin-syn. "In light of dramatic changes in the television market, including the significant increase in the number of channels available to most households today, we find no basis in the record to conclude that government regulation is necessary to promote source diversity," the FCC said.[32]

Nevertheless, Commissioner Copps wants the agency to address pending proposals from Hollywood for broadcast networks to devote 25 percent to 35 percent of their prime-time schedules to shows created by independent producers. "There's nothing left for protection against monopoly and . . . oligopoly," he says.

Some lawmakers, among them Senate Commerce Chairman John McCain, R-Ariz., and Sen. Ernest Hollings, D-S.C., support independent programmers. McCain and House Energy and Commerce Committee Chairman Billy Tauzin, R-La., are trying to forge a non-legislative resolution between producers and network executives. Lawmakers appear reticent to legislate because an appeals court ruled a decade ago that the FCC hadn't adequately justified its fin-syn rules. "It's clearly been declared unconstitutional by the courts," McCain said.[33]

"People are concerned about the gatekeepers," says PBS' Mitchell, who benefited from fin-syn when she worked earlier in her career as an independent producer. "If it's reached a point now where you've got to own the production as well as the distribution, then what's going to happen to people who are not in that chain? They're going to get left out, and they are getting left out," she says.

"We do need to have some regulatory policy in place," she adds.

CHRONOLOGY

1900-1940s *Government limits the influence of radio and television.*

1901 Italian inventor Guglielmo Marconi sends wireless signals across Atlantic Ocean, paving the way for radio.

1920 The first radio broadcast debuts at KDKA, in Pittsburgh.

1927 Philo T. Farnsworth, the inventor of television, demonstrates the technology for the first time. . . . Federal Radio Commission is established.

1934 Congress passes 1934 Communications Act, setting guidelines for regulating public airwaves.

1938 Orson Welles' realistic "War of the Worlds" radio broadcast about a Martian invasion creates pandemonium across the country.

1941 FCC issues National TV Ownership Rule barring companies from owning more than a few TV stations.

1946 FCC adopts Dual Network Rule, prohibiting companies from owning more than one radio network, later expanded to include TV.

1950s-1960s *Television enters its golden age.*

1950 Cable TV is introduced in rural Pennsylvania and Oregon. . . . FCC institutes the Fairness Doctrine.

1954 Color TV debuts.

1969 Public Broadcasting Service is created.

1970s *FCC seeks to limit media growth.*

1970 FCC prohibits companies from owning radio and TV stations in the same market.

1975 FCC bans cross-ownership of a broadcast and newspaper outlet in the same market.

1980s *New networks revolutionize television.*

1980 Media visionary Ted Turner creates Cable News Network, ushering in an era of 24-hour cable news.

1985 Australian media mogul Rupert Murdoch launches the Fox network, a feisty upstart to the Big 3.

1987 FCC eliminates Fairness Doctrine.

1990s *Media concentration accelerates after Congress deregulates telecommunications and eases media-ownership rules.*

1992 Cable Act requires cable systems to carry local broadcasters.

1995 FCC allows major TV networks to own production studios.

1996 Disney acquires Capitol Cities/ABC, combining a studio with a TV network. . . . Congress passes landmark Telecommunications Act, loosening broadcast-ownership restrictions and deregulating cable.

2000s *Rampant consolidation and FCC action to loosen ownership rules spark national debate.*

2000 Viacom merges with CBS, continuing the trend of "vertical integration."

2001 The largest merger in U.S. history joins AOL and Time Warner.

2002 Comcast and AT&T merge, forming the nation's largest cable company.

June 2, 2003 FCC loosens broadcast-ownership restrictions. Three months later, a federal court orders further review.

Sept. 2, 2003 NBC unveils plan to acquire the film, TV and theme-park assets of Vivendi Universal.

Oct. 6, 2003 Federal court in San Francisco rules that cable providers of high-speed Internet access must include competing Internet services on their systems. The FCC vows to appeal.

BACKGROUND

Regulating the Airwaves

The regulatory structure governing America's media industry was born in the early 1900s, when Congress saw a need to restrict the market power of burgeoning broadcasting companies.

The 1927 Federal Radio Act established the Federal Radio Commission, the precursor to the FCC. Seven years later, Congress passed the watershed 1934 Communications Act, creating the FCC as an independent agency and establishing guidelines for regulating the public airwaves — rules that remain the FCC's guiding principles today.

In the early 1940s, the FCC adopted the National TV Ownership Rule, which prevented networks from owning more than a handful of stations, and restricted their ability to buy radio outlets. In 1943, the FCC and the U.S. Supreme Court ordered NBC to divest one of its networks, which later became its competitor, ABC.

In yet another regulatory step, the FCC in 1946 adopted the Dual Network Rule, barring one radio network from owning another. Later amended to include television, it remains largely intact today, though the FCC amended it in the 1990s to let major networks buy smaller ones.

In the late 1940s, cable television emerged to provide TV service in mountainous and rural areas, but it would take three decades to become a serious competitor to broadcast TV.[34]

During a 1961 speech that was to become a harbinger of the regulatory and political battles ahead, FCC Chairman Newton Minnow, a Democrat, described TV as a "vast wasteland." A decade later, the FCC imposed cross-ownership restrictions designed to limit the influence of major media companies. Under the regulations, an individual media company was barred from owning a TV station and radio property in the same market, or a broadcast outlet and newspaper in the same market.

"It was a good rule for 1975," Dick Wiley, the Republican FCC chairman at the time, said recently of the newspaper-broadcast cross-ownership ban. "We were concerned that newspapers would dominate television, which people forget had only really [become popular] 20 years or so earlier. It's almost 30 years later, and many things are different." Wiley's influential Washington law firm represents clients that oppose the ban.[35]

Also in the '70s, with only three commercial networks and PBS available over-the-air, cable television became more competitive. As it grew in popularity, its fare would become more niche-oriented.[36]

Deregulation Begins

The era of deregulation began in earnest in the 1980s, under the Reagan administration and FCC Chairman Mark Fowler, a Republican who famously likened television to a toaster with pictures — simply another household appliance.

In 1981, the FCC ended its decades-old policy of "ascertainment" for radio stations. The policy required broadcasters to visit community groups and leaders to ascertain what types of programming they wanted and whether broadcasters were serving their needs. The FCC ended ascertainment for TV outlets in 1984. "We determined that it was excessive meddling on our part," says Robert Ratcliffe, deputy chief of the FCC's Media Bureau.

When the idea of requiring ascertainment is broached today with broadcast executives, "Those people jump up and down and say, 'Oh no, that's the heavy hand of regulation coming back. We can't consider something like that,' " Democratic FCC Commissioner Copps says.

In 1985, Fowler oversaw another deregulatory move: The FCC increased from seven to 12 the number of television stations that a single entity was permitted to own.[37]

Fowler also made it his mission to eliminate the Fairness Doctrine. Introduced in 1950, it gave citizens free airtime to reply to criticism leveled against them on TV or radio.[38] Journalists complained that the government should not be dictating editorial content, and the FCC decided that the abundance of media voices made the requirement obsolete. The FCC, which had already concluded that the policy might be unconstitutional, ended it in 1987 after a District of Columbia Circuit Court ruled the agency was no longer required to enforce it.[39]

The prime-time access rule was rescinded along with the Fairness Doctrine. It restricted local TV stations in the top 50 markets to airing only three hours of network programming during prime time, except on Sundays. The FCC had hoped the rule would encourage local public-affairs programming in time slots leading into prime time, but instead broadcasters often ran syndicated game shows, sitcom reruns and the like.[40]

Alternative Media on the Rise

By day, Tony Adragna toils for a Washington-area nonprofit and Will Vehrs works in Virginia's state government. But in their free time they're bloggers, filing constantly updated pontifications on their Web log, an online journal called "Shouting 'Cross the Potomac." This summer their log, at www.quasipundit.blogspot.com, garnered them enough attention to be interviewed on C-SPAN.

"Bloggers are a real window on the world, a really great supplement to reporters who may have trouble . . . getting to . . . a story," Vehrs said, noting that blogs (short for Web logs) provided instant coverage of the Sept. 11, 2001, terrorist attacks and the Aug. 14, 2003, blackout in the Northeast.[1]

Blogs and many other big-media alternatives that have surfaced in recent years don't meet the traditional definitions — or standards — of mainstream news outlets, often providing information that's largely unfiltered by professional editors. But that may be less important to citizens today because the major media — from *The New York Times* to the TV networks — have shown they can still get the facts wrong.[2]

While most blogs feature the writings, rantings and musings of everyday people who simply want to post their thoughts, some bloggers are media stars, such as former *New Republic* Editor Andrew Sullivan, whose "Daily Dish" blog can be found at www.andrewsullivan.com, and Glenn Reynolds, the creator of www.InstaPundit.com. Both sites feature continuously updated commentary on the latest news headlines and, in the case of Reynolds, links to other blogs.

The Economist estimates that 750,000 people now blog, and the number is expected to explode. As blogging becomes more popular, the London-based magazine reports, many are taking a closer look at the economic potential of the medium — i.e., charging for access and running ads.[3]

Seizing on the latest wave, the giant Internet service provider AOL now offers its subscribers blogging at no extra charge. And the Internet search engine Google purchased the company that makes Blogger, a free program to create blogs.[4]

Beyond Web logs, Americans also get their Internet news from sites operated by mainstream news organizations, such as CNN or *The Washington Post*, Internet-only magazines such as *Slate* and *Salon* and cybergossip Matt Drudge. Breaking e-mail news alerts are now commonplace, and for many Web users, the headlines on the Internet search engine Yahoo! are the first place they get news.

As competition from new and old news media grows, longtime players are becoming more flexible — and in the eyes of some, softening their standards. Consider Baltimore-based Sinclair Broadcasting, which relies on its Central Casting division to provide news and commentary to half of its 62 stations nationwide. From a studio near Baltimore, its news anchors provide newscasts to Pittsburgh, Raleigh, N.C., Flint, Mich., and other cities. Sinclair says Central Casting enables small, limited-resource stations to offer local news, but critics say the arrangement saves money at the expense of local coverage.[5]

Meanwhile, alternative news sites also have emerged. AlterNet.org, created in 1998 to provide its own brand of "investigative journalism," reaches more than 5 million readers through its Web and print publications.[6]

So far, however, the Internet is hardly a full-fledged alternative to traditional media. According to Nielsen ratings, the 20 most-popular Internet news sites are dominated by major media conglomerates, such as NBC and Microsoft, which co-own MSNBC.com, and CNN.com, operated by Time Warner.[7]

Apart from news, the Worldwide Web also provides alternative, low-cost publishing. Among the newest trends are "online content marketplaces," such as redpaper.com and Lulu.com. The sites provide little editing and let contributors set readership prices as low as pennies a page.

"It's great for grandpa doing his memoirs, and it's great for the family cookbook — people who can't get published anywhere else," said George Farrier, a 73-year old contrib-

---

As the broadcast industry was being progressively deregulated, Congress was turning its regulatory sights on the growing cable industry. In 1992, responding to consumer complaints, Congress passed legislation regulating cable rates and imposing other restrictions on cable monopolies. Meanwhile, direct-broadcast satellite (DBS), which made satellite-TV technology more accessible by offering consumers pizza-sized dishes for reception, was introduced in 1994.[41]

In 1995, when the FCC eliminated the fin-syn rules restricting network ownership of programming, it ushered in an era of vertical integration in which the major net-

utor to Lulu.com from Greenfield, Mo.[8] Lulu, which features lengthier writings, including many books, boasts to visitors that it "allows content to flow directly from creator to consumer. That means creators can keep 80 percent of the royalty from each sale, ownership of their work and the rights to sell it anywhere else."

In addition to alternative news and publishing, new technologies also offer alternative entertainment sources. About 250 low-power FM (LPFM) radio stations have cropped up across the country, mostly in small cities and rural areas. Another 600 or 700 of these 100-watt, non-commercial radio stations are expected to be operational soon.

Low-power radio gives a voice to nonprofits, such as religious groups, educational institutions and local governments, similar to the public access provided by local cable channels. Supporters hope LPFM will gain ground now that a recent study finds they would cause very little interference with commercial stations' signals.[9] Full-power radio broadcasters have opposed licensing LPFM stations in major markets because they feared interference, but supporters say the new report should silence those concerns.

Nevertheless, it could take a while for low-power FM to become a popular alternative to commercial radio. "Right now, a minuscule percentage of the public can tune in," says Michael Bracy, co-founder of the Future of Music Coalition, made up of radio and music interests who support LPFM expansion and oppose consolidation by Clear Channel and other big radio players.

Hedging their bets, some mainstream media companies are switching to newer technologies, or at least making investments in them. Clear Channel Communications, the dominant force in broadcast radio, has invested in XM Satellite Radio, the subscription service that offers 100 stations of music and other programming with few commercials and no cackling deejays. As part of the deal, XM carries some Clear Channel stations.[10]

Broadcast television is also evolving, as it slowly switches from analog to digital technology, which provides crisp, high-definition images and allows each broadcaster to offer multiple signals in each market. The transition, which was supposed to be complete by 2006, is expected to take much longer because of slow consumer demand, due in part to pricey digital sets and lack of awareness about digital TV. Squabbles with cable systems over signal carriage, industry bickering over copyright-protection standards and stations' difficulties raising capital to convert equipment have contributed to the delays.

In April 2002, the U.S. General Accounting Office (GAO) said many TV stations would not meet the May 2002 deadline for offering a digital signal.[11] Then in November, the GAO said more federal intervention will be needed for the digital transition to occur.[12]

Meanwhile, some Web-based alternative media have made the jump to more mainstream outlets. Thesmokinggun.com, known for obtaining controversial documents and photos, was born during the dot-com boom of the late 1990s and was later purchased by Court TV. This summer, it spawned "Smoking Gun TV," on Court TV, as well as a radio program carried by Infinity-owned stations. There's also a twice-monthly column in *People* magazine.[13]

---

[1] See transcript of C-SPAN's "Washington Journal," Aug. 15, 2003.

[2] For background, see Brian Hansen, "Combating Plagiarism," *The CQ Researcher*, Sept. 19, 2003, pp. 773-796.

[3] *The Economist*, "Golden Blogs," Aug. 16, 2003.

[4] *Ibid.*

[5] Jim Rutenberg and Micheline Maynard, "TV News That Looks Local, Even If It's Not," *The New York Times*, p. C1, June 2, 2003, p. C1.

[6] For more information, visit www.alternet.org.

[7] See "Top 20 Internet News Sites," Nielsen Media Research (see www.nielsen-netratings.com for more information), November 2002.

[8] Wailin Wong, "Web Sites Offer Unsung Writers Chance to Sing," *The Wall Street Journal*, Sept. 18, 2003, p. B1.

[9] Mitre Corp., "Experimental Measurements of the Third-Adjacent Channel Impacts of Low-Power FM Stations," released on June 30, 2003; http://hraunfoss.fcc.gov/edocs_public/attachmatch/DA-03-2277A1.doc.

[10] Frank Ahrens, "Why Radio Stinks," *The Washington Post Magazine*, Jan. 19, 2003, p. 24.

[11] "Many Broadcasters Will Not Meet May 2002 Digital Television Deadline," General Accounting Office (02-466), April 2002.

[12] "Additional Federal Efforts Could Help Advance Digital Television Transition," General Accounting Office (03-07), November 2002.

[13] Cesar G. Soriano, "The Smoking Gun Joins High-Caliber Media," *USA Today*, Aug. 18, 2003, p. 3D.

---

works merged with Hollywood studios. Also in the mid-'90s, after months of congressional hearings, debate and intensive lobbying by affected industry parties, Congress passed the sweeping 1996 Telecommunications Act, giving media companies a green light to consolidate and own more radio and TV properties in various markets.

The act also deregulated cable and expanded the audience reach of network-owned stations from 25 percent of U.S. households to 35 percent. In the ensuing years, broadcast TV networks and major cable companies would merge with other huge companies, transforming themselves into vertically integrated media giants controlling both the production and distribution of content.

In yet another loosening of its rules, the FCC in 1999 permitted more duopolies — the single ownership of two TV stations in a market — under certain conditions. Eight independent TV stations had to remain in the market after the combination, and none of the combined stations could be among the top four in the market. Before that, duopolies were permitted on a very limited basis, through waivers intended to aid struggling stations.

In June 2003, the FCC tweaked its duopoly rules again: If eight independent TV stations remain after the combination, a top-four TV station can combine with a non-top-four station in the same market.

Although industry executives insist that duopolies result in better-quality news because of the expanded resources available to the combined stations, critics say that's often not the case. "With the joining together of the two newsrooms, there's not a whole lot of original programming," complained Sylvia Teague, a former news executive and producer with the duopoly involving KCBS-TV and KCAL-TV in Los Angeles. She is now director of a project on broadcast political coverage at the University of Southern California's Annenberg School of Journalism.[42]

In October 2001, the two largest DBS companies — DirecTV and EchoStar — decided to merge, claiming the deal would create a formidable competitor to the cable-TV monopolies. But consumer groups said it would be anti-competitive to create a satellite monopoly. In the end, regulators blocked the deal. Now Murdoch's News Corp. is seeking to buy DirecTV, the nation's largest DBS provider.

Some 88 million Americans subscribe to multichannel video services such as cable and satellite, according to the FCC's 2002 report on video competition. The vast majority — 68.8 million — are cable subscribers.[43]

Complaints Increase

In recent years, the public has become increasingly dissatisfied with the media, fueled by concerns about everything from too much explicit sex and violence on TV to the botched predictions made by the networks the night of the 2000 presidential election to the recent journalism-fraud scandal at *The New York Times*.[44]

The public's cynicism was further fueled when big media outlets mostly ignored reporting on the FCC's

efforts to relax its media-ownership rules until the agency voted on June 2. Critics smelled a rat because many media properties lobbied in support of some or all of the new rules and stood to gain financially by their implementation.

"I just have to think there's something we should question about the lack of a national debate, the lack of editorials and really engaged reporting on an issue as important as this until the consumers themselves began to respond," says PBS' Mitchell, whose network was not affected by the FCC decision. The PBS program "Now with Bill Moyers" was among the few news shows that devoted significant coverage to the story.

Further exacerbating suspicions about big media companies, some recent studies suggest that media consolidation has taken a toll on news quality and depth of coverage. A five-year study of local television stations finds that despite the fact that network owned-and-operated stations (O&Os) have far more resources, smaller station groups produce better-quality news — by a "significant" margin.[45]

"Affiliates were more likely to air stories that affected everyone in the community, while O&Os were more likely to air national stories with no local connection — those car chases and exciting footage from far away," the report found.

Meanwhile, television stations have eliminated or dramatically reduced their election coverage. During the 2002 midterm elections, "almost six out of 10 top-rated news broadcasts contained no campaign coverage whatsoever," said Martin Kaplan, director of the Norman Lear Center at the Annenberg School, which surveyed election coverage by 10,000 local TV stations.

Of the stations that did cover the election, most focused only on the "horse race" during the final two weeks of the election and ignored the issues being debated. The average campaign story was less than 90 seconds, Kaplan said. "Fewer than three out of 10 campaign stories that aired included candidates speaking, and when they did speak, the average candidate sound bite was 12 seconds long."[46]

New Media Landscape

The raging controversy over the FCC's decision in June to relax its media-ownership rules has triggered plenty of comparisons between today's media marketplace and TV's so-called golden age a few decades ago.

"Even in small towns, the number of media outlets — including cable, satellite, radio, TV stations and newspapers — has increased more than 250 percent during the past 40 years," wrote FCC Chairman Powell.[47] But there are fewer media owners. For example, a decade ago there were 12,000 radio stations with 5,100 owners.[48] Today there are more radio stations — 13,000[49] — but only 3,800 owners.[50]

Two or three decades ago, there were more newspapers in large cities, says Kalb of Harvard's Shorenstein Center. Today there are roughly the same number of newspapers nationwide, but that's because there are more small suburban and small-town newspapers, he says. But today's small-town papers cover mostly local news and are not substitutes for major dailies, Kalb says.

Some industry observers are nostalgic for the days when there were only three major television networks because they feel the news coverage was more in-depth and less sensational. Robert J. Thompson, professor of television and popular culture at Syracuse University, said the comparative lack of choice when only three networks existed paradoxically served the public interest well.

"All three networks would carry presidential debates, State of the Union speeches and the national political conventions," he wrote.[51] Today, coverage of such events on broadcast TV is far more limited.

CURRENT SITUATION

TV Industry Split

The FCC's decision to raise the broadcast-ownership cap has cast a spotlight on an embarrassing schism within the television industry that threatens to undermine its lobbying muscle on ownership issues.

The networks want the cap upped to 45 percent or removed altogether. But local network affiliates want to preserve the cap at 35 percent, because they worry that if the networks own too many stations, they'll have too much sway over the programs the affiliates air. As the networks grow larger, it's more difficult for local affiliates to resist when the networks want to pre-empt local programming.

"The right to reject or pre-empt network programming must remain at the local level for stations to dis-

charge their duty to reflect what they believe is right for their individual communities," said Jim Goodmon, president and CEO of Capitol Broadcasting Co., which owns five TV stations and radio outlets in the Carolinas. Testifying before a Senate Commerce Committee hearing this year, Goodmon continued, "Whether it is to reject network programming based on community standards or whether it is to pre-empt national network programming in order to air a Billy Graham special, the Muscular Dystrophy Telethon or local sports, I can't imagine that anyone in this room really wants to take away local control over television programming."[52]

The spat has implications for the National Association of Broadcasters (NAB), the TV industry's fierce lobby, which has been abandoned in recent years by the influential Big Four networks over the ownership issue. The networks have indicated they may form a new lobbying organization to push their own deregulatory agenda.[53]

NAB opposed the FCC's decision to raise the cap and says it supports congressional efforts to roll it back to 35 percent. But it's now actively fighting bills that would do just that, because they contain additional language further regulating broadcasters. Some parties are disappointed with NAB's shifting positions.

"The NAB's decision to reverse itself on the issue of the national television-ownership cap is an unfortunate retreat from its proud history of support for localism, diversity and competition in the broadcast marketplace," said Rep. John Dingell, D-Mich.[54]

NAB spokesman Dennis Wharton insists there was no flip-flop or retreat: "If we can get a clean 35 percent rollback bill out of Congress and signed by the president, that is something we would support."

Reaction to Rules

Angered that the FCC relaxed the ownership rules too much, a growing chorus of lawmakers is aggressively moving to rescind at least key portions of it, including Senate Appropriations Committee Chairman Ted Stevens, R-Alaska, Sen. Minority Leader Tom Daschle, D-S.D., Sens. Dorgan and Hollings and Rep. Dingell.

Their top priority: to return the cap on the reach of broadcast network-owned TV stations to 35 percent of the nation's households.

To be sure, the FCC still has allies on the Hill, including House Appropriations Committee Chairman

C.W. Bill Young of Florida and House Commerce Committee Chairman Tauzin.

"Only in Washington, D.C., would those who ostensibly want to preserve free speech seek to do so by regulating broadcast rules," Tauzin said.[55]

On Sept. 16, the Senate passed a so-called "resolution of disapproval" — a little-used procedural device that rescinds the rule changes. Spearheaded by Sens. Dorgan, Lott, Feingold and Susan Collins, R-Maine, the vote was 55-40. But House Majority Leader Tom DeLay, R-Texas, warned the bill is dead on arrival in the lower chamber.

Hedging his bets, Dorgan said he'll also try to amend an appropriations bill with a rider to restore the ban on newspaper-television cross-ownership. But his prospects are uncertain because similar efforts have failed in the House.[56]

Putting a positive spin on the vote, Media Bureau Chief Ferree calls it a "huge victory" for the FCC. "This was a freebie for these guys. They know it's not going anywhere in the House." He adds, "I look at today's vote, and I say it's over."

"Were this to become law it would be a disaster," Ferree says. "It would just throw things into chaos. I don't know how we'd stop almost any transaction under old rules that have been questioned in court and new rules that we couldn't implement."

Ferree continues, "The point is trying to adopt measured, reasonable limits that we can defend in court, which I think we did. And if people on the Hill start to understand that, they'd come around, and we'd get more and more support."

In other action, the House this summer passed an appropriations bill by a vote of 400 to 21 that contained an amendment rolling the ownership cap back to 35 percent.

Stevens has added a similar measure to Senate appropriations legislation expected to be voted on this year. Republican leaders are vowing to strip out the rollback when the House and Senate spending bills go into conference negotiations. If the rollback is removed, it could be pushed by supportive lawmakers next year. The White House has threatened to veto any legislation rolling back the cap.

In addition, the Senate Commerce panel has approved legislation sponsored by Stevens and Hollings that returns the broadcast ownership cap to 35 percent and bars newspaper-broadcast cross-ownership.

Meanwhile, the FCC's new rules face a variety of court challenges. In a surprise 11th-hour move, a federal appeals court in Philadelphia stayed the FCC's June 2 announcement pending further judicial review. The court decision was in response to challenges to the rules filed by advocacy groups.

In addition, the NAB has appealed portions of the FCC decision that reduce the size of many radio markets and ban duopolies between TV stations in small markets. And a group representing local TV affiliates has appealed the raising of the ownership cap to 45 percent. Media General also is appealing because the FCC didn't relax restrictions on its ownership of both newspapers and broadcast outlets in small markets.[57]

Powell Under Fire

The controversy over ownership has focused on more than just regulation. FCC Chairman Powell is now under attack from both parties for shepherding the sweeping rule changes through his agency.

Critics say the FCC, which held only one official hearing on media concentration before it voted, rushed to adopt the changes and refused to compromise with Democratic FCC commissioners.[58] Powell counters that the agency issued 12 studies last fall examining the issues.

Critics insist Powell misjudged the guidance of the courts by developing relaxed ownership rules. In fact, a federal appeals court in Washington has struck down the last five media-ownership rules it has reviewed, tossing them back to the agency. Powell says the court told the FCC to get rid of the rules, but critics say the court instructed the agency to justify them, not discard them.

The FCC received at least 2 million e-mails, letters and postcards expressing opposition to the rule changes, though Powell is quick to point out that three-quarters of the messages were sent by NRA members.[59]

Constant rumors in the press that the chairman might resign have forced him to repeatedly deny he'll leave the FCC before his term expires.

The chairman has been fighting back with a series of op-eds in major newspapers and televised interviews to defend his positions. But he told C-SPAN earlier this year that it is difficult for the FCC, an independent agency, to battle with Capitol Hill on policy issues.

If the FCC is to fight lawmakers over policy issues, he said, "then I think there's a serious argument that we just belong in the administration. There ought to be a secretary of communications, it ought to be the president's policy, it ought to be in a political branch of government, and be treated that way."[60]

To stem the criticism, Powell this summer unveiled plans to promote localism among broadcasters, a key concern of his critics. In the end, the chairman's announcement didn't quiet his detractors, who think his initiative was intended to deflect anger over the agency's broader media policies.

Commissioner Copps says Powell's move should have occurred long before June 2. And he thinks it may not go far enough. "We require stations to keep a public file — we don't look at it when it comes time for license renewal. Can you imagine that?" He says license renewals are now mostly done by postcard. "Unless there is a gross character violation charge against you, you're going to get your license renewed," he says.

In response, Ratcliffe of the FCC's Media Bureau says the agency inspects the files when citizens file petitions against stations. "We constantly review how those things are working," he says.

Cable Debate

While broadcast and newspaper outlets have taken the brunt of the criticism lately, cable is not off the hook. If anything, it could be the next regulatory target, industry observers say. In a little-noticed move, the FCC said it wants to know if cable has met the so-called 70-70 test, which would trigger more regulation. The 70-70 threshold is reached if at least 70 percent of U.S. homes have access to cable, and 70 percent of those homes subscribe.[61]

According to a recent report by the consumer group U.S. PIRG, the top 10 cable operators serve about 85 percent of all cable subscribers and the top three — Comcast, Time Warner and Charter — serve about 56 percent, up 8 percent since 1996. Cable operators also dominate the high-speed Internet-access business, yet the cable industry operates largely unregulated.[62]

In 95 percent of all U.S. households, there is access to only one cable service.[63] In most markets, cable offers little in the way of local news, although regional cable-news channels have sprung up in some large metro areas.

Meanwhile, the FCC has to decide the fate of the cable-ownership cap, which a federal appeals court in Washington declared unconstitutional two years ago.[64] The cap limits a single cable company to reaching 30 percent of the national market. According to *USA Today*, the FCC is taking a "measured" approach toward a revised cable cap and would permit case-by-case reviews of cable mergers. In a draft proposal that could change, cable companies would be allowed to serve up to 45 percent of households, but the FCC would have the flexibility to block or approve deals at varying thresholds. AT&T Comcast, the nation's biggest cable provider, is just under the 30 percent cap.[65]

Meanwhile, the average monthly cable fee rose by 8.2 percent — from $37.06 to $40.11 — over the 12-month period ending July 1, 2002, according to the FCC.[66] In response, Commerce Committee Chairman McCain said, "The cable industry has risen to new heights in their apparent willingness and ability to gouge the American consumer."[67]

In a ruling on Oct. 6, a federal appeals court in San Francisco effectively required cable providers of high-speed Internet access to include competing Internet services on their systems. If it stands, the decision would be a blow to cable companies and the FCC, which fears such access would deter cable companies from investing heavily in super-fast Internet connections, or broadband. The FCC has vowed to appeal and may be able to override the decision through regulatory action.

Over the years, allegations have arisen that some cable companies play hardball with programmers and sometimes refuse to carry competing channels. Cox Communications, for example, which has a 25 percent stake in the parent of the Discovery Channel, doesn't carry the rival National Geographic Channel. "We carry more than 200 channels, and we own 10 of them, and we have 55 movie channels and own three," Cablevision spokesman Charles Schueler said. "To suggest that we favor our own programming is absurd."[68]

Robert Sachs, president and CEO of the National Cable and Telecommunications Association, added, "Since 1992, the percentage of program networks in which cable operators have any financial interest has plummeted from 48 percent to less than 21 percent. At the same time, the number of available channels has skyrocketed from 87 to 308. There are more than six times as many non-cable-owned channels as there were a decade ago."[69]

AT ISSUE

Are the major TV networks committed to localism?*

YES
Mel Karmazin
President and COO,
Viacom Inc.

From testimony before Senate Commerce,
Transportation and Science Committee, May 13, 2003

It is utterly unsupportable and unrealistic that broadcasters should be handcuffed in their attempts to compete for consumers at a time when Americans are bombarded with media choices via technologies never dreamed of even a decade ago, much less 60 years ago when some of these rules were first adopted. . . .

Most television stations in this country are held by multi-station groups owned by large corporations headquartered in cities located far from their stations' communities of license. What does it matter that Viacom's main offices are in New York? The corporate group owners are no more "local" in the cities where they own TV stations than is Viacom. Yet, like Viacom and all good broadcasters, group owners work hard to know what viewers want in each market where it has a media outlet. Localism is just good business.

Networks invest billions of dollars in programming, but most of the return on their investment is realized at the station level. Only two of the so-called "Big Four" networks are profitable in any year [compared] to television stations — run by networks and affiliates alike — which operate on margins anywhere from 20 percent to 50 percent.

If networks are precluded from realizing more of the revenue generated by stations, networks' ability to continue their multibillion-dollar programming investments will diminish, and more and more programming will migrate from broadcasting to cable and satellite TV, where regulation is less onerous. More Americans then will have to pay for what they now get for free.

[The] argument that affiliates provide more local news than do network-owned-and-operated stations is, again, false. In a study commissioned by Viacom, Fox and NBC, Economists Inc. found that the average TV station owned by a network provides more local news per week — 37 percent more — than the average affiliate, a finding consistent with the FCC's own independently conducted study. . . .

Nor is it true that affiliates stand as the bulwark against allegedly inappropriate network programming. . . . Pre-emptions based on content are rare. But in the handful of cases over the past years when an affiliate has determined that a program's subject may be too sensitive for its market — as was the case last week with our Providence affiliate with respect to the "CSI: Miami" episode dealing with fire hazards at nightclubs — we understand and accommodate. Our own stations would do the same thing for their markets' viewers.

NO
Tom Daschle, D-S.D.
Minority Leader, U.S. Senate

From a statement on the Senate floor, Sept. 16, 2003

Many argue there are an infinite number of media outlets today, especially given the huge growth in cable channels and Internet addresses.

But the vast majority of Americans get their news and information from television news and/or their local newspaper. None of the cable-news channels has anywhere near the viewership of the broadcast media, and most of the major cable and Internet news outlets are affiliated with the print and broadcast media already controlled in large part by just a handful of companies. Diversity of viewpoints is already in jeopardy, and the new rules would only exacerbate the situation. . . .

If many of those so-called diverse viewpoints are actually controlled by a handful of companies, then one can see that localism, too, is in trouble. The loss of localism in radio is well known, sometimes with dangerous consequences like the famous Minot, N.D., case.

In fact, the lack of localism in radio is so undeniable that even the FCC has agreed to address it in the one aspect of the proposed rules that makes sense.

But localism in television is also at risk — local entertainment choices as well as news. James Goodmon of Capitol Broadcasting in North Carolina explained it well in his testimony before the Commerce Committee.

He owns Fox and CBS stations in Raleigh. Out of respect for his local audience's sensibilities, he has refused to carry either network's "reality TV" shows, including "Temptation Island," "Cupid," "Who Wants to Marry a Millionaire" and "Married by America."

His actions have met with intense resistance from the networks, and he has expressed his grave concern that if the networks' ability to own more and more of the broadcast outlets goes unchecked, local stations and communities won't have any ability to choose their own programming. They will be forced to air the network fare, even when it is offensive to local viewers. . . .

Let me be clear: I don't blame the media companies for advocating for their own interests. They have every right to fight for their interests.

I do blame the chairman of the FCC and the other commissioners who voted for these rules for failing to give the rest of the country the consideration they deserved in this debate.

_____

* Localism refers to serving a community's needs and tastes.

OUTLOOK

More Mergers?

Before the current ownership brouhaha flared up, many observers were anticipating a new round of deals involving the broadcast television networks, individual TV stations and newspapers. Merrill Lynch and other Wall Street firms predicted TV-station acquisitions by Viacom, Disney, News Corp., Hearst Argyle, Sinclair Broadcasting and LIN TV, among others. "There may be a bantam wave of media mergers, but surely not the tsunami envisioned," Merrill media analyst Jessica Reif Cohen wrote recently.[70]

Several newspaper companies, including Tribune, Media General and Gannett, were widely expected to buy more TV properties. "The only people who can't own a TV or radio station are aliens, convicted felons and newspaper publishers," said Newspaper Association of America CEO John Sturm, before the FCC's announcement.[71]

Fallout from the FCC's decision, coupled with a court-imposed stay, has created considerable uncertainty and dampened the acquisition fervor. Nevertheless, a few transactions have been announced since the FCC's action, the largest being NBC's acquisition of Vivendi Universal's entertainment assets. Some deals were pending before the FCC decision, such as News Corp.'s bid to buy satellite-TV giant DirecTV and the recently approved merger of Univision and Hispanic Broadcasting Corp., which worries Democrats because Univision billionaire CEO Jerry Perenchio, a staunch Republican, would be at the helm.[72]

On Sept. 22, the FCC approved the Spanish-television merger, saying it would not harm diversity of programming for viewers of the networks. But it did require the companies to shed some radio properties to comply with new radio market rules adopted this past summer.[73]

Several Democratic presidential candidates have raised concerns about media consolidation, but it remains to be seen whether the subject will become a full-fledged election issue. Former Vermont Gov. Howard Dean and Sens. John Edwards, D-N.C., and John F. Kerry, D-Mass., have said they oppose the FCC changes. In recent years, Sen. Joseph I. Lieberman, D-Conn., has criticized the networks for airing too much gratuitous sex and violence.

Meanwhile, FCC Chairman Powell has repeatedly argued that free, over-the-air television is in danger of disappearing as programming — particularly sports, movies and children's fare — migrates to pay TV. Letting the broadcast networks own more stations would protect such programming, he said.

"There has been a steady migration of top programming to pay platforms and away from free TV," Powell said. "Free TV is being replaced by pretty low-cost budget programming, like reality TV."[74] If free TV cannot be made competitive with cable and satellite, he said later, "You're going to be wondering what happened [to it]."[75]

A recently released communications-industry forecast by the New York investment bank Veronis Suhler Stevenson indicates he may have a point. Over the next five years, it predicts, consumers seeking to avoid ads will spend more time with cable, DVDs, video games and other media with a pricetag and less time with free, over-the-air TV and radio.[76]

But critics emphasize that media companies reap healthy profits from their TV operations. "They're not a hardship case," FCC Commissioner Copps says. The cable and broadcast networks recently set records for commitments from advertisers for the upcoming television season. Ironically, media concentration helped to encourage the strong buying. "The consolidation of sellers and buyers has made it easy to move a market quickly," said Gene DeWitt, president of the Syndicated Network Television Association.[77]

Copps thinks if the consolidation trend continues, the Internet could be a future regulatory battleground. "I'm worried about the openness of the Internet, and companies having control over the gateways to the information there," he says.

After months of debate, politicking and saber rattling, some observers think there have been fundamental changes. "Something is definitely shifting in the country and in Washington. Where just a few years ago most people did not think about media as an issue . . . now there is a real dialogue going on," said Rep. Bernard Sanders, I-Vt.[78]

NOTES

1. Jim Rutenberg, "To Interview Former P.O.W., CBS Offers Stardom," *The New York Times*, June 16, 2003, p. A1.

2. Lynn Elber, "CBS May Have Erred in Pursuit of Lynch Interview, Executive Says," Associated Press/TBO.com, July 20, 2003.

3. For background, see Kenneth Jost, "The Future of Television," *The CQ Researcher*, Dec. 23, 1994, pp. 1129-1152.

4. Marc Fisher, "Sounds Familiar for a Reason," *The Washington Post*, May 18, 2003, p. B1.

5. Michael K. Powell, "New Rules, Old Rhetoric," *The New York Times*, July 28, 2003, p. A17.

6. Eric Boehlert, "Habla usted Clear Channel?" Salon.com, April 24, 2003.

7. From testimony before Britain's House of Lords, June 26, 2003.

8. "Annual Assessment of the Status of Competition in the Market for the Delivery of Video Programming, Ninth Annual Report," Federal Communications Commission, www.fcc.gov, Dec. 31, 2002, p. 3.

9. See "Mass Deregulation of Media Threatens to Undermine Democracy," Consumer Federation of America, June 3, 2003.

10. See "Report and Order," www.fcc.gov, July 2, 2003, p. 15.

11. Stephen Labaton, "Senate Debates Repeal of FCC Media Ownership Rules," *The New York Times*, Sept. 12, 2003, p. C3.

12. For background, see David Masci, "The Future of Telecommunications," *The CQ Researcher*, April 23, 1999, pp. 329-352.

13. For background, see "Minorities Lose Ground in Newsrooms" at www.rtnda.org. The survey was by the Radio and TV News Directors Association and Ball State University.

14. Paul Farhi, "Mega-Media: Better or More of the Same?" *The Washington Post*, June 3, 2003, p. C1.

15. Eli Noam, "The media concentration debate," *Financial Times*, July 31 2003, p. A16.

16. "FCC Chairman Powell Defends FCC Media Rules," FCC news release, July 23, 2003.

17. Adam Thierer and Clyde Wayne Crews Jr., "What Media Monopolies?" *The Wall Street Journal*, July 29, 2003, p. B2.

18. See "Free TV Swallowed by Media Giants: The Way It Really Is," Consumer Federation of America, Center for Digital Democracy, Sept. 15, 2003, p. 3.

19. Adam Lashinsky, "Americans Stupid? Media to Blame? Leading thinkers weigh in at Fortune's Brainstorm 2003 conference," *Fortune*, July 31, 2003.

20. See "Does Ownership Matter in Local Television News: A Five-Year Study of Ownership and Quality," Project for Excellence in Journalism, April 29, 2003.

21. See press release/statement, at http://lott.senate.gov/news, June 6, 2003.

22. See "Statement by Commissioner Adelstein before Minority Media & Telecommunications Council," July 22, 2003.

23. Catherine Yang, "FCC's Loner is No Longer So Lonely," *Business Week*, March 24, 2003, p. 78.

24. Labaton, *op. cit.*

25. Frank Ahrens, "FCC Rule Fight Continues in Congress," *The Washington Post*, June 4, 2003, p. E1.

26. See "Report and Order," *op. cit.*

27. For background, see Charles S. Clark, "Sex, Violence and the Media," *The CQ Researcher*, Nov. 17, 1995, pp. 1017-1040.

28. Meg James, "The Vivendi Deal; Creator of 'Law & Order' is Facing Chance of Being Outgunned in Talks," *Los Angeles Times*, Sept. 4, 2003, p. C1.

29. Bill Carter and Jim Rutenberg, "Deregulating the Media: Opponents, Shows' Creators Say Television Will Suffer in New Climate," *The New York Times*, June 3, 2003, p. C1.

30. Bill McConnell, "McCain Weighs in for Fin-Syn," *Broadcasting & Cable*, May 26, 2003, p. 2.

31. See petition for reconsideration filed at FCC by Center for the Creative Community and Association of Independent Video and Filmmakers, available at www.creativecommunity.us, Sept. 4, 2003, pp. 7-8.

32. See "Report and Order," *op. cit.*, p. 15.

33. McConnell, *op. cit.*

34. See "Data Gathering Weakness in FCC's Survey of Information on Factors Underlying Cable Rate Changes," General Accounting Office, May 6, 2003, p. 2.

35. Stephen Labaton, "Behind Media Rule and Its End, One Man," *The New York Times*, June 2, 2003, p. C1.

36. For background, see Adriel Bettelheim, "Public Broadcasting," *The CQ Researcher*, Oct. 29, 1999, pp. 929-952.

37. See "Media Regulations Timeline" at www.pbs.org/now/politics/mediatimeline.html.

38. *Ibid.*

39. *Ibid.*

40. Robert J. Thompson, "500 Channels, But No Clear Picture of What We Want," *The Washington Post*, May 25, 2003, p. B3.

41. See "Issues in Providing Cable and Satellite Television Services," General Accounting Office, Oct. 2002, p. 1.

42. Greg Braxton, "Rewriting the Rules: Synergies Emerge in TV Duopolies," *Los Angeles Times*, May 30, 2003, p. C1.

43. See FCC "Annual Assessment, *op. cit.*

44. For background, see Brian Hansen, "Combating Plagiarism," *The CQ Researcher*, Sept. 19, 2003, pp. 773-796, and Kathy Koch, "Journalism Under Fire," *The CQ Researcher*, Dec. 25, 1998, pp. 1121-1144.

45. Project for Excellence in Journalism, *op. cit.*

46. See testimony of Martin Kaplan of the USC Annenberg School of Communications before Senate Commerce Committee; www.senate.gov/~commerce/hearings, July 23, 2003.

47. Michael K. Powell, "Should Limits on Broadcast Ownership Change?" USAToday.com, Jan. 21, 2003, p. A11.

48. Frank Ahrens, "Why Radio Stinks," *The Washington Post Magazine*, p. 25, Jan. 19, 2003, p. W12.

49. "Broadcast station totals," FCC Audio Division, available at www.fcc.gov, June 30, 2003.

50. Ahrens, *op. cit.*

51. Robert J. Thompson, "500 Channels, But No Clear Picture of What We Want," *The Washington Post*, May 25, 2003, p. B3.

52. From testimony before Senate Commerce Committee, May 13, 2003.

53. Edmund Sanders, "Disney Quits Broadcasters Trade Group," *Los Angeles Times*, June 18, 2003, p. C1.

54. Bill McConnell, "Fritts: No Reversal on 35% Cap Legislation," *Broadcasting & Cable*, July 11, 2003.

55. See "Tauzin Issues Statement In Support of FCC's Media Ownership Process," May 29, 2003.

56. Frank Ahrens, "Senate Votes to Block FCC Media Rules, *The Washington Post*, Sept. 17, 2003, p. A1.

57. Edmund Sanders and Jube Shiver Jr., "ReWriting the Rules: FCC Relaxes Limits on Media Ownership," *Los Angeles Times*, June 18, 2003, p. A1.

58. Christopher Stern, "Bitter Atmosphere Envelops FCC: Under Chairman Powell, Panel Members Maneuver, Criticize," *The Washington Post*, June 3, 2003, p. E1.

59. Interview on C-SPAN's "Washington Journal," Sept. 3, 2003.

60. *Ibid.*

61. Dan Trigoboff, "FCC Eyes 70/70," www.Broadcastingandcable.com, Aug. 4, 2003.

62. See "The Failure of Cable Deregulation," at www.uspirg.org, U.S. PIRG, August 2003.

63. "Fighting Media Monopolies 2003," *Consumer Reports*, July 2003, p. 65.

64. For background, see "Judges Lift Cable Ownership Cap," www.broadcastingcable.com, March 4, 2001.

65. Paul Davidson, "FCC Fine-tuning Proposal to Relax Cable Ownership Limits," *USA Today*, July 25, 2003, p. B3.

66. See "Report on Cable Industry Prices," FCC 03-136, July 8, 2003.

67. Press release, July 8, 2003.

68. David Lieberman, "Media Moguls Have Second Thoughts," *USA Today*, June 2, 2003, p. B1.

69. See Robert Sachs, "Television Ownership" letter to the editor, *The New York Times*, Aug. 1, 2003, p. A20.

70. Sallie Hofmeister and Jube Shiver Jr., "Worry Over FCC Rules Not Shared on Wall Street," *Los Angeles Times*, June 4, 2003, p. C1.

71. David Lieberman, "Relaxing Rules Raises Concerns About Diverse Media Voices," *USA Today*, Jan. 15, 2003, p. B1.

72. Juliet Eilperin, "Democrats Fight Hispanic Media Merger, Republican Ownership Could Limit Access to Viewpoints, Groups Tell FCC," *The Washington Post*, May 25, 2003, p. A5.

73. Press release, Sept. 22, 2003.

74. Powell interview, *op. cit.*

75. See transcript of McLaughlin "One-on-One," Sept. 7, 2003.

76. Michael McCarthy, "Forecast: Public to turn to paid media," *USA Today*, Aug. 15, 2003, p. B12.

77. Stuart Elliott, "Trying to sort out the broader trends behind the big surge in spending on TV commercials," *The New York Times*, June 3, 2003, p. C10.

78. Quoted in Robert McChesney and John Nichols, "Media Democracy's Moment," *The Nation*, Feb. 24, 2003.

BIBLIOGRAPHY

Books

Klein, Alec, *Stealing Time: Steve Case, Jerry Levin and the Collapse of AOL Time Warner*, Simon & Schuster, 2003.
Reporter Klein describes how the bursting Internet bubble, conflicting management styles, accounting irregularities and other difficulties devalued the largest merger in American history and forced out top executives.

Articles

Fallows, James, "The Age of Murdoch," *The Atlantic*, September 2003.
Journalist Fallows argues that media baron Rupert Murdoch approaches his media empire as just another business — not one charged with serving the public interest.

Fisher, Marc, "Sounds Familiar for a Reason," *The Washington Post*, May 18, 2003, p. B1.
A *Post* columnist and the author of an upcoming book on the radio industry takes a critical look at radio giant Clear Channel Communications.

Kirkpatrick, David D., "Entertainment Industry Faces Problems Mergers Won't Solve," *The New York Times*, Sept. 8, 2003, p. C1.
Kirkpatrick explores whether NBC's proposed deal with Vivendi Universal signals the end of media mergers.

Noam, Eli, "The Media Concentration Debate," *Financial Times*, July 31, 2003, p. A11.
Telecom visionary and Columbia University Professor Eli Noam notes that while media companies are bigger, so is the sector. Local concentration is actually highest among newspapers, not TV stations, and radio-industry growth has slowed in recent years.

Thierer, Adam, and Clyde Wayne Crews Jr., "What Media Monopolies?" *The Wall Street Journal*, July 29, 2003, p. B2.
Analysts at the libertarian Cato Institute argue the broadcast networks are far from monopolies because audience share has decreased dramatically, and many non-network station groups own more TV outlets than networks.

Thompson, Robert J., "500 Channels, But No Clear Picture of What We Want," *The Washington Post*, May 25, 2003, p. B3.
Consumers have far more media choices today, but the quality of news and the quantity of civic-minded programming often pales compared to decades ago.

Reports and Studies

"Big Radio Rules in Small Markets: A few behemoths dominate medium-sized cities throughout the U.S.," Center for Public Integrity, Oct. 1, 2003.
Radio concentration is highest in small and medium-sized markets, where industry giant Clear Channel is a major player. FCC rules limit companies to owning eight radio outlets per market, but companies sidestep the limit by acquiring stations in adjacent markets that can be heard where they've reached the cap. For a copy, visit http://www.openairwaves.org/telecom/report.aspx?aid=63.

"Does Ownership Matter in Local Television News: A Five-Year Study of Ownership and Quality," Project for Excellence in Journalism, April 29, 2003.
This exhaustive study finds that small-station groups tend to produce better newscasts than large ones, and network affiliates tend to have better news than network-owned stations. Moreover, cross-ownership of a TV station and a newspaper in a market usually results in higher-quality news, but local ownership doesn't guarantee quality. Available at www.journalism.org.

"Free TV Swallowed by Media Giants: The Way It Really Is," Consumer Federation of America, Consumers Union and Center for Digital Democracy, Sept. 15, 2003.
Three watchdog groups challenge the argument that free TV is in jeopardy if the FCC's media-ownership rules are not relaxed, pointing out the broadcast networks are strong financially. Available at www.democraticmedia.org.

Halfon, Jay, and Edmund Mierzwinski, "The Failure of Cable Deregulation," U.S. PIRG, August 2003.
Cable rates have been rising three times faster than inflation, and even higher. Meanwhile, satellite-TV competition is not resulting in lower rates for cable. For a copy, visit www.uspirg.org.

"(Media Ownership) Report and Order and Notice of Proposed Rulemaking," Federal Communications Commission, (FCC 03-127), July 2, 2003.

This 256-page report provides extensive background on the FCC's decision to modify its media-ownership rules. The "Report and order" can be obtained at www.fcc.gov.

"Radio Deregulation: Has it Served Citizens and Musicians?" Future of Music Coalition, November 2002.

The rapid consolidation of the radio industry after deregulation in 1996 is documented in this 147-page report. Available at www.futureofmusic.org.

For More Information

Consumer Federation of America, 1424 16th St., N.W., Suite 604, Washington, DC 20036; (202) 387-6121; www.consumerfed.org. A vocal advocate of regulating the media; frequently issues reports detailing increased consolidation.

Consumers Union, 1666 Connecticut Ave., N.W., Suite 310, Washington, DC 20009-1039; (202) 462-6262; www.consumersunion.org. It has teamed with Consumer Federation to oppose further relaxation of the media-ownership rules.

Future of Music Coalition, 1615 L St., N.W., Suite 520, Washington, DC 20036; (202) 429-8855; www.futureofmusic.org. A nonprofit coalition of radio and music interests that opposes radio consolidation and supports fledgling low-power FM.

National Association of Broadcasters, 1771 N St., N.W., Washington, DC 20036; (202) 429-5300; www.nab.org. The main trade association representing television and radio broadcasters, though the Big Four TV networks are no longer members.

National Cable and Telecommunications Association, 1724 Massachusetts Ave., N.W., Washington, DC 20036; (202) 775-3550; www.ncta.com. The premier trade association for cable TV companies; many also offer high-speed Internet access.

Radio-Television News Directors Association & Foundation, 1600 K St., N.W., Suite 700, Washington, DC 20006-2838; (202) 659-6510; www.rtnda.org. Opposes curbs on press freedoms and promotes journalistic ethics.

14

Exporting Jobs

Mary H. Cooper

Workers at a call center in Bangalore, India, service customers from around the world 24 hours a day. U.S. and other firms are increasingly outsourcing their service operations to India, the Philippines, Russia and other sources of skilled, cheap labor. Proponents of so-called "offshoring" say it ultimately helps the U.S. economy, but critics say sending high-paying jobs overseas forces laid-off Americans into less desirable jobs.

From *The CQ Researcher*, February 20, 2004.

AP Photo/Indranil Mukherjee

Computer programmer Robin Tauch rode the technology boom to a salary of nearly $100,000 a year at Dallas-based Computer Sciences Corp. But the ride ended last August, when she joined legions of fellow computer professionals on the unemployment rolls.

"I've got tons of friends who are looking for work," she says. "We're all people who have been employed for 20-some years. For the first time in our lives, we've just been dumped on the street."

But losing her job was doubly painful to Tauch because she had to train the two technology workers brought in from India to replace her.

Similar scenarios are playing out across the United States. Eager to reduce labor costs, a U.S. firm imports qualified foreign information technology (IT) workers by obtaining temporary visas for the new employees. Once they learn the host company's specific needs, the foreign workers often return home to establish an IT department for the firm. Or they replace the workers who trained them.

India is one of several countries with relatively low-wage, highly educated, English-speaking populations — Ireland and the Philippines among them — benefiting from U.S. cost-cutting efforts.

Workers in such countries provide a broad range of business services, such as answering customer-service calls, accounting, reviewing insurance claims and processing bills.

The export of American jobs has touched so many sectors of the economy, in fact, that it has generated a new term to describe the trend — "offshoring," short for offshore outsourcing.

"A lot of these offshored positions replace very high-wage jobs," says Lester Thurow, dean of the Sloan School of Business at

Nearly 3 Million Factory Jobs Were Lost

More than 2.8 million U.S. factory jobs have been lost since 2000, mainly in the computer/electronics and textile industries. Offshoring accounted for about 10 percent of the losses, according to one estimate. In the next 15 years, other studies predict the loss of up to 14 million service jobs, such as answering customer calls, accounting, insurance claim review and bill processing.

Lost U.S. Manufacturing Jobs
Selected Industries, 2000-2003

Industry	Jobs Lost
Computers and electronics	455,000
Textiles and apparel	395,000
Machinery	301,000
Transportation equipment	297,000
Fabricated materials	288,000
Primary metals	154,000
Electrical equipment/appliances	135,000
Plastics	131,000
Printing	132,000
Furniture	107,000

Source: Labor Department, Bureau of Labor Statistics, Feb. 4, 2004; www.bls.gov.

Massachusetts Institute of Technology (MIT). "Here in Boston, for example, Massachusetts General Hospital is even outsourcing radiologists. Instead of having a $450,000 radiologist read an X-ray or an MRI here, they send it to India and have it read by a $50,000 radiologist."

Meanwhile, General Electric, Microsoft and other big firms are expanding their operations in India to include everything from basic customer service to high-end research and development.[1]

Business advocates say offshoring is nothing more than the latest cost-saving technique and that it will benefit Americans in the long run by allowing companies to be more efficient and to invest the savings in more valuable, cutting-edge U.S. jobs of the future.

Labor advocates counter that offshoring threatens U.S. living standards by forcing Americans whose jobs have gone overseas to take lower-wage positions. The debate over whether offshoring helps or hurts the economy also is emerging as a key issue in the coming presidential campaign.

U.S. job outsourcing began in the manufacturing sector in the 1980s, when disappearing worldwide trade barriers forced U.S. companies to compete with foreign manufacturers using cheap labor. To survive, U.S. manufacturers exported factory jobs from the higher-wage, heavily unionized Northeast and Midwest to Asia and Latin America, as well as to the largely non-unionized and lower-wage Southern United States.

In addition, many factory jobs fall victim to computerization and robotization.

As a result, many blue-collar workers and middle managers were "downsized," forcing many former assembly-line workers to seek lower-paid jobs in the rapidly expanding retail and business-service industries. Nearly 5 million U.S. factory jobs have been lost in the United States since 1979, more than half of them — 2.8 million — since 2000 alone.[2]

Lately, however, American businesses have been offshoring more of their highly paid professional staffs, who until now had been insulated from job insecurity by their specialized skills, usually acquired after years of costly college and graduate education.

"The Web makes it much easier for a skilled job to move to India, where you have plenty of people trained not just at MIT but at various high-tech Indian academic institutions," says Susan Aaronson, director of globalization studies at the University of North Carolina's Kenan Institute of Private Enterprise, in Washington, D.C. "The only thing that's new about this is that middle-class jobs are now being affected."

Estimates of the number of American jobs lost to the trend vary widely, largely because U.S. companies are not required to report their offshoring practices. One report blames offshoring for 300,000 of the 2.4 million total jobs lost since 2001. Various studies project that from

3 to 14 million service jobs could go overseas in the next 15 years.[3]

Economists say offshoring helps explain why the nation is undergoing its so-called jobless recovery. Since the last recession ended in 2001, the U.S. economy has rebounded — except for employment.

Last year, America's output of goods and services, or gross domestic product (GDP), rose by 3.1 percent, up from 2.2 percent in 2002 and just 0.5 percent in 2001.[4] Business investment and consumer spending also has picked up.[5] But employment, which typically improves during recoveries, has lagged: Only 112,000 new jobs were added to private payrolls in January, about 38,000 fewer than economists had expected.[6]

President Bush declared on Feb. 9, 2004, that "America's economy is strong and getting stronger" and predicted the creation of 2.6 million jobs this year, increasing non-farm payroll employment to 132.7 million. Last February, the White House predicted that 1.7 million jobs would be created in 2003. In fact, non-farm payrolls showed a small decline. Since Bush took office, the country has lost 2.2 million payroll jobs, as non-farm employment dipped to 130.2 million.

One explanation for the disappointing employment numbers lies in the economy's blistering productivity rate — 9.4 percent in the third quarter of last year.

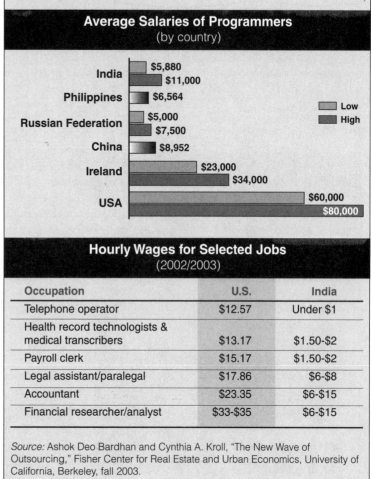

Outsourced Jobs Abroad Pay Lower Wages

Computer programmers in countries where U.S. companies are outsourcing their technology jobs earn far less than American programmers (top). Similarly, low wages are paid in other countries, like India, where U.S. firms also are outsourcing non-technology jobs (bottom).

Average Salaries of Programmers
(by country)

- India: $5,880 (Low) / $11,000 (High)
- Philippines: $6,564
- Russian Federation: $5,000 (Low) / $7,500 (High)
- China: $8,952
- Ireland: $23,000 (Low) / $34,000 (High)
- USA: $60,000 (Low) / $80,000 (High)

Hourly Wages for Selected Jobs
(2002/2003)

Occupation	U.S.	India
Telephone operator	$12.57	Under $1
Health record technologists & medical transcribers	$13.17	$1.50-$2
Payroll clerk	$15.17	$1.50-$2
Legal assistant/paralegal	$17.86	$6-$8
Accountant	$23.35	$6-$15
Financial researcher/analyst	$33-$35	$6-$15

Source: Ashok Deo Bardhan and Cynthia A. Kroll, "The New Wave of Outsourcing," Fisher Center for Real Estate and Urban Economics, University of California, Berkeley, fall 2003.

"Moving all the low-productivity stuff from the American economy to China or India raises the productivity level of what's left," Thurow says. "Outsourcing is the big reason why — even though we've got an economic recovery in terms of rate of growth — we don't have an economic recovery in terms of jobs."

Proponents of offshoring say it simply reflects the way the U.S. economy is evolving and that bumps in the road must be expected. "This trend of moving jobs to other locations, both onshore and offshore, started when we moved from an agrarian-based society to where we are today, and it's been a continuous evolution," says Robert Daigle, co-founder of Evalueserve, an offshoring company in Chappaqua, N.Y. Evalueserve's far-flung staff includes 270 people in India who conduct market research and write patent applications for corporate clients worldwide.

"Companies are outsourcing and offshoring to remain competitive."

Business representatives say that attempts to block the hiring of foreign workers would only hurt the economy, and eventually American workers. In addition to cutting labor costs, they say, globalizing work forces lets companies offer round-the-clock customer service, with workers in the Philippines and other overseas call centers answering customers when American employees are sleeping.

But critics say offshoring reflects the corporate quest for profits no matter the human cost. "Every time we hear a story like the one about the young lady [Tauch] in Texas, it just drives us crazy," says Mike Gildea, executive director of the AFL-CIO's Department for Professional Employees.

A job-seeker looks for tips at a state employment center in Arlington, Ill., last October. Although the economy is improving, economists call it a "jobless" recovery because of sluggish job growth. In December, manufacturers shed 26,000 jobs, bringing to 516,000 the number of U.S. factory jobs that disappeared last year. Moreover, a half-million tech jobs have been lost since 2001.

In addition, he says, offshoring could send a negative signal to the next generation of workers about the value of a college education. "These are American workers who have tried to do the right thing to get the American dream," Gildea says. "They've gone through years of schooling. Collectively, we're talking about billions of dollars invested in education going to waste. It makes no economic sense."

Nevertheless, offshoring is a $35-billion-a-year business and reportedly is growing 30-40 percent annually, gobbling up 1 percent of the world's service sector, according to the *Financial Times*.[7] As Nandan Nilekani, chief executive of Infosys Technologies, said at the World Economic Forum in Davos, Switzerland, recently: "Everything you can send down a wire is up for grabs."[8]

Still, offshoring advocates insist the threat to U.S. jobs has been overblown. According to the British information firm Datamonitor, only 2 percent of the world's 4 million call-center agents work outside the parent company's territory.[9]

Meanwhile, with the presidential campaign intensifying, candidates for the Democratic Party's nomination are beginning to blame offshoring for the loss of good jobs. And labor groups complain that a new immigration amnesty plan recently proposed by President Bush could flood the country with even more low-wage workers from Mexico, depressing U.S. wages for low-end jobs.

Here are some of the issues likely to fuel the coming debate:

Does offshoring threaten Americans' standard of living?

Traditionally during recessions, American workers were laid off with the implicit promise they would be rehired when demand for goods and services picked up again. Unemployment benefits generally lasted long enough to tide workers over until they returned to work, and pre-recession living standards were typically restored.

But the downsizing and offshoring trend of the past several decades marks a structural, or permanent, shift in the U.S. labor market, many economists say.[10] Domestic and offshore outsourcing often causes job losses. Unemployment benefits are no longer used to wait out recessions but to help workers retrain and find entirely different jobs — a process that frequently outlasts the benefits themselves.

Terminated workers frequently are forced to take jobs at much lower wages, forcing families to accept reduced living standards or compensate for the loss by sending a second family member to work. In the past, a single worker with a factory job could support a family, but today two-thirds of all working households are supported by two or more workers.[11] Even so, the shifting labor market is shutting many American workers out of the middle class: The Census Bureau reports that 67 percent of full-time workers earn less than $45,000 a year; half of all American workers make less than $33,636, hardly enough for a family to purchase the trappings of the American dream.[12]

But most economists cite the result of the 1980s downsizings — the economic boom of the 1990s — as evidence that offshoring will improve living standards for Americans and other workers over the long term.

"Globalization and the movement of jobs offshore are creating new markets for goods and services for U.S. companies," Daigle says. "In India, an emerging middle class lives the same lifestyle we Americans are familiar with; it didn't exist a decade or two ago. Not only are we bringing jobs to a place that sorely needs them, but there's a benefit to U.S. companies as well."

But critics of work force globalization say the benefits to developing countries and American companies are not trickling down to U.S. workers in all sectors of the economy. "We dispute the notion that workers have come out well in the end," Gildea says. "Any number of studies have shown that the lost manufacturing jobs have been replaced by jobs principally in the service sector, which are much, much lower-paying and have few, if any, benefits."

Workers' advocates say the same thing is happening to higher-paid technology specialists whose jobs are going overseas. "We are becoming a Wal-Martized country, where the only place you can afford to shop is at Wal-Mart, and the only thing you can get there is stuff made in China," says John A. Bauman, president of The Organization for the Rights of American Workers (T.O.R.A.W.), an advocacy group formed in 2002 to raise public awareness of IT offshoring. Bauman's job as a computer programmer was terminated in 2002, ending his 25-year career. Unable to find work, he says he delivered FedEx packages over the holidays.

Both sides agree on one thing: Globalization produces winners and losers. "Outsourcing doesn't threaten everybody's standard of living," says Josh Bivens, an economist at the Economic Policy Institute. "What it really does is redistribute a lot of income." Outsourcing boosts corporate profits, he explains, benefiting stockholders but not workers whose only income comes from wages.

Income redistribution already has widened the gap between rich and poor Americans. The share of aggregate income going to the wealthiest 5 percent of U.S. households has risen from 16 percent to 22 percent since 1980, while that received by the poorest 20 percent of all households has fallen by more than 80 percent, to just 3.5 percent of total U.S. income.[13]

Bivens says the trend is only likely to worsen as the offshoring of U.S. jobs escalates. "The winners are going to be people who own stock in large corporations," he says, "while people who get most of their money from a paycheck are going to see their standard of living hurt — the blue-collar workers who have had it rough for the past couple of decades."

Former U.S. Trade Representative Carla Hills likens the current anxiety about offshoring to the 1980s, when Americans feared the exodus of high-tech jobs to Japan. "They were going to make the computer chips, we were going to be left with the potato chips," she recalled. "But that didn't happen. Computer prices came down . . . and all of us, every business could afford a computer. We created jobs not only in computers, but across the spectrum."[14]

The new jobs may take longer than usual to materialize after the recent recession, she said, because the economy has undergone a major "structural change," and recovering from such changes "takes longer to get over the hump than when it's just cyclical."[15]

But Sen. Charles E. Schumer, D-N.Y., says the structural changes represent a fundamental, triple-threat, "paradigm shift" in the world economy, which may prevent classic economic theories from bearing fruit. First, capital flows more freely across borders, allowing American companies to invest in facilities abroad. Second, broadband allows information and jobs to be sent "around the world at no cost in the blink of an eye," he said.[16]

"Thirdly, and most importantly, we have 50 to 100 million well-educated, highly motivated Chinese and Indians coming on the market that can compete" with American workers, Schumer says. "If high-end jobs, middle-end jobs and low-end jobs can all be done better overseas, . . . what's left here?

"Yes, our companies will do better, but if 80 percent, 90 percent of their employees are overseas and if American wages are forced to go down in the new jobs [that are created], what do we do?" he asked.[17]

Craig R. Barrett, CEO of Intel, the world's leading computer chip maker, would seem to agree. "The structure of the world has changed," he said. "The U.S. no longer has a lock on high-tech, white-collar jobs."[18]

The solution, says Hills, is tax incentives to encourage "investment in human capital" so Americans could do the higher-end jobs that will be created in the coming decade.[19]

Manufacturers defend outsourcing as the only way they can stay in business and protect their remaining U.S. jobs. "Manufacturing, more than any other economic activity, is on the world stage," says Hank Cox, spokesman for the National Association of Manufacturers. "The service or retail companies compete with the business in the next block, but our guys compete with China, Korea and the rest of the world, so they face a relentless downward pressure on prices."

Cox says that while prices for manufactured goods have dropped by about 1 percent a year over the past seven years, production costs — including wages and especially health benefits — continue to rise. "A lot of our members have gone under, and we've lost a lot of jobs because of that. A lot of them have been faced with a choice between outsourcing and closing their doors."

Indeed, proponents of offshoring say Americans should embrace the practice, not deplore it. A study by the McKinsey Global Institute shows the U.S. economy gets up to $1.14 in profits for every dollar outsourced.[20]

Furthermore, the proponents say, given America's huge budget deficit, rather than restricting the offshoring of government jobs, the country should be shipping even more government jobs overseas — in order to save taxpayers money.[21]

Would better education and job training protect American jobs?

During the 1980s downsizing, factory workers were encouraged to retrain for the computer-related jobs the fledgling high-tech revolution was creating. While some did get retrained, others took service positions, though generally at lesser wages and benefits than their old jobs.

Now, as offshoring begins taking the jobs of higher-wage workers, many experts are once again urging unemployed Americans to retrain for the new, highly skilled positions expected to become available.

President Bush echoed the call. "Many of the fastest-growing occupations require strong math and science preparation, and training beyond the high school level," Bush said in his State of the Union address in January. "I propose increasing our support for America's fine community colleges, so they can train workers for the industries that are creating the most new jobs." The president announced a Jobs for the 21st Century proposal that would provide $100 million for education and training, including retraining of displaced workers, in fiscal 2005.[22]

But Bush's initiative ignores the plight of specialists with advanced degrees who are already unemployed or underemployed. The unemployment rate among science and engineering Ph.D.s stands at around 10 percent.[23] Gene Nelson, a biophysicist in Dallas, Texas, says he cannot find a job in his field that pays a living wage. "As a condition of being a postdoctoral worker, you must have a science or engineering doctorate, which is a very substantial investment of time and money," he says. "Postdocs today, by and large, are paid less than the high school graduate who manages the fast-food restaurant down the road. So there you are. You've earned your Ph.D., and there are no jobs; people are being trained for nonexistent positions at the Ph.D. level."

Nelson attributes the lack of demand for postdoctoral workers in part to an influx of foreign advanced-degree holders that followed dire warnings in the late 1990s that the United States was not graduating enough engineers and scientists.[24] Unless Congress increased the number of non-immigrant, H-1B, visas for skilled foreign workers, American firms argued, they could not maintain their competitive edge in the high-tech revolution. "Basically, we had a situation designed by employers and lobbied for by government agencies that was totally fraudulent," Nelson says, "because they alleged that we faced a looming shortage of scientists and engineers. Nothing could be further from the truth."

Thurow says the warnings were justified for IT specialists, but only temporarily. "In the late 1990s, there was a huge shortfall of IT professionals in the United States," he says. Even though many out-of-work, older programmers questioned whether there truly was a shortage, Congress expanded the temporary visa program for high-tech workers and those with advanced degrees. Between 1995 and 2000, millions of workers entered the country under the program.

But then the bubble burst. "When the dot-coms collapsed, they disgorged hundreds of thousands of experienced IT professionals," Thurow says. Today, about 800,000 American IT professionals are unemployed.[25]

Workers who lost IT jobs to off-shoring doubt education and training will ease their plight. After she lost her job at CSC, Tauch went to a community college to update her bachelor's degree in computer science. "But once you get the training and look for a job, they won't give it to you unless you have experience," she says. "President Bush keeps telling us to go to community college, but it's a joke."

Nevertheless, U.S. manufacturers agree with Bush on the need for a better-educated work force, particularly among high school graduates. "Our members say education is one of their biggest concerns," says the NAM's Cox. "They say the kids coming out of school today can't pass a writing test, can't pass a reading test, can't pass a math test and can't pass a drug test."

Cox supports Bush's community-college initiative and thinks it will help high school graduates transition to an increasingly demanding workplace. "The modern manufacturing workplace is like Star Trek," Cox says. "It's high-tech, and a dummy can't just go in there and handle it. These are advanced jobs that pay well, and we have to start directing some of our brightest young people into manufacturing."

Yet veterans of the labor-market turbulence of recent decades dispute the value of education and training, even for young people entering the job market. For instance, among computer programmers — the sector that has taken one of the biggest hits from outsourcing — unemployment has risen from just 1.6 percent two years ago to 7.1 percent today, significantly higher than the overall U.S. unemployment rate of 5.7 percent.[26]

"They tell you that if you take computer courses you're going to get a job in the computer field," says IT

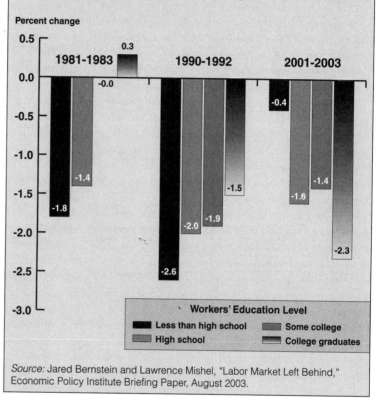

College Graduates Were Hit Hardest

Highly educated American workers suffered a greater drop in employment rates in the current economic recovery than less well-educated workers. In the previous two recoveries, by contrast, employment rates dropped farther for less-educated workers.

Changes in Employment Rates by Education Level

Source: Jared Bernstein and Lawrence Mishel, "Labor Market Left Behind," Economic Policy Institute Briefing Paper, August 2003.

specialist Bauman. "You can go and get an education, but for what jobs? Those of us who are already underemployed are working as FedEx drivers, selling cars and selling insurance. I've got two kids who have all their certifications, and they can't find jobs. It's all because they listened to Dad, and this is one time I wish they hadn't."

Do current work-visa rules hurt American workers?

Bringing foreign workers into the United States on a temporary basis is an indirect form of exporting American jobs, critics of U.S. work-visa programs say. Although the work contributes to the U.S. economy, many of the workers will likely return to their native lands when their visas expire. Although some end up getting green cards and working in the United States permanently, many are hired with the understanding that they will open satellite U.S. offices back home after their training in the United States.

"Importing visa workers facilitates the offshoring of American jobs," Bauman says. "The foreign workers learn about the technology from people here in the United States, figure out how to use that technology in their own countries and then take the jobs offshore." In the meantime, he says, the foreign workers are performing the computer support for which they were hired. "The Americans are already gone."

Temporary work-visa programs were created to satisfy employers' demands for workers during perceived labor shortages.[27] In the early 20th century, Mexican field hands entered the country under the "Bracero" program supported by Western farm interests, followed by Basque sheepherders, Caribbean sugar cane harvesters and academic researchers from Europe and Asia.

In 1990, responding to what industry said was an impending critical shortage of skilled high-tech workers, Congress passed the 1990 Immigration Act. It expanded several existing non-immigrant visas for technical professionals — notably the H-1B visa, granted to foreign professionals for up to six years to take jobs that employers said they could not find qualified U.S. workers to fill. The visa also has been used to import physical therapists and, more recently, elementary and kindergarten teachers. In addition, the L-1 visa program, introduced in 1970, permits foreign executives and managers of U.S.-based multinationals to work in the United States for up to seven years; workers with special knowledge of an employer's products can stay up to five years.

Last year, more than 217,000 work visas were approved for foreign nationals under the H-1B program.[28] Since 1985, more than 17 million H-1B foreign workers have been admitted to the United States, according to ZaZona.com, an online monitoring service run by a critic of the programs. It estimates that almost 900,000 H-1B workers were in the United States at the end of 2001.[29]

Industry supporters say the visas help ensure American competitiveness in the global marketplace. "Access to the best-educated engineering talent around the world is critical to [our] company's future success," said Patrick J. Duffy, human resources attorney for Intel

Corp. The U.S. semiconductor giant, with some $27 billion in revenues, employs almost 80,000 workers worldwide, and H-1B workers account for around 5 percent of its U.S. work force. "We expect . . . to sponsor H-1B employees in the future for the simple reason that we cannot find enough U.S. workers with the advanced education, skills and expertise we need."[30]

Moreover, supporters say, the visa programs help protect American jobs by keeping U.S. companies competitive. "When companies are competing in an international market, the inability to effectively manage their work force can mean the difference between gaining the edge and being put out of business," wrote Randel K. Johnson, a vice president of the U.S. Chamber of Commerce. "The result can mean even greater job losses in the long run."[31]

But critics say the visa programs simply have been used to replace American professionals with lower-wage foreigners. Although the visa law specifically says imported workers must receive prevailing wages, critics say enforcement is nearly nonexistent and that H-1B workers make between 15 and 33 percent less than their American counterparts.[32]

Dallas biophysicist Nelson says American universities took an early lead in promoting the visa programs, depressing wages for American scientists across the board. "This was all about bringing in cheap labor," he says.

Furthermore, Nelson says, because H-1B visa holders may only work for the employer who submitted their visa application, they are unlikely to object to adverse working conditions — such as lower pay scales or longer hours.

"This visa was designed to give the employer incredible leverage," Nelson says. "It is conditioned on the foreign national maintaining continuous employment. So if the employer gets unhappy and terminates that worker, the worker is immediately subject to deportation. In practice, it's been rarely done, but this is a very, very powerful tool."

That leverage extends beyond the foreign workers themselves, critics say. "By robbing the foreign workers of bargaining power, the visa program robs everyone else in the industry of that bargaining power as well," says the Economic Policy Institute's Bivens. If employers have access to cheaper labor, he explains, they can ignore American workers' demands for higher wages.

"There's nothing intrinsically wrong with guest workers, or even immigrants who wish to become citizens, having these jobs," Bivens adds. "What's wrong is the way the program is structured, which is quite bad for wages overall in these industries."

Many critics want work-visa programs eliminated altogether. "The H-1B program amounts to a government subsidy, because it provides economic benefits to a narrow class of entities, while the rest of us either have no benefit or — in the case of people like me — a negative benefit," Nelson says. "Our investment in our education, training and experience has been reduced to an economic value approaching zero."

In fact, he adds, because he's considered overqualified for most of the jobs now open — such as retail clerks and administrative assistants — "I've actually had to keep it a secret that I have a Ph.D."

BACKGROUND

Postwar Boom

As Western Europe, Japan and the Soviet bloc struggled to rebuild after World War II, U.S. manufacturing enjoyed a golden age. Expanding production and exports brought new jobs by the millions, feeding a rapidly growing American middle class.

Bolstered by union protections, a blue-collar wage earner in the leading manufacturing sectors — steel, appliances and automobiles — took home "family wages" sufficient to support an entire family, plus employer-provided health insurance and pensions. Even low-wage textile jobs offered opportunities for betterment to impoverished Southern farm workers.

For most of the 1950s and '60s, the United States was largely self-sufficient. As Europe and East Asia rebuilt their economies, they provided a vast market for U.S. goods while slowly emerging as significant trade competitors. Japan expanded its manufacturing sector by applying U.S. production techniques and became a leading exporter of plastic toys and other inexpensive products, and eventually high-end electronics and automobiles. Europe focused on exporting cars and other high-value manufactured goods to American consumers.

U.S. manufacturers began building factories in the South and overseas, where wages were much lower. The practice accelerated in the 1970s, when a series of energy crises signaled the beginning of the end of U.S. self-reliance in oil production — the basic fuel driving the U.S. economy. Rising energy prices caused a series of recessions, and steel- and automakers and other manufacturers laid off thousands of workers.

For their part, American consumers sought cheaper imported products, including the increasingly popular Japanese cars. Labor unions responded with "Buy-American" campaigns intended to shore up the beleaguered Midwest, which became known as the Rust Belt for its numerous shuttered factories.

But by the mid-1980s, rising production costs and growing foreign competition had prompted more and more industries to restructure. Many permanently downsized their work forces, often using automation. Others outsourced at least part of the production, either to lower-cost — non-union — domestic producers or overseas, where labor was cheaper still. The textile and apparel industries, usually in Southern mill towns, were among the first to export large numbers of American jobs, especially to emerging economies in Asia.

In the early 1980s, U.S. makers of auto and electronic equipment pioneered the overseas production of basic components for U.S. assembly — providing the technological foundation for other countries to develop their own industries.[33]

With Japan emerging as a major industrial power, Hong Kong, Taiwan, Malaysia, South Korea and Singapore assumed Japan's earlier role of low-cost producer of components shipped to the United States for assembly into finished products.

Meanwhile, to reduce the cost of transporting their own finished products to the U.S. market, foreign companies began opening factories in the United States, partly offsetting the loss of American jobs offshore. European and Japanese automakers, in particular, created thousands of new jobs for Americans in the late 1980s. But they mostly built their facilities outside the industrial heartland, hiring non-union workers for less pay than their unionized peers in the upper Midwest.

Wages also suffered as the manufacturing sector declined. Laid-off factory workers often took low-paying, non-union jobs in the burgeoning service sector as retail clerks and cashiers.

NAFTA and More

The export of U.S. manufacturing jobs accelerated in the 1990s, especially after Congress in 1993 approved the North American Free Trade Agreement (NAFTA),

CHRONOLOGY

1970s–1980s *Growing international competition prompts U.S. companies to reduce labor costs by moving factories to lower-wage countries.*

1970 Congress establishes the L-1 visa program to permit foreign executives and managers of U.S.-based multinationals to work in the United States.

1976 The Immigration and Nationality Act Amendments increase the number of visas allocated to foreign workers and their families.

1990s *Americans flock to information-technology (IT) jobs after government and industry vow that manufacturing jobs shifted overseas would be replaced by domestic computer jobs and warn of a coming high-tech labor shortage.*

1990 The Immigration Act expands the H-1B non-immigrant visa program. It permits up to 65,000 foreign technical professionals a year to work in the U.S. for up to six years at jobs employers claim cannot be filled by U.S. workers.

1993 Congress approves the North American Free Trade Agreement (NAFTA) removing trade barriers among the United States, Canada and Mexico. U.S. manufacturers set up plants just south of the border hiring low-wage Mexican workers.

1998 Congress expands the number of H-1B visas issued each year after U.S. businesses plead for more foreign computer specialists to help prevent widespread computer failures at the turn of the millennium.

2000s *High-tech unemployment increases after the "Y2K" crisis never materializes, the technology boom collapses and U.S. companies begin shifting high-tech and other white-collar jobs offshore.*

October 2000 Congress again raises the annual H-1B visa cap, to 195,000.

November 2001 The current "jobless" recovery begins, featuring rising stock prices, economic output and productivity, loss of manufacturing jobs and few new jobs.

2002 Recently fired technology professionals establish the Organization for the Rights of American Workers (T.O.R.A.W.) to raise public awareness of IT off-shoring. . . . Forrester Research predicts that 3.3 million service-sectors jobs will move offshore by 2015.

July 10, 2003 Rep. Rosa DeLauro, D-Conn., and Sen. Saxby Chambliss, R-Ga., introduce the L-1 Non-Immigrant Reform Act to address reported abuses of the L-1 visa program.

July 24, 2003 Sen. Christopher J. Dodd, D-Conn., and Rep. Nancy L. Johnson, R-Conn., introduce the USA Jobs Protection Act, which would beef up enforcement of the H-1B and L-1 visa programs to prevent companies from illegally replacing qualified American workers and underpaying foreign workers.

Sept. 30, 2003 Rising unemployment in the high-tech industry prompts Congress to slash the annual cap on H-1B visas from 195,000 to 65,000 in response to concern over the impact of guest workers on U.S. jobs.

December 2003 On the 10th anniversary of NAFTA, studies show that more U.S. jobs have been created than lost since the law was passed.

Jan. 7, 2004 President Bush proposes a plan to offer temporary legal status to illegal immigrants working in the United States.

Jan. 20, 2004 In his State of the Union address, Bush calls for a new education and job-retraining program to be based in the nation's community colleges.

Jan. 23, 2004 Bush signs into law a measure prohibiting American companies from subcontracting some government jobs to companies outside the United States.

Feb. 6, 2004 Labor Department reports that American employers added only 112,000 new jobs in January, about 38,000 fewer than economists had expected.

Poor Nations Thrive on Job Exporting

For all the controversy surrounding the offshore outsourcing of American white-collar jobs, one of its consequences is undisputed — higher living standards in developing countries that have just joined the global economy.

In the late 1980s, when U.S. corporations first began exporting "back-office" work like bill processing, they turned to developed countries with large English-speaking populations but lower prevailing wages, such as Ireland and Israel. Many were allies, reducing the political risks associated with outsourcing.

But by the 1990s, the end of the Cold War had opened up new labor markets in the former Soviet bloc, while the embrace of free markets and the gradual lowering of trade barriers by many formerly closed economies — such as India and China — made still more countries attractive targets for offshoring.[1]

Today, U.S. and European companies are shifting a growing array of white-collar jobs — 500,000 in the past five years — to poorer countries all over the world, from the Philippines to Russia and its former allies in Hungary, Romania and the Czech Republic — virtually any country with broadband Internet access and a technically literate work force.[2]

But no country has benefited more from recent white-collar job outsourcing by American industry than India, where such work now accounts for 2.5 per cent of gross domestic product.[3] After gaining independence in 1947, India missed out on the industrial revolution that had enriched its imperial overlord, Britain, remaining mired in poverty along with the rest of the Third World.

Successive Indian governments adopted protectionist policies to promote self-sufficiency as the engine of India's economy, but they also invested heavily in education, notably a large university system focusing on engineering and science. In addition, the colonial experience left most of India's 1 billion inhabitants with an enduring asset: proficiency in English.

In short, India offers highly educated, English-speaking workers for about a tenth of Americans' salaries. White-collar outsourcing has helped fuel a 33-percent increase in India's share of global economic output since 1991.[4]

Some of the newfound wealth is ending up in the pockets of Indian high-tech workers, whose wages are climbing.[5] Young college graduates are flocking to offshore centers such as Bangalore and Mumbai (formerly Bombay) and gaining the independence that comes with a generous paycheck. In addition, India's strict class and caste divisions are loosening, and a newly emerging middle class of young professionals is adopting the consumption habits of their American peers and casting aside such time-honored traditions as arranged marriages.

India may soon face stiff competition from such budding offshore locations as Bangladesh, Brazil, Singapore, Thailand, Venezuela and Vietnam, the United Nations reports.[6] As wages rise in India, it is likely to see competition from China, whose fast-growing industrial base and even bigger labor pool are making it a tempting alternative for cost-cutting American firms. China is likely to overcome its big shortcoming — a dearth of English speakers — as a new generation of workers graduates from China's schools, where English instruction is now mandatory.

Outsourcing of manufacturing jobs from the United States and other industrial countries has already benefited workers in special economic zones located along China's coastline that were opened to trade in the 1980s. "There are 300 million people in those eastern coastal provinces who have seen an extraordinary pickup in their standard of living," said Edmund Harriss, portfolio manager of the Guinness Atkinson China and Hong Kong Fund.[7]

In 2001, China was granted normal trade status by the United States after joining the World Trade Organization, two moves that forced it to significantly liberalize its trade policies. "You're seeing an economy that is just about to take wing because you now have consumers who were never able to participate in the economy before," Harriss said.

China's opening to foreign investment, including job offshoring, is being felt beyond the U.S. As a result of the 1993 North American Free Trade Agreement, Mexico enjoyed a decade of rapid job growth as U.S. firms seeking low-wage workers set up factories south of the border. But today Mexico is losing many of those jobs to even lower-wage countries, including China.

"Five years ago, Mexico was the logical place for manufacturers to go," said Jonathan Heath, an economist with LatinSource, a consulting firm in Mexico City. "Now China is logical."[8]

---

[1] See Andy Meisler, "Where in the World Is Offshoring Going?" *Workforce Management*, January 2004, p. 45.

[2] Christopher Caldwell, "A chill wind from offshore," *Financial Times*, Feb. 7, 2004.

[3] *Ibid.*

[4] International Monetary Fund, "IMF Survey," Feb. 2, 2004.

[5] See David E. Gumpert, "U.S. Programmers at Overseas Salaries," *Business Week Online*, Dec. 2, 2003.

[6] U.N. Conference on Trade and Development, "E-Commerce and Development Report 2003," Nov. 20, 2003.

[7] Quoted by Erika Kinetz, "Who Wins and Who Loses as Jobs Move Overseas?" *The New York Times*, Dec. 7, 2003, p. A5.

[8] Quoted by Chris Kraal, "NAFTA 10 Years Later," *Los Angeles Times*, Jan. 2, 2004, p. A1

which removed trade barriers among the United States, Canada and Mexico. U.S. companies seeking cheap labor close to the American market built hundreds of factories, called *maquiladoras*, just south of the border, employing tens of thousands of Mexicans. By 2000, American textile workers — already hit by outsourcing to Asia — had lost more than 80,000 additional jobs to Mexico as a result of NAFTA.[34]

But according to Mack McLarty, former chief of staff and special envoy for the Americas under President Bill Clinton, NAFTA created more U.S. jobs than it eliminated. While about 500,000 American factory jobs went to Mexico because of NAFTA, U.S. private-sector employment grew by 15 million jobs — with hourly wages up 10 percent — in the decade since the law went into effect, McLarty wrote recently.[35]

Even as traditional manufacturing jobs continued to disappear during the 1990s, increasing productivity transformed several U.S. manufacturing sectors. A newly organized American steel industry emerged, even after such industry leaders as Bethlehem Steel and LTV went under, crushed by lower-cost imports from Japan and other countries. Incorporating the latest technologies, International Steel Group and other new companies over the past two decades increased U.S. steel production from 75 million tons to 102 million tons. But they did so by increasing productivity, not jobs: Today there are

just 74,000 U.S. steelworkers, down from 289,000 in the early 1980s. And while wages remain high, at $18 to $21 an hour, the generous pension and health benefits their predecessors enjoyed are gone.[36]

Still, the enormous shift from traditional manufacturing to telecommunications, retail trade, finance and other industries continued apace. Between 1980 — when manufacturers began downsizing — and 2002, General Motors eliminated 53 percent of its work force, Kodak 46 percent and Goodyear 36 percent. Over the same period, United Parcel Service boosted its payroll by 224 percent, McDonald's by 253 percent and Wal-Mart by a whopping 4,715 percent.[37] A quarter of the factory workers who found new jobs took pay cuts of at least 25 percent, according to the Institute for International Economics.[38]

During the 1990s, makers of electronic equipment and computers began emulating older manufacturers by sending production overseas. Despite rapid productivity improvements — accompanied by high profits and rising stock prices — high-tech companies were eager to improve their competitive edge in a rapidly globalizing industry.

The service sector also sought cheaper labor overseas.[39] Software companies led the way, quickly establishing Bangalore, India, as a major U.S. outpost. Other countries benefited from U.S. offshoring as well. Ireland, which largely had missed Europe's postwar boom, blossomed in the 1990s as American corporations outsourced their billing and other "back-office" operations. The Philippines and Malaysia emerged as leading call-center locations, China became an important back-office service center, and Russia and Israel began providing customized software and computer systems.

Several unrelated developments further energized offshoring during the 1990s. Access to the Internet through high-speed broadband connection spread from the industrial countries to the developing world, enabling managers in the U.S. to communicate quickly and cheaply with satellite offices. The use of English as the *lingua franca* of businesses around the world enabled workers in India, the Philippines and other English-speaking countries to take part in the outsourcing boom. And locating offices in different time zones allowed call centers to service customers around the clock.

President Bush called for "stronger math and science preparation" in his State of the Union address in January. "I propose increasing our support for America's fine community colleges, so they can train workers for the industries that are creating the most new jobs," he said.

AFP/Getty Images/Luke Frazza

Y2K Impact

Before U.S. employers began exporting large numbers of IT and other white-collar jobs, they clamored for relaxation of the laws limiting non-immigrant visas. Fueling these efforts were dire predictions by the National Science Foundation and the conservative Hudson Institute that American universities were not turning out enough skilled technical professionals.[40]

Congress cited the studies in 1990, when it substantially increased the number of skilled workers allowed into the country. The Immigration Act of 1990 nearly tripled the number of permanent, work-based admissions allowed each year and created tens of thousands of slots for various types of temporary skilled workers, including 65,000 under the controversial H-1B program. The 1990 law also created new visas for other skilled temporary workers, including nurses, scientists, teachers and entertainers, and expanded the L-1 program enabling multinational corporations to bring key executives to the United States for up to seven years.

As the 20th century came to an end, there was widespread fear that computer systems would crash worldwide on Jan. 1, 2000, because their internal clocks were not set to change from 1999 to 2000.[41] As U.S. companies scrambled to hire extra workers to circumvent the so-called Y2K bug, programmers became scarce. Employers renewed their claims of a dire shortage of skilled American workers and brought in thousands of foreign programmers under the H-1B program.

Either the fears had been overblown — or enough computers had been fixed to avert the problem. In any event, the new century arrived without incident. But companies that had hired costly specialists to rewrite their codes were left with a new incentive to cut costs.

"When 2000 came, employers started laying off more employees," says T.O.R.A.W. President Bauman. "But the foreign visa workers, who were supposedly getting a fair wage, were costing them less." Seasoned professionals like Bauman received higher compensation than H-1B workers, who often were just out of college. "Employers were saving on salaries with foreign workers, and they decided to keep them on."

As the new millennium began, the elimination of U.S. high-tech jobs only accelerated when the nation went into recession after the telecom "bubble" burst. The economy took a further nosedive after the Sept. 11, 2001, terrorist attacks. U.S. employers decided to more fully tap India's vast, cheap, labor pool, setting up operations in Bangalore and other cities. The offshoring boom had begun.

Vietnamese computer programmers attend a job fair in Hanoi in April 2002. Vietnam has emerged as a major outsourcing base for U.S., European and Japanese high-tech firms.

CURRENT SITUATION

'Jobless' Recovery

The U.S. economy continues on its uneven path to recovery. The Dow Jones Industrial Average rose an encouraging 25 percent last year after two disappointing previous years. GDP growth — 8.2 percent in the third quarter and 4 percent in the fourth — suggests that the recovery, which officially began in November 2001, is finally picking up. Business investments in equipment and software are up, and inflation remains low, prompting the Federal Reserve to keep interest rates at their lowest levels in decades.[42]

"Exports are growing," Bush declared during his State of the Union address. "Productivity is high, and jobs are on the rise."

But Labor Department data show why economists call the recovery "jobless." A net total of just 1,000 jobs were added to industry payrolls in December. Temp agencies and other service companies hired 45,000 workers; construction workers and health-services workers also posted gains. But the new-job gains were offset by the continuing hemorrhaging of manufacturing jobs, which tend to pay middle-class wages and benefits. In December, manufacturers shed 26,000 jobs, bringing to 516,000 the number of U.S. factory jobs that disappeared last year. Moreover, in addition to the 2.8 million manufacturing jobs lost since July 2000, a half-million tech jobs have been lost since 2001.[43]

Although no figures are kept on how much of the job loss can be attributed to outsourcing or offshoring, economists are sure that outsourcing is a factor.

"It certainly plays a role in manufacturing," M.I.T.'s Thurow says. "A lot of the automobile components that used to be made in the United States are now made in various Third World countries. And that basically leads some blue-collar workers and their managers to lose their jobs. This outsourcing started back in the '90s, but the economy was growing so fast in the high-tech sector, we didn't notice it."

Former Labor Secretary Robert B. Reich contends most manufacturing jobs are not disappearing due to offshoring but because of the higher productivity that comes with enhanced efficiency and new technology. "I recently toured a U.S. factory containing two employees and 400 computerized robots," Reich wrote in *The Wall Street Journal*.[44]

Moreover, he noted, although more than 22 million factory jobs worldwide vanished between 1995 and 2002, the United States lost fewer than many other countries, both rich and poor. The United States lost 11 percent of its manufacturing jobs during the period, he noted, while Japan lost 16 percent, China 15 percent and Brazil 20 percent.[45]

Several business-research firms have estimated the extent of offshoring today and its likely growth in the future. The Information Technology Association of America found that 12 percent of its member companies had opened offshore operations, usually for programmers and software engineers.[46] Forrester Research predicts that 3.3 million U.S. service jobs — mostly IT-related positions like software developers and help-desk operators — will move offshore over the next 15 years.[47] Goldman Sachs estimates that 200,000 service jobs have been lost to offshoring so far — with 6 million more to follow over the next decade.[48] A University of California, Berkeley, study put the number at close to 14 million over the next 15 years.[49]

Lower costs for software and other services will allow "huge segments" of the economy to improve productivity, said former U.S. Trade Representative Hills, creating 20 million new American jobs in the coming decade. "That's faster than last decade," she said, noting that even the booming 1990s only created 15 million jobs. "Every metric study shows that . . . job growth [will rise]

faster than it did in the last decade. This is an amazing prospect."[50]

Some economists say the estimates ignore the economy's ability to absorb job losses. "The number of high-tech jobs outsourced abroad still accounts for a tiny proportion of America's 10-million strong IT work force," Reich also has noted. "When the U.S. economy fully bounces back from recession (as it almost certainly will within the next 18 months), a large portion of high-tech jobs that were lost after 2000 will come back in some form."[51]

But MIT's Thurow says white-collar outsourcing is still in its infancy — totaling only about $8 billion in a $400 billion, U.S.-dominated global software market. "White-collar outsourcing is rising very rapidly," Thurow says. "The issue is a little bit like rape. Not that many women have been raped, but you don't need a very large fraction of women who've been raped before everybody's worried about it."

Those fears seem likely to intensify as more American technology companies announce they are moving key jobs offshore. America Online reportedly is planning to hire additional Indian software engineers for its facility in Bangalore to help build its Internet software. Yahoo and Google may soon follow AOL's lead.[52] IBM plans to move as many as 4,730 white-collar jobs from the United States.[53] They would be joining the ranks of such American icons as AT&T, Dell, Microsoft, Proctor & Gamble and Verizon.

Legislative Action

Offshoring is turning into a hot political issue in this presidential election year, as the economic recovery fails to generate all the new jobs anticipated by the administration. The shortfall is prompting Congress and the states to consider proposals aimed at stemming the loss of American jobs.

A bipartisan measure pending in Congress would close what critics see as major loopholes in the H-1B and L-1 visa programs. The USA Jobs Protection Act, cosponsored by Democratic Sen. Christopher J. Dodd and GOP Rep. Nancy L. Johnson — both from Connecticut — would beef up federal enforcement of the programs to prevent companies from illegally replacing qualified American workers and underpaying the temporary workers.

Another proposal, sponsored in the House by Rep. Rosa DeLauro, D-Conn., and in the Senate by Sen. Saxby Chambliss, R-Ga., addresses reported abuses of the L-1 program. Since Sept. 30, 2003, when Congress slashed the annual cap on H-1B visas from 195,000 to 65,000, critics charge that companies have abused the L-1 program, which has no annual cap, to import non-managerial tech workers.

"The availability of the L-visa category to those applying under 'specialized knowledge' — a vague term at best open to multiple and elastic interpretations — has done clear harm to the American work force and contributed directly to the job loss since the most recent recession began," House International Relations Committee Chairman Henry J. Hyde, R-Ill., told a Feb. 4, 2004, committee hearing on visa reform. "Lax procedures, for L visas or any other category of non-immigrant visa, are clearly a prescription for chaos in both visa policy and border security. It is time for reform."

Business representatives counter that any attempt to restrict corporate America's ability to hire workers anywhere in the world would only hurt the U.S. economy, and eventually American workers. "The use of certain categories of visas, such as the H-1B or the L-1, by multinational companies has been an effective means of maintaining our competitive edge," the Chamber of Commerce's Johnson wrote. "In the long run, expansion of international trade and investment in the United States is in the best interests of all."[54]

"Unless U.S. and foreign companies are able to bring key personnel to their American operations, U.S. com-panies will be put at a competitive disadvantage and foreign companies will be unlikely to establish or expand their presence in our country," Harris N. Miller, president of the Information Technology Association of America, told the committee. "Foreign investment 'means more U.S. factories, offices and jobs, and the L-1 program facilitates these investments.'"

Another measure, introduced by Sens. John Kerry, D-Mass., the current front-runner for the Democratic presidential nomination, and Minority Leader Tom Daschle, D-S.D., seeks to help Americans understand how widespread the offshoring phenomenon really is by requiring employees at overseas call centers of U.S.-based companies to disclose the center's physical location.

On Jan. 23, President Bush signed into law a measure preventing American companies from subcontracting some government jobs to companies outside the United States. The ban, originally sponsored by Sens. George V. Voinovich, R-Ohio, and Craig Thomas, R-Wyo., was included in the fiscal 2004 omnibus appropriations bill. It remains uncertain how many of the 1.8 million civilians who work for the federal government will be affected. The Bush administration has accelerated the pace of outsourcing of federal jobs, and 102,000 jobs are currently slated to come up for competitive bidding.[55]

Some states that have been especially hard-hit by IT outsourcing are considering prohibiting government work from being contracted to non-Americans or barring employers from requiring workers slated for layoff to train their foreign replacements. Anti-outsourcing bills are now pending in a dozen legislatures, and up to 20 could consider such measures before the legislative season ends, according to Justin Marks, an analyst at the National Conference of State Legislatures (NCSL). Marks said eight states debated such bills last year, but none passed — largely due to Republican opposition.[56]

Even California — home to Silicon Valley companies that have been heavy users of offshoring and H-1B visas — is considering anti-offshoring legislation. A bill introduced by Assemblywoman Carol Liu, D-Pasadena, would prevent the use of overseas call centers for state services like welfare and food stamps. "There's a great irony here that we're telling people on welfare to find jobs, and the kind of jobs they could do are not here anymore," said Richard Johnson, Liu's legislative aide.[57]

> **Anti-outsourcing bills are now pending in a dozen legislatures, and up to 20 could consider such measures before the legislative season ends.**
>
> — **Justin Marks,**
> Analyst, National Conference of
> State Legislatures

Should the government slow the outsourcing of high-tech jobs?

YES — Ron Hira
Chairman, R&D Policy Committee, Institute of Electrical and Electronics Engineers

From testimony before the House Small Business Committee, Oct. 20, 2003

According to the most recent data from the Bureau of Labor Statistics, electrical, electronics and computer hardware engineers continue to face a higher unemployment rate than the general population, and over double the rate for other managers and professionals. The news for engineering managers is even worse, with an unemployment rate of 8 percent. . . .

To put this in historical context, in the 30-plus years that the Department of Labor has been collecting statistics, the past two years are the first in which unemployment rates for electrical, electronics and computer engineers are higher than the unemployment rate for all workers. . . . And throughout the 1980s, at a time when unemployment rates for all workers got as high as 9.5 percent, electrical and electronics engineering unemployment rates never rose above 2 percent. . . .

It is entirely misleading to describe offshore outsourcing as a "win-win" proposition for America and other countries, as free-trade advocates so often do. Those advocates [should be required] to demonstrate how workers who have been adversely affected will be compensated and helped to become productive citizens once again.

These advocates assume, as part of their argument, that displaced American workers will be redeployed. Instead of assuming, we should ensure that such workers are redeployed in equally high-skill and highly paid positions. . . .

The federal government must begin regularly tracking the volume and nature of the jobs that are moving offshore. Companies should be required to give adequate notice of their intentions to move work offshore, so displaced employees can make appropriate plans to minimize the financial hardship, and government support agencies can prepare to provide the necessary transition assistance. Congress should rethink how U.S. work force assistance programs can be designed to help displaced high-tech workers become productive again.

We are in a new era of work and lifelong learning, and new and more flexible methods are needed to provide meaningful assistance. Congress should strengthen H-1B and L-1 work force protections and their enforcement to ensure that the programs serve their respective purposes without adversely affecting employment opportunities for U.S. high-tech workers.

The United States needs a coordinated national strategy designed to sustain its technological leadership and promote job creation in response to the concerted strategies being used by other countries to attract U.S. industries and jobs.

NO — Harris N. Miller
President, Information Technology Association of America

From testimony before the House Small Business Committee, Oct. 20, 2003

In statistical terms, the trend towards offshore outsourcing is a cloud on the horizon, not a hurricane sweeping everything in its midst. We should keep our eye on how the weather pattern is changing, but we should not start boarding up our windows and stashing the patio furniture. The U.S. IT industry is facing new challenges, but it is not disappearing.

Over 10 million Americans earn their living in the IT work force . . . nine out of 10 of [them] employed by businesses outside of the IT industry: banks, law firms, factories, stores and the like. Eight out of 10 of these jobs are found in small businesses — the firms arguably least likely to [send their jobs offshore]. Even the most doom-and-gloom analysts predict that fewer than 500,000 computer-specific jobs will move offshore in the next 10 years. . . .

If we have seen any storm at all, it has been the three-year "perfect storm" of trends converging to depress the short-term demand for U.S. IT workers: the dot-com bust, the telecom collapse, the recession and jobless recovery and slow customer spending — domestically and globally — for new IT products and services. . . .

I do not mean to downplay the very real impacts of offshore competition to American IT workers or their families. Thousands of IT professionals have played by the rules: studied hard in school, worked long hours, made a sweat equity investment in the future of their companies, only to find themselves now unemployed or underemployed. A more vibrant economy and greater capital spending by the private sector will greatly help these individuals. Not all of the current concerns, however, can be attributed to the economy, and we need to better understand this new competitive reality, using logic — not emotion — as our filter. . . .

While it may be emotionally satisfying to try to protect jobs by throwing up barriers, free trade and global markets spark investment, trade and job creation. For Americans caught in the riptide of a transitioning job market, economic abstractions like positive trade balances and expanding free markets may be the source of cold comfort. I reject, however, the notion that offshore development is a zero sum game or that every job shipped offshore is a job permanently lost to an American worker. On the contrary, evidence abounds that the working capital that U.S. companies save by moving jobs and operations offshore results in new investment, innovation and job creation in this country.

At least one of the bills to be introduced in California is expected to apply to private employers that handle customers' confidential information. Controversies have erupted around the country in recent months when patients learned that insurance companies increasingly are having confidential medical records transcribed by companies overseas, where U.S. medical-privacy laws do not apply. During an employment dispute in October, a Pakistani contract worker handling confidential medical records from California threatened to disclose the information.[58]

Marks says political pressure to pass anti-outsourcing measures this year is growing in some states. "In any event, I think we'll see a ripple effect in policymaking," he said, "with greater efforts at local job creation in places most affected by outsourcing."[59]

Marks says offshoring public-sector jobs may not end up saving taxpayers money in the long run, because hidden long-term costs could outweigh short-term taxpayers' savings. "If you compare the savings to the loss in taxable income [from local workers laid off due to the offshoring] with the state's cost of paying unemployment benefits [to those laid off], it's possible states are not saving that much money," Marks said.[60]

Northeastern University labor economist Paul E. Harrington warns of another hidden, long-term cost: the erosion of a state's middle-class base. States that value "full employment, upward mobility and a solid middle class as an important and essential feature" of their economies should warn their companies to "think about this outsourcing issue," Harrington advised.[61]

Business spokesmen say anti-outsourcing measures amount to protectionism and will only hurt American workers. "The focus should be making sure that America stays a nimble, highly educated, forward-thinking, innovative economic presence, not one that's trying to hold onto things while the world around them is changing," says Daigle of Evalueserve. "That strategy is a going-out-of-business strategy."

But Bauman says displaced IT workers are counting on the offshoring bills. "If we don't see any action on this problem soon," he says, "we can kiss our careers goodbye forever."

Bush's Amnesty Plan

On Jan. 7, President Bush announced an initiative to permit the estimated 8 million illegal immigrants to remain in the United States for six years as long they are employed. The undocumented workers would receive identification cards enabling them to travel between the United States and their home countries. Employers also could bring in additional "guest workers" under the same conditions if they cannot find qualified American workers.

"We must make our immigration laws more rational and more humane," Bush said. "I believe we can do so without jeopardizing the livelihoods of American citizens."[62]

Critics say the proposal would worsen working conditions for American employees just as existing visa programs do — by tying a worker's legal status to steady employment with a single employer. "One of the ways you get ahead in the U.S. labor market is by making employers bid for you, and it doesn't sound like these guest workers are going to have that ability at all," says Bivens of the Economic Policy Institute. If employers can rely on low-wage immigrants to fill their job openings, he says, they will have no incentive to hire American workers who demand higher wages. "It doesn't really provide a big improvement over the status quo for the undocumented," Bivens says, "and it is one more way to subvert the bargaining power of other workers here."

Business groups welcome the proposal, saying immigrants would take jobs Americans don't want, not manufacturing or white-collar positions. "Manufacturing workers tend to be more sophisticated, higher-level workers," says Cox of the NAM. "Guys don't come here from Guatemala or Mexico and go to work in manufacturing. You have to know too much high-tech stuff."

But critics say similar efforts in other industrial countries offer little grounds for encouragement. "Guest-worker systems haven't worked anywhere in the world because eventually people just don't go home," MIT's Thurow says.

But Switzerland's program works, Thurow says, because every worker must return home for a certain period each year and is barred from bringing family members into the country. "The only way you can deport temporary workers is the way Switzerland does it," he says, "and they are just ferocious."

Few observers expect Congress to take up Bush's immigration plan this year. Many Republicans oppose any immigration initiative that rewards illegal immigrants for breaking the law, while many Democrats say the plan does not do enough to help them gain U.S. citizenship.

A bipartisan alternative presented on Jan. 21 by Sens. Daschle and Chuck Hagel, R-Neb., calls for eventual citizenship for illegal immigrants who meet a series of requirements and would admit no more than 350,000 new temporary workers each year.[63]

OUTLOOK

Election Debate

As presidential campaign rhetoric intensifies, many observers expect the globalization of American jobs to become an increasingly important issue, especially if offshoring continues to threaten white-collar jobs.

"If I were President Bush, professional white-collar outsourcing would give me nightmares," Thurow says. "When a factory moves to China or India, that's blue-collar jobs. They're Democratic voters anyway. But white-collar outsourcing? That's Republican voters."

The administration recently got a taste of how politically sensitive the offshoring issue is. N. Gregory Mankiw, chairman of the White House Council of Economic Advisers, stunned Democrats and Republicans alike when he recently described offshoring as "just a new way to do international trade. Outsourcing is a growing phenomenon, but it's something that we should realize is probably a plus for the economy in the long run."[64]

House Speaker J. Dennis Hastert, R-Ill., issued a stern rebuttal to his fellow Republican. "I understand that Mr. Mankiw is a brilliant economic theorist, but his theory fails a basic test of real economics," Hastert said. "An economy suffers when jobs disappear. Outsourcing can be a problem for American workers, and for the American economy. We can't have a healthy economy unless we have more jobs here in America."[65]

Mankiw subsequently hedged his statement. "It is regrettable whenever anyone loses a job," he wrote. "At the same time, we have to acknowledge that any economic change, whether arising from trade or technology, can cause painful dislocations for some workers and their families. The goal of policy should be to help workers prepare for the global economy of the future."

But the basic thrust of Bush's policy on outsourcing stands, as reflected in this year's "Economic Report of the President": "When a good or service is produced more cheaply abroad, it makes more sense to import it than to make or provide it domestically."[66]

President Bush asserts that his income-tax cuts, which the administration says will total $1.3 trillion over 10 years, are the key to speeding the recovery and stimulating job growth. "Americans took those dollars and put them to work, driving this economy forward," Bush said during his State of the Union address.

The president went on to ask Congress to fund new programs to improve science and math education at the middle- and high-school levels and help community colleges "train workers for the industries that are creating the most new jobs."

The job-export issue is creeping into the tax debate. Democratic candidates have lambasted a tax loophole that enables corporations to avoid paying U.S. taxes on offshore revenues that already have been taxed by foreign governments.

"George Bush continues to fight for incentives to encourage Benedict Arnold companies to ship jobs overseas at the same time he cuts job training for our workers and cuts help for small businesses that create jobs here at home," Kerry charged.[67]

But the campaign oratory does not impress T.O.R.A.W. President Bauman and other Americans who have lost their jobs to foreign workers.

"Neither side is addressing this problem adequately," Bauman says. "Some of the candidates have outwardly said they would do something, but nobody has come out and said exactly what they would do to stop offshoring. I don't want to wait until November. I want to see action now."

"The issue is going to be exaggerated and manipulated by both sides in the political debate," predicted Dean Davison, an analyst at the Meta Group, a technology research and advisory firm in Stamford, Conn.[68]

Former Trade Representative Hills warns, "We really must be very wary about making the wrong economic move, even when it's politically attractive to be sloganistic."[69]

NOTES

1. Saritha Rai, "Indians Fearing Repercussions Of U.S. Technology Outsourcing," *The New York Times*, Feb. 9, 2004, p. C4.
2. See Nelson D. Schwartz, "Will 'Made in USA' Fade Away?" *Fortune*, Nov. 24, 2003, p. 98, and

"Employees on Nonfarm Payrolls by Major Industry Sector, 1954 to Date," Bureau of Labor Statistics.

3. See Karl Schoenberger, "Kerry, Dean Compete to Stress Hot Issue," *San Jose Mercury News*, Jan. 30, 2004.

4. The Commerce Department released its most recent GDP data on Jan. 30, 2004.

5. See Nell Henderson, "Growth Again, but Slower," *The Washington Post*, Jan. 31, 2004.

6. See "Unemployment Rate Falls; Few Jobs Added," The Associated Press, Jan. 9, 2004.

7. Christopher Caldwell, "A chill wind from offshore," *Financial Times*, Feb. 7, 2004.

8. *Ibid.*

9. "Global Offshore Call Center Outsourcing: Who Will Be the Next India?" *Datamonitor*, Jan. 8, 2004.

10. See Erica L. Groshen and Simon Potter, "Has Structural Change Contributed to a Jobless Recovery?" *Current Issues in Economics and Finance*, Federal Reserve Bank of New York, August 2003.

11. Census Bureau, 2002. See Andrew Hacker, "The Underworld of Work," *The New York Review of Books*, Feb. 12, 2004, pp. 38-40.

12. *Ibid.*

13. U.S. Census Bureau, "Historical Income Tables — Income Equality," Table IE-3, www.census.gov. For background, see Mary H. Cooper, "Income Inequality," *The CQ Researcher*, April 17, 1998, pp. 337-360.

14. Quoted on ABC's "This Week," Feb. 15, 2004. Hills was citing a study by Catherine L. Mann, "Globalization of IT Services and White Collar Jobs: The Next Wave of Productivity Growth," International Economics Policy Briefs, Institute for International Economics, December 2003.

15. *Ibid.*

16. *Ibid.*

17. *Ibid.*

18. Quoted in Steve Lohr, "Many New Causes for Old problem of Jobs Lost Abroad," *The New York Times*, Feb. 15, 2004, p. A17.

19. ABC, *op. cit.*

20. www.mckinsey.com/knowledge/mgi/offshore/.

21. Caldwell, *op. cit.*

22. From Bush's State of the Union address, Jan. 20, 2004.

23. See Peter D. Syverson, "Coping with Conflicting Data: The Employment Status of Recent Science and Engineering Ph.D.s," Council of Graduate Schools, 1997.

24. See, for example, Committee for Economic Development, "Reforming Immigration: Helping Meet America's Need for a Skilled Workforce," 2001.

25. *Ibid.*

26. See Eric Chabrow, "The Programmer's Future," *InformationWeek*, Nov. 17, 2003, pp. 40-52.

27. For background, see Kathy Koch, "High-Tech Labor Shortage," *The CQ Researcher*, April 24, 1998, pp. 361-384.

28. U.S. Citizenship and Immigration Services Fact Sheet, "H-1B Petitions Received and Approved in FY 2003," Oct. 22, 2003. Citizenship and Immigration Services, part of the Department of Homeland Security, has administered work-visa programs since the department absorbed the Immigration and Naturalization Service in 2003.

29. Ron Sanchez administers ZaZona.com as a source of information on the H-1B program.

30. Duffy testified Sept. 16, 2003, before the Senate Judiciary Committee.

31. From a June 18, 2003, letter to House Small Business Committee Chairman Donald A. Manzullo, R-Ill.

32. Norman Matloff, "Needed Reform for the H-1B and L-1 Work Visas: Major Points," Feb. 5, 2003, http://heather.cs.ucdavis.edu/itaa.html.

33. See "The Impact of Global Sourcing on the U.S. Economy, 2003-2010," *Evalueserve*, 2003.

34. See Jane Tanner, "Future Job Market," *The CQ Researcher*, Jan. 11, 2002, p. 14.

35. See Mack McLarty, "Trade Paves Path to U.S. Prosperity," *Los Angeles Times*, Feb. 1, 2004, p. M2.

36. Schwartz, *op. cit.*

37. Hacker, *op. cit.*

38. See Steve Lohr, "Questioning the Age of Wal-Mart," *The New York Times*, Dec. 28, 2003.

39. Information in the following paragraphs is based on Ashok Deo Bardhan and Cynthia A. Kroll, "The New Wave of Outsourcing," Research Report, Fisher Center for Real Estate and Urban Economics, University of California, Berkeley, fall 2003.

40. Koch, *op. cit.*

41. For background, see Kathy Koch, "Y2K Dilemma," *The CQ Researcher*, Feb. 19, 1999, pp. 137-160.

42. See Bureau of Economic Analysis, Commerce Department, "Growth Moderates in Fourth Quarter but Is Up for the Year," Jan. 30, 2004.

43. Bureau of Labor Statistics, Department of Labor, "Employment Situation Summary," Jan. 9, 2004. Also see Jonathan Krim, "Grove Says U.S. Is Losing Edge in Tech Sector," Forbes.com, Oct. 10, 2003.

44. See Robert B. Reich, "Nice Work If You Can Get It," *The Wall Street Journal*, Dec. 26, 2003, p. A10.

45. *Ibid.*

46. Information Technology Association of America, "2003 IT Workforce Survey," May 5, 2003.

47. John C. McCarthy *et al.*, "3.3 Million U.S. Services Jobs to Go Offshore," *Forrester Tech Strategy Brief*, Nov. 11, 2002.

48. Andrew Tilton, "Offshoring: Where Have All the Jobs Gone?" Goldman, Sachs & Co., *U.S. Economics Analyst*, Sept. 19, 2003.

49. Bardhan, *op. cit.*

50. ABC, *op. cit.*

51. Robert Reich, "High-Tech Jobs Are Going Abroad! But That's OK," *The Washington Post*, Nov. 2, 2003, p. B3.

52. See Jim Hu and Evan Hansen, "AOL Takes Passage to India," CNET News.com, Dec. 22, 2003.

53. See William M. Bulkeley, "IBM to Export Highly Paid Jobs to India, China," *The Wall Street Journal*, Dec. 15, 2003, p. B1.

54. Johnson, *op. cit.*

55. Andrew Mollison, "GOP Ban on 'Offshoring' Federal Jobs Angers Business Groups," Cox News Service, Jan. 29, 2004.

56. Karl Schoenberger, "Legislator wants to keep jobs in state, limits sought on overseas contracts," *San Jose* [California] *Mercury News*, Feb. 5, 2004.

57. *Ibid.*

58. *Ibid.*

59. *Ibid.*

60. Quoted on "Marketplace," National Public Radio, Feb. 16, 2004.

61. *Ibid.*

62. Quoted in Mike Allen, "Bush Proposes Legal Status for Immigrant Labor," *The Washington Post*, Jan. 8, 2004, p. A1. For background, see David Masci, "Debate Over Immigration," *The CQ Researcher*, July 14, 2000, pp. 569-592.

63. See Helen Dewar, "2 Senators Counter Bush on Immigrants," *The Washington Post*, Jan. 22, 2004, p. A4.

64. Mankiw spoke as he released the "Economic Report of the President 2004" on Feb. 9, 2004.

65. Statement, "Hastert Disagrees With President's Economic Advisor On Outsourcing," Feb. 11, 2004, http://speaker.house.gov. See Mike Allen, "Hastert Rebukes Bush Adviser," *The Washington Post*, Feb. 12, 2004, p. A17.

66. "Economic Report of the President 2004," Chapter 12, International Trade and Cooperation.

67. From a Feb. 3, 2004, statement posted at Kerry's campaign Web site, johnkerry.com.

68. Quoted in Karl Schoenberger, "Offshore Job Losses on Voters' Agendas," *San Jose Mercury News*, Jan. 30, 2004.

69. ABC News, *op. cit.*

BIBLIOGRAPHY

Books

Bardhan, Ashok Deo, *et al.*, *Globalization and a High-Tech Economy*, Kluwer Academic Publishers, 2003.
High-tech U.S. firms are outsourcing white-collar jobs offshore to cut labor costs, according to a University of California, Berkeley, economist and his colleagues.

Thurow, Lester C., *Fortune Favors the Bold: What We Must Do to Build a New and Lasting Global Prosperity*, HarperBusiness, 2003.
The dean of MIT's business school calls on policymakers to take steps to reduce the threat of problems that could result from rapid globalization.

Articles

Cullen, Lisa Takeuchi, "Now Hiring!" *Time*, Nov. 24, 2003, p. 48.
The stagnant U.S. labor market is slowly improving, but the average job search today takes four to six months, while senior-level positions take more than a year.

Fox, Justin, "Where Your Job Is Going," *Fortune*, Nov. 10, 2003, p. 84.
Bangalore, India, has become a major center for call centers and computer services for U.S. businesses.

Hacker, Andrew, "The Underworld of Work," *The New York Review of Books*, Feb. 12, 2004, pp. 38-40.
Three recent books on U.S. employment trends describe the shift from high-wage manufacturing jobs to low-wage service jobs over the past 20 years.

Irwin, Douglas A., "'Outsourcing' Is Good for America," *The Wall Street Journal*, Jan. 28, 2004, p. A16.
Outsourcing gives consumers lower prices and employers higher profits that they can use to create high-skilled U.S. jobs.

Krugman, Paul, "For Richer," *The New York Times Magazine*, Oct. 20, 2003, pp. 62-142.
Tax policies favoring the wealthiest Americans are widening the income gap and worsening living standards for American workers.

Lind, Michael, "Are We Still a Middle-Class Nation?" *The Atlantic Monthly*, January/February 2004, pp. 120-128.
As the number of well-paid jobs shrinks, low-wage service jobs are growing, but the cost of living for middle-class workers is rising.

Overby, Stephanie, "U.S. Stays on Top," *CIO Magazine*, Dec. 15, 2003.
As companies continue to outsource computer jobs overseas, information-technology professionals will find high-level jobs in strategy, implementation and design.

Reich, Robert, "High-Tech Jobs Are Going Abroad! But That's OK," *The Washington Post*, Nov. 2, 2003, p. B3.
The former secretary of Labor explains why he believes the flow of high-tech jobs abroad is not a problem.

Risen, Clay, "Missed Target: Is Outsourcing Really So Bad?" *The New Republic*, Feb. 2, 2004, p. 10.
Instead of banning outsourcing, Congress should create a new program to retrain displaced manufacturing workers and help white-collar workers find alternative jobs.

Reports and Studies

Bernstein, Jared, and Lawrence Mishel, "Labor Market Left Behind," Briefing Paper, Economic Policy Institute, August 2003.
The current recovery has produced fewer jobs than any other during the post-World War II era.

Evalueserve, "The Impact of Global Sourcing on the U.S. Economy, 2003-2010," Oct. 9, 2003.
Some 1.3 million U.S. jobs will be shifted offshore from 2003-2010, compensating for the shrinking of the work force as the Baby Boomers retire.

Information Technology Association of America, "2003 IT Workforce Survey," May 5, 2003.
Twelve percent of U.S. information-technology companies outsourced jobs overseas, primarily programming jobs.

Matloff, Norman, "On the Need for Reform of the H-1B Non-Immigrant Work Visa in Computer-Related Occupations," *University of Michigan Journal of Law Reform*, Dec. 12, 2003.
In a special issue on immigration, a University of California expert on the H-1B visa program contends that employers abuse the program to import low-wage programmers and other professionals.

U.S. Department of Commerce, Economics and Statistics Administration, "Digital Economy 2003," December 2003.
The information-technology sector promises to continue on a modest, steady growth path, thanks in part to offshoring.

For More Information

Bureau of Labor Statistics, U.S. Labor Department, 2 Massachusetts Ave., N.E., Suite 4040, Washington, DC 20212-0001; (202) 691-5200; www.bls.gov.

Department for Professional Employees, AFL-CIO, 1025 Vermont Ave., N.W., Suite 1030, Washington, DC 20005; (202) 638-0320; www.dpeaflcio.org. This labor group representing more than 4 million white-collar workers calls for policy changes to stem the export of U.S. jobs.

Economic Policy Institute, 1660 L St., N.W., Suite 1200, Washington, DC 20036; (202) 775-8810; www.epinet.org. This nonprofit research group contends Americans lose jobs because of free-trade agreements.

National Association of Manufacturers, 1331 Pennsylvania Ave., N.W., Washington, DC 20004-1790; (202) 637-3000; www.nam.org. The 14,000-member organization defends outsourcing as essential to U.S. competitiveness.

Organization for the Rights of American Workers (T.O.R.A.W.), PO Box 2354, Meriden, CT 06450-1454; www.toraw.org. A worker-advocacy group demanding that U.S. jobs be preserved for American citizens and calling for legislation to limit offshoring and worker-visa programs.

U.S. Chamber of Commerce, 1615 H St., N.W., Washington, DC 20062-2000; (202) 659-6000; www.uschamber.com. The largest U.S. business lobby opposes legislative obstacles to offshore outsourcing.

15

Democracy in the Arab World

Kenneth Jost and Benton Ives-Halperin

Thousands of Shiite Muslims march through Baghdad on Jan. 19, demanding that Iraq's new government be selected through direct elections rather than caucuses, as the United States has proposed. Some monarchies in the Arab world have taken tentative steps toward electoral governance, but others continue to struggle under the grip of authoritarian regimes. President Bush recently called on all Arab states to join "the global democratic revolution."

AFP Photo/Ahmad Al-Rubaye

From *The CQ Researcher,*
January 30, 2004.

Egyptian sociologist Saad Eddin Ibrahim was lecturing in the United States last November when President Bush called for democratization in the Middle East. "I could not have written a better speech," Ibrahim, a longtime critic of Egyptian strongman Hosni Mubarak, wrote in *The Washington Post.*[1]

Back in Egypt, Ibrahim's op-ed remarks caused an uproar. Pro-government newspapers insinuated that he had actually written Bush's Nov. 6 speech — and that his entire trip was designed to embarrass Egypt and secure U.S. funding for Ibrahim's pro-democracy center in Cairo. Declared a headline in the pro-government weekly *Al-Osbou:* "Saad in Washington to incite the U.S. against Egypt and the Arab world."[2]

Political dissidents in many countries can shrug off newspaper innuendoes. But government critics in Egypt must take care. Ibrahim himself served more than a year in prison and was twice convicted of receiving foreign funds for his Ibn Khaldun Center without permission — a $225,000 grant from the European Union for voter-awareness projects — and spreading defamatory information about Egypt. The convictions sparked international protests that died down only after Ibrahim won a reversal and subsequent acquittal in March 2003. The center, which the government had ordered closed, reopened in November.

Hafez Abu Saada, head of the Egyptian Organization for Human Rights, was arrested five years ago and charged with similar offenses. He was never tried, but he says the government can revive the case any time in the next 15 years. Meanwhile, he has been waiting for more than six months to find out whether the Egyptian Ministry of Social Affairs will allow his group to accept a grant from the

U.S.-government-funded National Endowment for Democracy to help pay for its human rights monitoring work.

Egypt's law regulating non-governmental organizations is just one of the many statutes tightly controlling civic life in a country that is a critical American partner in the Middle East and — with about 75 million people — the most populous nation in the Arab world. According to the U.S.-based human rights group Freedom House, a government committee must license all political parties, and the Ministry of the Interior must approve public demonstrations in advance. In addition, the government owns all the broadcast media, along with three major daily newspapers, whose editors are appointed by the president. Direct criticism of the president, his family or the military can result in imprisonment of journalists or closure of publications.

Egypt has an elected president and a bicameral legislature with an elected lower house and a mostly elective upper chamber. But Mubarak — who has ruled by decree since taking office after the assassination of President Anwar el-Sadat in 1981 — is nominated by parliament and then voted on in a single-candidate referendum for a five-year term. Further, the political licensing laws combine with what Freedom House calls "systematic irregularities" in election procedures to assure the ruling National Democratic Party (NDP) a lock on governmental power. "Egyptians cannot change their government democratically," the group concludes.[3]

As in Egypt, so in the rest of the Arab world — which stretches across North Africa, south through the Arabian peninsula and east to Iraq. (*See map, p. 347*) With around 300 million people, the 22 members of the League of Arab States include only one rated by Freedom House as "free" — tiny Djibouti on the Horn of Africa. None of the other members allows a free election to choose the national leader, and only one — Kuwait — has a parliament with effective power to control the executive branch of government.

"There is no substantial and significant movement toward full democracy in any of the majority-Arab countries," says Adrian Karatnycky, a senior counselor and former president of Freedom House.

Other human rights advocates and experts agree. "Legitimate democracy is non-existent in the Arab world," says James Phillips, a Mideast expert at the conservative Heritage Foundation.

Thomas Carothers, vice president of the more liberal Carnegie Endowment for International Peace, says, "There is very little democratic trend in the region."

Arab leaders, however, profess support for democracy and claim to see progress toward the goal in many countries in the region. "More than a few people are committed to the democratization process, committed to widening and consolidating political participation," says Nassif Hitti, a diplomat in the Paris mission of the League of Arab States. "It's a process. It's moving on, perhaps not as fast as one would like to see it. It's moving on at different speeds depending on different cases."

A leading American spokesman for Arab-Americans also sees advancing democratization in the region. "It's proceeding apace," says James Zogby, president of the Arab American Institute. "While there are problems, to be sure, changes have been occurring that should not be ignored but all too frequently are ignored."

A major 2002 human rights report by a leading Arab development group, however, takes a more critical view. "The wave of democracy . . . has barely reached the Arab States," the Arab Fund for Economic and Social Development said in a 2002 report co-published by the United Nations Development Program. Representative democracy "is not always genuine and sometimes absent," the group said, while freedoms of expression and association are "frequently curtailed."[4]

Bush raised the profile of the issue in his Nov. 6 speech marking the 20th anniversary of the National Endowment for Democracy, calling on the Middle East and North Africa to join what he called "the global democratic revolution." Bush cataloged signs of democratization in many Arab lands — from the first-ever parliamentary elections in the island emirate of Bahrain and planned elections in Saudi Arabia to a new constitution in Qatar and a call by Morocco's king to extend rights to women.

In a widely noted passage, Bush also directly criticized the United States and other Western nations for supporting autocratic governments in the past. "Sixty years of Western nations excusing and accommodating the lack of freedom in the Middle East did nothing to make us safe," Bush said, "because in the long run, stability cannot be purchased at the expense of liberty."[5]

Bush also vowed to press on with building a democracy in Iraq following last year's U.S.-led invasion and ouster of the country's former dictator, Saddam Hussein.[6]

Political Freedom Rare in the Arab World

Only one member of the 22-member League of Arab States — tiny Djibouti on the Horn of Africa — is rated "free" by the human-rights group Freedom House. No other Arab country allows free elections of national leaders, and only Kuwait has a parliament that can effectively control the executive branch. Yemen is the only Arab country whose freedom status improved over the past year.

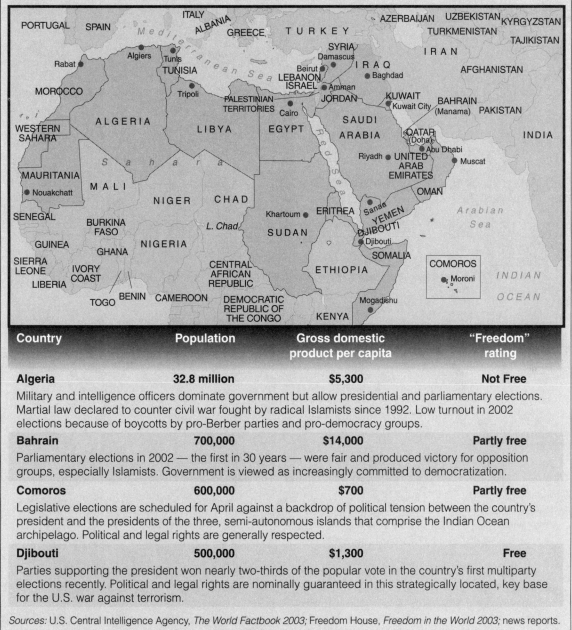

Country	Population	Gross domestic product per capita	"Freedom" rating
Algeria	32.8 million	$5,300	**Not Free**

Military and intelligence officers dominate government but allow presidential and parliamentary elections. Martial law declared to counter civil war fought by radical Islamists since 1992. Low turnout in 2002 elections because of boycotts by pro-Berber parties and pro-democracy groups.

Bahrain	700,000	$14,000	**Partly free**

Parliamentary elections in 2002 — the first in 30 years — were fair and produced victory for opposition groups, especially Islamists. Government is viewed as increasingly committed to democratization.

Comoros	600,000	$700	**Partly free**

Legislative elections are scheduled for April against a backdrop of political tension between the country's president and the presidents of the three, semi-autonomous islands that comprise the Indian Ocean archipelago. Political and legal rights are generally respected.

Djibouti	500,000	$1,300	**Free**

Parties supporting the president won nearly two-thirds of the popular vote in the country's first multiparty elections recently. Political and legal rights are nominally guaranteed in this strategically located, key base for the U.S. war against terrorism.

Sources: U.S. Central Intelligence Agency, *The World Factbook 2003;* Freedom House, *Freedom in the World 2003;* news reports.

Country	Population	Gross domestic product per capita	"Freedom" rating
Egypt	**74.7 million**	**$3,900**	**Not free**
President Hosni Mubarak has ruled under a continuous state of emergency since assuming office in 1981 after the assassination of Anwar el-Sadat but said he supports limited reforms drafted by a party committee headed by his son Gamal. Some easing of previous crackdowns on internal dissent has occurred; Islamic militancy is seen as fueled by socioeconomic problems.			
Iraq	**24.7 million**	**$2,400**	**Not free**
The United States is pressing transition to democratic self-rule after a U.S.-led coalition ousted Saddam Hussein last spring. Captured in December 2003, Hussein faces trial by an Iraqi tribunal. L. Paul Bremer III — administrator of the American-led occupation — is working to transfer power to Iraqi entities; elections possible in 2004.			
Jordan	**5.5 million**	**$4,300**	**Not free**
King Abdullah II promises to continue pushing democratic reforms following victory for allies in previously postponed parliamentary elections in June 2003. He dissolved parliament in 2001 to counter Islamist opposition to pro-Western foreign policy he continued after 1999 death of his father, King Hussein.			
Kuwait	**2.2 million**	**$15,000**	**Partly free**
Fundamentalist Muslims and supporters of the royal-backed cabinet improved their standing in parliamentary elections last June; the aging emir appointed his 74-year-old brother as prime minister in July in an apparent effort to boost economic and political reforms, but succession issues still cloud prospects.			
Lebanon	**3.7 million**	**$5,400**	**Not free**
Opposition to Syrian military occupation increasing, although Syria downsized its military presence in 2001. The elected, pro-Syrian government continues to hold power since winning control after the end of Christian-Muslim civil war in 1990.			
Libya	**5.5 million**	**$7,600**	**Not free**
Muammar el-Qaddafi has ruled by decree since seizing power in 1969. Independent political parties and non-authorized Islamic groups are banned. Qaddafi recently has been seeking U.S. goodwill by cooperating in the war against terrorism, while domestic support wanes.			
Mauritania	**2.9 million**	**$1,700**	**Partly free**
Longtime President Maaouiya Ould Taya was re-elected in November after his main opponent was charged with plotting a coup d'etat. Elections in October 2001 were seen as generally fair and open, but Ould Taya's political control was left undisturbed.			
Morocco	**31.7 million**	**$3,900**	**Partly free**
King Mohammed VI instituted political and economic liberalization after assuming the throne in 1999. Free and fair elections for parliament were held in 2002, but turnout was low. Palace still holds decision-making power.			
Oman	**2.8 million**	**$8,300**	**Not free**
An 83-member advisory council was elected by universal-suffrage election in October; parliamentary elections planned in 2004. Political liberalization and economic modernization have been pushed since 1990s by Sultan Qaboos, who overthrew his father in 1970.			
Palestinian Territories	**3.2 million**	**$930**	**Not free**
Progress toward limited self-rule by the Palestinian Authority in the Israeli-occupied West Bank and Gaza Strip has stalled following the outbreak of the Palestinian intifada (uprising) in September 2000, a continuing dispute over Israeli settlements and a stalemate in peace talks. The first popular election in 1996 was seen as legitimate; municipal elections have been postponed since 1998.			

Country	Population	Gross domestic product per capita	"Freedom" rating
Qatar	800,000	$21,500	Not free

Parliamentary elections have been promised for 2004. Liberalization has been directed by the ruling emir, who overthrew his father in 1995. The government's Al-Jazeera all-news satellite TV station and close military ties with the United States have raised the country's profile.

| Saudi Arabia | 24.3 million | $10,500 | Not free |

Crown Prince Abdullah favors political and economic liberalization but faces family opposition. Popular discontent among religious and liberal dissidents fueled by declining living standards has been put down by harsh measures. Under U.S. pressure, the government is moving against al-Qaeda terrorist activities.

| Somalia | 8 million | $600 | Not free |

Delegates to a peace conference agreed in July 2003 to create a new federal government after more than a decade of civil war and virtual anarchy, but the plan has yet to be implemented. The breakaway Republic of Somaliland in the north has not won diplomatic recognition.

| Sudan | 38.1 million | $1,420 | Not free |

The Arab Muslim government reached a cease-fire agreement in September with black African rebels in the south in 20-year-old civil war that has claimed 2 million lives. Accord envisions a six-year transition to autonomy for the southern region and Islamic law in north.

| Syria | 17.6 million | $3,500 | Not free |

President Bashar Assad has mixed record on reform since the death of his autocratic father, Hafez al-Assad, in 2000. Bashar allowed reform movement to form during "Damascus Spring" but began clamping down in February 2001. Calls for reform were renewed last September, but broad political change is seen as unlikely.

| Tunisia | 10 million | $6,500 | Not free |

President Zine el-Abidine Ben Ali gained power in a 1987 coup and won 99 percent approval in a 2002 referendum to seek election for a fourth five-year term. Elections for parliament are heavily orchestrated. The country has a strong, diversified market economy, but political and civil liberties are restricted.

| United Arab Emirates | 2.5 million | $22,000 | Not free |

Council of seven dynastic families have ruled the federation since its formation in 1971. No elections have been held and political parties are banned. The diversified modern economy supports high per capita income. The federation has a moderate foreign policy stance and new anti-money laundering laws to stem terrorism financing.

| Western Sahara | 300,000 | N/A | Not free |

Morocco virtually annexed the country in late 1970s, but the territory is still contested by the so-called Polisario guerrillas; guerrilla activities continued sporadically until a U.N.-monitored cease-fire on Sept. 6, 1991.

| Yemen | 19.3 million | $840 | Partly free |

President Ali Abdullah Saleh, in office since unification of North and South Yemen in 1990, won approval in a 2001 referendum to extend presidential and parliamentary terms. Elections for parliament were deemed free and fair, but it exercises little power. Under U.S. pressure, government is cracking down on al-Qaeda cells and radical Islamist schools.

"This work is not easy," he said. But, he added, "We will meet this test."

Egypt merited a mention in the speech, with the president hailing a "great and proud nation" but calling on it to "show the way toward democracy in the Middle East." President Mubarak answered the next month by insisting that Egypt is already a democracy. "We do not need any pressure from anyone to adopt democratic principles," he told a news conference in December.[7]

Indeed, many Arabists say the United States should not try to impose democracy on the Arab world. "It might be considered by many as an interference, for right

President Bush has urged Egyptian President Hosni Mubarak, left, and other Arab leaders to allow more democracy in the Middle East. "For too long, many people in that region have been victims and subjects — they deserve to be active citizens," Bush said in a Nov. 6 speech.

or wrong reasons, and this might frustrate at some times the progress of this process," Hitti says.

Mubarak's son Gamal, in fact, heads an NDP committee that has called for revising the political licensing laws and invited legal opposition parties and nongovernmental organizations to join a "national dialogue." Most Egyptian democracy advocates are unimpressed. "I find all policies unchanged," Abu Saad says. As for Mubarak's assessment, Abu Saad flatly disagrees: "You can't say we have democracy at all."

As the debate on democratic reforms continues in Egypt and elsewhere in the Arab world and in Washington, here are some of the questions being considered:

Is democracy taking root in the Arab world?

The U.S.-led liberation of Kuwait in the first Gulf War in 1991 raised hopes for democratic changes in the oil-rich emirate. Pressure from Washington helped persuade the ruling al-Sabah family to restore the previously suspended national assembly.

Today, Kuwait's parliament is regarded as the only legislative body in an Arab country with the power to check decisions by the executive branch. The parliament's most notable use of that power came in 1999 when it nullified a decree by the ruling emir to allow women the right to vote. And the prospect for further reforms is clouded by fractiousness within the ruling family and the strong showing by Islamist, or Muslim

fundamentalist, forces in the most recent parliamentary elections in 2003.

Kuwait's al-Sabah regime serves as one example of the many obstacles to democratization in the Arab world. While historic, cultural and religious factors are all cited as important, the Carnegie Foundation's Carothers says the most important obstacle is political: the power and survival skills of existing, undemocratic governments.

"These are well-entrenched, non-democratic regimes that have learned to survive over the years and are able to mobilize resources — either oil or foreign aid — to co-opt opposition movements, to repress and to tell their peoples that they are forces of order that are necessary to keep societies together," Carothers says.

Arab League diplomat Hitti acknowledges that established regimes are part of the problem. "The official elements are in many instances part of the constraining factors," he says. But he declines to comment on specific countries or leaders.

Contemporary political conditions, however, have developed from a history largely without democratic institutions or procedures. The Heritage Foundation's Phillips says Arab culture itself is ill disposed toward democracy. For example, the Arab word for politics translates most closely as "control," he points out, while the English word derives from a Greek root meaning cooperation.

"Arabs in general don't handle equality very well because in their system you're either giving orders or taking orders," Phillips says.

"The Muslim and Arab countries do not have a culture or heritage or traditions of democratic practices or liberties as such," says Laith Kubba, an Iraqi-born U.S. citizen who is senior program officer for the Middle East and North Africa at the National Endowment for Democracy. "They have more traditional tribal cultures, where consensus is valued and dissent is not appreciated or welcome."

The 2002 Arab human rights report itself acknowledges that "traditional Arab culture and values" are often "at odds with those of the globalizing world."[8] The report calls for Arab countries to adopt an attitude of "openness and constructive engagement" toward other cultures, but Carothers says outside influences are generally unwelcome. "There is a sense in the Arab world that there is a particular Arab way to do things, and they should resist change from the outside," he says.

Arabs and Arab-Americans say cultural factors are less important in inhibiting democracy than historical factors — specifically, the legacy of colonial rule, first by the Ottoman Empire and then by European powers beginning in the 19th century. "During the colonial era, whatever existed before was wiped out," says Radwan Masmoudi, a Tunisian-born U.S. citizen who heads the Center for the Study of Islam and Democracy in Washington.

After independence in the early 20th century, Masmoudi continues, "the new states were created in an ad hoc fashion. They weren't established to represent the will of the people or even to serve the people."

Zogby agrees. "You've got a region that for the last 150 years has not controlled its own destiny," he says. "This region was not free to advance and develop at its own rate, and that's never a positive factor in promoting democracy."

The region's largely Muslim population and character are often cited as another barrier to democratization, but the relationship between Islam and democracy is complex and susceptible to what the Arab League's Hitti calls "contradictory interpretations." Many experts see support for democracy in Islam's central tenets, while others view Islam's fusion of religion and the state as antithetical to democracy.

For his part, President Bush insisted in his Nov. 6 speech that Islam and democracy are not in conflict. And Arab and U.S. experts alike stress the multiplicity of views among Muslims themselves. "There are versions of Islam that are pretty anti-democratic, but they're just versions," Carothers says.

But Abdelwahab El-Affendi, a senior research fellow at the Centre for the Study of Democracy at the University of Westminster, in London, says the strong differences among Muslims themselves are part of the problem. "The many visions are often incompatible," says El-Affendi, a Sudanese. "The holders of each vision are not ready to negotiate."

The Arab human rights report cataloged a host of factors underlying what it called the "freedom deficit" in the region. It listed high rates of illiteracy and low rates of economic development as important factors, along with such political conditions as the unchecked power of executive branches of government, little popular participation and limited freedom of expression or association. "Remedying this state of affairs," the report concluded, "must be a priority of national leaderships."[9]

Will democracy help promote economic development in the Arab world?

Saudi Arabia may be oil-rich, but the kingdom is beset with economic problems, according to Freedom House's most recent annual country profile. The report blames "declining oil prices," "rampant corruption within the royal family" and "gross economic mismanagement" for a steep decline in living standards — represented by a 50 percent drop in per capita income since the 1980s. Meanwhile, unemployment is estimated at 35 percent and expected to rise in coming years.[10]

Saudi Arabia provides just one example — though the most dramatic — of the paradoxical economic conditions in the Arab world. Arab nations control about half of the world's oil reserves, but the region has higher unemployment and poverty than much of the developing world. Unemployment averages 15 percent, according to the Arab human rights report, and more than one out of five people live on less than $2 per day. Combined, the Arab states' gross national product is less than that of Spain — which has less than one-seventh of the Arab world's population.[11]

The region's economic problems are widely seen as an obstacle to democratization, which in turn is viewed as one of the keys to improved economic performance. "Opening up markets is tied directly to opening up the political process," says diplomat Hitti. "There is a direct relationship between the issues."

Many advocates and experts say the region's dependence on oil as its primary source of wealth has had a negative effect on democratization. "Energy-rich societies have been able to use oil and wealth to buy quiescence and consent from portions of their population, and they've used repression to deal with the balance," says Freedom House's Karatnycky.

"Oil is an incredibly corrupting influence," says Stephen Krasner, director of the Center on Democracy, Development and the Rule of Law at Stanford University's Institute of International Studies, in Palo Alto, Calif.

In states with oil wealth, Krasner explains, "People want to get control of the state [because] the state gives you resources that you can use to repress your enemies. You don't have to compromise. You don't have to think about responsive fiscal systems. It's a huge problem."

Michael Ross, a political scientist at the University of California, Los Angeles, says oil dependence also

Are Islam and Democracy Incompatible?

Politics and religion are a volatile mix in many countries, but nowhere more so than in the Arab world. Islam has a special status in Arab states — not only because it is the nearly universal faith but also because many Muslims view Islam as an essential source of government law.

Even in non-Arab Islamic countries, fundamentalists, or Islamists, often claim a religious basis for repressive policies against political opponents, women and other religions — notably, in Iran after the Islamic revolution of 1979 and in Afghanistan under the now-deposed Taliban. In addition, Islamist groups bring a sometimes deadly religious zeal to their battles against secular Arab regimes, not to mention Israel and the United States.

As a result, many Westerners regard Islam and democracy as inherently incompatible. Muslims in and outside the Arab world resent that view, and human rights advocates take pains to try to refute it.

"Islam, per se, is not an obstacle to democracy," says Thomas Carothers, director of the Project on Democracy and the Rule of Law at the Carnegie Endowment for International Peace. But, Carothers adds, "there are certain patterns of Islam that are inhospitable to democracy."

"There is a long tradition of people who want to combine liberalism with Islam," says Abdelwahab El-Affendi, coordinator of the Project on Democracy in the Muslim World at the University of Westminster in London and a native Sudanese. But he concedes that groups with "illiberal" Islamic views have more adherents in the Arab world today. "They say if liberalism and Islam conflict, then the Islamic way should be supreme," he explains.

In its most recent annual survey, the human rights group Freedom House says there is "no inexorable link between Islam and political repression."[1] Nearly half of the world's 1.5 billion Muslims live in countries with elective democracies, according to the survey. The list includes such majority-Muslim countries as Bangladesh, Nigeria and Turkey as well as more religiously diverse nations like India, Indonesia and the United States.

Nevertheless, the survey reports, "The largest freedom gap exists in countries with a majority-Muslim population, especially in the Arab world." Out of 44 majority-Muslim countries, only eight are electoral democracies — none of them Arab states. And only two are classified as "free": Mali and Senegal in West Africa. The other 42 countries — home to more than 1 billion Muslims — are rated either as "partly free" or "not free."

Human rights advocates blame the limited advance of democracy in the Islamic world more on history and politics than on religion. Radwan Masmoudi, the founding president of the Center for the Study of Islam and Democracy in Washington, says that European colonial rulers of the early 20th century were succeeded by ideologues of various stripes — Arab nationalists, communists and Baathists — who adopted authoritarian policies to hold power.

Properly understood, Islam has been fully consistent with democracy, according to Masmoudi, a Tunisian-born U.S. citizen who founded the center partly with U.S.-government funding in 1999. "From a historical perspective, Islam has been a fairly tolerant religion," Masmoudi says, ever since its birth with the teachings of Muhammad in the seventh century A.D. "The sayings of the Prophet are clearly for freedom, democracy and tolerance," he explains.

Other experts also see support for democratic government in such Islamic principles as consultation (*shurah*), consensus (*ijma*) and independent judgment (*itjihad*). But John Esposito, director of the Center for Christian-Muslim Understanding at Georgetown University in Washington, notes that Islamic thinkers adapt these concepts in ways that reflect criticisms of what they see as the secularism and materialism of Western-style democracy.[2]

Other U.S. scholars, however, say that fundamentalists interpret Islam in ways that are antithetical to democracy. "For [fundamentalists], the truth is knowable, and so there is no need to discuss it in an open forum," says Daniel Pipes, director of the Middle East Forum, a think tank in Philadelphia. "That strikes me as undemocratic."[3]

Islamic fundamentalists "regard liberal democracy as a corrupt and corrupting form of government," writes Bernard Lewis, a leading historian of the Middle East. "They are willing to see it, at best, as an avenue to power,

hampers democratization because it fails to produce the kind of social modernization usually associated with democratic change, such as urbanization, education and occupational specialization. Without those changes, Ross writes in a detailed examination of the issue, the public is "demobilized" — ill equipped to organize and communicate and unaccustomed to thinking for itself.[12]

but an avenue that runs one way only."[4]

Masmoudi and others say that U.S. policymakers must accept that secularism and separation of church and state will not be accepted by most Muslims. "People tend to think that democracy is equal to secularism, that religion will play no role in society whatsoever," he explains. If people view Islam and democracy in conflict, Masmoudi says, "Eighty percent of them will say, 'We want to be good Muslims. We don't care about good democracy — if it is against Islam, we don't want it.' "

"The Islamists in the Middle East are there to stay," says Mohamed Ben-Ruwin, an assistant professor of political science at Texas A&M International University in Laredo. "You have to engage them in some kind of dialogue."[5]

"We should have a dialogue of civilizations, not 'a clash of civilizations,' " Ben-Ruwin adds, referring to the widely discussed book by Harvard political scientist Samuel Huntington forecasting an increasing threat of violence from countries and cultures with religiously based policies and traditions.[6]

Democracy advocates point to the success of a moderate Islamic party in Turkey as a promising example for majority-Muslim countries. Since taking office after an overwhelming election victory in November 2002, the Justice and Development Party has moved to expand political rights in a nation founded in 1923 as a secular republic.

"Turkey shows us that Islamists in a democratic environment modify their policies over time," says Adrian Karatnycky, counselor and former president of Freedom House. "Just because this is a religiously informed movement doesn't mean it is going to be anti-democratic."

Shiite Muslim Iraqis have become increasingly vocal in supporting their spiritual leader Grand Ayatollah Ali al-Sistani's unrelenting call for direct elections. The majority Shiites were repressed by the ruling Sunnis during the regime of deposed President Saddam Hussein.

AFP Photo/Getty Images/Hani al-Obeidi

In Iran, the reform-minded Mohammad Khatami won election as president in 1997 and re-election in 2001 after reformers had also won the overwhelming majority of parliamentary seats in 2000. But hard-line conservatives still dominate the judiciary and security services — producing a stalemate between pro- and anti-liberalization forces.[7]

Many Arab leaders resist free elections by pointing to the danger of a victory for extremist Islamist groups — a fear shared though not always voiced among U.S. policymakers. Masmoudi says the danger is exaggerated.

"I trust the people," he says. "The Islamist parties that will win are not against democracy. I believe it will be the moderate Islamists, not the radical Islamists who are opposed to democracy."

---

[1] "Global Freedom Gains Amid Terror, Uncertainty," Freedom House, Dec. 18, 2003 (www.freedomhouse.org).

[2] See John L. Esposito and John O. Voll, *Islam and Democracy* (1996), pp. 27-32.

[3] Quoted in David Masci, "Islamic Fundamentalism," *The CQ Researcher*, March 24, 2000, pp. 241-264.

[4] Bernard Lewis, "A Historical Overview," in Larry Diamond, Marc F. Plattner and Daniel Brumberg (eds.), *Islam and Democracy in the Middle East* (2003), p. 210.

[5] See Mohamed Berween, "Leadership Crisis in the Arab Countries and the Challenge of the Islamists," *Middle East Affairs Journal*, Vol. 7, No. 1-2 (winter/spring 2001), pp. 121-132.

[6] Samuel P. Huntington, *The Clash of Civilizations and the Remaking of World Order* (2000).

[7] For background, see David Masci, "Reform in Iran," *The CQ Researcher*, Dec. 18, 1998, pp. 1097-1120.

The 2002 Arab human rights report viewed government policies as unhelpful to economic development. "[T]he state's role in promoting, complementing and regulating markets for goods, services and factors of pro-duction has been both constrained and constraining," the 2002 report stated. As a result, "the private sector's contribution to development has often been hesitant and certainly below expectations."[13]

Today, however, Hitti claims that Arab governments are adopting free-market policies. "Almost all of our countries are moving along market economic lines," he says.

Some experts say they expect democratic changes will encourage more economic development. "You may liberate a lot of economic free-wheeling activity," says the Heritage Foundation's Phillips. "The Arabs are great traders and merchants, but the problem is that the merchant class has been kept down except in Kuwait, where the merchants run the place."

Other experts, however, caution against expecting democratic change alone to solve the region's economic problems. "No statistical relationship can be shown between democracy and economic growth," Krasner says. He puts greater emphasis on instilling "decent levels of governance," including reducing corruption, adopting a "reasonable level of rule of law" and delivering government services more effectively.

For Saudi Arabia itself, broad democratic changes would have "a huge positive effect" on economic development, says Jean-Francois Seznec, an adjunct professor at Georgetown University's Center for Contemporary Arab Studies, in Washington. "If you have democratization, the private sector will be much more able to invest."

Seznec notes that Saudi Arabia has been developing an industrial base — notably, in petrochemical manufacturing. The Saudi Ministry of Labor is calling for investing $200 billion a year in further industrialization. But investment is hampered by the government's tight control of the economy and the lack of an independent judiciary.

"Right now, the civil service controls the economy, and the royal family is above the law," Seznec explains. An independent judiciary, he says, "would allow people to invest more freely, and there's plenty of money to invest."

Without democratization, Seznec concludes, economic changes "will occur, but very, very slowly."

Should the United States do more to promote democracy in Arab countries?

As Secretary of State Colin L. Powell prepared to visit Morocco, Algeria and Tunisia last December, human rights groups urged him to lobby their leaders for democratic reforms. "Secretary Powell should make bold and specific statements calling for the countries in the region to take serious steps to enhance the rule of law, strengthen independent media and expand democratic freedoms," Freedom House Executive Director Jennifer Windsor urged.

Powell did raise the issue in each country. He praised Morocco's holding of parliamentary elections in 2002, called on Algeria to ensure "free and fair" elections for the national assembly in April 2004 and pressed Tunisia's longtime president, Zine el-Abidine Ben Ali, to move faster on political reforms. But Powell was careful to soften any implied criticism. In Tunis, for example, Powell said that Tunisia "has accomplished so much that people are expecting more to happen."

Human rights groups had mixed reactions. Human rights "was not a major theme of his public statements," Freedom House's Karatnycky commented afterwards. But Tom Malinowski, Washington advocacy director for Human Rights Watch, was more impressed. "Human rights were raised in a manner in which they haven't been raised in the past by the United States in these countries," he remarked.

Powell's careful diplomacy illustrates the recurrent tension between

Anti-U.S. Views Dominate Arab World

Unfavorable attitudes about the United States were twice as prevalent, on average, as favorable attitudes, according to a poll in five Arab nations.

Country	Favorable	Unfavorable
Lebanon	41%	40%
Kuwait	28	41
Jordan	22	62
Morocco	22	41
Saudi Arabia	16	64
Total	26%	50%

Note: Percentages are not included for respondents with neither favorable nor unfavorable attitudes.

Source: Gallup Organization, poll of nearly 10,000 residents, February 2002.

human rights advocacy and present-day strategic considerations. "We still need and value our close cooperation with some of the non-democratic governments in the region — like Egypt and Saudi Arabia — on security matters as well as on economic matters like oil," says the Carnegie Endowment's Carothers. "It's hard for us to take a genuinely tough line toward governments that know we need them."

But human rights advocates and experts also stress that the United States is hampered in pushing for democratic change in the region because of its past record of supporting autocratic Arab governments. "The United States has been, over time, interested in stability and generally indifferent to democracy," Karatnycky says.

"We have very little credibility as a pro-democratic actor," Carothers says. "We will have to earn that credibility by word and deed over a sustained period of time."

Arab-American advocates make the same point, even more critically. "We've never been a supporter of democracy in this region," Zogby says. "We lack both the moral authority and credibility at this point to be an agent for that kind of change."

For their part, Arab governments and Arab-American advocates also say that U.S. support for Israel undermines the United States' position in pushing for democratic changes. "The American position — particularly as it pertains to the Arab-Israeli conflict — has been damaging," Hitti says. He complains today of U.S. "immobilism" in peacemaking efforts in the Mideast.[14]

Bush's Nov. 6 speech drew mixed reactions from U.S. experts and advocates. The Heritage Foundation's Phillips calls it a "great speech," but Joe Stork, acting director for the Middle East and North Africa at Human Rights Watch, is more restrained. "It was a positive signal, but now we have to see if he can walk the walk," Stork says.

"The rhetoric is very dramatic," Karatnycky says, "but as yet the programmatic resources are relatively modest, and the pressure [from the U.S.] is still very, very mild."

The administration's vehicle for pro-democracy programs in the region is the Middle East Partnership Initiative, a State Department program that was headed by Elizabeth Cheney, daughter of the vice president, until her resignation in December 2003 to join President Bush's re-election campaign. Funding for the initiative was $129 million for 2002 and 2003 and up to $120 million for 2004.[15]

For his part, the Arab League's Hitti says Bush's speech failed to resolve concerns about U.S. hypocrisy in pushing for democratization. "There is a great feeling in the region that there is a double standard in America," he says. "You use democracy in certain aspects and not in other aspects."

Apart from any questions about the administration's sincerity, some experts also say that the push for democratization may be too narrowly focused on elections rather than on the full range of political reforms needed to sustain democratic government. Daniel Brumberg, an associate professor of government at Georgetown and a senior associate at the Carnegie Endowment, complains that Bush's speech lacked "any discussion of fundamental constitutional reforms." He points in particular to the need for Arab governments to create what none of them now has: legislative bodies "with the authority and power to speak for elected majorities."[16]

"We are deeply hamstrung by thinking that we must only focus on having free elections," Stanford's Krasner says. "What we should be talking about is good governance and accountability, of which democracy is a part, but only one part."

Despite those criticisms, Kubba at the National Endowment for Democracy believes the United States is on the way to becoming a positive force for democratization — not only for moral reasons but also for national self-interest, particularly after the Sept. 11, 2001, attacks on New York's World Trade Center and the Pentagon by Arab terrorists.

"There has been a genuine shift after Sept. 11 toward supporting democracy in the Middle East," Kubba says, "because [the administration] now believes that democracy-building enhances not only the security and stability in the region but also America's interest and security."

BACKGROUND

A Vast Empire

The earliest known Arab governments were established during a period of imperial expansion in the seventh century — shortly after the Islamic religion was established.[17] Led initially by the prophet Muhammad, nomadic peoples of the Arabian Peninsula conquered a vast empire stretching from Spain and North Africa to the Middle East and present-day Pakistan, spreading their religion, language and culture throughout the

C H R O N O L O G Y

Before 1900 *Arab empire extends from Spain to India; Ottoman Turks conquer the Arabs in 15th century; European powers gain foothold in 1800s.*

1900-1945 *Britain, France establish "mandates" after defeating Ottomans in World War I; House of Saud establishes kingdom on Arabian peninsula.*

1946-1970 *Arab nationalism grows with independence after World War II and creation of Israel; U.S. bolsters sitting leaders to protect oil supplies, aid Cold War struggle.*

1948-1949 Israel established as Jewish homeland, defeats Arab states in nine-month war; 960,000 Palestinians displaced.

1952 Gamal Abdel Nasser becomes Egypt's president after military coup, promotes pan-Arab unity but loses prestige after Arab defeat in Six-Day War with Israel in 1967.

1967 Israel occupies Gaza Strip, West Bank after victory in Six-Day War.

1968 Sadaam Hussein assumes power in Iraq as leader of Baath Party.

1970s-1980s *Oil, terrorism raise U.S. stakes in Arab lands.*

1973 Saudi Arabia leads oil embargo against U.S. by Organization of Petroleum Exporting Countries (OPEC).

1981 Egyptian President Anwar el-Sadat assassinated; new president, Hosni Mubarak, institutes rule by decree that continues to present day.

1990s *U.S. role in Iraq grows after Iraq's defeat in Gulf War; radical Islamist movements advance.*

1990-1991 Iraq's Hussein invades Kuwait; U.S. leads United Nations coalition in Gulf War to force withdrawal, but President George Bush, the current president's father, decides not to seek Hussein's ouster.

1992 Algerian military cancels legislative elections to forestall victory by radical Islamic Salvation Front, touching off protracted civil war.

1996 With King Fahd ailing, Crown Prince Abdullah gains authority in Saudi Arabia; he later pushes for reforms but faces opposition from other members of royal family.

1999 Jordan's King Hussein, key U.S. ally, dies; his son, Abdullah, succeeds him, continues pro-U.S. policies while promoting limited political reform.

2000-Present *Democracy makes limited gains in region; U.S. promotes democracy after ousting Iraq's Hussein.*

2000 Syrian President Hafez al-Assad dies, succeeded by his son, Bashar, who adopts, then backs off from, limited reforms.

2001 Terrorist attacks against U.S. by Osama bin Laden's al-Qaeda leave nearly 3,000 dead; President Bush promises war against global terror.

2002 Bahrain holds first parliamentary elections in 30 years . . . Parliamentary elections in Morocco . . . Arab report criticizes "freedom deficit" in Arab world.

2003 U.S.-led invasion ousts Hussein in Iraq . . . Bush vows transition to democracy, promotes democracy for all Middle East on Nov. 6 . . . Gamal Mubarak, president's son, pushes limited reforms in Egypt.

2004 Democratic elections planned in many Arab states; Saudi Arabia eyes balloting for municipal councils . . . U.S. plans for handoff to Iraqi authorities by June 30 roiled by dispute over timing of elections. . . . Thousands of Shiites march through Baghdad and other major cities on Jan. 19, demanding direct elections to choose a new government. . . . U.N. Secretary-General Kofi Annan announces on Jan. 27 he will send a fact-finding mission to determine whether early elections are feasible.

region. Islam reached Central Asia and the South Caucasus Mountains in the eighth century and spread to India and Indonesia in the 12th and 13th centuries, largely via Muslim traders and explorers.

Arab leaders exercised a tolerant but absolutist rule over their empire. Democratic governance was largely non-existent. Although the empire collapsed in the 15th century, Arabs have remained the principal power in the Middle East well into the modern era.

Pre-imperial Arab society had been organized around tribal allegiances, with little central authority or government and no common legal system. Most Arabs were nomadic shepherds, tending herds of goats, sheep or camels. All males were expected to be warriors, and competition over scarce resources often led to conflict between various tribal groups. Despite their differences, most Mideast tribes shared Arabic as a common language, and overland trade routes required inter-tribal cooperation and interaction.

The emergence of Islam ("surrender" in Arabic), a new monotheistic religion, on the Arabian Peninsula in 622 A.D. heralded the beginning of the transformation of the Arabs from desert nomads to a world power. Established by an Arab merchant known only as Muhammad, Islam provided a framework for running early Arabian society. The *Koran* — Islam's holy book and a record of God's revelations to Muhammad — provided rules for business contracts, marriages, inheritance and other societal institutions.

Under Muhammad's spiritual and military leadership, early Arab-Islamic society rose to prominence in Arabia, gaining control of religious and trade centers like Mecca and Medina. Muhammad exercised supreme authority over his nascent empire.

Following Muhammad's death in 632 A.D., two factions struggled for control of Arab-Islamic society, producing a schism in Islam. Sunni Arabs believed that a politically selected successor, or caliph, should become ruler. Shiites, on the other hand, claimed that the direct descendents of Muhammad, called imams, were the legitimate rulers of Islam. Sunnis won the power struggle, and the secular caliphs dominated the Arab empire until the 16th century, with Shiite imams wielding only negligible power.

By the middle of the eighth century, the caliphs ruled from Spain to the Indian subcontinent. In theory, a central Arab ruler governed outlying territories with absolute secular and Islamic authority. In practice, the size and breadth of the sprawling empire made direct governance difficult, so Arab rulers often left local administrative and governmental structures intact. Nonetheless, occasional uprisings produced breakaway caliphates in places like North Africa and Egypt.

During the heyday of the Arab-Islamic empire — generally from the eighth to the 10th centuries — poetry, agriculture, trade and intellectual pursuits flourished. Arab scholars made valuable contributions to trigonometry, algebra and philosophy. Religious scholars developed the five pillars of Islam, a framework of prayers and rituals that formed a common and universal religious experience for Arabs.

By the standards of its day, the Islamic empire showed remarkable religious tolerance. Other monotheistic faiths like Christianity or Judaism were protected under the *Koran*. While early caliphs discriminated against non-Arab Muslim converts, later rulers universalized Islam and granted all Muslims equal rights.

Eventually, the increasingly diverse Arab empire proved difficult to govern with only the *Koran* for guidance. Arab leaders and intellectuals developed Sharia, a "legal system that would recognize the requirements of imperial administration and the value of local customs while remaining true to the concept of a community guided by divine [Islamic] revelation," writes William Cleveland, in his book, *A History of the Modern Middle East*. Sharia allowed Islamic officials to interpret Islamic principles to mediate situations not explicitly covered by the *Koran*.

By the 11th century, the central power of the Arab caliphate in Baghdad began to wane. Turkish nomads from Asia — who had converted to Islam — carved out large dynasties of their own within the Arab empire, previewing the coming Ottoman Empire. European crusaders invaded Arab lands and maintained a tenuous occupation of some Arab territory for 200 years. Ultimately, though, the crusades had minimal impact on the Middle East.[18]

Later foreign invasions spelled the end of the Arab empire. In the 13th century, Mongol conquerors from Asia sacked Baghdad and killed the caliph, ending 500 years of Arab imperial rule. And, at the beginning of the 15th century, the armies of Timur Lang (Tamerlane) swept over the empire, splintering it into several, smaller and weakened dynasties.

Women Benefit From Top-Down Reforms

Women's groups are working in many Arab countries to change what an Arab development group describes as a "glaring deficit in women's empowerment" in the region. But recent advances in voting rights and family law in some countries amount to "top-down" reforms pushed by progressive-minded leaders rather than victories for grass-roots women's movements, experts say.

Qatar and Bahrain recently extended the right to vote for women, thanks to changes pushed by the ruling emirs in the tiny Persian Gulf states. Jordan and Morocco have recently given women limited rights to divorce at the behest of their ruling monarchs: King Abdullah II in Jordan and Mohamed VI in Morocco.

Egypt similarly enacted a "personal status" law in 2000 giving women the right to divorce if they relinquish financial rights. Women's associations "indirectly contributed" to passage of the law, according to a 2002 human rights report by the Arab Fund for Economic and Social Development, but the reform ultimately "was decided by the political powers."[1]

"Most of the progress in women's rights has come from progressive-minded rulers or rulers who want to be considered progressive and have tried to impose top-down reforms on society," says Amy Hawthorne, an expert on Mideast politics at the Carnegie Endowment for International Peace in Washington.

Arab countries rank below every other world region except sub-Saharan Africa on a "gender-empowerment measure," according to the Arab human rights report. The statistical measure — created by the United Nations Development Program — combines women's per capita income and the percentages of professional and technical positions and parliamentary seats held by women.[2]

"Women have a lower social and political status" in Arab countries compared to the rest of the world, Hawthorne says. But she also notes that women's status "varies considerably" through the region. She notes that women have had the right to vote in most Arab countries for some time — even if elections in many of those countries are blatantly undemocratic.

Diane Singerman, a professor of political studies at American University in Washington, also says that women are not subjected to second-class status throughout the Arab world. Women's illiteracy is high because education is not encouraged for women, she says, and unemployment is high — especially among educated women.

On the other hand, "there are a lot of very high-powered, very serious professional women," Singerman says. "In many cases, when women do well, they're not discriminated against in ways that are common" in the United States.

Islamic groups inhibit advances for women's rights. Moroccan women's groups mounted a demonstration with some 800,000 marchers in the capital city of Rabat in March 2000 in support of the proposed divorce law. But on the same day, some 2 million people took to the streets of Casablanca, warning that the proposal was a

Ottoman Empire

Beginning in the 15th century, Ottoman Turks established a new empire that encompassed almost all of the Arabic-speaking lands in the Middle East.* But Ottoman imperial rule failed under external pressure from the rising European powers, and after World War I the Middle East fell under European control. Following World War II, the region struggled to shed the yoke of European dominance and adopt independent governments, even as new concepts of Arab identity emerged.

By the late 17th century, the sultans — supreme monarchs of the Ottoman Empire — ruled lands that stretched from Hungary in Europe to Algiers in North Africa to Baghdad in the Middle East. The empire was an agrarian, absolutist monarchy, with a strong bureaucracy of educated ruling elites. The sultans implemented Sharia throughout the empire and conferred with a counsel of advisers on policy issues.[19]

The Ottomans employed a flexible system of imperial governance — similar to earlier Arab empires — that allowed local authorities to retain traditional customs, so long as they supplied adequate tax revenue to the Ottoman rulers. The Ottomans also continued Arab traditions of religious tolerance, granting non-

---

* The Ottomans were Turks who organized under Osman I, a tribal chieftain who lived from 1290-1326.

threat to Islam. Religious conservatives relented only after the king's intervention.[3]

Islamist-minded legislators led the successful opposition to granting women the right to vote in Kuwait in 1999. The strict school of Islam known as Wahhabism serves as the basis for a host of restrictions on women in Saudi Arabia — such as a ban on driving.

Egypt passed its new divorce law, however, after women's groups claimed the *Koran* itself approved dissolving a marriage if a woman gave up financial rights created by the marital contract. "What's happening throughout the area is that women and other people in the region are saying that Islam may say something else," Singerman says. "It's a revisionist history of the record instead of a patriarchal interpretation."

Improving the status of women is "a critical aspect of human freedom," according to the Arab human rights report.[4]

Getty Images/Salah Malkawi

A veiled Jordanian woman casts her ballot. Women have limited voting rights in the Arab world. Bahrain became the first of the Persian Gulf states to allow women to vote in 2002. Kuwait's parliament nullified a decree by the ruling emir in 1999 that would have allowed women to vote.

But Hawthorne cautions against assuming that granting women political rights will necessarily lead to political change. Some of the countries with broadest rights for women — for example, Syria — are also among the most autocratic of Arab states, she says.

"In the long run, any country that is going through a genuine process of democratization needs to include the empowerment of women," Hawthorne says. "But the addition of women won't necessarily result [right away] in increased democratization."

---

[1] United Nations Development Program/Arab Fund for Economic and Social Development Report, "Arab Human Development Report 2002," p. 117.

[2] *Ibid.*, p. 28.

[3] See Kent Davis-Packard, "Morocco Pushes Ahead," *The Christian Science Monitor*, Nov. 12, 2003, p. 15.

[4] "Arab Human Development Report," *loc. cit.*

Muslims significant civil rights and powers of self-governance.

In the 18th and 19th centuries, faced with the rise of European economic and military might, the Ottoman Empire entered a period of governmental reform and Europeanization. Ottoman officials who knew European languages and supported reforms were promoted, while old-style Ottoman institutions, like the *ulama* (religious scholars), increasingly were bypassed.

The first Ottoman constitution was adopted in 1876, providing for the election of government deputies and an appointed senate. But constitutional reforms proved short-lived, and the sultan reclaimed absolute authority in 1878.

But with central Ottoman authority weakened, several Islamic reformist movements emerged on the rural outskirts of the empire. In Arabia, the puritanical Wahhabi movement rose to power, advocating a return to strict interpretation of the *Koran* and adherence to Sharia.

European 'Mandates'

Elsewhere, intellectuals and scholars called for an Arab cultural renaissance, which reinvigorated the Arabic language and Arab identity, producing a kind of proto-Arab nationalism. And in 1916, an Arab insurrection — supported by the British — founded a short-lived Arab kingdom centered in Damascus.

Although the Ottomans reinstated a constitution in 1908, World War I doomed the empire. The victorious Allies partitioned the empire — which had been allied with Germany — into European-controlled "mandates." Britain maintained control of Egypt — which it had held since 1914 — and gained control over Iraq, Palestine and Transjordan (later called Jordan). France assumed control of Syria.

Under international agreement, Britain and France were expected to guide the Arab mandates toward self-governance. In actuality, the mandates allowed the British and French to protect their interests in the Middle East through the end of World War II.[20]

Not surprisingly, the Arabs chafed under the mandates, and many grew to distrust European-imposed political reforms. In Egypt, the Wafd — a political group opposed to British rule — established a secularist parliamentary constitution in 1924. But continued British influence over Wafd governments spawned popular opposition groups, most notably the fundamentalist Muslim Brotherhood, which advocated a return to an Islamic Egyptian state.

Nominally, Iraq achieved early independence in 1932, with a constitutional monarchy and bicameral legislature, as Britain had little interest in governing Iraq's volatile population of Sunnis, Shiites and ethnic Kurds. But Iraqi nationalists battled British-backed governments until 1958, when they succeeded in evicting the monarch.

Transjordan achieved independence in 1946, although the constitutional monarchy owed much of its authority to British support. In Syria, the French retained almost total control over the government until 1946, despite attempts by the Syrians to form a popular government.

Meanwhile, in Arabia — an area outside of European interest — a strong Islamic government took root in the wake of the Ottoman Empire. The Arabian tribal chief Abd al-Aziz ibn Saud, in an alliance with the Wahhabis, founded the kingdom of Saudi Arabia. Saud gained control of key Islamic religious sites, like Mecca and Medina and instituted strict Sharia law.

Some historians say the period of British and French control in the Middle East marked a high point for Arab democracy. "The Anglo-French domination also gave the Middle East an interlude of liberal economy and political freedom. The freedom was always limited and sometimes suspended but . . . it was on the whole more extensive than anything experienced before or after," writes noted historian Bernard Lewis, in his book, *The Middle East*.[21]

But other historians say Anglo-French domination merely installed a new class of ruling elites. "The same elite that had enjoyed power and prestige before 1914 — the European-educated landed and professional classes in Egypt and the traditional notables in Syria, Lebanon and Palestine — continued to exercise their privileges during the 1920s and 1930s," Cleveland writes.[22]

With the twin failures of Ottoman imperialism and European-backed governments in the Middle East, Arabs increasingly looked to nationalism and Islamism as political organizing principles.

Arab Nationalism

After World War II, the creation of Israel threw much of the Middle East into turmoil. Arab efforts to dislodge the Jewish state failed, and military coups replaced many of the defeated Arab governments. Although Arab military leaders espoused reform and pan-Arabism in the 1960s and '70s, they steadily moved toward authoritarianism. Meanwhile, the Cold War extended U.S. influence throughout the Middle East, and the Arabian oil boom cemented U.S. interests in the region. By the new millennium, Arab governments had stymied democratic reform, and radical Islamic groups increasingly targeted the United States for supporting the autocratic regimes.

After the Nazi Holocaust killed millions of Jews in World War II, international support for a Jewish state rose dramatically, culminating with Israel declaring its independence in 1948. Members of the Arab League — a federation of Arab states including Syria, Egypt and Jordan — promptly declared war on the new state.

Following a nine-month war, Arab forces were defeated, and hundreds of thousands of Arabs fled or were forced out of Palestine. By 1950, more than 960,000 Palestinians were refugees.[23] The Arab League later sponsored the Palestine Liberation Organization (PLO), a resistance group that battled Israel and became a Palestinian government in exile.

After the 1948 war, many post-imperial Arab governments were swept away by military regimes promising democratic and social reforms. But the new governments reverted to authoritarianism, which some historians attribute to a legacy of authoritarian rule under the European mandates.[24]

In Egypt, a military coup in 1952 led by Col. Gamal Abdel Nasser ousted the old Wafd government and brought some constitutional reforms, including an elected legislature. But Nasser quickly consolidated power and undermined democratic measures by adopting broad presidential powers.

Nasser also championed the cause of pan-Arab unity, hoping to unite all the Arab countries under a single Egyptian-Arab authority. Nasser achieved some success: Egypt and Syria united as a single nation for a short while, and strong Arab alliances formed in opposition to Israel. But the crushing defeat of Egypt (along with Syria and Jordan) by Israel in 1967 — during the so-called Six-Day War — damaged Nasser's reputation and derailed his hopes for pan-Arabism.

Nasser's successor, Sadat, renewed efforts to liberalize Egyptian politics. But Sadat's Western-style reforms failed to satisfy calls for democratic reform. Resistance groups, including the Muslim Brotherhood, called for a return to the successful theocratic governments of the past, and Muslim dissidents assassinated Sadat in 1981. Hosni Mubarak's autocratic government, which assumed power after Sadat's death, continued to control the electoral process and brutally suppress rising Islamic dissent.

In other Arab nations, radical nationalist movements — more focused on ejecting Western-influenced leaders and social reform than in democratization — installed similarly autocratic regimes. A series of military coups in Syria eventually empowered the radical Baath Party, which advocated social reform, pan-Arab unity and nationalism. But Baathist rule brought little reform, prompting militant Islamic groups to battle with the government for power throughout the 1980s and '90s.

Baathist radicals — under Hussein's leadership — assumed power in Iraq in 1968. Hussein's regime produced some social reforms, like increased literacy, but opposition and dissent were violently snuffed out.

Democratic reforms also remained elusive in Arab countries that avoided military insurrection. Jordan's King Hussein assumed power in 1953 and ruled over a monarchy until his death in 1999 — a longevity often attributed to Western support. In Lebanon — a state carved out of Syria by the French — democratic governance was pushed aside by Syrian occupation in 1976.

Muslims and Freedom

The vast majority of people in Muslim-majority nations are only "partly free" or "not free," according to Freedom House.

Freedom Status in Muslim-Majority Nations

Free Population	Partly Free Population	Not Free Population
20.4 million	577.1 million	532.4 million

Source: CIA Factbook, www.islamicpopulations.com; Freedom House.

And in Algeria's 1991 free elections, voters overwhelmingly chose an Islamic government that vowed a return to Sharia. Military leaders quickly halted the elections, sparking a civil war between radical fundamentalists and the government.

Many of the Arab autocracies received aid from the superpowers during the Cold War. The U.S. provided billions of dollars in military and economic assistance to Israel, Jordan and Iran, while the Soviets armed Syria, Egypt and Iraq. But continued U.S. support for Israel after the Cold War further inflamed anti-American Arab sentiment, even though since 1979 Egypt has been the second-largest recipient of U.S. foreign aid, after President Jimmy Carter brokered the Egypt-Israeli "Camp David" peace accord the year before.[25]

On the Arabian peninsula, the discovery in the early 20th century of vast oil reserves transformed the desert monarchies into world powers. By 1973, Saudi Arabia was producing 13 percent of the world's crude oil, and surging oil wealth strengthened Arabian monarchs' grip on power, enabling them to sidestep democratic reforms.

The monarchies turned to petroleum-hungry Western powers for military protection, particularly the United States. When Hussein invaded the Kuwaiti monarchy in 1990 and threatened Saudi oil fields, a U.S.-led coalition destroyed Iraq's army.[26]

After the Persian Gulf War, popular resistance to the monarchies grew. Radical Islamic groups objected to Western military and social influence in Saudi Arabia — home of Islam's holiest cities and shrines — and secular interests pushed for more democracy. In Egypt, radicals battled to overthrow the government, while moderates called for democratic reforms.

A demonstrator outside No. 10 Downing Street in London, the official residence of British Prime Minister Tony Blair, protests Egypt's arrests, torture and detentions of Islamic activists, scholars and civilians. Egypt's ruling National Democratic Party recently has proposed some democratic reforms, but not competitive presidential elections.

In the 1990s, America's ties to autocratic regimes and its continued support for Israel led militant Islamic radicals to launch terrorist attacks against American targets. In 1993, Islamic terrorists bombed New York's World Trade Center, killing six and injuring 1,000. And in 1998, hundreds were killed — including 12 Americans — when U.S. embassies in Kenya and Tanzania were bombed by terrorists linked to the al-Qaeda Islamic terrorist organization run by Saudi dissident Osama bin Laden.

Calls for Reform

In response to the murders of nearly 3,000 people in the Sept. 11 terrorist attacks, many Arab governments helped the United States hunt down the bin Laden followers who had helped put the plan to hijack four airliners into action.[27] Under mounting internal and external pressure, some Arab governments also unveiled new democratization efforts, but widespread reform faltered. Israeli-American ties continued to undermine Arab support for U.S. policies in the Middle East, even though the United States and Britain overthrew the murderously repressive Hussein and tried to establish democracy in Iraq.

The Arab world's initial reaction to the Sept. 11 attacks was mixed. Some news reports showed Arabs celebrating in the Palestinian territories. But heads of Arab governments unanimously condemned the carnage.[28]

American officials pressured Arab governments to crack down on Islamic extremists, and Arab states formerly antagonistic to the U.S. — including Syria, Libya and Sudan — provided intelligence and assistance to the Americans. In Yemen, U.S. forces assassinated a suspected al-Qaeda leader with the government's tacit approval.[29] Security forces in Saudi Arabia — the homeland of 15 of the 19 hijackers — began restricting the activities of Islamic militants.[30]

Some Arab liberals renewed calls for electoral reform, suggesting that political oppression might have been partly responsible for inspiring the hijackers.[31] Even some members of the Arab ruling elite said democratic reforms could curtail extremism. "If people speak more freely and get more involved in the political process, you can really contain them and make them part of the process," said Saudi Prince Walid bin Talal.[32]

A combination of internal dissent and U.S. pressure inspired some Arab democratization efforts after Sept. 11. Reformers gained some ground in Egypt when Mubarak tentatively backed a democratization package put forward by his son, Gamal. Under pressure from the United States, Egypt also freed and later acquitted Egyptian-American democracy advocate Ibrahim, who had been imprisoned by Mubarak's government, some say in an effort to intimidate critics.

On the Arabian Peninsula, some of the monarchies took tentative steps toward electoral governance. Saudi Arabian officials promised municipal elections but did not set a firm date. In Bahrain, parliamentary elections in 2002 established strong support for opposition candidates, particularly Islamists. Qatar approved a constitution in 2003, opening the way for parliamentary elections later this year.

But other Arab states continue to struggle under the grip of authoritarian regimes. Bashar Assad has maintained strict control over Syria since the death of his father in 2000. Pro-democracy groups boycotted the 2002 elections convened by the military in Algeria.

Recent remarks by Jordan's King Abdullah II seem to represent a growing Arab interest in governmental reform. "We are at the beginning of a new stage in terms of democracy and freedom," said Abdullah at a September breakfast with human rights and democracy activists in Washington. "If we are successful, if we can get our act together, we can be an agent other Arabs can use."[33]

AT ISSUE

Should the United States increase pressure on Arab countries to democratize?

YES
Adrian Karatnycky
Counselor, Senior Scholar, Freedom House

Written for The CQ Researcher, January 2004

Over the last 30 years, nearly 50 countries have established democratic governments rooted in the rule of law. Today, countries that provide basic freedoms represent nearly half the world's 192 states. Democracies can be found on all continents, among all races and creeds. They include prosperous and expanding economies as well as poor countries. Yet not one is part of the Arab world.

There are compelling reasons to try to end this Arab exceptionalism and for the United States to press Arab regimes to change by supporting non-violent democratic civic power.

First, it is in the U.S.'s national security interests to do so. It is no coincidence that much global terrorism originates in the least democratic part of the world. The absence of open discourse means ill-informed and misinformed populations fall under the sway of the disinformation of anti-liberal ideas. As a result, extremists prosper. In short, the war on terrorism cannot be won without waging a war of ideas against the extremist ideologies that fuel terror.

Second, Arabs are the main victims of tyrannical regimes and extremist movements, which wreak mayhem on ordinary people and suppress their basic rights. This is why recent polling data show that Arabs strongly favor government elected by and accountable to the people.

Opponents of a U.S. role in promoting democracy in the Arab world suggest that we are hated in that region and our pressure would be counterproductive. Yet, anti-Americanism is rampant because official media in Arab autocracies preach anti-U.S. messages. We are also disliked because over the years, the United States has been indifferent to the massive violations of the basic rights of Arabs.

Others argue that pressing for democracy would only destabilize the Arab world and empower Islamist extremists. Yet the opening of formerly closed societies to genuine freedom of the press, civic activism and electoral competition has served to moderate Islamist political movements — as last year's elections in Turkey showed.

No one says the promotion of democracy in the Arab world will be easy. It will require working with the region's democratic voices to develop a strong latticework of free and diverse media, political parties, civic organizations and think tanks.

But if we fail to exert constructive pressure, we will only help perpetuate the very political environments that produce the fanatics who threaten our well-being today.

NO
James Zogby
President, Arab American Institute

Written for The CQ Researcher, January 2004

Sadly, given our current foreign policy in the Middle East, I do not believe the United States can, at this time, make a meaningful and positive contribution to democratic transformation in the Arab world.

Positive changes are occurring in many Arab countries, largely in response to the evolving circumstances in those countries and independent of U.S. involvement. In some instances, the United States has served as an impediment to this process: As public opinion has turned against the United States, some Arab governments have become more defensive and resistive to democratic change.

The United States lacks credibility and legitimacy when it claims to support democracy and human rights. While Arabs view U.S. values — democracy, freedom and education — positively, they view U.S. Middle East policy so negatively that overall attitudes toward the United States drop into the single digits.

In other words, Arabs like our values, but do not believe that we have their best interests at heart, especially in Palestine — the central, defining issue of Arab attitudes. We are viewed as biased toward Israel and insensitive to Palestinians' needs and rights. This harms not only our overall standing in the region but also our friends' standings and our ability to function as a partner in the Arab world.

For too long, we have not appreciated Arab history. The current state of affairs for the Arab people is the culmination of more than 100 years of a loss of control. During the past century, some Arab areas were colonized by the West. Others were victims of imperial powers that occupied the region, created states out of whole cloth and implanted regimes.

The neo-conservative "idealism" that sees us establishing democracy in this region is, at best, counterproductive, and, at worst, damaging. Our unilateral occupation of Iraq and our behavior vis-à-vis the Palestinians has us viewed today as a continuation of the Western machinations of the last century. If we fail to understand this, we put ourselves at great risk.

If the United States were to do an about-face on Palestine — for example, by directly and dramatically challenging Israeli expansion on the West Bank — our relationship with the region would improve dramatically. It would significantly contribute to our peacemaking ability, as well as our ability to play a more constructive role as an agent for change in the region.

Some experts say Arab autocrats use Mideast resentment about U.S. support for Israel as a way to divert anger toward the slow rate of reform in their own countries. "The continuing conflict between Israel and Palestine gives [autocratic] regimes an excuse to deflect people's attention away from their own shortcomings," the Carnegie Endowment's Carothers says.

Others say Arab feelings of frustration over the Palestinian issue are more than an excuse. "People see the issue of Palestine as symbolic of their lives," says Zogby, of the Arab American Institute. "It's ever-present, it's very real and it's deeply felt. It's not a game that's being played on them."

The 2003 U.S.-led military campaign to depose Hussein thrust the issue of Arab democracy into the spotlight. While arguing the case for war at the United Nations in September 2002, President Bush said, "Liberty for the Iraqi people is a great moral cause and a great strategic goal." And after a quick and decisive military victory, the U.S. occupying authority established a 25-member Iraqi governing council and organized municipal elections in many Iraqi cities and towns.

But conflict between Iraq's majority-Shiite population and the minority Sunnis has marred efforts to form a popular government. A continued insurgency, thought to be the work of Baathist loyalists, has killed hundreds of American soldiers and further hindered U.S. efforts to democratize Iraq.

Nonetheless, President Bush in his November speech called for more democracy in the Middle East, noting that past U.S. efforts to turn a blind eye to the lack of freedom in the Middle East has made neither America nor the Middle East safer.[34]

But many Arab commentators frostily rejected Bush's calls for reform. "The fundamental problem remains that of Palestine and the scandalous U.S. bias in favor of Israel and against the Arabs, their interests and their aspirations," wrote Lebanese columnist Sahar Baasiri.[35]

CURRENT SITUATION

Casting Ballots

Sometime this year, Saudi Arabia will give its people their first opportunity to elect government officials in four decades. But the balloting will be for only half the nation's municipal councils — which have only limited power anyway.

"It's very symbolic," says Georgetown's Seznec. "It doesn't mean anything, especially in terms of democratization per se."

Still, the planned elections — not yet scheduled but likely to be held in the fall — represent a concession by the ruling House of Saud to the need for some form of public participation in a country beset by economic ills and shaken by violent protests, including a deadly terrorist bombing in Riyadh that left 17 people dead in November.

"There is a strong logic to expanding participation for these ruling families," says Michael Herb, an assistant professor of political science at Georgia State University. "It allows them to hear what their people actually have to say, to show a more liberal face to the outside world and to let off steam — all without the risk of actually losing power."

The Saudi elections — the first since similar balloting in the 1950s and '60s — come as more Arab states are allowing their citizens to vote for government officials. As in Saudi Arabia, however, the elections fall far short of full democracy. Women are barred from voting in most countries, political parties often are restricted or prohibited and the media are either government-controlled or tightly regulated.

As President Bush noted in his November speech, some of the strongest stirrings of democracy are in the smallest Arab states: the Persian Gulf emirates of Kuwait, Bahrain, Oman and Qatar. But Bush did not mention the limitations. In Kuwait, for example, voting for the national assembly is limited to less than one-sixth of the population, and political parties are banned. Western-style liberals fared badly in the most recent parliamentary elections in June 2003, winning only three of 50 seats.

Elsewhere, Bahrain became the first of the Gulf states to allow women to vote, but some opposition groups boycotted the 2002 parliamentary elections because of limits on the national assembly's power. As in Kuwait, Islamists led the balloting. Oman is now preparing for universal suffrage parliamentary elections in 2004 following balloting for an advisory council in October 2003. But Herb says that a ban on campaigning makes it impossible to evaluate the results. Qatar is also preparing for legislative elections sometime in 2004, but the constitution approved by voters in 2003 gives the parliament little power, he says.

Outside the Gulf, democracy is less advanced even when voting is allowed. Morocco and Jordan — two countries praised by Bush — held relatively free parliamentary elections in 2002 and 2003, respectively. But King Mohammed VI in Morocco and Jordan's Abdullah both have supreme power, including the right to dissolve parliament and appoint the prime minister and cabinet. Yemen has held free, universal-suffrage elections, but the elected House of Representatives has never exercised its power to initiate legislation.

In Tunisia, balloting for the presidency is highly orchestrated: President Zine el-Abidine Ben Ali claimed 99.4 percent of the vote in 1999 and won approval of a constitutional change in May 2003 to allow him to seek fourth and fifth five-year terms in 2004 and 2009. Syrian President Assad won 97 percent of the vote in a 2000 referendum after succeeding his father. In Algeria, the electoral process is viewed as highly flawed: All of the rivals to President Abdelaziz Bouteflika withdrew from the 1999 campaign, claiming fraud.

In other countries, elections are simply lacking. Libya's Muammar el-Qaddafi rules by decree, with no signs to date of following his recent moves out of international disgrace with an easing of his domestic powers. The seven ruling families of the United Arab Emirates choose a president and vice president every five years, with no popular elections or political parties. Lebanon holds elections, but Syria effectively controls the government after more than a decade of military occupation.

Democracy also lags in the handful of Arab-minority African countries — all preponderantly Muslim — that belong to the Arab League. Sudan is ravaged by a civil war between the Arab minority in the north and the insurgent black minority in the south, while a secession movement by northern clans racks Somalia. Djibouti — the only Arab League country rated as "free" by Freedom House — held successful multiparty elections in January. A four-party opposition alliance won slightly more than one-third of the vote.

In Egypt, meanwhile, talk of reform is increasing, but the outcome remains uncertain. In a signed editorial, Ibrahim Nafie, editor in chief of the semi-official *Al-Ahram*, praises the ruling National Democratic Party for having taken "big steps" toward reform, but he cautions against moving too fast. Rights advocate Abu Saada notes that the reform package does not call for competitive presidential elections.

In Saudi Arabia as well, experts caution against expecting too much in terms of reform. Former *Washington*

Egyptian-American human rights activist Saad Eddin Ibrahim, a sociology professor at Cairo's American University, enters Egypt's highest court on Feb. 4, 2003, with his wife. After spending more than a year in jail, he was acquitted of tarnishing Egypt's image with his writings on democracy and human rights.

Post Mideast correspondent Thomas Lippman, author of a new book on Saudi Arabia, notes that the country's "basic law" — adopted in 1993 — locks in rule by the House of Saud.

"You can talk about the trappings of democracy, various democratic forms, ways in which certain forms of communication with the rulers might be structured to allow more public participation," Lippman says, "but you're not talking about democracy."[36]

Building Democracy?

The United States has what seems an unparalleled opportunity to advance democracy in the Arab world in Iraq, where an American administrator heads a U.S.-led military occupation in consultation with an Iraqi advisory council handpicked by the United States. But forging a stable government — much less a working democracy — is treacherous in a country with longstanding ethnic and religious factionalism and present-day anti-American insurgency.

Bush sees success as important, not only for domestic political reasons but also for the worldwide advance of democracy. "The establishment of a free Iraq at the heart of the Middle East," he said in his November speech, "will be a watershed event in the global democratic revolution."

As 2004 began, however, the administration found itself pressured by the leading cleric of Iraq's majority Shiite Muslims to allow direct elections sooner than envisioned under the U.S. timetable. The United States, citing the difficulties of holding elections, planned instead to hold caucuses around the country to select an interim legislature and executive that would assume responsibility for governing Iraq by June 30. But Grand Ayatollah Ali al-Sistani rejected the plan on Jan. 11, repeating demands he has made since November for direct elections before a U.S. transfer of power.

"The planned transitional assembly cannot represent the Iraqis in an ideal manner," Sistani said after meeting with a delegation of the U.S.-appointed governing council. Sistani described elections as "the ideal mechanism" and insisted balloting could be held in the near future "with an acceptable degree of credibility and transparency."[37]

During voting in Qatar last April 29, Qataris approved the gas-rich monarchy's first written constitution, paving the way for parliamentary elections later this year.

"It's interesting to see Islamic clerics giving the United States lessons in how to conduct democracy," says the Carnegie Endowment's Carothers. "It's funny to see them pushing for early elections and the United States resisting."

Carothers acknowledges that national elections in Iraq would present "huge logistical obstacles," given the lack of security and destruction of Iraqi infrastructure in the invasion. But the dispute is more than procedural. Iraq's 15 million Shiites comprise about 60 percent of the population, but they were politically disadvantaged under Hussein, a Sunni Muslim. The Shiites hope to make political gains with early elections, while the Sunnis and the ethnic Kurds in northern Iraq fear early voting will weaken the influence they currently have with the American-led occupation.

The timing of elections is one of several contentious questions that U.S. Administrator L. Paul Bremer III is grappling with while trying to meet the accelerated timetable for transferring power. One issue — what to do with former members of the ruling Baath Party — appeared in January to be moving toward resolution. The 18-member Governing Council adopted new guidelines that give lower-level party members a better chance to appeal their dismissals or to apply for pensions than under the U.S. "de-Baathification" procedures. American officials were quoted as approving the shift.[38]

The United States appears less content with developments so far on the issue of the Kurds' status in a new Iraq. The Kurds — a non-Arab ethnic group comprising about 17 percent of Iraq's population — were essentially autonomous in Hussein's final 12 years in office following Iraq's defeat in the first Gulf War. They want to maintain their autonomy — or, more ambitiously, gain independence. While the United States supports some form of self-rule, it fears a fragmented Iraq or a weak central government.[39]

Other difficult issues loom in the drafting of the constitution, notably the role of religion. Shiites are widely seen as religiously conservative, the Sunnis and Kurds more liberal. But fears of a religious theocracy appear to have been eased with a formula drawn up by the Governing Council that declares Iraq to be a majority-Muslim community that protects minority rights and in which Islamic law is one — but not the only — source of legislation.[40]

The elections dispute, meanwhile, forced Bremer to return to Washington on Jan. 16 for conferences on how to salvage the administration's timetable. With thousands of Iraqis rallying in the streets demanding prompt elections — the largest protest since the U.S. occupation of Iraq last March — Bremer told reporters that the United States was willing to consider changing the planned method for selecting the interim government.

The administration and the Governing Council also asked the United Nations on Jan. 19 to help broker an agreement with Sistani on transition plans. U.N. Secretary-General Kofi Annan said on Jan. 27 he would send a team to Baghdad to determine whether early elections are feasible.

OUTLOOK

Slow Process

Talk of democracy is spreading in the Arab world, but Arab leaders are resisting outside pressure and insisting on definitions and timetables of their own choosing. The result seems all but certain to be slower and less thoroughgoing change than sought by pro-democracy advocates in and outside the Arab world.

Arab ambivalence can be seen in the proceedings of a recent pro-democracy conference, hosted by Yemen and cosponsored by the European Union (EU) and the U.N. Development Program.[41] The January conference in the Yemeni capital of Sanaa drew 600 delegates from 40 countries, including government representatives and democracy activists from most Arab states.

The conference ended with adoption of a declaration embracing the major tenets of so-called Western-style democracy — from elective legislatures and independent judiciaries to fair-trial guarantees and protection of women's rights.

"Democracy is the choice of the modern age for all people of the world and the rescue ship for political regimes," Yemeni President Ali Abdulla Saleh said as he opened the conference.

But Amr Moussa, secretary-general of the Arab League, said democracy should be viewed "as a process, not a decision imposed by others," a point echoed by U.N. Secretary-General Annan. Democracy, Annan told the conference, "cannot be imposed from the outside."

Human rights advocates both in and outside the Arab world discern mounting political pressures for change from the social and economic gaps between Arab countries and the rest of the world. On a variety of socio-economic measures, Arab states lag behind developing countries in other parts of the world, as well as the United States and other industrialized nations.

Demographics add to the pressure. Population growth rates in all but one of the Arab League states exceed the worldwide average of 1.4 percent per year. Population increases can be "an engine of material development," notes the 2002 Arab human rights report, if other factors are conducive to economic growth — but a "force for immiserization" if not.[42]

Arab leaders say political changes are necessary to respond to the discontent bred by what others more bluntly describe as deteriorating socioeconomic conditions. "There is a great sense in the Arab world about the necessity of having a new social pact," the Arab League's Hitti says. "Democracy is part and parcel of this process."

Still, human rights advocates are generally cautious, at best, in predicting the pace of democratization. "I would be very surprised to see much genuine movement toward democracy in the next five years," says the Carnegie Endowment's Carothers. "The question is whether we can help foster a trend in the next five years. That would be a realistic goal."

Similarly, the Heritage Foundation's Phillips expects little change over the next few years.

Others are somewhat more optimistic. "You've got a little bit of a trend developing," Freedom House's Karatnycky says. He sees prospects for more liberalization in the gulf countries and some larger states, such as Jordan and Morocco. "There's more of a chance for a liberal trend than a retrenchment or some new dark age of anti-liberal ideologies or more repressive regimes," he concludes.

The University of Westminster's El-Affendi also sounds optimistic. "The undemocratic forces are a spent force," he says. "The desire for democracy is very widespread, and the disillusionment with undemocratic governments is at a very high level, and increasing at all times."

El-Affendi says support for democratization from the United States and the European Union is helpful. Others disagree. U.S. pressure, Hitti says, "might fire back." Zogby of the Arab American Institute says American influence has fallen because of increasingly unfavorable public opinion about America due to the invasion of Iraq, the stalemate in the Arab-Israeli peace process and the mistreatment of people of Muslim or Arab backgrounds in the U.S. war on terror.[43]

Apart from government policies, however, El-Affendi says broader global changes — including the Arab peoples' increased exposure to the world beyond — impel democratic advances in the long run.

"The trend is moving in this direction," he says. "It's now very difficult for any ruler in the Muslim world to just hope that he's going to stay in power forever without being responsive to the people. It's just not going to work."

NOTES

1. See Saad Eddin Ibrahim, "A Dissident Asks: Can Bush Turn Words Into Action?" *The Washington Post*, Nov. 23, 2003, p. A23. The article and other background can be found on the Web site of the Ibn Khaldun Center: www.democracy-egypt.org.
2. See "Flimsy on Facts," *Al Ahram Weekly*, Nov. 27, 2003 (http://weekly.ahram.org.eg). *Al Ahram Weekly* is an English-language version of the Arabic-language daily *Al Ahram*.
3. Freedom House, "Freedom in the World 2004" (www.freedomhouse.org).
4. United Nations Development Programme/Arab Fund for Economic and Social Development, "Arab Human Development Report 2002," p. 2.
5. For coverage, see David E. Sanger, "Bush Asks Lands in Mideast to Try Democratic Ways," *The New York Times*, Nov. 7, 2003, p. A1; Dana Milbank and Mike Allen, "Bush Urges Commitment to Transform Mideast," *The Washington Post*, Nov. 7, 2003, p. A1.
6. For background, see David Masci, "Rebuilding Iraq," *The CQ Researcher*, July 25, 2003, pp. 625-648 and David Masci, "Confronting Iraq," *The CQ Researcher*, Oct. 4, 2002, pp. 793-816.
7. Quoted in Glenn Frankel, "Egypt Muzzles Calls for Democracy," *The Washington Post*, Jan. 6, 2004, p. A1.
8. United Nations Development Programme, *op. cit.*, p. 8.
9. *Ibid.*, p. 9.
10. Country profile in "Freedom in the World 2003," www.freedomhouse.org.
11. United Nations Development Programme, *op. cit.*, pp. 4-6.
12. Michael Ross, "Does Oil Hinder Democracy?" *World Politics*, Vol. 53 (April 2001), pp. 336-337.
13. United Nations Development Programme, *op. cit.*, p. 4.
14. For background, see David Masci, "Prospects for Middle East Peace," *The CQ Researcher*, Aug. 30, 2002, pp. 673-696, and David Masci, "Israel at 50," *The CQ Researcher*, March 6, 1998, pp. 193-215.
15. See Glenn Kessler and Robin Wright, "Realities Overtake Arab Democracy Drive," *The Washington Post*, Dec. 3, 2003, p. A22.
16. See Daniel Brumberg, "Bush Policy or Bush Philosophy," *The Washington Post*, Nov. 16, 2003, p. B3.
17. Background drawn from William Cleveland, *A History of the Modern Middle East* (2000) and Albert Hourani, *A History of the Arab Peoples* (1992).
18. Cleveland, *op. cit.*, p. 36.
19. Bernard Lewis, *The Middle East* (1995), p. 147.
20. Hourani, *op. cit.*, pp. 315-323.
21. Lewis, *op. cit.*, p. 355.
22. Cleveland, *op. cit.*, p. 170.
23. Cleveland, *op. cit.*, p. 261.
24. Shibley Telhami, *The Stakes* (2004), p. 161.
25. For background, see Mary H. Cooper, "Foreign Aid After Sept. 11," *The CQ Researcher*, April 26, 2002, pp. 361-392, and Masci, "Prospects for Mideast Peace," *op. cit.*
26. For background, see Mary H. Cooper, "Oil Diplomacy," *The CQ Researcher*, Jan. 24, 2003, pp. 49-62.
27. For background, see David Masci and Kenneth Jost, "War on Terrorism," *The CQ Researcher*, Oct. 12, 2001, pp. 817-848.
28. See Mary H. Cooper, "Hating America," *The CQ Researcher*, Nov. 23 2001, pp. 969-992.
29. David Johnston and David Sanger, "Fatal Strike in Yemen Was Based on Rules Set Out by Bush," *The New York Times*, Nov. 6, 2002, p. A16.
30. Douglas Jehl, "Holy War Lured Saudis As Rulers Looked Away," *The New York Times*, Dec. 27, 2001, p. A1.
31. *Ibid.*
32. Douglas Jehl, "A Saudi Prince With an Unconventional Idea: Elections," *The New York Times*, Nov. 28, 2001, p. A3.
33. Jackson Diehl, "Jordan's Democracy Option," *The Washington Post*, Sept. 21, 2003, p. B7.

34. Sanger, *op. cit.*

35. Neil MacFarquhar, "Mideast View: Bush Spoke More to U.S. Than to Us," *The New York Times*, Nov. 8, 2003, p. A9.

36. See Thomas W. Lippman, *Inside the Mirage: America's Fragile Partnership with Saudi Arabia* (2004).

37. Quoted in Daniel Williams, "Top Shiite Cleric Hardens Call for Early Iraqi Vote," *The Washington Post*, Jan. 12, 2004, p. A12. See also Edward Wong, "Direct Election of Iraq Assembly Pushed by Cleric," *The New York Times*, Jan. 12, 2004, p. A1; Steven R. Weisman, "Bush Team Revising Planning for Iraqi Self-Rule," *The New York Times*, Jan. 13, 2004, p. A1.

38. See Pamela Constable, "Iraqis Revise Policy on Ex-Baath Members," *The Washington Post*, Jan. 12, 2004, p. A12.

39. Robin Wright, "Kurds' Wariness Frustrates U.S. Efforts," *The Washington Post*, Jan. 9, 2004, p. A13.

40. *Ibid.*

41. Account drawn from John R. Bradley, "Arab Leaders See Democracy Ascendant," *The Washington Times*, Jan. 13, 2004, p. A13. A summary of the conference declaration can be found on the Ibn Khaldun Center's Web site: www.democracy-egypt.org.eg.

42. United Nations Development Programme, *op. cit.*, pp. 37-38.

43. For background, see Kenneth Jost, "Civil Liberties Debates," *The CQ Researcher*, Oct. 24, 2003, pp. 893-916.

BIBLIOGRAPHY

Books

Brynen, Rex, Baghat Kornay and Paul Noble, *Political Liberalization and Democratization in the Arab World: Theoretical Perspectives* (Vol. 1), Lynne Rienner, 1996; Brynen, Rex, Baghat Kornay and Paul Noble, *Political Liberalization and Democratization in the Arab World: Comparative Experiences* (Vol. 2), Lynne Rienner, 1998.

Various experts provide an overview of democratization in the region (vol. 1) and the status of democratization in 10 specific countries (vol. 2). Brynen and Noble are McGill University professors; Kornay is now at the American University in Cairo.

Cleveland, William L., *A History of the Modern Middle East* (2d ed.), Westview Press, 2000 (1st edition, 1994).

A professor of Arab political history at Simon Fraser University in Vancouver traces the history of the Middle East, from the rise of Islam through the radical Islamist movements.

Diamond, Larry, Marc F. Plattner and Daniel Brumberg (eds.), *Islam and Democracy in the Middle East*, Johns Hopkins University Press, 2003.

An anthology of *Journal of Democracy* articles by U.S. and Middle Eastern experts examines the status of democratization in the Mideast and the relationship between Islam and democracy.

Esposito, John L., and John O. Voll, *Islam and Democracy*, Oxford University Press, 1996.

The director (Esposito) and assistant director (Voll) of Georgetown University's Center for Muslim-Christian Understanding examine the "heritage and global context" of Islam and democracy, along with the status of democratization in major Islamic countries.

Humphreys, R. Stephen, *Between Memory and Desire: The Middle East in a Troubled Age*, University of California Press, 1999.

A professor of Islamic and Middle Eastern history at the University of California, Santa Barbara, focuses on four basic conditions in the Middle East: economic stagnation, weakness in the international arena, political instability and ideological confusion.

Lewis, Bernard, *What Went Wrong? Western Impact and Middle Eastern Response*, Oxford University Press, 2002 (reissued by Perennial, 2003, with subtitle *The Clash Between Islam and Modernity in the Middle East*).

A distinguished U.S. historian provides a trenchant critique of the Islamic world's failure to modernize. For a comprehensive history of the region, see *The Middle East: A Brief History of the Last 2,000 Years* (Touchstone, 1995).

Magnarella, Paul J. (ed.), *Middle East and North Africa: Governance, Democratization, Human Rights*, Ashgate, 1999.

Experts examine the status of democratization in major Arab countries, Turkey, Israel and the West Bank and

Gaza Strip. Magnarella is a professor of anthropology at the University of Florida.

Telhami, Shelby, *The Stakes: America and the Middle East — The Consequences of Power and the Choice for Peace*, Westview Press, 2002.
A professor of government at the University of Maryland and a senior fellow at the Brookings Institution examines public opinion in the Middle East toward the United States and U.S. policy in the Middle East.

Reports and Studies

Ottaway, Marina, *et al.*, "Democratic Mirage in the Middle East," Carnegie Endowment for International Peace, October 2002.
A policy brief forecasts a "long, hard, and slow" path to democratization in the Middle East.

United Nations Development Programme, Arab Fund for Economic and Social Development, "Arab Human Development Report 2002: Creating Opportunities for Future Generations," 2002.

Human development in Arab countries is hampered by "deficits in popular freedoms and in the quality of Arab governance institutions," say the authors. A second report, "Arab Human Development Report 2003: Building a Knowledge Society," focuses on education, communication and technology. Available at www.un.org/publications or www.miftah.org.

Articles

Anderson, Lisa, "Arab Democracy: Dismal Prospects," *World Policy Journal*, Vol. 18, No. 3 (fall 2001), p. 53.
The dean of Columbia University's School of International and Public Affairs critically examines prospects for Arab democracy. For a more favorable assessment by the Arab League's representative to the U.S., see Hussein A. Hassouna, "Arab Democracy: The Hope," *ibid.*, p. 47.

For More Information

Arab American Institute, 1600 K St. N.W., Suite 601, Washington, DC 20006; (202) 429-9210; www.aaiusa.org.

Arab Information Center/Arab League, 1100 17th St., N.W., Washington, DC 20036; (202) 265-3210; www.arableagueonline.org.

Carnegie Endowment for International Peace, 1779 Massachusetts Ave. N.W., Washington DC 20036-2103; (202) 483-7600; www.ceip.org.

Center for the Study of Islam and Democracy, 1050 Connecticut Ave., N.W., Suite 1000, Washington, DC 20036; (202) 772-2022; www.islam-democracy.org.

Freedom House, 120 Wall St., 26th floor, New York, NY 10005; (212) 514-8040; www.freedomhouse.org.

Heritage Foundation, 214 Massachusetts Ave., N.W., Washington, DC 20002-4999; (202) 546-4400; www.heritage.org.

Human Rights Watch, 350 Fifth Ave. 34th floor, New York, NY 10118-3299; (212) 290-4700; www.hrw.org; Washington office: 1630 Connecticut Ave., N.W., Suite 500, Washington, DC 20009; (202) 612-4321.

National Endowment for Democracy, 1101 15th St., N.W., Suite 700, Washington, DC 20005; (202) 293-9072; www.ned.org.

16

Nuclear Proliferation and Terrorism

Mary H. Cooper

Terrorist leader Osama bin Laden, left, with his deputy, Ayman al-Zawahiri, has said he wants to use a nuclear bomb against the West. The recent sale of black-market nuclear-weapons technology to North Korea and Iran and the terrorist bombing of passenger trains in Madrid, killing more than 190 people, have intensified concerns about nuclear weapons falling into the hands of "rogue" states or terrorists.

From *The CQ Researcher*,
April 2, 2004.

Concern about nuclear terrorism rose to new levels when A.Q. Khan, the revered father of Pakistan's nuclear bomb, confessed recently to peddling nuclear weapons technology to Libya and other rogue states.

Khan's dramatic confession punctured any remaining illusions that 60 years of nonproliferation efforts had kept the world's most dangerous weapons out of the hands of countries hostile to the United States and its allies. Moreover, he enhanced fears that terrorist groups bent on destroying the United States — like Osama bin Laden's al Qaeda network — may be closer than anyone had realized to acquiring nuclear weapons.

"A nuclear 9/11 in Washington or New York would change American history in ways that [the original] 9/11 didn't," says Graham Allison, director of Harvard University's Belfer Center for Science and International Affairs. "It would be as big a leap beyond 9/11 as 9/11 itself was beyond the pre-attack illusion that we were invulnerable."

Khan's January confession followed the revelation that he had operated a busy black-market trade in centrifuges, blueprints for nuclear-weapons equipment to enrich uranium into weapons-grade fuel and missiles capable of delivering nuclear warheads. Khan's vast network involved manufacturers in Malaysia, middlemen in the United Arab Emirates and the governments of Libya, North Korea and Iran.[1]

Several countries in Khan's network were known to have violated the 1968 Nuclear Non-Proliferation Treaty (NPT) and hidden their weapons programs from inspectors for the U.N.'s International Atomic Energy Agency (IAEA).[2] NPT signatories promise

Russia Has Most Nuclear Warheads

Russia and the United States have most of the more than 28,000 nuclear warheads stockpiled today. India, Israel and Pakistan — which have not signed the Nuclear Non-Proliferation Treaty (NPT) — have enough nuclear materials to produce more than 300 warheads. North Korea and Iran are both thought to be developing nuclear bombs. It is unknown whether terrorist groups have or are developing nuclear weapons.

Worldwide Nuclear Stockpiles

Country	Nuclear Weapons (estimated)
NPT Signatories	
China	410
France	350
Russia	18,000
United Kingdom	185
United States	9,000
Non-NPT Signatories *	
India	95 (max.)
Israel	200 (max.)
Pakistan	52 (max.)
Maximum total	28,292

* The number of warheads that could be produced with the amount of weapons-grade nuclear material these countries are thought to possess. The total number of assembled weapons is not known.

Source: Carnegie Endowment for International Peace, 2004.

to forgo nuclear weapons in exchange for help from the world's five official nuclear powers — the United States, Russia, China, France and Britain — in building civilian nuclear power plants.

In fact, North Korea has bragged that it is developing nuclear weapons, Iraq tried for years to produce weapons-grade fuel, and Iran recently barred IAEA inspections from its nuclear facilities amid allegations that it was developing a bomb. Libya's admission in December that it, too, had tried to build the bomb blew the cover on Khan's network. (*See sidebar, p. 382.*)

But the extent of Khan's black-market activities stunned even the most seasoned observers. "I was surprised by the level of commerce in the supporting supply network," says Charles B. Curtis, president of the Nuclear

Threat Initiative, an advocacy group that calls for stronger measures to stop the spread of nuclear weapons. "While there had been suggestions that the Pakistanis were nefariously engaged in both Iran and North Korea, the extent of the engagement in Libya and indications that there was an attempt to market proliferation technology in Syria exceeded the darkest suspicions of the intelligence community."

Given the grim realities of the post-9/11 world, fear of nuclear terrorism has dominated the international response to Khan's revelations. President Bush has proposed several measures to strengthen international anti-proliferation efforts. "In the hands of terrorists, weapons of mass destruction would be a first resort," Bush said. "[T]hese terrible weapons are becoming easier to acquire, build, hide and transport. . . . Our message to proliferators must be consistent and must be clear: We will find you, and we're not going to rest until you're stopped."[3]

But many experts say the president's proposals will not provide adequate safeguards against these lethal weapons. Wade Boese, research director of the Arms Control Association, a Washington think tank, commends the administration for emphasizing proliferation and pointing out that it is the most serious threat facing the United States today. However, he notes, since 9/11, the Bush administration has only "maintained the status quo" on funding for programs that deal with the threat of nuclear proliferation.

"The Khan network underscores the fact that we're in a race to tighten down security around [nuclear-weapons technology] so the terrorists can't get it," Boese says. "If this is such an urgent priority, which it is, why not fund it like it is and recognize that we're in a race with the terrorists?"

During the Cold War, both the United States and the Soviet Union understood that using nuclear weapons would amount to mass suicide. The doctrine of mutual assured destruction — MAD — ensured that a nuclear attack by one superpower would unleash a full-scale response by the other, resulting in annihilation on a national, if not global, scale. Consequently, the theory went, rational leaders would avoid using nuclear weapons at all costs.

But al Qaeda and other radical Islamist organizations don't appear to operate under such constraints. Their suicide bombers embrace death as martyrdom in their quest to destroy the "Great Satan."[4] And because they operate in a number of countries and have no permanent, identifiable headquarters, terrorist groups also have no "return address" to target for a counterattack.

As a result, keeping weapons-grade plutonium and highly enriched uranium out of the hands of terrorists is the only sure way to block terrorists from building nuclear bombs, many experts say.

"The essential ingredients of nuclear weapons are very hard to make and don't occur in nature," notes Matthew Bunn, a nuclear-terrorism expert at the Belfer Center. "But once a well-organized terrorist group gets hold of them, it could make at least a crude nuclear explosive."

Instructions for making a nuclear bomb are not secret; they are even on the Internet. "The secret is in making the nuclear material," Bunn points out, "and that, unfortunately, is the secret that A.Q. Khan was peddling."

While the ability of terrorists to stage a full-scale nuclear attack is of paramount concern, experts say the use of a conventional explosive device containing radioactive waste — a so-called dirty bomb — is far more likely. A dirty bomb in an urban area could contaminate dozens of city blocks, fomenting panic and costing tens of billions of dollars in lost revenues and devalued real estate, even if it claimed no human lives.[5]

"A dirty bomb is pretty likely to happen," says Leonard S. Spector, director of the Center for Nonproliferation Studies' Washington office, a part of the Monterey Institute of International Studies. A dirty bomb can be made easily with radioactive materials, such as cesium, used in X-ray machines and other commonplace diagnostic equipment. Moreover, he points out, civilian nuclear-waste facilities are much easier to penetrate than weapons facilities.

"We have to do our best to control as much of the radioactive material as possible," he says, "but it's already the subject of criminal activities. So we're recommending that people get ready for this one."

As policymakers examine the impact of Khan's nuclear black marketeering on U.S. counterproliferation policy, these are some of the questions being considered:

Is the Non-Proliferation Treaty still an effective shield against the spread of nuclear weapons?

The United States launched the atomic age when it detonated the first atomic bomb in 1945. But After Britain, China, France and the Soviet Union developed their own nuclear weapons, the great powers sought to put the nuclear genie back in the bottle. The landmark 1968 Non-Proliferation Treaty embodied a "grand bargain," by which the five countries with nuclear arsenals agreed to help the rest of the world develop nuclear power for peaceful uses in exchange for the non-nuclear states' promise to forgo nuclear weapons. The IAEA was to oversee compliance with the treaty, which enjoyed near universal support.

However, India, Israel and Pakistan — all of which have since developed nuclear weapons — never signed the treaty. And North Korea, which signed but later renounced the treaty, recently boasted that it is on the threshold of developing nuclear weapons.

The absence of universal adherence to the NPT reveals the treaty's basic weakness. "The fact that a very small number of individuals — nobody believes that A.Q. Khan was acting alone — can create a network that provides some of the most worrisome states on the planet with the technology needed to produce nuclear weapons

Protesters in Seoul, South Korea, burn a North Korean flag and an effigy of Kim Jong Il on Dec. 28, 2003, calling on North Korea's leader to end the country's efforts to build a nuclear bomb.

A Chronology of Nuclear Close Calls

The superpowers came close to using nuclear weapons several times during the Cold War, sometimes due to tensions that might have escalated, and sometimes due to simple accidents or mistakes. The end of the Cold War in 1991, however, did not end the threat of nuclear conflict.

First year of Korean War, 1950-51 — President Harry S. Truman sends atomic weapons to Guam for possible use against North Korea; Strategic Air Command makes plans to coordinate an atomic strike. Gen. Douglas MacArthur pushes for attacks on China, possibly using atomic weapons.[1]

The Offshore Islands Crises, 1954-55, 1958 — Testing America's resolve, China bombs Quemoy and Matzu, two Nationalist-held islands near the mainland. U.S. officials warn they will use atomic weapons to defend the islands.[2]

Mistake in Greenland, October 1960 — The American early-warning radar system in Thule, Greenland, mistakenly reports a "massive" Soviet missile launch against the United States. A reflection on the moon 250,000 miles away is thought to be a missile launch 2,500 miles away.[3]

Flashpoint Berlin, 1961 — Soviet threats regarding West Berlin prompt President John F. Kennedy to consider a nuclear first-strike against the U.S.S.R. if it attacks the city.[4]

Cuban Missile Crisis, October 1962 — President Kennedy considers invading Cuba to remove Soviet nuclear missiles, unaware the Soviets plan to respond with nuclear weapons. The Strategic Air Command goes to Defense Condition 2 (DEFCON 2), the second-highest state of readiness, for the only time in U.S. history. After an American naval quarantine of the island, Soviet Premier Nikita Khrushchev withdraws the missiles.[5]

B-52 Crash in Greenland, January 1968 — A B-52 carrying four thermonuclear bombs crashes near the U.S. early-warning base in Greenland. If the bombs' safety features had failed, the detonation could have been viewed as a surprise attack on America's early-warning system, prompting nuclear retaliation.[6]

Sino-Soviet Conflict, 1969 — Soviet Defense Minister Andrei Grechko advocates a nuclear strike against China to deal with what is perceived as an inevitable future war. Fearing the U.S. reaction, the Soviets refrain.[7]

Yom Kippur War, October 1973 — Egypt and Syria attack Israel, and after initial successes face military disaster. The Soviet Union indicates it might intervene to rescue its client states if Israel continues to refuse a cease-fire; Soviet airborne forces are put on alert, and U.S. military forces also go on alert. Israel agrees to a cease-fire and the superpower crisis ends.[8]

War Game Turns 'Real' at NORAD, 1979-80 — In November 1979, a technician at the North American Air Defense (NORAD) facility in Cheyenne Mountain, Colo., accidentally places a training tape simulating a

---

is very troubling," Bunn says. "It shows that the NPT regime is only as strong as its weakest links. We can secure 90 percent of the nuclear material to very high levels, but if the other 10 percent is vulnerable to theft, we still won't have solved the problem because we're dealing with intelligent adversaries who will be able to find and exploit the weak points."

In fact, some experts say that weaknesses doom the NPT to failure. "Arms-control regimes are not capable of dealing with the hard cases," says John Pike, a defense policy expert and founding director of GlobalSecurity.org, a nonprofit organization that studies emerging security threats.

"The logic of the NPT just doesn't get you very far in Tehran [Iran] or Pyongyang [North Korea]," Pike says. "It's not going to matter to India or Pakistan, which have

their own fish to fry. And the Israelis are not going to let go of their arsenal until there is a just and lasting peace in the Middle East," Pike says. "I'm afraid we're rapidly approaching a situation in which there are more nuclear-weapons states outside the NPT than inside, and the treaty itself provides no way whatsoever of addressing that problem."

The nonproliferation regime also lacks adequate verification and enforcement provisions, critics say. "The NPT was a confidence-building measure, not a true arms-control treaty," says C. Paul Robinson, director of Sandia National Laboratories, a division of the Energy Department's National Nuclear Security Administration. Robinson also was chief U.S. negotiator of the U.S.-Soviet Threshold Test Ban and Peaceful Nuclear Explosions Treaties, both ratified in 1990. None of the

nuclear attack on the United States into the base computer system. The mistake is corrected in six minutes — but after the president's airborne command post is launched. Twice in June 1980, false attack warnings caused by faulty computer chips send bomber crews racing for their planes.[9]

Tension in Europe, Early 1980s — After the Soviet Union deploys new nuclear missiles in Europe, the United States follows suit. Soviet leader Yuri Andropov fears NATO is planning a nuclear first-strike and orders Soviet intelligence to find the non-existent evidence. Tension in Europe decreases when Mikhail Gorbachev replaces Andropov.[10]

Soviet Pacific Fleet, August 1984 — A rogue officer at the Soviet Pacific Fleet in Vladivostok broadcasts an unauthorized war alert to Soviet naval forces, which, like American vessels, are armed with nuclear weapons. Soviet, U.S. and Japanese forces all prepare for battle. After 30 minutes, the alert is determined to be false.[11]

Norwegian Sea, January 1995 — Russian radar detects an inbound missile over the Norwegian Sea, and President Boris N. Yeltsin opens his nuclear command briefcase and confers with his military commanders. The missile turns out to be a Norwegian weather rocket.[12]

Kargil, Kashmir, May-July 1999 — A year after nuclear tests by India and Pakistan, Pakistan invades Kargil, in Indian-controlled Kashmir, and battles Indian forces from May until July. The crisis between the two rival nuclear powers is described as "warlike." Pakistan withdraws in July under heavy international pressure.[13]

Attack on the Indian Parliament, December 2001-January 2002 — Islamic militants probably connected to Pakistan's intelligence service attack India's Parliament. India demands that Pakistan cease supporting Islamic fighters. Hundreds of thousands of troops face off at the Indo-Pakistani border; both sides discuss a possible nuclear exchange. Tensions ease after Pakistan cracks down on Islamist groups.[14]

— Kenneth Lukas

[1] Burton Kaufman, *The Korean Conflict* (1999).

[2] John W. Garver, *Foreign Relations of the People's Republic of China* (1993), pp. 50-60.

[3] Center for Defense Information (CDI), www.cdi.org/Issues/NukeAccidents/accidents.htm.

[4] Fred Kaplan, "JFK's First Strike Plan," *The Atlantic Monthly*, October 2001, pp. 81-86.

[5] Graham Allison and Philip Zelikow, *Essence of Decision* (1999).

[6] Scott D. Sagan, *The Limits of Safety* (1993), pp. 180-193.

[7] Garver, *op. cit.*, pp. 305-310.

[8] P. R. Kumaraswamy (ed.), *Revisiting the Yom Kippur War* (2000).

[9] Sagan, *op. cit.*, pp. 228-233.

[10] Christopher Andrew and Vasili Mitrokhin, *The Sword and the Shield* (1999).

[11] CNN, www.cnn.com/SPECIALS/cold.war/episodes/12/spotlight/.

[12] CNN, *op. cit.*

[13] Yossef Bodansky, "The Kargil Crisis in Kashmir Threatens to Move into a New Indo-Pak War, With PRC Involvement," *Defense & Foreign Affairs Strategic Policy*, May/June 1999, p. 20.

[14] Seymour M. Hersh, "The Getaway," *The New Yorker*, Jan. 28, 2002, p. 36.

requirements normally found in arms-control treaties to verify compliance were included in the NPT, he says. "So there's nothing in the original NPT designed to catch cheaters."

After the 1991 Persian Gulf War, the nuclear nonproliferation community was surprised to learn that Iraq had been secretly developing nuclear weapons. So an "Additional Protocol" was added to the NPT allowing for more thorough inspections of suspected weapons facilities, but only 38 countries have ratified it. In any case, Robinson dismisses the protocol as little more than a "Band-Aid."

Even IAEA Director Mohamed ElBaradei said the NPT regime does not prevent nuclear proliferation. "You need a complete overhaul of the export-control system," he said. "It is not working right now."[6]

But the Bush administration says if the NPT and the IAEA oversight powers are strengthened, nonproliferation can remain a credible goal. On Feb. 11, Bush outlined seven steps designed to make the regime more effective in dealing with the threat of what the State Department calls "rogue" states and nuclear terrorism, including U.S. Senate approval of the Additional Protocol (*see p. 386*).

Other analysts say world dynamics have changed so dramatically since the NPT took effect that the nonproliferation regime needs a revolutionary overhaul. "The treaty was about controlling states and governments, not rogue individuals or terrorists who get their hands on these weapons," says Boese of the Arms Control Association. "The nonproliferation regime needs to be modified to better address this gap."

"The system has been pretty remarkable and successful, but is now in sufficient need of radical repair that we need a big jump forward," says Allison of the Belfer Center, who as assistant Defense secretary oversaw the Clinton administration's efforts to reduce the former Soviet nuclear arsenal. "We should now build a global alliance against nuclear terrorism, and the core of its strategy should be the doctrine of what I call the three 'Nos:' "[7]

- "No loose nukes" — Allison coined the phrase a decade ago to describe weapons and weapons-grade materials inadequately secured against theft. "These weapons and materials must be protected to a new security standard adequate to prevent nuclear terrorists from attacking us," he says. Under Allison's proposal, all nuclear states would have to be certified by another member of the nuclear club that all their nuclear materials had been adequately secured. The NPT has no such requirement.

- "No new nascent nukes" — New production of highly enriched uranium and plutonium would be barred. "If you don't have either one of them, you don't have a nuclear weapon," Allison says.

- "No new nuclear weapons" — Noting North Korea's nuclear ambitions, Allison acknowledges that this is the most difficult but potentially most important goal. "To accept North Korea as a new member of the nuclear club would be catastrophic," Allison says, "because North Korea historically has been the most promiscuous proliferator on Earth."

North Korea has sold nuclear-capable missiles to Iraq, Pakistan and other would-be nuclear powers. If Pyongyang develops a nuclear arsenal, most experts agree, other countries in the region, including South Korea, Japan and Taiwan, would be tempted to jettison the NPT and develop their own arsenals in defense, setting off a potentially disastrous regional arms race. "A nuclear North Korea," Allison says, "would blow the lid off the previous arms control and nuclear proliferation regime."

Is the United States doing enough to halt nuclear proliferation?

Since the fall of the Soviet Union in 1991, the United States has concentrated its nonproliferation efforts on preventing the theft or sale of nuclear weapons and materials left in Russia, Ukraine and other former Soviet republics. The 1991 Soviet Nuclear Threat Reduction Act — renamed the Cooperative Threat Reduction (CTR) program in 1993 — was designed to help former Soviet satellite countries destroy nuclear, chemical and biological weapons and associated infrastructure. Nicknamed Nunn-Lugar after the law's original sponsors (Sens. Sam Nunn, D-Ga., and Richard G. Lugar, R-Ind.), it also established verifiable safeguards against the proliferation of such weapons.

Recent U.S. efforts to control the worldwide supply of nuclear weapons and materials have focused almost solely on the CTR program: More than 50 former Soviet nuclear-storage sites have been secured and new security systems installed. Besides locking up nuclear materials and establishing security perimeters around the storage sites, says Robinson of Sandia Labs, the CTR program installs detection equipment to warn of any movement of the guarded material. "This material is being locked up and safeguarded," Robinson says. Sandia designs and installs the nuclear-security systems and trains foreign technicians on their use.

But critics say the agreement is woefully inadequate. "Very, very little progress has taken place," says Curtis of the Nuclear Threat Initiative, which Nunn co-founded. "There is an inertia that simply must be overcome with presidential leadership in all the participant countries."

The Bush administration recognizes the importance of securing Russia's nuclear stockpiles. In 2002, the United States, along with Britain, France, Canada, Japan, Germany and Italy, agreed to spend $20 billion over 10 years to support CTR programs — with half of it, or $1 billion a year, to come from the United States.

But that amounts to only about a quarter of 1 percent of the current Defense Department budget of about $401 billion, Bunn points out. "Amazingly," he adds, despite the new terrorist threats throughout the world, U.S. funding for the CTR programs "hasn't increased noticeably since Sept. 11."

Bunn is not alone. A task force led by former Sen. Howard H. Baker Jr., R-Tenn., and former White House Counsel Lloyd Cutler in January 2001 called for a tripling in annual CTR spending — to $3 billion a year.[8]

Inadequate funding has slowed the pace of securing Russia's nuclear sites, critics say. "We're not doing all that we know how to do and all that we must to keep these weapons and materials safe," Curtis says. After more than a decade of Nunn-Lugar efforts, only half of Russia's nuclear weapons have been adequately secured, Curtis points out.

Critics of the war against Iraq suggest that the campaign to topple Saddam Hussein expended precious resources that could have gone toward halting the spread of nuclear materials. The first order of business in combating nuclear terrorism, Allison says, is to list potential sources of nuclear weapons, in order of priority. "Saddam clearly had nuclear ambitions, and the CIA said that over the course of a decade he might realize them," Allison says. "So he deserved to be on the list somewhere down there, but he wasn't in the top dozen for me."

The nuclear weapons and materials that remain vulnerable to theft in Russia are at the top of Allison's list, primarily because of the magnitude of the problem. "We've still got 120 metric tons of highly enriched uranium and plutonium in Russia alone that we haven't even begun security upgrades on," Curtis points out.

Second on Allison's list is North Korea. By repudiating the Clinton administration's "Agreed Framework" with North Korea and refusing to engage in negotiations with the regime until it renounces its nuclear program, Allison says the Bush administration has allowed "North Korea to just about declare itself a nuclear-weapons state. For the past three years, they have been given a pass. And what have they been doing while they got a pass? They've been creating more plutonium every day, as they are today." Recent six-party talks in Beijing aimed at halting North Korea's nuclear-weapons program ended without significant progress.[9]

Third on Allison's priority list is Pakistan. Because it is not a party to the NPT, Pakistan's nuclear-weapons inventory is unknown. But according to a recent CIA analysis, Pakistan's Khan Research Laboratories has been providing North Korea with nuclear fuel, centrifuges and warhead designs since the early 1990s.[10] No one knows how many other customers Khan supplied over the past decade.

"A coherent strategy has got to deal with the most urgent potential sources of supply to terrorists first," Allison says. "When all this other stuff has been happening, why was Iraq the focus of attention for two years?"

Although no evidence that Iraq had recently pursued nuclear weapons has been found since the United States invaded the country over a year ago, Bush continues to defend his decision to overthrow Hussein's regime in the name of counterproliferation.

"The former dictator of Iraq possessed and used weapons of mass destruction against his own people," Bush said on Feb. 11. "For 12 years, he defied the will of the international community. He refused to disarm or account for his illegal weapons and programs. He doubted our resolve to enforce our word — and now he sits in a prison cell, while his country moves toward a democratic future."

Although Russia and Pakistan are widely regarded as the biggest potential sources of nuclear proliferation, the United States has a mixed record on safeguarding its own nuclear materials. The United States exported highly enriched uranium to 43 countries for nearly four decades as part of the Atoms for Peace program, sanctioned by the NPT, to help other countries acquire nuclear technology for peaceful purposes. The uranium was supposed to be returned to the United States in its original form or as spent fuel. But according to a recent report by the Energy Department's inspector general, the United States has made little headway in recovering the uranium, which is enough to make about 1,000 nuclear weapons.[11]

"While we should be locking up materials at risk wherever we can and recovering them when needed, the Department of Energy has been leisurely pursuing its program to recover highly enriched uranium at risk in research facilities around the world," Curtis says. "This is a leisure that we can ill afford."

Should nonproliferation policy aim to eliminate all nuclear weapons?

Article VI of the NPT requires countries with nuclear weapons to take "effective measures" to end the arms race and work toward nuclear disarmament. This was an essential component of the "grand bargain" used to lure the rest of the world to forgo nuclear arms.

As the sole remaining superpower, the United States plays a key role in leading the world toward disarmament. "Nonproliferation strategies have always been linked to U.S. efforts to reduce reliance on its nuclear forces, so there's always been an arms control link to the NPT as part of the essential bargain," says Curtis of NTI. "The world community also considers it a prerequisite for the United States to exercise its moral leadership on nonproliferation, that it be seen to be living up to its side of that bargain."

During the Cold War, the United States and the Soviet Union, which had amassed vast nuclear arsenals, signed a series of treaties that first limited, and then began to reduce, the number of nuclear weapons on each side.[12] On May 24, 2002, President Bush and Russian

Defusing North Korea and Iran

The good news: Only two so-called rogue nations are suspected of trying to build nuclear weapons. (Libya recently promised to end its bomb-making efforts, and Iraq never was close to having a bomb, U.N. inspectors say.) The bad news: The two rogue nations are North Korea and Iran.

North Korea is considered the more immediate threat. The shaky truce that ended the bloody Korean War (1950-53) has not removed the threat of hostilities between the reclusive, authoritarian regime and U.S.-supported South Korea, which relies on a large U.S. military presence for much of its defense.

Under the 1994 Agreed Framework brokered by President Bill Clinton, North Korea agreed to freeze production of plutonium — needed in the production of some nuclear weapons — in exchange for U.S. energy assistance and improved diplomatic relations. That agreement fell apart in October 2002, when the Bush administration accused North Korean leader Kim Jong Il of trying to enrich uranium in violation of the Non-Proliferation Treaty (NPT).

In January 2003, North Korea withdrew from the NPT and kicked out U.N. International Atomic Energy Agency (IAEA) inspectors. North Korea has continued to deny it has a uranium-enrichment program but openly acknowledges its plutonium program, which may already have produced one or two nuclear weapons.

North Korean leader Kim Jong Il

The most recent talks aimed at ending North Korea's nuclear-weapons ambitions, held in late February 2004 in Beijing, also involved China, Russia, Japan and South Korea. The talks failed to overcome the impasse between the Bush administration, which insists on the "complete, verifiable and irreversible dismantlement " of North Korea's nuclear programs before the United States will agree to improve bilateral relations, provide economic and energy assistance and offer "security guarantees" that it will not invade North Korea.

Prospects for the success of follow-up talks soured further on March 20, when North Korea warned it would expand its nuclear-weapons program if the yearly U.S.-led military exercises in South Korea proceed as scheduled in late March.[1]

Iran's nuclear ambitions raised concern two years ago with the discovery of a large uranium-enrichment plant south of Tehran, the capital. Iran, a signatory to the NPT, claims its nuclear program is used purely to generate electricity. In mid-March, after the IAEA censured Tehran for not fully disclosing its nuclear program, Iran temporarily barred the agency from the country. Inspections were set to resume on March 27.

Meanwhile, IAEA Director Mohamed ElBaradei has appealed to President Bush to launch talks with Iran aimed at improving bilateral relations, which have remained hostile since Islamic clerics wrested control of Iran from the U.S.-supported regime of Shah Mohammed Reza Pahlavi in 1979.

Ending Iran's and North Korea's nuclear ambitions will require convincing both countries that they don't need nuclear weapons to defend themselves, experts say. "To strengthen the international nonproliferation regime, we're going have to provide security assurances as well as economic aid," says Matthew Bunn, a nuclear-weapons expert at Harvard University's Belfer Center for Science and International Affairs. "There's going to have to be some kind of security assurance that the United States isn't going to invade Iran and overthrow its government. That's the center of the discussion with North Korea as well."

Failure to do so may lead to regional arms races that could quickly get out of control. If North Korea produces a nuclear arsenal, predicts John Pike of GlobalSecurity.org, Japan may feel sufficiently threatened to transform some of its civilian power-plant nuclear materials to build nuclear weapons in self-defense. "Then South Korea is going to need them, and Taiwan's going to need them," he says. "That will make China want to have more, which will prompt India to need more, and then Pakistan will, too."

[1] United Press International, "N. Korea Warns U.S. over War Exercises," March 20, 2004.

President Vladimir V. Putin signed the latest of these, the Strategic Offensive Reductions Treaty (SORT). It called on the two countries to reduce their current number of strategic nuclear warheads by nearly two-thirds by Dec. 31, 2012 — to 1,700-2,200 warheads.

"President Putin and I have signed a treaty that will substantially reduce our strategic nuclear warhead arsenals to . . . the lowest level in decades," Bush declared at the Moscow signing ceremony. "This treaty liquidates the Cold War legacy of nuclear hostility between our countries."

But critics say the so-called Moscow Treaty will be far less effective in ridding the world of nuclear weapons than the president's comments suggest. "The agreement doesn't require the destruction of a single warhead or a single delivery vehicle," says Boese of the Arms Control Association. Warheads that are removed from deployment could be disassembled or stored rather than destroyed. "Also, the agreement's limit is actually in effect for just one day — Dec. 31, 2012," Boese says. "Because neither side has to destroy anything after that day, presumably they could then rebuild their arsenals."

After the Sept. 11 terrorist attacks, the Bush administration toughened U.S. policy on nuclear weapons and other weapons of mass destruction (WMD). The new national strategy to combat nuclear, biological and chemical weapons, issued in December 2002, called for strengthening "traditional measures — diplomacy, arms control, multilateral agreements, threat-reduction assistance and export controls." But for the first time, the United States openly warned that it would pre-emptively attack adversaries thought to be preparing to use weapons of mass destruction against the United States.

"U.S. military forces . . . must have the capability to defend against WMD-armed adversaries, including, in appropriate cases, through pre-emptive measures," the administration declared. "This requires capabilities to detect and destroy an adversary's WMD assets before these weapons are used."[13]

Meanwhile, the administration's latest Nuclear Posture Review, sent to Congress on Dec. 31, 2001, called for research into new types of nuclear weapons and outlined new uses for them.[14] As part of that policy, the administration has initiated research into the "bunker buster," a missile armed with a low-yield (less than five kilotons) nuclear warhead designed to penetrate and destroy enemy arsenals or other targets buried deep

underground. To enable research to proceed, Congress last year overturned a Clinton-era ban on research and development of low-yield nuclear weapons.[15]

"The reason it was important to reduce or get rid of the prohibition on low-yield nuclear weapons was not because we're trying to develop or are developing low-yield nuclear weapons," said National Nuclear Security Administrator Linton Brooks. "That's a misconception. . . . What we said was that the amendment was poorly drawn and it prohibited research that could lead to a low-yield nuclear weapon."[16] In fact, research on high-powered "bunker buster" bombs commenced in 2003, after Congress overturned the ban.[17]

Since taking office, the administration has rejected arms control as an essential tool for reducing the nuclear threat. Shortly after being sworn into office, Bush said he would not resubmit the 1996 Comprehensive Test Ban Treaty to the Senate for ratification. He also abrogated the 1972 U.S.-Soviet Anti-Ballistic Missile Treaty, which barred signatories from building national defense systems to protect against ballistic-missile attack — a move designed to discourage the superpowers from building more nuclear weapons to overcome such defenses.

Bush instead announced he would pursue earlier plans to build a National Missile Defense System while seeking a "new strategic framework" for dealing with Russia that would focus on reductions in nuclear weapons.[18] The first U.S. anti-missile defense facility, scheduled for deployment in Alaska this summer, has faced criticism for its technical flaws and for undermining the United States' credibility as a strong advocate of nuclear disarmament.[19]

"The current U.S. approach to proliferation emphasizes non-treaty methods and military means, including the effort to deploy a national missile defense system," said John Cirincione, director for nonproliferation at the Carnegie Endowment for International Peace. "The system faces formidable technical challenges and is unlikely to be militarily effective anytime in this decade. Every system within the missile-defense program is behind schedule, over budget and underperforming."[20]

While supporters of the administration's nuclear policy say the changes were needed to protect the United States in a new era of uncertainty, critics say they undermine the administration's credibility in its calls to strengthen global anti-proliferation measures.

"If you're trying to build a consensus [on halting proliferation] while at the same time saying we need a few more different nuclear weapons, I would say those are inconsistent arguments," Allison says. "I've negotiated on behalf of the U.S. government many times when I felt I had a weak hand, but I couldn't imagine keeping a straight face in trying to argue these two goals at the same time."

BACKGROUND

Manhattan Project

The nuclear age traces its origins to 1938, when scientists in Nazi Germany split the nucleus of a uranium atom, releasing heat and radiation. The potential of nuclear fission, as the process was called, to produce weapons of unparalleled power prompted a recent refugee from Germany — Albert Einstein — to alert President Franklin D. Roosevelt. "[T]he element uranium may be turned into a new and important source of energy in the immediate future," the already-legendary physicist wrote. ["T]his new phenomenon," he added, could lead "to the construction of bombs . . ., extremely powerful bombs of a new type."[21]

In 1939, even before the United States entered World War II or realized the full implications of Einstein's warning, Roosevelt established the first federal uranium-research program. Fission research led to further advances, including the 1940 discovery of the element plutonium by physicists at the University of California, Berkeley. After the United States entered the war against Japan, Germany and Italy in December, the race to beat Germany in developing an atomic bomb accelerated under a secret Army Corps of Engineers program known as the Manhattan Project.*

By September 1944, after less than two years of work, Manhattan Project researchers had begun producing plutonium for weapons. On July 16, 1945, they detonated an experimental atomic bomb known as "the Gadget" from a tower in the New Mexico desert. Less than three weeks later, on Aug. 6, U.S. airmen dropped an atom bomb nicknamed "Little Boy" on Hiroshima, followed on Aug. 9 by the detonation of "Fat Man" over Nagasaki.

---

* Atomic weapons get their energy from the fission, or breaking apart, of the nucleus of an atom of uranium or plutonium. Hydrogen — or thermonuclear — weapons get their energy largely from fusion, the formation of a heavier nucleus from two lighter ones. Both types of weapons are known collectively as nuclear weapons.

Two days later, Japan surrendered. World War II was over and the "Atomic Age" had begun. Within weeks of the bombings, the death toll had climbed to more than 100,000 people — mainly civilians.

The enormous loss of civilian lives sparked intense debate over the future of atomic weapons. The Manhattan Project cost the U.S. government almost $20 billion (in today's dollars), including the construction of reactors and lab facilities at more than 30 sites, such as Los Alamos, N.M., Oak Ridge, Tenn., and Hanford, Wash. In 1946, the American representative to the newly created United Nations Atomic Energy Commission, Bernard M. Baruch, proposed the elimination of atomic weapons, but the Soviet Union rejected the proposal. In 1947, Congress replaced the Manhattan Project with the civilian Atomic Energy Commission, which assumed control over atomic research and weapons facilities around the country.

The postwar deterioration of relations with the Soviet Union effectively ended the nuclear debate in the United States and prompted the administration of President Harry S Truman to intensify production of nuclear weapons, especially the next generation of more powerful, thermonuclear weapons. The first Soviet atomic bomb test and the rise of communism in China in 1949, followed the next year by the outbreak of the Korean War, fueled U.S. policymakers' support of the weapons program. By the early 1950s, both sides in the rapidly escalating Cold War had developed hydrogen bombs.

With momentum building for still more nuclear research, calls to abandon the new technology ran into resistance from those promoting nuclear power as a cheap, virtually inexhaustible source of energy. Fission releases large amounts of heat, which can be harnessed to power a steam turbine to generate electricity.

On Dec. 8, 1953, President Dwight D. Eisenhower presented his "Atoms for Peace" proposal to the United Nations, calling for creation of an international atomic energy agency "to devise methods whereby this fissionable material would be allocated to serve the peaceful pursuits of mankind."

The Soviet Union beat the United States in the race to introduce nuclear power, starting up the world's first plant in 1954. With federal support and AEC oversight, General Electric, Westinghouse Electric and other U.S. companies invested heavily in the new technology. On May 26, 1958, Eisenhower opened the first U.S. nuclear power plant, at Shippingport, Pa.

1930s-1980s *Atomic Age begins and evolves into the Cold War.*

1938 Scientists in Nazi Germany split the nucleus of a uranium atom. A year later, the U.S. Manhattan Project enters the race to create an atomic bomb.

Aug. 6, 1945 U.S. drops an atomic bomb on Hiroshima, Japan, followed on Aug. 9 by another on Nagasaki, killing a total of more than 250,000 people. Two days later, Japan surrenders, ending World War II.

1949 The Soviet Union tests its first atomic weapon.

Dec. 8, 1953 President Dwight D. Eisenhower's "Atoms for Peace" proposal calls for using fissionable material "to serve the peaceful pursuits of mankind."

1957 International Atomic Energy Agency (IAEA) is created to promote peaceful use of nuclear energy.

May 26, 1958 Eisenhower opens first U.S. nuclear power plant, at Shippingport, Pa.

1964 China joins the United States, Soviet Union, Britain and France in the "nuclear club" of officially recognized nuclear-weapons states.

July 1, 1968 Nuclear Non-Proliferation Treaty (NPT) is signed by 98 countries after a decade of talks.

1969 Treaty of Tlatelolco bars nuclear weapons from Latin America. Brazil and Argentina are the last nations to sign, in the 1990s.

1981 Israel destroys an Iraqi nuclear reactor, claiming it was being used to produce fuel for weapons.

1990s *Cold War ends, posing new proliferation threats.*

1991 Soviet Union collapses. . . . Persian Gulf War against Iraq, an NPT signatory, reveals that Saddam Hussein had been trying to develop nuclear weapons. . . . Soviet Nuclear Threat Reduction Act sponsored by Sens. Sam Nunn, D-Ga., and Richard G. Lugar, R-Ind., authorizes the United States to help former Soviet-bloc countries destroy nuclear, chemical and biological weapons and establishes verifiable safeguards against their proliferation.

1993 Nunn-Lugar program is broadened and renamed the Cooperative Threat Reduction (CTR) program. . . . South Africa becomes first country with nuclear weapons to renounce its nuclear program and join the NPT.

October 1994 North Korea agrees to freeze its plutonium production in exchange for U.S. assistance in producing energy.

1996 President Bill Clinton signs the Comprehensive Test Ban Treaty.

1998 India and Pakistan join Israel on the list of non-NPT signatories with nuclear weapons.

2000s *Massive terrorist attacks raise the specter of nuclear terrorism.*

Sept. 11, 2001 Suicide airline hijackers linked to Osama bin Laden's al Qaeda terrorist group kill nearly 3,000 people in the worst terrorist attacks in U.S. history.

2002 President Bush disavows the U.S. pact with North Korea and calls on Kim Jong Il to renounce his nuclear ambitions as a condition of the resumption of U.S. aid.

March 19, 2003 U.S. troops invade Iraq but find no weapons of mass destruction.

Dec. 19, 2003 Libya agrees to terminate its nuclear-weapons program, revealing evidence of a Pakistan-based black market in nuclear technology.

Feb. 6, 2004 Pakistani President Pervez Musharraf pardons Abdul Qadeer Khan, founder of Pakistan's nuclear-weapons program, for selling nuclear technology to Iran, North Korea, Libya and possibly others.

Feb. 11, 2004 President Bush responds to the revelations about Khan's network with a seven-point plan to strengthen the NPT and IAEA's enforcement powers.

Fall of a Nuclear Black Marketeer

As A. Q. Khan tells it, the horrors of religious intolerance he witnessed as a 10-year-old Muslim in India turned him into the world's leading black-market merchant of nuclear-bomb materials.[1]

"I can remember trains coming into the station full of dead Muslims," Khan recalled recently, describing the sectarian violence that broke out in Bhopal following Indian independence from Britain. "The [Hindu] Indian authorities were treating the Muslims horribly."[2]

Six years later, Khan fled north to the newly independent Islamic nation of Pakistan. But the slaughter he had seen as a youngster left Khan with an enduring enmity toward India and shaped his life's work, spurring him to develop Pakistan's nuclear bomb.

In the 1960s, Khan pursued postgraduate studies in metallurgy in Western Europe and later worked in the Netherlands at a uranium-enrichment plant run by Urenco, a Dutch-British-German consortium. There he learned about uranium enrichment and the design of sophisticated centrifuges needed to produce weapons-grade nuclear fuel.

Khan reportedly smuggled Urenco's centrifuge designs into Pakistan in the mid-1970s after Prime Minister Zulfikar Ali Bhutto invited him to establish the country's nuclear-weapons program. A Dutch court in 1983 convicted him in absentia of attempted espionage for stealing the designs, but the conviction was overturned.

As the director of Pakistan's nuclear program, Khan became adept at procuring equipment and technology — both legally and on the black market — and did little to conceal his activities. He even published a brochure with a photo of himself and a list of nuclear materials available for sale or barter, including intermediate-range ballistic missiles. Investigators say Khan's network stretched from Europe to Turkey, Russia and Malaysia. Khan himself traveled to North Korea at least 13 times to swap his nuclear technology for Korean missile technology, and U.N. inspectors have discovered documents in Iraq suggesting that he offered to help Saddam Hussein build a nuclear weapon in 1990, just before the first Gulf War.[3]

By 1998, when India first tested nuclear devices, Khan was quick to follow suit. Now the bitter adversaries were both in the "nuclear club."

Khan became an instant hero to Pakistanis, whose hatred of India permeates the national culture. Schools, streets and children were named after him. Indeed, most Pakistanis appeared forgiving when Khan confessed in February following revelations he had illegally supplied nuclear technology to North Korea, Libya and Iran.

But Khan's admissions — and the fact that he was not punished for selling nuclear secrets to rogue states — infuriated many Americans and others in the West. "It sends a horrible signal," said David Albright, president of the Institute for Science and International Security, a nonpartisan think tank dedicated to educating the public on scientific issues affecting international security. "It basically says, 'Yeah, your wrists will be slapped, but, boy, you're

---

For the next 20 years — until the partial meltdown at Pennsylvania's Three Mile Island nuclear plant in 1979 and the catastrophic accident at the Soviet plant at Chernobyl in 1986 — nuclear power accounted for a growing percentage of the world's electricity.

Today nuclear power accounts for 16 percent of global electricity generated at some 440 plants in 30 countries.[22] A handful of countries depend on nuclear power for more than half of their electricity, but only about 20 percent of the power generated in the United States comes from nuclear reactors.

Nonproliferation Efforts

Eisenhower's Atoms for Peace proposal bore fruit in 1957, when the IAEA was established as an independent U.N. body charged with promoting the peaceful use of nuclear energy. The agency was responsible for inspecting nuclear research facilities and power plants to ensure that they were not being used to build nuclear weapons.[23]

It already was becoming clear, however, that stronger measures were needed to prevent nuclear proliferation. Britain, which had participated in the U.S. nuclear development program, tested its first nuclear device in 1952 and quickly built several hundred warheads. France developed its nuclear capability independently and began building a nuclear arsenal in 1960. In 1964, China tested its first nuclear weapon, becoming the fifth and last nuclear-weapon state recognized under the NPT.

Faced with the prospect of dozens more countries acquiring the bomb within a few decades, the United

going to make millions of dollars.' "[4]

Khan professes bewilderment at the outrage his proliferation activities have engendered. "They dislike me and accuse me of all kinds of unsubstantiated and fabricated lies because I disturbed all their strategic plans, the balance of power and blackmailing potential in this part of the world," he said. "I am not a madman or a nut. . . . I consider myself a humble, patriotic Pakistani who gave his best for his country."

Indeed, while Islamic extremism is rising in Pakistan, the moderate Khan is married to a Dutch national, and neither she nor their daughters wear the veil typically worn by conservative Muslims.

Kahn's enduring popularity helps explain why Pakistani President Pervez Musharraf pardoned him — and why the Bush administration accepted Musharraf's claim that he knew nothing of Khan's illicit activities. Others say the United States did not push Musharraf to punish Khan because of a deal in which Pakistan would

AFP Photo

Pakistani nuclear scientist Abdul Qadeer Khan

help U.S. troops find terrorist leader Osama bin Laden, thought to be hiding in Pakistan's northwest territories (*see p. 386*).

(see p. 386)

"They correctly judged that the United States would blow hot and cold on the question of nuclear proliferation, depending on the temper of the times," says defense-policy analyst John Pike, director of Global-Security.org, a nonprofit organization studying emerging security threats. "Blaming the black market all on A.Q. Khan and letting Musharraf say he had no idea what was going on is just a way for everybody to have their cake and eat it, too."

[1] Unless otherwise noted, information in this section is based on Peter Grier, Faye Bowers and Owais Tohid, "Pakistan's Nuclear Hero, World's No. 1 Nuclear Suspect," *The Christian Science Monitor*, Feb. 2, 2004.

[2] Khan was interviewed by the Human Development Foundation, an expatriate Pakistani group in Shaumburg, Ill., www.yespakistan.com.

[3] "The Black Marketeer," "Nightline," ABC News, March 8, 2004.

[4] *Ibid*

States and 17 other countries began talks in 1958 aimed at halting the further spread of nuclear weapons. A proposal by Ireland envisioned a commitment by all nuclear-weapons states not to provide the technology to other countries. In theory, non-nuclear countries would benefit from such an arrangement because it would ensure that their neighbors would also remain nuclear-free. But non-nuclear states called for more incentives to accept this permanent state of military inferiority.

In 1968, after a decade of negotiations, 98 countries signed the Nuclear Non-Proliferation Treaty (NPT). The agreement recognized the original five nuclear-weapons states — the United States, the Soviet Union, France, the United Kingdom and China — defined as countries that had "manufactured and exploded a

nuclear weapon or other nuclear explosive device prior to 1 January 1967." The IAEA was charged with monitoring compliance with the treaty. Countries that signed the treaty agreed to refrain from producing, obtaining or stockpiling nuclear weapons.

The treaty expanded on the Irish resolution by offering more incentives to refrain from building nuclear weapons. The nuclear states agreed to help other countries develop civilian nuclear power plants and also, under Article X, to take "effective measures" to end the arms race and work toward nuclear disarmament.

But the treaty set no timetables for disarmament, enabling the nuclear powers to keep their arsenals virtually indefinitely. The NPT's Article X contains another important loophole — it allows signatories to withdraw

EPA/Wade Payne

Components from Libya's nuclear weapons program are displayed by Secretary of Energy Spencer Abraham at the Y-12 National Security Complex in Oak Ridge, Tenn., on March 15, 2004. Libyan leader Muammar el-Qaddafi ended the country's isolation by renouncing weapons of mass destruction and joining the world nonproliferation regime.

from the treaty without penalty for unspecified "supreme interests."

With 188 parties, the NPT has the broadest support of any arms control treaty. Only three countries — India, Israel and Pakistan — have not signed the pact and are believed to possess finished nuclear weapons or components that could be rapidly assembled. Israel began developing its nuclear capability in the 1950s with French assistance. The United States has refrained from pressing its chief Middle Eastern ally on its nuclear program, and Israel has never acknowledged its arsenal, thought to number 98-172 warheads. In 1998, India and Pakistan — engaged in a longstanding border dispute — acknowledged their nuclear status. Both India with (50-90 warheads) and Pakistan (30-50 warheads) are believed to store their nuclear weapons in the form of separate components that can be assembled at short notice.[24]

Over the past decade, the international nonproliferation regime has scored some important successes. In the 1990s, Argentina and Brazil agreed to abandon their nuclear-weapons ambitions, signed the NPT and became the last two Latin American countries to sign the 1969 Treaty of Tlatelolco, which barred nuclear weapons from the 33-nation region. After the Soviet Union's collapse, the former Soviet republics of Belarus, Kazakhstan and Ukraine voluntarily relinquished to Russia all the nuclear weapons Moscow had deployed on their territory

during the Cold War. And, in 1993, after the fall of apartheid, South Africa became the first nuclear-armed country to voluntarily dismantle its entire nuclear-weapons program.

Mushrooming Nukes

For all the NPT's success in containing nuclear weapons, it has failed to keep non-signatories, and even some "renegade states" that signed the treaty, from pursuing nuclear capabilities. Almost as soon as it signed the NPT in 1968, Iraq began developing nuclear weapons with help from France and Italy, presumably to counter Israel's arsenal. Israel destroyed an Iraqi reactor in 1981, claiming it was being used to produce fuel for weapons. Nevertheless, Iraq continued its clandestine program, as weapons inspectors discovered upon entering Iraq after its defeat in the 1991 Gulf War.

After the war, U.S.-led condemnation of Iraq's nuclear-weapons program resulted in U.N. sanctions that prohibited trade with Iraq. The sanctions were later eased to allow Iraq to sell a limited amount of oil to buy food and medical supplies, but by the end of the 1990s, Iraq was in the throes of an economic crisis.

Although the Bush administration cited evidence that Iraq had continued its nuclear-weapons program to justify last year's invasion and toppling of Hussein, recent inspections have turned up no signs Hussein was pursuing nuclear weapons. "It turns out we were all wrong," said former weapons inspector David Kay of U.S. suspicions that Iraq possessed weapons of mass destruction. "And that is most disturbing."[25]

Another NPT "renegade," North Korea is considered to pose a far greater risk. A party to the NPT since 1985, North Korea launched a clandestine nuclear program centered on production of plutonium, which could be used to make nuclear weapons. Although North Korea insisted that its program was intended only to generate electricity, in 1993 it barred IAEA inspectors from viewing its facilities, precipitating a crisis in the nonproliferation regime. In October 1994, the Clinton administration brokered an "Agreed Framework," whereby North Korea agreed to freeze plutonium production in exchange for U.S. assistance to compensate for any energy lost due to the reactor shutdown. President Bush disavowed the pact in 2002 as bowing to nuclear blackmail and called on North Korea's Kim Jong Il to renounce his nuclear ambitions as a condition of resuming aid to the impoverished country.

Concerned that nuclear weapons or weapons-grade materials might fall into the hands of renegade states or terrorist groups, the United States, the Soviet Union and 38 other countries with nuclear technology established the Nuclear Suppliers Group in 1985, agreeing to control exports of civilian nuclear material and related technology to non-nuclear-weapon states. And to restrict the proliferation of nuclear-capable missiles, the United States and six other countries in 1987 set up the Missile Technology Control Regime, a voluntary agreement that has since been expanded to more than 30 countries.

The collapse of the Soviet Union signaled the end of both the Cold War and the nuclear standoff dominated by the military doctrine of mutual assured destruction. But the post-Cold War peace, welcome as it was, ushered in a new era of uncertainty in which concern over nuclear proliferation took the place of superpower nuclear brinkmanship. The resulting economic and political upheavals left Russia — the Soviet successor state — poorly equipped to maintain security over the vast nuclear arsenal it inherited.

Recognizing the proliferation risk posed by Russia's arsenal, Congress passed the so-called Nunn-Lugar measure. Since it became law in 1991, the United States has helped Russia deactivate some 6,000 nuclear warheads, retrain 22,000 nuclear-weapons scientists and remove all the nuclear weapons deployed in the former Soviet republics of Belarus, Kazakhstan and Ukraine. Nunn-Lugar also has helped destroy hundreds of Soviet missiles, seal nuclear test facilities and dismantle submarine-based nuclear warheads.

CURRENT SITUATION

Black Market Revealed

A.Q. Khan's black market in nuclear weapons and materials began to unravel on Dec. 19, 2003, when Libya told the United States and Britain it would terminate its nuclear-weapons program. Although the North African country had not developed warheads, it was found to have imported numerous key components, including sophisticated centrifuges needed to enrich uranium into fuel for bombs.

The Bush administration claims much of the credit for this unexpected victory in the fight against nuclear proliferation. "The success of our mission in Libya underscores the success of this administration's broader nonproliferation efforts around the world," said Energy Secretary Spencer Abraham at a special press tour of seized Libyan nuclear materials and equipment on display at the department's Oak Ridge labs on March 15. "What you have witnessed represents a big, big victory in the administration's efforts to combat weapons of mass destruction."

Administration critics dispute this claim, citing reports that Libyan leader Muammar el-Qaddafi had been convinced by his son and presumptive heir, 31-year-old Saif al-Islam Qaddafi, to end the country's isolation by renouncing weapons of mass destruction and joining the world nonproliferation regime.[26] Libya has suffered severe economic privation since coming under U.N.-sponsored economic sanctions for its involvement in the 1988 bombing of a Pan-Am flight over Lockerbie, Scotland, which killed 270 people.

U.N. sanctions, imposed in 1992, were lifted in September 2003, after Libya accepted responsibility for the bombing and agreed to pay $2.7 billion in compensation to families of the Pan Am victims. Although the Bush administration lifted a ban on travel to Libya after it renounced its nuclear program, other U.S. economic sanctions remain in place.[27]

"Muammar's son thought his dad had run the country into a ditch," says Pike of GlobalSecuirity.Org. "But

Vehicles entering the United States from Canada pass through radiation detectors at the Blaine, Wash., border crossing. Experts say terrorists are far more likely to deploy a small, easily transported conventional explosive device containing radioactive waste — a so-called dirty bomb — than to explode a nuclear bomb.

AP Photo/Ted S. Warren

when the dynastic handoff of a country from father to son becomes the primary determinant of our disarmament success, then we're running on a pretty thin reed."

When they entered Libyan facilities in January, IAEA inspectors said they discovered crates of nuclear equipment that only could have come from sources with advanced nuclear programs of their own. Subsequent investigations uncovered a complex web of international transactions that led to a factory in Malaysia, transshipment facilities in Dubai, an intercepted cargo ship in Italy, shipments to Iran and ultimately to Khan himself. In January, after acknowledging his role in establishing the nuclear black market, Khan was pardoned by Pakistani President Pervez Musharraf, who claimed he knew nothing of Khan's undercover business.

Nuclear experts dismiss Musharraf's disavowal as ludicrous. Khan's prominent role as the father of Pakistan's nuclear arsenal made him a highly visible national hero who made no attempt to conceal his lavish lifestyle in his impoverished country and who actually had published brochures describing nuclear materials and equipment that were for sale from his lab for more than a decade.

"The pattern of activity was at such a large scale that it's inconceivable that the Pakistani government didn't know about this all along," Pike says. "It's like asking me to believe that [U.S. nuclear pioneer] Ed Teller was secretly selling hydrogen bombs out of the back of a pickup truck."

But the Bush administration did not question Musharraf's disavowal of knowledge about Khan's activities. Since the Pakistani leader emerged as an outspoken ally of the United States in its war on terrorism after Sept. 11, the administration clearly has been loath to undermine his standing in an Islamic country where anti-American feelings and support for al Qaeda run high. Musharraf has narrowly escaped two assassination attempts, attributed to al Qaeda, in recent months.[28]

Moreover, the Bush administration needs Musharraf's cooperation in order to find al Qaeda leader Osama bin Laden — considered by some to be the mastermind of the 9/11 attacks — and his top lieutenants. Some observers suggest that the Bush administration decided to accept Musharraf's denial of knowledge about Khan's network in exchange for permission for U.S. forces to enter the rugged area on the Pakistani side of the border with Afghanistan, believed to be a key stronghold of al

Qaeda militants and possibly bin Laden himself.[29] Up to now, U.S. forces have had to limit their searches to the Afghan side of the border.

Although administration spokesmen deny the existence of such a deal, American military officials have announced plans for a "spring initiative" on the Afghan side of the border.[30] Already, signs are emerging that an offensive is under way. On March 16, on the eve of a visit to Pakistan by Secretary of State Colin L. Powell, Pakistani troops suffered numerous casualties in gun battles in the border region.[31]

Bush's Response

President Bush responded to the revelations about Khan's network with a seven-point plan to strengthen the NPT and IAEA's enforcement powers. On Feb. 11, the president called for the expansion of his Proliferation Security Initiative, a year-old international effort to seize nuclear materials on the high seas while in transit to or from rogue states. In 1999 and 2000, years before Bush's initiative, Indian and British authorities seized two North Korean shipments of missile components and related equipment en route to Libya.[32]

Bush also called on the U.N. Security Council to adopt a resolution requiring all states to criminalize proliferation of components that could be used to make weapons of mass destruction and to strengthen export controls on them. And he proposed expanding U.S. efforts to secure Russia's nuclear weapons and materials under the Nunn-Lugar program.

In addition, Bush called for closing the loophole in the NPT that allows aspirants to the nuclear club to enrich and reprocess fuel used in civilian nuclear reactors and proposed that only signatories of the Additional Protocol be allowed to import equipment for civilian reactors. To strengthen the IAEA, Bush proposed a new measure to beef up the agency's safeguards and verification powers. Finally, he recommended barring countries being investigated for alleged NPT violations from holding positions of influence in the IAEA.

"We've shown that proliferators can be discovered and can be stopped," Bush said. "Terrorists and terror states are in a race for weapons of mass murder, a race they must lose."

Weapons analysts praised Bush's recommendations. "It was a very important speech," says Curtis of the Nuclear Threat Initiative. "It addressed a number of

AT ISSUE

Will U.S. policies keep nuclear weapons away from terrorists?

YES   President George W. Bush

From a speech at the National Defense University, Feb. 11, 2004

On Sept. 11, 2001, America and the world witnessed a new kind of war. We saw the great harm that a stateless network could inflict upon our country, killers armed with box cutters, mace and 19 airline tickets. Those attacks also raised the prospect of even worse dangers — of other weapons in the hands of other men. The greatest threat before humanity today is the possibility of secret and sudden attack with chemical or biological or radiological or nuclear weapons. . . .

America, and the entire civilized world, will face this threat for decades to come. We must confront the danger with open eyes, and unbending purpose. I have made clear to all the policy of this nation: America will not permit terrorists and dangerous regimes to threaten us with the world's most deadly weapons. . . .

We're determined to confront those threats at the source. We will stop these weapons from being acquired or built. We'll block them from being transferred. We'll prevent them from ever being used. One source of these weapons is dangerous and secretive regimes that build weapons of mass destruction to intimidate their neighbors and force their influence upon the world. These nations pose different challenges; they require different strategies. . . .

I propose to expand our efforts to keep weapons from the Cold War and other dangerous materials out of the wrong hands. In 1991, Congress passed the Nunn-Lugar legislation. Sen. [Richard] Lugar had a clear vision, along with Sen. [Sam] Nunn, about what to do with the old Soviet Union. Under this program, we're helping former Soviet states find productive employment for former weapons scientists. We're dismantling, destroying and securing weapons and materials left over from the Soviet . . . arsenal. . . .

Over the last two years, a great coalition has come together to defeat terrorism and to oppose the spread of weapons of mass destruction — the inseparable commitments of the war on terror. We've shown that proliferators can be discovered and can be stopped. We've shown that for regimes that choose defiance, there are serious consequences. The way ahead is not easy, but it is clear. We will proceed as if the lives of our citizens depend on our vigilance, because they do.

Terrorists and terror states are in a race for weapons of mass murder, a race they must lose. Terrorists are resourceful; we're more resourceful. They're determined; we must be more determined. We will never lose focus or resolve. We'll be unrelenting in the defense of free nations, and rise to the hard demands of dangerous times.

NO   Natural Resources Defense Council

From a statement, Feb. 12, 2004, www.nrdc.org.

Nunn-Lugar funds are not being used to "dismantle and destroy" Russian nuclear weapons (as opposed to missile silos and obsolete strategic bombers and submarines). In fact, the recently signed Moscow Treaty between the United States and Russia allows Russia to keep SS-18 "heavy" strategic ballistic missile systems that would otherwise have been destroyed under the START II and START III treaties.

Despite years of cooperation, the United States still has no firm idea of how many and which types of Russian nuclear warheads and bombs have been dismantled. As former Sen. Sam Nunn has indicated, the Nunn-Lugar program suffers from inadequate funding. President Bush cites the 2002 G-8 Summit agreement to provide $20 billion over 10 years, but even here the participating countries used accounting tricks to avoid increasing previous commitments. Moreover, some of this money is earmarked to build a plutonium fuel-fabrication plant in Russia that many observers believe will increase the potential that plutonium will be diverted and used for illicit purposes.

President Bush so far has refused to commit to destroying more than a few hundred of the more than 10,000 nuclear weapons still in the United States' nuclear weapons stockpile. The Strategic Offensive Reduction Treaty (SORT) negotiated with Russia in 2002 — the Moscow Treaty — does not require the elimination of a single nuclear missile silo, submarine, missile warhead, bomber or bomb. . .

President Bush failed to address the longer-term problem, and long-term proliferation pressures, arising from a world permanently and inequitably divided into declared nuclear weapons states under the Non-Proliferation Treaty (NPT), de-facto nuclear weapon states outside the treaty (India, Pakistan and Israel), non-weapon states that have abandoned the treaty (North Korea) and states with varying degrees of nuclear expertise (Iran) that are presently bound by their treaty commitment not to acquire nuclear weapons but could elect to withdraw from the NPT at any time.

Nor did President Bush discuss how and when the United States and other nuclear weapon states would take further steps to fulfill their Non-Proliferation Treaty commitments to eliminate their nuclear arsenals. On the contrary, the Bush administration is spending record amounts revitalizing the U.S. nuclear weapons complex. . . .

There are two distinct kinds of threats facing the United States, one having to do with the proliferation of [weapons of mass destruction] by nation states and the second with threats posed by terrorists. The president's proposals focused on threats posed by the spread of nuclear weapons, materials and technologies to nation states rather than those by terrorists.

areas that require U.S. leadership and international cooperation."

But Curtis also says the United States needs to do more to dispel the perception that it holds itself to a different standard than the rest of the world regarding proliferation. "Missing from the speech was some meaningful initiative on addressing the strategic nuclear weapons that the United States and Russia still maintain in very large numbers and, under the Treaty of Moscow, may retain into the indefinite future," Curtis says.

To others, Bush's speech exemplified the administration's unilateral approach to pursuing U.S. interests. "President Bush's speech was a series of measures that would constrain everybody else," says Bunn of Harvard's Belfer Center. "There was no mention of anything that would constrain the United States."

In Pike's view, the Bush administration's nuclear policies have left the United States with few viable options. "Right now, our declaratory policy is one of attacks to disarm our enemies' weapons infrastructure, followed up by military invasion and regime change," he says. That's the policy that led to the war in Iraq, which did not yet possess nuclear weapons. But the same policy cannot be applied to a state like North Korea, which may harbor nuclear weapons, for fear of igniting a global holocaust. "So we have an extraordinarily alarming declaratory policy that's basically frightened the living daylights out of the rest of humanity, [but which] we're not prepared to implement. That puts us in the worst of all possible worlds."

OUTLOOK

Crumbling Coalition?

The March 11 bombing of commuter trains in Madrid has lent further urgency to the international war on terrorism. Ten separate explosions at the rush hour ripped through the trains, killing more than 190 commuters and wounding some 1,400.[33] After initially blaming Basque separatists for the attacks, the government announced two days later that it had arrested five people with suspected links to al Qaeda.

The next day, March 14, Spaniards went to the polls and removed Prime Minister José Maria Aznar, a staunch U.S. ally in the war against terrorism, from office. Spain's new leader, Socialist José Luis Rodríguez Zapatero, renewed Spain's commitment to fight terrorism. But he promised to fulfill a campaign pledge to withdraw Spain's 1,300-man contingent of peacekeepers in Iraq by June 30. He is one of Europe's most outspoken critics of the war.

Calling the occupation of Iraq "a fiasco," Zapatero has outlined an approach to fighting terrorism that relies on international cooperation, which he says differs sharply from the administration's tactic. "Fighting terrorism with Tomahawk missiles isn't the way to defeat terrorism," he said. "I will listen to Mr. Bush, but my position is very clear and very firm. . . . Terrorism is combated by the [rule] of law."[34]

Zapatero may be expressing the views of more than a demoralized Spanish electorate. According to a new international survey, opposition to the war in Iraq and U.S. international policies has intensified in Europe. A growing percentage of Europeans polled said they want to distance their fate from the United States by adopting independent foreign and security policies through the European Union. More than half support a European foreign policy independent from that of the United States. Even in Britain, the administration's strongest war on terrorism ally, support for an independent European foreign policy has risen from 47 percent in April 2002 to 56 percent in the current poll.[35]

The Bush administration has downplayed any notion of a rift between the United States and its European allies. "We don't think countries face a choice — being European or being trans-Atlantic," said an administration official following Secretary of State Powell's March 24 trip to Spain to attend a memorial service for victims of the Madrid bombing. "All of us, especially in the NATO alliance, are almost by definition both. . . . European nations don't have to choose between good relations with Europe and good relations with the United States."

Foiling Nuclear Terror

The Madrid bombing — the worst incident of terrorist violence in Europe since the Pan Am bombing — coming as it did on the heels of the exposure of Khan's nuclear-smuggling network, will likely intensify debate over how to deal with the threat of nuclear terrorism. Bin Laden has made no secret of his desire to use a nuclear bomb as the ultimate weapon against the West, and weapons experts say events are fast outpacing policies deigned to avert such a catastrophe.

"The Bush administration and the president himself have rightly said that the ultimate specter is al Qaeda with a nuclear weapon," says Harvard's Allison. "But this administration has no coherent strategy for preventing nuclear terrorism. That's a pretty serious charge, but I think it's correct."

Administration supporters reject that view. "President Bush has transported the fight the terrorists began back to their land," wrote former Sen. Alfonse M. D'Amato, R-N.Y. "He refuses to allow them to contaminate our soil with their hatred. He has stood firm in the face of the terrorist threat, despite constant harping from critics who would second-guess his leadership."[36]

Still, IAEA Director General ElBaradei paints a grim picture of nuclear proliferation's future and calls for a revolutionary overhaul of international systems and policies to prevent nuclear terrorism. "Eventually, inevitably, terrorists will gain access to such materials and technology, if not actual weapons," he wrote. "If the world does not change course, we risk self destruction."

ElBaradei calls for globalization of worldwide security. "We must abandon the traditional approach of defining security in terms of boundaries — city walls, border patrols, racial and religious groupings," he wrote recently in *The New York Times*. "The global community has become irreversibly interdependent, with the constant movement of people, ideas, goods and resources.

"In such a world, we must combat terrorism with an infectious security culture that crosses borders — an inclusive approach to security based on solidarity and the value of human life. In such a world, weapons of mass destruction will have no place."[37]

NOTES

1. See Ellen Nakashima and Alan Sipress, "Insider Tells of Nuclear Deals, Cash," *The Washington Post*, Feb. 21, 2004, p. A1.

2. For background, see Mary H. Cooper, "Non-Proliferation Treaty at 25," *The CQ Researcher*, Jan. 27, 1995, pp. 73-96.

3. From a speech at the National Defense University in Washington, D.C., Feb. 11, 2004.

4. For background, see Mary H. Cooper, "Hating America," *The CQ Researcher*, Nov. 23, 2001, pp. 969-992, and David Masci and Kenneth Jost, "War on Terrorism," *The CQ Researcher*, Oct. 12, 2001, pp. 817-840.

5. See Michael A. Levi and Henry C. Kelly, "Weapons of Mass Disruption," *Scientific American*, November 2002, pp. 76-81.

6. ElBaradei spoke at IAEA headquarter in Vienna, Feb. 5, 2004. See Peter Slevin, "U.N. Nuclear Chief Warns of Global Black Market," *The Washington Post*, Feb. 6, 2004, p. A18.

7. For a detailed description, see Graham Allison, "How to Stop Nuclear Terrorism," *Foreign Affairs*, January/February 2004, pp. 64-74.

8. Howard Baker and Lloyd Cutler, "A Report Card on the Department Of Energy's Nonproliferation Programs with Russia," Jan. 10, 2001.

9. See Steven R. Weisman, "Lasting Discord Clouds Talks on North Korean Nuclear Arms," *The New York Times*, March 14, 2004. For background, see Mary H. Cooper, "North Korean Crisis," *The CQ Researcher*, April 11, 2003, pp. 321-344.

10. See David E. Sanger, "U.S. Sees More Arms Ties between Pakistan and Korea," *The New York Times*, March 14, 2004, p. A1.

11. See Joel Brinkley and William J. Broad, "U.S. Lags in Recovering Fuel Suitable for Nuclear Arms," *The New York Times*, March 7, 2004, p. A8.

12. For a list of nuclear arms-control treaties and their provisions, see "Treaties and Agreements," U.S. State Department, www.state.gov, and Nuclear Threat Initiative, "WMD411," www.nti.org. For background, see Mary H. Cooper, "Weapons of Mass Destruction," *The CQ Researcher*, March 8, 2002, pp. 193-116.

13. "National Strategy to Combat Weapons of Mass Destruction," The White House, December 2002, p. 3.

14. "Findings of the Nuclear Posture Review," U.S. Department of Defense, released Jan. 9, 2002; www.defenselink.mil.

15. The measure was included in the 1994 Defense Authorization Act.

16. From an interview with *Arms Control Today*, January/February 2004; www.armscontrol.org.

17. See Joseph C. Anselmo, "Opponents See New Arms Race in Push for Nuclear Research," *CQ Weekly*, Feb. 21, 2004, pp. 498-500.

18. For background, see Mary H. Cooper, "Bush's Defense Policy," *The CQ Researcher*, Sept. 7, 2001, pp. 689-712.

19. See Bradley Graham, "Missile Defense Still Uncertain," *The Washington Post*, March 12, 2004.

20. Cirincione testified before a special meeting of the Danish Parliament, April 24, 2003.

21. For the text of Einstein's letter, see Robert C. Williams and Philip L. Cantelon, eds., *The American Atom* (1984), cited in Stephen I. Schwartz, ed., *Atomic Audit* (1998). Unless otherwise noted, information in this section is based on Schwartz.

22. Data from www.iaea.org and the Nuclear Energy Institute, www.nei.org.

23. For background, see David Masci, "The United Nations and Global Security," *The CQ Researcher*, Feb. 27, 2004, pp. 173-196.

24. For background, see David Masci, "Emerging India," *The CQ Researcher*, April 19, 2002, pp. 329-360.

25. Kay testified before the Senate Armed Services Committee, Jan. 28, 2004.

26. See Michael Evans, "Libya Knew Game Was Up Before Iraq War," *The Times* (London), March 23, 2004, p. 8.

27. See "Top U.S. Official Visits Libyan Leader," The Associated Press, March 23, 2004.

28. See Salman Masood, "Link to Qaeda Cited in Effort to Assassinate Pakistan Chief," *The New York Times*, March 17, 2004.

29. See Seymour M. Hersh, "The Deal," *The New Yorker*, March 8, 2004, pp. 32-37.

30. See David Rohde, "U.S. Announces New Offensive Against Taliban and al Qaeda," *The New York Times*, March 14, 2004, p. 4.

31. See Sulfiqar Ali, "Firefight in Pakistan Claims 32 Lives; Troops Hunting for Militants Clash with Tribesmen in a Region Bordering Afghanistan," *Los Angeles Times*, March 17, 2004, p. A13.

32. See J. Peter Scoblic, "Indefensible," *The New Republic*, March 8, 2004, p. 14.

33. See Aparisim Ghosh and James Graff, "Terror on the Tracks," *Time*, March 22, 2004, p. 32.

34. From an interview on radio Onda Cero quoted in "New Spain PM Firm on Troop Withdrawal," The Associated Press, March 17, 2004.

35. Pew Research Center for the People & the Press, "A Year After Iraq War, Mistrust of America in Europe Ever Higher, Muslim Anger Persists," March 16, 2004; people-press.org.

36. Alfonse D'Amato, "Bush Will Win War on Terrorism," *Newsday*, March 22, 2004.

37. Mohamed ElBaradei, "Saving Ourselves from Self-Destruction," *The New York Times*, Feb. 12, 2004, p. A37.

BIBLIOGRAPHY

Books

Allison, Graham, *Nuclear Terrorism: The Ultimate Preventable Catastrophe,* Henry Holt, 2004.
A former Defense Department official outlines his strategy for strengthening the nuclear nonproliferation regime to prevent the spread of nuclear weapons to terrorists.

Blix, Hans, *Disarming Iraq,* Pantheon, 2004.
The head of the U.N. weapons inspection team in Iraq asserts that the inspectors would have proved conclusively that Iraq no longer possessed weapons of mass destruction had the Bush administration given them more time before invading.

Frum, David, and Richard Perle, *An End to Evil: How to Win the War on Terror,* Random House, 2003.
A former Bush speechwriter (Frum) and a former administration Defense official call current policies in the war on terrorism a choice between "victory or holocaust."

Weissman, Steve, and Herbert Krosney, *The Islamic Bomb,* Times Books, 1981.
Two authors describe how Pakistan and Iraq launched programs to develop nuclear weapons more than two decades ago.

Articles

Cirincione, Joseph, and Jon B. Wolfsthal, "North Korea and Iran: Test Cases for an Improved Non-

proliferation Regime?" *Arms Control Today*, December 2003.

Innovative measures to strengthen anti-proliferation measures may be needed to keep North Korea and Iran from developing nuclear weapons.

Hersh, Seymour, "The Deal," *The New Yorker*, March 8, 2004, pp. 32-37.

President Bush may have accepted Pakistani President Pervez Musharraf's pardon of his top nuclear scientist's black marketing activities in exchange for letting U.S. troops pursue al Qaeda inside Pakistan.

Kagan, Robert, and William Kristol, "The Right War for the Right Reasons," *The Weekly Standard*, Feb. 23, 2004.

Although weapons of mass destruction have not been uncovered, two conservative commentators say that ridding the world of Saddam Hussein more than justifies the war against Iraq.

Pollack, Kenneth M., "Spies, Lies, and Weapons: What Went Wrong," *The Atlantic Monthly*, January/February 2004, pp. 78-92.

A former CIA analyst examines how U.S. intelligence wrongfully concluded that Saddam Hussein's regime was actively pursuing nuclear, biological and chemical weapons.

Sokolski, Henry, "Taking Proliferation Seriously," *Policy Review*, October/November 2003.

A conservative analyst argues the United States should call for strong measures to close loopholes in the Nuclear Non-Proliferation Treaty.

Weisman, Steven R., "Lasting Discord Clouds Talks on North Korea Nuclear Arms," *The New York Times*, March 14, 2004, p. 10.

A proposal to overcome an impasse in six-party talks to end North Korea's nuclear-weapons program has failed to gain acceptance, forcing a postponement of future talks.

Reports and Studies

Baker, Howard, and Lloyd Cutler, "A Report Card on the Department of Energy's Nonproliferation Programs with Russia," Russia Task Force, Secretary of Energy Advisory Board, Jan. 10, 2001.

The panel calls for greater efforts to keep nuclear weapons and materials in the former Soviet Union out of the hands of terrorists.

Cochran, Thomas B., and Christopher E. Paine, "The Amount of Plutonium and Highly-Enriched Uranium Needed for Pure Fission Nuclear Weapons," Natural Resources Defense Council, April 15, 1995.

The environmental-protection advocacy organization questions the standards the International Atomic Energy Agency (IAEA) uses to determine the amount of weapons-grade material needed to build a nuclear weapon.

Federation of American Scientists, Natural Resources Defense Council and Union of Concerned Scientists, "Toward True Security: A U.S. Nuclear Posture for the Next Decade," June 2001.

Three organizations that support arms control say drastically reducing the U.S. nuclear arsenal is essential to countering nuclear proliferation.

Ferguson, Charles D., *et al.*, "Commercial Radioactive Sources: Surveying the Security Risks," Center for Nonproliferation Studies, Monterey Institute of International Studies, January 2003.

Numerous sources of commercial radioactive material are vulnerable to terrorist theft. The authors call for an education campaign to prepare the public for a "dirty-bomb" attack.

The White House, "National Strategy to Combat Weapons of Mass Destruction," December 2002.

The Bush administration's post-Sept. 11 strategy contemplates preemptively attacking adversaries armed with nuclear, chemical or biological weapons before they can attack the United States.

For More Information

Arms Control Association, 1150 Connecticut Ave., N.W., Suite 620, Washington, DC 20036; (202) 463-8270; www.armscontrol.org. A nonpartisan membership organization dedicated to promoting support for effective arms-control policies.

Belfer Center for Science and International Affairs, John F. Kennedy School of Government, Harvard University, 79 JFK St., Cambridge, MA 02138; (617) 495-1400; http://bcsia.ksg.harvard.edu. Provides information on technical and political aspects of nonproliferation policy.

Bureau of Nonproliferation, U.S. Department of State, 2201 C St., N.W., Washington, DC 20520; (202) 647-4000; www.state.gov/t/np. Administers policies to prevent the spread of weapons of mass destruction.

Center for Nonproliferation Studies, Monterey Institute of International Studies, 460 Pierce St., Monterey, CA 93940; (831) 647-4154; http://cns.miis.edu. A nongovernmental organization devoted to research and training on nonproliferation issues.

GlobalSecurity.org, 300 N. Washington St., Suite B-100, Alexandria, VA 22314; (703) 548-2700; www.globalsecurity.org. A Web site maintained by veteran defense-policy analyst John Pike containing exhaustive information on U.S. defense policies, including nonproliferation strategy.

Nonproliferation Policy Education Center, 1718 M St., N.W., Suite 244, Washington, DC 20036; (202) 466-4406; www.npec-web.org. A project of the Institute for International Studies that promotes understanding of proliferation issues.

Nuclear Threat Initiative, 1747 Pennsylvania Ave., N.W., 7th Floor, Washington DC 20006; (202) 296-4810; www.nti.org. Seeks to increase global security by reducing the risk from nuclear, biological and chemical weapons. The Web site contains a wealth of information.

Nuclear Cities Initiative, U.S. Department of Energy, NA-24, 1000 Independence Ave., S.W., Washington, DC 20585; (202) 586-1007; www.nnsa.doe.gov/na-20/nci/index.shtml. Helps the Russian Federation downsize its nuclear weapons complex by establishing private business opportunities for nuclear scientists living in three of the former Soviet Union's closed cities.